WHAT EVERY VETERAN SHOULD KNOW

85th EDITION

BOOK PRICE - $28.00 – INCLUDES SHIPPING

This is the 85th Edition of the book "WHAT EVERY VETERAN SHOULD KNOW," a service officer's guide since 1937.

Monthly supplements are available from the publisher, which provide updates to the information contained in this book. A one-year subscription to the supplement service is $36.00.

The material herein covers veterans' benefits, rights, privileges, and services over which the Department of Veterans Affairs has jurisdiction. All references to "VA" pertain to the Department of Veterans Affairs. Revised and new laws passed by the 116th Congress as of December 31, 2020, are incorporated in this text.

This guide was prepared solely for convenient reference purposes and does not have the effect of law. Although diligent effort has been made to ensure its accuracy, in the event of any conflict between this book and any regulation, the latter is, of course, controlling.

Veterans and the dependents of deceased veterans are advised to contact their local veterans organization service officers or the nearest Veterans Administration Office, for help in completing any valid claim.

VETERANS INFORMATION SERVICE
P.O. Box 111
East Moline, Illinois 61244-0111
Telephone: (309) 757-7760
Fax: (309) 278-5304
Email: help@vetsinfoservice.com
www.vetsinfoservice.com

ASK FOR YOUR **FREE** SAMPLE COPY OF THE
MONTHLY SUPPLEMENT,
DESIGNED TO KEEP THIS BOOK UP TO DATE.
ONE-YEAR SUPPLEMENT SERVICE: $36.00

WHAT EVERY VETERAN SHOULD KNOW

VETERANS INFORMATION SERVICE
P.O. Box 111
East Moline, Illinois 61244-0111

Phone: (309) 757-7760
Fax: (309) 278-5304
E-mail: help@vetsinfoservice.com
www.vetsinfoservice.com

3 3113 03707 3030

A NOTE TO THE READER:

Revised and new laws passed by the 116th Congress as of December 31, 2020, are incorporated in the text of this book. Chapter 1 of the book contains a brief summary of some of the important legislative changes affecting veterans' benefits during 2020.

You will find a Table of Contents, listing the main subject headings. For your convenience there is also a complete index in the back of the book, as well as an Edge Index on the back cover.

We hope you enjoy this edition of **WHAT EVERY VETERAN SHOULD KNOW**. Any comments or suggestions for future improvements are welcome.

© 2021
What Every Veteran Should Know
Library of Congress Cataloging in Serials
ISSN 1532-8112
ISBN 978-0-9600887-1-3

Publisher:
Veterans Information Service
P.O. Box 111
East Moline, IL 61244-0111

TABLE OF CONTENTS

VA PHONE NUMBERS

Main VA Phone Numbers

Where to Call	Toll-Free Number
MyVA411 (main information line for VA)	800-698-2411
Telecommunications Relay Service Using TTY	744

VA Health Care

Where to Call	Toll-Free Number
Health Care Benefits	877-222-8387
My HealtheVet Help Desk	877-327-0022
Civilian Health and Medical Program of the Department of Veterans Affairs (CHAMPA)	800-733-8387
CHAMPVA Meds by Mail	888-385-0235 or 866-229-7389
Foreign Medical Program (FMP)	877-345-8179
Quit Vet (Get Help from a Counselor to Quit Smoking)	855-784-8838
MISSION Act	844-698-2311, Option 1
Spina Bifida Health Care Benefits Program	888-820-1756
Caregiver Support Line	855-260-3274

VA Benefits

Where to Call	Toll-Free Number
VA Benefits Hotline	800-827-1000
GI Bill Hotline	888-442-4551
Students Outside the U.S.	+1-918-781-5678
National Pension Call Center	877-294-6380
Support for SGLI or VGLI	800-419-1473
All Other VA Life Insurance Programs	800-669-8477
Special Issue Hotline (Blue Water Navy Act, Gulf War, Agent Orange, and Other Information)	800-749-8387

Burials and Memorials

Where to Call	Toll-Free Number
National Cemetery Scheduling Office	800-535-1117
Headstones and Markers	800-697-6947

Other VA Support

Where to Call	Toll-Free Number
Women Veterans Hotline	855-829-6636
eBenefits Technical Support	800-983-0937
Debt Management Center (Collection of Nonmedical Debt)	800-827-0648
Vets Center Call Center	877-327-8387
White House VA Hotline	855-948-2311
Veterans Crisis Line	800-273-8255

QUICK GUIDE—
APPLYING FOR BENEFITS

The following are guides to applying for the most commonly used benefits and services for veterans.

Apply for VA Health Care

Collect the following:
- Discharge papers (DD214 member-4 or equivalent)
- Your most recent tax return
- Social security numbers for yourself and your dependents
- Account numbers for insurance programs you're enrolled in
- If applicable, your VA Disability Rating Decision

Application
- Apply by completing the health care application form (VA Form 10-10EZ) in one of a few ways.
  - Visit online
  - Call 877-222-8387 and press 1
  - Visit in person at a VA medical center
  - Print out and mail the completed form to the Health Eligibility Center (2957 Clairmont Rd. Suite 200 Atlanta, GA 30329)
  - Call 877-222-8387 and press 0 if you haven't heard back from the VA within one week of submitting your application
- If approved, take steps to access your benefits.
  - Review your priority assignment group and personalized benefits handbook, mailed to you by the VA after enrollment.
  - Contact your local VA Medical Center to set up an appointment.
  - Make an appointment to obtain your Veterans Health Identification Card (VHIC).
- You are eligible for VA health care if:
  - VA rated you for a service-connected disability.
  - You received a purple heart, or you are a former POW.
  - You are a combat veteran who separated within the last five years.
  - You are eligible for Medicaid.
  - Your family income is below the income threshold.
  - You served in Vietnam, Southwest Asia during the Gulf War or Camp Lejeune during certain periods.

To Apply Online (The Equivalent of the VA Form 10-10 EZ):

If you're not signed into your account on the VA's health care website, you'll need to sign into your account. If you sign in, it can make the process faster because parts of the application can be pre-filled with account details. If you do it this way, you can also save your progress and finish filling out the form later. You have 60 days from the date you start or update your application to submit the form. After 60 days, your form isn't saved, and you'll have to start over.

If you need help filling out an application, you can work with an accredited representative such as a Veterans Service Officer.

You may also qualify for vision and dental benefits as part of your VA health care benefits.

When you apply for VA health care, you're assigned to 1 of 8 priority groups. Then, the systems that need immediate help can get signed up quickly. Veterans with a service-connected disability are assigned the highest priority. Veterans who earn a higher income and don't have a service-connected disability are assigned a lower priority level.

If you're applying in person, you fill out the 10-10EZ and then bring it to your nearest VA medical center or clinic.

If you're using a power of attorney, you need to submit a copy of the Power of Attorney with the application

If you sign with an X, you must have two witnesses who also sign and print their name on the form.

Getting Started with Mental Health Services

If you need help right now, you can call, text, or chat online with responders at the Veterans Crisis Line. Many responders are also veterans. The line is always open. To connect call 1-800-273-8255 and Press 1.

You can also text a message to 838255.

You can go online at veteranscrisisline.net and click chat.

If you need emergency mental health care, you can go directly to your local VA medical center, regardless of discharge status or enrollment in other VA health care.

If you don't need immediate health care but would like to learn more about VA mental health care, you may be eligible for services.

All former servicemembers can access emergency VA mental health care.

Apply for a Disability Rating

A rating is between 0% and 100%. A rating may give you access to VA benefits like health care and compensation.

Collect the documents you'll need to file a claim, which includes:
- Discharge papers (DD214 member-4 or equivalent)
- Military medical records
- Hospital reports and VA medical records related to your disability
- Private medical records and hospital reports related to your disability
- Any other medical evidence related to your injury or illness
- Apply by submitting all documents in one of two ways—submitting a claim online or completing a claim form in person at a VA Regional Office
- Track your status at va.gov/claim-or-appeal-status
- If requested, provide more information or documentation
- Attend a VA medical exam if requested
- If you're approved, review your award letter for your rating

You may be able to file a claim if you are a veteran, servicemember preparing to separate from the military, or you're a survivor or family member. Veterans Service Organizations can file a claim on your behalf as well.

Apply for VA Pension as a Veteran

The Veterans Pension Program provides monthly payments to wartime veterans who meet certain age or disability requirements and who have income and net worth within certain limits. If you are eligible, you'll need the following information:
- Social Security number or VA file number
- Military history
- Financial information and financial information of dependents
- Work history
- Medical information
- Bank account direct deposit information

You can apply online or by mail. You need to fill out an Application for Pension (VA Form 21P-527EZ).

If you're applying by mail, you'll send it to:
Department of Veterans Affairs
Pension Intake Center
PO Box 5365
Janesville, WI 53547-5365

You can also bring your application to a nearby VA regional office or work with an accredited representative to complete it.

You can start by submitting an intent to file while you gather documents to send in with your pension application. If you submit at intent to file before you file your claim, you may get retroactive payments.

You can submit an intent to file by phone by calling 800-827-1000. You can also download and submit an Intent to File a Claim for Compensation and/or Pension, Survivors Pension, and/or DIC (VA Form 21-0966).

Using Community Care

You may be eligible to see a community provider if you meet one of six eligibility criteria:
- Service is unavailable: You need a service not available at VA.
- Facility unavailable: You live in a state or territory without a full-service VA medical facility.
- Grandfathered choice: You were eligible for community care under the Veterans Choice Program distance criteria.
- Medical interest: Your VA provider determines it's in your best medical interest to be referred to a community provider.
- Quality standards: You need care from a VA medical service that VA determines is not providing care that complies with VA's quality standards.
- Access standards: You meet the access standards for average drive time or wait time for a VA appointment.

You may be eligible to see a community provider if your average drive time from home to a VA medical facility that provides the service you need takes more than:
- 30 minutes travel time to receive primary care, mental health, and non-institutional extended care services including adult home day care
- 60 minutes travel time to receive specialty care services

You may be eligible if the wait time for an appointment at a VA medical facility that provides the service you need exceeds:
- 20 days for primary care, mental health, and non-institutional extended care services
- 28 days for specialty care from the date of request with certain exceptions

Accessing Urgent Care

VA offers eligible veterans an urgent care benefit for treating minor injuries and illnesses at retail and urgent care providers who are part of VA's contracted network. The urgent care benefit is offered to veterans and urgent care and same-day services VA provides through its medical facilities.

To be eligible for the urgent care benefit, you must be enrolled in the VA healthcare system, and you must have received care through VA from either a VA or a community provider within the last 24 months. To find an urgent care facility, use the VA Facility locator at www.va.gov/find-locations. You can also call your local VA medical facility to find an in-network urgent care provider. When you arrive, tell the provider you would like to use your VA urgent care benefit and confirm they're part of the VAs network.

Apply for Education Benefits

Education benefits include the Post-9/11 GI Bill, the Montgomery GI Bill, career counseling, and on-the-job training. To get started, decide on the type of education benefit you want to use, and learn about schools that offer VA-approved programs. You can utilize the online GI Bill Comparison tool to compare school statistics and your out-of-pocket costs.

Once you decide on a program, you will need your discharge papers and your orders if activated from the Guard or Reserves.

You can submit your application online or complete an application in person at a VA regional office. You will work with your school's VA certifying official.

If you have questions, you can call the Education Call Center at 888-442-4551.

Some of the types of education benefits include:
- Post-9/11 GI Bill: You must have qualifying active service on or after 9/11/01. It includes payment for 40-100% of tuition and stipends for housing and books.
- Montgomery GI Bill—Active Duty: This requires qualifying active service and a high school diploma or GED. The benefit includes a monthly stipend for tuition and fees.
- Montgomery GI Bill—Selected Reserve: This requires a six-year commitment to Selected Reserve, and it's usable only while serving. There's a monthly stipend for tuition and fees.
- Survivors and Dependents' Educational Assistance: This is for a spouse or dependent of a qualifying veteran, and it includes a monthly stipend for tuition and fees.

Apply for Burial in a VA National Cemetery and Memorial Products

To start, decide whether a burial will be in a VA national cemetery, state, or tribal veterans' cemetery. You might also decide on a private cemetery. From there, decide on the desired memorial products.

For burial in a VA national cemetery, a private cemetery, or for a Presidential Memorial Certificate, you will need to submit the following with your application, if available:

- Discharge documents (DD214 member-4) or equivalent
- Orders if activated by Executive Federal Order from the National Guard or Reserves
- Pre-need determination approval letter if previously completed

Apply for burial in a VA national cemetery by:

- Faxing discharge documents to 866-900-6417 or
- Scanning discharge documents to NCA.Scheduling@va.gov and
- Calling the National Cemetery Scheduling Office at 800-535-1117

Apply for a government-furnished headstone, marker, or medallion for placement in a private cemetery by submitting a:

- VA Form 40-1330, Claim for Standard Government Headstone or Marker or
- VA Form 40-1330M, Claim for Government Medallion for Placement in a Private Cemetery

Apply for a Presidential Memorial Certificate by submitting a VA Form 40-0247, Presidential Memorial Certificate Request Form.

Apply for a burial flag by submitting a VA Form 27-2008, Application for United States Flag for Burial Purposes.

A funeral director can assist a family by gathering and providing the VA's documents, calling the National Cemetery Scheduling Office to schedule the burial, acquiring a burial flag, requesting Military Funeral Honors from the Department of Defense, and serving as a liaison between the family and VA.

Request Your Military Service Records (Including DD214)

The best way to begin to request your military service records is to use the milConnect website. You will need to sign into milConnect to get your service records. To do this, you will need a Premium DS Logon account. You can't use your My HealtheVet or ID.me credentials. You will have to go to milConnect to sign up, register, and upgrade your account to premium.

Once you have done that, you can take the following steps to request your military service records:

- From the homepage where you are signed in, click or tap on Correspondence/Documentation
- Select Defense Personnel Records Information (DPRIS) from the drop-down menu
- Choose the Personnel File tab
- Select Request My Personnel File
- Fill out the form

- In the Document Index section, check the boxes next to the documents you want to request
- Click or tap the Create and Send Request button

You can request the following by taking the above steps:
- DD214
- DD215
- Report of Separation
- Other release papers
- Orders and endorsements
- Performance reports
- Awards and decorations
- Qualifications, licenses, and certificates
- Security clearance

Once you submit your request, you'll get an email letting you know the request is being processed. You'll receive a second email when your request is complete and your files are ready to be viewed and downloaded. You can also check your request's status by signing into milConnect and going to the Personnel File tab in the Defense Personnel Records Information section.

If you prefer, you can also request your military records in other ways. These options include:
- Mail or fax a Request Pertaining to Military Records (Standard Form SF 180) to the National Personnel Records Center (NPRC)
- Write a letter to the NPRC at 1 Archives Drive, St. Louis, Missouri 63138
- Visit the NPRC in person
- Contact your state or county veteran's agency

If you want to request someone else's military records because you're planning a burial for a veteran in a VA national cemetery, you can contact the National Scheduling Office at (800) 535-1117. You can also request records by mailing or faxing a request to NPRC at the address above or taking any of the other steps named above.

If you are not next of kin for the veteran and the veteran was discharged more than 62 years ago, you can order a copy of their military records from the National Archives. If the veteran was discharged less than 62 years ago, you might be able to request limited information from their Military Personnel File.

Applying for Disability Compensation

How to prepare to file a claim for disability compensation:
- Find out if you're eligible
- Gather any evidence and supporting documents you'll submit
- Make sure your claim is filled out completely

- Find out if you need any supplemental forms with your claim

Evidence can include:

- VA medical records and hospital records relating to claimed illnesses or injuries
- Private medical records and hospital reports that relate to your claimed illnesses or injuries
- Supporting statements you want to provide from friends, family members, clergy members, law enforcement, or people you served with

You should also know that you have up to a year from the date the VA receives your claim to turn in any evidence. If you start your application and need time to gather more supporting documents, you can save your application and come back later to finish it. The VA will recognize the date you started your application as your date of claim as long as you complete it within 365 days.

The best way to apply for disability compensation is by obtaining an eBenefits account and applying online. When applying for compensation benefits, you must have access to the following information:

- Discharge or separation papers (DD214 or equivalent)
- Medical evidence (doctor and hospital reports)
- Dependency records (marriage and children's birth certificates)
- Alternatively, you may print and mail-in VA Form 21-526EZ, Application for Disability Compensation and Related Compensation Benefits, or call VA at 1-800-827-1000 to have the form mailed to you.

Service members may be able to receive disability compensation benefits sooner if you apply before your discharge from service through the Benefits Delivery at Discharge (BDD) or Quick Start pre-discharge programs.

Dependency and Indemnity Compensation (DIC) VA Form 21P-534EZ, Application for DIC, Death Pension, and/or Accrued Benefits and mail it to your nearest VA regional office.

Special Monthly Compensation VA will automatically award special monthly compensation if your disability qualifies. To apply for SMC, if you are housebound or required the aid and attendance of someone to perform daily living functions complete VA Form 21-2680 and mail it to your nearest VA regional office.

How to File an Appeal

In 2019, elements of the Veterans Appeals Improvement and Modernization Act of 2017 (Public Law 115-55) went into effect. This modernizes the current claims and appeals process and includes three review options for disagreements with decisions. It requires improved notification of VA decisions, provides earlier claim resolution, and ensures you receive the earliest effective date possible.

Supplemental Claim

If you are adding new and relevant evidence, you can choose to file a Supplemental Claim. A reviewer looks at the evidence and determines whether it changes the decision. You can file a supplemental claim anytime if you have new evidence. The recommendation is that you file within one year from the date of your decision letter. To file a supplemental claim, you will use VA Form 20-0995: Supplemental Claim.

Higher-Level Review

If you request a higher-level review, you're asking for someone to review the same evidence. A senior reviewer will look at your case and determine if the decision can be changed. You can't submit any evidence, but either you or your representative can speak with the reviewer on the phone and tell them why you think the decision should be changed.

To follow this option, you would use VA Form 20-0996: Higher-Level Review. There is a deadline of one year from the date on your decision letter to request a higher-level review.

Please note, the below steps are only applicable for VA decisions received before February 19, 2019.

- After the Veterans Benefits Administration decides on your claim, you can appeal some or all of the decision if you don't agree with it. You can have a representative help you with your appeal. This person could be a lawyer, claims agent, or Veterans Service Officer.
- The first step in the process requires filing a Notice of Disagreement (NOD). When you file a NOD, you begin the appeals process. This needs to be filed within one year of the date on the letter notifying you of the claim decision. The NOD is VA Form 21-0958.
- You can fill out the NOD and mail it to the address on the VA claim decision notice you receive. You can also bring it to your local regional office.
- An accredited representative can help you file a NOD.
- After the VA receives your NOD, it's reviewed by a Decision Review Officer. If they don't determine there's enough evidence to grant your appeal, they send you findings in what's called a Statement of the Case. At that point, you can decide whether to continue your appeal to the Board of Veterans' Appeals.
- When you receive the Statement of the Case in the mail, you also get VA Form 9. VA Form 9 needs to be returned to the Board of Veterans' Appeals within 60 days if you want to continue your appeal.
- You can submit new evidence at any time in the process.
- The case is sent to the Board of Veterans Appeals when the Decision Review Officer finishes the review.
- If you have a serious illness, are in financial distress, or have sufficient cause, you can apply for your appeal Advanced on Docket. If you're older

than 75, your appeal automatically receives this status.

- You have the option to request a hearing with a Veterans Law Judge, but the judge doesn't make a decision at the hearing.
- The board reviews your appeal and provides a decision on each issue. There are three ways it can be decided—allowed, remanded, meaning more evidence is needed or denied.
- If you disagree with the Board's decision, you can appeal to the Court of Appeals for Veterans Claims.

How to Apply for a VA Home Loan Certificate of Eligibility (COE)

The first step to get a VA direct or VA-backed home loan is to apply for a Certificate of Eligibility. This indicates and confirms to the lender that you qualify for the VA home loan benefit.

The information you'll need to apply for your COE is listed below:

- Veteran: You will need a copy of your discharge or separation papers (DD214)
- Servicemember: Servicemembers need a statement of service signed by a commander, adjutant, or personnel officer. It should include your Social Security number, date of birth, the date you entered duty, duration of any lost time, and the name of the command providing the information
- Current or Former Activated National Guard or Reserve Member: You'll need your discharge or separation papers (DD214)
- Discharged member of the National Guard Who Was Never Activated: You'll need your Report of Separation and Record of Service (NGB Form 22) for each period of service OR your Retirement Points Statement (NGB Form 23) and proof of the character of service
- Surviving Spouse of a Veteran Who Died on Active Duty or Who Had a Service-Connected Disability: You'll need the veteran's discharge documents (DD214) if available, AND you'll need to fill out VA form 26-1817 (Request for Determination of Loan Guaranty Eligibility—Unremarried Surviving Spouses), OR if you don't receive DIC benefits, you'll need to fill out VA Form 21P-534EZ and have a copy of your marriage license and the veteran's death certificate.

You can then use the eBenefits service online to apply for your COE. You can also apply through the Web LGY system—ask a lender about this option. If you want to apply by mail, you can complete a Request for Certificate of Eligibility (VA Form 26-1880) and mail it to the address on the form. This option will take the longest.

How to File for Increased Disability Compensation

To apply for increased disability compensation, a veteran can use VA Form 21-526-EZ (Application for Disability Compensation and Related Compensation Benefits).

Veterans can also sign into the VA's website using their DS Logon, My HealtheVet, or their ID.me account. They can then begin the disability application. When the button is clicked to begin the process online, it is declaring intent to file. This reserves a potential effective date for when you could begin getting benefits. You have a year from the day you submit your intent to file to complete an application.

The following are the steps to file a claim for increased disability compensation:
- When you file for a disability increase, you'll need to provide evidence to support your claim. This evidence can include VA medical and hospital records, private medical and hospital records, or support statements.
- The VA advises that you check to see if you're already receiving the maximum disability rating for your claimed condition before filing for an increase.
- After applying, you receive a confirmation message, which should be printed for your records.
- The VA then processes the applications in the order they're received.
- Once it's received, you receive a notice in the mail with the decision.

Applying for VA Survivor Benefits

To begin, learn more about the different survivor benefits and services that may be available. Collect the necessary paperwork including:
- Veteran's discharge paperwork—DD214 or other separation documents
- Veteran's death certificate
- Proof of your relationship to the veteran (marriage or birth certificate)

Apply by submitting all required documents, including the applicable VA Form and the veteran's death certificate to the required servicing location. You can mail it to the VA office that serves your state.

You can also work with an accredited Veterans Service Organization or directly to your VA Regional Office for assistance.

For Life Insurance Claims, call 800-669-8477.

Surviving family members can learn whether they are eligible for survivor benefits by contacting the Office of Survivors' Assistance at 202-461-1077 or contacting the VBA directly at 800-827-1000.

Benefits may include:

- Internment in a National Cemetery
- Memorialization and Legacy Programs
- Financial Burial Benefits—VA Form 21P-530
- Dependency and Indemnity Compensation (VA Form 21P-534EZ)
- Parents' Dependency and Indemnity Compensation (VA Form 21P-535)
- Survivors' Pension (VA Form 21P-534EZ)
- Dependent's Educational Assistance Program (VA Form 22-5490_
- Fry Education Scholarship
- VA Home Loan Benefits
- Civilian Health and Medical Program of the Department of Veterans Affairs (CHAMPVA)

Types of Veteran ID Cards

There are different types of veteran ID cards you can use to show you're a veteran. The following are those cards and instructions on getting them.

Department of Defense ID Card

A Department of Defense ID Card is used to show your military status and to get access to services at military bases. You can also use the card to get veteran discounts. If you have a DoD ID Card, you don't need another type of photo ID to prove you're a veteran.

You'll need to fill out an Application for Identification Card/DEERS Enrollment (DD Form 1172-2). Then, turn your completed application into a Real-Time Automated Personnel Identification System (RAPIDS) office for processing.

Veteran Health Identification Card

When you're enrolled in VA health care, you can get a Veteran Health Identification Card (VHIC) that you use to check into your appointments at VA medical centers. You can also use a VHIC to get veterans' discounts at restaurants, stores and other businesses. If you have a VHIC, you don't need to request another type of photo ID card to prove you're a veteran. To get this card, you need to be enrolled in VA health care.

Veteran ID Card

A Veteran ID Card (VIC) is a form of photo ID you can use to get military discounts, so you don't have to bring your military discharge papers with you wherever you go.

To be eligible, you must have served on active duty in the Reserves or the National Guard, including the Coast Guard. You must have also received an honorable discharge or a general discharge. If you received other-than-honorable, bad conduct or dishonorable character of discharge, you aren't eligible for a Veteran ID Card.

You can apply for the card online using your DS Logon, My HealtheVet, or Id.me account.

Veteran's Designation on a State-Issued Driver's License or ID

Currently, all 50 states and Puerto Rico offer a veteran designation printed on state-issued driver's licenses or IDs. Most states will ask you to provide a copy of your discharge papers, such as your DD214, to get this designation. Some states may also require other documents. You should talk to your local DMV about what you need to apply for a veteran's designation in your state.

Filing a Pre-Discharge Claim

If you have an illness or injury you believe was caused or made worse by active-duty service, you can file a claim for disability benefits 180 to 90 days before leaving the military. This may help speed up the claims decision process so that you can get benefits sooner.

You must be a service member on full-time active duty, have a known separation date, and that date must be in the next 180 to 90 days.

If you have 180 to 90 days left, you'll apply through the Benefits Delivery at Discharge (BDD) program. To do so, you'll need to submit your service treatment records along with your application. You'll need to be available for 45 days from the date you apply for a VA medical exam and finish all phases of the VA/DoD medical separation examination process before your military release.

2020 UPDATES

Following is a brief summary of some of the important legislative changes and VA policy changes affecting veterans' benefits during 2020.

VA Patient Statement Portal Now Available Online

The U.S. Department of Veterans Affairs (VA) announced on December 18 that veterans now have digital access to patient statements through AccessVA using their secure information for DS Logon, ID.me or MyHealtheVet Premium.

Veterans receiving VA care for non-service-connected conditions can view, download, and print their patient statements using the Veteran Patient Statement selection on the AccessVA homepage.

"VA is committed to leveraging technology to help veterans access their patient information quickly and conveniently," said VA Secretary Robert Wilkie. "We believe these advancements will help veterans manage their healthcare in more efficient ways."

Patient statements are available on AccessVA for up to six months and include a summary of services veterans receive at any VA medical facility. VA will continue to mail veterans paper statements.

VA Announces New Direct Deposit Options

The U.S. Department of Veterans Affairs (VA), in partnership with the Association of Military Banks of America (AMBA), launched the Veterans Benefits Banking Program (VBBP), available as of December 20, 2019.

The program provides veterans and their beneficiaries the chance to safely, reliably, and inexpensively receive and manage their VA monetary benefits through participating banks' financial services.

"VBBP offers another way to simplify banking choices to help eligible veterans select the right bank for themselves and their families," said VA Secretary Robert Wilkie. "The VA and AMBA are proud to provide this opportunity to connect veterans with banks that understand their needs."

According to the VA, its collaboration with AMBA will leverage its consortium of military-friendly financial institutions that cater to service members. AMBA is the only trade association representing banking institutions specializing in providing services for military personnel, veterans, and their families worldwide. VBBP leverages participating AMBA institutions and banks operating within the gates of installations of all branches of service and National Guard and Reserve components.

"AMBA and its member banks welcome the opportunity to provide our nation's veterans additional financial services options to help them achieve greater financial independence, resiliency, and literacy," said AMBA president and Air Force veteran Steve Lepper. "We hope that as veterans recognize the benefits of working with the banks to achieve financial stability, more veterans, banks, and credit unions will join this effort."

The currently available banking options include direct deposit into an existing bank account, electronic funds transfer into a Direct Express pre-paid debit card and mailing of a paper check for pre-approved beneficiaries. VBBP introduces new financial resources to veterans and their beneficiaries.

The program is an effort to address the problems some veterans experience using these payment methods. VBBP offers these VA beneficiaries – including many who have been unable to open bank accounts in the past – the opportunity to deposit their benefit funds directly into existing or new bank accounts offered by participating AMBA member banks.

Neither VA nor AMBA is endorsing any particular bank or requiring veterans and other beneficiaries to use them. It does not require veterans satisfied with their current financial situation to change how they receive their VA monetary benefits.

All veterans and other beneficiaries – who currently receive more than $118 billion in financial benefits through VA – are eligible to access this program. There are approximately 250,000 veterans and beneficiaries who receive their VA benefits through a pre-paid debit card or paper check who may not have a bank account. VA's Veterans Banking Benefits and AMBA's Veterans Benefits Banking Program websites have details for identifying participating banks.

To have your federal benefits electronically transferred to a veteran's designated financial institution (e.g., bank), VA beneficiaries interested in changing direct deposit options can also call 1-800-827-1000 with their relevant banking information.

VA Announces Change to Urgent Care Community Network

The U.S. Department of Veterans Affairs (VA) is transitioning its urgent care network manager, effective March 18, from TriWest Healthcare Alliance to Optum Public Sector Solutions, Inc. (Optum), which is part of UnitedHealth Group, Inc., in Community Care Network Region 1.

The change will result in new urgent care providers being added to VA's contracted network, while others will be removed.

These changes in veterans' urgent care are part of the VA Maintaining Internal Systems and Strengthening Outside Networks Act of 2018 or MISSION Act. Veterans have the option for urgent care treatment of minor injuries and illnesses such as colds, sore throats, and minor skin infections at in-network non-VA urgent care providers. Additionally, veterans can receive same-day urgent care treatment at VA medical centers.

"VA is working to ensure veterans in Region 1 understand how this change will affect them," said VA Secretary Robert L. Wilkie.

"The goal is to provide veterans a seamless transition when seeking urgent care in their communities."

Not all urgent care providers currently in the Region 1 network will be authorized to provide care after March 18. Conversely, new providers who are not currently authorized through the TriWest network will be available through Optum's network beginning March 18. VA can only pay for urgent care if the provider is part of VA's contracted network. If veterans go to an out-of-network urgent care provider, they will be required to pay the full cost of care.

The change in network management will also affect pharmacies. Veterans who require urgent care prescriptions of 14 days or less can find an authorized in-network provider or contact their local VA medical facility to identify a VA network pharmacy to avoid paying out-of-pocket costs.

Community providers within Region 1 who want to provide urgent care services to Veterans after March 18 must establish a contract with Optum.

The change will impact veterans in the following locations: Connecticut, Delaware,

Maine, Maryland, Massachusetts, New Hampshire, New Jersey, New York, North Carolina, Pennsylvania, Rhode Island, Vermont, Virginia, Washington, D.C., and West Virginia. Veterans in these states who need urgent care should use VA's facility locator or contact their local VA medical facility for help identifying in-network urgent care providers.

VA Publishes Proposed Caregiver Regulations

The U.S. Department of Veterans Affairs (VA) will publish a proposed rule in the Federal Register on March 6 to improve and standardize VA's Program of Comprehensive Assistance for Family Caregivers (PCAFC) and ensure the program regulations reflect changes required by the VA MISSION Act of 2018.

A component of the Caregiver Support Program, the PCAFC was established in 2011 to provide additional benefits, including a monthly stipend for qualifying family caregivers of eligible veterans who were seriously injured in the line of duty on or after September 11, 2001.

In the proposed rule, VA seeks to standardize eligibility by expanding the definition of serious injury to include any service-connected disability — regardless of whether it resulted from an injury, illness, or disease — defining what it means to need personal care services, and ensuring that the eligibility criteria capture the personal care service needs of veterans and servicemembers with cognitive or neurological impairment or mental health conditions, among other things.

Additionally, VA proposes changes to the stipend payment methodology, definitions for financial planning and legal services, and procedures for revocation and discharge to include advance notice requirements aimed at improving communication between VA and PFAFC participants.
"This proposed regulation would improve the assistance we provide to help ensure our most vulnerable veterans can stay in their homes with their loved ones for as long as possible," said VA Secretary Robert Wilkie.

The regulations are part of a broad effort to strengthen PCAFC in advance of a planned expansion under the MISSION Act, which expanded eligibility for PCAFC to eligible veterans from all eras.

VA Introduces Simplified Travel Reimbursement System

The U.S. Department of Veterans Affairs (VA) announced the rollout of a way for veterans and eligible beneficiaries to submit and track transportation reimbursement claims using VA's secure web-based portal, Access VA.

The Beneficiary Travel Self-Service System (BTSSS), which is accessible 24/7, 365 days a year, will simplify how eligible veterans and beneficiaries claim mileage reimbursement for travel to and from both VA health care or VA authorized non-VA health care service locations.

"VA is working diligently to find new ways to innovate and simplify how we serve Veterans and their beneficiaries," said VA Secretary Robert Wilkie. "Streamlining the Beneficiary Travel Self-Service System will help our Veterans get their travel reimbursements more securely and efficiently."

BTSSS enables veterans and caregivers to submit claims for reimbursement of costs from a personally owned vehicle, common carrier, meals and/or lodging, and other travel-related expenses such as tolls, parking and luggage.

The national implementation across Veterans Integrated Service Networks (VISN) will run in phases through November. The first phase will start in July and includes VA Salt Lake City Health Care System, Kansas City VA Medical Center, Bay Pines VA Health Care System, Bay Pines, FL, and Minneapolis VA Health Care System. The implementation will continue in phases beginning on the following dates:

September 8: VISN's 1, 9, 12, 17, 21, 22
October 5: VISN's 2, 6, 10, 15, 20
November 2: VISN's 4, 5, 7, 8, 16, 19, 23

VA Digitizes Deck Logs for Blue Water Veterans

As part of a collaboration between VA and National Archives and Records Administration, the deck logs for Blue Water Navy veterans are now completely digitized. NARA has made the newly digitized records available to researchers, veterans advocates, and other groups. The innovation will significantly impact Vietnam Navy Veterans. With ship deck log information now completely online, Blue Water Navy veterans' disability claims may move through VA faster because the ships' locations and exposure to toxins during the Vietnam War can be more easily established.

Support for Veterans in Effective Apprenticeship Act of 2019 (Public Law 116-134)

This bill requires the Department of Labor to revise its registered apprenticeship programs to include additional program requirements for increasing the access of veterans and their survivors or dependents to such programs.

Labor must acquire written assurance that sponsors of apprenticeship programs (1) are aware of the availability of educational assistance for veterans, and eligible individuals for use in such programs, (2) will make a good faith effort to obtain approval for such educational assistance for at least each program location that employs or recruits such recipients, and (3) will not deny a qualified applicant to avoid making a good faith effort to obtain approval for educational assistance.

In addition, Labor must (1) require program sponsors to provide standards that contain provisions to grant advanced standing or credit, (2) provide increased wages commensurate to such standing or credit for veterans or individuals eligible for educational assistance, and (3) provide a copy of the approved apprenticeship program's certificate of registration to the state approving agency.

Fallen Warrior Battlefield Cross Memorial Act (Public Law 116-106)

This bill provides that the Department of Veterans Affairs authorizes a Fallen Soldier Display in any national cemetery. A Fallen Soldier Display is a memorial monument in honor of deceased members of the Armed Forces.

VA Tele-Hearing Modernization Act (Public Law 116-1337)

This bill authorizes appellants in cases before the Board of Veterans' Appeals to appear at a hearing by picture and voice transmission (e.g., Skype) from locations other than Department of Veterans Affairs (VA) facilities. The bill requires the VA to report specified statistics and information related to hearings held by picture and voice transmission.

Ryan Kules and Paul Benne Specially Adaptive Housing Improvement Act of 2019 (Public Law 116-154)

An Act To amend title 38, United States Code, to provide for improvements to the specially adapted housing program and educational assistance programs of the Department of Veterans Affairs, and for other purposes.

Veteran Treatment Court Coordination Act of 2019 (Public Law 116-153)

This bill directs the Department of Justice to establish a Veterans Treatment Court

Program to provide grants and technical assistance for state, local, and tribal governments to develop and maintain veteran's treatment courts.

Commander John Scott Hannon Veterans Mental Health Care Improvement Act of 2019 (Public Law 116-171)

This bill makes updates related to the Department of Veterans Affairs (VA) transition assistance, mental health care, care for women veterans, and telehealth care.
COVID-19 Vaccines
The FDA has authorized the first two COVID-19 vaccines. The VA has a limited amount of the vaccines to start, but they have worked with the CDC and other federal partners to create a phased plan.

The vaccine is initially being offered to veterans living in long-term care facilities and VA health care personnel.

After those two groups, the VA will open up vaccine availability to more veterans at risk of severe illness from COVID-19. If you're eligible to get a vaccine, your VA health care team will contact you. You don't need to reserve a vaccine or come to a VA facility to request or receive a vaccine until you're contacted. The VA staff will only provide vaccines to veterans currently eligible based on VA and CDC risk criteria.

When more vaccines become available, the VA says they plan to offer a free COVID-19 vaccine to all veterans receiving VA health care who want one.

VA Launches Single Access Point to All VA Contact Centers

The U.S. Department of Veterans Affairs (VA) announced the formal launch of 1-800-MyVA411 (1-800-698-2411), a single access point to all VA contact centers. The number is available 24 hours-a-day, 365 days-a-year to serve veterans, their families, caregivers and survivors. Responding to veteran feedback on the challenges of knowing the right number for VA assistance, 1-800-MyVA411, serves all members of the veteran community seeking information or help. Veterans and their families can still reach the Veterans Crisis Line directly at 1-800-273-8255 and pressing 1, by Chat or by texting 838255. The White House VA Hotline is also still available at 1-855-948-2311 for veterans and their families to share compliments and concerns.

CHAPTER 2

BENEFITS FOR ELDERLY VETERANS

According to data from the U.S. Department of Veterans Affairs, around 34 percent of the country's veterans are age 70 and above. These veterans served in conflicts worldwide, including World War II, the Korean War, the Vietnam War, and even in the Persian Gulf War. As veterans age, the Department of Veterans Affairs (VA) will provide benefits and services that address a variety of issues including the changing health risks they face and financial challenges through VA benefits and health services.

Blue Water Navy Act of 2019

On January 1, 2020, the Blue Water Navy Act of 2019 went into effect. The Act was signed into law on June 25, 2019 and extends the presumption of herbicide exposure such as Agent Orange to Blue Water Navy veterans who served as far as 12 nautical miles from the shore of Vietnam and have since developed one of 14 conditions related to exposure. These 14 conditions believed to be diseases related to Agent Orange include:

> **Key Takeaways**
> Elderly veterans may be eligible for a variety of benefits including disability compensation, pension, education and training, home loans, insurance and burial.
>
> Geriatrics is health care for elderly veterans with complex needs.
>
> If you are eligible for or receiving a VA pension benefit, you may be eligible for Aid and Attendance or Housebound, both of which are increased monthly pension amounts paid if you meet certain criteria.

- Chronic B-cell leukemia
- Hodgkin's disease
- Multiple myelomas
- Non-Hodgkin lymphoma
- Prostate cancer
- Respiratory cancer, including lung cancer
- Soft tissue sarcomas other than osteosarcoma, chondrosarcoma, Kaposi's sarcoma, or mesothelioma
- AL amyloidosis
- Chloracne
- Diabetes mellitus type 2
- Ischemic heart disease
- Parkinson's disease
- Peripheral neuropathy
- Porphyria cutanea tarda
- Peripheral

Veterans may be eligible for disability compensation and other benefits. Additionally, if you're a veteran who served in the Korean Demilitarized Zone (DMZ) between September 1, 1967, and August 31, 1971, you may qualify for compensation and benefits for yourself and your family members.

You can file an initial claim that hasn't been previously decided by VA by submitting form 21-526EZ, Application for Disability Compensation and Related Compensation Benefits.

VA will be using the new law to automatically review claims currently with the VA review process or under appeal. However, if you had an herbicide exposure claim with one or more presumptive conditions denied in the past, you are urged to file a new claim.

When you begin the claims process, be sure to provide or identify any new and relevant information regarding your claim, such as the dates the vessel you were serving on traveled through the offshore waters of the Republic of Vietnam or updated medical information.

Submit a VA Form 20-0995, Decision Review Request: Supplemental Claim.

If you are deemed eligible, you may receive a monthly disability compensation payment and free healthcare related to your disability. The amount of compensation you may receive is determined by your diagnosed condition and level of disability.

Another important component of the Blue Water Navy Act includes changes to the VA Home Loan program. VA now allows the no-down-payment option on guaranteed home loans, regardless of the mortgage amount for ALL Veterans. In addition, there is a reduction in the funding fee required for Reservists and National Guard borrowers and other changes.

Veterans over the age of 85 who have life-threatening illnesses will have priority in claims processing.

Thailand Military Bases and Agent Orange Exposure

Vietnam-era Veterans whose service involved duty on or near the perimeters of military bases in Thailand anytime between February 28, 1961 and May 7, 1975 may have been exposed to herbicides and may qualify for VA benefits.

The following veterans may have been exposed to herbicides:
- U.S. Air Force veterans who served on Royal Thai Air Force (RTAF) bases at U-Tapao, Ubon, Nakhon Phanom, Udorn, Takhli, Korat, and Don Muang, near the air base perimeters anytime between February 28, 1961 and May 7, 1975.
- U.S. Army veterans who provided perimeter security on RTAF bases in Thailand anytime between February 28, 1961, and May 7, 1975.
- U.S. Army veterans who were stationed on some small Army installations in Thailand anytime between February 28, 1961, and May 7, 1975. However, the Army veteran must have been a member of a military (MP) unit or assigned an MP military occupational specialty whose duty placed him/her at or near the base perimeter.

To receive benefits for diseases associated with herbicide exposure, these veterans must show on a factual basis that they were exposed to herbicides during their service as shown by evidence of daily work duties, performance evaluation reports, or other credible evidence.

Parkinson's Disease

Veterans with suspected movement disorders are typically referred to a PADRECC or a Consortium Center by a consult from their VA primary care provider or general neurologist.

Veterans diagnosed with Parkinson's disease who served in-country or on the inland waterways of Vietnam between January 9, 1962, and May 7, 1975 are presumed exposed to Agent Orange or other herbicides and are eligible for presumptive service-connection.

VA Benefits

There are a wide variety of benefits available to all military veterans, including benefits for elderly veterans. Some of these benefits include disability compensation, pension,

25

education and training, health care, home loans, insurance, vocational rehabilitation, and burial.

Aid & Attendance

Aid and Attendance (A&A) is a monthly pension that's paid if veterans meet certain conditions listed below. This VA program is designed to provide an additional amount of money for elderly veterans eligible for or are receiving a VA Pension benefit. Aid & Attendance is not a separate benefit but is instead provides additional monthly income over and above the Basic Monthly Pension. To be eligible for this, you must also meet the requirements for Basic Pension.

Eligibility conditions include:
- The veteran is required to have help performing daily functions including bathing, eating, or dressing
- The veteran is bedridden
- The veteran is a patient in a nursing home
- The veteran has eyesight limited to a corrected 5/200 visual acuity or less in both eyes, or concentric contraction of the visual field to 5 degrees or less

Housebound

Housebound is an increased monthly pension amount paid if a veteran is substantially confined to their immediate premises because of a permanent disability. This is for veterans with a disability rating of 100%, preventing them from leaving their home.

How to Apply for Aid & Attendance and Housebound

A veteran may apply for Aid and Attendance or Housebound benefits by writing to the Pension Management Center (PMC) that serves their state. Veterans can also visit their local, regional benefits offices to file a request.

Copies of included evidence should include, if possible, a report from an attending physician validating the need for Aid and Attendance or Housebound type care. The report should include sufficient detail to determine whether a disease or injury is producing physical or mental impairment, loss of coordination, or conditions affecting the ability to dress and undress, feed oneself, attend to sanitary needs, and to keep oneself ordinarily clean and presentable.

Regardless of whether the claim is for Aid and Attendance or Housebound, the report should indicate how well the applicant gets around, where the applicant goes and what the applicant is able to do during a typical day. It's also important to determine whether the claimant is confined to the home or immediate premises.

VA Health Care for Elderly Veterans

Geriatrics is health care for elderly Veterans with complex needs. Extended care – also known as long term care – is a program for Veterans of all ages who need the daily support and assistance of another individual. Elderly Veterans can receive geriatric and long-term care programs at home, at VA medical centers, or in the community.

Geriatrics and Extended Care Services

Geriatrics and Extended Care Services (GEC) is committed to optimizing the health and well-being of Veterans with multiple chronic conditions, life-limiting illness, frailty, or disability associated with chronic disease, aging or injury. Below are some of the main options for care in these categories.

Adult Day Care

Adult Day Health Care is a veteran's program that can include daytime care, social activities, peer support, companionship, and recreation. It's designed for veterans who need skilled services, case management and help with daily living activities. Health services including care from nurses, therapists, social workers, and others may be available.

Adult Day Care can provide respite care for a family caregiver and help veterans and their caregivers gain skills to manage the veteran's care at home.
The program may be provided at VA medical centers, State Veterans Homes, or community organizations.

Home-Based Health Care

Home Based Primary Care is health care services provided to veterans in their home, with supervision from a VA physician who manages a health care team delivering services. Home Based Primary Care is for Veterans who have complex health care needs for whom routine clinic-based care isn't effective.

The program is for veterans who need skills services, case management and help with activities of daily living. The program is also for veterans who are isolated or who have a caregiver experiencing burden.

Hospice Care

Hospice Care is comfort care provided to you and your family if you have a terminal condition, with less than six months to live, and are no longer seeking treatment other than palliative care. Hospice Care can be provided at home, in an outpatient clinic, or an inpatient setting.

Hospice is a benefit that the VA offers to qualified veterans in the final phase of their lives, typically six months or less. This multi-disciplinary team approach helps Veterans live fully until they die. The VA also works very closely with community and home hospice agencies to provide care in the home.

Other geriatric care options include homemaker and home health aide care, palliative care, respite care, skilled home health care, and tele-healthcare.

Residential Settings

Another option for elderly veterans in terms of long-term care is residential settings.

These can include community residential care, medical foster homes, adult family homes and assisted living.

There are also nursing homes, including community living centers and community nursing homes, and State Veterans Homes.

State Veterans Homes are facilities providing nursing homes, domiciliary or adult day care. They're owned, operated and managed by state governments. To participate in the State Veterans Home program, the VA must formally recognize and certify a facility as a State Veterans Home. The VA then surveys all facilities each year to make sure they meet VA standards.

Eligibility for State Veterans Homes is based on clinical need and setting availability, and each individual state establishes eligibility and admissions criteria for the homes. Some State Veterans Homes may admit non-Veteran spouses and gold star parents, while others may admit only veterans.

Paying for Long-Term Care

Home and Community-Based Services are part of the VA Medical Benefits Package. All enrolled veterans are eligible for these services. However, to get the service, you must have a clinical need for it, and the service must be available in your location.

VA Standard Benefits Package includes:

- Geriatric Evaluation to assess your care needs and to create a care plan
- Adult Day Health Care
- Respite Care
- Skilled Home Health Care

Some Home and Community Based Services may be prioritized based on your level of VA service-connected disability. Nursing Home and Residential Settings have different eligibility requirements for each setting. The VA does not pay for room and board in residential settings such as Assisted Living or Adult Family Homes. However, you may receive some Home and Community Based Services while living in a residential setting.

The VA will provide Community Living Center (VA Nursing Home) or community nursing home care IF you meet certain eligibility criteria involving your service-connected status, level of disability, and income.

Service-Connected Disability

A "service-connected disability" is a disability that is related to your active military service. Your disability is assigned a rating (0% to 100%) based on how severely it impacts your daily life. The greater your disability, the higher your rating.

VA Disability Compensation

VA Disability Compensation is a monthly tax-free payment to Veterans who have a service-connected disability. The higher your rating, the higher your monthly payments will be.

However, having a disability caused by your active military service does NOT automatically start disability compensation payments. You need to APPLY for those benefits. It is important to do this because your service-connected disability status affects how much you pay for VA health care services, what programs you are eligible for, and your priority in receiving certain services

How Do I Apply for VA Disability Compensation?

There are several ways to apply for your service-connected disability status. You can:

- Complete and mail VA Form 21-526EZ to your Veterans Benefits Administration (VBA) regional office. To find your VBA regional office, visit the facility locator site, or
- Complete the application online using an eBenefits account, or
- Work with a representative, such as a Veterans Service Officer. You can search for a representative here or visit your local VBA office for assistance.

Your disability needs to be reviewed by staff at VBA and assigned a rating before you can receive payments.

Other Available Monthly Compensation

If you receive VA compensation for a service-connected disability, you may be eligible to receive additional monthly monetary benefits if you ALSO:

- Require significant help with your personal care needs by another person because of your disability, or
- Are bedridden because of your disabilities

Veterans Pension

Veterans Pension is a sometimes-tax-free monetary benefit paid to low-income wartime Veterans who are ALSO:

- 65 or older, or
- Totally and permanently disabled, or
- Living in a nursing home receiving skilled nursing care, or
- Receiving Social Security Disability Insurance, or
- Receiving Supplemental Security Income Low-income guidelines are set by Congress. Additional income is allowed if you have dependents.

How much does it pay?

Your payments will raise your income to the Maximum Annual Pension Rate and not exceed it. Pension benefits are paid monthly.

How do I apply?

Complete and mail VA Form 21P-527EZ to your Veterans Benefits Administration (VBA) regional office.

To find your VBA regional office:

- Visit the facility locator site, or
- Complete the application online using an eBenefits account, or
- Work with an accredited representative or agent, such as a Veterans Service Officer. You can search for representatives here or visit your local VBA office for assistance.

World War II Veterans

World War II (WWII) was the most widespread war in history, with more than 100 million people serving in military units. About 16 million Americans served during WWII, and many veterans are now receiving VA benefits including Pension and Health Care. WWII Veterans who were a part of the Occupation Forces assigned to Hiroshima and Nagasaki, Japan soon after the detonation of Atomic-Bombs over those respective cities, and those American prisoners of war (POWs) who were housed close to those cities are sometimes called "Atomic Veterans.

VA Benefits

World War II Veterans may be eligible for a wide variety of benefits available to all U.S. military Veterans. VA benefits include disability compensation, pension, education and training, health care, home loans, insurance, vocational rehabilitation and employment, and burial. The following sections provide information tailored to the experiences of World War II Veterans to help you better understand specific VA benefits for which you may qualify.

Benefits for World War II Veterans Exposed to Ionizing Radiation

World War II-era Veterans might qualify for health care and compensation benefits if exposed to ionizing radiation during military service. Health care services include an Ionizing Radiation Registry health exam and clinical treatment at VA's War Related Illness and Injury Study Centers. You may also be entitled to disability compensation benefits if you have certain cancers due to exposure to ionizing radiation during military service.

Benefits for World War II Veterans Who Participated in Radiation-Risk Activities

World War II-era veterans may qualify for health care and compensation benefits if you participated in certain radiation-risk activities, such as nuclear weapons testing, during military service. These Veterans may be informally referred to as "Atomic Veterans." Health care services include an Ionizing Radiation Registry health exam and clinical treatment at VA's War Related Illness and Injury Study Centers. You may also be entitled to disability compensation benefits if you have certain cancers as a result of your participation in a radiation-risk activity during military service

Benefits for Survivors of Veterans with Radiation Exposure

Surviving spouses, dependent children, and dependent parents of Veterans who died due to diseases related to radiation exposure during military service may be eligible for survivors' benefits.

Korean War Veterans

Approximately 5.7 million Veterans served in the Korean War. Korean War Veterans are more prone to suffer from disabilities related to cold injures due to exposure to severe cold climates. Cold weather accounted for 16% of Army non-battle injuries and over 5,000 U.S. casualties of cold injury required evacuation from Korea during the winter of 1950-1951. In many instances, servicemembers could not seek or were unable to obtain medical care for cold injuries because of battlefield conditions.

VA Benefits

Korean War veterans may be eligible for a range of benefits available to all U.S. military veterans, including disability compensation, pension, education and training, health care, home loans, insurance, vocational rehabilitation and employment and burial.

Benefits for Veterans Who Experience Cold Injuries

Veterans who experienced cold injuries may have medical conditions resulting from a cold-related disease or injury.

Examples of cold-related medical conditions include:

- Skin cancer in frostbite scars;
- Arthritis;
- Fallen arches;
- Stiff toes;
- Cold sensitization.

These cold-related problems may worsen as Veterans grow older and develop complicating conditions such as diabetes and peripheral vascular disease, which place them at higher risk for late amputations.

Benefits for Korean War Veterans Exposed to Ionizing Radiation

Korean War-era veterans may qualify for health care and compensation benefits if exposed to ionizing radiation during military service. Health care services include an Ionizing Radiation Registry health exam and clinical treatment at VA's War Related Illness and Injury Study Centers. You may also be entitled to disability compensation benefits if you have certain cancers due to exposure to ionizing radiation during military service. Korean War-era veterans may qualify for health care and compensation benefits if you participated in certain radiation-risk activities, such as nuclear weapons testing, during military service. These Veterans may be informally referred to as "Atomic Veterans."

Health care services include an Ionizing Radiation Registry health exam and clinical treatment at VA's War Related Illness and Injury Study Centers. You may also be entitled to disability compensation benefits if you have certain cancers due to your participation in a radiation-risk activity during military service.

Vietnam Veterans

United States military involvement in the Vietnam War officially began on August 5, 1964; however, the first U.S. casualty in Vietnam occurred on July 8, 1959.

Approximately 2.7 million American men and women served in Vietnam. During the war, over 58,000 U.S. military members lost their lives, and 153,000 were wounded. There were 766 prisoners of war of which 114 died in captivity.

VA Benefits for Vietnam Veterans

Vietnam Veterans may be eligible for a wide variety of benefits available to all U.S. military Veterans. VA benefits include disability compensation, pension, education and training, health care, home loans, insurance, vocational rehabilitation and employment, and burial.

Disability Compensation for Veterans Exposed to Agent Orange

VA presumes that some disabilities diagnosed in certain Veterans were caused by exposure to Agent Orange during military service.

Children of Veterans with Exposure to Agent Orange

Children of Veterans exposed to Agent Orange who have a birth defect including spina bifida, a congenital birth defect of the spine, and certain other birth defects may be entitled to VA benefits. These include monetary benefits, health care, and vocational rehabilitation services.

CHAPTER 3

BENEFITS FOR YOUNGER VETERANS

Younger veterans are often referred to as Gulf War Veterans. More than 650,000 Service members served in Operation Desert Shield and Desert Storm from August 2, 1990, to July 31, 1991. For VA benefits eligibility purposes, the Gulf War period is still in effect. This means that anyone who served on active duty from August 2, 1990, to present is considered a Gulf War Veteran. For example, the Veterans Pension benefit requires service during a wartime period. Therefore, any veteran who served on active military service for any period from August 2, 1990, to the present meets the wartime service requirement.

Solid Start Program

The VA, in collaboration with the Departments of Defense and Homeland Security, introduced VA Solid Start, which will proactively contact all newly separated service members at least three times during their first year of transition from the military. The program is part of Executive Order 13822, which was issued to improve mental health care and access to suicide prevention

> **Key Takeaways**
> Certain illnesses and diseases are "presumed" by VA to be related to your military service in designated areas of Southwest Asia and may entitle you to VA disability compensation benefits. For Gulf War Veterans, these presumptive diseases include:
>
> Medically unexplained illnesses (popularly called "Gulf War Syndrome").
> Certain infectious diseases.
> Amyotrophic lateral sclerosis (ALS) diagnosed in all Veterans who had 90 days or more continuous active military service.

resources available to transitioning uniformed service members in the year following discharge, separation, or retirement.

Concierge for Care

In 2018, the VA announced the launch of the Concierge for Care program. This health care enrollment initiative is intended to help connect former service members shortly after they separate from service.

It was designed as research showed more than a third of veterans aren't aware of VA healthcare benefits. A quarter of veterans don't know how to apply for these benefits.

The Concierge for Care program allows VA staff members to directly contact recently separated service members to answer questions, process their health enrollment applications over the phone, and help schedule their first VA medical appointment if needed. The goal is to make contact with veterans within a month of discharge.

Veterans who served in a theater of combat operations can enroll and receive cost-free health care for medical conditions related to their military service during the five years after discharge.

Transitioning Service Members

As part of the U.S. Department of Veterans Affairs (VA) ongoing efforts to help transitioning service members navigate and understand VA's various benefits, the agency recently updated VA's briefing portion of the Transition Assistance Program (TAP) – an interagency initiative authorized as a voluntary program in 1991 under the National Defense Authorization Act and made mandatory under the VOW to Hire Heroes Act in 2011 to help service members adjust to civilian life.

The new VA briefing is more collaborative and stimulating, helping service members make informed decisions about their health care, employment, housing, and other benefits.

Because no two transitions are the same, the updates deliver elements relevant to service members based on where they are in their career and life. The redesign will encourage whole-health support for service members and their family members, to include relevant information about Veterans Service Organizations (VSOs), and allow time to identify local VSO representatives.

The updates incorporated suggestions made by veterans, VSOs, and post-9/11 veterans' groups, including taking a more holistic view of a service member's new life and the psychosocial aspects of the transition to civilian life.

VA will now work to integrate TAP objectives into the military lifecycle fully, and as an added benefit, will begin implementing a post-transition veteran survey.

VA Benefits

Gulf War veterans may be eligible for a wide variety of benefits available to all U.S. military veterans, including disability compensation, pension, education and training, health care, home loans, insurance, vocational rehabilitation and employment, and burial.

Gulf War Veterans' Illnesses

Certain illnesses and diseases are presumed by the VA to be related to military service in designated areas of Southwest Asia and may entitle the veteran to VA disability compensation benefits. For Gulf War veterans, these presumptive diseases include:

- Medically unexplained illnesses often called "Gulf War Syndrome."
- Certain infectious diseases
- Amyotrophic lateral sclerosis (ALS) diagnosed in all veterans who had 90 days or more continuous active military service

Veterans discharged under conditions other than dishonorable who served in the Southwest Asia theater of military operations, which includes the areas specified by regulation, but not Afghanistan, may be entitled to disability compensation for certain undiagnosed illnesses, certain diagnosable chronic disability patterns, and certain presumptive diseases (as described below) even though these disorders did not become manifest during qualifying service.

Veterans who served in Afghanistan on or after September 19, 2001, may be entitled to disability compensation for certain presumptive diseases.

Eligibility Requirements

Qualifying undiagnosed illnesses or diagnosable chronic disability patterns that appeared either during a qualifying period of active service or prior to December 31, 2021 must meet the following conditions:

- There must be no other cause for your disability or illness than service in the Southwest Asia theater of military operations.
- Your disability existed for six months or more, AND
- If your disability or illness did not appear during active duty in the Southwest Asia theater of military operations, then it must have appeared before December 31, 2021, to the degree that is at least 10-percent disabling (for VA rating purposes).

The disability must be one or more of the following:

- Undiagnosed illnesses. These are illnesses that may include but are not limited to: abnormal weight loss, fatigue, cardiovascular disease, muscle and joint pain, headache, menstrual disorders, neurological and psychological problems, skin conditions, respiratory disorders, and sleep disturbances.
- Diagnosable functional gastrointestinal disorders. Functional gastrointestinal

disorders are a group of conditions characterized by chronic or recurrent symptoms that are unexplained. These disorders may include but are not limited to irritable bowel syndrome, functional dyspepsia, functional vomiting, functional constipation, functional bloating, functional abdominal pain syndrome, and functional dysphagia.

- Diagnosable Chronic Fatigue Syndrome
- Diagnosable Fibromyalgia

Certain presumptive diseases will be considered to have been incurred in or aggravated by service even if there is no evidence of such disease during active service. With three exceptions (see asterisks), one of the following must have become manifest to a degree of 10 percent or more within one year of the date of separation from a qualifying period of active service:

- Brucellosis
- Campylobacter jejuni
- Coxiella burnetii (Q fever)
- Malaria* (if not 10 percent or more within one year of separation, may be 10 percent or more at a time when standard or accepted treatises indicate that the incubation period commenced during a qualifying period of service)
- Mycobacterium tuberculosis* (no time limit)
- Nontyphoid Salmonella
- Shigella
- Visceral leishmaniasis* (no time limit)
- West Nile Virus

Evidence Requirements

- The evidence must show you served in the Southwest Asia theater of military operations, as defined by regulation, or served in Afghanistan on or after September 19, 2001, for benefits associated with certain presumptive diseases.
- Medical evidence of treatment of the claimed disability or illness.
- If there is no medical evidence that you have been previously treated for a disability pattern and the only significant evidence is a lay statement describing the disability pattern, a VA examination may be needed (VA will request an examination).
- For undiagnosed illness claims, the evidence may be medical evidence or nonmedical indications that can be independently observed or verified, such as lost time from work, changes in appearance, changes in physical abilities, and changes in mental or emotional attitudes (**Note:** Independently verified means it must be possible for VA to obtain verification of the nonmedical indicators from an independent source).

Blended Retirement

A new retirement system was introduced in 2017, which is known as the "Blended Retirement System" or BRS. The blending is of two primary sources of retirement income. One of these is the existing annuity provision for people retiring after 20 or more years of service, in addition to the Thrift Savings Plan (TSP), which is a government-operated 401(k) retirement account allowing members to invest their own money in stocks or government securities and also receive a contribution to that account from their employer.

BRS will use the annuity formula currently in place: the average of the servicemember's highest 36 months of basic pay times 2.5% of their years of service - - but the 2.5% is adjusted downward by half of a percentage point, from 2.5 to 2%.

To make up for this reduction, the government will contribute to a member's TSP. After the first 60 days in the service, all members will be enrolled in TSP and receive an automatic government contribution of 1% of basic pay into their account each month. Additionally, the servicemember will be automatically enrolled to contribute 3% of their basic pay to the TSP each month.

After two years of service, the government will match the member's contributions up to an additional 4%.

So, after two years, members can get up to a 5% government contribution on top of what they contribute each month.
Therefore, if a member contributes 5% of their basic pay, the government will match it, making a total contribution to the TSP of 10% of their basic pay.

BRS also includes a mid-career continuation pay at about 12 years of service as a further incentive to continue serving toward the traditional 20 years to qualify for monthly military retired pay.

When you retire (at age 60 for guard/reserve members), you will be given the option to take your full retirement pay, or you can take a lump-sum payment of either 25% or 50% of your gross estimated retired pay and receive a reduced monthly annuity until the age of 67 when your retirement pay goes back up to the full amount.

Current members who have less than 12 total years of service when the new plan was effective in 2018 will be able to switch over to the new system. There will be no back pay, but matching contributions will begin on enrollment.

Active-Duty Eligibility for the New Retirement System

If you joined active duty:
- Before January 1, 2006 - you will remain in your current retirement system

- After December 31, 2005, but before January 1, 2018 - you can choose either your current retirement system or the BRS
- After December 31, 2017 - you will be enrolled in the BRS

The opt-in/election period for the Blended Retirement System begins January 1, 2018, and concludes on December 31, 2018.

Reserve Component Member Eligibility

Reserve Component members with more than 4,320 retirement points will remain under their current retirement system. Reserve Component members with less than 4,320 retirement points as of December 31, 2017, will have the choice of whether to opt into the new Blended Retirement System or remain in the legacy retirement system. New accessions after January 1, 2018, will automatically be enrolled in the new Blended Retirement System. The opt-in/election period for the Blended Retirement System begins January 1, 2018 and concludes on December 31, 2018.

The mid-career continuation pay for reserve component members is 0.5x monthly basic pay (of active duty).

Transition Assistance Program

The Transition Goals, Plans, Success program, known as Transition GPS, was created by the Department of Defense and the Department of Defense and other partnering agencies. The goal is to provide in-depth services to servicemembers as they transition to work, life, and home after the military.

Earned Services

Transition GPS delivers information about the benefits and services servicemembers have earned. Some of the offerings include:

- Pre-Separation Counseling: Before leaving the military, servicemembers can receive individual assessments and one-on-one counseling with military service representatives who specialize in the transition process.
- Enhanced VA benefits briefings: Trained instructors lead training sessions to cover what the VA offers to servicemembers, veterans, family members, and services.
- Education and employment programs are offered to strengthen job skills and jump-start careers.
- VA benefits and services are offered to improve overall quality of life.
- There are other benefits designed to help transitioning service members maintain a stable home environment.

Personalized Plans

The Transition GPS program is designed to make adjusting to post-military life easier, and all transitioning servicemembers are required to participate in the program. This includes Guard and Reserve members demobilizing after 180 days or more of active service.

Services include individual transitioning planning to create a customized roadmap that will outline career goals and steps necessary to achieve them.

Employment workshops are designed to show transitioning service members what civilian employers are looking for in applicants.

There are tailored tracks that include three optional workshops to prepare servicemembers for separation or retirement.

Through two briefings—VA Benefits I and II—learn what you need to know about VA benefits and services in a highly interactive, activity-based class attended by your peers.

Information is provided through these briefings:
VA Benefits I. This is a four-hour briefing providing information on education, health care, compensation, life insurance, and home loans, as well as vocational rehabilitation and employment benefits information and counseling. The program assists you in developing a personal plan of action for using VA benefits.

It's open to 50 attendees per class; spouses and family members are encouraged to attend.

VA Benefits II. This two-hour supplemental briefing with video presentations provides an overview of the eBenefits portal and further information on VA health care benefits and services and the disability compensation process.

Pre-Discharge

The VA recommends disability compensation claims are submitted before separation, retirement, or release from active duty or demobilization. Processing times tend to be significantly shorter for claims submitted pre-discharge as opposed to after discharge. Pre-discharge programs provide servicemembers with the chance to file claims for disability compensation up to 180 days before separation or retirement from active duty or full-time National Guard or Reserve duty.

Benefits Delivery at Discharge (BDD)

Benefits Delivery at Discharge (BDD) lets a service member submit a claim for disability compensation 60 to 180 days before separation, retirement, or release from active duty or demobilization. BDD can help veterans receive VA disability benefits sooner, with the goal of within 60 days after release or discharge.

BDD requires a minimum of 60 days to allow sufficient time to complete the medical examination process (which may involve multiple specialty clinics) before separation from service. If you are closer than 60 days to separation from service, you can submit a QuickStart claim. BDD is available nationwide and open to all Servicemembers on full-time active duty, including members of the National Guard and Reserve. Members of the Coast Guard may also participate.

To file a pre-discharge claim under BDD, do one of the following:

- Submit your application online using eBenefits and follow the instructions about where to submit your service treatment records
- Complete the VA Form 21-526EZ, Application for Disability Compensation and Related Compensation Benefits, and submit it with copies of your service treatment records to the VA location nearest you.
- Call VA toll-free at 1-800-827-1000 to have the claim form mailed to you
- Visit your local VA regional office. For the VA regional office nearest you, call VA toll-free at 1-800-827-1000.

Quick Start Program

Quick Start lets a servicemember submit a claim for disability compensation 1 to 59 days before separation, retirement, or release from active duty or demobilization. Submitting a claim before discharge makes it possible to receive VA disability benefits as soon as possible after separation, retirement or demobilization.

Servicemembers with 1-59 days remaining on active duty or full-time Reserve or National Guard service or servicemembers who don't receive BDD criteria requiring availability for all examinations before discharge may apply through Quick Start.

The program is available nationwide and open to all servicemembers on full-time active duty including members of the National Guard and Reserves.

Integrated Disability Evaluation System

The "Integrated Disability Evaluation System (IDES) Examination" is used to determine a Servicemember's fitness for duty. The Departments of Defense (DoD) and Veterans Affairs (VA) worked together to make disability evaluation seamless, simple, fast, and fair. If the Servicemember is found medically unfit for duty, the IDES gives them a proposed VA disability rating before leaving the service. IDES participants may be entitled to Vocational Rehabilitation and Employment services.

Post-9/11 GI Bill

The Post 9/11 GI-Bill can help pay for education and housing to those who:

- Have been discharged honorably.
- Have at least 90 days of aggregate service on or after September 11, 2001.
- Discharged with a service-connected disability after 30 days.

What Does the Bill Cover?

- Tuition and fees paid directly to the school are based on the maximum in-state tuition rate at a public institution of higher learning. That is the maximum coverage unless Yellow Ribbon comes into play.

- Monthly housing allowance.
- Living expense stipend based on E-5 BAH with dependents based on the zip code of your school.
- Annual books and supplies stipend up to $1,000 paid proportionately based on enrollment.
- Can transfer to eligible dependents.

If you have served on or called to active duty after September 11, 2001:

- **100%** benefit if you have at least 36 months of duty
- **100%** benefit if you have 30 days service and were discharged with a service-connected disability
- **90%** 30 to 36 month of duty
- **80%** 24 to 30 months of duty
- **70%** 18 to 24 months of duty
- **60%** 12 to 18 months of duty
- **50%** 6 to 12 months of duty
- **40%** 90 days to 6 months of duty

Readjustment Counseling Services

The VA operates 300 community-based counseling Vet Centers. Many providers at Vet Centers are Veterans of combat themselves. Vet Centers provide readjustment counseling and outreach services to all Veterans who served in any combat zone. Military sexual trauma counseling and bereavement counseling are also provided. Services are available for family members for military-related issues, and bereavement counseling is offered for parents, spouses, and children of Armed Forces, National Guard, and Reserves personnel who died in the service of their country. Veterans have earned these benefits through their service, and all are provided at no cost to the Veteran or family.

Substance Abuse Programs

Some Veterans who return from combat have problems with the use of alcohol, tobacco, or drugs. This can include use of street drugs as well as using prescription medications in ways they weren't prescribed. Such substance use can harm health, cause mood and behavior problems, hurt social relationships, and cause financial problems. Available treatments address all types of problems related to substance use, from unhealthy use of alcohol to life-threatening addictions.

A patient coming to VA can expect to find the following types of care:

- First-time screening for alcohol or tobacco use in all care locations;
- Short outpatient counseling including a focus on motivation;
- Intensive outpatient treatment;

- Residential (live-in) care;
- Medically managed detoxification (stopping substance use safely) and services to get stable;
- Continuing care and relapse prevention;
- Marriage and family counseling;
- Self-help groups;
- Drug substitution therapies and newer medicines to reduce cravings.

How to Get Help

- Speak with your existing VA healthcare provider;
- Contact the OEF/OIF Coordinator at your local VA Medical Center;
- Contact your local Vet Center;
- Call 1-800-827-1000, VA's general information hotline.

Home Loans

VA helps Servicemembers, Veterans, and eligible surviving spouses become homeowners. As part of our mission to serve you, VA provides a home loan guaranty benefit and other housing-related programs to help you buy, build, repair, retain, or adapt a home for your own personal occupancy.

VA Home Loans are provided by private lenders, such as banks and mortgage companies. VA guarantees a portion of the loan, enabling the lender to provide you with more favorable terms.

Purchase Loans help you purchase a home at a competitive interest rate often without requiring a down payment or private mortgage insurance. Cash-Out Refinance loans allow you to take cash out of your home equity to take care of concerns like paying off debt, funding school, or making home improvements.

Interest Rate Reduction Refinance Loan (IRRRL): also called the Streamline Refinance Loan, can help you obtain a lower interest rate by refinancing your existing VA loan.

Native American Direct Loan (NADL) Program: helps eligible Native American Veterans finance the purchase, construction, or improvement of homes on Federal Trust Land, or reduce the interest rate on a VA loan.

Adapted Housing Grants: help Veterans with a permanent and total service-connected disability purchase or build an adapted home or to modify an existing home to account for their disability.

Other Resources: many states offer resources to Veterans, including property tax reductions to certain Veterans.

VA Caregiver Support—Caring for Seriously Injured Post 9/11 Veterans

The Program of Comprehensive Assistance for Family Caregivers offers enhanced support for Caregivers of eligible veterans seriously injured in the line of duty on or after September 11, 2001.

Enhanced services for eligible participants may include a financial stipend, access to health care insurance, mental health services and counseling, caregiver training, and respite care.

Veterans eligible for this program must:

- Have sustained or aggravated a serious injury — including traumatic brain injury, psychological trauma or other mental disorder — in the line of duty, on or after September 11, 2001; and
- Be in need of personal care services to perform one or more activities of daily living and/or need supervision or protection based on symptoms or residuals of neurological impairment or injury.

Participating veterans may appoint one primary caregiver and up to two secondary caregivers who serve as back-up. The support available to caregivers will depend on their designation—primary or secondary—and the needs of the veteran.

For more information, contact your local Caregiver Support Coordinator. Caregiver Support Coordinators are available at every VA Medical Center to assist veterans and their caregivers with the application process. Additional application assistance is available at 1-877-222 VETS (8387).

See Chapter 12 (Nursing Home and Long-Term Care Benefits) to learn more about caregiver programs.

CHAPTER 4

DISABILITY COMPENSATION FOR SERVICE-CONNECTED DISABILITIES

In grateful recognition of their dedication and sacrifice, the United States, through the Veterans Administration has provided its former servicemen and women with compensation and pension programs designed to assist disabled veterans and their dependents. The disability compensation program provides financial assistance to veterans with service-connected disabilities to compensate them for the loss of, or reduction in earning power resulting from comparable injuries and disease in civil life.

Disability compensation payments vary in amount, depending on the impairment of earning capacity suffered by the veteran. The degree is assessed in multiples of 10, from 10 percent to 100 percent, with special statutory rates for such disabilities as blindness and loss of use of limbs.

The VA shall adopt and apply a schedule of ratings in reductions in earning capacity from specific injuries or combination of

> **Key Takeaways:**
> There was a 1.3% COLA increase in 2020.
>
> VA disability compensation (pay) offers a monthly tax-free payment to Veterans who got sick or injured while serving in the military and to Veterans whose service made an existing condition worse.
>
> You may qualify for VA disability benefits for physical conditions (like a chronic illness or injury) and mental health conditions (like PTSD) that developed before, during, or after service. Find out how to apply for and manage the veterans disability benefits you've earned.

injuries. The rating shall be based, as far as practicable, upon the average impairments of earning capacity resulting from such injuries in civil occupations. The Administrator shall from time to time readjust this schedule or ratings in accordance with experience.

The rates of compensation payments are not automatically adjusted for inflation, and they can be increased only if Congress passes specific enabling legislation.
However, almost without exception, each Congress has acted to grant an increase equal to the consumer price that determines the social security old-age increases. If a veteran is evaluated as having a service-connected disability of 30 percent or more, the veteran is entitled to additional allowances for his or her dependents. In addition, in cases where a veteran has suffered certain severe disabilities, the veteran may be entitled to special monthly compensation (SMC), which can provide compensation payments at a rate much greater than the 100 percent rate.

Severely disabled veterans in need of regular aid and attendance or daily health-care services may be eligible for additional compensation.

HAVEN ACT

The Honoring American Veterans in Extreme Need Act of 2019 went into effect. Also called the HAVEN Act, this law excludes certain benefits paid to veterans or their family members from the definition of Current Monthly Income (CMI) found in the Bankruptcy Code. 11 U.S.C. 101 (10A). The types of compensation excluded from CMI under the Act include but are not limited to:

- Disability and death benefits paid by the Veterans Administration under title 38 of the United States Code
- Monthly special compensation for catastrophic injuries or illnesses paid to servicemembers under 37 U.S.C. § 439
- Any combat-related special compensation paid by the Department of Defense under 10 U.S.C. § 1413a.
- Disability severance pay paid by the Department of Defense under 10 U.S.C. § 1212.
- Any payment by the Department of Defense to a survivor in connection with the death of a member of the uniformed services.
- See 10 U.S.C. §§ 1431-1456.
- Disability-related military retired pay paid by the Department of Defense to a servicemember retired under 10 U.S.C. §§ 1201-1202, 1204-1205, except that such payments are excluded from CMI only to the extent that they exceed the military retired pay that the servicemember would have received if the servicemember had retired without a disability.

It should be noted, however, that certain benefits to current servicemembers are included in the CMI calculation, for example, monthly special compensation from DOD and retirement pay for people on the temporary disability retired list.

Question: How does the Act affect enforcement under section 707(b)(2) of the Bankruptcy Code and the determination of whether the presumption of abuse arises for veterans or their family members filing for chapter 7 relief under the Bankruptcy Code?

Answer: Veterans or their family members who file for bankruptcy relief under chapter 7 should exclude income covered by the Act from the calculation of CMI. The calculation of CMI is the starting point for determining whether a chapter 7 bankruptcy case is presumed abusive under section 707(b)(2).

Question: How does the Act affect chapter 13 cases?

Answer: Veterans and their family members who file for bankruptcy relief under chapter 13 should exclude income covered by the Act from the calculation of CMI, which may affect the determination of projected disposable income available for a chapter 13 plan.

Question: Will the USTP require debtors to produce documentation to support any veterans' benefits that they exclude from the calculation of CMI?

Answer: The USTP will limit its requests for documents related to income excluded from CMI under the HAVEN Act so as not to unduly burden debtors. The USTP does not routinely request from debtors' documents not otherwise required by the Bankruptcy Code or Rules without a specific need for additional information.

Question: How does the Act affect the USTP's enforcement under section 707(b)(3) of the Bankruptcy Code (bad faith and the totality of the circumstances) and the determination of a debtor's actual ability to repay creditors?

Answer: By modifying the definition of "current monthly income," the HAVEN Act does not directly impact section 707(b)(3)'s provisions providing for dismissal of cases based on the debtor's bad faith or under the totality of the circumstances.

Disability Rating Schedule for Infectious Diseases, Immune Disorders and Nutritional Deficiencies

As of August 11, 2019, the VA updated portions of the VA Schedule for Rating Disabilities that evaluate infectious disease, immune disorders, and nutritional deficiencies. The collection of federal regulations used by the Veterans Benefits Administration helps claims processors evaluate the severity of disabilities and assign disability ratings. Claims filed prior to August 11 will be considered under both the old and new rating criteria, whichever is more favorable to a veteran will be applied. Claims filed on or after August 11 will be rated under the new rating schedule.

Since 2017, VA says it has updated schedules for:

- Dental and oral health concerns
- Endocrine system conditions
- Gynecological conditions
- Breast disorders
- Eye diseases
- Skin conditions
- Hematologic and lymphatic system issues

Court Rules Chronic Pain is a VA Disability

A ruling by the U.S. Court of Appeals for Veterans Claims found in April 2018 that pain, without an underlying disability, may be a reason for awarding VA compensation benefits.

The ruling stemmed from a case with Gulf War veteran Melba Saunders. During her time in service, Saunders suffered a knee injury and was treated by military doctors and diagnosed with patellofemoral pain syndrome, which is essentially knee pain.

The VA initially said she had no real disability, and there was no injury qualifying her for compensation. The VA said pain was not in and of itself a disability.

The law (38 U.S.C. § 1110) says that VA shall award compensation benefits "for disability resulting from personal injury suffered...in line of duty."

The court cited the definition of a disability as "an impairment in the enjoyment of life or earning ability." The court said that "pain is a form of functional impairment." So the pain can be considered a disability by itself, without any diagnosed injury.

VA Updates the Disability Rating Schedule Related to Skin Conditions

Effective August 13, 2018, the VA updated portions of the VA Schedule for Rating Disabilities (VASRD or Rating Schedule) that evaluate conditions related to the skin.

The VASRD is the collection of federal regulations used by Veterans Benefits Administration claims processors to evaluate the severity of disabilities and assign disability ratings.

VA is in the process of updating all 15 body systems of the VASRD to reflect modern medicine more accurately and provide clearer rating decisions.

No conditions were removed from the new skin rating schedule. However, several diagnostic codes were restructured or revised. The complete list of updates to the rating schedule for skin conditions is now available online. Claims pending prior to August 13 will be considered under both the old and new rating criteria, and whichever criteria are more favorable to the Veteran will be applied. Claims filed on or after August 13 will be rated under the new rating schedule.

By updating the rating schedule for skin conditions, VA claims processors can make more consistent decisions with greater ease and ensure veterans understand these decisions.

VA Expands Provision of TBI Benefits

The VA has officially put new regulations in place, making it easier for some veterans diagnosed with traumatic brain injury (TBI) to receive additional disability compensation. The VA announced the implementation of a new regulation that impacts some veterans living with TBI who also have Parkinson's disease, certain types of dementia, depression, unprovoked seizures or certain diseases of the hypothalamus and pituitary glands.

Elimination of Income Reporting Requirement

The VA announced the removal of the annual income reporting requirement for most veterans enrolled in the VA healthcare system. Beginning in March 2014, the VA began utilizing income information as reported from the IRS and Social Security Administration.

Same-Sex Married Couples

The Obama administration announced a decision to extend veteran benefits to same-sex married couples as a result of the Supreme Court's decision to strike down the Defense of Marriage Act. Veterans' spouses are now eligible to collect benefits, regardless of sexual orientation.

Veterans with Spinal Cord Injuries

There are 24 VA-operated Spinal Cord Injury Centers (SCI) that provide services for Veterans with spinal cord injuries and disorders (SCI/D). Comprehensive rehabilitation, SCI/D specialty care, medical, surgical, primary, preventive, psychological, respite, and home care are provided at these centers by interdisciplinary teams which include physicians, nurses, therapists (physical, occupational, Kinesio therapists, therapeutic recreation), psychologists, social workers, vocational counselors, dieticians, respiratory therapy, and other specialists as needed.

There are five SCI centers that provide long-term care for Veterans with SCI/D. In VA facilities that do not have SCI centers, there is a designated team that consists of a physician, nurse, and social worker to address primary care needs for Veterans with SCI/D and to make referrals to SCI Centers. These SCI Centers and the teams in facilities that do not have centers comprise VA SCI System of Care. Some of the services provided in this system of care include rehabilitation, prosthetics and durable medical equipment, orthotics, sensory aids, assistive technology, environmental modifications, telehealth, ventilator weaning and care, chronic pain management, mental health treatment, drivers training, peer counseling, substance abuse treatment, vocational counseling, and caregiver training and support.

There is a long-standing memorandum of agreement between VA and the Department of Defense (DoD) to provide specialized care at VA medical facilities for Active Duty Servicemembers who have sustained a spinal cord injury. Ongoing collaboration and education between VA and DoD ensure continuity of care and services.

Wartime Disability Compensation

Eligibility

A veteran may be entitled to VA disability compensation for any medical condition or injury incurred in or aggravated by his or her military service. The veteran must have been discharged or released under conditions other than dishonorable from the period of service in which the injury or disease was incurred or aggravated. No compensation shall be paid if the disability is a result of the person's own willful misconduct or abuse of alcohol or drugs.

There is no time limit for applying for VA disability compensation. However, veterans are encouraged to apply within one year of release from active duty. If a claim is filed within this period, entitlement may be established retroactively to the date of separation from service. If a claim is filed beyond one year of release from active duty, the effective date of eligibility for benefits will be based upon the date of the claim, not the date of separation.

Individual Unemployability

There is a benefit administered by the U.S. Department of Veterans Affairs (VA) that is payable under certain conditions when a veteran has one or more service-connected disabilities rated less than 100% that interfere with his or her ability to secure or retain employment. This benefit is known as Individual Unemployability (I.U.). I.U. must be established on a factual basis. establishes entitlement to compensation at the 100% disability rate even though a veteran's combined disabilities are less than a scheduler 100% rating.

Eligibility Requirements

- You must be a veteran
- You must have at least one service-connected disability rated at least 60% or

- Two or more service-connected disabilities at least one disability ratable at 40 percent or more with a combined rating of 70 percent or more
- You must be unable to maintain substantially gainful employment as a result of service-connected disabilities (marginal employment, such as odd jobs, is not considered substantial gainful employment for VA purposes)

Evidence Requirements

- Evidence of at least one service-connected disability AND
- That the service-connected disability or disabilities are sufficient, without regard to other factors, to prevent performing the mental and/or physical tasks required to get or keep substantially gainful employment AND
- That one disability is ratable at 60% or more OR
- If more than one disability exists one disability is ratable at 40% or more with a combined rating of 70% or more.

Under exceptional circumstances, this benefit may be granted with a lower disability rating than noted above provided the evidence shows the service-connected disability or disabilities present such an exceptional or unusual disability picture, due to such factors as marked interference with employment or frequent periods of hospitalization, that applying the normal disability requirements is impractical.

To apply for I.U. benefits VA Form 21-8940, Application for Increased Compensation Based on Unemployability, must be submitted to the VA with current medical evidence on the extent of the service-connected disabilities.

VA's definition of substantial gainful employment is basically any amount earned above the annual poverty limit for one person set by the U.S. Census Bureau.
Amounts earned below the Census Bureau's annual poverty limit are considered marginal employment and do not affect receipt of I.U. benefits.

Each year after the U.S. Census Bureau sets the new poverty limit, VA publishes a notice in the Federal Register.

VA Pension Benefits

Occasionally, a veteran may be entitled to both VA Compensation benefits and VA Pension benefits. The VA is prohibited from paying both benefits concurrently. In the event a veteran is entitled to both, the VA will typically pay the higher of the monetary amount of the two.

Selected Reserve and National Guard

Since September 11, 2001, numerous members of the Armed Forces Reserves have been called to active duty. Some of these individuals had already filed claims for VA compensation, based on earlier periods of active service. In September 2004, the VA

General Counsel issued a precedent opinion that discussed the effect of a return to active service on a pending disability compensation claim.

In general, a veteran's return to active duty does not affect his or her claim for VA benefits and does not alter either the veteran's right or the VA's duty to develop and adjudicate the claim. If the veteran is temporarily unable to report for a medical examination, or take some other required action because of his or her return to active duty, the VA must defer processing the claim until the veteran can take the required action. The VA cannot deny a claim because a veteran is temporarily unavailable due to a return to active duty.

A veteran is not entitled to receive both active duty pay and VA disability compensation for the same period of time. However, the higher monetary benefit is usually paid. If a veteran with a pending claim dies on active duty before the claim is decided, an eligible survivor may be entitled to any accrued benefits payable.

Fully Developed Claims

The Fully Developed Claims (FDC) program is an optional new initiative that offers Servicemembers, Veterans, and survivors faster decisions from VA on compensation, pension, and survivor benefit claims.

Veterans, Servicemembers, and survivors simply submit all relevant records in their possession, and those records which are easily obtainable, such as private medical records, at the time they make their claim and certify that they have no further evidence to submit. VA can then review and process the claim more quickly.

By filing an FDC, Veterans, Servicemembers and survivors take charge of their claim by providing all the evidence at once. By then certifying that there is no more evidence, VA can issue a decision faster.

File an FDC without risk. Participation will not affect the attention your claim receives from qualified VA rating staff or the benefits to which you're entitled. If VA determines other records exist and are required to decide a claim, VA will remove the claim from the FDC program and process it through the traditional claims process. Once you initiate your FDC, you'll have up to one year to complete it. Should VA approve your claim, you'll be paid back to the day you initiated your claim.

Types of Claims

There are many types of claims for disability compensation. For example, if you're filing a VA claim for the very first time, you have an original claim. A reopened claim means you have new and material evidence, and you want VA to reconsider a claim it once denied. There are also new claims, secondary claims, and special claims.

Who Can File a Claim?

Veterans may file an FDC for disability compensation for the following reasons:

- An injury, disability, or condition believed to have occurred or been aggravated by military service.
- A condition caused or aggravated by an existing service-related condition.
- Servicemembers may use the Benefits Delivery at Discharge (BDD) program at eBenefits.va.gov to submit a Fully Developed Claim before discharge.

The BDD program is available nationwide to all Servicemembers on full-time active duty, including members of the National Guard, Reserve, and Coast Guard.

Servicemembers who do not meet the BDD criteria or have 1-59 days remaining in service should submit a Quick Start claim on eBenefits.va.gov.

What's the Best Way to File An FDC?

The best way to file an FDC is electronically at eBenefits.va.gov. Once you log on to your account, VA recommends you appoint an accredited Veterans Service Officer to help you initiate your claim, gather the required medical records and evidence, and submit your claim.

If you prefer to file your FDC by paper, complete VA Form 21-526EZ, and visit your local regional office. While there, you can appoint an accredited Veterans Service Officer to help you prepare and submit your claim. You can also appoint your accredited Veterans Service Officer online at eBenefits.va.gov.

Military Retired Pay

Historically, veterans were not permitted to receive **full** military retirement pay and VA compensation benefits at the same time. Veterans who were entitled to both had to either select one of the benefits or waive the amount of retirement pay which equaled the amount of VA disability compensation to which he or she was entitled. This issue was commonly known as "concurrent receipt."

Because there was often a tax advantage to receive VA disability compensation, which is tax-free, rather than military retirement pay, most disabled retirees chose to have a $1 reduction in their retired pay for each $1 of VA disability compensation they received. Since this type of rule against "concurrent receipt" does not apply to any other group of federal or state retirees, many individuals and service organizations felt this was unfair discrimination against disabled military retirees.

This has been a very hot topic for the last several years, and Congress and the President have taken several steps toward eliminating the bar to concurrent receipt of full military retired pay and full disability compensation.

Details of CRSC Payments

As a result of the current disability process, a retiree can have both a DOD and a VA disability rating and these ratings will not necessarily be the same percentage. The percentage determined by DOD is used to determine fitness for duty and may result in the medical separation or disability retirement of the service member. The VA rating, on the other hand, was designed to reflect the average loss of earning power.

CRSC is not subject to taxation. Individuals must apply for CRSC.
For detailed information, individuals should contact the following:

Army
DEPARTMENT OF THE ARMY
U.S. Army Physical Disabilities Agency/ Combat-Related Special Compensation (CRSC) 200 Stovall Street
Alexandria, VA 22332-0470
(866) 281-3254

Navy and Marine Corps
Department of Navy Naval Council of Personnel Boards Combat-Related Special Compensation Branch
720 Kennon Street S.E., Suite 309
Washington Navy Yard, DC
20374-5023
(877) 366-2772

Air Force
United States Air Force Personnel Center Disability Division (CRSC)
550 C Street West, Suite 6
Randolph AFB TX 78150-4708
(800) 525-0102

Details of Concurrent Receipt
As veterans, military retirees can apply to the VA for disability compensation. A retiree may (1) apply for VA compensation any time after leaving the service and (2) have his or her degree of disability changed by the VA as the result of a later medical reevaluation, as noted above. Many retirees seek benefits from the VA years after retirement for a condition that may have been incurred during military service, but that does not manifest itself until many years later. Typical examples include hearing loss, some cardiovascular problems, and conditions related to exposure to Agent Orange.

Until 2004, the law required that military retired pay be reduced dollar-for-dollar by the amount of any VA disability compensation received. This procedure was generally referred to as an "offset." If, for example, a military retiree who received $1,500 a month in retired pay and was rated by the VA as 70% disabled (and therefore entitled to approximately $1,000 per month in disability compensation), the offset would operate to pay $500 monthly in retired pay and the $1,000 in disability compensation.

What If a Retiree Is Eligible for Both?
Retirees eligible for both programs will be able to make an election between the two

programs, depending on which one is more advantageous.

Because the CRSC program provides full payment immediately, versus the 10—year phase-in for concurrent receipt, the election can be changed each year. (This recognizes that a retiree who is 100% disabled, but only 60% of that is due to combat-related conditions, may find it advantageous to elect full CRSC payments for a few years until the concurrent receipt payment rises to a level that exceeds the CRSC payment. Because CRSC payments are tax-free, and non-disability retired pay is not, this could also figure into a retiree's election decision.

Detailed Rates of Disability Compensation

Rates Effective December 1,2020

Dependent Status	Disability Rating									
	10%	20%	30%	40%	50%	60%	70%	80%	90%	100%
Veteran Alone	$144.14	$284.93	$441.35	$635.77	$905.04	$1146.39	$1444.71	$1679.35	$1887.18	$3146.42
Veteran & Spouse	$144.14	$284.93	$493.35	$705.77	$92.04	$1251.39	$1566.71	$1819.35	$2044.18	$3321.85
Veteran, Spouse & 1 Child	$144.14	$284.93	$532.35	$756.77	$1056.04	$1328.39	$1656.71	$1922.35	$2160.18	$3450.32
Veteran, No Spouse & 1 Child	$144.14	$284.93	$476.35	$681.77	$963.14	$1216.39	$1526.71	$1772.35	$1992.18	$3263.74
	10%	20%	30%	40%	50%	60%	70%	80%	90%	100%
Veteran & Spouse & No Children and 1 parent	$144.14	$284.93	$535.35	$761.77	$1062.04	$1335.39	$1644.17	$1931.35	$2170.18	$3462.64
Veteran & Spouse & 1 Child & 1 parent	$144.14	$284.93	$574.35	$812.77	$1126.04	$1412.39	$1754.71	$2034.35	$2286.18	$3591.11
Veteran & Spouse & No Child & 2 Parents	$144.14	$284.93	$577.35	$817.77	$1132.04	$1419.39	$1762.71	$2043.45	$2296.18	$3603.43
Veteran & Spouse & 1 Child & 2 Parents	$144.14	$284.93	$616.35	$868.77	$1196.04	$1496.39	$1852.71	$2146.35	$2412.18	$3731.90
Veteran & No Spouse & No Children & 1 Parent	$144.14	$284.93	$483.35	$691.77	$975.04	$1230.39	$1542.71	$1791.35	$2013.18	$3287.21
Veteran & No Spouse & 1 Child & 1 Parent	$144.14	$284.93	$518.35	$737.77	$1033.04	$1300.39	$1624.71	$1884.35	$2118.18	$3404.53
Veteran & No Spouse & No Children & 2 Parents	$144.14	$284.93	$525.35	$747.77	$1045.04	$1314.39	$1640.71	$1903.35	$2139.18	$3428.00
Veteran & No Spouse & 1 Child & 2 Parents	$144.14	$284.93	$560.35	$793.77	$1103.04	$1384.39	$1722.71	$1996.35	$2244.18	$3545.32

Benefits Rates for Service-Connected Disability Compensation

VA compensation and pension benefits cost of living allowance (COLA) is paid based on the Social Security Administration (SSA) COLA. By statute, compensation COLA may not be more than the SSA COLA; and pension COLA is equal to the SSA COLA.

This year SSA increased COLA by 1.3%

Basic Rates of Disability Compensation Effective December 1, 2020		
	Disability Rating	Monthly Benefit
(a)	10 percent	$144.14
(b)	20 percent	$284.93
(c)	30 percent	$441.35
(d)	40 percent	$635.77
(e)	50 percent	$905.04
(f)	60 percent	$1146.39
(g)	70 percent	$1444.71
(h)	80 percent	$1679.35
(i)	90 percent	$1887.18
(j)	100 percent	$3146.42

Additional Amounts Payable for Spouse Requiring Aid & Attendance Rates Effective December 1, 2020								
Disability Rating	30%	40%	50%	60%	70%	80%	90%	100%
Monthly Benefit	$48	$64	$81	$96	$113	$129	$145	$160.89

56

Additional Amount Payable for Each Additional Child Under 18 Rates Effective December 1, 2020								
Disability Rating	30%	40%	50%	60%	70%	80%	90%	100%
Monthly Benefit	$26	$34	$43	$52	$61	$69	$78	$87.17

Additional Amount Payable for Each Additional Child Over Age 18 Attending School Rates Effective December 1, 2020								
Disability Rating	30%	40%	50%	60%	70%	80%	90%	100%
Monthly Benefit	$84	$112	$140	$168	$197	$225	$253	$281.57

Notes: Rates for Children over age 18 attending school are shown separately in the above chart. All other entries in the above charts reflect rates for children under age 18, or helpless.

All references in the preceding charts to parents refer to parents who have been determined to be dependent by the Secretary of Veterans Affairs.

Higher Statutory Awards for Certain Multiple Disabilities

Additional Compensation for Dependents

(38 USC 1115)

TITLE 38, USC 1114 SUBSECTION (K)

If a veteran, as the result of a service-connected disability, has suffered the anatomical loss or loss of use of one or more creative organs, or one foot, or one hand, or both buttocks, or 25 percent or more tissue from a single breast or from both breasts in combination (loss by mastectomy or partial mastectomy or following radiation treatment), or blindness of one eye, having only light perception, or has suffered complete organic aphonia with constant inability to communicate by speech, or deafness of both ears, having absence of air and bone conduction, the rate of compensation shall be $111.74 per month for each such loss or loss of use.

In the event the veteran has suffered one or more of the disabilities previously specified in this subsection, in addition to the requirement for any of the rates specified in subsections (l) through (n), described below, the rate of compensation shall be increased by $111.74 per month for each such loss or loss of use.

TITLE 38, USC 1114 SUBSECTION (L)

If the veteran, as the result of a service-connected disability, has suffered the anatomical loss or loss of use of both feet, or of one hand and one foot, or is blind in both eyes, with 5/200 visual acuity or less, or is permanently bedridden or so helpless as to be in need of regular aid and attendance, the monthly compensation shall be $3915.14

TITLE 38, USC 1114 SUBSECTION (M)

If the veteran, as the result of a service-connected disability, has suffered the anatomical loss or loss of use of both hands, or of both legs at a level, or with complications, preventing natural knee action with prostheses in place, or of one arm and one leg at levels, or with complications, preventing natural elbow and knee action with prostheses in place, or has suffered blindness in both eyes, having only light perception, or has suffered blindness in both eyes, rendering such veteran so helpless as to be in need of regular aid and attendance, the monthly compensation shall be $4,320.76.

TITLE 38, USC 1114 SUBSECTION (N)

If the veteran, as the result of a service-connected disability, has suffered the anatomical loss or loss of use of both arms at levels, or with complications, preventing natural elbow action with prostheses in place has suffered the anatomical loss of both legs so near the hip as to prevent the use of prosthetic appliances, or has suffered the anatomical loss of one arm and one leg so near the shoulder and hip as to prevent the use of prosthetic appliances, or has suffered the anatomical loss of both eyes, or has suffered blindness without light perception in both eyes, the monthly compensation shall be $4,915.17.

TITLE 38, USC 1114 SUBSECTION (O)

If the veteran, as the result of a service-connected disability, has suffered disability under conditions which would entitle such veteran to two or more of the rates provided in one or more subsections (l) through (n) of this section, no condition being considered twice in the determination, or if the veteran has suffered bilateral deafness (and the hearing impairment in either one or both ears is service-connected) rated at 60% or more disabling, and the veteran has also suffered service-connected total blindness with 5/200 visual acuity or less, or if the veteran has suffered service-connected total deafness in one ear or bilateral deafness (and the hearing impairment in either one or both ears is service-connected) rated at 40% or more disabling, and the veteran has also suffered service-connected blindness having only light perception or less, or if the veterans has suffered the anatomical loss of both arms so near the shoulder as to prevent the use of prosthetic appliances, the monthly compensation shall be $5,611.27.

TITLE 38, USC 1114 SUBSECTION (P)

In the event a veteran's service-connected disabilities exceed the requirements for any of the rates previously prescribed in this section, the Secretary of Veterans Affairs may allow the next higher rate or an intermediate rate, but in no event in excess of $5,611.27.

In the event a veteran has suffered service-connected blindness with 5/200 visual acuity or less, and (1) has also suffered bilateral deafness (and the hearing impairment in either one or both ears is service-connected) rated at no less than 30% disabling, the Secretary of Veterans Affairs shall allow the next higher rate, or (2) has also suffered service-connected total deafness in one ear or service-connected anatomical loss or loss of use of one hand or one foot, the Secretary shall allow the next intermediate rate, but in no event in excess of $5,611.27.

In the event a veteran has suffered service-connected blindness, having only light perception or less, and has also suffered bilateral deafness (and the hearing impairment in either one or both ears is service-connected) rated at 10 or 20% disabling, the Secretary shall allow the next intermediate rate, but in no event in excess of $5,611.27.

In the event a veteran has suffered the anatomical loss or loss of use, or a combination of anatomical loss and loss of use, of three extremities, the Secretary shall allow the next higher rate or intermediate rate, but in no event in excess of $5,611.27.

Any intermediate rate under this subsection shall be established at the arithmetic mean, rounded down to the nearest dollar, between the two rates concerned.

TITLE 38, USC 1114 SUBSECTION (R)

If a veteran is entitled to compensation under (o) of this section, at the maximum rate authorized under (p) of this section, or at the intermediate rate authorized between the rates authorized under subsections (n) and (o) of this section and at the rate authorized under subsection (k) of this section, is in need of regular aid and attendance, then, in addition to such compensation:

The veteran shall be paid a monthly aid and attendance allowance at the rate of $7,967.75 or 9,121.96.

If the veteran, in addition to such need for regular aid and attendance, is in need of a higher level of care, such veteran shall be paid a monthly aid and attendance allowance at the rate of $160.89, in lieu of the allowance authorized in the previous paragraph. Need for a higher level of care shall be considered to be need for personal health-care services provided daily in the veteran's home by a person who is licensed to provide such services or who provides such services under the regular supervision of a licensed health-care professional. The existence of the need for such care shall be determined by a physician employed by the VA, or in areas where no such physician is available, by a physician carrying out such function under contract or fee arrangement based on an examination by such physician.

TITLE 38, USC 1114 SUBSECTION (S)

- If a veteran has a service-connected disability rated as total, and:
- Has additional service-connected disability or disabilities independently ratable at 60% or more; or
- By reason of such veteran's service-connected disability or disabilities, is permanently housebound, and then the monthly compensation shall be $3,639.17.

For this subsection, the requirement of "permanently housebound" will be considered to have been met when the veteran is substantially confined to such veteran's house (ward or clinical areas, if institutionalized) or immediate premised due to a service-connected disability or disabilities which it is reasonably certain will remain throughout such veteran's lifetime.

Adjustment to Individual VA Awards

There will be no adjustment of VA awards. Special Compensation paid under 10 USC 1413 is provided under chapter 71, title 10, USC, "Computation of Retired Pay." However, it is NOT RETIRED PAY. It is to be paid from funds appropriated for pay and allowances of the recipient member's branch of service. Eligible retirees in receipt of VA disability compensation may receive this special compensation in addition to their VA disability compensation.

Presumptions

Presumption of Sound Condition

Every veteran will be assumed to have been in sound medical condition when examined, accepted, and enrolled for service, except any defects, infirmities, or disorders noted at the time of the examination, acceptance, and enrollment, or if there is clear and unmistakable evidence showing that the injury or disease did exist before acceptance and enrollment, and the injury or disease was not aggravated by such service.

Presumptions of Service-Connection Relating to Certain Chronic Diseases and Disabilities

In the case of any veteran who served for 90 days or more during a period of war, any of the following shall be considered to have been incurred in, or aggravated by such service, notwithstanding there is no record of evidence of such disease during the period of service:

A chronic disease (detailed below), becoming manifest to a degree of 10% or more within one year from the date of separation from such service.

A tropical disease (detailed below), and the resultant disorders or disease originating because of therapy, administered in connection with such diseases, or as a preventative thereof, becoming manifest to a degree of 10% or more within one year from the date of separation from such service. Additionally, if it is shown to exist at a time when standard and accepted treatises indicate that the incubation period thereof commenced during active service, it shall be deemed to have incurred during such service.

Active tuberculosis disease developing a 10% degree of disability or more within three years from the date of separation from such service.

Multiple sclerosis developing a 10% degree of disability or more within seven years from the date of separation from such service.
Hansen's disease developing a 10% degree of disability or more within three years from the date of separation from such service.

Chronic Diseases

- Amyotrophic lateral sclerosis (ALS)
- Anemia, primary
- Arteriosclerosis
- Arthritis
- Atrophy, progressive muscular
- Brain hemorrhage
- Brain thrombosis
- Bronchiectasis
- Calculi of the kidney, bladder, or gallbladder
- Cardiovascular-renal disease, including hypertension
- Cirrhosis of the liver
- Coccidioidomycosis
- Diabetes mellitus
- Encephalitis lethargica residuals
- Endocarditis
- Endocrinopathies
- Epilepsies
- Hansen's disease
- Hodgkin's disease
- Leukemia
- Lupus erythematosus, systemic
- Myasthenia gravis
- Myelitis Myocarditis
- Nephritis
- Organic diseases of the nervous system
- Osteitis deformans (Paget's disease)
- Osteomalacia
- Palsy, bulbar
- Paralysis agitans
- Psychoses

61

- Purpura idiopathic, hemorrhagic
- Raynaud's disease
- Sarcoidosis
- Scleroderma
- Sclerosis, amyotrophic lateral Sclerosis,
- multiple Syringomyelia
- Thromboangiitis obliterans (Buerger's disease)
- Tuberculosis, active
- Tumors, malignant, or of the brain or spinal cord or peripheral nerves
- Ulcers, peptic (gastric or duodenal)
- Other chronic diseases the Secretary of Veterans Affairs may add to this list.

Tropical Diseases
- Amebiasis
- Blackwater fever
- Cholera
- Dracontiasis
- Dysentery
- Filariasis
- Hansen's disease
- Leishmaniasis, including kala-azar
- Loiasis
- Onchocerciasis
- Oroya fever
- Pinta
- Plague Schistosomiasis
- Yaws
- Yellow fever
- Other tropical diseases the Secretary of Veterans Affairs may add to this list.

Presumptions of Service-Connection Relating to Certain Diseases and Disabilities for Former Prisoners of War

In the case of any veteran who is a former prisoner of war, and who was detained or interned for not less than thirty days, any of the following which became manifest to a degree of 10% or more after active military, naval or air service, shall be considered to have been incurred in or aggravated by such service, notwithstanding that there is no record of such disease during the period of service:

In the case of any veteran who is a former prisoner of war, and **who was detained or interned for not less than thirty days,** any of the following which became manifest to a degree of 10% or more after active military, naval or air service, shall be considered to have been incurred in or aggravated by such service, notwithstanding that there is no record of such disease during the period of service:

- Avitaminosis

- Beriberi (including beriberi heart disease, which includes Ischemic Heart Disease-coronary artery disease-for former POWs who suffered during captivity from edema-swelling of the legs or feet- also known as "wet" beriberi)
- Chronic dysentery
- Helminthiasis
- Malnutrition (including optic atrophy associated with malnutrition)
- Pellagra
- Any other nutritional deficiency
- Peripheral neuropathy, except where directly related to infectious causes
- Irritable bowel syndrome
- Peptic ulcer disease
- Cirrhosis of the liver (This condition was added as part of Public Law 108- 183, The Veterans Benefits Act of 2003.)
- Atherosclerotic heart disease or hypertensive vascular disease (including hypertensive heart disease) and their complications (including myocardial infarction, congestive heart failure, and arrhythmia). These conditions were added as part of Public Law 109-233.
- Stroke and its complications; this condition was added as part of Public Law 109-233.
- The Veterans Benefits Improvement Act added osteoporosis to the list of disabilities presumed to be service-connected (and therefore compensable through VA disability compensation) in the case of veterans who are former prisoners of war, if the Secretary determines that such veteran has post-traumatic stress disorder (PTSD).

In the case of any veteran who is a former prisoner of war, and **who was detained or interned for any period of time,** any of the following which became manifest to a degree of 10% or more after active military, naval or air service, shall be considered to have been incurred in or aggravated by such service, notwithstanding that there is no record of such disease during the period of service:

- Psychosis
- Any of the anxiety states
- Dysthymic disorder (or depressive neurosis)
- Organic residuals of frostbite, if the VA determines the veteran was interned in climatic conditions consistent with the occurrence of frostbite.
- Post-traumatic osteoarthritis

Presumptions Relating to Certain Diseases Associated with Exposure to Radiation
VA may pay compensation for radiogenic diseases under two programs specific to radiation-exposed veterans and their survivors:

Statutory List
Veterans who participated in nuclear tests by the U.S. or its allies, who served with the

occupation forces in Hiroshima or Nagasaki, Japan, between August 1945 and July 1946, or who were similarly exposed to ionizing radiation while a prisoner of war in Japan, are eligible for compensation for cancers specified in legislation.

The definition of radiation-risk activities was expanded in March 2002 to include service at Amchitka Island, Alaska, prior to January 1, 1974, if a veteran was exposed while performing duties related to certain underground nuclear tests.

The new definition also included service at gaseous diffusion plants located in Paducah, Ky., Portsmouth, Ohio, and an area known as K25 at Oak Ridge, Tenn.

The types of cancer covered by these laws are:
 All forms of leukemia
Cancer of the thyroid,
Cancer of the breast,
Cancer of the pharynx,
Cancer of the esophagus,
Cancer of the stomach,
Cancer of the small intestine,
Cancer of the pancreas,
Cancer of the bile ducts,
Cancer of the gall bladder,
Cancer of the salivary gland,
Cancer of the urinary tract,
Lymphomas (except Hodgkin's disease),
Multiple myelomas,
Primary liver cancer.
Bone Cancer
Brain Cancer
Colon Cancer
Lung Cancer
Ovary Cancer

The rules apply to those veterans who participated in "radiation-risk activities" while on active duty, during active duty for training or inactive duty training as a member of a reserve component.

Regulatory List
Disability compensation claims of veterans who were exposed to radiation in service and who develop a disease within specified time periods not specified in the statutory list are governed by regulation. Under regulations, various additional factors must be considered in determining service-connection, including the amount of radiation exposure, duration of exposure, and elapsed time between exposure and onset of the disease. VA regulations identify all cancers as potentially radiogenic, as well as

certain other non- malignant conditions: posterior subcapsular cataracts, non-malignant thyroid nodular disease, parathyroid adenoma, and tumors of the brain and central nervous system.

A final rule that expanded the regulatory list from more than a dozen specific cancers to add "any other cancer" (any malignancy) was published September 24, 1998. The rulemaking began following a 1995 review of the radiogenic of cancer generally by the Veterans Advisory Committee on Environmental Hazards. It concluded that, based on current scientific knowledge, exposure to ionizing radiation could be a contributing factor in the development of any malignancy. VA also will consider evidence that diseases other than those specified in regulation may be caused by radiation exposure

Presumptions of Service-Connection for Diseases Associated with Exposure to Certain Herbicide Agents

A disease specified below, becoming manifest in a veteran, who, during active military, naval, or air service, served in the Republic of Vietnam during the period beginning on January 9, 1962, and ending on May 7, 1975, shall be considered to have been incurred in or aggravated by such service, notwithstanding that there is no record of evidence of such disease during the period of such service.

In 2011, the Department of Veterans Affairs published a final regulation expanding the dates when illnesses caused by herbicide exposure can be presumed to be related to Agent Orange.

Under the final regulation, published in the Federal Register, the VA will presume herbicide exposure for any Veteran who **served between April 1, 1968, and August 21, 1971, in** an area in or near the Korean demilitarized zone in which herbicides were applied.

The diseases referred to above are:

Acute and Subacute Peripheral Neuropathy

A nervous system condition that causes numbness, tingling, and motor weakness. Under VA's rating regulations, it must be at least 10% disabling within one year of exposure to Agent Orange and resolve within two years after the date it began.

AL Amyloidosis

A rare disease caused when an abnormal protein, amyloid, enters tissues or organs.

B Cell Leukemias

Cancers which affect B cells, such as hairy cell leukemia.

Chloracne (or Similar Acneform Disease)

A skin condition that occurs soon after dioxin exposure and looks like common forms of acne seen in teenagers. Under VA's rating regulations, chloracne (or another acneform disease similar to chloracne) must be at least 10% disabling within one year of exposure to Agent Orange.

Chronic Lymphocytic Leukemia
A disease that progresses slowly with increasing production of excessive numbers of white blood cells.

Diabetes Mellitus (Type 2)
A disease characterized by high blood sugar levels resulting from the body's inability to respond properly to the hormone insulin.

Hodgkin's Disease
A malignant lymphoma (cancer) characterized by progressive enlargement of the lymph nodes, liver, and spleen, and by progressive anemia.

Ischemic Heart Disease
A disease characterized by a reduced supply of blood to the heart.

Multiple Myeloma
A cancer of specific bone marrow cells that is characterized by bone marrow tumors in various bones of the body.

Non-Hodgkin's Lymphoma
A group of cancers that affect the lymph glands and other lymphatic tissue.

Parkinson's Disease
A motor system condition with symptoms that include trembling of the limbs and face and impaired balance.

Porphyria Cutanea Tarda
A disorder characterized by liver dysfunction and by thinning and blistering of the skin in sun-exposed areas. Under VA's rating regulations, it must be at least 10% disabling within one year of exposure to Agent Orange.

Prostate Cancer
Cancer of the prostate; one of the most common cancers among men

Respiratory Cancers
Cancers of the lung, larynx, trachea, and bronchus.

Soft Tissue Sarcoma (other than Osteosarcoma, Chondrosarcoma, Kaposi's sarcoma, or Mesothelioma)

A group of different types of cancers in body tissues such as muscle, fat, blood and lymph vessels, and connective tissues.

Each additional disease (if any) that the Secretary of the VA determines warrants a presumption of service-connection because of having positive association with exposure to an herbicide agent becomes manifest within the period (if any) prescribed in such regulations in a veteran who, during active military, naval, or air service, served in the Republic of Vietnam during the period beginning on January 9,

1962 and ending on May 7, 1975, and while so serving was exposed to that herbicide agent.

Veterans having a disease referred to above shall be presumed to have been exposed during such service to an herbicide agent containing dioxin or 2,4-dichlorophenoxyacetic acid and may be presumed to have been exposed during such service to any other chemical compound in an herbicide agent unless there is affirmative evidence to establish that the veteran was not exposed to any such agent during that service.

If the Secretary of the VA later determines that a previously established presumption of service connection for one of the above diseases is no longer warranted, all veteran currently awarded compensation based on the presumption shall continue to be entitled to receive compensation. Additionally, all survivors of any such veterans who were awarded dependency and indemnity compensation shall continue to be entitled to receive dependency and indemnity compensation on that basis.

Presumptions of Service-Connection for Illnesses Associated with Service in the Persian Gulf during the Persian Gulf War

Like all other veterans, veterans of the Persian Gulf War can receive service-connected compensation for mental and physical disabilities that were incurred during, or aggravated by their service in the armed forces
Recent legislation also authorized disability compensation for Persian Gulf veterans with chronic, **undiagnosed** illness resulting in a permanent disability that developed after they left the Persian Gulf.

Congress created this legislation after many Persian Gulf War veterans reported they were suffering from multi-symptom disabilities that are poorly understood by the medical profession and may be classified as "undiagnosed" by one physician, or referred to as "chronic fatigue syndrome" by another physician.
Public Law 107-103, signed by then-President Bush on December 27, 2001, extended the presumptive period for disabilities associated with Persian Gulf War service until December 31, 2011, or such later date as prescribed by VA.

To be entitled to disability compensation due to an undiagnosed illness, the claimant must meet the following requirements:

The veteran must qualify as a Persian Gulf War veteran.
VA considers an individual to be a Persian Gulf War veteran if he or she served on active military, naval, or air service in the Southwest Asia theater of operations during

67

the Persian Gulf War. This includes service in Iraq, Kuwait, Saudi Arabia, the neutral zone between Iraq and Saudi Arabia, Bahrain, Qatar, the United Arab Emirates, Oman, the Gulf of Aden, the Gulf of Oman, the Persian Gulf, the Arabian Sea, the Red Sea, and the airspace above these locations.

The veteran's period of service must have included service in the designated area after August 2, 1990. Since members of the armed services are still serving in the area of operations, they qualify as Persian Gulf veterans because the end date for the Persian Gulf War has not been set.

The veteran must suffer from a "qualifying chronic disability."
A "qualifying chronic disability" can be any of the following (or combination of the following):
- An undiagnosed illness;
- A medically unexplained chronic multi-symptom illness (such as chronic fatigue syndrome, fibromyalgia, or irritable bowel syndrome) that is defined by a cluster of signs or symptoms;
- Any diagnosed illness that the VA Secretary determines warrants a presumption of service connection.

VA considers disabilities to be chronic if they have existed for six months or more, or if they have exhibited intermittent episodes of improvement and worsening over six months. The six months is measured from the earliest date that the signs or symptoms manifest.

The "qualifying chronic disability" must have appeared either during active duty in the Southwest Asia Theater of Operations during the Gulf War or it must have manifested to a degree of at least 10 percent during the presumptive period.

The following symptoms may be manifestations of an undiagnosed illness:

Fatigue

Skin disorders

Headaches

Muscle pain

Joint pain

Neurological symptoms

Neuropsychological symptoms

Symptoms involving the respiratory system

Sleep disturbances

Gastrointestinal symptoms

Cardiovascular symptoms

Abnormal weight loss

Menstrual disorders

Any poorly defined chronic multi-symptom illness of unknown etiology characterized by two or more of the above symptoms.

Rates of compensation depend upon the degree of disability and follow a payment schedule that is adjusted annually and applies to all veterans. Please refer to the charts detailed earlier in this chapter for the current rates payable.

Presumptive Illnesses in Iraq, Afghanistan

In late 2010, VA the VA established new presumptions of service connection for nine specific infectious diseases associated with military service in Southwest Asia beginning on or after the start of the first Gulf War on August 2, 1990, through the conflict in Iraq and on or after September 19, 2001, in Afghanistan.

The nine diseases are Brucellosis, Campylobacter jejuni, Coxiella burnetii (Q fever), Malaria, Mycobacterium tuberculosis, Nontyphoid Salmonella, Shigella, Visceral leishmaniasis and West Nile virus.

A veteran now only has to show service in Southwest Asia or Afghanistan and that he or she had one of the nine diseases within a certain time after service, and has a current disability as a result of that disease, subject to certain time limits for seven of the disease.

Lou Gehrig's Disease Amyotrophic Lateral Sclerosis (ALS)

ALS is a rapidly progressive, totally debilitating, and irreversible motor neuron disease that results in muscle weakness leading to a wide range of serious disabilities, including impaired mobility. VA adapted its rules, so veterans with service-connected ALS no longer have to file multiple claims with VA for increased benefits as their condition progresses.

Before the new Specially Adapted Housing (SAH) regulatory change, many Veterans and Servicemembers who were rated by VA for service-connected ALS, but who did not yet have symptoms debilitating enough to affect their mobility to the degree required for SAH grant eligibility, were unable to begin the process of modifying their homes to accommodate their often rapidly progressing conditions. Veterans with Lou Gehrig's or ALS are eligible for monthly VA disability compensation benefits because of a presumption of service connection established in 2008. VA amended its disability rating scale in January 2012 to assign a 100% disability evaluation for any veteran with service-connected ALS. In 2014 the VA announced military personnel and veterans with service-connected ALS would also be presumed medically eligible for grants to adapt their homes, making them eligible for the maximum grant amount.

Presumptions Rebuttal

If there is affirmative evidence to the contrary, or evidence to establish that an intercurrent injury or disease which is a recognized cause of any of the diseases or disabilities mentioned in the above sections, has been suffered between the date of separation from service and the onset of any such diseases or disabilities, or if the disability is due to the veteran's own willful misconduct, payment of compensation shall not be made.

Special Provisions Relating to Claims Based Upon Effects of Tobacco Products

Effective June 10, 1998, a veteran's death or disability will not be considered to have resulted from personal injury suffered, or disease contracted in the line of duty if the injury or disease is attributable to the use of tobacco products by the veteran during the veteran's service.

Peacetime Disability Compensation

Basic Entitlement

A veteran may be entitled to VA disability compensation for any medical condition or injury that was incurred in or aggravated by his or her military service during any period other than a period of war. The veteran must have been discharged or released under conditions other than dishonorable from the period of service in which the injury or disease was incurred or aggravated.

No compensation shall be paid if the disability is a result of the person's own willful misconduct or abuse of alcohol or drugs.

Presumption of Sound Condition

Every person employed in the active military, naval, or air service during any period other than a period of war, for six months or more, will be assumed to have been in sound medical condition when examined, accepted, and enrolled for service, except any defects, infirmities, or disorders noted at the time of the examination, acceptance, and enrollment, or if there is clear and unmistakable evidence showing that the injury or disease did exist before acceptance and enrollment, and the injury or disease was not aggravated by such service.

Presumptions Relating to Certain Diseases

If a veteran who served in the active military, naval, or air service after December 31, 1946, during any period other than a period of war, for six months or more, contracts any of the following, it shall be considered to have been incurred in, or aggravated by such service, notwithstanding there is no record of evidence of such disease during the period of service:

- A chronic disease, becoming manifest to a degree of 10% or more within one year from the date of separation from such service.
- Tropical disease and the resultant disorders or disease originating because of therapy, administered in connection with such diseases, or as a preventative thereof, becoming manifest to a degree of 10% or more within one year from the date of separation from such service. Additionally, if it is shown to exist at a time when standard and accepted treatises indicate that the incubation period thereof commenced during active service, it shall be deemed to have incurred during such service.
- Active tuberculosis disease developing a 10% degree of disability or more within three years from the date of separation from such service.
- Multiple sclerosis developing a 10% degree of disability or more within seven years from the date of separation from such service.
- Hansen's disease developing a 10% degree of disability or more within three years from the date of separation from such service.

In the case of any veteran who served for 90 days or more during a period of war, service- connection will not be granted in any case where the disease or disorder is shown by clear and unmistakable evidence to have had its inception before or after active military, naval, or air service.

Presumptions Rebuttal

If there is affirmative evidence to the contrary, or evidence to establish that an intercurrent injury or disease which is a recognized cause of any of the diseases or disabilities mentioned in the above sections, has been suffered between the date of separation from service and the onset of any such diseases or disabilities, or if the disability is due to the veteran's own willful misconduct, payment of compensation shall not be made.

Rates of Peacetime Disability Compensation

The compensation payable shall be the same as the compensation payable for Wartime Disability Compensation. Please refer to the charts presented earlier in this chapter.

Additional Compensation for Dependents

Any veteran entitled to peacetime disability compensation, and whose disability is rated as 30% or greater, will be entitled to additional monthly compensation for dependents in the same amounts payable for Wartime Disability Compensation. Please refer to the charts presented earlier in this chapter.

General Disability Compensation Provisions

How to Apply for Disability Compensation Benefits

The Department of Veteran Affairs (VA) has announced the elimination of the need for veterans to complete the Eligibility Verification Report (EVR) annually. According to the VA, this is a way of cutting the red tape for veterans and working toward eliminating the claims backlog. The VA reports that it will implement a new process to confirm veterans' benefits eligibility, and staff members that had previously been responsible for processing the old form will now focus on eliminating the compensation claims backlog.

Previously, beneficiaries had been required to complete an EVR each year to ensure the continuation of pension benefits. With the new change in eligibility confirmation, the VA says it will work with the Internal Revenue Service (IRS) and the Social Security Administration (SSA) to confirm eligibility for benefits.

To apply for disability compensation benefits from the VA, **Form 21-526EZ, Application for Disability Compensation and Related Compensation Benefits**, must be completed and returned to the VA Regional Office serving the veteran's area (refer to Chapter 36 for a listing of regional offices). In addition to the application, the following documents must be submitted:

- Service Medical Records: To expedite processing of the claim, if an applicant has his or her service medical records, they should be submitted with the application. If not included with the application, VA will contact the veteran's service department to obtain them.
- Other Medical Records: Any medical records from private doctors or hospitals pertaining to the claim should be submitted along with the application.
- Dependency Documents: Copies of pertinent birth, marriage, death, and divorce certificates should be submitted along with the application.
- Military Discharge / DD Form 214-Copy 4-Member Copy: To expedite processing of the claim, if an applicant has a copy of his or her DD-214, it should be submitted with the application. If not included with the application, VA will attempt to obtain verification from the veteran's service department. Copies of missing DD Forms 214 may be obtained from:

National Personnel Records Center
1 Archives Dr.
St. Louis, MO 63138

If any of the pertinent supporting evidence is not immediately available, the applicant should send in the application anyway. The date VA receives the application is important! If VA approves the claim, benefit payments usually begin from the date the application is received, regardless of when the claim is approved.

Adjudication

Adjudication means a judicial decision made by the Veterans Administration in claims filed within their jurisdiction. There is an Adjudication Division in each regional office, under the direction of an adjudication officer, who is responsible for the preparation of claims.

Upon the receipt of an original application in the Adjudication Division, it will be referred to the Authorization Unit for review and development in accordance with established procedures. All reasonable assistance will be extended a claimant in the prosecution of his or her claim, and all sources from which information may be elicited will be thoroughly developed before the submission of the case to the rating board. Every legitimate assistance will be rendered a claimant in obtaining any benefit to which he or she is entitled, and the veteran will be given every opportunity to substantiate his or her claim. Information and advice to claimants will be complete and will be given in words that the average person can understand.

VA personnel must always give to claimants and other properly interested and recognized individuals courteous and satisfactory service, which is essential to good public relations. It is incumbent upon the claimant to establish his or her case following the law. This rule, however, should not be highly technical and rigid in its application. The general policy is to give the claimant every opportunity to substantiate the claim, to extend all reasonable assistance in its prosecution, and to develop all sources from which information may be obtained. Information and advice to claimants will be complete and expressed, so far as possible, in plain language, which can be easily read and understood by persons not familiar with the subject matter.

Benefits for Persons Disabled by Treatment or Vocational Rehabilitation

Compensation shall be awarded for an additional qualifying disability or a qualifying death of a veteran in the same manner as if such additional disability or death were service connected, provided:

The disability or death was caused by hospital care, medical or surgical treatment, or examination was furnished under any law administered by the VA, either by a VA employee, on a VA facility, and the proximate cause of the disability or death was:
- Carelessness, negligence, lack of proper skill, error in judgment, or similar instance of fault on the part of the VA in furnishing the hospital care, medical treatment, surgical treatment, or examination; or
- An event not reasonably foreseeable.
- The disability or death was proximately caused by the provision of training and rehabilitation services by the VA (including a service-provider used by the VA) as part of an approved rehabilitation program.

Effective December 1, 1962, if an individual is awarded a judgment against the United States in a civil action brought pursuant to Section 1346(b) of Title 28, or enters into a settlement or compromise under Section 2672 or 2677 of Title 28 by reason of a disability or death treated pursuant to this section as if it were service-connected, then no benefits shall be paid to such individual for any month beginning after the date such judgment, settlement, or compromise on account of such disability or death becomes final until the aggregate amount of benefits which would be paid out for this subsection equals the total amount included in such judgment, settlement, or compromise.

LGBT Veterans

The Obama administration announced a decision to extend veteran benefits to same sex married couples as a result of the Supreme Court's decision to strike down the Defense of Marriage Act. Veterans' spouses are now eligible to collect benefits, regardless of sexual orientation.

LGBT Veterans are eligible for the same VA benefits as any other veteran and will be treated in a welcoming environment. Comprehensive health services are available to LGBT veterans, including primary care, specialty care, mental health care, residential treatment, and reproductive health care services. VA provides management of acute and chronic illnesses, preventive care, contraceptive and gynecology services, menopause management, and cancer screenings.

Transgender veterans will be treated based upon their self- identified gender, including room assignments in residential and inpatient settings. Eligible transgender Veterans can receive cross-sex hormone therapy, gender dysphoria counseling, preoperative evaluations, as well as post-operative and long-term care following sex reassignment surgeries.

Person Heretofore Having a Compensable Status

The death and disability benefits outlined in this chapter, shall, notwithstanding the service requirements thereof, be granted to persons heretofore recognized by law as having a compensable status, including persons whose claims are based on war or peacetime service rendered before April 21, 1898.

Aggravation

A preexisting injury or disease will be considered to have been aggravated by active military, naval, or air service, if there is an increase in disability during such service unless there is a specific finding that the increase in disability is due to the natural progress of the disease.

Consideration to be Accorded Time, Place and Circumstances of Service

Consideration shall be given to the places, types, and circumstances of each veteran's service. The VA will consider the veteran's service record, the official history of each organization in which such veteran served, such veteran's medical records, and all pertinent medical and lay evidence. The provisions of Public Law 98-542 – Section 5 of the Veterans' Dioxin and Radiation Exposure Compensation Standards Act shall also be applied.

In the case of any veteran who engaged in combat with the enemy in active service with a military, naval, or air organization of the United States during a period of war, campaign, or expedition, the Secretary shall accept as sufficient proof of service-connection of any disease or injury alleged to have been incurred in or aggravated by such service, if consistent with the circumstances, conditions, or hardships of such service. This provision will apply even if there is no official record of such incurrence or aggravation in such service. Every reasonable doubt in such instances will be resolved in favor of the veteran.

The service-connection of such injury or disease may be rebutted only by clear and convincing evidence to the contrary. The reasons for granting or denying service-connection in each case shall be recorded in full.

Disappearance

If a veteran who is receiving disability compensation disappears, the VA may pay the compensation otherwise payable to the veteran to such veteran's spouse, children, and parents. Payments made to such spouse, child, or parent should not exceed the amounts payable to each if the veteran died from a service-connected disability.

Combination of Certain Ratings

If the VA finds that a veteran has multiple disabilities, they use a Combined Ratings Table to calculate combined disability rating. Disability ratings are not additive, meaning that if a veteran has one disability rated 60% and a second disability 20%, the combined rating is not 80%. This is because subsequent disability ratings are applied to an already disabled veteran, so the 20% disability is applied to a veteran who is already 60% disabled. The following outlines how the VA combines ratings for more than one disability:

The disabilities are first arranged in the exact order of their severity, beginning with the greatest disability combined with use of the Combined Ratings Table. The degree of one disability will be read in the left column of the table, and the degree of the other in the top row, whoever is appropriate. The figures appearing in the space where the column and row intersect will represent the combined value of the two. This combined value is rounded to the nearest 10%. If there are more than two disabilities, the combined value for the first two will be found as previously described for two disabilities. The exact combined value—without yet rounding—is combined with the degree of the third disability. The process continues for subsequent disabilities, and the final number is rounded to the nearest 10%.

Example of Combining Two Disabilities: If a veteran has a 50 percent disability and a 30 percent disability, the combined value will be found to be 65 percent, but the 65 percent must be converted to 70 percent to represent the final degree of disability. Similarly, with a disability of 40 percent, and another disability of 20 percent, the combined value is found to be 52 percent, but the 52 percent must be converted to the nearest degree divisible by 10, which is 50 percent.

Example of Combining Three Disabilities: If there are three disabilities ratable at 60 percent, 40 percent, and 20 percent, respectively, the combined value for the first two will be found opposite 60 and under 40 and is 76 percent. This 76 will be found in the left column, then the 20 rating in the top row. The intersection of these two ratings is 81. Thus, the final rating will be rounded to 80%.

Tax Exemption

Compensation and pension may not be assigned to anyone, and are exempt from taxation (including income tax). No one can attach, levy, or seize a compensation or pension check either before or after receipt. Property purchased with money received from the government is not protected.

Disabled veterans may be eligible to claim a federal tax refund based on an increase in the veteran's percentage of disability from the Department of Veterans Affairs (which may include a retroactive determination) or the combat-disabled veteran applying for, and being granted, Combat-Related Special Compensation, after an award for Concurrent Retirement and Disability.

To do so, the disabled veteran will need to file the amended return, Form 1040X, Amended U.S. Individual Income Tax Return, to correct a previously filed Form 1040, 1040A, or 1040EZ. An amended return cannot be e-filed. It must be filed as a paper return. Disabled veterans should include all documents from the Department of Veterans Affairs and any information received from Defense Finance and Accounting Services explaining proper tax treatment for the current year.

Please note: It is only in the year of the Department of Veterans Affairs reassessment of disability percentage (including any impacted retroactive year) or the year that the CRSC is initially granted or adjusted that the veteran may need to file amended returns.

Under normal circumstances, the Form 1099-R issued to the veteran by Defense Finance and Accounting Services correctly reflects the taxable portion of compensation received. No amended returns would be required since it has already been adjusted for any non-taxable awards.

If needed, veterans should seek assistance from a competent tax professional before filing amended returns based on a disability determination. Refund claims based on an incorrect interpretation of the tax law could subject the veteran to interest and/or penalty charges.

Protection of Service Connection

Service connection for any disability or death granted under this title which has been in force for ten or more years shall not be severed on or after January 1, 1962, unless it is shown that the original grant of service connection was based on fraud, or it is clearly shown from military records that the person concerned did not have the requisite service or character of discharge. The mentioned period shall be computed from the date determined by the VA as the date on which the status commenced for rating purposes.

Preservation of Ratings

Public Law 88-445, approved August 19, 1964, effective the same date, amends Section 110, Title 38, U.S. Code as follows:

The law provides that a disability that has been continuously rated at or above a given percentage for 20 years or longer for service connection compensation under laws administered by the VA shall not after that be rated at any lesser percentage except upon showing that the rating was based on fraud.

Special Consideration for Certain Cases of Loss of Paired Organs or Extremities

If a veteran has suffered any of the following, the VA shall assign and pay to the veteran the applicable rate of compensation, as if the combination of disabilities were the result of a service-connected disability:

- Blindness in one eye as a result of a service-connected disability, and blindness in the other eye as a result of a non-service-connected disability not the result of the veteran's own willful misconduct; or
- The loss or loss of use of one kidney as a result of a service-connected disability, and involvement of the other kidney as a result of a non-service connected disability not the result of the veteran's own willful misconduct; or
- Total deafness in one ear as a result of a service-connected disability, and total deafness in the other ear as the result of non-service-connected disability not the result of the veteran's own willful misconduct; or
- The loss or loss of use of one hand or one foot as a result of a service-connected disability and the loss or loss of use of the other hand or foot as a result of non- service-connected disability not the result of the veteran's own willful misconduct; or
- Permanent service-connected disability of one lung rated 50% or more

disabling, in combination with a non-service-connected disability of the other lung that is not the result of the veteran's own willful misconduct.

If a veteran described above receives any money or property of value according to an award in a judicial proceeding based upon, or a settlement or compromise of, any cause of action for damages for the non-service-connected disability, the increase in the rate of compensation otherwise payable shall not be paid for any month following a month in which any such money or property is received until the total of the amount of such increase that would otherwise have been payable equals the total of the amount of any such money received, and the fair market value of any such property received.

Payment of Disability Compensation in Disability Severance Cases

The deduction of disability severance pay from disability compensation, as required by Section 1212(c) of Title 10, shall be made at a monthly rate, not more than the rate of compensation to which the former member would be entitled based on the degree of such former member's disability, as determined on the initial Department rating.

Trial Work Periods and Vocational Rehabilitation for Certain Veterans with Total Disability Ratings

The disability rating of a qualified veteran who begins to engage in a substantially gainful occupation after January 31, 1985, may not be reduced based on the veteran having secured and followed a substantially gainful occupation unless the veteran maintains such an occupation for 12 consecutive months.

("Qualified Veteran" means a veteran who has a service-connected disability or disabilities, not rated as total, but who has been awarded a rating of total of disability because of inability to secure or follow a substantially gainful occupation as a result of such disability or disabilities.)

Counseling services, placement, and post-placement services shall be available to each qualified veteran, whether or not the veteran is participating in a vocational rehabilitation program.

Asbestos Exposure

Veterans who were exposed to asbestos while in service and developed a disease related to asbestos exposure may receive service-connected compensation benefits. If you served in any of the following occupations, you may have been exposed to asbestos: mining, milling, shipyard work, insulation work, demolition of old buildings, carpentry and construction, the manufacturing and installation of products such as flooring, roofing, cement sheet, pipe products, or the servicing of friction products such as clutch facings and brake linings.

Additionally, if you served in Iraq or other countries in that region, you could have been exposed to asbestos when older buildings were damaged, and the contaminant was released into the air.

Eligibility Requirements

- You must be a Veteran who was discharged under conditions other than dishonorable.
- You must have been exposed to asbestos while in military service.
- You must have a disease or disability related to the asbestos exposure that occurred in military service.

Evidence Requirements

The evidence must show asbestos exposure while in military service. This may include your military occupation specialty and/or where you were stationed

The evidence must show you have a disease or disability related to asbestos and a relationship exists between the exposure to asbestos in military service and the disease/disability.

Note: You must claim a disease or disability. Exposure, in and of itself, is not a condition that is subject to service connection.

Normally, VA will initiate a VA medical examination and request an opinion regarding the relationship of the disease or disability to asbestos exposure that occurred during military service.

Naturalization

Veterans who served before September 11, 2001, are eligible to file for naturalization based on their U.S. military service. An applicant who served three years in the U.S. military and is a lawful permanent resident is excused from any specific period of required residence, period of residence in any specific place, or physical presence within the United States if the application for naturalization is filed while the applicant is still serving in the military or within six months of honorable discharge. Applicants who file for naturalization more than six months after termination of three years of U.S. military service may count any periods of honorable service as residence and physical presence in the United States.

Aliens and non-citizen nationals with honorable service in the U.S. armed forces during specified periods of hostilities may be naturalized without having to comply with the general requirements for naturalization. This is the only section of the Immigration and Nationality Act, as amended, which allows persons who have not been lawfully admitted for permanent residence to apply for naturalization.

Any person who has served honorably during qualifying time may apply at any time in his or her life if, at the time of enlistment, reenlistment, extension of enlistment or induction, such person shall have been in the United States, the Canal Zone, American Samoa or Swain's Island, or, on or after November 18, 1997, aboard a public vessel owned or operated by the United States for non-commercial service, whether or not lawful admittance to the United States for permanent residence has been granted. Certain applicants who have served in the U.S. Armed Forces are eligible to file for naturalization based on current or prior U.S. military service. Such applicants should file the N-400 Military Naturalization Packet.

CHAPTER 5

MISCELLANEOUS BENEFITS—
AUTOMOBILES, ADAPTIVE EQUIPMENT, HOUSING GRANTS, CLOTHING ALLOWANCE AND MEDAL OF HONOR PENSION

Commissary Access

According to the Department of Defense, starting January 1, 2020, all service-connected Veterans, Purple Heart recipients, former prisoners of war (POW), and individuals approved and designated as the primary family caregivers of eligible Veterans under the Department of Veterans Affairs Program of Comprehensive Assistance for Family Caregivers (PCAFC) can use commissaries, exchanges, and morale, welfare, and recreation (MWR) retail facilities, in-person and online.

Who Is Eligible?

Eligible people include veterans who are Purple Heart recipients, former prisoners of war, and veterans with 0-90% service-connected disability ratings. On January 1, 2020, individuals approved and designated as the primary family caregiver of an eligible veteran under the PCAFC are eligible for these privileges.

Required Credentials

Veterans

- On January 1, Veterans eligible solely under this act who are eligible to

> **Key Takeaways**
> In 2020, commissaries and exchanges opened up for four million more people.
>
> The new benefit was authorized by law for all veterans with VA service-connected disability ratings, Purple Heart recipients, veterans who are former prisoners of war and primary family caregivers of eligible veterans under the VA caregiver program.
>
> Veterans should use their Veterans Health Identification Card (VHIC) to gain access to military installations, to shop and to use MWR facilities.

obtain a Veteran Health Identification Card must use this credential for in-person installation and privilege access. The card must display the Veteran's eligibility status (i.e., PURPLE HEART, FORMER POW, or SERVICE CONNECTED).

- Veterans eligible solely under this act who are not enrolled in or are not eligible to enroll in VA health care, or who are enrolled in VA health care, but do not possess a Veteran Health Identification Card will not have access to DoD and Coast Guard installations for in-person commissary, exchange, and MWR retail privileges, but will have full access to online exchanges and American Forces Travel.
- Medal of Honor recipients and Veterans with 100% service-connected disability ratings are eligible for DoD credentials under DoD policy.

Caregivers

Eligible caregivers will receive an eligibility letter from VA's Office of Community Care. If you are a primary family caregiver under the PCAFC and lose your eligibility letter, please call 1-877-733-7927 to request a replacement. Please allow two weeks for processing.

Automobile Assistance Program

The VA offers an automobile assistance program for eligible veterans, or eligible members of the Armed Forces serving on active duty who are suffering from a disability as described below if such disability is the result of an injury incurred or disease contracted in or aggravated in the line of duty in the active military, naval, or air service. Following are highlights of the VA program:

Financial Assistance

Qualified veterans may receive a **one-time** payment from VA of up to **$21,795.57** to be used toward the purchase of an automobile or other conveyance. The law requires that this amount be adjusted annually by the percentage increase in the Consumer Price Index.

This is available beginning October 1, 2020. You must have VA approval before purchasing an automobile or adaptive equipment

Eligibility Requirements for Receipt of One-Time Payment

Veterans or service members who are entitled to Disability Compensation under Chapter 11 of Title 38 due to one of the following service-connected losses:

- The loss or permanent loss of use of one or both feet; or
- The loss or permanent loss of use of one or both hands; or
- The permanent impairment of vision of both eyes of the following status:
    - Central visual acuity of 20/200 or less in the better eye, with corrective glasses, or central visual acuity of more than 20/200 if there is a field defect in which the peripheral field has contracted to such an extent that the widest diameter

of visual field subtends an angular distance no greater than twenty degrees in the better eye.

Adaptive Equipment

In addition to the one-time payment described above, VA will also pay for installation of adaptive equipment deemed necessary to ensure that the eligible veteran will be able to safely operate the vehicle and to satisfy the applicable state standards of licensure.

VA will also repair, replace, or reinstall adaptive equipment determined necessary for the operation of a vehicle acquired under this program, or for the operation of a vehicle an eligible veteran may previously or subsequently have acquired.

Eligibility Requirements for Receipt of Adaptive Equipment

- The loss or permanent loss of use of one or both feet; or
- The loss or permanent loss of use of one or both hands; or
- The permanent impairment of vision of both eyes of the following status:
  - Central visual acuity of 20/200 or less in the better eye, with corrective glasses, or central visual acuity of more than 20/200 if there is a field defect in which the peripheral field has contracted to such an extent that the widest diameter of visual field subtends an angular distance no greater than twenty degrees in the better eye; or
  - Ankylosis (immobility) of one or both knees; or
  - Ankylosis (immobility) of one or both hips.

Adaptive Equipment Available for Installation

The term adaptive equipment generally means any equipment which must be part of or added to a vehicle manufactured for sale to the general public to make it safe for use by the claimant and to assist him or her in meeting the applicable standards of licensure of the proper licensing authority.

Following is a partial list of adaptive equipment available under this program:

- Power steering;
- Power brakes;
- Power window lifts;
- Power seats;
- Special equipment necessary to assist the eligible person into and out of the automobile or other conveyance;
- Air-conditioning equipment, if such equipment is necessary to the health and safety of the veteran and the safety of others, regardless of whether the automobile or other conveyance is to be operated by the eligible person or is

to be operated for such person by another person;

- Any modification of the size of the interior space of the automobile or other conveyance if necessary, for the disabled person to enter or operate the vehicle;
- Other equipment, not described above, if determined necessary by the Chief Medical Director or designee in an individual case.

Eligible veterans are not entitled to adaptive equipment for more than two vehicles at any one time during any four years. (In the event an adapted vehicle is no longer available for use by the eligible veteran due to circumstances beyond his or her control, loss due to fire, theft, accident, etc., an exception to this four-year provision may be approved.

Specially Adapted Housing Grant

There are three types of grants that may be payable:

Specially Adapted Housing Grants (SAH)
Special Housing Adaptations Grants (SHA)
Temporary Residence Adaptation Grants (TRA)
Specially Adapted Housing Grant (SAH)

The VA may approve a grant of not more than 50% of the cost of building, buying, or remodeling adapted homes or paying indebtedness on homes previously acquired, up to a maximum of **$100,896.**

Public law 110-289 directed that the maximum grant amount will be adjusted annually. The amount will either increase or stay the same each year – it cannot decrease.

To qualify for this grant, veterans must be entitled to compensation for permanent and total service-connected disability due to:

- Loss or loss of use of both lower extremities, which prevents movement without the aid of braces, crutches, canes, or a wheelchair; or

Disability which includes:

- Blindness in both eyes, having only light perception; **with** Loss or loss of use of one lower extremity; or
- Loss or loss of use of one lower extremity together with:
- Residuals of organic disease or injury; **or**
- The loss or loss of use of one upper extremity, which so affects the functions of balance or propulsion as to preclude locomotion without using braces, canes, crutches, or a wheelchair.
- Loss of, or loss of use, of both upper extremities such as to preclude the use of the arms at or above the elbows.
- A severe burn injury (as so determined.)

84

Eligibility for Active-Duty Members

Public Law 108-183, The Veterans Benefits Act of 2003, which became law on December 16, 2003, extended eligibility for the $100,896 grant to members of the Armed Forces serving on active duty who are suffering from a disability as described above if such disability is the result of an injury incurred or disease contracted in or aggravated in the line of duty in the active military, naval, or air service.

Public Law 110-289, the Economic and Housing Recovery Act of 2008, dated July 30, 2008, extended eligibility for active duty servicemembers to the same extent, and made them subject to the same limitations, as veterans.

An eligible veteran or active-duty service member can use his or her benefit up to three times, as long as the aggregate amount of assistance does not exceed the maximum amounts allowable.

This benefit extends to previous grant recipients; however, they cannot obtain a subsequent grant(s) to pay for adaptations made before June 15, 2006, or to reduce an existing mortgage principal balance for properties acquired before June 15, 2006.

Special Housing Adaptation Grant (SHA)

VA may approve a grant for the actual cost, up to a maximum of $20,215, for adaptations to a veteran's residence that are determined by VA to be reasonably necessary. Public Law 110-289 directed that the maximum grant amount will be adjusted annually, based on a cost-of-construction index. The amount will either increase or stay the same each year- it cannot decrease.

The grant may also be used to assist veterans in acquiring a residence that has already been adapted with special features for the veteran's disability.

To qualify for this grant, veterans must be entitled to compensation for permanent and total service-connected disability due to:

- Blindness in both eyes, with 5/200 visual acuity or less; or
- Anatomical loss or loss of use of both hands

Temporary Residence Adaptation Grant (TRA)

Eligible veterans and servicemembers who are temporarily residing in a home owned by a family member may also receive a Temporary Residence Adaptation (TRA) grant to help the veteran or servicemember adapt the family member's home to meet his or her special needs. While the SAH and SHA grants require ownership and title to a house, in creating the TRA, Congress recognized the need to allow veterans and active-duty members who may not yet own homes to have access to the adaptive housing grant

85

program.

VA may provide a TEMPORARY RESIDENCE ADAPTATION GRANT of up to
$40,637 (for those eligible for the $100,896 to assist a veteran in adapting a family member's home to meet the veteran's special needs.

VA may provide a TEMPORARY RESIDENCE ADAPTATION GRANT of up to
$7,256 (for those eligible for the $20,215 grant) to assist a veteran in adapting a family member's home to meet the veteran's special needs.

Specially Adapted Housing Assistive Technology Grant Program

VA through its Specially Adapted Housing Assistive Technology (SAHAT) Grant Program is authorized to award grants of up to $200,000 per fiscal year to persons or entities to encourage the development of specially adapted housing assistive technologies. The FY2020 grant solicitation period is to be determined but may open mid-December and close late February.

Program Purpose

There are many emerging technologies that could improve home adaptions or enhance a veteran's or servicemember's ability to live independently, such as voice-recognition and voice-command operations, living environment controls, and adaptive feeding equipment. VA has defined "new assistive technology" as an advancement that could aid or enhance the ability of a veteran or servicemember to live in an adapted home.

Please note: SAHAT funding does not support the construction or modification of residential dwellings for accessibility. Veterans and servicemembers interested in adapting their home for barrier-free living are encouraged to review this factsheet to identify Home Adaptation programs offered by VA.

Amount of Funding

For FY2020, VA is authorized to award up to $1 million in grant funds for the SAHAT Grant Program. The number of grants VA will fund will be based on application quality and funding availability. The maximum grant award is limited to $200,000 per grant recipient.

How to Apply

Interested applicants must register and apply through www.grants.gov during the application period stated on the Notice of Funding Availability (NOFA). Applications will not be accepted outside of the application period and each application must meet the requirements provided in the NOFA and at www.grants.gov. To locate the funding opportunity on www.grants.gov, click here or search using the following terms: Opportunity Title: Specially Adapted Housing Assistive Technology Grant, or

Opportunity Number (FY2020): VA-SAHAT-20-05, or Catalog of Federal Domestic Assistance (CFDA) Number: 64.051

To be eligible for federal contracts and grants, organizations must register for a Dun & Bradstreet DUNS Number and a System for Award Management (SAM) account: For DUNS registration, see: http://fedgov.dnb.com/webform/ For SAM registration, see: https://sam.gov/SAM/

Please note: For the sam.gov link, if you are using Internet Explorer, you must use version greater than 11. The URL has been tested using Mozilla Firefox and Google Chrome.

The SAHAT Grant Program transfers grants funds through the Department of Health and Human Services Payment Management System (PMS). SAHAT grant recipients will need to register with the PMS in order to access SAHAT grant funds. For information on the PMS, please refer to: https://pms.psc.gov/ For more information on the SAHAT Grant Program, please write to SAHAT.VBAVACO@va.gov

Supplemental Financing—Loan Guaranty

Veterans who have available loan guaranty entitlement may also obtain a guaranteed loan or possibly a direct loan from VA to supplement the grant to acquire a specially adapted home.

Clothing Allowance

In 2011, a final regulation was published in the Federal Register, expanding the eligibility criteria for veterans with multiple prosthetic and orthopedic devices or those who use prescription medications for service-related skin conditions.

The new regulation provides the criteria for more than one annual clothing allowance in situations where distinct garments are affected. Payment for more than one clothing allowance for eligible veterans began in 2012.

The VA shall pay a clothing allowance of $841.36 per year (rate effective December 1, 2020, and payable beginning August 1, 2021) to each veteran who:
- Because of a service-connected disability, wears or uses a prosthetic or orthopedic appliance (including a wheelchair) which the VA determines tends to wear out or tear the clothing of the veteran; or
- Uses medication prescribed by a physician for a skin condition that is due to a service-connected disability, and which the VA determines causes irreparable damage to the veteran's outer garments.

Medal of Honor Pension

The law further states that VA shall pay, in a lump sum, to each person who is in receipt of the Medal of Honor Pension, an amount equal to the total amount of special pension that the person would have received during the period beginning on the 1st day of the 1st month beginning after the date of the act for which the person was awarded the Medal of Honor, and ending on the last day of the month preceding the month in which the person's special pension commenced.

For each month of a period referred to in the previous paragraph, the amount of special pension payable shall be determined using the rate of special pension that was in effect for such month.

The Secretary of the Department of the Army, the Department of the Navy, the Department of the Air Force, or the Department of Transportation will determine the eligibility of applicants to be entered on the Medal of Honor Roll and will deliver to the Secretary of the Department of Veterans Affairs a certified copy of each certificate issued in which the right of the person named in the certificate to the special pension is set forth. The special pension will be authorized based on such certification.

The special pension will be paid in addition to all other payments under laws of the United States. However, a person awarded more than one Medal of Honor may not receive more than one special pension.

The Medal of Honor Pension rate was changed 12/01/2020 to $1,406.73.

CHAPTER 6

PENSION: NON-SERVICE-CONNECTED DISABILITY

Non-Service-Connected Disability Pension is a Department of Veterans Affairs benefits program that provides financial support to wartime veterans having limited income. The amount payable under this program depends on the type and amount of income the veteran and family members receive from other sources. Monthly payments are made to bring a veteran's total annual income (including other retirement and Social Security income) to an established support level. (Unreimbursed medical expenses may reduce countable income.)

Indian Wars: means the campaigns, engagements, and expeditions of the United States military forces against Indian tribes or nations, service in which has been recognized heretofore as pensionable service.

World War I: means the period April 6, 1917, through November 11, 1918. In the case of a veteran who served with the United States military forces in Russia, the ending date is April 1, 1920. Service after November 11, 1918, and before July 2, 1921

> ## Key Takeaways
> You may be eligible for the Veterans Pension program if you meet the requirements listed below. Both of these must be true:
>
> You didn't receive a dishonorable discharge, and Your yearly family income and net worth meet certain limits set by Congress. Your net worth includes all personal property you own (except your house, your car, and most home furnishings), minus any debt you owe. Your net worth includes the net worth of your spouse.
>
> To apply, you can fill out VA Form 21P-527EZ Application for Pension.

is considered World War I for compensation or pension purposes if the veteran served in the active military, naval, or air service after April 5, 1917, and before November 12, 1918.

Civil War Veteran: includes a person who served in the military or naval forces of the Confederate States of America during the Civil War, and the term "active military or naval service" includes active service in those forces.

Period of War: means the Mexican border period, World War I, World War II, the Korean conflict, the Vietnam era, the Persian Gulf War, and the period beginning on the date of any future declaration of war by the Congress and ending on the date prescribed by Presidential proclamation or concurrent resolution of the Congress.

Permanently and Totally Disabled: for the purposes of this chapter, a person shall be permanently and totally disabled if such person is unemployable because of disability reasonably certain to continue throughout the life of the disabled person, or:

- Suffering from any disability which is sufficient to render it impossible for the average person to follow a substantially gainful occupation, but only if it is reasonably certain that such disability will continue throughout the life of the disabled person; or
- Suffering from any disease or disorder determined by the VA Secretary to be of such a nature or extent as to justify a determination that persons suffering is permanently and totally disabled; or
- Is a patient in a nursing home for long-term care because of disability; or
- Is disabled, as determined by the Social Security Administration (SSA) for purpose of benefits administered by the SSA; or
- Is unemployable, because of suffering from any disability which is sufficient to render it impossible for the average person to follow a substantially gainful occupation, but only if it is reasonably certain that such disability will continue throughout the life of the person, or otherwise justifying a determination of permanent and total disability.

Regular Aid and Attendance: for the purposes of this chapter, a person shall be considered to require regular aid and attendance if such person is:

- A patient in a nursing home; or
- Helpless or blind, or so nearly helpless or blind as to need or require the aid and attendance of another person.

Permanently Housebound: for the purposes of this chapter, the requirement of "permanently housebound" will be considered to have been met when the veteran is substantially confined to such veteran's house (ward or clinical areas, if institutionalized) or immediate premises due to a disability or disabilities, which it is reasonably certain will remain throughout such veteran's lifetime.

Annual Income: In determining annual income under this chapter, all payments of any kind or from any source (including salary, retirement or annuity payments, or similar income, which has been waived, irrespective of whether the waiver was made according to statute, contract, or otherwise) shall be included except:

- Donations from public or private relief or welfare organizations;
- Payments under this chapter;

- Amounts equal to amounts paid by a spouse of a veteran for the expenses of such veteran's last illness, and by a surviving spouse or child of a deceased veteran for:
    - Such veteran's just debts;
    - The expenses of such veteran's last illness; and
    - The expenses of such veteran's burial to the extent such expenses are not reimbursed through Chapter 23 of Title 38, United States Code (Burial Benefits);

Amounts equal to amounts paid:

- By a veteran for the last illness and burial of such veteran's deceased spouse or child; or
- By the spouse of a living veteran or the surviving spouse of a deceased veteran for the last illness and burial of a child of such veteran;
- Reimbursements of any kind for any casualty loss, but the amount excluded under this clause may not exceed the greater of the fair market value or reasonable replacement value of the property involved at the time immediately preceding the loss;
- Profit realized from the disposition of real or personal property other than in the course of a business.
- Amounts in joint accounts in banks and similar institutions acquired by reason of the death of other joint owner;
- Amounts equal to amounts paid by a veteran, veteran's spouse, or surviving spouse, or by or on behalf of a veteran's child for unreimbursed medical expenses, to the extent that such amounts exceed 5% of the maximum annual rate of pension (including any amount of increased pension payable on account of family members but not including any amount of pension payable because a person is in need of regular aid and attendance, or because a person is permanently housebound) payable to such veteran surviving spouse, or child.
- In the case of a veteran or surviving spouse pursuing a course of education or vocational rehabilitation or training, amounts equal to amounts paid by such veteran or surviving spouse for such course of education or vocational rehabilitation or training, including:
- Amounts paid for tuition, fees, books, and materials; and
    - In the case of such a veteran or surviving spouse in need of regular aid and attendance, unreimbursed amounts paid for unusual transpiration expenses in connection with the pursuit of such course of education or vocational rehabilitation or training, to the extent that such amounts exceed the reasonable expenses which would have been incurred by a nondisabled person using an appropriate means of transportation (public transportation, if reasonably available); and

- In the case of a child, or any current-work income received during the year, to the extent that the total amount of such income does not exceed an amount equal to the sum of:

  - The lowest amount of gross income for which an income tax return is required under section 6012(a) of the Internal Revenue Code of 1986, to be filed by an individual who is not married, is not a surviving spouse, and is not a head of household; and

  - If the child is pursuing a course of postsecondary education or vocational rehabilitation or training, the amount paid by such child for such course of education or vocational rehabilitation or training, including the amount paid for tuition, fees, books, and materials.

Eligibility

Veteran was discharged from service under other than dishonorable conditions, and the veteran served 90 days or more of active duty with at least one day during a period of wartime. However, 38 CFR 3.12a requires that anyone who enlisted after 9/7/80 generally has to serve at least 24 months or the full period for which a person was called or ordered to active duty to receive any benefits based on that period of service; and veteran is permanently and totally disabled, or is age 65 or older; and veteran's countable family income is below a yearly limit set by law.

Improved Pension Annual Rates Effective December 1, 2020	
STATUS OF VETERAN:	ANNUAL LIMIT
Permanently & totally disabled veterans:	
Veteran alone	$13,931.00
Veteran with one dependent	$18,243.00
Each additional dependent child	$2,382.00
Veteran – Aid and Attendance:	
Veteran alone	$23,238.00
Veteran with one dependent	$27,549.00
Each additional dependent child	$2,382.00
Veteran –Housebound:	
Veteran alone	$17,024.00
Veteran with one dependent	$21,337.00
Each additional dependent child	$2,382.00
Two veterans married to one another:	$18,243.00
Each additional dependent child	$2,382.00
Child Earned Income Exclusion effective 1-1-2020–$12,550.00	

If eligible, VA pays the difference between a recipient's countable family income and the annual income limit set by law (see following charts) for his or her status. This difference is generally paid in 12 equal monthly installments.

Family Income Limits:

Maximum Annual Income Limitations for Protected Pensions Effective December 1, 2020

If you're entitled to benefits as of December 31, 1978, and don't receive a pension under the Improved Pension Program, may continue to receive pension benefits at the rates they were entitled to receive on December 31, 1978, or June 30, 1960, as long as they remain permanently and totally disabled, do not lose a dependent, and their income does not exceed the income limitation, adjusted annually.

Pension Law in Effect December 31, 1978 (Section 306):	
The rate entitled to on December 31, 1978, may be continued if the recipients IVAP for 2020 is below the following limits:	
Status of Recipient:	**Annual Income Limitation:**
Veteran/widow with no dependents	$15,845.00 or less
Veteran/widow with one or more dependent	$21,298.00 or less
Child (no entitled veteran or surviving spouse)	$12,956.00 or less
Veteran with no dependents in receipt of A&A	$16,415.00 or less
Veteran with one dependent in receipt of A&A	$21,866.00 or less
Surviving spouse's income exclusion	$5,060.00

Pension Law in Effect June 30, 1960 (Old Law):	
The rate entitled to on June 30, 1960, may be continued if the recipients IVAP for 2020 is below the following limits:	
Status of Recipient:	**Annual Income Limitation:**
Veteran/widow with no dependents	$13,875.00
Veteran/widow with one or more dependents	$19,997.00
Child /no entitled veteran or surviving	$13,875.00

Monthly benefit payable to eligible veterans receiving disability pension under laws in effect June 30, 1960 or December 31, 1978	
Veteran's Entitlement:	**Rate Payable:**
Basic Rates	$66.15
10 Years or Age 65	$78.75
If Entitled to Aid & Attendance	$135.45
If Entitled to Housebound	$100.00

Veterans can apply for a Pension by completing VA **Form 21P-527EZ.** If available, the applicant should attach copies of dependency records (marriage and children's birth certificates) and current medical evidence (doctor and hospital reports).

The completed form should be sent to the veteran's VA Regional Office. If any of the pertinent supporting evidence is not immediately available, the applicant should apply anyway. The date VA receives the application is important!

If VA approves the claim, benefit payments usually begin from the date the application is received, regardless of when the claim is approved.

Net Worth Limitation

Net worth means the net value of the assets of the veteran and dependents. It includes such assets as bank accounts, CDs, stocks, bonds, mutual funds, and any real estate other than the personal residence and a reasonable lot area. There is no set limit on how much net worth a veteran and dependents can have, but net worth cannot be excessive. Each case is decided individually. The life expectancy of the claimant, the available income, and the cost of unreimbursed medical and care costs are taken into consideration.

Combination of Ratings

The VA shall provide that, for the purpose of determining whether or not a veteran is permanently and totally disabled, ratings for service-connected disabilities may be combined with ratings for non-service-connected disabilities. Where a veteran is found to be entitled to a Non-Service-Connected Disability Pension and is also entitled to Service-Connected Disability Compensation, the VA shall pay the veteran the greater benefit.

Vocational Training for Certain Pension Recipients

In the case of a veteran who is awarded a Non-Service-Connected Disability Pension, the VA shall base on information on file with the VA, make a preliminary finding whether such veteran, with the assistance of a vocational training program, has a good potential for achieving employment. If such potential is found to exist, the VA shall solicit from the veteran an application for vocational training. If the veteran after that applies for such training, the VA shall provide the veteran with an evaluation, which may include a personal interview, to determine whether the achievement of a vocational goal is reasonably feasible.

If the VA, based on the evaluation, determines that the achievement of a vocational goal by a veteran is reasonably feasible, the veteran shall be offered and may elect to pursue a vocational training program.

If the veteran elects to pursue such a program, the program shall be designed in consultation with the veteran to meet the veteran's individual needs and shall be outlined in an individualized written plan of vocational rehabilitation.

A vocational training program under this section:

- May not exceed 24 months unless, based on a determination by the VA that an extension is necessary for the veteran to achieve a vocational goal identified in the written plan formulated for the veteran, the VA grants an extension for a period not to exceed 24 months.
- May not include the provision of any loan or subsistence allowance or any adaptive automobile equipment.
- May include a program of education at an institution of higher learning, only in a case in which the Secretary of the VA determines that the program involved is predominantly vocational in content.
- When a veteran completes a vocational training program, the VA may provide the veteran with counseling, placement, and post-placement services for a period not to exceed 18 months.

A veteran may not begin pursuit of a vocational training program under this chapter after the later of:

- December 31, 1995; or
- The end of a reasonable period of time, as determined by the VA, following either the evaluation of the veteran or the award of pension to the veteran.

In the case of a veteran who has been determined to have a permanent and total non- service-connected disability and who, not later than one year after the date the veteran's eligibility for counseling under this chapter expires, secures employment within the scope of a vocational goal identified in the veteran's individualized written plan of vocational rehabilitation (or in a related field which requires reasonably developed skills, and the use of some or all of the training or services furnished the veteran under such plan), the evaluation of the veteran as having a permanent and total disability may not be terminated because of the veteran's capacity to engage in such employment until the veteran first maintains such employment for a period of not less than 12 consecutive months.

Protection of Healthcare Eligibility

In the case of a veteran whose entitlement to pension is terminated after January 31, 1985, because of income from work or training, the veteran shall retain for a period of three years, beginning on the date of such termination, all eligibility for care and services that the veteran would have had if the veteran's entitlement to pension had not been terminated.

Disappearance

When a veteran receiving a non-service-connected disability pension from the VA disappears, the VA may pay the pension otherwise payable to such veteran's spouse and children. Payments made to a spouse or child shall not exceed the amount to which each would be entitled if the veteran died of a non-service-connected disability.

CHAPTER 7

SURVIVOR BENEFITS

Dependence and Indemnity Compensation for Service-Connected Deaths May Be Available For:

- Surviving spouses who have not remarried
- Surviving spouses who remarry after attaining age 57
- Unmarried Children under 18; Helpless children;
- Children between 18 and 23, if attending a VA- approved school; and
- Low-income parents of deceased servicemembers or veterans.

Definitions

Veteran: in this chapter, the term includes a person who died in the active military, naval, or air service.

Social Security Increase: in this chapter, the term means the percentage by which benefit amounts payable under Title II of the Social Security Act (42 U.S.C. 401 et seq.) are increased for any fiscal year as a result of a determination under section 215(i) of such Act (42 U.S.C. 415(i)).

Key Takeaways

If you're the surviving spouse, child or parent of a service member who died in the line of duty or the survivor of a veteran who died from a service-related injury or illness, you may be able to get a tax-free monetary benefit called VA Dependency and Indemnity Compensation (DIC).

If the VA denied your Blue Water Navy Veteran's service-connected disability claim in the past, you may be eligible for DIC benefits based on the Blue Water Navy Vietnam Veterans Act of 2019.

Permanently Housebound: for the purposes of this chapter, the requirement of "permanently housebound" will be considered to have been met when the individual is substantially confined to such individual's house (ward or clinical areas, if institutionalized) or immediate premises due to a disability or disabilities, which it is reasonably certain will remain throughout such individual's lifetime.

Eligibility

To receive Dependency and Indemnity Compensation (DIC), an individual must be an eligible survivor of a veteran who died from:
- A disease or injury incurred or aggravated while on active duty or active duty for training; or
- An injury incurred or aggravated in the line of duty while on inactive duty training; or
- A disability compensable by VA.

The death cannot be a result of the veteran's willful misconduct.

DIC also may be authorized for survivors of veterans who at the time of death, were determined to be totally disabled as a result of military service, even though their service-connected disabilities did not cause their deaths. The survivor qualifies if:
- The veteran was continuously rated totally disabled for a period of 10 or more years immediately preceding death; or
- The veteran was so rated for a period of at least five years from the date of military discharge; or
- The veteran was a former prisoner of war who died after September 30, 1999, and who was continuously rated totally disabled for a period of at least one year immediately preceding death.

To qualify as an eligible survivor, an individual must have proof of the following:
- Proof that he or she was married to the veteran for at least one year (Note: If a child was born, there is no time requirement); AND
- Proof that the marriage was VALID; AND
- Proof that he or she lived with the veteran continuously until his/her death or, if separated, the surviving spouse wasn't at fault; AND
- Proof that he or she did not remarry. (Note: The remarriage of the surviving spouse of a veteran shall not bar the furnishing of DIC if the remarriage is terminated by death, divorce, or annulment unless the VA determines that the divorce or annulment was secured through fraud or collusion.)

Public Law 108-183, The Veterans Benefits Act of 2003, restored DIC eligibility, effective January 1, 2004, for surviving spouses who remarry after age 57. Qualifying spouses who remarried at age 57 or older before the enactment of this bill had until December 16, 2004 to apply for reinstatement of these benefits. No retroactive benefits will be paid for any period before January 1, 2004.
OR
The individual is an unmarried child of a deceased veteran; AND
The individual is under age 18 or between the ages of 18 and 23 and attending school.

Note: Certain helpless adult children and some parents of deceased veterans are entitled to DIC. Call VA at (800) 827-1000 for the eligibility requirements for these survivors.

DIC Eligibility for Bluewater Survivors

Veterans who served on a Blue Water Navy vessel offshore of the Republic of Vietnam, or on another U.S. Navy or Coast Guard ship operating in the coastal waterways of Vietnam between January 9, 1962, and May 7, 1975, are now entitled to a presumption of service connection for illnesses related to Agent Orange exposure. This is a result of Public Law 116-23, also known as the Blue Water Navy Vietnam Veterans Act of 2019.

Amount of DIC Payments to Surviving Spouses

Surviving spouses of veterans who died after January 1, 1993, receive a basic monthly rate of $1,357.56 (effective December 1, 2020)

Surviving spouses entitled to DIC based on the veteran's death before January 1, 1993, receive the greater of:

- The basic monthly rate of **$1,357.56 or**
- An amount based on the veteran's pay grade. (See following sections for Pay Grade tables and Determination of Pay Grade.)

There are additional DIC payments for dependent children. (Refer to the following charts.)

Additional Allowances for Surviving Spouses

Add **$288.27** to the basic monthly rate if, at the time of the veteran's death, the veteran was in receipt of or entitled to receive compensation for a service-connected disability rated totally disabling (including a rating based on individual unemployability) for a continuous period of at least eight years immediately preceding death, AND the surviving spouse was married to the veteran for those same eight years.

Add **$336.32** per child to the basic monthly rate for each dependent child under age 18. If the surviving spouse is entitled to Aid & Attendance, add **$336.32** to the basic monthly rate. If the surviving spouse is Permanently Housebound, add **$157.55** to the basic monthly rate.

Surviving Spouse DIC Rates If Veteran's Death was Prior to January 1, 1993			
	Monthly Rate	Pay Grade	Monthly Rate
E-1*:	$1357.56	W-4**:	$1623.49
E-2*:	$1357.56	O-1**:	$1433.56
E-3*(see footnote#1):	$1357.56	O-2**:	$1482.72
E-4*:	$1357.56	O-3**:	$1584.38
E-5*:	$1357.56	O-4:	$1679.35
E-6*:	$1357.56	O-5:	$1848.08
E-7**:	$1404.49	O-6:	$2083.85
E-8**:	$1482.72	O-7:	$2249.19
E-9**(see footnote#2):	$1546.55 or $1669.31	O-8:	$2470.44
W-1**:	$1433.56	O-9:	$2642.50
W-2**:	$1490.53	O-10 (see footnote#3):	$2898.37 or $3110.67
W-3**:	$1534.11		

Footnotes to Table:

* Add $288.27 if veteran rated totally disabled eight continuous years before death and surviving spouse was married to veteran those same 8years.

A surviving spouse of an Aviation Cadet or other services not covered by this table is paid the DIC rate for enlisted E-3 under 34. $1669.31 is for a veteran who served as Sergeant Major of the Army or Marine Corps, Senior Enlisted Advisor of the Navy, Chief Master Sergeant of the Air Force, or Master Chief Petty Officer of the Coast Guard. $3110.67 is for a veteran who served as Chairman of the Joint Chiefs of Staff, Chief of Staff of the Army or Air Force, Chief of Naval Operations, or Commandant of the Marine Corps.

Determination of Pay Grade

With respect to a veteran who died in the active military, naval, or air service, such veteran's pay grade shall be determined as of the date of such veteran's death, or as of the date of promotion after death, while in a missing status.

With respect to a veteran who did not die in the active military, naval, or air service, such veteran's pay grade shall be determined as of:

- The time of such veteran's last discharge or release from active duty under conditions other than dishonorable; or
- The time of such veteran's discharge or release from any period of active duty for training or inactive duty training, if such veteran's death results from a service-connected disability incurred during such period, and if such veteran was not thereafter discharged or released under conditions other than dishonorable from active duty.
- If a veteran has satisfactorily served on active duty for a period of six months or more in a pay grade higher than that specified in the previous paragraphs of this section, and any subsequent discharge or release from active duty was under conditions other than dishonorable, the higher pay grade shall be used if it will result in greater monthly payments to such veteran's surviving spouse under this chapter. The determination as to whether an individual has served satisfactorily for the required period in a higher pay grade shall be made by the Secretary of the department in which such higher pay grade was held

DIC Payments to Children

Whenever there is no surviving spouse of a deceased veteran entitled to DIC, DIC shall be paid in equal shares to the children of the deceased veteran at the following monthly rates (effective December 1, 2020):

Number of Children	Total Payable (to be divided in equal shares):
1	$573.20
2	$824.59
3	$1076.01
4	$1280.49
5	$1484.97
6	$1689.45
7	$1893.93
8	$2098.41

If DIC is payable monthly to a person as a surviving spouse, and there is a child (of such person's deceased spouse) who has attained the age of 18, and who, while under such age, became permanently incapable of self-support, DIC shall be paid monthly to each such child, concurrently with the payment of DIC to the surviving spouse, in the amount of **$565.84**

If DIC is payable monthly to a person as a surviving spouse, and there is a child (of such person's deceased spouse) who has attained the age of 18 and who, while under the age of 23, is pursuing a course of instruction at a VA-approved educational institution, DIC shall be paid monthly to each such child, concurrently with the payment of DIC to the surviving spouse, in the amount of **$284.57.**

DIC Payments for Parents

Parents whose child died in-service or from a service-connected disability may be entitled to DIC if they are in financial need. Parents may be biological, step, adopted, or in loco parentis. The monthly payment for parents of deceased veterans depends upon their income.

The following 3 charts outline the monthly rates payable, **effective December 1, 2020,** under various conditions.

Chart #1 Sole Surviving Parent Unremarried or Remarried Living with Spouse			
Income Not Over:	Monthly	Income Not Over:	Monthly Rate:
$ 800	$672	$ 2,500	$536
900	$664	2,600	$528
1,000	$656	2,700	$520
1,100	$648	2,800	$512
1,200	$640	2,900	$504
1,300	$632	3,000	$496
1,400	$624	3,100	$488
1,500	$616	3,200	$480
1,600	$608	3,300	$472
1,700	$600	3,400	$464
1,800	$592	3,500	$456
1,900	$584	3,600	$448
2,000	$576	3,700	$440
2,100	$568	3,800	$432
2,200	$560	3,900	$424
2,300	$552	4,000	$416
2,400	$544	4,100	$408

$4,200	$400	$6,300	$232
4,300	$392	6,400	$224
4,400	$384	6,500	$216
4,500	$376	6,600	$208
4,600	$368	6,700	$200
4,700	$360	6,800	$192
4,800	$352	6,900	$184
4,900	$344	7,000	$176
5,000	$336	7,100	$168
5,100	$328	7,200	$160
5,200	$320	7,300	$152
5,300	$312	7,400	$144
5,400	$304	7,500	$136
5,500	$296	7,600	$128
5,600	$288	7,700	$120
5,700	$280	7,800	$112
5,800	$272	7,900	$104
5,900	$264		
6,000	$256	If A&A add:	$364
6,100	$248	If living w/ spouse: $21,298	
6,200	$240	**If not living w/ spouse: $15,845	

Chart#2- One of Two Parents Not Living with Spouse			
Income Not Over:	Monthly Rate:	Income Not Over:	Monthly Rate:
$800	$487	$3,600	$263
900	$479	3,700	$255
1,000	$471	3,800	$247
1,100	$463	3,900	$239
1,200	$455	4,000	$231
1300	$447	4,100	$223
1,400	$439	4,200	$215
1,500	$431	4,300	$207
1,600	$423	4,400	$199
1,700	$415	4,500	$191
1,800	$407	4,600	$183
1,900	$399	4,700	$175
2,000	$391	4,800	$167
2,100	$383	4,900	$159
2,200	$375	5,000	$151
2,300	$367	5,100	$143
2,400	$359	5,200	$135
2,500	$351	5,300	$127
2,600	$343	5,400	$119
2,700	$335	5,500	$111
2,800	$327	5,600	$103
2,900	$319	5,700	$95

3,000	$311	5,800	$87	
3,100	$303	5,900	$79	
3,200	$295	6,000	$71	
3,300	$287	$6,825 to $15,845		None
3,400	$279			
3,500	$271	If A&A add:		$364

Chart #3 1 of 2 Parents Living with Spouse or Other Parent			
Income Not Over:	Monthly Rate:	Income Not Over:	Monthly Rate:
$1,000	$458	$4,000	$263
1,100	$455	4,100	$255
1,200	$452	4,200	$247
1,300	$449	4,300	$239
1,400	$445	4,400	$231
1,500	$441	4,500	$223
1,600	$437	4,600	$215
1,700	$432	4,700	$207
1,800	$427	4,800	$199
1,900	$422	4,900	$191
2,000	$416	5,000	$183
2,100	$410	5,100	$175
2,200	$404	5,200	$167
2,300	$397	5,300	$159
2,400	$390	5,400	$151
2,500	$383	5,500	$143
2,600	$375	5,600	$135
2,700	$367	5,700	$127
2,800	$359	5,800	$119
2,900	$351	5,900	$111

3,000	$343	6,000	$103
3,100	$335	6,100	$95
3,200	$327	6,200	$87
3,300	$319	6,300	$79
3,400	$311	6,400	$71
3,500	$303	6,500	$63
3,600	$295	6,600	$55
3,700	$287	6,800	$47
3,800	$279	6,900	$39
3,900	$271	If A&A add:	$364

Miscellaneous Information Regarding Income Limitations for Parents

The VA may require, as a condition of granting or continuing DIC to a parent that such parent, other than one who has attained 72 years of age and has been paid DIC during two consecutive calendar years, file for a calendar year with the VA, a report showing the total income which such parent expects to receive in that year, and the total income which such parent received in the preceding year. The parent or parents shall notify the VA whenever there is a material change in annual income.

In determining income under this section, all payments of any kind, or from any source shall be included except:
- Payments of a death gratuity.
- Donations from public or private relief or welfare organizations.
- Payments under this chapter (DIC), Chapter 11 of Title 38, United States Code (Disability Compensation), and Chapter 15 of Title 38, United States Code (Non- Service-Connected Disability/Death Pension);
- Payments under policies of servicemembers group life insurance, United States Government life insurance, or national service life insurance, and payments of servicemen's indemnity.
- 10% of the number of payments to an individual under public or private retirement, annuity, endowment, or similar plans or programs;

Amounts equal to amounts paid by a parent of a deceased veteran for:
- A deceased spouse's just debts.
- The expenses of the spouse's last illness, to the extent such expenses are not reimbursed under Chapter 51 of Title 38 of the United States Code.
- The expenses of the spouse's burial to the extent that such expenses are not reimbursed under Chapter 23 or Chapter 51 of Title 38 of the United States Code.
- Reimbursements of any kind for any casualty loss (as defined in regulations which the VA shall prescribe), but the amount excluded under this clause may not exceed the greater of the fair market value or the reasonable replacement value of the property involved at the time immediately preceding the loss.

Amounts equal to amounts paid by a parent of a deceased veteran for:
- The expenses of the veteran's last illness, and expenses of such veteran's burial, to the extent that such expenses are not reimbursed under Chapter 23 of Title 38 of the United States Code.
- Profit realized from the disposition of real or personal property other than during business.
- Payments received for discharge of jury duty or obligatory civic duties.
- Payments of annuities elected under Subchapter I of Chapter 73 of Title 10.

Where a fraction of a dollar is involved, annual income shall be fixed at the next lower dollar. The VA may provide by regulation for the exclusion from income under this section of amounts paid by a parent for unusual medical expense

Special Provisions Relating to Surviving Spouses

No Dependency and Indemnity Compensation shall be paid to the surviving spouse of a veteran dying after December 31, 1956, unless such surviving spouse was married to such veteran:

- Before the expiration of 15 years after the termination of the period of service in which the injury or disease causing the death of the veteran was incurred or aggravated; or
- For one year or more; or
- For any period of time if a child was born of the marriage or was born to them before the marriage.

Applying for Dependency and Indemnity Compensation

Eligible surviving spouses and dependent children can apply for DIC by completing VA Form 21P-534ez, "Application for Dependency and Indemnity Compensation or Death Pension by Surviving Spouse or Child." If available, copies of dependency records (marriage records, divorce records, & children's birth certificates) should be attached to the application. A copy of the veteran's DD Form 214 and a copy of the veteran's death certificate should also be included with the completed application.

The completed form should be sent to the applicable VA Regional Office.

CHAPTER 8

SURVIVOR BENEFITS: DEATH PENSIONS

A Death Pension is a benefit paid to eligible dependents of deceased wartime veterans.

Definitions

Veteran: as used in this chapter, includes a person who has completed at least two years of honorable active military, naval, or air service, as certified by the appropriate authority, but whose death in such service was not in line of duty.

Indian Wars: means the campaigns, engagements, and expeditions of the United States military forces against Indian tribes or nations, service in which has been recognized heretofore as pensionable service.

World War I: means the period April 6, 1917, through November 11, 1918. In the case of a veteran who served with the United States military forces in Russia, the ending date is April 1, 1920. Service after November 11, 1918 and before July 2, 1921 is considered World War I for compensation or pension purposes if the veteran served in the active military, naval, or air service after April 5, 1917, and before November 12, 1 9 1 8.

> **Key Takeaways**
>
> The Survivors' Pension Benefit, which may also be referred to as Death Pension, is a tax-free monetary benefit available to low-income, un-remarried surviving spouses and/or unremarried child(ren) of a deceased veteran with wartime service.
>
> Survivors Pension is based on your yearly family income which must be less than the amount set by Congress to Quality.
>
> To apply for Survivors Pension, download and complete VA Form 21P-534EZ, Application for DIC, Death Pension and/or Accrued Benefits.

Civil War Veteran: includes a person who served in the military or naval forces of the Confederate States of America during the Civil War, and the term "active military or naval service" includes active service in those forces.

Period of War: means the Mexican border period, World War I, World War II, the Korean conflict, the Vietnam era, the Persian Gulf War, and the period beginning on the date of any future declaration of war by the Congress and ending on the date prescribed by Presidential proclamation or concurrent resolution of the Congress.

Regular Aid and Attendance: for the purposes of this chapter, a person shall be considered to require regular aid and attendance if such person is:

- A patient in a nursing home; or
- Helpless or blind, or so nearly helpless or blind as to need or require the aid and attendance of another person.

Permanently Housebound: for the purposes of this chapter, the requirement of "permanently housebound" will be considered to have been met when the surviving spouse is substantially confined to such surviving spouse's house (ward or clinical areas, if institutionalized) or immediate premises due to a disability or disabilities, which it is reasonably certain will remain throughout such surviving spouse's lifetime.

Eligibility Requirements

Eligible dependents may qualify for a Death Pension if:

- For service on or before September 7, 1980, the veteran must have served at least 90 days of active military service, with at least one day during a wartime period
- If he or she entered active duty after September 7, 1980, generally he or she must have served at least 24 months or the full period for which called or ordered to active duty with at least one day during a wartime period
- Was discharged from service under other than dishonorable condition
- The dependent is the surviving spouse (spouse must not have remarried), or the unmarried child of the deceased veteran (children must be under age 18, or under age 23 if attending a VA-approved school); **AND**
- The dependent's countable income is below an annual limit set by law (See below for 2020 annual income limitations.)

(Children who become incapable of self-support because of a disability before age 18 may be eligible for a pension as long as the condition exists unless the child marries, or the child's income exceeds the applicable limit.

Annual Income Limitations

Death Pension Rate Tables for Surviving Spouses and Children	
Rates Effective December 1, 2020	
Maximum Annual Pension Rate (MAPR)Category	Annual Income Must Be Less Than:
Surviving Spouse Alone (No Dependent Child):	$9,344.00
Surviving Spouse with One Dependent Child:	$12,229.00
Child Alone:	$2,382.00
Housebound Spouse Without Dependents:	$11,420.00
Housebound Spouse with One Dependent:	$14,300.00
Surviving Spouse in Need of Aid and Attendance (No Dependent Child):	$14,934.00
Surviving Spouse in Need of Aid and Attendance with One Dependent Child:	$17,815.00
For Each Additional Child:	$2,382.00
Child Earned Income Exclusion Effective 1/1/2021:	$12,550.00

Maximum Annual Income Limitations for Protected Pensions

Effective December 1, 2020

Pensioners entitled to benefits as of December 31, 1978, who do not elect to receive a pension under the Improved Pension Program, may continue to receive pension benefits at the rates they were entitled to receive on December 31, 1978, or June 30, 1960, as long as they remain permanently and totally disabled, do not lose a dependent, and their income does not exceed the income limitation, adjusted annually.

Pension Law In Effect on December 31,1978 (Section 306): The rate entitled to on December 31, 1978, may be continued if the recipient's IVAP for 2020 is below the following limits:		
Status of Recipient		Annual Income Limitation
Surviving spouse with no dependents		$15,845.00
Surviving spouse with one or more dependents		$21,298.00
Child (no entitled veteran or surviving spouse)		$12,956.00
Pension Law in Effect on June 30,1960 (Old Law): The rate entitled to on June 30, 1960 may be continued if the recipient's IVAP for 2020 is below the following limits:		
Status of Recipient		Annual Income Limitation
Surviving spouse with no dependents		$13,875.00
Surviving spouse with one or more dependents		$19,997.00
Child only (no entitled veteran or surviving spouse)		$13,875.00

Note: Some income is not counted toward the yearly limit (for example, welfare benefits, some wages earned by dependent children, and Supplemental Security Income).

In determining the annual income of a surviving spouse, if there is a child of the veteran in the custody of the surviving spouse, that portion of the annual income of the child that is reasonably available to or for the surviving spouse shall be considered to be income of the surviving spouse, unless in the judgment of the VA, to do so would work a hardship on the surviving spouse..

Net Worth Limitation

The VA shall deny or discontinue payment of pension to a surviving spouse when the corpus of the estate of the surviving spouse is such that under all the circumstances, including consideration of the income of the surviving spouse and the income of any child from whom the surviving spouse is receiving increased pension, it is reasonable that some part of the corpus of such estate be consumed for the surviving spouse's maintenance.

The VA shall deny or discontinue the payment of increased pension on account of a child when the corpus of such child's estate is such that under all the circumstances, including consideration of the income of the surviving spouse and such child and the income of any other child for whom the surviving spouse is receiving increased pension, it is reasonable that some part of the corpus of the child's estate be consumed for the child's maintenance. During the period, such denial or discontinuance remains in effect, such child shall not be considered as the surviving spouse's child for purposes of this chapter.

The VA shall deny or discontinue payment of pension to a child when the corpus of the state of the child is such that under all the circumstances, including consideration of the income of the child, the income of any person with whom such child is residing who is legally responsible for such child's support, and the corpus of the estate of such person, it is reasonable that some part of the corpus of such estate be consumed for the child's maintenance.

Applying for Death Pension Benefits

Eligible surviving spouses and dependent children can apply for Death Pension benefits by **completing** VA **Form 21P-534EZ**, "Application for Dependency and Indemnity Compensation or Death Pension by Surviving Spouse or Child." If available, copies of dependency records (marriage & children's birth certificates) should be attached to the application. A copy of the veteran's DD Form 214 and a copy of the veteran's death certificate should also be included with the completed application.

The completed forms should be sent to the applicable VA Regional Office.

CHAPTER 9

SURVIVOR BENEFITS:

MISCELLANEOUS BENEFITS FOR SURVIVING SPOUSES AND CHILDREN

Survivor Benefit Plan (SBP)

Military retired pay stops upon death of a retiree, and the Survivor Benefit Plan (SBP), allows a retiree to ensure after death a continuous lifetime annuity for their dependents. The annuity is based on a percentage of retired pay and is called SBP—which is paid to an eligible beneficiary. It pays your eligible survivors an inflation-adjusted monthly income. A military retiree pays premiums for SBP coverage upon retiring. Premiums are paid from gross retired pay, so they don't count as income. This means less tax and less out-of-pocket costs for SBP. The premiums are partially funded by the government, and the costs of operating the program are absorbed by the government, so the average premiums are well below the cost for a conventional insurance policy. For most retirees, SBP is a good choice, but the government contribution is based on assumptions in average cases and may not apply equally to every situation.

The maximum SBP annuity for a spouse is based on 55 percent of the member's retired pay (or in the case of a member who retires

> **Key Takeaways**
> The Survivor Benefit Plan is an elective program providing monthly income to survivors of retired military personnel.
>
> The Special Survivor Indemnity Allowance (SSIA) was set to expire in 2018 but is now permanent.
>
> Certain surviving spouses of military retirees who didn't participate in the Survivor Benefit plan and who died before September 21, 1973 are eligible for the SBP-MIW.
>
> There are benefits available for the children of women Vietnam veterans born with certain birth defects.

under REDUX, the retired pay the member would have received if under the high-three retirement system). However, a smaller amount may be elected. Your base amount can be any amount from full coverage down to as little as $300 a month. Full coverage is based on your full retired pay meaning your spouse will receive **55%** of your retirement pay. If you select lesser coverage, then your spouse will receive 55% percent of your elected "base amount."

Note: A surviving spouse's SBP annuity is reduced when they reach age 62 and become eligible for Social Security. This is called the Social Security offset. In the past the offset reduced the SBP annuity to 35 percent of the base amount. The offset created a need for members to purchase a Supplemental Survivor Benefit Plan (SSBP) policy. Fortunately, the National Defense Authorization Act of 2005 established a phase-out of the offset by 2008, thus eliminating the need for the SSBP. Details of the National Defense Authorization Act of 2005 are described below.

Phased-In Increase in Basic Annuity

One major provision of the Ronald W. Reagan FY2005 National Defense Authorization Act included an increase in the minimum SBP annuity for survivors age 62 and older from 35% to 55% over three years.

The FY 2005 Defense Authorization Act included provisions to eliminate the social security offset under SBP by increasing the annuities paid to survivors of military retirees who are 62 or older from 35 percent of retired pay to the percentages indicated below:

For months after September 2005 and before April 2006: 40%

For months after March 2006 and before April 2007: 45%

For months after March 2007 and before April 2008: 50%

For months after March 2008: 55%

Note: Public Law 108-183, The Veterans Benefits Act of 2003 provided that, for surviving spouses who remarry after attaining age 57, Dependency and Indemnity Compensation (DIC) be paid with no reduction of certain other Federal benefits to which a surviving spouse might be entitled. This provision, in essence, eliminates the requirement for DIC to offset military SBP annuities, as was required under prior law. In other words, concurrent receipt of DIC and SBP without an offset of either is now allowed for surviving spouses who remarry after attaining age 57.

What is the Difference Between DIC and SBP?

Dependents Indemnity Compensation (DIC) is an entitlement benefit paid to eligible survivors, including spouses and married children of certain deceased servicemembers and veterans. The DIC benefit is managed by the Department of Veterans Affairs and is dispersed to surviving family members that meet specific criteria. The Survivor Benefits Program is a voluntary annuity program managed by the Department of Defense.

What is the SBP/DIC Offset?

DIC is a payment made by the Department of Veteran Affairs (DVA) to the spouse of a member who dies due to a service-connected illness or injury. The DVA determines entitlement to and the amount of the DIC award. If DIC is awarded, the SBP/RCSBP annuity must be reduced by the amount of the DIC award. The SBP/RCSBP annuity is terminated if the DIC is greater than the SBP/RCSBP. However, if an annuitant receives DIC based on a member other than the one providing SBP/RCSBP, there will not be a DIC reduction.

Each annuitant signs a DIC authorization statement when they submit their annuity application. This allows DFAS to establish their SBP/RCSBP annuity before notification from the DVA regarding their entitlement to DIC. This prevents delays in SBP/RCSBP payments.

If DIC is awarded, the following conditions apply:

- If the monthly DIC benefit exceeds the SBP/RCSBP monthly annuity, the amount of the SBP/RCSBP annuity paid before notification of the DIC award, not including the month of death, is an overpayment. If the DIC monthly benefit does not exceed the SBP/RCSBP monthly annuity, the amount of SBP overpayment will be the amount of DIC awarded prior to notification. See number 3 for more information on overpayments.
- Once Defense Finance and Accounting Services (DFAS) receives all of the necessary information from the DVA, the annuitant will be due a refund of all or part of the SBP/RCSBP costs paid into the plan by the member (SBP/RCSBP cost refund) if the DIC award is made retroactive to the date of death. The SBP/RCSBP cost refund will be applied to any SBP/RCSBP overpayment or other indebtedness, and a check for the remaining balance, if any, will be forwarded to the annuitant. The SBP/RCSBP cost refund might be taxable if the retiree paid the SBP/RCSBP costs from the retired pay taxable income. Any taxable portion of the cost refund will be included as taxable income on the TD Form 1099-R annuitants receive at the end of the year.
- Depending on the amount of the overpayment, it will either be collected from the SBP/RCSBP cost refund, referred to the DVA for collection from the annuitant's DIC payment, or combination of both. Annuitants will be advised of the method of collection and sent an account statement showing the SBP/RCSBP cost refund less any overpayment collected when the SBP/RCSBP cost refund is processed.
- Annuitant's taxable income will be increased by the taxable portion of the cost refund and reduced by the amount applied to the overpayment. The taxable income will be adjusted when the overpayment is collected. An annuitant may receive a tax deduction or tax credit, as appropriate, if the overpayment occurred.
- Since SBP/RCSBP costs are not paid by members who die while on active

duty, or by Reservist who dies before retirement, there will be no refund of costs. The overpayments will be referred to the DVA for collection from the annuitant's DIC.

- Annuitants can reduce the amount of the SBP/RCSBP overpayment by notifying DFAS at once when DIC has been awarded. Please furnish DFAS with a copy of the award letter from the DVA.
- Since DIC benefits are nontaxable, VA encourages annuitants to apply for DIC if they have not done so.
- If the DIC effective date is past the first day of the month after the member's death and the annuitant has received a benefit from receipt of the SBP/RCSBP, no cost refund is due.

Special Survivor Indemnity Allowance (SSIA)

Section 644 of the National Defense Authorization Act (NDAA) for Fiscal Year 2008 created the Special Survivor Indemnity Allowance (SSIA). This allowance is payable to all Survivor Benefit Plan (SBP) annuitants whose annuity has been offset for receipt of Dependency and Indemnity Compensation (DIC) from the Department of Veterans Affairs (DVA).

SSIA Is Now Permanent

SSIA is now a permanent benefit. The benefit will now be paid at $310 per month plus a cost-of-living adjustment each calendar year. The cost-of-living adjustment will begin in 2019. When a spouse is eligible to receive SBP and DIC, and those payments are subject to the SBP/DIC offset, the spouse will also receive the Special Survivor Indemnity Allowance (SSIA). This allowance is taxable. Your DIC payment address will be used for your SSIA payment. If you are currently receiving your DIC payment from the DVA at your home address, your SSIA payment will also be sent there. If your DIC payment is paid via electronic funds transfer (EFT) by the DVA, your DIC electronic payment address will be used for the SSIA payment.

Survivor Benefit Plan – Minimum Income Annuity

Eligible surviving spouses of military retirees who did not participate in the plan, and who died prior to September 21, 1973, are eligible for SBP-MIW (Survivor Benefit Plan – Minimum Income Annuity). To be eligible, the surviving spouse must not be remarried, must be eligible for VA death pension, and must have income for VA purposes, excluding any SBP annuity, of less than the MIW- SBP annuity limitation. **Effective December 1, 2020, the SBP-MIW annuity limitation is $9,344**

Benefits for Children of Women Vietnam Veterans Born with Certain Birth Defects

Section 401 of P.L. 106-416, which became law on November 1, 2000 directed the Secretary of VA to identify birth defects of children of female Vietnam veterans that: (1) are associated with service during the Vietnam era; and (2) result in the permanent physical or mental disability of such children. The law excludes from such defects familial or birth-related defects or injuries.

Children of Women Vietnam Veterans Born with Certain Birth Defects (P.L 106-419)- Rates Effective December 1, 2020	
Disability Level	Monthly Allowance
Level I	$159.00
Level II	$341.00
Level III	$1162.00
Level IV	$1979.00

The law further directs the Secretary to provide to such children the necessary health care to address the defect and any associated disability. It authorizes the Secretary to provide vocational training to such a child if the achievement of a vocational goal is reasonably feasible.

The law also directs the Secretary to pay a monthly allowance to such a child, the amount to be determined through a schedule rating the various defects and disabilities and their degrees. The receipt of such allowance shall not infringe upon the right to receive any other benefit to which the individual is entitled. Such allowance shall not be considered income for purposes of other veterans' benefits for which income limitations exist.

In the case of an eligible child whose only covered birth defect is spina bifida, a monetary allowance shall be paid under these provisions only. An eligible individual shall be provided only one program of vocational training.

The monthly allowance is set at four levels, depending upon the degree of disability suffered by the child.

Survivors' Frequently Asked Questions

How do I apply for benefits?
The application for VA Survivors Benefits involves the claimant completing the appropriate forms and supplying the necessary documentation. Applications are then sent to the appropriate VA Regional Office or Pension Management Center for processing.

It is strongly recommended that claimants make duplicate copies of their application for their own records.

How do I reinstate my previous benefit?
If your DIC benefit as a surviving spouse was terminated because you remarried, but the subsequent marriage has since ended due to death, divorce, or annulment, you might file to have your previous Survivor's benefit reinstated.

To do so, you will be asked to complete VA Form 21-4138 and submit it to your local VA Regional Office along with documentation supporting the claim that your subsequent marriage has ended (i.e., divorce decree or death certificate). After doing so, call the Veterans Benefits Administration directly at **800-827-1000** to confirm that your materials have been received and to find out the status of your reinstatement.

Is there someone that can help me file my claim?
Yes. You have two options available. You may seek assistance at your local VA regional office. Another option is to locate a Veteran Service Organizations (VSO) or County Veteran Service Officers (CVSO) throughout the United States. Many VSOs offer to surviving families' benefits counseling and assistance with the application process, and often have local chapters.
It is strongly recommended that surviving family members consult with the VSO of their choice when applying for VA Survivor Benefits.

As a survivor, am I eligible for my loved one's month of death compensation?
The Department of Veterans Affairs (VA) announced immediate actions to quickly identify and pay surviving spouses who are eligible to receive the deceased veteran's VA compensation or pension benefit for the month of the veteran's death.

This benefit is only payable to surviving spouses of veterans who were receiving VA compensation or pension benefits at the time of their death.
Because VA does not always know if a veteran is survived by a spouse, some surviving spouses have not received the month-of-death benefit to which they are entitled.

As a surviving spouse, am I eligible for VA medical care?
The Department of Veterans Affairs offers CHAMPVA healthcare coverage to family members that meet specific eligibility criteria. The Civilian Health and Medical Program of the Department of Veterans Affairs (CHAMPVA) is a comprehensive health care program in which the VA shares the cost of covered health care services and supplies with eligible beneficiaries. The program is administered by Health Administration Center and our offices are located in Denver, Colorado.

Due to the similarity between CHAMPVA and the Department of Defense (DoD) TRICARE program (sometimes referred to by its old name, CHAMPUS), the two are often mistaken for each other. CHAMPVA is a Department of Veterans Affairs program whereas TRICARE is a regionally managed health care program for active duty and retired members of the uniformed services, their families, and survivors.

In some cases, a veteran or survivor may look to be eligible for both/either program on paper. However, if you are a military retiree or the spouse of a veteran who was killed in action, you are and will always be a TRICARE beneficiary, you cannot choose between the two.

CHAPTER 10

BURIAL AND MEMORIAL BENEFITS

Veteran Burial Benefits

VA burial allowances are flat-rate monetary benefits. They help cover eligible veterans' burial and funeral costs. Generally, they are paid at the maximum amount allowed by law. A 2014 VA regulation change helped simplify the program. Eligible surviving spouses are now paid automatically. This happens upon notification of the veteran's death. There is no need to submit a claim. However, VA may grant additional benefits after receiving a claim. These include plot or interment allowance and transportation allowance.

Burial, Headstone and Plot Rate Tables Effective 10/1/2020

Benefits	Rate	Date Rate Changed	Public Law
Headstone/Marker	$231	10-01-2020	PL 95-476
Service-Connected Burial	*$2,000 $1,500	12-1-2001 04-01-1988	PL 107-103 PL 100-322
Non-Service-Connected Burial	$807	10-01-2020	PL 111-275 PL 111-275 PL 100-322
Plot Allowance	$807	10-01-2020	PL 111-275 PL 107-103 PL 100-322
State Cemetery Plot Allowance	$807	10-01-2020	PL 111-275 PL 107-103 PL 100-322

Note 1: The P.L. 107-103 service-connected burial rate applies in cases where death occurred on or after 9/11/01.

Note 2: The headstone/marker allowance is payable only if the veteran died between 10/18/78 and 11/1/90. The rate payable is determined by when the headstone/marker was purchased.

Note 3: For non-service connected deaths, VA will pay up to $807 toward burial and funeral expenses (if hospitalized by VA at time of death), or $300 toward burial and funeral expenses (if not hospitalized by VA at time of death).

Pre-Need Burial Eligibility

The Department of Veterans Affairs (VA) implemented the pre-need burial eligibility determination program to assist anyone who would like to know if they are eligible for burial in a VA national cemetery. VA is promoting pre-need eligibility determinations to encourage Veterans and their eligible family members to plan in advance to use VA burial benefits that Veterans have earned through their military service. Planning in advance for a Veteran's or loved one's final resting place can eliminate unnecessary delays and reduce stress on a family at a difficult time. Veteran families will have increased confidence that their loved ones are eligible for burial in a VA national cemetery at their time of need.

Upon request, VA will make eligibility determinations for burial in a VA national cemetery in advance of need. Eligible individuals are entitled to burial in any open VA national cemetery, which includes opening/closing of the grave, a government-furnished grave liner, perpetual care of the gravesite, and a government-furnished upright headstone or flat marker or niche cover all at no cost to the family. Veterans are also eligible for a burial flag and Presidential Memorial Certificate.

Burial in a VA national cemetery is open to all members of the armed forces and Veterans who have met minimum active duty service requirements, as applicable by law, and were discharged under conditions other than dishonorable. Members of the reserve components of the armed forces who die while on active duty under certain circumstances or who die while on training duty are also eligible for burial, as are service members and former service members who were eligible for retired pay at the time of their death. Spouses, minor children and, under certain conditions, dependent unmarried adult children are also eligible for burial even if they predecease the Veteran.

The Department of Veterans Affairs (VA) has implemented this pre-need eligibility program so that Veterans, spouses and unmarried dependent adult children may better prepare for burial in a VA national cemetery before the time of need. Interested individuals may submit VA Form 40-10007, Application for Pre-Need Determination of Eligibility for Burial in a VA National Cemetery, along with a copy of supporting documentation of military service such as a DD214, if readily available, by Toll-free fax at 1-855-840-8299; or mail to the National Cemetery Scheduling Office, P.O. Box 510543, St. Louis, MO 63151.

Authorized representatives can also apply on behalf of eligible claimants. An authorized agent or representative is an individual authorized by the claimant to make decisions on the claimant's behalf. An authorized representative first needs to be recognized by VA as an authorized representative or agent by filing a VA Form 21-22 Appointment of Veterans Service Organization As Claimant Representative or VA Form 21-22a Appointment of Attorney or Agent As Claimant Representative.

You can access the forms at www.vba.va.gov/pubs/forms/VBA-21-22-ARE.pdf and VA Form 21-22a at www.vba.va.gov/pubs/forms/VBA-21-22A-ARE.pdf. Written authorization should be included with the VA Form 40-10007, Application for Pre-Need Determination of Eligibility for Burial in a VA National Cemetery, if available. A notarized statement is not required.

VA will review pre-need burial applications and provide written notice of a determination of eligibility. VA will store the pre-need application, supporting documentation, and the decision letter to expedite burial arrangements at the time of need. We encourage you to keep the decision letter with supporting documentation with your important papers in a safe place and to discuss your burial wishes and final arrangements with your loved ones or other representatives. Submission of a pre-need burial eligibility application does not obligate the Veteran or family member to burial in a VA national cemetery.

Applicants may indicate a preference for a VA national cemetery on the application form, but a pre-need determination of eligibility does not guarantee burial in a specific VA national cemetery or a specific gravesite. VA assigns gravesites in cemeteries with available space once death has occurred, and the burial is scheduled.

At your time of need, your next-of-kin, funeral home or another representative responsible for making your final arrangements should contact the National Cemetery Scheduling Office at (800) 535-1117 to request burial. VA will locate your pre-need decision letter and validate our determination. Because laws affecting VA burial eligibility and individual circumstances may change, upon receipt of a burial request, VA will verify pre-need decisions in accordance with the laws in effect at that time including bars to receipt of burial benefits.

Burial Benefits

Beginning July 7, 2014, VA changed its monetary burial benefits regulations to simplify the program and pay eligible survivors more quickly and efficiently. These regulations will authorize VA to pay, without a written application, most eligible surviving spouses basic monetary burial benefits at the maximum amount authorized in law through automated systems rather than reimbursing them for actual costs incurred.

The new burial regulations will permit VA to pay, at a flat rate, burial, and plot or interment allowances, thereby enabling VA to automate payment of burial benefits to most eligible surviving spouses and more efficiently process other burial benefit claims. The burial allowance for a non-service-connected death is $300, and $2,000 for a death connected to military service.

Service-related Death

VA will pay up to $2,000 toward burial expenses for deaths on or after September 11, 2001, or up to $1,500 for deaths before September 11, 2001. If the Veteran is buried in a VA national cemetery, some or all of the cost of transporting the deceased may be reimbursed.

Non-service-related Death

VA will pay up to $796 toward burial and funeral expenses for deaths on or after October 1, 2019 (if hospitalized by VA at time of death), or $300 toward burial and funeral expenses (if not hospitalized by VA at time of death), and a $796 plot-interment allowance (if not buried in a national cemetery).

For deaths on or after December 1, 2001, but before October 1, 2011, VA will pay up to $300 toward burial and funeral expenses and a $300 plot-interment allowance. For deaths on or after April 1, 1988, but before October 1, 2011, VA will pay $300 toward burial and funeral expenses (for Veterans hospitalized by VA at the time of death).
An annual increase in burial and plot allowances for deaths occurring after October 1, 2011, begins in fiscal year 2013 based on the Consumer Price Index for the preceding 12- month period.

Eligibility Requirements

- You paid for a Veteran's burial or funeral, AND
- You have not been reimbursed by another government agency or some other source, such as the deceased Veteran's employer, AND
- The Veteran was discharged under conditions other than dishonorable, AND
- The Veteran died because of a service-related disability, OR
- The Veteran was receiving VA pension or compensation at the time of death,
- OR The Veteran was entitled to receive VA pension or compensation, but decided not to reduce his/her military retirement or disability pay, OR
- The Veteran died while hospitalized by VA, or while receiving care under VA contract at a non-VA facility, OR
- The Veteran died while traveling under proper authorization and at VA expense to or from a specified place for the purpose of examination, treatment, or care, OR
- The Veteran had an original or reopened claim pending at the time of death and has been found entitled to compensation or pension from a date prior to the date of death, OR
- The Veteran died on or after October 9, 1996, while a patient at a VA-approved state nursing home.

NOTE: VA does not pay burial benefits if the deceased:

- Died during active military service, OR
- Was a member of Congress who died while holding office, OR
- Was a Federal prisoner

Evidence Requirements:

- Acceptable proof of death as specified in 38 CFR 3.211, AND
- Receipted bills that show that you made payment in whole or part, OR
- A statement of account, preferably on the printed billhead of the funeral director or cemetery owner.

The statement of account must show:

- The name of the deceased Veteran for whom the services and merchandise were furnished, AND
- The nature and cost of the services and merchandise, AND
- All credits, AND
- The amount of the unpaid balance, if any

You can apply online at Vets.gov or submit a paper application by completing VA Form 21P-530, Application for Burial Allowance. When completed, mail it to the Pension Management Center that serves your state. You can also work with an accredited representative or go to your local, regional benefit office.

Dignified Burial of Unclaimed Veterans Act

On December 30, 2012, the Dignified Burial of Unclaimed Veterans Act of 2012 was sent to the President for signature into law. The law contains the following provisions:

Cemetery Matters: The bill authorizes the Secretary of Veterans Affairs (VA) to furnish a casket or urn for a deceased veteran with no known living kin.

Veterans Freedom of Conscience Protection: Under the bill, in cases where family or the next of kin of a deceased veteran can be identified, the bill requires the VA to ensure that the expressed wishes of the next of kin are met with regards to memorial service, funeral or interment at a national cemetery.

Improved Communication Between Department of Veterans Affairs And Medical Examiners and Funeral Directors: The bill requires the VA to obtain information from the relevant medical examiner, funeral director, service group, or other entity regarding the steps taken to determine if the deceased has no next of kin.

Identification and Burial of Unclaimed or Abandoned Human Remains: The VA will be required to cooperate with veterans service organizations to assist entities in possession of unclaimed or abandoned remains of veterans, with the department authorized to determine whether such remains are eligible for burial in a national cemetery.

Restoration, Operation and Maintenance of Clark Veterans Cemetery by American Battle Monuments Commission: The bill authorizes the appropriation of $5 million for site preparation and construction at the Clark Veterans Cemetery located in the Philippines. The bill directs the American Battle Monuments

Commission to restore and operate the cemetery once a cooperative agreement is reached with the government of the Philippines.

Reimbursement: The Veterans Benefits Administration administers a burial benefit program designed to assist claimants in meeting the funeral and burial costs of a deceased veteran. The type and amount of benefits payable depend on the veteran's individual service record and cause of death.

Service-Connected Death: If a veteran's death is service-connected, the VA will pay a burial allowance of up to $2,000 (for deaths on or after 9-11-2001 - prior to 9-11-2001, the burial allowance was $1,500). If the veteran is buried in a VA national cemetery, some or all of the cost of moving the deceased to the national cemetery nearest the veteran's home may also be reimbursed. There is no time limit for applying for a service-connected burial allowance. The person who bore the veteran's burial expense may claim reimbursement from any VA regional office.

Unpaid Balance Due Persons Who Performed Services: If there is an unpaid balance due the person who performed burial, funeral, and transportation services, such claim as a creditor for the statutory burial allowance will be given priority over any claim for reimbursement based on use of personal funds unless there is executed by such creditor a waiver in favor of the person or persons whose personal funds were used in making the partial payment of the account. No reimbursement may be made to a State, County, or other governmental subdivision.

Veteran's Estate: The representative of a deceased person's estate might file a claim for reimbursement if estate funds were used to pay the expenses of the veteran's burial, funeral, and transportation. Accordingly, if otherwise in order, reimbursement may be made to the estate, regardless of whether such person pre-deceased the veteran or was deceased at the time the expenses were incurred or paid, or burial of the veteran actually occurred.

Death of Active-Duty Personnel: The VA does not pay a burial or plot interment allowance if a veteran dies while on active military duty. However, such veteran is entitled to certain benefits from the military. Information should be obtained from the branch of the armed forces in which the person served at the time of death.

Correction of Discharge to Honorable Conditions: Public Law 88-3 (H.R. 212) provides that where burial allowance was not payable at the time of a veteran's death because of the nature of his discharge from service, but after death, his discharge is corrected by competent authority to reflect a discharge under conditions other than dishonorable, claim may be filed within two years from the date of correction of the discharge.

Legal Execution: The execution of a veteran as a lawful punishment for a crime does not of itself preclude payment of the statutory burial allowances.

State Burial Allowance: There are some burial allowances allowed by states or counties for the burial of needy veterans, and in some instances, of their dependents. Check with the veteran's state or county of residence for specific information.

Assistance to Claimants: It is incumbent upon the claimant to establish his case in accordance with the law. This rule, however, will not be highly technical or rigid in its application. The general policy of the VA is to give the claimant every opportunity to substantiate his claim, to extend all reasonable assistance in its prosecution, and develop all sources from which information may be obtained. Assistance may also be secured from post, state, and national service officers or veterans' organizations.

Miscellaneous: If the deceased veteran is entitled to payment in full of burial expenses by the Employees' Compensation Commission, Workman's Compensation, or employer, the Veterans Administration will make no payment.

Appeal: An appeal may be made within one year from the date of the denial of a claim. The appeal must be sent to the regional VA office that denied the claim.

Burial Flags

The VA shall furnish a United States flag, at no cost, for burial or memorial purposes in connection with the death of an eligible veteran who served honorably in the U.S. Armed Forces. Public Law 105-261, added eligibility for former member of the Selected Reserve who:

- Completed at least one enlistment as a member of the Selected Reserve or, in the case of an officer, completed the period of initial obligated service as a member of the Selected Reserve; or
- Was discharged before completion of the person's initial enlistment as a member of the Selected Reserve or, in the case of an officer, period of initial obligated service as a member of the Selected Reserve, for a disability incurred or aggravated in the line of duty; or
- Who died while a member of the Selected Reserve.

Burial flags may not be furnished on behalf of deceased veterans who committed capital crimes. After the burial of the veteran, the flag shall be given to his next of kin. If no claim is made for the flag by the next of kin, it may be given, upon request, to a close friend or associate of the deceased veteran. If a flag is given to a close friend or associate of the deceased veteran, no flag shall be given to any other person on account of the death of such veteran.

When burial is in a national, state or post cemetery, a burial flag will automatically be provided. When burial is in a private cemetery, an American flag may be obtained by a service officer, an undertaker or another interested person from the nearest Veterans Administration office or most U.S. Post Offices. VA Form 27-2008, "Application for United States Flag for Burial Purposes," must be completed and submitted along with a copy of the veteran's discharge papers. Generally, the funeral director will help the next of kin with this process.

The proper way to display the flag depends upon whether the casket is open or closed. VA Form 27-2008 provides the proper method for displaying and folding the flag. The burial flag is not suitable for outside display because of its size and fabric.

After burial of a veteran, the flag should be folded in military style and presented to the next of kin at the cemetery. Local veteran organizations, when presenting the flag, usually say something like this: "In the name of the United States government and name of a veterans organization (such as A.L., D.A.V., V.F.W., and American Veterans of World War II, etc.), we present you this flag, in loving memory of our departed comrade."

Presenting of the flag is sometimes a difficult task when there is a disagreement in the family. However, the Veterans Administration gives the following order of preference to be followed:
- Widow or widower (even if separated but not divorced)
- Children according to age (minor child may be issued flag on an application signed by guardian)
- Father, including adopted, step and foster father
- Mother, including adopted, step and foster mother
- Brothers or sisters, including brothers and sisters of half-blood. Uncles or aunts
- Nephews or nieces
- Cousins, grandparents, etc. (but not in-laws)
- If two relatives have equal rights, the flag will be presented to the elder one.

Following a veteran's burial, the United States flag received by the next of kin may be donated to the VA for use on national holidays at VA national cemeteries. If the next of kin choose to make such a donation, it should be given or mailed to the Director of any national cemetery selected by the donor with a written request that the flag is flown at that location.

If the flag is brought into a Veterans Service Division, it will be accepted and forwarded to the cemetery chosen by the donor. A Certificate of Appreciation is presented to the donor for providing their loved ones' burial flag to a national cemetery. Please note that VA cannot provide flag holders for placement on private headstones or markers. These flag holders may be purchased from private manufacturing companies.

The law allows the VA to issue one flag for a veteran's funeral. The VA cannot replace it if it is lost, destroyed, or stolen. However, if this occurs, a local veteran's organization or another community group may be able to assist you in obtaining another flag.

Headstones and Markers in Private Cemeteries

Ordering Grave Marker Medallion

In 2012 the VA introduced a new form, VA **Form 40-1330**, which is now used as the sole form for families to order a grave marker medallion. Prior to the change, families of the deceased used a form to order the medallion that was the same as the form used to order a government headstone or grave marker. The medallion is given instead of a traditional government headstone or marker, specifically for veterans whose death occurred on or after November 1, 1990. The medallion is intended for use for those veterans whose grave is located in a private cemetery and marked with a privately purchased headstone or marker.

The VA is required to furnish an appropriate headstone or marker for the graves of eligible veterans buried in private cemeteries, whose deaths occur on or after December 27, 2001, regardless of whether the grave is already marked with a non-government marker. Headstones or markers may not be furnished on behalf of deceased veterans who committed capital crimes.

For all deaths occurring before September 11, 2001, the VA may provide a headstone or marker only for graves that are not marked with a private headstone.

Spouses and dependents buried in a private cemetery are not eligible for a Government-provided headstone or marker.

Flat markers in granite, marble, and bronze, and upright headstones in granite and marble are available. The style chosen must be consistent with existing monuments at the place of burial. Niche markers are also available to mark columbaria used for cremated remains.

Government-furnished headstones and markers must be inscribed with the name of the deceased, branch of service, and the year of birth and death, in this order. Headstones and markers also may be inscribed with other items, including an authorized emblem of belief and, space permitting, additional text including military-grade, rate or rank, war service such as "World War II," complete dates of birth and death, military awards, military organizations, and civilian or veteran affiliations. To apply, and to obtain specific information on available styles, contact the cemetery where the headstone or marker is to be placed.

When burial occurs in a private cemetery, an application for a government-furnished headstone or marker must be made to VA. The government will ship the headstone or marker free of charge but will not pay for its placement. To apply, complete VA Form 40-1330 (**application form updated in 2012**), and forward it along with a copy of the veteran's military discharge documents (do not send original discharge documents, as they will not be returned) to:

Memorial Products Service (41B)
Department of Veterans Affairs
5109 Russell Road
Quantico, VA 22134-3903

Bronze Medallion

VA made available a new medallion to be affixed to an existing privately purchased headstone or marker to signify the deceased's status as a veteran.

If requested, the medallion will be furnished in lieu of a traditional government headstone or marker for veterans that died on or after November 1, 1990, and whose grave is marked with a privately purchased headstone or marker.

The medallion is currently available in three sizes, 5 inches, 3 inches, and 1 ½ inches. Each medallion will be inscribed with the word VETERAN across the top and the Branch of Service at the bottom. Appropriate affixing adhesive, instructions, and hardware will be provided with the medallion.

Important: This benefit is only applicable if the grave is marked with a privately purchased headstone or marker. In these instances, eligible veterans are entitled to either a traditional government-furnished headstone or marker, or the new medallion, but not both.

Eligibility Rules for a Government Headstone Or Marker in a Private Cemetery

Veterans and Members of the Armed Forces (Army, Navy, Air Force, Marine Corps, Coast Guard):

- Any veterans or members of The Armed Forces who die while on active duty.
- Any veteran who was discharged under conditions other than dishonorable. With certain exceptions, service beginning after September 7, 1980, as an enlisted person, and service after October 16, 1981, as an officer, must be for a minimum of 24 months or the full period for which the person was called to active duty. (Examples include those serving less than 24 months in the Gulf War or Reservists that were federalized by Presidential Act.) Undesirable, bad conduct and any other type of discharge other than honorable may or may not qualify the individual for veterans' benefits, depending upon a determination made by a VA Regional Office. Cases presenting multiple discharges of varying character are also referred for adjudication to a VA Regional Office

Members of Reserve Components and Reserve Officers' Training Corps:

- Reservists and National Guard members who, at time of death, were entitled to retired pay under Chapter 1223, Title 10, United States Code, or would have been entitled, but for being under the age of 60.
  - Members of reserve components who die while hospitalized or undergoing treatment at the expense of the United States for injury or disease contracted or incurred under honorable conditions while performing active duty for training or inactive

131

duty training or undergoing such hospitalization or treatment.

- Members of the Reserve Officers' Training Corps of the Army, Navy, or Air Force who die under honorable conditions while attending an authorized training camp or on an authorized cruise, while performing authorized travel to or from that camp or cruise, or while hospitalized or undergoing treatment at the expense of the United States for injury or disease contracted or incurred under honorable conditions while engaged in one of those activities.

- Members of reserve components who, during a period of active duty for training, were disabled or died from a disease or injury incurred or aggravated in the line of duty or, during a period of inactive duty training, were disabled or died from an injury incurred or aggravated in the line of duty

Commissioned Officers, National Oceanic, and Atmospheric Administration:

- A commissioned officer of the National Oceanic and Atmospheric Administration (formerly titled the Coast and Geodetic Survey and the Environmental Science Services Administration) with full-time duty on or after July 29, 1945
- A commissioned officer who served before July 29, 1945, and:
- Was assigned to an area of immediate military hazard while in time of war, or of a Presidentially declared national emergency as determined by the Secretary of Defense; or
- Served in the Philippine Islands on December 7, 1941, and continuously in such islands thereafter; or
- Transferred to the Department of the Army or the Department of the Navy under the provisions of the Act of May 22, 1917 Public Health Service
- A Commissioned Officer of the Regular or Reserve Corps of the Public Health Service who served on full-time duty on or after July 29, 1945. If the service of the particular Public Health Service Officer falls within the meaning of active duty for training, as defined in section 101(22), title 38, United States Code, he or she must have been disabled or died from a disease or injury incurred or aggravated in the line of duty.

A Commissioned Officer of the Regular or Reserve Corps of the Public Health Service who performed full-time duty before July 29, 1945:

- In time of war;
- On detail for duty with the Army, Navy, Air Force, Marine Corps, or Coast Guard; or,
- While the Service was part of the military forces of the United States pursuant to Executive Order of the President.
- A Commissioned Officer serving on inactive duty training as defined in section 101(23), title 38, United States Code, whose death resulted from an injury incurred or aggravated in the line of duty.

World War II Merchant Mariners

United States Merchant Mariners with oceangoing service during the period of armed conflict, December 7, 1941, to December 31, 1946. Prior to the enactment of Public Law 105-368, United States Merchant Mariners with oceangoing service during the period of armed conflict of December 7, 1941, to August 15, 1945, were eligible.

With the enactment of Public Law 105-368, the service period is extended to December 31, 1946, for those dying on or after November 11, 1998. A DD-214 documenting this service may be obtained by applying Commandant (G-MVP- 6), United States Coast Guard, 2100 2nd Street, SW, Washington, DC 20593.

Notwithstanding, the Mariner's death must have occurred after the enactment of Public Law 105-368, and the interment not violate the applicable restrictions while meeting the requirements held therein.

Persons Not Eligible for a Headstone or Marker

Disqualifying Characters of Discharge

A person whose only separation from the Armed Forces was under dishonorable conditions or whose character of service results in a bar to veterans' benefits.

- Discharge from Draft: A person who was ordered to report to an induction station but was not actually inducted into military service.
- Person Found Guilty of a Capital Crime: Eligibility for a headstone or marker is prohibited if a person is convicted of a federal capital crime and sentenced to death or life imprisonment, or is convicted of a state capital crime, and sentenced to death or life imprisonment without parole. Federal officials are authorized to deny requests for headstones or markers to persons who are shown by clear and convincing evidence to have committed a Federal or State capital crime but were not convicted of such crime because of flight to avoid prosecution or by death before trial.
- Subversive Activities: Any person convicted of subversive activities after September 1, 1959, shall have no right to burial in a national cemetery from and after the date of commission of such offense, based on periods of active military service commencing before the date of the commission of such offense, nor shall another person be entitled to burial on account of such an individual. Eligibility will be reinstated if the President of the United States grants a pardon.
- Active or Inactive Duty for Training: A person whose only service is active duty for training or inactive duty training in the National Guard or Reserve Component, unless the individual meets the following criteria.

Reservists and National Guard members who, at time of death, were entitled to retired pay under Chapter 1223, title 10, United States Code, or would have been entitled, but for being under the age of 60. Specific categories of individuals eligible for retired pay are delineated in section 12731 of Chapter 1223, title 10, United States Code.

Members of reserve components who die while hospitalized or undergoing treatment at the expense of the United States for injury or disease contracted or incurred under honorable conditions while performing active duty for training or inactive duty training or undergoing such hospitalization or treatment.

Members of the Reserve Officers' Training Corps of the Army, Navy, or Air Force who die under honorable conditions while attending an authorized training camp or on an authorized cruise, while performing authorized travel to or from that camp or cruise, or while hospitalized or undergoing treatment at the expense of the United States for injury or disease contracted or incurred under honorable conditions while engaged in one of those activities.

Members of reserve components who, during a period of active duty for training, were disabled or died from a disease or injury incurred or aggravated in the line of duty or, during a period of inactive duty training, were disabled or died from an injury incurred or aggravated in line of duty.

Other Groups
Members of groups whose service has been determined by the Secretary of the Air Force under the provisions of Public Law 95-202 as not warranting entitlement to benefits administered by the Secretary of Veterans Affairs.

Burial in National Cemeteries

In 2012 the VA announced plans to move forward with plans to provide burial options for veterans who live in rural areas, where no national, state or tribal cemeteries are available. The plan is part of the Rural Initiative Plan, in which the VA will work to build small National Veterans Burial Grounds that will be located inside existing rurally located public or private cemeteries. These burial grounds will also be located where the unserved veteran population is 25,000 or less, within a 75-mile radius.

The VA announced plans to open eight National Veteran Burial Grounds. A National Veterans Burial Ground will consist of a small area of three to five acres, located within the existing public or private cemetery that will be managed by the VA. The VA will provide a full range of burial options and be responsible for the maintenance and operation of the burial lots. These sections will be held to the national shrine standards that are in place at VA national cemeteries.

The National Cemetery Administration honors Veterans with a final resting place and lasting memorials that commemorate their service to our nation.

Veterans and service members who meet the eligibility requirements and their eligible dependents may be buried in one of the VA's national cemeteries. The National Cemetery Administration currently includes 122 national cemeteries. The Department of the Army administers two national cemeteries, and the Department of the Interior administers 14 national cemeteries. There are also numerous state cemeteries for veterans throughout the U.S. For a listing of all national cemeteries as well as state veterans' cemeteries refer to the listing at the end of this chapter.

Effective under Public Law 112-154, reservations for more than one space at Arlington National Cemetery will no longer be accepted, and reservations will not be honored until the time of death unless there is a case of extraordinary circumstances.

Honoring America's Veterans and Caring for Camp Lejeune Families Act of 2012

This law, signed into effect by then-President Obama, provided sweeping legislation for veterans, including limitations on protestors at military funerals. The law prohibits protestors at military funerals from protesting two hours before or after a military funeral, and the must hold their protests at least 300 feet from the site of the funeral.

Respect for America's Fallen Heroes Act

On May 29, 2006, then-President Bush signed the Respect for America's Fallen Heroes Act into law. This law does the following:

Prohibits a demonstration on the property of a cemetery under the control of the National Cemetery Administration or the property of Arlington National Cemetery unless the demonstration has been approved by the cemetery superintendent or the director of the property on which the cemetery is located.

Prohibits, with respect to the above cemeteries, a demonstration during the period beginning 60 minutes before and ending 60 minutes after a funeral, memorial service, or ceremony is held, which:

- Takes place within 150 feet of a road, pathway, or other route of ingress to or egress from such cemetery property; or
- Is within 300 feet of such cemetery and impedes access to or egress from such cemetery.

The term "Demonstration" includes the following:

- Any picketing or similar conduct.
- Any oration, speech, use of sound amplification equipment or device, or similar conduct that is not part of a funeral, memorial service, or ceremony.
- The display of any placard, banner, flag, or similar device, unless the display is part of a funeral, memorial service, or ceremony.
- The distribution of any handbill, pamphlet, leaflet, or other written or printed matter other than what is distributed as part of a funeral, memorial service, or ceremony. Amends the federal criminal code to provide criminal

penalties for violations of such prohibitions.

- Express the sense of Congress that each state should enact similar legislation to restrict demonstrations near any military funeral.

Eligibility

The VA national cemetery directors have the primary responsibility for verifying eligibility for burial in VA national cemeteries. A dependent's eligibility for burial is based upon the eligibility of the veteran. To establish a veteran's eligibility, a copy of the official military discharge document bearing an official seal or a DD 214 is usually sufficient. The document must show that release from service was under conditions other than dishonorable. A determination of eligibility is usually made in response to a request for burial in a VA national cemetery.

The cemeteries administered by the National Cemetery Administration and the Department of the Interior use the eligibility requirements that follow. The Department of the Interior can be contacted at:

Department of the Interior National Park Service
1849 C Street, N.W.
Washington, D.C. 20240
(202) 208-4621

The Department of the Army should be contacted directly for inquiries concerning eligibility for interment in either of the two cemeteries under its jurisdiction (call (703) 695-3250).

Eligibility requirements for burial in state veterans cemeteries are the same, or similar, to the eligibility requirements that follow. However, some states also have residency and other more restrictive requirements. Please contact the specific state cemetery for its eligibility requirements.

The following veterans and members of the Armed Forces (Army, Navy, Air Force, Marine Corps, Coast Guard) are eligible for burial in a VA national cemetery:

- Any member of the Armed Forces of the U.S. who dies on active duty.
- Any citizen of the U.S. who, during any war in which the U.S. has been engaged, served in the Armed Forces of any U.S. ally during that war, whose last active service was terminated honorably by death or otherwise, and who was a citizen of the U.S. at the time of entry into such service and at the time of death.
- Any veteran discharged under conditions other than dishonorable and who has completed the required period of service. With certain exceptions, service beginning after September 7, 1980, as an enlisted person, and service after October 16, 1981, as an officer, must be for a minimum of 24 months or the full period for which the person was called to active duty.

Members of Reserve Components and Reserve Officers' Training Corps

- Reservists and National Guard members with 20 years of qualifying service, who are entitled to retired pay, or would be entitled, if at least 60 years of age.

- Members of reserve components who die under honorable conditions while hospitalized or undergoing treatment at the expense of the U.S. for injury or disease contracted or incurred under honorable conditions while performing active duty for training, or inactive duty training, or undergoing such hospitalization or treatment.
- Members of the Reserve Officers' Training Corps of the Army, Navy, or Air Force who die under honorable conditions while attending an authorized training camp or cruise, or while traveling to or from that camp or cruise, or while hospitalized or undergoing treatment at the expense of the U.S. for injury or disease contracted or incurred under honorable conditions while engaged in one of those activities.
- Members of reserve components who, during a period of active duty for training, were disabled or died from a disease or injury incurred or aggravated in the line of duty, or, during a period of inactive duty training, were disabled or died from an injury incurred or aggravated in the line of duty.

Commissioned Officers, National Oceanic and Atmospheric Administration

- A Commissioned Officer of the National Oceanic and Atmospheric Administration with full-time duty on or after July 29, 1945.
- A Commissioned Officer of the National Oceanic and Atmospheric Administration who served before July 29, 1945, and:
- Was assigned to an area of immediate hazard described in the Act of December 3, 1942 (56 Stat. 1038; 33 U.S.C. 855a), as amended
- Served in the Philippine Islands on December 7, 1941, and continuously in such islands thereafter.

Public Health Service

- A Commissioned Officer of the Regular or Reserve Corps of the Public Health Service who served on full-time duty on or after July 29, 1945. If the service of such an Officer falls within the meaning of active duty for training, he must have been disabled or died from a disease or injury incurred or aggravated in the line of duty.
- A Commissioned Officer of the Regular or Reserve Corps of the Public Health Service who performed full-time duty prior to July 29, 1945:
- In the time of war; or
- On detail for duty with the Army, Navy, Air Force, Marine Corps, or Coast Guard, or While the service was part of the military forces of the U.S. under Executive Order of the President.
- A Commissioned Officer of the Regular or Reserve Corps of the Public Health Service serving on inactive duty training as defined in Section 101 (23), title 39, U.S. Code, whose death resulted from an injury incurred or aggravated in the line of duty.

World War II Merchant Mariners

U.S. Merchant Mariners with oceangoing service during the period of armed conflict, December 7, 1941, to December 31, 1946. Prior to the enactment of Public Law 105-368, United States Merchant Mariners with oceangoing service during the period of armed conflict of December 7, 1941, to August 15, 1945, were eligible. With enactment of Public Law 105-368, the service period is extended to December 31, 1946, for those dying on or after November 11, 1998. Merchant Mariners who served on blockships in support of Operation Mulberry during WWII.

The Philippine Armed Forces

Any Philippine veteran who was a citizen of the United States or an alien lawfully admitted for permanent residence in the United States at the time of their death, and resided in the United States at the time of their death; and:

Was a person who served before July 1, 1946, in the organized military forces of the Government of the Commonwealth of the Philippines, while such forces were in the service of the Armed Forces of the United States pursuant to the military order of the President dated July 26, 1941, including organized guerilla forces under commanders appointed, designated, or subsequently recognized by the Commander in Chief, Southwest Pacific Area, or other competent authority in the Army of the United States who dies on or after November 1, 2000; or

Was a person who enlisted between October 6, 1945, and June 30, 1947, with the Armed Forces of the United States with the consent of the Philippine government, pursuant to Section 14 of the Armed Forces Voluntary Recruitment Act of 1945, and who died on or after December 16, 2003.

Spouses and Dependents

The spouse or surviving spouse of an eligible veteran is eligible for interment in a national cemetery even if that veteran is not buried or memorialized in a national cemetery. In addition, the spouse or surviving spouse of a member of the Armed Forces of the United States whose remains are unavailable for burial is also eligible for burial.

The surviving spouse of an eligible veteran who had a subsequent remarriage to a non- veteran and whose death occurred on or after January 1, 2000, is eligible for burial in a national cemetery, based on his or her marriage to the eligible veteran.

The minor children of an eligible veteran. For the purpose of burial in a national cemetery, a minor child is a child who is unmarried and:

- Under 21 years of age; or
- Under 23 years of age and pursuing a full-time course of instruction at an approved educational institution.
- An unmarried adult child of an eligible veteran if the child became permanently physically or mentally disabled and incapable of self-support before reaching 21 years of age, or before reaching 23 years of age if pursuing

a full-time course of instruction at an approved educational institution.

- Any other persons or classes of persons as designated by the Secretary of Veterans Affairs or the Secretary of the Air Force.

The Veterans' Benefits Act of 2010 contains a provision that allows a parent whose child gave their lives in service to our country to be buried in a national cemetery with that child when their veteran child has no living spouse or children.

The following are not eligible for burial in a VA National Cemetery:

- A former spouse of an eligible individual whose marriage to that individual has been terminated by annulment or divorce, if not otherwise eligible.
- Family members other than those specifically described above.
- A person whose only separation from the Armed Forces was under dishonorable conditions, or whose character of service results in a bar to veterans benefits.
- A person ordered to report to an induction station, but not actually inducted into military service.
- Any person found guilty of a capital crime. Interment or memorialization in a VA cemetery or in Arlington National Cemetery is prohibited if a person is convicted of a federal capital crime and sentenced to death or life imprisonment, or is convicted of a state capital crime, and sentenced to death or life imprisonment without parole. Federal officials are authorized to deny burial in veterans' cemeteries to persons who are shown by clear and convincing evidence to have committed a federal or state capital crime but were not convicted of such crime because of flight to avoid prosecution or by death prior to trial. The Secretary is authorized to provide aid to states for the establishment, expansion and/or improvement of veterans cemeteries on the condition that the state is willing to prohibit interment or memorialization in such cemeteries of individuals convicted of federal or state capital crimes, or found by clear and convincing evidence to have committed such crimes, without having been convicted of the crimes due to flight to avoid prosecution or death prior to trial.
- Any person convicted of subversive activities after September 1, 1959, shall have no right to burial in a national cemetery from and after the date of commission of such offense, based on periods of active military service commencing before the date of the commission of such offense, nor shall another person be entitled to burial on account of such an individual. Eligibility will be reinstated if the President of the United States grants a pardon.

Requests for Gravesites in National Cemeteries

Under Public Law 112-154 the Secretary of the Army will be responsible for decisions regarding organizations wishing to place monuments honoring the service of a group or individual at Arlington. This became law in 2012.

An eligible veteran or family member may be buried in the VA national cemetery of his choice, provided space is available. A veteran may not reserve a gravesite in his name prior to his death. However, any reservations made under previous programs will be honored. The funeral director or loved one making the burial arrangements must apply for a gravesite at the time of death. No special forms are required when requesting burial in a VA national cemetery. The person making burial arrangements should contact the national cemetery in which burial is desired at the time of need.

If possible, the following information concerning the deceased should be provided when the cemetery is first contacted:
- Full name and military rank;
- Branch of service;
- Social security number;
- VA claim number, if applicable;
- Date and place of birth;
- Date and place of death;
- Date of retirement or last separation from active duty; and
- Copy of any military separation documents (such as DD-214)

When a death occurs, and eligibility for interment in a national cemetery is determined, grave space is assigned by the cemetery director in the name of the veteran or family member

One gravesite is permitted for the internment of all eligible family members unless soil conditions or the number of family decedents necessitate more than one grave. There is no charge for burial in a national cemetery.

The availability of grave space varies among each National Cemetery. In many cases, if a national cemetery does not have space for a full-casket burial, it may still intern cremated remains. Full-casket gravesites occasionally become available in such cemeteries due to disinterment or cancellation of prior reservations. The cemetery director can answer such questions at the time of need.

Most national cemeteries do not typically conduct burials on weekends. However, weekend callers trying to make burial arrangements for the following week will be provided with the phone number of one of three strategically located VA cemetery offices that remain open during weekends.

Burial at Sea

The National Cemetery Administration cannot provide burial at sea. For information, contact the United States Navy Mortuary Affairs office toll-free at 866-787-0081.

Furnishing and Placement of Headstones and Markers

In addition to the gravesite, burial in a VA national cemetery also includes furnishing and placement of the headstone or marker, opening and closing of the grave, and perpetual care. Many national cemeteries also have columbaria or gravesites for cremated remains. (Some state veterans' cemeteries may charge a nominal fee for placing a government-provided headstone or marker.)

Special Notes:

For persons with 20-years' service in the National Guard or Reserves, entitlement to retired pay must be subsequent to November 1, 1990, in order to qualify for a government-provided headstone or marker. A copy of the Reserve Retirement Eligibility Benefits Letter must accompany the application. Active duty service while in the National Guard or Reserves also establishes eligibility.

Service prior to World War I require detailed documentation to prove eligibility such as muster rolls extracts from State files, military or State organizations where served, pension or land warrants, etc.

Flat bronze, granite, or marble grave markers and upright marble or granite headstones are available to mark graves in the style consistent with existing monuments in the national cemetery. Niche markers are also available for identifying cremated remains in columbaria. The following is a brief description of each type:

- Upright Marble and Upright Granite: 42 inches long, 13 inches wide, 4 inches thick, approximately 230 pounds.
- Flat Bronze: 24 inches long, 12 inches wide, ¾ inch rise, approximately 18 pounds. Anchor bolts, nuts, and washers for fastening to the base are supplied with marker. The government does not provide the base.
- Flat Granite and Flat Marble: 24 inches long, 12 inches wide, 4 inches thick, approximately 130 pounds.
- Bronze Niche: 8 ½ inches long, 5 ½ inches wide, 7/16-inch rise, approximately 3 pounds. Mounting bolts and washers are supplied with the marker.

There are also two special styles of upright marble headstones and flat markers available - one for those who served with the Union Forces during the Civil War or the Spanish- American War, and one for those who served with the Confederate forces during the Civil War.

Inscriptions

Headstones and markers are inscribed with the name of the deceased, branch of service, year of birth, and year of death. The word "Korea" may be included on government headstones and markers for the graves of those members and former members of the United States Armed Forces who served within the areas of military operations in the Korean Theater between June 27, 1950, and July 27, 1954; and for

141

headstones and markers for active duty decedents who lost their lives in Korea or adjacent waters as a result of hostile action subsequent to the 1953 Armistice

The word "Vietnam" may be included on government headstones and markers for the graves of those members and former members of the United States Armed Forces who died in Vietnam or whose death was attributable to service in Vietnam, and on the headstones and markers of all decedents who were on active duty on or after August 5, 1964. The words "Lebanon" or "Grenada" may be included on government headstones and markers for those killed as a result of those military actions.

The words "Panama" and "Persian Gulf" may be included on government headstones and markers for those killed as a result of those military actions
If desired, the following inscriptions can also be made (space permitting):

Military grade
Military rank
Military rate
Identification of war service
Months and days of birth and death
An authorized emblem of religious belief (see the following list of available emblems)
Military awards (documentation of award must be provided)
Military organizations
Civilian or veteran affiliations

With the VA's approval, terms of endearment that meet acceptable standards of good taste may also be added. Most optional inscriptions are placed as the last lines of the inscription. No other graphics are permitted on government-provided headstones and markers, and inscriptions will be in English text only. Civilian titles such as "Doctor or Reverend" are not permitted on the name line of government-provided headstones and markers.

Available Emblems of Belief for Placement on Government Headstones and Markers:

Christian Cross
Buddhist (Wheel of Righteousness)
Hebrew (Star of David)
Presbyterian Cross
Russian Orthodox Cross
Lutheran Cross
Episcopal Cross
Unitarian Church (Flaming Chalice)
United Methodist Church

Aaronic Order
Church Mormon (Angel Moroni)
Native American Church of North America
Serbian Orthodox
Greek Cross
Bahai (9 Pointed Star)
Atheist
Muslim (Crescent and Star)
Hindu
Konko-Kyo
Faith Community of Christ
Sufism Reoriented Tenrikyo Church
Seicho-No-Ie
Church of World Messianity (Izunome)
United Church of Religious Science
Christian Reformed Church
United Moravian Church
Eckankar
Christian Church United Church of Christ
Christian & Missionary Alliance
Humanist Emblem Of Spirit
Presbyterian Church (USA)
Izumo Taishakyo Mission Of Hawaii
Soka Gakkai International - USA Sikh (Khanda)
Christian Scientist (Cross and Crown)
Muslim (Islamic 5-Pointed Star)

Ordering a Headstone or Marker

For burial of a veteran in a national, state veteran, or military post cemetery, the cemetery will order the headstone or marker and can give loved one's information on style, inscription, and shipment. Shipment and placement of the headstone or marker is provided at no cost.

When burial is in a private cemetery, VA Form 40-1330, "Application for Standard Government Headstone or Marker" must be submitted by the next of kin or a representative, such as funeral director, cemetery official or veterans' counselor, along with the veteran's military discharge documents, to request a Government-provided headstone or marker. Do not send original documents, as they will not be returned.

Headstones and Markers for Families and Children

The VA will issue a headstone or marker for an eligible spouse or child buried in a national, state veteran or military post cemetery. However, the VA cannot issue a headstone or marker for a spouse or child buried in a private cemetery.

The applicant can, however, request to reserve inscription space below the veteran's inscription, so that the non-veteran's commemorative information can be inscribed locally, at private expense, when the non-veteran is buried. The applicant may also choose to have his/her name and date of birth added at Government expense when the headstone or marker is ordered. The date of death may then be added, at private expense, at the time of his/her death.

Commemoration of Unidentified Remains

Many national cemeteries have areas suitable to commemorate veterans whose remains were not recovered or identified, were buried at sea, or are otherwise unavailable for interment. In such instances, the VA will provide a memorial headstone or marker to be placed in that section of the cemetery. The words "In Memory of" must precede the authorized inscription.

Checking Order Status

To check the status of a previously ordered headstone or marker for placement in a private cemetery, applicants may call the VA's Applicant Assistance Line at (800) 697-6947. The line is open weekdays, from 8:00 A.M. to 5:00 P.M., Eastern Standard Time

Replacement of Headstones and Markers

The government will replace a previously furnished headstone or marker if it becomes badly damaged, is vandalized, is stolen, becomes badly deteriorated, the inscription becomes illegible, is different from that ordered by the applicant, becomes damaged in transit, or the inscription is incorrect.

Government headstones or markers in private cemeteries damaged by cemetery personnel will not be replaced at government expense.

If a marble or granite headstone or marker is permanently removed from a grave, it must be destroyed. Bronze markers must be returned to the contractor.

Military Honors

The rendering of Military Funeral Honors is a way to show the nation's deep gratitude to those who have faithfully defended our country in times of war and peace. It is the final demonstration a grateful nation can provide to the veterans' families.

The following service members are eligible for Military Funeral Honors:

- Military members on active duty or in the Selected Reserve at time of death;
- Former military members who served on active duty and departed under conditions other than dishonorable;
- Former military members who completed at least one term of enlistment or period of initial obligated service in the Selected Reserve, and departed under conditions other than dishonorable;
- Former military members discharged from the Selected Reserve due to a disability incurred or aggravated in the line of duty.

144

All eligible veterans receive basic Military Funeral Honors if requested by the deceased veteran's family. As provided by law, an honor guard detail for the burial of an eligible veteran shall consist of not less than two members of the Armed Forces. One member of the detail shall be a representative of the parent Service of the deceased veteran. The honor detail will, at a minimum, perform a ceremony that includes the folding and presenting of the American flag to the next of kin, and the playing of Taps. Taps will be played by a bugler, if available, or by electronic recording.

The ceremonial bugle consists of a small cone-shaped device inserted deep into the bell of a bugle that plays an exceptionally high-quality rendition of Taps that is virtually indistinguishable from a live bugler. The ceremonial bugle will be offered to families as an alternative to the pre-recorded Taps played on a stereo, but will not be used as a substitute for a live bugler when one is available. Live buglers will continue to play at veterans' funerals whenever available.

Funeral Directors have the responsibility of assisting loved ones in requesting military honors. A toll-free telephone number has been established for funeral directors requesting military honors. That number is 1-800-535-1117.
The Department of Defense (DOD) has provided registered funeral home directors with a military funeral honors kit and information on how to contact the appropriate military organization to perform the honors ceremony.
Questions about the Military Funeral Honors program should be sent to Deputy Assistant Secretary of Defense
(Military Community and Family Policy)
4000 Defense Pentagon, Room 5A726
Washington DC 20380

Preparations Which Can Be Made Prior to Death

It is suggested that veterans and their families prepare in advance by discussing cemetery options, collecting the veteran's military information (including discharge papers), and by contacting the cemetery where the veteran wishes to be buried. If burial will be in a private cemetery and a government headstone or marker will be requested, VA Form 40-1330 can be completed in advance and placed with the veteran's military discharge papers for use at the time of need.

Burial Location Assistance

The VA National Cemetery Administration can provide limited burial location assistance to family members and close friends of descendants thought to be buried in a VA national cemetery.

The National Cemetery Administration will research its records to determine if the decedent is buried in one of VA's national cemeteries. A request can include a maximum of ten specific names to locate. The National Cemetery Administration does not have information on persons buried in cemeteries other than its national cemeteries. Its records do not contain any personal, military or family information – only information regarding whether or not an individual is buried in a VA national cemetery, and if so, where, can be provided

The "Gravesite Locator" tool is available online at the VA's website.

If the online tool is not available or helpful, you may submit a written request. No form is required to request this information, and no fee is charged. The following information should be provided.

- Full name, including any alternate spellings, of descendent;
- Date and place of birth;
- Date and place of death;
- State from which the individual entered active duty;
- Military service branch;
- Mailing address and phone number of individuals requesting the information.

Allow approximately 4 weeks for a reply.

Requests should be sent to:
U.S. Department of Veterans Affairs
National Cemetery Administration (41C1)
Burial Location Request
810 Vermont Avenue, N.W.
Washington, D.C. 20420

U.S. Military Cemeteries and Monuments Overseas

The American Battle Monuments Commission (ABMC) a small, independent agency of the government's executive branch, maintains 24 American military cemeteries, and 27 memorials, monuments, or markers. (The VA is not responsible for maintaining cemeteries and monuments honoring deceased veterans buried on foreign soil.)

ABMC Services

The ABMC can provide interested parties with:
Name, location, and information on cemeteries and memorials.
Plot, row and grave number or memorialization location of Honored War Dead.
Best in-country routes and modes of travel to cemeteries or memorials.
Information on accommodations near cemeteries or memorials.
Escort service for relatives to grave and memorial sites within the cemeteries.
Letters authorizing fee-free passports for members of the immediate family traveling overseas to visit a grave or memorialization site.

Black and white photographs of headstones and Tablets of the Missing on which the names of dead or missing are engraved.

Arrangements for floral decorations placed at graves and memorialization sites.

An Honor Roll Certificate containing data on a Korean War casualty suitable for framing.

Polaroid color photographs of donated floral decorations in place.

The Andrews Project

The commission also provides friends and relatives of those interred in its cemeteries or memorialized on its Tablets of the Missing with color lithographs of the cemetery or memorial on which is mounted a photograph of the headstone or commemorative inscription. The Andrews Project, named in honor of its sponsor, the late Congressman George W. Andrews, is ABMC's most popular service.

For further information, contact the ABMC at:
American Battle Monuments Commission
Arlington Court House Plaza II
2300 Clarendon Blvd., Suite 500
Arlington, VA 22201
(703) 696-6897

Passports to Visit Overseas Cemeteries

Family members who wish to visit overseas graves and memorial sites of World War I and World War II veterans are eligible for "no-fee" passports. Family members eligible for the "no-fee" passports include surviving spouses, parents, children, sisters, brothers and guardians of the deceased veteran buried or commemorated in American military cemeteries on foreign soil. For further information contact the American Battle Monuments Commission at the address and phone number indicated in the previous section.

Presidential Memorial Certificate

Under Public Law 112-154, service members who die on active duty are eligible for Presidential Memorial Certificates. A Presidential Memorial Certificate is an engraved paper certificate that has been signed by the current president, honoring the memory of any honorably discharged deceased veteran. Presidential Memorial Certificates may be distributed to a deceased veteran's next of kin and loved ones. More than one certificate can be provided per family, and there is no time limit for applying for the certificate. Presidential Memorial Certificates may not be furnished on behalf of deceased veterans who committed capital crimes.

2020 Update

In 2020, the VA will automatically present a PMC to a veteran's next of kin at the burial, when the veteran is buried in a national cemetery. If the family or close friends would like to request more than one PMC, they can apply for more copies using the Presidential Memorial Certificate Request Form (VA Form 40-0247).

If the veteran is eligible for burial in a national cemetery, but is instead buried in a private cemetery, the family member or close friend can still apply to get a PMC. Fill out the Presidential Memorial Certificate Request Form (VA Form 40-0247); again, more than one PMC can be requested. To speed up the processing of the claim, submit the veteran's military discharge documents and death certificate. Don't send original documents, as they won't be returned.

Presidential Memorial Certificates (41A1C)
Department of Veterans Affairs
5109 Russell Road
Quantico, VA 22134-3903

List of National Cemeteries

Some national cemeteries can bury only cremated remains or casketed remains of eligible family members of those already buried. Contact the cemetery director for information on the availability of space

Department of Veterans Affairs National Cemeteries

ALABAMA

Alabama National Cemetery
3133 Highway 119
Montevallo, AL 35115
(205) 665-9039

Fort Mitchell National Cemetery
553 Highway 165
Ft. Mitchell, AL 36856
(334) 855-4731

Mobile National Cemetery
1202 Virginia Street
Mobile, AL 36604
(850) 453-4635
Burial Space- Closed

ALASKA

Fort Richardson National Cemetery
Building #58-512,
Davis Highway
Fort Richardson, AK 99505
(907) 384-7075

Sitka National Cemetery
803 Sawmill CreekRoad
Sitka, AK 99835
(907) 384-7075

ARIZONA

National Memorial Cemetery of Arizona
23029 North Cave Creek Road
Phoenix, AZ 85024
(480) 513-3600

Prescott National Cemetery
500 Highway 89 North
Prescott, AZ 86303
(928) 717-7569
Cremation Only

ARKANSAS

Fayetteville National Cemetery
700 Government Avenue
Fayetteville, AR 72701
(479) 444-5051

Fort Smith National Cemetery
522 Garland Avenue
Fort Smith, AR 72901
(479) 783-5345

Little Rock National Cemetery
2523 Springer Blvd.
Little Rock AR 72206
(479) 783-5345
Closed

CALIFORNIA

Baker National Cemetery
30338 East Bear Mountain Blvd.
Arvin, CA 93203
(661) 867-2250

Fort Rosecrans National Cemetery
Cabrillo Memorial Dr.
San Diego, CA 92106
(619) 553-2084
Closed

Golden Gate National Cemetery
1300 Sneath Lane
San Bruno, CA 94066
(650) 589-7737
Closed

Los Angeles National Cemetery
950 South Sepulveda Boulevard
Los Angeles, CA 90049
(310) 268-4675
Closed

Miramar National Cemetery
5795 Nobel Dr.
San Diego, CA 92122
(858) 658-7360

Riverside National Cemetery
22495 Van Buren Boulevard
Riverside, CA 92518
(951) 653-5233

Sacramento Valley National
Cemetery
5810 Midway Road
Dixon, CA 9562
(707) 693-2460
Closed

San Francisco National Cemetery
1 Lincoln Blvd.
Presidio of San Francisco
San Francisco, CA 94129
(650) 589-7737
Closed

San Joaquin Valley National
Cemetery
32053 West McCabe Road
Santa Nella, CA 95322
(209) 854-1040

COLORADO
Fort Logan National Cemetery
4400 W. Kenyon Ave.
Denver, CO 80236
(303) 761-0117

Fort Lyon National Cemetery
15700 County Road HH
Las Animas, CO 81054
(303) 761-0117

FLORIDA
Barrancas National Cemetery
1 Cemetery Rd.
Pensacola, FL 32508
(850) 453-4108

Bay Pines National Cemetery
1000 Bay Pines Boulevard North
St. Petersburg, FL 33708
(727) 319-6479
Cremation Only

Florida National Cemetery
6502 SW 102nd Avenue
Bushnell, FL 33513
(352) 793-7740

Jacksonville National Cemetery
4083 Lannie Road
Jacksonville, FL 32218-1247
(904) 766-5222

Sarasota National Cemetery
9810 State Hwy 72
Sarasota, FL 34241
(877) 861-9840

South Florida National Cemetery
6501 S. State Road
Lake Worth, FL 33449
(561) 649-6489

St. Augustine National Cemetery
104 Marine Street
St. Augustine, FL 32084
(904) 766-5222
Closed

Tallahassee National Cemetery
5015 Apalachee Parkway
Tallahassee, FL 32311
(850) 402-8941

GEORGIA
Georgia National Cemetery
1080 Scott Hudgens Drive
Canton, GA 30114
(866) 236-8159

Marietta National Cemetery
500 Washington Avenue
Marietta, GA 30060
(866) 236-8159
Closed

HAWAII
National Memorial Cemetery of the
Pacific
2177 Puowaina Drive
Honolulu, HI 96813-1729
(808) 523-3720
Cremation Only

ILLINOIS
Abraham Lincoln National Cemetery
20953 W. Hoff Road
Elwood, IL 60421
(815) 423-9958

Alton National Cemetery
600 Pearl Street
Alton, IL 62003
(314) 845-8320

Camp Butler National Cemetery
5063 Camp Butler Road
Springfield, IL 92707-9722
(217) 492-4070

Danville National Cemetery
1900 East Main Street
Danville, IL 61832
(217) 554-4550

Mound City National Cemetery
141 State Highway 37
Mound City, IL 62963
(618) 748-9107

Quincy National Cemetery
36th and Maine Street
Quincy, IL 62301
(309) 782-2094
Closed

Rock Island National Cemetery
Bldg. 118
Rock Island Arsenal
Rock Island, IL 61299-7090
(309) 782-2094

Confederate Mound
Oak Woods Cemetery
1035 E. 67th St.
Chicago IL 60637
(815) 423-9958
Closed

North Alton Confederate Cemetery
635 Rozier St.
Alton, IL 62003
(314) 845-8355
Closed

151

Rock Island Confederate Cemetery
Rodman Avenue
Rock Island Arsenal
Rock Island, IL 61299
(309) 782-2094
Closed

INDIANA
Crown Hill National Cemetery
700 West 38th
Street Indianapolis, IN 46208
(765) 674-0284
Closed

Marion National Cemetery
1700 East 38th Street
Maion, IN 46952
(765) 674-0284

New Albany National Cemetery
1943 Ekin Avenue
New Albany, IN 47150
(502) 893-3852
Cremation Only

Crown Hill Cemetery Confederate
Plot
700 West 38th St.
Indianapolis, IN 46208
(765) 674-0284
Closed

Woodlawn Monument site
North 3rd St. and 4th Avenue
Terre Haute, IN 47802
(815) 423-9958
Closed

IOWA
Keokuk National Cemetery
1701 J Street
Keokuk, IA 52632
(319) 524-1304

KANSAS
Fort Leavenworth Natl Cemetery
395 Biddle Blvd.
Fort Leavenworth, KS 66027
(913) 758-4105
Cremation Only

Fort Scott National Cemetery
900 East National Avenue
Fort Scott, KS 66701
(620) 223-2840

Leavenworth National Cemetery
150 Muncie Rd.
Leavenworth, KS 66048
(913) 758-4136

Baxter Springs City Cemetery
Baxter Springs, KS 66713
(913)758-4136
Closed

Mound City Cemetery Soldiers' Lot
Woodland Cemetery
Mound City, KS 66506
(913) 758-4105

KENTUCKY
Camp Nelson National Cemetery
6980 Danville Road
Nicholasville, KY 40356
(859) 885-5727

Cave Hill National Cemetery
701 Baxter Avenue
Louisville, KY 40204
For information please contact:
Zachary Taylor National Cemetery
(502) 893-3852
Closed

Danville National Cemetery
277 North First Street
Danville, KY 40442
(859) 885-5727
Closed

Lebanon National Cemetery
20 Highway 208
Lebanon, KY 40033
(270) 692-3390

Lexington National Cemetery
833 West Main Street
Lexington, KY 40508
(859) 885-5727
Closed

Mill Springs National Cemetery
9044 West Highway 80
Nancy, KY 42544
(859) 885-5727

Zachary Taylor National Cemetery
4701 Brownsboro Road
Louisville, KY 40207
(502) 893-3852
Closed

Evergreen Cemetery Soldiers' Lot
25 South Alexandria Pike
Southgate, KY 41071
(859) 885-5727
Closed

LOUISIANA
Alexandria National Cemetery
209 East Shamrock Street
Pineville, LA 71360
(601) 445-4891
Closed

Baton Rouge National Cemetery
220 North 19th Street
Baton Rouge, LA 70806
(225) 654-1988
Closed

Louisiana National Cemetery
303 W. Mount Pleasant Rd.
Zachary, LA 70791
(225) 654-1988

Port Hudson National Cemetery
20978 Port Hickey Road
Zachary, LA 70791
(225) 654-3767
Cremation Only

MAINE
Togus National Cemetery
VA Medical and Regional Office
Center
Togus, ME 04330
(508) 563-7113
Closed

MARYLAND
Annapolis National Cemetery
800 West Street
Annapolis, MD 21401
(410) 644-9696
Closed

Baltimore National Cemetery
5501 Frederick Avenue
Baltimore, MD 21228
(410) 644-9696
Cremation Only

Loudon Park National Cemetery
3445 Frederick Avenue
Baltimore, MD 21228
(410) 644-9696

MASSACHUSETTS
Massachusetts National Cemetery
Connery Ave.
Bourne, MA 02532
(508) 563-7113

MICHIGAN
Fort Custer National Cemetery
15501 Dickman Road
Augusta, MI 49012
(269) 731-4164

Great Lakes National Cemetery
4200 Belford Road
Holly, MI 48842
(866) 348-8603

MINNESOTA
Fort Snelling National Cemetery
7601 34th Avenue
South Minneapolis, MN 55450-1199
(612) 726-1127

MISSISSIPPI
Biloxi National Cemetery
400 Veterans Avenue
Bld. 1001
Biloxi, MS 39535-4968
(228) 388-6668

Corinth National Cemetery
1551 Horton Street
Corinth, MS 38834
(901) 386-8311

Natchez National Cemetery
41 Cemetery Road
Natchez, MS 39120
(601) 445-4981

MISSOURI
Jefferson Barracks National
Cemetery
2900 Sheridan Road

St. Louis, MO 63125
(314) 845-8320

Jefferson City National Cemetery
1024 East McCarty Street
Jefferson City, MO 65101
(314) 845-8320
Closed

Springfield National Cemetery
1702 East Seminole Street
Springfield, MO 65804
(417) 881-9499
Cremation Only

NEBRASKA
Fort McPherson National Cemetery
12004 South Spur 56A
Maxwell, NE 69151
(308) 582-4433

Omaha National Cemetery
14250 Schram Rd.
Omaha, NE 68138
(402) 253-3949

NEW JERSEY
Beverly National Cemetery
916 Bridgeboro Rd.
Beverly, NJ 08010
(215) 504-5610
Closed

Finn's Point National Cemetery
454 Fort Mott Road,
Pennsville, NJ 08070
(215) 504-5610
Cremation only

NEW MEXICO
Fort Bayard National Cemetery
200 Camino De Paz
Fort Bayard, NM 88036
(505) 988-6400

154

Santa Fe National Cemetery
501 North Guadalupe Street
Santa Fe, NM 87501
(505) 988-6400

NEW YORK
Bath National Cemetery
San Juan Avenue
Bath, NY 14810
(607) 664-4853

Calverton National Cemetery
210 Princeton Boulevard
Calverton, NY 11933-1031
(631) 727-5410

Cypress Hills National Cemetery
625 Jamaica Avenue
Brooklyn, NY 11208
(631) 454-4949
Closed

George B.H. Solomon Saratoga
National Cemetery
200 Duell Rd.
Schuylerville, NY 12871
(631) 454-4949
Cremation Only

Long Island National Cemetery
2040 Wellwood Avenue
Farmingdale, NY 11735-1211
(631) 454-4949
Cremation Only

Woodlawn National Cemetery
1825 Davis Street
Elmira, NY 14901
(607) 732-5411
Cremation Only

NORTH CAROLINA
New Bern National Cemetery
1711 National Avenue
New Bern, NC 28560
(252) 637-2912
Closed

Raleigh National Cemetery
501 Rock Quarry Road
Raleigh, NC 27610
(252) 637-2912d
Closed

Salisbury National Cemetery
501 Statesville Blvd.
Salisbury, NC 28144
(704) 636-2661

Wilmington National Cemetery
2011 Market Street
Wilmington, NC 28403
(910) 815-4877
Closed

OHIO
Dayton National Cemetery
4400 West Third St.
Dayton, OH 45428-1008
(937) 268-2221

Ohio Western Reserve National
Cemetery
10175 Rawiga Road
Seville, OH 44273
(330) 335-3069

OKLAHOMA
Fort Gibson National Cemetery
1423 Cemetery Road
Fort Gibson, OK 74434
(918) 478-2334

Fort Sill National Cemetery
2648 NE Jake Dunn Rd.
Elgin, OK 73538
(580) 492-3200

OREGON
Eagle Point National Cemetery
2763 Riley Road
Eagle Point, OR 97524
(541) 826-2511

Roseburg National Cemetery
913 NW Garden Valley Blvd.
Roseburg, OR 97471
(541) 671-3152

Willamette National Cemetery
11800 S.E. Mt. Scott Boulevard
Portland, OR 97086
(503) 273-5250

PENNSYLVANIA
Indiantown Gap National Cemetery
Indiantown Gap Rd.
Annville, PA 17003-9618
(717) 865-5254

National Cemetery of the Alleghenies
1158 Morgan Road
Bridgeville, PA 15017
(724) 746-4363

Philadelphia National Cemetery
Haines Street and Limekiln Pike
Philadelphia, PA 19138
(215) 504-5611
Closed

PUERTO RICO
Puerto Rico National Cemetery
Avenue Cementario Nacional
#50 Bayamon, PR 00960
(787) 798-8400

SOUTH CAROLINA
Beaufort National Cemetery
1601 Boundary Street
Beaufort, SC 29902
(843) 524-3925

Florence National Cemetery
803 East National Cemetery Road
Florence, SC 29501
(843) 669-8783

Fort Jackson National Cemetery
4170 Percival Rd
Columbia, SC 29229
(866) 577-5248

SOUTH DAKOTA
Black Hills National Cemetery
20901 Pleasant Valley Dr.
Sturgis, SD 57785
(605) 347- 3830

Fort Meade National Cemetery
Old Stone Road
Sturgis, SD 57785
(605) 347-3830
Closed

Hot Springs National Cemetery
VA Medical Center
Hot Springs, SD 57747
(605) 347-3830
Closed

TENNESSEE
Chattanooga National Cemetery
1200 Bailey Avenue
Chattanooga, TN 37404
(423) 855-6590

Knoxville National Cemetery
939 Tyson Street, N.W.
Knoxville, TN 37917
(423) 855-6590
Cremation Only

Memphis National Cemetery
3568 Townes Avenue
Memphis, TN 38122
(901) 386-8311
Cremation Only

Mountain Home National Cemetery
53 Memorial Avenue
Mountain Home, TN 37684
(423) 979-3535

Nashville National Cemetery
1420 Gallatin Road S
Madison, TN 37115-4619
(615) 860-0086
Cremation Only

TEXAS
Dallas-Fort Worth National Cemetery
2000 Mountain Creek Parkway
Dallas, TX 75211
(214) 467-3374

Fort Bliss National Cemetery
5200 Fred Wilson Road
El Paso, TX 79906
(915) 564-0201

Fort Sam Houston National
Cemetery
1520 Harry Wurzbach Road
San Antonio, TX 78209
(210) 820-3891

Houston National Cemetery
10410 Veterans Memorial Drive
Houston, TX 77038
(281) 447-8686

Kerrville National Cemetery
3600 Memorial Boulevard
Kerrville, TX 78028
(210) 820-3891
Closed

San Antonio National Cemetery
517 Paso Hondo Street
San Antonio, TX 78202
(210) 820-3891
Cremation Only

VIRGINIA
Alexandria National Cemetery
1450 Wilkes Street
Alexandria, VA 22314
(703) 221-2183
Cremation Only

Balls Bluff National Cemetery
Route 7
Leesburg, VA 22075
(540) 825-0027
Closed

City Point National Cemetery
10th Avenue and Davis Street
Hopewell, VA 23860
(804) 795-2031
Closed

Cold Harbor National Cemetery
6038 Cold Harbor Rd.
Mechanicsville, VA 23111
(804) 795-2031
Closed

Culpeper National Cemetery
305 U.S. Avenue
Culpeper, VA 22701
(540) 825-0027

Danville National Cemetery
721 Lee Street
Danville, VA 24541
(704) 636-2661
Cremation Only

Fort Harrison National Cemetery
8620 Varina Road
Richmond, VA 23231
(804) 795-2031
Closed

Glendale National Cemetery
8301 Willis Church Road
Richmond, VA 23231
For information please contact:
Fort Harrison National Cemetery
(804) 795-2031

Hampton National Cemetery Road at
Marshall Avenue
Hampton, VA 23667
(757) 723-7104

Hampton National Cemetery
VA Medical Center
Emancipation Drive
Hampton, VA 23667
(757) 723-7104

Quantico National Cemetery
P. O. Box 10
18424 Joplin Road (Route 619)
Triangle, VA 22172
(703) 221-2183 (local)

Richmond National Cemetery
1701 Williamsburg Road
Richmond, VA 23231
For information please contact: Fort
Harrison National Cemetery
(804) 795-2031

Seven Pines National Cemetery
400 East Williamsburg Road
Sandston, VA 2315
For information please contact: Fort
Harrison National Cemetery
(804) 795-2031

Staunton National Cemetery
901 Richmond Avenue
Staunton, VA 24401
(540) 825-0027

Winchester National Cemetery
401 National Avenue
Winchester, VA 22601
For information please contact:
Culpeper National Cemetery
(540) 825-0027

WASHINGTON
Tahoma National Cemetery
18600 Southeast 240th Street
Kent, WA 98042-4868
(425) 413-9614

WEST VIRGINIA
Grafton National Cemetery
431 Walnut Street
Grafton, WV 26354
For information please contact:
West Virginia National Cemetery
(304) 265-2044

West Virginia National Cemetery
Route 2, Box 127
Grafton, WV 26354
(304) 265-2044

WISCONSIN
Wood National Cemetery
5000 W National Ave, Bldg 1301
Milwaukee, WI 53295-4000
(414) 382-5300

DEPARTMENT OF THE INTERIOR
NATIONAL CEMETERIES

DISTRICT OF COLUMBIA
Battleground National Cemetery
C/O Superintendent,
Rock Creek Park
3545 Williamsburg Lane, NW
Washington, DC 20008
(202) 282-1063

GEORGIA
Andersonville National Historic Site
Route 1, Box 800
Andersonville, GA 31711
(912) 924-0343

LOUISIANA
Chalmette National Cemetery C/O
Jean Lafitte National Historical Park
and Preserve
365 Canal Street, Suite 2400
New Orleans, LA 70130
(504) 589-3882
(504) 589-4430

MARYLAND
Antietam National Battlefield
Box 158
Sharpsburg, MD 21782-0158
(301) 432-5124

MISSISSIPPI
Vicksburg National Military Park
3201 Clay Street
Vicksburg, MS 39180
(601) 636-0583

MONTANA
Little Bighorn Battle National
Monument Custer National
Cemetery
P. O. Box 39
Crow Agency, MT 59022

PENNSYLVANIA
Gettysburg National Military Park
97 Taneytown Road
Gettysburg, PA 17325-2804
(717) 334-1124

TENNESSEE
Andrew Johnson National Historic
Site
P. O. Box 1088
Greeneville, TN 37744
(423) 638-3551

Fort Donelson National Battlefield
P. O. Box 434
Dover, TN 37058
(615) 232-5348

Shiloh National Military Park
Route 1, Box 9
Shiloh, TN 38376-9704
(901) 689-5275

Stones River National Battlefield
3501 Old Nashville Highway
Murfreesboro, TN 37129
(615) 893-9501

VIRGINIA
Fredericksburg and Spotsylvania
County Battlefields Memorial
National Military Park
120 Chatham Lane
Fredericksburg, VA 22405
(540) 371-0802

Poplar Grove National Cemetery
Petersburg National Battlefield
1539 (Yorktown Battlefield Cemetery
Colonial National Historical Park
P. O. Box 210
Yorktown, VA 23690
(757) 898-3400

**DEPARTMENT OF THE ARMY
NATIONAL CEMETERIES**

United States Soldiers' &
Airmen's Home National
Cemetery
21 Harewood Road, NW
Washington, DC 20011
(202) 829-1829

STATE VETERANS CEMETERIES

ALABAMA
Alabama State Veterans Memorial
Cemetery At Spanish Fort
34904 State Highway 225
Spanish Fort, AL 36577

ARIZONA
Southern Arizona Veterans Memorial
14317 Veterans Drive
Camp Navajo
PO Box 16419
Bellemont, AZ
(928) 214-3474

ARKANSAS
Arkansas Veterans Cemetery
1501 W Maryland Avenue
North Little Rock, AR 72120
(501) 683-2259

CALIFORNIA
Veterans Memorial Grove Cemetery
Veterans Home of California
Yountville, CA 94599
(707) 944-4600

Northern California Veterans
Cemetery
P.O. Box 76
11800 Gas Point Road
Igo, CA 96047
(866) 777-4533

COLORADO
Colorado State Veterans Cemetery At
Homelake
3749 Sherman Avenue
Monte Vista, CO 81144
(719) 852-5118

Veterans Memorial Cemetery Of
Western Colorado
2830 D Road
Grand Junction, CO 81505
(970) 263-8986

CONNECTICUT
Colonel Raymond F. Gates Memorial
Cemetery Veterans Home and
Hospital
287 West Street
Rocky Hill, CT 06067
(860) 721-5838

Spring Grove Veterans Cemetery
Darien, CT C/O Veterans Home and
Hospital
287 West Street
Rocky Hill, CT 06067
(860) 721-5838

Middletown Veterans Cemetery C/O
Veterans Home and Hospital
287 West Street
Rocky Hill, CT 06067
(860) 721-5838

DELAWARE

Delaware Veterans Memorial
Cemetery
2465 Chesapeake City Road
Bear, DE 19701
(302) 834-8046

Delaware Veterans Memorial
Cemetery-Sussex County
RD 5 Box 100
Millsboro, DE 19966
(302) 934-5653

GEORGIA

Georgia Veterans Memorial
Cemetery
2617 Vinson Highway
Milledgeville, Georgia 31061
(478) 445-3363

Georgia Veterans Memorial
Cemetery
8819 U.S. Highway 301
Glennville, Georgia 30427
(912)-654-5398

HAWAII

Director, Office of Veterans Services
459 Patterson Road
E-Wing, Room 1-A103
Honolulu, HI 96189
(808) 433-0420

Hawaii State Veterans Cemetery
45-349 Kamehameha Highway
Kaneohe, HI 96744
(808) 233-3630

East Hawaii Veterans Cemetery
No. I County of Hawaii
25 Aupuni Street
Hilo, HI 96720
(Island of Hawaii)
(808) 961-8311

East Hawaii Veterans Cemetery
-No. II
County of Hawaii
25 Aupuni Street
Hilo, HI 96720
(Island of Hawaii)
(808) 961-8311

Kauai Veterans Cemetery County of
Kauai Public Works
3021 Umi Street
Lihue, HI 96766
(Island of Kauai)
(808) 241-6670

Maui Veterans Cemetery
1295 Makawao Avenue,
Box 117
Makawao, HI 96768 (Island of Maui)
(808) 572-7272

Hoolehua Veterans
Cemetery (Molokai)
P. O. Box 526
Kauna Kakai, HI 96748
(Island of Molokai)
(808) 553-3204

Lanai Veterans Cemetery Maui
County (Island of Lanai)
PO Box 630359
Lanai City, Hawaii 96763

IDAHO
Idaho Veterans Cemetery
10101 North Horseshoe Bend Road
Boise, ID 83714
(208) 334-4796

ILLINOIS
Sunset Cemetery Illinois Veterans
Home
1707 North 12th Street
Quincy, IL 62301
(217) 222-8641

INDIANA
Indiana State Soldiers Home
Cemetery
3851 North River Road
West Lafayette, IN 47906-3765
(765) 463-1502

Indiana Veterans Memorial Cemetery
1415 North Gate Road
Madison, IN 47250
(812) 273-9220

IOWA
Iowa Veterans Home and Cemetery
13th & Summit Streets
Marshalltown, IA 50158
(641) 753-4309

Iowa Veterans Cemetery
34024 Veterans Memorial Drive
Adel, Iowa 50003-3300
(515) 996-9048

KANSAS
Kansas Veterans Cemetery At Fort
Dodge
714 Sheridan, Unit #66
Fort Dodge, KS 67801
(620) 338-8775

Kansas Veterans Cemetery At
Wakeeney
P.O. Box 185
4035 13th Street
Wakeeney, KS 67672
(785) 743-5685

Kansas Veterans Cemetery At
Winfield
1208 North College
Winfield, KS 67156
(620) 229-2287

KENTUCKY
Kentucky Veterans Cemetery
Central
1111 Louisville Road
Frankfort, Kentucky
(502) 564-9281

Kentucky Veterans Cemetery
North 205 Eibeck Lane
P.O. Box 467
Williamstown, Kentucky 41097
(859)-823-0720

Kentucky Veteran's Cemetery West
5817 Fort Campbell Boulevard
Hopkinsville, Kentucky 42240
(270) 707-9653

LOUISIANA
Northwest Louisiana Veterans
Cemetery
7970 Mike Clark Road
Keithville, Louisiana 71047
(318) 925-0612

MAINE
Maine Veterans Memorial
Cemetery (Closed)
Civic Center Drive
Augusta, Maine

Maine Veterans Memorial Cemetery-
- Mt. Vernon Rd.
163 Mt. Vernon Road
Augusta, ME 04330
(207) 287-3481

Northern Maine Veterans Cemetery-
Caribou
37 Lombard Road
Caribou, ME 04736
(207)-492-1173

MARYLAND
Maryland State Veterans Cemeteries
Federal Building- 31 Hopkins Plaza
Baltimore, MD 21201
(410) 962-4700

Cheltenham Veterans
Cemetery
11301 Crain Highway
P. O. Box 10
Cheltenham, MD 20623
(301) 372-6398

Crownsville Veterans Cemetery
1080 Sunrise Beach Road
Crownsville, MD 21032
(410) 987-6320

Eastern Shore Veterans Cemetery
6827 East New Market Ellwood Road
Hurlock, MD 21643
(410) 943-3420

Garrison Forest Veterans Cemetery
11501 Garrison Forest Road
Owings Mills, MD 21117
(410) 363-6090

Rocky Gap Veterans Cemetery
14205 Pleasant Valley Road, NE
Flintstone, MD 21530
(301) 777-2185

MASSACHUSETTS
Massachusetts State Veterans
Cemetery (Agawam & Winchendon)
1390 Main Street
Agawam, MA 01001
(413) 821-9500

Winchendon Veterans Cemetery
111 Glenallen Street
Winchendon, MA 01475
(978) 297-9501

MICHIGAN
Grand Rapids Home for Veterans
Cemetery
3000 Monroe, NW
Grand Rapids, MI 49505
(616) 364-5400

MINNESOTA
MN State Veterans Cemetery
15550 HWY 15
Little Falls, MN 56345
(320) 616-2527

MISSOURI
St. James Missouri Veterans Home
Cemetery
620 North Jefferson
St. James, MO 65559
(573) 265-3271

Missouri Veterans Cemetery
20109 Bus. Hwy. 13
Higgensville, MO 64037
(660) 584-5252

Missouri Veterans Cemetery
Springfield, MO
5201 South Southwood Road
Springfield, MO 65804
(417) 823-3944

Missouri State Veterans Cemetery
Bloomfield
17357 Stars and Stripes Way
Bloomfield, Missouri 63825
(573) 568-3871

Missouri State Cemetery
Jacksonville
1479 County Road 1675
Jacksonville, Missouri 65260
(660) 295-4237

MONTANA
State Veterans Cemetery
Fort William H. Harrison Box 5715
Helena, MT 59604
(406) 324-3740

State Veterans Cemetery Miles City
Highway 59
Miles City, MT 59301
(406) 324-3740

Montana Veterans Home Cemetery
P. O. Box 250
Columbia Falls, MT 59912
(406) 892-3256

NEBRASKA
Nebraska Veterans Home Cemetery
Burkett Station
Grand Island, NE 68803
(308) 385-6252, Ext. 230

NEVADA
Commissioner of Veterans Affairs
1201 Terminal Way, Room 108
Reno, NV 89520
(775) 688-1155

Northern Nevada Veterans
Memorial Cemetery
14 Veterans Way
Fernley, NV 8940
(775) 575-4441

Southern Nevada Veterans Memorial
Cemetery
1900 Buchanan Boulevard
Boulder City, NV 89005
(702) 486-5920

NEW HAMPSHIRE
NH State Veterans Cemetery
110 Daniel Webster Hwy, Route 3
Boscawen, NH 03303
(603) 796-2026

NEW JERSEY
Brigadier General William C. Doyle
Veterans Memorial Cemetery
350 Provenceline Road,
Route #2
Wrightstown, NJ 08562
(609) 758-7250

164

New Jersey Memorial Home
Cemetery (Closed)
524 N.W. Boulevard
Vineland, NJ 08360
(609) 696-6350

NORTH CAROLINA
Western Carolina State Veterans
Cemetery
962 Old Highway 70,
West Black Mountain, NC 28711
(828) 669-0684

Coastal Carolina State Veterans
Cemetery
P. O. Box 1486
Jacksonville, NC 28541
(910) 347-4550 or 3570

Sandhills State Veterans Cemetery
P. O. Box 39
400 Murchison Road
Spring Lake, NC 28390
(910) 436-5630 or 5635

NORTH DAKOTA
North Dakota Veterans Cemetery
1825 46th Street
Mandan, ND 58554
(701) 667-1418

OHIO
Ohio Veterans Home Cemetery
3416 Columbus Avenue
Sandusky, OH 44870
(419) 625-2454, Ext. 200

OKLAHOMA
Oklahoma Veterans Cemetery
Military Department (OKFAC)
3501 Military Circle N.E.
Oklahoma City, OK 73111-4398
(405) 228-5334

PENNSYLVANIA
Pennsylvania Soldiers and Sailors
Home Cemetery
P. O. Box 6239
560 East Third Street
Erie, PA 16512-6239
(814) 871-4531

RHODE ISLAND
Rhode Island Veterans Cemetery
301 South County
Trail Exeter, RI 02822-9712
(401) 268-3088

SOUTH CAROLINA
M.J. "Dolly" Cooper Veterans
Cemetery
140 Inway Drive
Anderson, SC 29621
(864) 332-8022

SOUTH DAKOTA
SD Veterans Home Cemetery
2500 Minnekahta Avenue
Hot Springs, SD 57747
(605) 745-5127

TENNESSEE
East Tennessee State Veterans
Cemetery
5901 Lyons View Pike
Knoxville, TN 37919
(865) 594-6776

Middle Tennessee Veterans
Cemetery
7931 McCrory Lane
Nashville, TN 37221
(615) 532-2238

West Tennessee Veterans Cemetery
4000 Forest Hill/Irene Road
Memphis, TN 38125
(901) 543-7005

TEXAS
Central Texas State Veterans
Cemetery
11463 South Highway 195
Killeen, Texas 76542
(512) 463-5977

Rio Grande Valley
State Veterans Cemetery
2520 South Inspiration Road
Mission, TX 78572
(956) 583-7227

UTAH
Utah State Veterans Cemetery
Utah Parks and Recreation
17111 South Camp Williams Road
Bluffdale, UT 84065
(801) 254-9036

VERMONT
Vermont Veterans Home War
Memorial Cemetery
325 North Street
Bennington, VT 05201
(802) 442-6353

Vermont Veterans Memorial
Cemetery
120 State Street
Montpelier, VT 05602-4401
(802) 828-3379

VIRGINIA
Virginia Veterans Cemetery
10300 Pridesville Road
Amelia, VA 23002
(804) 561-1475

Albert G. Horton, Jr. Memorial
Veterans Cemetery
5310 Milner's Road
Suffolk, Virginia 23434
(757) 334-4731

WASHINGTON
Washington Soldiers Home Colony
and Cemetery
1301 Orting-Kapowsin Highway
Orting, WA 98360
(360) 893-4500

Washington Veterans Home
Cemetery
P.O. Box 698
Retsil, WA 98378
(360) 895-4700

WISCONSIN
Northern Wisconsin Veterans
Memorial Cemetery
N4063 Veterans Way
Spooner, WI 54801
(715) 635-5360

Wisconsin Veterans Memorial
Cemetery
Wisconsin Veterans Home
N2665 Highway QQ
King, WI 54946
(715) 258-5586

Southern Wisconsin Veterans
Memorial Cemetery
21731 Spring Street
Union Grove, WI 53182

WYOMING
Oregon Trail Veterans Cemetery
89 Cemetery Road, Box 669
Evansville, WY 82636
(262) 878-5660

TERRITORIES
Guam Veterans Cemetery
490 Chalan Palayso
Agatna Heights, Guam 96910
(671) 475-8388

CHAPTER 11

HEALTHCARE BENEFITS

Individuals are encouraged to contact the nearest VA benefits or healthcare facility to obtain the latest information regarding healthcare benefits. Legislation often changes the specific regulations regarding healthcare and nursing home care.

Community Care

In 2019, the VA released final rules related to its revamped health care program, which provides more choice in health care providers for veterans. Currently, some of the provisions apply only to certain regions.

The final rules are related to the implementation of the VA Mission Act of 2018, which consolidated the VA's community care programs into a new community care program known as the Veterans Community Care Program. The VA Choice program is consolidated into the Community Care Program.

Veterans are no longer eligible for community care under certain Veterans Choice Program eligibility criteria because of the expiration of the program. Veterans who were eligible for community care under the Choice Program should talk to their VA care team or a VA staff member at their local VA medical facility about their eligibility for community care.

Key Takeaways
A Veteran's eligibility for community care depends on his/her individual health care needs or circumstances.

Veterans must receive approval from VA prior to obtaining care from a community provider, in most circumstances.
Veterans must either be enrolled in VA health care or be eligible for VA care without needing to enroll to be eligible for community care.
Eligibility for community care will continue to be dependent upon a Veteran's individual health care needs or circumstances.
VA staff members generally make all eligibility determinations.

Veterans may be eligible for care through a provider in their local community, depending on their health care needs or circumstances, and if they meet specific eligibility criteria. Even if a veteran is eligible for community care, they generally still have the option to receive care from a VA medical facility.

In most cases, veterans must receive approval from VA before receiving care from a community provider to avoid being billed for the care. VA staff members generally make all eligibility determinations for community care.

Eligibility

A veteran's eligibility for community care depends on his/her individual health care needs or circumstances. Veterans must receive approval from the VA before obtaining care from a community provider in most circumstances; veterans must either be enrolled in VA health care or be eligible for VA care without needing to enroll to be eligible for community care. Eligibility for community care will continue to be dependent upon a veteran's individual health care needs or circumstances. VA staff generally make all eligibility determinations.

Six criteria can qualify a veteran to receive community care. Veterans only have to meet ONE to be eligible. These criteria are:

- The veteran needs a service not available at a VA medical facility. To meet this criterion, a veteran would require a specific type of service or care not provided in-house by the VA at any of its medical facilities.
- Veteran lives in a U.S. state or territory without a full-service medical facility.
- VA can't provide care within certain designated access standards. This situation means that the VA wouldn't be able to schedule an appointment that is both within the average driving time standards and wait time standards. The access standards are a 30-minute average drive time for primary care, mental health, and non-institutional extended care services, including adult day health care. The access standard is a 60-minute average drive time for specialty care. For appointment wait times at a specific VA medical facility, the accent standards are 20 days for primary care, mental health care and non-institutional extended care services, unless the veteran agrees to a later day in consultation with their VA health care provider, and 28 days for specialty care from the date of request, unless the veteran agrees to a later date in consultation with their VA health care provider.
- Veteran qualifies under the "Grandfather" provision related to distance eligibility for VCP. For this element, there are a few different ways that a veteran could be eligible for community care. Initially, there are two requirements that must be met in every case. First, the veteran was eligible under the 40-mile criterion under the Veterans Choice Program on the day before the VA MISSION Act was enacted into law (June 6, 2018), and the veteran continues to reside in a location that would qualify them under that criterion. If both of these requirements have been met, a veteran may be

eligible if one of the following is also true: the veteran lives in North Dakota, South Dakota, Montana, Alaska or Wyoming, or the veteran lives in another state, received care between June 6, 2017 and June 6, 2018 and requires care before June 6, 2020.

- It is in the veteran's best medical interest.
- VA service line doesn't meet certain quality standards.

Appointments

Veterans eligible for community care generally have the option of choosing to receive care from a VA medical facility or community provider. For veterans who choose to receive community care, a VA staff member will discuss with them their preferences for getting care from a community provider.

Veterans can either choose their preferred community provider, or a VA staff member can help select one. The selected community provider must be part of VA's network.

If there is a specific community provider a veteran would like to see that is not in VA's network, VA may be able to add them to its network. In some cases, a VA staff member will work with the veteran to find other options when:

- A community provider cannot be found that meets the veteran's health care needs
- A community provider was but is no longer part of VA's network
- An existing community provider is no longer available

Once a community provider is selected, an appointment can be scheduled based on the veteran's preferences and the community provider's availability.

Scheduling Appointments

Before scheduling an appointment, it is important for the veteran to confirm with a VA staff member that they are eligible and authorized for community care.

Once authorized to receive community care, they have several options for scheduling an appointment with a community provider, depending on the type of care they need. A veteran may be able to:

- Directly schedule an appointment and inform a VA staff member about the appointment
- Use VA Online Scheduling to request an appointment for certain types of routine services
- Have a VA staff member schedule the appointment
- Have VA's Third-Party Administrator (TPA) schedule the appointment

VA will send the veteran and the selected community provider a referral. VA will also send the veteran's medical documentation to the community provider to ensure proper care coordination between their VA care team and the community provider.

Getting Care

When a veteran arrives for the appointment, the community provider should have the appointment, VA referral, and medical documentation on file. If a veteran needs a follow-up appointment, the community provider should check to make sure the VA has authorized additional care before scheduling the appointment.

Surgery

Prior to undergoing surgery at a community provider facility, veterans and their family members may access information about the surgeon performing the surgery. Information required to be available includes the surgeon's education, training, licensure, registration, and certification by the authorizing state and national entity.

Prescription Medicine

If prescription medication is needed, the prescription should usually be sent to and filled by the nearest VA pharmacy. Veterans can receive short-term prescription medication for a 14-day or fewer supply that can be filled at a non-VA pharmacy. A prescription for more than a 14-day supply must be filled by VA.

Billing and Payments

After receiving care from a community provider, veterans may have to pay a copayment for nonservice-connected care, just as the veteran would if care was received at a VA medical facility. For urgent care, copayments depend on the veteran's assigned priority group and the number of times the veteran visits an urgent care provider in a calendar year.

Community providers cannot bill or collect a VA copayment directly from veterans, including for urgent care. All VA copayments are billed as part of VA's billing process.

Community Care FAQs

These are a collection of some of the most commonly asked questions as far as the new community care program.

Q: Am I Eligible for Community Care Under the New Criteria?

A: A veteran is eligible for community care based on the six eligibility criteria named above. Briefly, to repeat, these community care eligibility criteria are:

1. Veteran needs a service not available at VA;
2. Veteran resides in a U.S. state or territory without a full-service VA medical facility;
3. Veteran qualifies under the "Grandfather" provision meaning, the veteran was eligible under the 40-mile distance criteria under the Veterans Choice Program on the day before the VA MISSION Act was enacted into law and the veteran continues to reside in a location that would qualify them under that criterion;
4. Veterans must meet specific accessibility standards for average drive time or appointment wait times. The designated access criteria are not based on

a veteran's preferred location but instead on the wait times and average drive times to any VA facility that provides the service needed;

5. A veteran and their referring clinician agree that it's in the best interest of the veteran to be referred to a community provider;

6. A veteran needs care from a VA medical service line that VA determines is not providing care complying with VA quality standards;

The new eligibility criteria for community care became effective on June 6, 2019.

Q: How Does VA Determine If I am Eligible for Community Care?

A: The VA provider for a veteran and the VA medical staff members work with a veteran to determine whether or not they're eligible for community care.

Q: Is the Process for Getting Prescription Medicines Different?

A: There are no changes to the processing of prescriptions for veterans receiving community care. As part of an authorized visit with a community provider, veterans can receive a short-term supply of 14 days or fewer days, urgent prescription medication in their community. Long-term prescription medications longer than a 14-day supply must be filled by VA.

Q: Do I Pay a Copayment for Community Care?

A: Copayment charges are the same for community care as care at a VA medical facility. This usually means veterans who are required to pay copayments will be charged a copayment for the treatment of their non-service-connected conditions. Copayment bills are sent by the VA, not the community provider. For the urgent care benefit, veterans may owe a copayment that would be different from their usual VA copayment, depending on their assigned veteran priority group and the number of urgent care visits per calendar year.

Q: What Is the Difference Between the Veterans Choice Program (VCP) and the VA Mission Act?

A: The Veterans Choice Program (VCP) is the name of a federal program launched in 2014 to expand access to care for veterans. VCP ended on June 6, 2019. The VA MISSION Act is a federal law that established a new community care program.

Urgent Care

VA offers urgent care services to eligible Veterans at VA medical facilities or at in-network urgent care clinics closer to home.

Use VA's urgent care benefit to treat minor injuries and illnesses that are not life-threatening, such as colds, strep throat, sprained muscles, and skin and ear infections.

To make sure you have a smooth experience, please review the information on this page to understand the requirements and limitations associated with this benefit. To access an in-network care provider, you must be eligible, go to an in-network urgent care provider, and pay a VA copayment if applicable after the visit, billed separate by VA.

To be eligible you must be enrolled in the VA health care system and have received care through VA from either a VA or community provider within the last 24 months. To check your eligibility, contact or local VA medical facility or call 844-MyVA311, select option one and then select option one again.

Covered services include colds, minor injuries, some lab testing and diagnostic services, and therapeutic vaccines. Urgent care is not a replacement for emergency or preventative care.

To find an in-network urgent care provider, you can use the online VA facility locator, or contact your local VA medical facility. You can also call 877-881-7618 to reach the OCC National Contact Center.

VA can only pay for urgent care if the provider is part of the VA contracted network. Veterans may be required to pay the full cost of care if they go to an out-of-network urgent care provider. By law, VA can't pay claims for urgent care from providers that are not part of the VA contracted network.

If you are getting care, you should bring a valid government-issued photo ID.

Inform the provider you would like to use your VA urgent care benefit to receive care. The urgent care provider will confirm your eligibility. Don't pay a copayment at the time of your visit.

You may be charged a copayment for urgent care that is different from other VA medical copayments.

Copayments depend on the veteran's assigned priority group and the number of times an urgent care provider is visited in a calendar year. Copayment charges are billed separately by VA as part of the VA billing process. There is no limit to the number of times a veteran can go to an urgent care provider.

Keep in mind that urgent care is for non-life-threatening illnesses and injuries like pink eye or strep throat. Emergency care is for severe illnesses or injuries.

VA will reimburse beneficiary travel for eligible veterans that travel to receive community care. Payment will be made for the distance to either the nearest VA or community medical facility that could have provided the care or services. Payment will only be made on a one-way basis for unscheduled care.

Only eligible veterans can use this benefit. The benefit is non-transferrable and doesn't extend to family members.

Health ID Cards

When you're enrolled in VA health care, you'll use your Veteran Health Identification Card (VHIC) to check in to your appointments at VA medical centers. This secure ID card keeps your personal information safe while giving us the information we need to easily access your VA health record.

You may also use this card to get discounts offered to Veterans at many stores, businesses, and restaurants. If you have a VHIC, you don't need to request another type of photo ID card to prove you're a Veteran or to get retail or business discounts.

Note: You can't use your VHIC as a credit card or insurance card. It doesn't pay copays or authorize care at non-VA health facilities.

After you receive your VA health care welcome call, you should contact the VA medical center closest to you and ask to speak with the enrollment coordinator. The enrollment coordinator can arrange to get your picture taken for your VHIC.

When you arrive for your picture, you will need to bring your current unexpired state-issued driver's license, or U.S. passport or passport card, or another government ID issued by a federal, state or local government agency.

The ID must show your picture and date of birth. If it doesn't include your address you'll need to bring a separate document to confirm your address. After your picture is taken, VA will process your VHIC and send it to you by mail. It should arrive within 10 days.

You can request a replacement card at the VA medical center where you had your picture taken. You'll need to bring your driver's license, passport, or other government ID or be able to answer a series of challenge questions so we can verify your identity before we give you a new card.

If you've changed your medical center since getting your original card, you can contact the medical center where you currently receive care. Or, call VA at 877-222-8387, Monday through Friday, 8:00 a.m. to 8:00 p.m. ET. The staff will need to verify your identity with a series of challenge questions before we can send a new card.

Camp Lejeune Water Contamination Health Issues

If you served at Marine Corps Base Camp Lejeune or Marine Corps Air Station (MCAS) New River in North Carolina, you may have had contact with contaminants in the drinking water there. Scientific and medical evidence has shown an association between exposure to these contaminants during military service and development of certain diseases later on. If you have qualifying service at Camp Lejeune and a current diagnosis of one of the conditions listed below, you may be able to get disability benefits.

As a part of the Caring for Camp Lejeune Families Act of 2012, qualifying veterans can receive all their health care (except dental care) from VA if they served on active duty at Camp Lejeune for at least 30 days between August 1, 1953 and December 31, 1987, even if they don't have a health condition that is presumed to be related to exposure. For individuals with one of the 15 medical conditions presumed to be related to exposure, there is no charge for care. For other health conditions, Veterans will have a co-pay, depending on income and health eligibility priority category.

In accordance with the 2020 Camp Lejeune health care law, VA provides cost-free health care for certain conditions to veterans who served at least 30 days of active duty at Camp Lejeune from August 1, 1953 and December 31, 1987. Qualifying health conditions include:

- Esophageal cancer
- Breast cancer
- Kidney cancer
- Multiple myeloma
- Renal toxicity
- Female infertility
- Scleroderma
- Non-Hodgkin's lymphoma
- Lung cancer
- Bladder cancer
- Leukemia
- Myelodysplastic syndromes
- Hepatic steatosis
- Miscarriage
- Neurobiological effects

Veterans eligible for health care under the 2012 Camp Lejeune health care law may enroll in VA health care and receive medical services for the 15 covered health conditions at no cost including copayments. If you aren't enrolled in VA health care, you can call 1-877-222-8287 and ask for help.

Family Member Health Care Reimbursement

Family members of veterans who also resided at Camp Lejeune during the qualifying period are eligible for reimbursement of out-of-pocket medical expenses related to the 15 covered health conditions. VA can only pay treatment costs that remain after payment from other health plans. Call 1-866-372-1144 for help. To apply for the Camp Lejeune Family Member Program, you can complete a paper application and fax it to (512) 460-5536 or mail it to:

Department of Veterans Affairs
Financial Services Center
PO Box 149200
Austin, TX 78714-9200

VA will need evidence that you were both a legal dependent of the veteran and that you were a resident at Camp Lejeune for at least 30 days between the dates of august 1, 1953 and December 31, 1987. Evidence to show legal dependency could include:

- Marriage certificate
- Birth certificate
- Adoption papers or
- Other legal documents

Proof of Camp Lejeune residence documents could include:

- Military orders
- Base housing records
- Utility bill
- Pay stub
- Tax forms

It's a good idea to provide a Camp Lejeune Family Member Program Treating Physician Report (VA Form 10-10068b). Your doctor will need to fill it out and sign it before it's submitted to the VA. It's not required, but it can help the process.

Am I Eligible for Disability Benefits from VA?

You may be eligible for disability benefits if you meet all of the requirements listed below:

Both of these must be true. You:

- Served at Camp Lejeune or MCAS New River for at least 30 cumulative days from August 1953 through December 1987, and
- Didn't receive a dishonorable discharge when you were separated from the military

And you must have a diagnosis of one or more of these presumptive conditions:

- Adult leukemia
- Aplastic anemia and other myelodysplastic syndromes
- Bladder cancer
- Kidney cancer
- Liver cancer
- Multiple myeloma
- Non-Hodgkin's lymphoma
- Parkinson's disease

Veterans, reservists and guardsmen are covered. Benefits available include health care and compensation. Presently, the only conditions that the VA says have sufficient scientific and medical evidence to support the creation of presumptions are the ones above. The VA says they will continue to review information as it becomes available.

Veterans experiencing other health conditions they think may be related to contaminated water at Camp Lejeune are encouraged to contact their primary care provider and file a claim. VA reviews and decides disability compensation claims on a case-by-case basis.

To file a claim for disability compensation, you will need to provide the evidence (supporting documents) listed below:

- Your military records showing you served at Camp Lejeune or MCAS New River for at least 30 days from August 1953 through December 1987 while on active duty or in the National Guard or reserves, and
- Medical records stating that you have one or more of the eight illnesses on the presumptive conditions list

When you file, make sure you're applying for one or more of the presumed Camp Lejeune illnesses and upload evidence like a doctor's report or medical test results.

You can file a claim online at VA.gov, or at eBenefits.com. You can also file a claim by getting help from a veterans service officer or accredited representative, or by getting help at a VA regional office.

Telehealth

The Department of Veterans Affairs has been working on offering more telehealth options. In 2020, this became a priority because of the COVID-19 pandemic.

VA offers telehealth options in hospitals to help VA providers collaborate to improve care. You can connect with VA health specialists across the country from a VA clinic located near your home. You can also meet with VA providers virtually and send health data from your home, using your mobile device or computer.

If you don't already use VA for your health care, you can apply online, by phone or by mail. If you're already enrolled, you can get started with telehealth by having a conversation with your VA provider.

Each VA Medical Center has staff who can tell you about the available telehealth options and help you enroll. VA offers telehealth services in more than 50 specialty care areas. VA also lends telehealth devices to veterans including tablets and devices like blood pressure monitors, blood oximeters, and thermometers.

Remote Patient Monitoring

Telehealth technologies can collect and send health data such as vital signs to your care team. Providers receive the information they need to manage your care, while you are comfortable at home. Health data isn't collected without your informed consent. If you're interested in remote patient monitoring, you are first assessed for Home Telehealth remote monitoring services. If they find it appropriate, VA will provide a device to fit your needs and train you on how to use it.

VA assigns you a Home Telehealth remote monitoring care coordinator. Your care coordinator contacts VA hospitals and providers and helps you arrange treatment changes, clinic appointments and hospital admissions.

VA Video Connect

With VA Video Connect, you can meet providers in virtual medical rooms using the camera on a smartphone, computer or tablet. You will work together with your provider to schedule online video appointments. You can also have family members and caretakers join the session.

If you're interested, speak to your doctor to see if VA Video Connect could be part of your care plan. You'll receive an email link for your VA Video Connect session when it's scheduled. At the time of your appointment, you click on the link, enter your information and launch the session. If you're using an Apple device, you have to download the VA Video Connect app to connect.

VA Mobile Health

VA Mobile aims to improve veteran health by providing technologies to expand clinical care beyond the traditional office visit.

Annie App For Veterans

Annie is a VA service that sends automated texts to veterans to help them stay focused on self-care. This could include health-related notifications, reminders or motivational messages. Annie also empowers veterans to play an active role in their care, by prompting them to provide health data such as weight or blood pressure.

VA Online Scheduling

VA Only Scheduling accesses a veteran's VA Electronic Health Record and requires that you enter ID.me, DS Logon, or My HealtheVet account credentials. VA Online Scheduling is a secure, online way to request and self-schedule appointments at VA and Community Care facilities. With VA Online Scheduling you can also view details about upcoming appointments.

To request an appointment through VA Online Scheduling, you must be enrolled in VA health care. You also have to be scheduling your appointment with a VA health facility using online scheduling and you have to have registered at that facility or have had an appointment there before.

My HealtheVet

Through the My HealtheVet portal, you can refill your VA prescriptions, track delivery, and view a list of your VA medications and other details.

You can keep track of upcoming VA medical appointments and get email reminders. You can communicate securely online with your VA health care team, and you can view, print or download a copy of your VA medical record information or enter your own health information.

Veteran Health Registries

Certain veterans can participate in a VA health registry and receive free medical examinations, including laboratory and other diagnostic tests, when determined necessary by an examining clinician.

Gulf War Registry:

For veterans who served in the Gulf War and Operation Iraqi Freedom.

Depleted Uranium Registries:

VA maintains two registries for veterans possibly exposed to depleted uranium. The first is for veterans who served in the Gulf War, including Operation Iraqi Freedom. The second is for veterans who served elsewhere, including Bosnia and Afghanistan.

Agent Orange Registry:

For veterans possible exposed to dioxin or other toxic substances in herbicides used during the Vietnam War, while serving in Korea in 1968 or 1969, or as a result of testing, transporting, or spraying herbicides for military purposes.

Ionizing Radiation Registry:

For veterans possibly exposed to atomic radiation during the following activities:
Atmospheric detonation of a nuclear device;
Occupation of Hiroshima or Nagasaki from August 6, 1945, through July 1, 1946;
Internment as a prisoner of war in Japan during WWII;
Serving in official military duties at the gaseous diffusion plants at Paducah, KY;
Portsmouth, OH; or the K-25 area at Oak Ridge, TN for at least 250 days before February 1, 1992, or in Longshot, Milrow or Cannikin underground nuclear tests at Amchitka Island, Alaska, before January 1, 1974; or
Treatment with nasopharyngeal (NP) radium during military service.

Eligibility

The primary factor in determining a veteran's eligibility to receive VA health care benefits is "veteran status." "Veteran status" is established by active duty service in the military, naval, or air service and a discharge or release from active military service under other than dishonorable conditions.

The veteran's length of service may also matter. It depends on when he or she served. There is no length of service requirement for:
- Former enlisted persons who started active duty before September 8, 1980; or
- Former officers who first entered active duty before October 17, 1981.
- All other veterans must have 24 months of continuous active-duty military service or meet one of the exceptions described below.

179

Exceptions to the 24-Month Active-Duty Rule

The 24 continuous months of active-duty service requirement does not apply to:

- Reservists who were called to Active Duty and who completed the term for which they were called, and who were granted an "other than dishonorable" discharge; or
- National Guard members who were called to Active Duty by federal executive order, and who completed the term for which they were called, and who were granted an "other than dishonorable" discharge; or
- Veterans requesting a benefit for, or in connection with, a service-connected condition or disability; or
- Veterans who were discharged or released from active duty under section 1171 or 1173 of title 10; or
- Veterans who were discharged or released from active duty for a disability incurred or aggravated in the line of duty; or
- Veterans who have been determined by VA to have compensable service-connected conditions; or
- Veterans requesting treatment for and/or counseling of sexual trauma that occurred while on active military service, for treatment of conditions related to ionizing radiation or for head or neck cancer related to the nose or throat radium treatment while in the military.

Enrollment

The very first step in obtaining access to your VA Health Benefits is to apply for enrollment. Effective immediately, veterans who served in a theater of combat operations after November 11, 1998, can complete applications for enrollment in VA health care by telephone without the need for a signed paper application.

All other Veterans may apply by phone effective since July 5, 2016. In addition, VA sends each new enrollee an introductory letter and personalized Veterans Health Benefits Handbook in the mail.

All veterans seeking VA healthcare are required to be enrolled unless they are in one of the following categories:

- VA rated the individual as having a service-connected disability of 50% or more;
- It has been less than one year since the veteran was discharged from military service for a disability that the military determined was incurred or aggravated in the line of duty, and has not yet been rated by VA;
- Veteran is seeking care from VA for a service-connected disability only.

As part of the enrollment process, a veteran may select any VA health care facility to serve as his or her primary treatment facility. There are three ways a veteran can apply to enroll in healthcare benefits. The first is to obtain the enrollment form, "10-10EZ" from their local VA Medical Center or Clinic, in person. The second way is telephone; by calling (877) 222-VETS (8387) Monday through Friday between 8:00 a.m. and 8:00

p.m. Eastern Time. The third way to apply is online through the VA's website.

The application will be processed and forwarded to the VA Health Eligibility Center in Atlanta, GA. The Health Eligibility Center will notify the veteran of his or her status.

Once enrolled, most veterans will remain enrolled from year to year without further action on their part. However, certain veterans are required to provide income information to determine their priority level. These veterans will be mailed a "VA Form 10-10 EZ" for completion for re-enrollment on an annual basis, or they can renew their benefits by visiting the VA's website.

A veteran may choose not to be re-enrolled, or changes in VA funding may reduce the number of priority groups VA can enroll in a given fiscal year. If VA cannot renew enrollment for another year, the veteran will be notified in writing before their enrollment period expires.

Priority Groups

The number of veterans who can be enrolled in the health care program is determined by the amount of money Congress gives VA each year. Since funds are limited, VA set up priority groups to make sure that certain groups of veterans are able to be enrolled before others.

Once a veteran applies for enrollment, his or her eligibility will be verified. Based on the individual's specific eligibility status, he or she will be assigned a priority group.

The priority groups range from 1-8 with 1 being the highest priority for enrollment. Some veterans may have to agree to pay copay to be placed in certain priority groups.

A veteran may be eligible for more than one Enrollment Priority Group. In that case, VA will always place him or her in the highest priority group that he or she is eligible for. Under the Medical Benefits Package, the same services are generally available to all enrolled veterans.

The priority groups are complicated and some reference financial thresholds.

Priority Group 1
- Veterans with service-connected disabilities rated 50% or more disabling
- Veterans determined by VA to be unemployable due to service-connected conditions.
- Veterans who have been awarded the Medal of Honor (MOH)

Priority Group 2
- Veterans with service-connected disabilities rated 30% or 40% disabling.

Priority Group 3

- Veterans who are former POWs;
- Veterans whose discharge was for a disability that was incurred or aggravated in the line of duty;
- Veterans with service-connected disabilities rated 10% or 20% disabling;
- Veterans who are Purple Heart recipients (unless eligible for a higher Priority Group);
- Veterans awarded special eligibility classification under Title 38, U.S.C., Section 1151, "benefits for individuals disabled by treatment or vocational rehabilitation".

Priority Group 4

- Veterans who are receiving aid and attendance or housebound benefits from VA
- Veterans who have been determined by VA to be catastrophically disabled.

Priority Group 5

- Nonservice-connected veterans and service-connected veterans rated 0% disabled whose annual income and net worth are below the established dollar threshold. (Veterans in this priority group must provide VA with information on their annual income and net worth in order to determine whether they are below the "means test" threshold; or agree to co- payment requirements. The threshold is adjusted annually, and announced in January. In making the assessment, the veteran's household income is considered.);
- Veterans receiving VA pension benefits; Veterans eligible for Medicaid benefits.

Priority Group 6

- Veterans with a compensable 0% service-connected disability.
- Veterans exposed to ionizing radiation during atmospheric testing or during the occupation of Hiroshima and Nagasaki.
- Project 112/SHAD participants.
- Veterans of the Mexican border period or of World War I
- Veterans who served in the Republic of Vietnam between January 9, 1962, and May 7, 1975.
- Veterans of the Persian Gulf War who served between August 2, 1990, and November 11, 1998.
- Veterans who served on active duty at Camp Lejeune for at least 30 days between August 1, 1953, and December 31, 1987.
- Currently enrolled Veterans and new enrollees who served in a theater of combat operations after November 11, 1998, and those who were discharged from active duty on or after January 28, 2003, are eligible for the enhanced benefits for five years post discharge

182

Priority Group 7
- Veterans with incomes below the geographic means test (GMT) income thresholds and who agree to pay the applicable copayment

Priority Group 8
- Veterans with gross household incomes above the VA national income threshold and the geographically-adjusted income threshold for their resident location and who agrees to pay copays
- Veterans eligibility for enrollment:
- Noncompensable 0% service-connected and:
  - Subpriority a: Enrolled as of January 16, 2003, and who have remained enrolled since that date and/or placed in this subpriority due to changed eligibility status
  - Subpriority g: Enrolled on or after June 15, 2009 whose income exceeds the current VA National Income Thresholds or VA National Geographic Income thresholds by 10% or less

Veterans eligibility for enrollment:
- Non-service-connected and:
- Subpriority c: Enrolled as of January 16, 2003, and who remained enrolled since that date and or/placed in this subpriority due to changed eligibility status
- Subpriority d: Enrolled on or after June 15, 2009 and whose income exceeds the current VA National Income Thresholds or VA National Geographic Income thresholds by 10% or less

Veterans not eligible for enrollment: veterans not meeting the criteria below:
- Subpriority e: Noncompensable 0%service-connected
- Subpriority f: Non-service-connected

Special Access to Care

Service-Disabled Veterans

Veterans who are 50 percent or more disabled from service-connected conditions, unemployable due to service-connected conditions, or receiving care for a service-connected disability receive priority in scheduling of hospital or outpatient medical appointments.

Financial Assessment

A financial assessment is a means of collecting the veteran's household income information which is used to determine whether a veteran is eligible for enrollment and whether or not the veteran would be required to pay copays for care or prescription medication. VA is required by law to collect this information.

There is no change in VA's long-standing policy to provide no-cost care to veterans who cannot afford to pay for their care, veterans with catastrophic medical conditions, veterans with a disability rating of 50 percent or higher, or for conditions that are officially rated as "service-connected."

Veterans Required to Provide a Financial Assessment

Not all veterans are required to provide their income information to VA when applying for enrollment. Only certain veterans who do not have a VA-rated service-connected disability, who do not receive a VA pension payment or have a special eligibility, such as a recently discharged combat veteran or a Purple Heart recipient, must provide their gross household income (which includes spouse/partner and dependent children, if applicable) for the previous year when applying for enrollment for VA health care. This part of the application process is called an 'income assessment or financial assessment" (also formerly called a means test) and is used to determine if these veterans are eligible for enrollment and whether or not they have to pay copays for their health care or prescription medication.

Enrolled veterans are no longer required to provide their financial assessment on an annual basis if they had a current financial assessment on file as of March 24, 2014. This means veterans can enjoy their VA health care benefits without worrying about having to submit updated income information to VA every year.

If the enrolled veteran does not have a financial assessment on file as of March 24, 2014, the veteran will be required to provide updated income information. Veterans may update their financial assessment when they visit their VA facility at their next appointment. Veterans may also update their information by submitting VA Form 1010EZR, which is available online, at their local VA medical center or by contacting 1-877-222-VETS (8387), to have the form mailed. This form is available online at https://www.1010ez.med.va.gov.

Income Updates from IRS and SSA

VA securely receives income information from the IRS and SSA to confirm veterans' continued enrollment eligibility. VA will contact the Veteran (and spouse/partner and dependents, if applicable) only if the income information received from IRS and SSA indicates a change in the Veteran's eligibility or copay requirements. Veterans will still have access to care during the period of review should they do not agree with the information VA receives from IRS and SSA.

Existing Healthcare Coverage

Since VA health care depends primarily on annual congressional appropriations, veterans are allowed to keep their current healthcare coverage and are encouraged to do so. Veterans with private insurance or other coverage such as DoD, Medicare, or Medicaid may find these coverages to be a supplement to their VA enrollment. The use of other available healthcare coverage does not affect a veteran's enrollment status. VA does not charge the veteran for insurance company co-payments and deductibles.

When applying for medical care, all veterans will be asked to provide information pertaining to health insurance coverage, including policies held by spouses. VA is obligated to submit claims to insurance carriers for the recovery of costs for medical care provided to nonservice-connected veterans and service-connected veterans for nonservice-connected conditions.

Copayment Requirements

While many veterans qualify for free healthcare services based on a VA compensable service-connected condition or other eligibility, most veterans are required to complete a financial assessment or means test at the time of enrollment to determine if they qualify for free health care services. Veterans whose income exceeds VA income limits, as well as those who choose not to complete the financial assessment at the time of enrollment, must agree to pay required copays for health care services to become eligible for VA health care services.

Veterans Not Required to Make Copays

Some veterans qualify for free healthcare and/or prescriptions based on special eligibility factors including but not limited to:

- Former Prisoner of War status
- 50% or more compensable VA service-connected disabilities (0-40% may take copay test to determine prescription copay status)
- Veterans deemed catastrophically disabled by a VA provider

Services Exempt from Inpatient and Outpatient Copays

- Special registry exams offered by VA to evaluate health risks associated with service
- Compensation and Pension exams
- Counseling and care for Military Sexual Trauma
- Care related to a VA-rated service-connected disability
- Readjustment counseling and related mental health services
- Care that is part of a VA research project
- Care for cancer of head or neck caused by nose or throat radium treatments received while in the military
- Care potentially related to combat service for veterans that served in a theater of combat operations after November 11, 1998
- Laboratory and electrocardiograms
- Hospice care

Copayment Rates – Current as of January 2021

Outpatient Services	
Basic Services – Services provided by a primary care clinician	$15/visit
Specialty Care Services –services provided by a clinical specialist such as surgeon, radiologist, audiologist, optometrist, cardiologist, and specialty tests such as magnetic resonance imagery (MRI), computerized axial tomography (CAT) scan, and nuclear medicine studies	$50 /visit
Footnotes for outpatient services: Copayment amount is limited to a single charge per visit regardless of the number of health care providers seen in a single day. The copayment amount is based on the highest level of service received. There is no copayment requirement for preventive services such as screenings and immunizations.)	
Medications	
Veterans in Priority Groups 2-6, for each 30-day supply of medication for treatment of nonservice-connected conditions	$8/prescription
(The total amount paid annually by veterans in Priority Groups 2 through 6 is limited to $960.)	
Effective July 1, 2010, Veterans in Priority Groups 7-8, for each 30- day supply of medication for treatment of nonservice-connected conditions	$9/prescription
(Veterans in Priority Groups 7-8 do not qualify for medication copay annual cap.)	
Veterans in Priority Group 1 do not pay for medications.	
Inpatient Services	
Priority Group 8 and certain other Veterans are responsible for VA's full inpatient copay rate. Inpatient Copay for the first 90 days of care during a 365-day period	$1,484+$10 charge per day

Priority Group 8 and certain other Veterans are responsible for VA's full inpatient copay rate. Inpatient Copay for each additional 90 days of care during a 365- day period	$742+$10 charge per day
Per Diem Charge Daily Charge for Priority Group 8 and Other Certain Veterans	$10/day $10/day
Priority Group 7 and certain other Veterans are responsible for paying 20 percent of VA's inpatient copay rate. Inpatient Copay for the first 90 days of care during a 365-day period	$296.80 + $2 charge per day
Priority Group 7 and certain other Veterans are responsible for paying 20 percent of VA's inpatient copay rate. Inpatient Copay for each additional 90 days of care during a 365- day period	$148.40 + $2 charge per day
Priority Group 7 And Other Certain Veterans Daily Charge	$2/day
Long-Term Care	
Nursing Home Care / Inpatient Respite Care / Geriatric Evaluation	Maximum of $97/day Adult
Day Health Care / Outpatient Geriatric Evaluation / Outpatient Respite Care	Maximum of $15/day
Domiciliary Care	Maximum of $5/day

Footnote for inpatient services:

**Copayments for Long-Term Care services start on the 22nd day of care during any 12-month period — there is no copayment requirement for the first 21 days. Actual copayment charges will vary from Veteran to Veteran depending upon financial information submitted on VA Form 10-10EC.

Hardship Determination

If gross household income decreases, a veteran may be eligible for a hardship which may qualify them for copayment exemption for the remaining calendar year and enrollment in a higher priority group.

To request a hardship determination, veterans should send a letter explaining the financial hardship their copayment charges will cause them and a completed Request for Hardship Determination (VA **Form10-10HS**).

Letters and forms can be submitted in person at a local Veteran Affairs Medical Center Business Office or Health Administration Office.

They can also be sent by mail to the Business Office/Health Administration Service at a local VA Medical Center.

Medicare Prescription Benefits

Beginning January 1, 2006, Medicare prescription drug coverage (Medicare Part D) became available to everyone with Medicare Part A or B coverage. The Medicare prescription drug coverage is wholly voluntary on the part of the participant. Each individual must decide whether to participate based on his or her own circumstances.

How This Affects Veterans

Each veteran must decide whether to enroll in a Medicare Part D plan based on his or her own situation. An individual's VA prescription drug coverage will not change based on his or her decision to participate in Medicare Part D. VA prescription drug coverage is considered by Medicare to be at least as good as Medicare Part D coverage. (Therefore, it is considered to be creditable coverage.

Refer to the following section for more information regarding creditable coverage. If an individual's spouse is covered by Medicare, he or she must decide whether to enroll in a Medicare Part D plan regardless of the veteran's decision to participate.

Creditable Coverage

Most entities that currently provide prescription drug coverage to Medicare beneficiaries, including VA, must disclose whether the entity's coverage is "creditable prescription drug coverage."

Enrollment in the VA health care system is creditable coverage. This means that VA prescription drug coverage is at least as good as the Medicare Part D coverage. Because they have creditable coverage, veterans enrolled in the VA health care program who chose not to enroll in a Medicare Part D plan before May 15, 2006 will not have to pay a higher premium on a permanent basis ("late enrollment penalty") if they enroll in a Medicare drug plan during a later enrollment period.

However, if an individual un-enrolls in VA health care or if he or she loses his or her enrollment status through no fault of his/her own (such as an enrollment decision by VA that would further restrict access to certain Priority Groups), he or she may be subject to the late enrollment penalty unless he or she enrolls in a Medicare Part D plan within 62 days of losing VA coverage.

If a veteran becomes a patient or inmate in an institution of another government agency (for example, state veterans home, a state institution, a jail, or a corrections facility), he or she may not have creditable coverage from VA while in that institution.

For further information, individuals should contact the institution where the veteran resides, the VA Health Benefits Service Center at (877) 222-VETS, or the local VA medical facility.

Covered Services—Standard Benefits

VA's medical benefits package provides the following health care services to all enrolled veterans:

Preventative Care Services
- Immunizations
- Physical Examinations (including eye and hearing examinations)
- Health Care Assessments
- Screening Tests
- Health Education Programs

Ambulatory (Outpatient) Diagnostic and Treatment Services
- Emergency outpatient care in VA facilities
- Medical
- Surgical (including reconstructive/plastic surgery as a result of disease or trauma)
- Chiropractic Care
- Bereavement Counseling
- Mental Health
- Substance Abuse

Hospital (Inpatient) Diagnostic and Treatment
- Emergency inpatient care in VA facilities
- Medical
- Surgical (including reconstructive/plastic surgery as a result of disease or trauma)
- Mental Health
- Substance Abuse

Limited Benefits

The following is a partial listing of acute care services which may have limitations and special eligibility criteria:
- Ambulance Services
- Dental Care (refer to Chapter 11 of this book for additional details.)
- Durable Medical Equipment
- Eyeglasses (see footnote below)
- Hearing Aids (see footnote below)
- Home Health Care
- Homeless Programs
- Maternity and Parturition Services—usually provided in non-VA contracted hospitals at VA expense, care is limited to the mother (costs associated with the care of newborn are not covered)

Non-VA Healthcare Services
- Orthopedic, Prosthetic, and Rehabilitative Devices

189

- Rehabilitative Services
- Readjustment Counseling
- Sexual Trauma Counseling

Footnote: To qualify for hearing aids or eyeglasses, the individual must have a VA service-connected disability rating of 10% or more. An individual may also qualify if he or she is a former prisoner of war, Purple Heart recipient, require this benefit for treatment of a 0% service-connected condition, or are receiving increased pension based on the need for regular aid and attendance or being permanently housebound.

General Exclusions

The following is a partial listing of general exclusions:

- Abortions and abortion counseling
- Cosmetic surgery except where determined by VA to be medically necessary for reconstructive or psychiatric care
- Gender alteration
- Health club or spa membership, even for rehabilitation
- Drugs, biological, and medical devices not approved by the Food and Drug Administration unless part of formal clinical trial under an approved research program or when prescribed under a compassionate use exemption.
- Medical care for a veteran who is either a patient or inmate in an institution of another government agency if that agency has a duty to provide the care or services.
- Services not ordered and provided by licensed/accredited professional staff
- Special private duty nursing

Services That Don't Require a Co-Pay

You don't have to pay a copay for any of the services listed below, regardless of your disability rating or what priority group you're in:

- Readjustment counseling and mental health services
- Counseling and care for issues related to military sexual trauma
- Exams to determine your risk of health problems linked to your military service
- Care that may be related to combat service for veterans who served in a theater of combat operations after November 11, 1998
- VA claim exams—also called compensation and pension or C&P exams
- Care related to a VA-rated service-connected disability
- Care for cancer of head or neck caused by nose or throat radium treatments received while in the military
- Individual or group programs to help you quit smoking or lose weight
- Care that's part of a VA research project
- Lab tests
- Electrocardiograms (EKGs or ECGs) to check for heart problems and heart disease

- VA health initiatives that are open to the public, such as health fairs

Emergency Care

Revised Regulations for Emergency Treatment Reimbursement

in 2018, the Department of Veterans Affairs announced through a Federal Registrar notice that there are revised regulations relating to payment or reimbursement for emergency treatment for non-service-connected conditions at non-VA facilities.

The VA announced it would begin processing claims for reimbursement of reasonable costs that were only partially paid by the veterans other health insurance OHI. These costs may include hospital charges, professional fees, and emergency transportation such as ambulances. Effective January 9, 2018, the VA updated a portion of its regulations in response to an April 2016 U.S. Court of Appeals for Veterans Claims decision stating the VA can no longer deny reimbursement when OHI pays a portion of the treatment expenses.

VA will apply the updated regulations to claims pending with VA on or after April 8, 2016, and to new claims. By law, VA may still not reimburse veterans for the costs of copayments, cost shares and deductibles required by their OHI. VA will work directly with community providers to get additional information needed to review and process these claims. Previous claims do not have to be resubmitted unless requested by the VA.

What Is a Medical Emergency?

A medical emergency is defined as a condition of such nation that it would be expected that a delay in immediate medical attention would be life-threatening. With VA medical care, a veteran may receive emergency care at a non-VA health care facility at VA expense when a VA facility or other federal health care facility with which the VA has an agreement can't furnish economical care due to your distance from the facility, or when the VA is unable to furnish the needed emergency services.

VA Payment for Emergency Care

Since payment may be limited to the point when your condition is stable enough for you to travel to a VA facility, you need to contact the nearest VA medical facility as possible. VA may pay for your non-VA emergency care based on the following situations

- If you are service-connected: The VA may pay for your non-VA emergency care for a rated service-connected disability, or for your non-service-connected condition associated with and held to be aggravating for your service- connected condition, or any condition if you are an active participant in the VA Chapter 31 Vocational Rehabilitation program, and you need treatment to make possible your entrance into a course of training or to prevent interruption of a course of training or other approved reason for any condition if you were rated as having a total disability permanent in nature resulting from your service-connected disability

VA Payment for Emergency Care of Non-Service- Connected Conditions Without Prior Authorization

VA may pay for emergency care provided in a non-VA facility for treatment of a non-service-connected condition only if all the following conditions are met:

If you are service-connected, not permanently and totally disabled, or nonservice-connected, then the VA may pay for your non-VA emergency care for treatment of a non- service-connected condition if all of the following conditions are met:

- The episode of care can't be paid for under another VA authority, and
- Based on an average knowledge of health and medicine you reasonably expected that a delay in seeking immediate medical attention for have been hazardous to life or health and
- A VA or other federal facility/provider wasn't feasibly available and
- You receive VA medical care within a 24-month period preceding the non-VA emergency care and
- The services were furnished by an emergency department, or similar facility held out to provide emergency care to the general public and
- You are financially liable to the health care provider for emergency care and
- You have no other coverage under a health plan including Medicare, Medicaid and Worker's Compensation and
- You have no contractual or legal recourse against a third party that would, in whole, extinguish your liability

FAQs About Veteran Emergency Care

What Is an Emergency?

A medical emergency is defined as an injury or illness so severe that without immediate treatment, it threatens your life or health. Your situation is an emergency if you believe your life or health is in danger. If you believe your life or health is in danger, call 911 or go to the ER immediately. You don't need to call the VA before calling an ambulance or going to the ER.

When Should I Contact the VA About an ER Visit?

You, your family, friends, or hospital staff should call the closest VACM as possible, and it's best if this happens within 72 hours of an emergency. The VA will need information about your emergency and the services being provided, and the VA can provide guidance on what charges are covered.

If the Doctor Wants Me to Be Admitted to the Hospital, Do I Need Advance Approval from the VA?

If you are being admitted because of an emergency, an advanced approval isn't required, but prompt VA notification is important.

If I Am Admitted to the Hospital As a Result of An Emergency, How Much Will VA Pay?

Depending on your VA eligibility, VA may pay all, some or none of the charges. Since payment may be limited to the point when your condition is stable enough for you to travel to a VA facility, you need to contact the nearest VA medical facility as soon as possible. An emergency is deemed to have ended at the point when a VA provider has determined that, based on sound medical judgment, you should be transferred from the non-VA facility to a VA medical center.

If you are service-connected the VA may pay for your non-VA emergency care for a rated Service-connected disability, or for your Nonservice-connected condition associated with and held to be aggravating your Service-connected condition, or any condition, if you are an active participant in the VA Chapter 31 Vocational Rehabilitation program, and you need treatment to make possible your entrance into a course of training or to prevent interruption of a course of training or other approved reason or any condition if you are rated as having a total disability permanent in nature resulting from your Service-connected disability.

If you are service-connected, not permanently and totally disabled, or non-service connected, then VA may pay for non-VA emergency care for treatment of a nonservice-connected condition if all the following conditions are met:

- The episode of care can't be paid under another VA authority and
- Based on an average knowledge of health and medicine, you reasonably expected that delay in seeking immediate medical attention would have been hazardous to your life or health and
- A VA or other federal facility or provider was not feasibly available and
- You received VA medical care within a 24-month period preceding the non-VA emergency care and
- The services were furnished by an Emergency Department or similar facility held out to provide emergency care to the general public and
- You have no other coverage under a health plan including Medicare, Medicaid and Worker's Compensation and
- You have no contractual resource against a third party that would in whole extinguish your liability

Ambulance Transport

The Department of Veterans Affairs may provide or reimburse for land or air ambulance transport of certain eligible veterans in relation to VA care or VA-authorized community care.

VA pays for ambulance transport when the transport has been preauthorized and in certain emergency situations without preauthorization. Two criteria must be met for the VA to pay for ambulance transport.

First, the claimant must meet appropriate administrative eligibility, and a VA provider must determine medical need for ambulance transport. VA must be providing medical care or paying a community care provider for medical care in order to pay for the transport in relation to that care.

Preauthorized Ambulance Transport

Transport is arranged for eligible veterans before inpatient or outpatient care. To qualify a veteran must meet the following administrative requirements:

- Has a single or combined service-connected rating of 30 percent or more, or
- Veteran is in receipt of VA pension, or
- Previous calendar year income does not exceed maximum VA pension rate, or
- Projected income in travel year does not exceed maximum VA pension rate, or
- Projected income in travel year does not exceed maximum VA pension rate, or
- Travel is in connection with care for a service-connected disability, or
- Travel is for a Compensation and Pension exam, or
- Travel is to obtain a service dog, and
- A VA clinician must determine and document that special mode transportation is medically required

Unauthorized Ambulance Transport

Transport must be preauthorized by VA unless it is in relationship to a medical emergency. Veterans do not have to contact VA in advance of a medical emergency and are encouraged to call 911 or go to the nearest medical emergency room.

VA may pay for ambulance transport that's not preauthorized in the following situations:

- Transport from point of community emergency to a VA facility if the veteran meets administrative and eligibility criteria noted under "Preauthorized ambulance transport"
- Transport from point of community emergency to a community care facility if VA pays for the emergency care in the community care facility under the nonservice-connected or service-connected authorities detailed below
- VA is contacted within 72 hours of care at a community care facility and retroactively authorizes the community care, and the veteran meets administrative and medical travel eligibility noted under "preauthorized ambulance transport."

In order for VA to pay for unauthorized ambulance transport, the care associated with the transport must meet one of the following authorities for VA payment:

Emergent care for nonservice-connected conditions (38 United States Code (U.S.C.) 1725 ["Mill Bill"])

- Based on average knowledge of health and medicine, it is reasonably expected that a delay in seeking immediate medical attention would have been hazardous to life or health and
- The episode of care can't be paid under another VA authority and
- A VA or other federal facility/provider was not feasibly available and

- VA medical care was received within 24 months prior to the episode of emergency care and
- The services were furnished by an Emergency Department or similar facility that provides emergency care to the general public and
- Veteran is financial liable for the emergency care and
- Veteran has no other coverage under a health care plan including Medicare, Medicaid or Worker's Compensation, and
- There is no contractual or legal recourse against a third party that could, in whole, extinguish liability

Emergent Care for Service-Connect Conditions (38 U.S.C. 1728)

- Care is for a service-connected disability or
- Care is for a nonservice-connected condition associated with and aggravating a service-connected condition or
- Care is for any condition of an active participant in the VA Chapter 31 Vocational Rehabilitation program and is needed to make a possible entrance into a course of training or to prevent interruption of a course of training, or
- Care is for any condition of a veteran rated as having a total disability permanent in nature resulting from a service-connected disability and
- Based on an average knowledge of health and medicine, it is reasonably expected that delay in seeking immediate medical attention would have been hazardous to life or health and
- A VA or other federal facility/provider was not feasibly available

Retroactive Preauthorization (38 CFR 17.54)

In case of an emergency which existed at the time of treatment, VA may retroactively preauthorize the care if:

- An application for VA payment of care provided is made within 72 hours after the emergency care initiated and
- Veteran meets the eligibility criteria for community care at VA expense of 38 U.S.C. 1703

Reimbursement Considerations

- If the emergency room visit and/or admission meets eligibility for VA reimbursement, and the veteran meets beneficiary travel requirements, the ambulance will be paid from the scene of the incident to the first community care facility providing necessary care
- If a veteran arrives via ambulance but leaves the hospital before being treated by a physician, the ambulance is not guaranteed to be covered by VA regardless of eligibility
- Accepted VA payments are payments in full. Balance due billing of VA or veterans is prohibited. VA pays the authorized amount or not at all.

Documents Needed to Process Claims

In order to consider a claim for VA payment of emergency care provided and associated ambulance transport, VA needs the following documents:

- Documented request or application for VA payment of emergency transportation (usually a Health Care Financing Administration form or a bill). Unless transport is preauthorized, the application must be made within 30 days of transport.

- Ambulance trip report documenting circumstances of medical event and care provided by the ambulance service.
- Invoice from ambulance service and community care provider.
- Community care facility records of care provided to the veteran—VA will request these from the facility.

All required documents must be received prior to payment consideration. Payment for associated ambulance transport can't occur unless VA is providing or paying for emergency care.

Appeals

If a claim does not meet VA payment criteria (is not payable,) then it's denied and both the community care provider and veteran are provided an explanation of denial and notified of the right to appeal the decision (VA Form 4107, Notification of Rights to Appeal Decision).

Veterans Transportation Program

The Veterans Transportation Service (VTS) provides safe and reliable transportation to veterans who require assistance traveling to and from VA health care facilities and authorized non-VA health care appointments. VTS also partners with service providers in local communities to serve veteran's transportation needs. Partners include Veterans Service Organizations (VSOs), local and national non-profit groups, and federal, state and local transportation services.

VA recognizes Veterans who are visually impaired, elderly or immobilized due to disease or disability, and particularly those living in remote and rural areas face challenges traveling to their VA health care appointments. Veterans Transportation Service (VTS) is working to establish Mobility Managers at each local VA facility to help Veterans meet their transportation needs.

VTS has established a network of transportation options for Veterans through joint efforts with VA's Office of Rural Health and organizations, such as Veterans Service Organizations (VSOs); community transportation providers; federal, state and local government transportation agencies; non-profits and Veterans Transportation Community Living Initiative (VTCLI) grantees.

Veterans who are eligible for VA health care benefits and have a VA-authorized appointment are eligible for transportation through the VTS program based on the availability and guidelines in place at their local facility. Each local VA authorized facility has ridership guidelines based on their capabilities.

Highly Rural Transportation Grants

Highly Rural Transportation Grants (HRTG) is a grant-based program that helps veterans in highly rural areas travel to VA or VA-authorized health care facilities. This program provides grant funding to Veteran Service Organizations and State Veterans Service Agencies to provide transportation services in eligible counties. HRTGs provide transportation programs in counties with fewer than seven people per square mile. There is no cost to participate in the program for veterans who live in an area where HRTG is available.

Grantee Organization Name	Details
North Dakota Department of Veterans Affairs	**Eligible Counties**: Adams, Billings, Bottineau, Bowman, Burke, Cavalier, Divide, Dickey, Dunn, Emmons, Foster, Golden Valley, Grant, Griggs, Hettinger, Kidder, Lamoure, Logan, McHenry, McIntosh, McKenzie, McLean, Mountrail, Nelson, Oliver, Pierce, Renville, Sargent, Sheridan, Sioux, Slope, Steele, Towner **Call for Transportation Services**: 1-800-920-9595
North Dakota-Robert Tovsrud VFW Post 757	**Eligible Counties**: Benson, Eddie, Wells Call for Transportation Services: 701-438-2192
South Dakota-American Legion Stanley Post 20	**Eligible Counties**: Clark, Dewey, Hand, Hyde, Haakon, Jerauld, Jones, Kingsbury, Lyman, Miner, Potter, Sandborn, Spink, Stanley, Sully, Ziebach. **Call for Transportation Services**: 605-945-2360 or Toll Free at 1-877-587-5776 **Eligible Counties**: Butte, Custer, Fall River **Call for Transportation Services**: 605-642-6668 or Toll Free at 1-877-673-3687
Washington State Department of Veterans Affairs	**Eligible County**: Skamania **Call for Transportation Services**: 509-427-3990 **Eligible County**: Ferry **Call for Transportation Services**: 1-800-776-9026 or 509-684-2961
Nevada Department of Veterans Services	**Eligible County**: Elko

-	**Call for Transportation Services**: 775-777-1428 **Eligible County**: Nye **Call for Transportation Services**: 775-572-VETS (8387)
California-VFW Post 8988	**Eligible County**: Mono, Inyo **Call for Transportation Services**: 760-873-7850
Texas Veterans Commission	**Eligible County**: Duval **Call for Transportation Services**: 361-279-6219 **Eligible County**: Hansford **Call for Transportation Services**: 806-659-4100 **Eligible County**: Kimble **Call for Transportation Services**: 325-396-4682 **Eligible County**: Jim Hogg **Call for Transportation Services**: 361-527-5845 **Eligible County**: McMullen **Call for Transportation Services**: 361-279-6219 **Eligible County**: Briscoe **Call for Transportation Services**: 806-823-2131 **Eligible County**: Cochran **Call for Transportation Services**: 806-266-5508 **Eligible County**: Kent **Call for Transportation Services**: 806-237-3373 **Eligible County**: Menard **Call for Transportation Services**: 325-396-4682
Texas-American Legion Post 142	**Eligible Counties**: Baylor, Cottle, Foard, Hardeman Call for Transportation Services: 1-800-633-0852
Texas VFW Post 7207	**Eligible Counties**: Borden, Crane, Glasscock, Loving, Martin, Pecos, Reeves, Terrell

	Call for Transportation Services: 1-800-245-9028 **Eligible counties**: Brewster, Culberson, Hudspeth, Jeff Davis, Presidio **Call for Transportation Services**: 1-855-879-8729
Maine Veterans of Foreign Wars of the U.S.	**Eligible County**: Piscataquis **Call for Transportation Services**: Bangor Clinic: 207-561-3637 or Lincoln Clinic: 207-403-2012
Montana-American Legion Rocky Boy Post 67	**Eligible Counties**: Blaine, Chouteau, Hill **Call for Transportation Services**: 406-395-5610
Idaho-American Legion Post 12	**Eligible County**: Boise **Call for Transportation Services**: 208-392- 9934 or 9935
Oregon Department of Veterans Affairs	**Eligible Counties & the number to call for Transportation Services**: Baker, 541-523-6591 Gilliam, 541-384-2252 Grant, 541-575-2721 Malheur, 541-881-0000 Morrow, 541-922-6420 Sherman 541-565-3553 Wallowa, 541-426-3840 Wheeler 541-468-2859
Alaska Department of Military and Veterans Affairs	Interior Alaska Bus Southwest Fairbanks **Call for Transportation Services**: 1-800-770-6652 Valley People Mover **Eligible County**: Matanuska-Susitna **Call for Transportation Services**: 907-892-8800 Alaska Marine Highway System **Eligible Counties**: Kodiak Island, Kenai Peninsula Call for Transportation Services: 1-800-642-0066 Inter-Island Ferry **Eligible County**: Prince of Wales-

	Hyder Call for Transportation Services: 1-866-308-4848

Beneficiary Travel

The Beneficiary Travel program provides eligible veterans and other beneficiaries mileage reimbursement, common carrier, or when medically indicated, special mode transport for travel to and from VA health care or VA authorized non-VA healthcare for eligible veterans.

A veteran may be eligible for Beneficiary Travel Service if the following criteria are met:

- You have a service-connected rating of 30 percent or more, or
- You are traveling for treatment of a service-connected condition, or
- You receive a VA pension, or your income does not exceed the maximum annual VA pension rate, or
- Your income does not exceed the maximum annual VA pension rate, or
- You are traveling for scheduled compensation or pension

You qualify for special mode transportation (ambulance, wheelchair, van, etc.) if:

- You meet one of the eligibility criteria above, and
- Your medical condition requires an ambulance or specially equipped van as determined by a VA clinician, and
- The travel is pre-authorized (authorization is not required for emergencies if a delay would be hazardous to life or health

---

In Vitro Fertilization (IVF)

The VA announced fertility regulations would be expanded to include in vitro fertilization. The new benefit makes IVF available as an option for eligible veterans with service-connected disabilities that result in infertility. The benefit also provides spouses of eligible veterans with access to assisted reproductive technologies, including IVF.

The Office of Women's Health Services (10P4W) is responsible for the contents of this VHA directive. Questions may be referred to the Director of Reproductive Health at 202-461-0373.

This Veterans Health Administration (VHA) directive establishes policy and procedures for the Department of Veterans Affairs (VA) health care systems for the evaluation and treatment of infertility as authorized under the VA medical benefits package for eligible Veterans enrolled in the VA health care system.

NOTE: Except for certain Veterans who have a service-connected disability that results in their inability to procreate without the use of assisted reproductive technology (ART), and their spouses, VA cannot perform or pay for in vitro fertilization

(IVF) because it is specifically excluded from the VA medical benefits package (Title 38 Code of Federal Regulations (CFR) 17.38). VA may also provide ART and fertility counseling and treatment that is available under the medical benefits package to spouses of Veterans authorized to receive IVF. AUTHORITY: Title 38 United States Code (U.S.C.) 7301(b), Public Law 114-223 section 260, 38 CFR §§ 17.38, 17.380, and 17.412.

The Office of Women's Health Services (Reproductive Health), in collaboration with experts designated by the National Surgery Office (NSO), will be available to assist with Veterans Integrated Service Network (VISN) level consultations when the medical standards for providing services and treatment related to gamete (sperm or oocyte) cryopreservation or other infertility services are unavailable or unclear. Women's Health Services (WHS) may need to involve Spinal Cord Injury/Disorders (SCI/D) National Program Office, National Center for Ethics in Health Care, and the NSO).

Eligibility

Veterans eligible to receive health care under the medical benefits package may receive VA-covered infertility evaluation, management, and treatment. IVF is specifically excluded from the medical benefits package.

However, ART including IVF is authorized under 38 CFR 17.380 for certain Veterans who have a service-connected disability that results in the inability of the Veteran to procreate without the use of assisted reproductive technology (ART).

The spouse of a Veteran authorized to receive IVF may be provided with fertility counseling and treatment that is available under the medical benefits package, as well as ART, including IVF (38 CFR 17.412). The aforementioned ART/IVF benefit for certain Veterans and their spouse is further delineated in VHA Directive 1334, Assisted Reproductive Technology (ART) Services for the Benefit of Veterans with Service-Connected Illness or Injury Resulting in Infertility, pending publication.

Otherwise, non-Veteran partners (spouses or significant others), if applicable, are not eligible to receive infertility treatment services from VA unless they are eligible for the Civilian Health and Medical Program of the Department of Veterans Affairs (CHAMPVA), which allows VA to provide infertility services and treatment to certain family members of Veterans under 38 CFR 17.270- 278.

In cases where a non-Veteran partner is not eligible for VA-covered infertility services, the Veteran and non-Veteran partner must be informed that payment for such service to the community provider is the responsibility of the Veteran and non-Veteran partner. These requirements must be discussed with the Veteran before any treatment course is undertaken.

Exclusions

The following procedures or services are not covered VA medical benefits: (1) Gestational surrogacy treatment; (2) Costs of obtaining, transporting, and storing donor sperm and oocytes; (3) IVF procedures, except for certain Veterans who have a service-connected disability that results in the inability of the Veteran to procreate without the use of assisted reproductive technology (ART) (38 CFR 17.380). The spouse of a Veteran authorized to receive IVF may be provided with fertility counseling and treatment that is available under the medical benefits package, as well as IVF (38 CFR 17.412). (4) Costs of cryopreservation, storage, and transport of embryo(s), except for certain Veterans who have a service-connected disability that results in the inability of the Veteran to procreate without the use of ART and their non-Veteran spouses. (38 CFR 17.380 and 17.412); and (5) Infertility, evaluation, and management of non-Veteran partners except for the spouse of certain Veterans who have a service-connected disability that results in the inability of the Veteran to procreate without the use of assisted reproductive technology (ART), including IVF.

CHAPTER 12

NURSING HOME AND LONG-TERM CARE BENEFITS

Standard Benefits

The following long-term care services are available to all enrolled veterans:

Geriatric Evaluation

A geriatric evaluation is the comprehensive assessment of a veteran's ability to care for him/herself, his/her physical health, and the social environment, which leads to a plan of care. The plan could include treatment, rehabilitation, health promotion, and social services. These evaluations are performed by inpatient Geriatric Evaluation and Management (GEM) Units, GEM clinics, geriatric primary care clinics, and other outpatient settings.

Adult Day Health Care

The adult day health care (ADHC) program is a therapeutic daycare program, providing medical and rehabilitation services to disabled veterans in a combined setting.

Respite Care

Respite care provides supportive care to veterans on a short-term basis to give the caregiver a planned period of relief from the physical and emotional demands associated with providing care. Respite care can be

> **Key Takeaways**
> Long-term care services include nursing and medical care, physical therapy, help with daily tasks, comfort care and support for caregivers.
>
> To access these benefits, you must be signed up for VA health care and VA must conclude you need a specific service to help you with your ongoing treatment and personal care.
> To find out how to access these services, you can contact your VA social worker or call the toll-free hotline at (877) 222-8387.

provided in the home or other noninstitutionalized settings.

Home Care

Skilled home care is provided by VA and contract agencies to veterans that are homebound with chronic diseases and include nursing, physical/occupational therapy, and social services.

Hospice/Palliative Care

Hospice/palliative care programs offer pain management, symptom control, and other medical services to terminally ill veterans or veterans in the late stages of the chronic disease process. Services also include respite care as well as bereavement counseling to family members.

Financial Assessment for Long-Term Care Services

For veterans who are not automatically exempt from making copayments for long-term care services, a separate financial assessment must be completed to determine whether they qualify for cost-free services or to what extent they are required to make long term care copayments. For those veterans who do not qualify for cost-free services, the financial assessment for long term care services is used to determine the copayment requirement. Unlike copayments for other VA health care services, which are based on fixed charges for all, long-term care copayment charges are individually adjusted based on each veteran's financial status.

Limited Benefits

Nursing Home Care

While some veterans qualify for indefinite nursing home care services, other veterans may qualify for a limited period of time. Among those that automatically qualify for indefinite nursing home care are veterans whose service-connected condition is clinically determined to require nursing home care and veterans with a service-connected rating of 70% or more. Other veterans—with priority given to those with service-connected conditions—may be provided short-term nursing home care if space and resources are available.

The Department of Veterans Affairs (VA) provides both short-term and long-term care in nursing homes to veterans who aren't sick enough to be in the hospital but are too disabled or elderly to take care of themselves. Priority is given to veterans with service- connected disabilities.

Priority Groups

The VA is required to provide nursing home care to any veteran who

- Needs nursing home care because of a service-connected disability
- Has a combined disability rating of 70% or more, or

- Has a disability rating of at least 60% and is:
  - Deemed unemployable, or
  - Has been rated permanently and totally disabled.

Other veterans in need of nursing care will be provided services if resources are available after the above groups are taken care of.

Types of Nursing Care Available

Community Living Centers

Some VA Medical Centers have Community Living Centers (these used to be called Nursing Home Care Units or VA Nursing Homes). These centers are typically located within the VA Medical Center itself or in a separate building.

Contract Nursing Home Care

Nursing home care in public or private nursing homes is also available to some veterans. Stays in these nursing homes can be limited; however, for veterans with ratings less than 70% and for veterans who do not need care due to a service-connected disability.

State Veterans Homes

State Veterans Homes are nursing homes run by the state and approved by the VA. Sometimes the VA will pay for part of the care a veteran gets at a state veterans' home.

Eligibility for Community Living Centers (CLCS)

To receive care in a Community Living Center/VA nursing home, a veteran must:
- Be enrolled in the VA Health Care System
- Be psychiatrically and medically stable
- Provide documentation specifying whether short or long-term care is needed, an estimation of how long the stay will be, and when discharge occurs, and
- Show priority for a stay in a CLC.

However, meeting the above criteria does not automatically ensure admission. CLCs make decisions about whether to admit a veteran based on the following factors:
- Availability of services in the CLC
- What sort of care the veteran needs, and
- Whether the CLC can competently provide the type of care the veteran needs.

Co-Pays

Veterans required to make co-pays are typically those:
- Without a service-connected disability rated at least 10%, and
- Whose income is higher than the VA's maximum annual pension rate.

How to Apply for CLC Care

Typically, a veteran's physician will submit the application requesting care in a CLC. Veterans who are not exempt from co-pays must complete VA Form 10-10EC, Application for Extended Care Services.

Eligibility for Contract Nursing Home Care
Any veteran who needs Contract Nursing Home Care for a service-connected disability or is receiving VA home health care after discharge from a VA hospital is eligible for direct admission. To be admitted, all that is required is for a VA physician or authorized private physician to determine that nursing home care is needed. Veterans rated 70%, or more service-connected should also be eligible.

Other veterans are eligible to be transferred into Contract Nursing Home Care (also called a Community Nursing Home) if the VA determines the care is needed and:

- The veteran is in a VA hospital, nursing home, domiciliary, or has been receiving VA outpatient care, or
- An active member of the Armed Forces who was in a DOD hospital needs nursing care and will be an eligible veteran upon discharge.

Time Limits for Contract Nursing Home Care
Veterans who are not in the priority groups are technically limited to six months of care, but this may be reduced to 30 to 60 days if resources are limited. Veterans in the priority groups are technically entitled to unlimited free care but again may receive shorter stays due to a lack of funding and resources to accommodate them.

Many veterans can extend their stay by relying on payments from Medicare and Medicaid.

How to Apply for Contract Nursing Home Care
Typically, an application will be made by a veterans' doctor, social worker or nurse, using VA Form 10-0415, Geriatrics and Extended Care (GEC) Referral.

Eligibility for State Veterans Homes

In some cases, the VA will help pay for a veteran's care at a State Veterans Home. The payments the VA will make are called per diem aid. A home must meet the VA standards for nursing home care to receive per diem aid. In addition, the VA will not pay more than half the cost of the veteran's care.

State homes provide hospital care, nursing home care, domiciliary care, and sometimes adult daycare. To receive per diem aid, veterans must meet VA eligibility requirements for the type of care they will receive.

States usually have their own eligibility requirements, in addition to the VA's requirements, such as residency requirements. The veterans' home will apply for VA aid for a veteran's care by submitting VA Form 10-10EZ, Application for Medical Benefits. The VA will pay per diem aid for a veteran's care indefinitely.

Basic State Home Per Diem Rates

The Basic State Home Per Diem Rates for Fiscal Year (FY) 2020 are as follows:

Adult Day Health Care: 89.52 per day

Domiciliary: $48.50 per day

Nursing Homes: $112.36 per resident per day

Reduction in Pension

A veteran who begins to receive nursing home care will have his or her monthly pension payment reduced to $90 if:

- The veteran has no dependents
- The veteran is living in a Medicaid-approved nursing facility, and
- The nursing home care is paid for by Medicaid.

Domiciliary Care

Domiciliary care provides rehabilitative and long-term, health maintenance care for veterans who require some medical care, but who do not require all the services provided in nursing homes. Domiciliary care emphasizes rehabilitation and return to the community. VA may provide domiciliary care to veterans whose annual income does not exceed the maximum annual rate of VA pension or to veterans who have no adequate means of support.

Services for Blind Veterans

Veterans with corrected central vision of 20/200 or less in both eyes, or field loss to 20 degrees or less in both eyes are considered to be blind.

Blind veterans may be eligible for many of the benefits detailed throughout this book, including, but not limited to: Disability Compensation, Health Insurance, Adaptive Equipment, and Training & Rehabilitation. In addition to these benefits, there are a number of miscellaneous benefits due veterans of all wars who were blinded as the result of their war service. Many individual states offer special programs and benefits for the blind.

Services are available at all VA medical facilities through Visual Impairment Services Team (VIST) coordinators.

The VIST Coordinator is a case manager who has major responsibility for the coordination of all services for legally blind veterans and their families. Duties include providing and/or arranging for appropriate treatment, identifying new cases of blindness, providing professional counseling, resolving problems, arranging annual healthcare reviews, and conducting education programs relating to blindness.

Blind veterans may be eligible for services at a VA medical center or for admission to a VA blind rehabilitation center or clinic. In addition, blind veterans entitled to receive disability compensation may receive VA aids for the blind, which may include:

- A total health and benefits review by a VA Visual Impairment Services team;
- Adjustment to blindness training;
- Home Improvements and Structural Alterations to homes (HISA Program);
- Specially adapted housing and adaptations;
- Low-vision aids and training in their use;
- Electronic and mechanical aids for the blind, including adaptive computers and computer-assisted devices;
- Guide dogs, including the expense of training the veteran to use the dog, and the cost of the dog's medical care;
- Talking books, tapes, and Braille literature, provided from the Library of Congress.

Guide Dogs/Service Dogs

As previously mentioned, VA may provide guide dogs to blind veterans. Additionally, Public Law 107-135 (signed by then-President Bush January 23, 2002) states that VA may provide:

- Service dogs trained for the aid of the hearing impaired to veterans who are hearing impaired, and are enrolled under Section 1705 of Title 38; and

- Service dogs trained for the aid of persons with spinal cord injury or dysfunction or other chronic impairment that substantially limits mobility to veterans with such injury, dysfunction, or impairment who are enrolled under section 1705 of Title 38.

- VA may also pay travel and incidental expenses for the veteran to travel to and from the veteran's home while becoming adjusted to the dog.

The VA operates nine blind rehabilitation centers in the United States and Puerto Rico. Rehabilitation centers offer comprehensive programs to guide individuals through a process that eventually leads to maximum adjustment to the disability, reorganization of the person's life, and return to a contributing place in the family and community. To achieve these goals, the rehabilitation centers offer a variety of skill courses to veterans, which are designed to help achieve a realistic level of independence. Services offered at rehabilitation centers include:

- Orientation and mobility;
- Living skills;
- Communication skills;
- Activities of daily living;
- Independent daily living program;
- Manual skills;
- Visual skills;
- Computer Access Training Section;
- Physical conditioning;
- Recreation;
- Adjustment to blindness;

extended family member or be someone who lives with the
[vetera]n full-time or will do so if designated as a Family caregiver
[be a]ssessed by VA as being able to complete caregiver education

caregiver training and demonstrate the ability to carry out specific
[personal] care services, core competencies and additional care
[requireme]nts

[In additio]n, there must be no determination by VA of any abuse or neglect of
[the eligib]le veteran by the caregiver

[As a Pri]mary Family Caregiver, you may qualify to receive a monthly stipend,
[at] one of two levels:
[If the vet]eran meets all seven eligibility requirements, then VA must determine
[wheth]er the VA is unable to self-sustain in the community
[Level] One: If VA determines that a veteran is not unable to self-sustain in the
[com]munity, the designated Primary Family Caregiver will receive the lower-
[leve]l stipend payment.
[Lev]el Two: If VA determines the veteran is unable to self-sustain in the
[co]mmunity, the designated Primary Family Caregiver will receive the higher-
[lev]el stipend payment.
[S]elf-sustain in the community means that each time the veteran completes
[one or m]ore of the seven activities of daily living (ADL) listed above, personal care
[services a]re required. The veteran would be fully dependent on a caregiver to
[complete] the ADLs or the veteran has a need for supervision, protection or instruction
[on a cont]inuous basis.

[You and] the veteran (if you're the potential caregiver) will need to apply together and
[bot]h participate in the application process to determine if you are eligible for the
[Progra]m of Comprehensive Assistance for Family Caregivers.

[Any] time the veteran wants to add a new family caregiver, the veteran and the new
[care]giver will need to submit a new application. You can fill out a joint Application for
[the P]rogram of Comprehensive Assistance for Family Caregivers (VA Form 10-10CG).

[Mai]l the form and any supporting documents to:
[Pro]gram of Comprehensive Assistance for Family Caregivers
[He]alth Eligibility Center
[29]57 Clairmont Rd. NE Suite 200
[A]tlanta, GA 30329-1647

If you want to apply in person, you can bring the completed VA Form 10-10CG to your
local VA medica center's Caregiver Support Coordinator. To find the name of your
local coordinator, call 855-260-3247.

- Group meetings.

The VA also employs Blind Rehabilitation Outpatient Specialists (BROS) in several areas, including:

Albuquerque, NM
Ann Arbor, MI
Bay Pines / St. Petersburg, FL
Baltimore, MD
Boston, MA
Cleveland, OH
Dallas, TX
Gainesville, FL
Los Angeles, CA
Phoenix, AZ
Portland, OR
San Antonio, TX
San Juan, PR
Seattle, WA
West Haven, CT

Home Improvements and Structural Alterations (HISA)

The HISA program provides funding for disabled veterans to make home improvements necessary for the continuation of treatment or for disability access to the home, essential lavatory and sanitary facilities.

Disabled veterans may be eligible for HISA when it is determined medically necessary or appropriate for the effective and economical treatment of the service-connected disability.

Veterans who are rated 50% or higher are not required to prove their service-connected disability is the reason for their HISA request, although veterans rated less than 50% must demonstrate their disability is the cause of the HISA improvements.

Lifetime home improvement benefits may not exceed $6,800 (U.S.). Any costs that exceed $6,800 (U.S.) will be the veteran's responsibility. This amount is provided to veterans with a service-connected condition or a non-service-connected condition of a veteran rated 50 percent or more service-connected. Home improvement benefits of up to $2,000 may be provided to all other veterans registered in the VA healthcare system.

To apply, veterans must submit the following documentation:
- A letter from describing the physical disability and a description of the request home improvement and/or structural alteration;

- A statement from the attending physician or therapist. This statement should describe the physical condition/disability, why the home modification(s) are medically necessary or appropriate for the effective and economical treatment of the service-connected disabling condition;
- A drawing of the work to be undertaken. This drawing can be hand sketched. It should include the height, width and length dimensions. It does not have to be a formal blueprint or architectural drawing;
- A completed, signed home ownership or a rental lease form with a letter from the landlord agreeing with the modifications if required;
- A completed and signed "VA Form 10-0103", Veterans Application for Assistance;
- Documentation verifying that the provider/contractor is licensed/bonded;
- An itemized cost estimate of the proposed improvement and/or structural alteration from the provider/contractor.

Preauthorization must be obtained before beginning any alterations, otherwise, HISA benefits will be denied.

VA Caregiver Support

The Program of Comprehensive Assistance for Family Caregivers (PCAFC) is for eligible veterans who have incurred or aggravated a serious injury in the line of duty on or before May 7, 1975 or after September 11, 2001. This program provides resources, education, support, a financial stipend, and health insurance if eligible, beneficiary travel if eligible, to caregivers of eligible veterans.

Veterans may be eligible for this clinical program if they:
Sustained or aggravated a serious injury (now includes a serious illness) in the line of duty on or before May 7, 1975 or on or after 9/11/2001; and meet both of the following criteria to be eligible for PCAFC. Among other applicable eligibility criteria, the veteran must:

- Have a single or combined service-connected disability rating by the Department of Veterans Affairs of 70% or more. This requirement is included in the definition of serious injury; and
- Be in need of personal care services for a minimum of six continuous months based on either an inability to perform an activity of daily living or a need for supervision, protection or instruction.

Changes were made to the program based on the "Program of Comprehensive Assistance for Family Caregivers Improvements and Amendments Under the VA Mission Act of 2018," Final Rule, RIN 2900-AQ48 effective October 1, 2020.

The changes included expanding eligibility for the PCAFC, offerings legal and financial services for designated Primary Family Caregivers of eligible veterans in 2021, and making other changes affecting program eligibility and VA's evaluation of PCAFC applications.

The inability to perform an AD' personal care services each time below:
- Dressing or undressing on
- Bathing
- Grooming to keep oneself cle
- Adjusting any special prosthe the particular disability can't be
- Toileting or attending to toileting
- Feeding oneself due to loss of c extremities, extreme weakness, in oral means of nutrition
- Mobility such as walking or going up

Requiring assistance with ADL only some of the inability to perform an ADL.

If approved for this program, veterans can select o to two secondary caregivers. Secondary caregivers primary caregiver when needed. The services you re are the primary or secondary caregiver.

If you are the primary caregiver, you may receive:
- A monthly stipend paid directly to you as the care
- Access to health care insurance through the Ci Program of the Department of Veterans Affairs already have health insurance
- Mental health counseling
- Certain beneficiary travel benefits when traveling appointments
- At least 30 days of respite care per year for the veteran. R relief for someone else to care for the veteran while you ta

If you are the secondary caregiver, you may receive:
- Mental health counseling
- Certain beneficiary travel benefits when traveling with th appointments
- At least 30 days of respite care per year for the veteran

Call the VA's Caregiver Support Line at 1-855-260-3247 to learn more support available to you and for assistance connecting with the Caregive Coordinator at your local VA Medical Center.

Family Caregiver Eligibility Requirements
For you to be eligible to be a Family Caregiver, you must:
- Be at least 18 years old
- Be either the eligible veteran's spouse, son, daughter, parent, stepfam

member or
eligible vete
Be initially
and training
Complete
personal
requireme
In additio
the eligib

Stipend Levels
As an eligible Pri
which is paid at
- If a ve wheth
- Leve com leve
- Lev co le

Unable to three or m services complete on a con

You an will bo Progra

Each care the

Ma
Pr
H

CHAPTER 13

DENTAL BENEFITS

VA Outpatient Dental Benefits

Eligibility and benefits for veteran dental care are restricted by law and categorized into VA dental classifications or classes. If you just got out of the service, you may be entitled to a one-time course of dental care. You must apply for dental care within 180 days of your discharge, and your discharge must be under conditions under than dishonorable, from a period of active duty of 90 days or more.

If not eligible for VA Dental Care, the national VA Dental Insurance Program gives enrolled Veterans and CHAMPVA beneficiaries the opportunity to purchase dental insurance at a reduced cost.

The eligibility for outpatient dental care isn't the same as for most other VA medical benefits and is categorized into classes. If you are eligible for VA dental care under Class I, IIA, IIC, or IV, you are eligible for any necessary dental care to maintain or restore oral health and masticatory function, including repeat care. Other classes have time and/or service limitations.

If You:	You Are Eligible For:	Through:
Have a service-connected compensable dental disability or condition	Any needed dental care	Class I
Are a former prisoner of war	Any needed dental care disability, convalescence or pre-stabilization are not eligible for comprehensive outpatient dental services based on this temporary rating)	Class IIC

Apply for dental care within 180 days of discharge or release (under conditions other than dishonorable) from a period of active duty of 90 days or more during the Persian Gulf War era	One-time dental care if your DD214 certificate of discharge does not indicate that a complete dental examination and all appropriate dental treatment had been rendered prior to discharge	Class II
Have a service-connected noncompensable dental condition or disability resulting from combat wounds or service trauma	Any dental care necessary to provide and maintain a functioning dentition. A Dental Trauma Rating (VA Form 10-564-D) or VA Regional Office Rating Decision Letter (VA Form 10-7131) identifies the tooth/teeth/conditions that are trauma rated	Class IIA
Have a dental condition clinically determined by VA to be associated with and aggravating a service-connected medical condition	Dental care to treat the oral conditions that are determined by a VA dental professional to have a direct and material detrimental effect to your service-connected medical condition	Class III
Are actively engaged in a 38 USC Chapter 31 vocational rehabilitation program	Dental care to the extent necessary as determined by a VA dental professional to: Make possible your entrance into a rehabilitation program Achieve the goals of your program Prevent interruption of your program Hasten the return to a rehabilitation program if you are in interrupted or leave status Hasten the return to a rehabilitation program of a veteran placed in discontinued status because of illness, injury or	Class V

	a dental condition, or secure and adjust to employment during the period of employment assistance, or enable you to achieve maximum independence in daily living	

VA Dental Insurance Program

VA offers the comprehensive VA Dental Insurance Program (VADIP) as a way for enrolled veterans and CHAMPVA beneficiaries the chance to purchase dental insurance through Delta Dental and MetLife at a reduced cost. Participation is voluntary and purchasing a dental plan doesn't impact a veteran's eligibility for VA dental services and treatments. Covered services include diagnostic, preventative, surgical, emergency and endodontic/restorative treatment. Delta Dental and MetLife offering multiple plans.

Each participant pays the fixed monthly premiums for coverage and any copayments required, depending on the type of plan selected.

Dependents of veterans, except for those eligible under CHAMPVA, are not authorized to participate in VADIP. These individuals may be eligible for separate dental insurance coverage offered by these carriers.

TRICARE Retiree Dental Program

RDP ended in 2018 and was replaced by the Office of Personnel Management's Federal Employees Dental and Vision Insurance Program (FEDVIP). If you were eligible for TRDP, you might be able to enroll in a FEDVIP dental plan.

You must enroll in FEDVIP dental during the 2020 Open Season or after a FEDVIP Qualifying Life Event.

FEDVIP is a voluntary, enrollee-pay-all dental and vision program available to Federal employees and annuitants and certain uniformed service members. It is sponsored by the U.S. Office of Personnel Management (OPM) and offers eligible participants a choice between ten dental and four vision carriers.

BENEFEDS is the government-authorized and OPM-sponsored enrollment portal that eligible participants use to enroll in and manage their FEDVIP coverage. BENEFEDS also manages the billing systems and customer service functions necessary for the collection of FEDVIP premiums.

FEDVIP dental plans provide comprehensive dental coverage, including in-network preventive services covered 100%; no deductibles when using in-network dentists; no waiting period for major services such as crowns, bridges, dentures, and implants; and no 12-month waiting period or age limit for orthodontic coverage under some plans.

TRICARE Selected Reserve Dental Program Benefits

Individuals with at least one year of service commitment remaining who are serving in the Army Reserve, Naval Reserve, Air Force Reserve, Marine Corps Reserve, Coast Guard Reserve, Army National Guard or Air National Guard, may be eligible to enroll in the Tricare Selected Reserve Dental Program (TSRDP).

The Department of Defense works in conjunction with Humana Military Healthcare Services to offer and administer the TRICARE Selected Reserve Dental Program.

Coverage remains available as long as an individual maintains his or her Reserve status and is shown as eligible on the DEERS record.

The information provided in this section is intended only as a brief overview. Humana Military Healthcare Services has a staff of trained Beneficiary Services Representatives who are available to answer your questions.

TRICARE Dental Program Survivor Benefit Plan

If your sponsor died while serving on active duty, you may qualify for the TRICARE Dental Program Survivor Benefit Plan.

This includes 100% payment of monthly premiums, and TRICARE pays for cost shares for covered service.

If you were using the TRICARE Dental Program when your sponsor died, you're automatically transferred to the Survivor Benefit Plan. If not, you can enroll at any time. After three years, surviving spouses lose eligibility for the TRICARE Dental Program. They can purchase the TRICARE Retiree Dental Program only if their sponsor died while on active duty for more than 30 days.

Surviving children can remain enrolled in the TRICARE Dental Plan until they lose TRICARE eligibility for other reasons.

CHAPTER 14

CHAMPVA

The Civilian Health and Medical Program of the Department of Veterans Affairs (CHAMPVA) is a comprehensive health care program where the VA shares the cost of covered health care services and supplies with eligible beneficiaries. The program is administered by the Veterans Health Administration Office of Community Care (VHA CC) in Denver, Colorado.

CHAMPVA is similar to the Department of Defense TRICARE program, but CHAMPVA is a VA program, while TRICARE is a regionally managed care program for active duty and retired members of the military, their family and their survivors.

Under CHAMPVA, VA shares the cost of covered healthcare services and supplies with eligible beneficiaries.

Eligibility Requirements

> **Key Takeaways**
>
> If you are the spouse or surviving spouse of, or a child of a veteran with disabilities or a veteran who died, and you don't qualify for TRICARE (the Department of Defense's health care program for active-duty and retired service members and their families), you may be able to get health insurance through the Civilian Health and Medical Program of the Department of Veterans Affairs (CHAMPVA).
>
> Through this program, VA will cover the cost of some of your health care services and supplies. This is called cost sharing.

To be eligible for CHAMPVA, you cannot be eligible for TRICARE/CHAMPUS, and you must be in one of these categories:

- The spouse or child of a veteran who has been rated permanently and totally disabled for a service-connected disability by a VA regional office; or
- The surviving spouse or child of a veteran who died from a VA-rated service-connected disability; or

- The surviving spouse or child of a veteran who was at the time death rated permanently and totally disabled from a service connected disability ; or
- The surviving spouse or child of a military member who died in the line of duty, not due to misconduct (in most of these cases, these family members are eligible for TRICARE, not CHAMPVA).

An eligible CHAMPVA sponsor may be entitled to receive medical care through the VA health care system based on his or her own veteran status. Additionally, as the result of a recent policy change, if the eligible CHAMPVA sponsor is the spouse of another eligible CHAMPVA sponsor, both may now be eligible for CHAMPVA benefits. In each instance where the eligible spouse requires medical attention, he or she may choose the VA health care system or coverage under CHAMPVA for his/her health care needs. If you have been previously denied CHAMPVA benefits and you believe you would now be qualified, please call (800)733-8387.

Benefits

In general, CHAMPVA covers most healthcare services and supplies that are medically and psychologically necessary. Upon confirmation of eligibility, applicants will receive program material that specifically addresses covered and non-covered services and supplies.

CHAMPVA General Exclusions

- Services determined by VA to be medically unnecessary;
- Care as part of a grant, study, or research program;
- Care considered experimental or investigational;
- Care for persons eligible for benefits under other government agency programs, except Medicaid and State Victims of Crime Compensation programs;
- Care for which the beneficiary is not obligated to pay, such as services obtained at a health fair;
- Custodial, domiciliary, or rest cures;
- Dental care (except treatment related to certain covered medical conditions);
- Medications that do not require a prescription (except insulin);
- Personal comfort and convenience items;
- Services rendered by providers suspended or sanctioned by other Federal entities.

Retention of CHAMPVA For Surviving Spouses Remarrying After Age 55

Eligibility for CHAMPVA ends at midnight on the date of your remarriage if you remarry prior to age 55. However, Public Law 107-330 (signed by then-President Bush on December 6, 2002) contained a provision stating that:

"For marriages occurring on or after February 4, 2003, the remarriage after age 55 of the surviving spouse of a veteran shall not bar the furnishing of benefits under CHAMPVA to such person as the surviving spouse of the veteran".

The law also contained a provision allowing those widows who remarried prior to February 4, 2003 and were over the age of 55 and lost their CHAMPVA benefits, to apply to have their medical benefits reinstated. However, such widows had to apply for reinstatement of benefits by February 4, 2004. (The deadline was later extended to December 16, 2004.)

Termination of Remarriage

If a widow(er) of a qualifying sponsor remarries, and the remarriage is later terminated by death, divorce, or annulment, he or she may reestablish CHAMPVA eligibility. The beginning date of re-eligibility is the first day of the month after termination of the remarriage or December 1, 1999, whichever date is later. To reestablish CHAMPVA eligibility, copies of the marriage certificate and death, divorce, or annulment documents (as appropriate) must be provided.

Applying for CHAMPVA and Filing Claims

To apply for CHAMPVA, applicants should submit the following documents
- Application for CHAMPVA Benefits, VA Form 10-10d
- Other Health Insurance (OHI) Certification, VA Form 10-7959c or Forma 10-7959c
- For individuals who are eligible for Medicare for any reason, a copy of their Medicare card is also needed
- If you are 65 or older and not entitled to Medicare, you must send documentation from the Social Security Administration confirming you're not entitled to Medicare benefits under anyone's Social Security number

Optional Documents

If you want to speed up the processing of your application, you can send copies of the following:
- Birth certificate/adoption papers for children.
- The page from the VBA rating decision showing permanent and total disablement or death rating for a survivor
- If you are a remarried widow/widower and are again single, provide a copy of the legal documentation terminating the marriage. The document may be a divorce decree, death certificate, or annulment decree.
- Veteran's DD214 or if a WWII or Korean Veteran, the Report of Separation.
- School certification of full-time enrollment for children ages 18-23 Sign and date the application, and send it to the following address:

VHA **Office of Community Care**
CHAMPVA **Eligibility PO Box 469028**
Denver, CO 80246-9028
Fax: (303) 331-7809

CHAMPVA As Secondary Payer

CHAMPVA is intended to serve as a safety net in the event other coverage is not available—rather than being the primary carrier. While families with other health insurance are not disqualified from CHAMPVA benefits, CHAMPVA's safety net protection only kicks in after the application of all other policies—including benefits available from the enrollment in a health maintenance organization (HMO).

Exceptions to CHAMPVA's secondary payer status are supplemental CHAMPVA policies, Medicaid, and State Victims Compensation Programs—CHAMPVA assumes primary payer in these cases.

Beneficiaries enrolled in an HMO cannot elect to waive the HMO benefits without forfeiting their CHAMPVA benefits. CHAMPVA benefits, however, do apply to covered services that are not covered by the HMO.

Healthcare Services at VA Facilities

Under the CHAMPVA In-house Treatment Initiative (CITI for short), CHAMPVA beneficiaries may receive cost-free healthcare services at participating VA facilities.

Although some VA facilities are not CITI participants due to the volume of veterans, they are responsible for serving, most are. **The CITI program is not available to beneficiaries with Medicare or with an HMO insurance plan.**

CHAMPVA and the Affordable Care Act

The Affordable Care Act designates CHAMPVA as fulfilling the minimum essential coverage requirement. If you are enrolled in CHAMPVA, you don't need to take additional steps to meet health care coverage standards. The ACA does not change CHAMPVA benefits or out-of-pocket costs. CHAMPVA will send IRS Form 1095-B, Health Coverage annually.

Medicare Impact

If a person is eligible for CHAMPVA, under age 65 and enrolled in both Medicare Parts A & B, SSA documentation of enrollment in both Parts A&B is required.

CHAMPVA is always the secondary payer to Medicare.

For benefits to be extended past age 65, the individual must meet the following conditions:

- If he or she turned 65 before June 5, 2001, and only has Medicare Part A, he or she will be eligible for CHAMPVA without having to have Medicare Part B coverage.
- If he or she turned 65 on/or before June 5, 2001 and has Medicare Parts A and B, he or she must keep both Parts to be eligible.
- If he or she turned 65 on or after June 5, 2001, he or she must be enrolled in Medicare Parts A and B to be eligible.

CHAMPVA Frequently Asked Questions

Q. What is CHAMPVA?

The Civilian Health and Medical Program of the Department of Veterans Affairs (CHAMPVA) is a health benefits program in which the Department of Veterans Affairs (VA) shares the cost of certain health care services and supplies with eligible beneficiaries.

CHAMPVA is managed by the Veterans Health Administration Office of Community Care (VHA OCC) in Denver, Colorado. We verify CHAMPVA eligibility, authorize benefits, and process medical claims.

Q. Who is Eligible for CHAMPVA?

To be eligible for CHAMPVA, the beneficiary cannot be eligible for TRICARE. CHAMPVA provides coverage to the spouse or widow(er) and to the children of a veteran who:

- is rated permanently and totally disabled due to a service-connected disability, or
- was rated permanently and totally disabled due to a service-connected condition at the time of death, or
- died of a service-connected disability, or
- died on active duty and the dependents are not otherwise eligible for Department of Defense TRICARE benefits.

Effective October 1, 2001, CHAMPVA benefits were extended to those age 65 and older. To be eligible for CHAMPVA, you must also meet the following conditions:

- If the beneficiary was 65 or older prior to June 5, 2001, and was otherwise eligible for CHAMPVA, and was entitled to Medicare Part A coverage, then the beneficiary will be eligible for CHAMPVA without having to have Medicare Part B coverage.
- If the beneficiary turned 65 before June 5, 2001, and has Medicare Parts A and B, the beneficiary must keep both Medicare Parts A & B to be eligible for CHAMPVA.
- If the beneficiary turned age 65 on or after June 5, 2001, the beneficiary must be enrolled in Medicare Parts A and B to be eligible for CHAMPVA.

Q. What is the difference between CHAMPVA and TRICARE?

Although similar, CHAMPVA is a separate program with a totally different beneficiary population than TRICARE — a Department of Defense health care program formerly called CHAMPUS. While the benefits are similar, the programs are administered separately with significant differences in claim filing procedures and preauthorization requirements.

Q. Are healthcare services at VA facilities available to CHAMPVA beneficiaries?

Under the CHAMPVA In-House Treatment Initiative, CHAMPVA beneficiaries may receive cost-free health care services at participating VA facilities.

CHAPTER 15

TRICARE AND TRICARE FOR LIFE

TRICARE is the Department of Defense's worldwide health care program for active duty and retired uniformed services members and their families. TRICARE offers several health plan options to meet your specific needs.

TRICARE For Life
TRICARE Global Remote Overseas
TRICARE Prime
TRICARE Prime Overseas
TRICARE Prime Remote
TRICARE Reserve Select
TRICARE Standard and Extra
TRICARE Standard Overseas
Family Health Plan
TRICARE Young Adult

TRICARE For Life

TRICARE For Life (TFL) is TRICARE's Medicare-wraparound coverage available to all Medicare-eligible TRICARE beneficiaries, regardless of age, provided they have Medicare Parts A and B. While Medicare is your primary insurance, TRICARE acts as your secondary payer minimizing your out-of-pocket expenses. TRICARE benefits include covering Medicare's coinsurance and deductible.

Key Takeaways

Since 1995, all VA health care facilities have participated as TRICARE Network Providers.

TRICARE is the Department of Defense health care program, and eligibility is determined by military service.

VA can provide care for active-duty service members, military retirees and family members under their TRICARE benefit on a space available basis.

Each VA health care facility can serve as a primary care manager for TRICARE beneficiaries, but more often, TRICARE referrals are used for specialty care.

Key Features of TRICARE for Life

- Minimal **out-of-pocket costs** (aside from Medicare Part B Premium).
- No enrollment fees for TFL. But, you must purchase Medicare Part B and pay monthly premiums to be eligible for TFL.
- Coordination of benefits between Medicare and TRICARE.
- TRICARE is the secondary payer for all services covered by both TRICARE and Medicare.
- TRICARE is the primary payer for those services covered only by TRICARE. Additional steps may be required in order to coordinate benefits if you have other health insurance in addition to TRICARE and Medicare.
- Freedom to manage your own health care.
- No assigned primary care manager.
- Visit any Medicare provider.
- Receive care at a military treatment facility on a space-available basis.
- No claims to file (in most cases).
- Your provider files your claim with Medicare.
- Medicare processes the claims.
- Medicare forwards it electronically to TRICARE.
- TRICARE pays similarly to TRICARE Standard in those overseas locations where Medicare is not available.

Eligibility

TFL is available to all Medicare-eligible TRICARE beneficiaries, regardless of age, including retired members of the National Guard and Reserve who are in receipt of retired pay, family members, widows and widowers, and certain former spouses. Dependent parents and parents-in-law are not eligible for TFL.

Note: If you're under age 65, have Medicare Part B, and live in a TRICARE Prime service area, you have the option to enroll in **TRICARE Prime**; TRICARE waives your TRICARE Prime enrollment fee.

You should confirm that your Medicare status is current in the **Defense Enrollment Eligibility Reporting System** (DEERS). Your uniformed services ID card and your Medicare card, which must reflect enrollment in Medicare Part B, are evidence of your TFL eligibility.

TRICARE Global Remote Overseas

TRICARE Global Remote Overseas (TGRO) is a TRICARE Prime option offered in designated remote overseas locations for active-duty service members and their families. TRICARE has partnered with International SOS to identify the best local providers and facilities and develop a network of licensed, qualified physicians in remote overseas areas. The TGRO contractor's careful selection of providers is the first step in ensuring quality care.

Only physicians who are licensed and who have graduated from an accredited medical school are included in the core network. To access a list of TGRO providers, please visit the TGRO Provider Directory. The TGRO network is updated daily.

Key Features

- Enrollment is required, but there are no enrollment fees.
- Fewer out-of-pocket costs than TRICARE Standard Overseas.
- You receive most care from your primary care manager (PCM).
- Your PCM or TGRO Call Center refers you to specialists when necessary and will tell you when you need to go to another city, country or the U.S. for quality care.
- No claims to file (in most cases).

Eligibility

In general, TGRO is available to the following beneficiaries:

- Permanently assigned active-duty service members are living in designated remote locations.
- Command-sponsored active-duty family members living with their active-duty sponsor in designated remote locations.
- Activated National Guard and Reserve members living in designated remote locations when their orders are for more than 30 consecutive days.
- Command-sponsored family members of activated National Guard and Reserve living with their sponsors in designated remote locations.

TRICARE Prime

TRICARE Prime is a managed care option offering the most affordable and comprehensive coverage. TRICARE Prime is available in Prime Service Areas in each TRICARE Region. To find out if you live in a Prime Service Area, contact your regional contractor. If you don't, you may be eligible for TRICARE Prime Remote, or you may use TRICARE Standard and Extra.

Key Features

- Enrollment is required.
- Fewer out-of-pocket costs than other TRICARE options.
- Enhanced vision and preventive coverage.
- Priority access for care at military treatment facilities.
- Receive most care from an assigned primary care manager (PCM).
- Your PCM refers you to specialists when necessary.
- No claims to file (in most cases).
- Easy to transfer enrollment when you move.
- Time and distance access standards for care, including wait times for urgent, routine and specialty care.

Eligibility

You may enroll in TRICARE Prime as long as you are not entitled to Medicare based on age (65). (At age 65, you become eligible for TRICARE For Life as long as you have

Medicare Parts A and B). The following beneficiaries who live in a Prime Service area may enroll in TRICARE Prime:

- Active-duty service members* and their families.
- Retired service members and their families.
- Surviving family members (widowed spouses, children)
- Eligible former spouses.
- Activated National Guard/Reserve members* and their families.
- Retired National Guard and Reserve members and their families (upon reaching age 60).
- Medal of Honor recipients and their families.
- *Active-duty service members and activated National Guard/Reserve members must enroll in one of the TRICARE Prime options (includes TRICARE Prime, TRICARE Prime Remote, TRICARE Prime Overseas and TRICARE Global Remote Overseas)

TRICARE Prime Overseas

TRICARE Prime Overseas is a managed care plan for active duty service members and their eligible family members residing together in overseas locations in which TRICARE Prime Overseas is available. Retirees and retiree family members are not eligible for TRICARE Prime Overseas.

Key Features

- Enrollment required, but no enrollment fees.
- Fewer out-of-pocket costs than TRICARE Standard Overseas.
- Enhanced coverage for vision and clinical preventive services.
- You receive most care from your primary care manager (PCM).
- Your PCM refers you to specialists when necessary.
- No claims to file (in most cases).
- Easy to transfers from one overseas area to another or back to the United States.
- Time and distance access standards for care, including wait times for urgent, routine and specialty care.
- Point of service option available (in certain circumstances) to receive care without requesting a referral from your PCM (resulting in higher out-of- pocket costs).

Eligibility

In general, TRICARE Prime Overseas is available to the following beneficiaries:

- Active-duty service members residing in overseas areas in which Prime is offered.
- Active-duty family members who:
    - Accompany their sponsor;
    - Are command-sponsored on their permanent change of station orders or relocate on service sponsored/funded orders;
    - Are eligible in the Defense Enrollment Eligibility Reporting

    System; and

    o   Enroll through the nearest TRICARE Service Center.

TRICARE Prime Remote

TRICARE Prime Remote (TPR) is a managed care option similar to TRICARE Prime for active-duty service members and their eligible family members while they are assigned to remote duty stations in the United States.

Remote locations are those that are 50 miles or an hour drive time from a military treatment facility and the ZIP code areas are pre-determined.

Note: TRICARE Global Remote Overseas is a similar program available in remote locations outside of the United States

Key Features

- Enrollment required to participate
- Active-duty service members must enroll
- Active-duty family members have the option to enroll or use TRICARE Standard and Extra
- Flexible enrollment options:
    - Online via the Beneficiary Web Enrollment Web Site
    - Submit a TRICARE Prime Enrollment and PCM Change Form through the mail
    - Receive most care from an assigned network primary care manager (PCM) who will provide referrals for specialty care.
    - If a network PCM is not available, care is received from any TRICARE- authorized provider.
- Fewer out-of-pocket costs.
- Eligible for travel reimbursement if referred for medically necessary care far from home.
- Enhanced coverage for vision and clinical preventive services.
- Time and distance access standards for care.
- No claims to file (in most cases).
- Easy to transfer enrollment when moving to another location in your TRICARE region or to a new TRICARE region.

TRICARE Reserve Select

TRICARE Reserve Select (TRS) is a premium-based health plan that qualified National Guard, and Reserve members may purchase. TRS, which requires a monthly premium, offers coverage similar to TRICARE Standard and Extra.

Key Features

- Available worldwide to most Selected Reserve members (and families) when not on active-duty orders or covered under the Transitional Assistance Management Program.

- Few out-of-pocket costs (similar to TRICARE Prime).
- You do not access Medicare providers, military treatment facilities (MTFs) or TRICARE network providers, but instead, receive your care from a primary care physician that you select from a network of private physicians affiliated with one of the not-for-profit health care systems offering the plan. Your primary care physician assists you in getting appointments with specialists in the area and coordinates your care.
- You will benefit from the same level of prescription coverage as that available under the TRICARE program and at the same costs. However, you may only use your US Family Health Plan's list of retail or on-site pharmacies and the US Family Health Plan mail order service instead of TRICARE retail, mail-order or MTF pharmacies.
- If you move or un-enroll from the US Family Health Plan, you may choose any TRICARE program that you are eligible for, and that is available in your area.
- Each US Family Health Plan site offers enhanced benefits and services such as discounts for eyeglasses, hearing aids and dental care. These enhancements will vary by US Family Health Plan site.
- There are no claims to file when plan-approved providers are used.
- Enrollment is required. You may enroll at any time throughout the year and enrollment is automatically renewed each year unless you take action to un-enroll. Enrollment fees, if applicable, may transfer to another US Family Health Plan location or to TRICARE Prime.
- You are encouraged to enroll in the US Family Health Plan as a complete family unit, but you may enroll on an individual basis. When you enroll in the US Family Health Plan, you are committing to the plan for one year unless moving out of the area or un-enrolling for another qualified reason.

Eligible beneficiaries include:

- Active-duty family members.
- Retirees and their eligible family members.
- Survivors.
- Former spouses.
- Medal of Honor recipients and their families.
- Family members of activated National Guard or Reserve Members.

Should I Get Medicare Part B?

You do not need to have Medicare Part B to enroll in the US Family Health Plan. However, if you do not enroll in Medicare Part B when first eligible, and subsequently choose to do so, you will pay (in addition to the normal Medicare Part B monthly premium) an annual 10% penalty for each year you were eligible to enroll in Medicare Part B and did not.

In addition, you will only be able to in Medicare Part B enroll during the general enrollment period, January 1-March 31, of each year, and your Part B benefits will not be effective until July 1 of that year. You are encouraged to enroll in Medicare Part B when first eligible.

If you are entitled to Medicare Part A and decide to un-enroll from the US Family Health Plan, you will then be able to use the TRICARE For Life benefit, but only if you also are enrolled in Medicare Part B. Additionally, if you subscribe to Medicare Part B, you pay only copayments for prescription drugs and your annual enrollment fee is waived. Medicare Part B also adds coverage for End-Stage Renal Disease, a condition that usually involves kidney failure. Medicare Part B is not required for the US Family Health Plan, but you should carefully consider whether or not it is in your best interest to enroll.

TRICARE Young Adult

TRICARE Young Adult is a premium-based health care plan that qualified dependents may purchase. TRICARE Young Adult provides medical and pharmacy benefits, but dental coverage is not included. The plan allows dependent adult children to purchase TRICARE coverage after eligibility for "regular" TRICARE coverage ends at age 21 (or age 23 if enrolled in a full course of study at an approved institution of higher learning). There are two options to select from at enrollment: Prime and Standard.

Eligibility
You may be eligible if you are:
- An adult child of an eligible sponsor.
- Eligible sponsors include:
- Active duty servicemembers
- Retired servicemembers
- Activated Guard/Reserve members
- Non-activated Guard/Reserve members using TRICARE Reserve Select
- Retired Guard/Reserve members using TRICARE Retired Reserve
- Unmarried
- At least age 21, but not yet age 26 (If you are enrolled in a full course of study at an approved institution of higher learning, and your sponsor provides 50 percent of your financial support, your eligibility may not begin until age 23 or upon graduation, whichever comes first.)
- Not eligible to enroll in an employer-sponsored health plan based on your own employment
- Not otherwise eligible for TRICARE program coverage

Key Features
- In the United States, the Prime Option is available only in Prime Service Areas to children of active duty and retired service members.
- If you live in an area where the US Family Health Plan is offered, you may enroll in the US Family Health Plan for your prime option.
- If your sponsor is on active duty, you may also select the Prime Option when you live with your sponsor:
  - In remote U.S. Zip Codes, if your sponsor is enrolled in TRICARE

> Prime remote and; Anywhere overseas if you are command-sponsored.
>   o If your sponsor is using TRICARE Reserve Select or TRICARE Retired Reserve, the Prime Option is not available to you.

- With the Prime Option, you will have an assigned primary care manager (PCM), either at a military treatment facility (MTF) or in the TRICARE network, who will provide the majority of your care.
- Your PCM will refer you to a specialist for care when he or she is unable to provide that care. Your PCM will also coordinate with your regional contractor for authorization, to find a specialist in the network, and will file claims on your behalf.
- Other benefits include enhanced vision and preventative services and travel reimbursement for some specialty care.
- Children of active duty servicemembers pay no out-of-pocket costs for any type of care as long as care is received from PCM or with a referral.

Key Features of TRICARE Young Adult Standard Option

All dependent children who qualify for TRICARE Young Adult may select the Standard Option. You may visit any TRICARE-authorized provider, network or non-network. Care at military treatment facilities is available on a space-available basis only. You do not need a referral for any type of care but some services may require prior authorization.

The type of provider determines how much you'll pay out-of-pocket. If you're visiting a network provider, you'll pay less out-of-pocket, and the provider will file claims for you.

Transitional Assistance Management Program

The Transitional Assistance Management Program (TAMP) provides 180 days of transitional health care benefits upon separation from active-duty service. Service members who meet the criteria below are eligible for TRICARE benefits for themselves and their family members.

- A member who is involuntarily separated from active duty.
- A member of a reserve component who is separated from active duty to which called or ordered in support of a contingency operation if the active duty is for a period of more than 30 days.
- A member who is separated from active duty for which the member is involuntarily retained under Section 12305 (also referred to as "stop loss") of Title 10, U.S.C., in support of a contingency operation.
- A member who is separated from active duty served pursuant to a voluntary agreement of the member to remain on active duty for a period of less than one year in support of a contingency operation.

For those who qualify, the 180-day TAMP period begins upon the sponsor's separation. During TAMP, sponsors and family members are eligible to use one of the following health plan options:

- TRICARE Prime (enrollment required) TRICARE Standard and Extra
- TRICARE Prime Overseas (enrollment required) TRICARE Standard Overseas

Continued Health Care Benefit Program (CHCBP)

The Continued Health Care Benefit Program (CHCBP) is a premium-based health care program administered by Humana Military Health Care Services, Inc. (Humana Military). CHCBP offers temporary transitional health coverage (18-36 months) after TRICARE eligibility ends. If you qualify, you can purchase CHCBP within 60 days of loss of eligibility for either regular TRICARE or Transitional Assistance Management Program (TAMP) coverage.

CHCBP acts as a bridge between military health benefits and your new civilian health plan. CHCBP benefits are comparable to TRICARE Standard with the same benefits, providers, and program rules. The main difference is that you pay premiums to participate.

Who Is Eligible?

Under certain circumstances, the following beneficiaries may be eligible:

- Former active-duty service members released from active duty (under other than adverse conditions) and their eligible family members. Coverage is limited to 18 months.
- Un-remarried former spouses who were eligible for TRICARE on the day before the date of the final decree of divorce, dissolution or annulment. Coverage is usually limited to 36 months however some un-remarried former spouses may continue coverage beyond 36 months if they meet certain criteria. Contact Humana Military for details.
- Children who cease to meet the requirements to be an eligible family member and were eligible for TRICARE on the day before ceasing to meet those requirements. Coverage is limited to 36 months.
- Certain unmarried children by adoption or legal custody. Coverage is limited to 36 months.

For more information about CHCBP, call (800) 444-5445. Contact your regional contractor or a Beneficiary Counseling and Assistance Coordinator (BCAC) to discuss your eligibility for this program.

Extended Care Health Option

The TRICARE Extended Care Health Option (ECHO) provides financial assistance to eligible beneficiaries who qualify based on specific mental or physical disabilities and offers an integrated set of services and supplies not available through the basic

TRICARE program. TRICARE ECHO doesn't replace basic TRICARE programs; it supplements the benefits of the TRICARE program option that eligible beneficiaries use.

ECHO benefits are only available to qualified active duty family members (including family members of activated National Guard or Reserve members). Active-duty family members must qualify for ECHO through ECHO case managers in each TRICARE region.

Eligibility

The TRICARE Extended Care Health Option (ECHO) is available **only to active-duty family members** who have a qualifying condition.

Qualifying conditions include:
- Moderate or severe mental retardation
- A serious physical disability
- An extraordinary physical or psychological condition of such complexity that the beneficiary is homebound
- A diagnosis of a neuromuscular developmental condition or other condition in an infant or toddler that is expected to precede a diagnosis of moderate or severe mental retardation or a serious physical disability
- Multiple disabilities, which may qualify if there are two or more disabilities affecting separate body systems

If you or your provider believes a qualifying condition exists, talk to a case manager or with your regional contractor or TRICARE Area Office (if stationed overseas) to determine eligibility for TRICARE ECHO benefits.

To begin using TRICARE ECHO, qualifying family members must be enrolled in the Exceptional Family Member Program and must be registered for TRICARE ECHO with their regional contractor or TRICARE Area Office. There is no enrollment fee for TRICARE ECHO.

Pre-Activation Benefit for National Guard and Reserve

National Guard and Reserve members who are issued delayed-effective-date active-duty orders for more than 30 days in support of a contingency operation may qualify for "early eligibility for TRICARE" beginning on the later of:
- the date their orders were issued; or
- 90 days before they report to active duty.

National Guard and Reserve members who qualify for the pre-activation benefit are covered as "active-duty service members" and receive active-duty medical and dental benefits.

Additionally, when National Guard or Reserve members qualify for pre-activation benefits, family members who are registered in the Defense Enrollment Eligibility Reporting System are also covered under TRICARE up to 90 days before the sponsor's active-duty service begins. Family members become covered by TRICARE as "active-duty family members during the pre-activation period and while the sponsor is activated.

The member's Service personnel office will tell members if they are eligible for pre-activation benefits when they receive their delayed-effective-date active duty orders.

Pharmacy Benefits

TRICARE prescription drug coverage is available to all TRICARE-eligible beneficiaries who are enrolled in the Defense Enrollment Eligibility Reporting System (DEERS). Prescription drug coverage is the same regardless of which health plan option you are using, and it is available worldwide.

Eligible beneficiaries include:

- Active-duty service members and their families
- Activated National Guard and Reserve members and their families (on Title 10 or Title 32 [federal]orders)
- Retired service members and their families
- Retired National Guard and Reserve members and their families (age 60 and above and receiving retired pay)
- Survivors, widows/widowers and certain former spouses
- Medal of Honor recipients and their families
- Beneficiaries enrolled in TRICARE Reserve Select or the Continued Health Care Benefit Program
- Other beneficiaries listed in DEERS as eligible for TRICARE, including foreign force members and their families.

Chiropractic Care

In 2001, the National Defense Authorization Act established the Chiropractic Health Care Program. The program is currently available to active duty service members (including activated National Guard and Reserve members) at designated military treatment facilities (MTFs) throughout the United States.

Eligibility

Active-duty service members and activated National Guard or Reserve members must obtain chiropractic care at a designated MTF and must receive a referral from their primary care manager (PCM).

Family members, retirees and their family members, un-remarried former spouses and survivors **are not eligible** for this program. They may be referred to non-chiropractic health care services in the Military Health System (e.g., physical therapy

TRICARE program. TRICARE ECHO doesn't replace basic TRICARE programs; it supplements the benefits of the TRICARE program option that eligible beneficiaries use.

ECHO benefits are only available to qualified active duty family members (including family members of activated National Guard or Reserve members). Active-duty family members must qualify for ECHO through ECHO case managers in each TRICARE region.

Eligibility

The TRICARE Extended Care Health Option (ECHO) is available **only to active-duty family members** who have a qualifying condition.

Qualifying conditions include:
- Moderate or severe mental retardation
- A serious physical disability
- An extraordinary physical or psychological condition of such complexity that the beneficiary is homebound
- A diagnosis of a neuromuscular developmental condition or other condition in an infant or toddler that is expected to precede a diagnosis of moderate or severe mental retardation or a serious physical disability
- Multiple disabilities, which may qualify if there are two or more disabilities affecting separate body systems

If you or your provider believes a qualifying condition exists, talk to a case manager or with your regional contractor or TRICARE Area Office (if stationed overseas) to determine eligibility for TRICARE ECHO benefits.

To begin using TRICARE ECHO, qualifying family members must be enrolled in the Exceptional Family Member Program and must be registered for TRICARE ECHO with their regional contractor or TRICARE Area Office. There is no enrollment fee for TRICARE ECHO.

Pre-Activation Benefit for National Guard and Reserve

National Guard and Reserve members who are issued delayed-effective-date active-duty orders for more than 30 days in support of a contingency operation may qualify for "early eligibility for TRICARE" beginning on the later of:
- the date their orders were issued; or
- 90 days before they report to active duty.

National Guard and Reserve members who qualify for the pre-activation benefit are covered as "active-duty service members" and receive active-duty medical and dental benefits.

Additionally, when National Guard or Reserve members qualify for pre-activation benefits, family members who are registered in the Defense Enrollment Eligibility Reporting System are also covered under TRICARE up to 90 days before the sponsor's active-duty service begins. Family members become covered by TRICARE as "active-duty family members during the pre-activation period and while the sponsor is activated.

The member's Service personnel office will tell members if they are eligible for pre-activation benefits when they receive their delayed-effective-date active duty orders.

Pharmacy Benefits

TRICARE prescription drug coverage is available to all TRICARE-eligible beneficiaries who are enrolled in the Defense Enrollment Eligibility Reporting System (DEERS). Prescription drug coverage is the same regardless of which health plan option you are using, and it is available worldwide.

Eligible beneficiaries include:

- Active-duty service members and their families
- Activated National Guard and Reserve members and their families (on Title 10 or Title 32 [federal]orders)
- Retired service members and their families
- Retired National Guard and Reserve members and their families (age 60 and above and receiving retired pay)
- Survivors, widows/widowers and certain former spouses
- Medal of Honor recipients and their families
- Beneficiaries enrolled in TRICARE Reserve Select or the Continued Health Care Benefit Program
- Other beneficiaries listed in DEERS as eligible for TRICARE, including foreign force members and their families.

Chiropractic Care

In 2001, the National Defense Authorization Act established the Chiropractic Health Care Program. The program is currently available to active duty service members (including activated National Guard and Reserve members) at designated military treatment facilities (MTFs) throughout the United States.

Eligibility

Active-duty service members and activated National Guard or Reserve members must obtain chiropractic care at a designated MTF and must receive a referral from their primary care manager (PCM).

Family members, retirees and their family members, un-remarried former spouses and survivors **are not eligible** for this program. They may be referred to non-chiropractic health care services in the Military Health System (e.g., physical therapy or orthopedics) or may seek chiropractic care in the local community at their own expense.

Access to Chiropractic Care

During the course of treatment, the service member's PCM will determine if specialty care (traditional or chiropractic care) is required. If chiropractic care is considered an option, the service member will undergo a screening process to rule out any medical conditions that would prohibit chiropractic care. If appropriate, the PCM will refer the service member to a chiropractic provider for treatment.

While receiving chiropractic care, the service member will continue to see his or her PCM and the duration/frequency of the chiropractic services will be determined by the PCM and follow the usual referral process.

Chiropractic care received outside of the designated locations is not covered under the Chiropractic Health Care Program.

TRICARE Catastrophic Cap

The TRICARE catastrophic cap limits the amount of out-of-pocket expenses a family will have to pay for TRICARE-covered medical services. The cap applies to the allowable charges for covered services—annual deductibles, Prime enrollment fees, pharmacy co-pays, and other cost shares based on TRICARE-allowable charges. Out-of-pocket expenses paid under the TRICARE Prime point-of-service (POS) option (deductibles and cost-shares) are not applied to the annual enrollment year catastrophic cap. Additionally, any POS charges incurred after the catastrophic cap has been met are the beneficiary's financial responsibility.

The catastrophic cap amount depends on an individual's profile and should be obtained from TRICARE directly.

TRICARE Regions

North

TRICARE's North region includes Connecticut, Delaware, the District of Columbia, Illinois, Indiana, Kentucky, Maine, Maryland, Massachusetts, Michigan, New Hampshire, New Jersey, New York, North Carolina, Ohio, Pennsylvania, Rhode Island, Vermont, Virginia, West Virginia, and Wisconsin (and some zip code areas in Iowa, Missouri, and Tennessee). Health Net Federal Services, Inc. is the new regional contractor providing health care services and network-provider support in the TRICARE North Region.

Health Net's customer service representatives are available Monday – Friday, 8 a.m. to 7 p.m. in all North region time zones, at (877) 874-2273.

South

TRICARE's South region includes Alabama, Arkansas, Florida, Georgia, Louisiana, Mississippi Oklahoma, South Carolina, and Tennessee (excluding 35 Tennessee zip codes in the Fort Campbell, KY area), and Texas (excluding, only, the extreme southwestern El Paso-area). Humana-Military is the regional contractor providing health care services and network provider support in the TRICARE South Region.

Humana's customer service representatives are available Monday – Friday, 8 a.m. to 6 in all South region time zones, at (800) 444-5445.

West

TRICARE's West region includes Alaska, Arizona, California, Colorado, Hawaii, Idaho, Iowa (except 82 Iowa zip codes that are in the Rock Island, Illinois area), Kansas, Minnesota, Missouri (except the St. Louis area), Montana, Nebraska, Nevada, New Mexico, North Dakota, Oregon, South Dakota, Texas (the southwestern corner, including El Paso, only) Utah, Washington, and Wyoming. TriWest Healthcare Alliance is the regional contractor providing health care services and network-provider support in the TRICARE West region.

TriWest's customer service representatives are available Monday – Friday, 8 a.m. to 6 p.m. in the West Region time zone in which you reside, at (888) 874-9378.

Europe Area

The TRICARE Europe area is managed by the TAO Europe located at Sembach Air Base in Germany and includes Europe, Africa and the Middle East.

Customer service representatives can be reached at (888) 777-8343.

Latin America and Canada Area

The TRICARE Latin America and Canada (TLAC) area is managed by the TAO TLAC located at Fort Gordon, Georgia and includes Central and South America, the Caribbean Basin, Canada, Puerto Rico, and the Virgin Islands.

Customer service representatives can be reached at (888) 777-8343.

Pacific Area

The TRICARE Pacific area is managed by the TAO Pacific located at Camp Lester in Okinawa, Japan, and includes Guam, Japan, Korea, Asia, New Zealand, India, and Western Pacific remote countries.

Customer service representatives can be reached at (888) 777-8343.

Affordable Care Act

The Affordable Care Act, also known as the health care law, was created to expand access to coverage, control health care costs and improve health care quality and care coordination. The health care law does not change VA health benefits or Veterans' out-of-pocket costs.

Three things you should know:

- VA wants all Veterans to receive health care that improves their health and well-being.

- If you are enrolled in VA health care, you don't need to take additional steps to meet the health care law coverage standards. The health care law does not change VA health benefits or Veterans' out-of-pocket costs.

- If you are not enrolled in VA health care, you can apply at any time.

Veterans Enrolled in VA Health Care

Veterans enrolled in VA health care programs have health coverage that meets the new health care law's standard. You do not have to take any additional steps to have health coverage.

Veterans Not Enrolled in VA Health Care

Veterans not currently enrolled in VA health care programs can apply for enrollment at any time.

Family Members

VA offers health care benefits for certain family members of Veterans through programs such as the Civilian Health and Medical Program of the Department of Veterans Affairs (CHAMPVA) and the Spina Bifida program. Your family members who are not enrolled in a VA health care program should use the Marketplace to get coverage.

CHAPTER 16

VA'S FIDUCIARY PROGRAM

VA's Fiduciary Program was established to protect Veterans and other beneficiaries who, due to injury, disease, or due to age, are unable to manage their financial affairs. VA will only determine an individual to be unable to manage his or her financial affairs after receipt of medical documentation or if a court of competent jurisdiction has already made the determination.

Upon determining a beneficiary is unable to manage his or her financial affairs, VA will appoint a fiduciary. The fiduciary, normally chosen by the beneficiary, must undergo an investigation of their suitability to serve. This investigation includes a criminal background check, review of credit report, personal interview, and recommendations of character references. Only after a complete investigation is a fiduciary appointed to manage a beneficiaries VA benefits.

The fiduciary is responsible to the beneficiary and oversees financial management of VA benefit payments. Generally, family members or friends serve as fiduciaries for beneficiaries; however, when friends and family are not able to serve, VA looks for qualified individuals or organizations to serve as a fiduciary.

> **Key Takeaways**
>
> The VA Fiduciary Program was established to protect veterans and other beneficiaries.
>
> To become a fiduciary for a family member or friend, you must submit a request with the beneficiary's name and VA file number and your name and contact information to the VA regional office nearest you.
>
> The fiduciary selection is based on an assessment of the qualifications of the proposed fiduciary.

What is the Fiduciary Program?

The purpose of the Department of Veterans Affairs (VA) Fiduciary Program is to protect Veterans and beneficiaries who are unable to manage their VA benefits through the appointment and oversight of a fiduciary.

If you have been determined unable to manage your VA benefits, the VA will conduct a field examination to appoint a fiduciary to assist you.

VA Field Examination

A VA field examination will be scheduled for the purpose of appointing a fiduciary to assist you in managing your VA benefits. During the field examination, please have the following information available for review by the field examiner:

- Photo identification.
- The source and amount of all monthly bills, recurring expenses (annual, bi-annual, quarterly, etc.), and income.
- A list of all assets, to include bank accounts, owned property, stocks, bonds, life insurance, burial plans,etc.
- A list of all current medications.
- Name, phone number, and address of your primary care doctor. Name, phone number, and address of your next of kin.

Selection Process

During the selection process, the VA will first seek to qualify the individual you desire to serve as your fiduciary.

The fiduciary selection is based on an assessment of the qualifications of the proposed fiduciary. When seeking a fiduciary, the following individuals may be considered:

- A spouse or family member
- Court-appointed fiduciaries
- Another interested party,or
- A professional fiduciary

An assessment of the qualifications of a proposed fiduciary includes, but is not limited to:

- The willingness to serve and abide by all agreements
- An interview with a VA representative
- Credit report review
- An inquiry into the criminal background, and
- Interviews with character witnesses

What Are My Rights?

The determination that you are unable to manage your VA benefits does not affect your non-VA finances, or your right to vote or contract.

You have the right to appeal VA's decision finding that you are unable to manage your VA benefits. You also have the right to appeal VA's selection of the fiduciary. If you disagree with the VA on either of these matters you may:

- Appeal to the Board of Veterans' Appeals (Board) by telling them you disagree with their decision and want the Board to review it, or
- Give them evidence they do not already have that may lead us to change their decision.

How to Apply

To become a fiduciary for a family member or friend, submit a request with the beneficiary's name and VA file number, and your name and contact information to the VA regional office nearest you.

To become a professional fiduciary, submit your resume with a cover letter to the following e-mail address: VA_Fiduciary@va.gov. Include your name, the name of your organization (if applicable), mailing address, and e-mail address with your request.

Responsibilities

Any individual appointed as a VA fiduciary is responsible for managing the beneficiary's VA income and ensuring the beneficiary's just debts are paid. Additional, responsibilities of the fiduciary include, but are not limited to the following:

1. Utilizing the funds for the daily needs (e.g., food, clothing, housing, medical expenses, and personal items) of the beneficiary and his/her recognized dependents.
2. Never borrowing, loaning, or gifting funds belonging to the beneficiary.
3. Reporting any of the following changes to the Fiduciary Activity immediately:

    1. Change in address or phone number of the beneficiary or fiduciary
    2. Change in income or dependents
    3. Incarceration of the beneficiary
    4. Hospitalization of the beneficiary in a VA or state facility, and
    5. Death of the beneficiary or the beneficiary's dependents
4. Establishing a properly titled bank account as follows: (Beneficiary's Name) by (Fiduciary's Name, Federal Fiduciary).
5. Never commingling the beneficiary's funds with those of another.
6. Never withdrawing cash from the beneficiary's account by counter check or ATM withdrawal.
7. Timely submitting periodic accountings when required.

8. Keeping accurate, complete records and receipts, regardless of any requirement to submit periodic accountings.

9. Conserving excess funds in a federally or state insured interest-bearing account or United States savings bonds.

10. Registering saving bonds to reflect proper ownership and the existence of the fiduciary relationship, as follows: (Beneficiary's Name), (Social Security No.), under custodianship by the designation of the Department of Veterans Affairs.

11. Reporting any event that affects the beneficiary's payment or entitlement to benefits and promptly returning any payment that the beneficiary is not due.

12. Notifying VA of any changes or circumstances that would affect your performance as a payee or your decision to continue to serve as a payee (e.g., you sell or transfer your business).

13. Returning any funds owed by the beneficiary to VA if you stop serving as the fiduciary.

14. Notifying the VA if the beneficiary's condition improves to a point where you believe he or she no longer needs a fiduciary.

15. Protecting the beneficiary's funds from the claims of creditors since the beneficiary's funds are protected by law.

CHAPTER 17

VOCATIONAL READINESS AND EMPLOYMENT SERVICES FOR VETERANS WITH SERVICE-CONNECTED DISABILITIES

You may receive Vocational Readiness and Employment (VR&E) services to help with job training, employment accommodations, resume development, and job-seeking skills coaching. Other services may be provided to assist Veterans in starting their own businesses or independent living services for those who are severely disabled and unable to work in traditional employment. VR& E was formerly known as Vocational Rehabilitation and Employment.

Services that may be provided by the VR&E Program include:

- Comprehensive evaluation to determine abilities, skills, and interests for employment
- Vocational counseling and rehabilitation planning for employment services
- Employment services such as job training, job-seeking skills, resume development, and other work readiness assistance

> **Key Takeaways**
>
> You may receive Veteran Readiness and Employment (VR&E) services to help with job training, employment accommodations, resume development, and job seeking skills coaching.
>
> Other services may be provided to assist Veterans and Servicemembers in starting their own businesses or independent living services for those who are severely disabled and unable to work in traditional employment.

- Assistance finding and keeping a job, including the use of special employer incentives and job accommodations
- On the Job Training (OJT), apprenticeships, and non-paid work experiences
- Post-secondary training at a college, vocational, technical or business school
- Supportive rehabilitation services including case management, counseling, and medical referrals
- Independent living services for veterans unable to work due to the severity of their disabilities

Eligibility

Active Duty Servicemembers are eligible if they:

- Expect to receive an honorable or other than dishonorable discharge upon separation from active duty
- Obtain a memorandum rating of 20% or more from the Department of Veterans Affairs (VA), and
- Apply for VR&E services

Or (until December 31, 2017)

- Are participating in the Integrated Disability Evaluation System (IDES) or are certified by the military as having a severe injury or illness that may prevent them from performing their military duties
- Apply for VR&E services, and
- Report for an evaluation with a VR&E counselor before separating from active duty

Veterans are eligible if they:

- Have received a discharge that is other than dishonorable
- Have a service-connected disability rating of at least 10% from VA
- Apply for VR&E services

Basic Period of Eligibility

The basic period of eligibility ends 12 years from the date of notification of one of the following:

- Date of separation from active military service, or
- Date, the veteran, was first notified by VA of a service-connected disability rating.

The basic period of eligibility may be extended if a Vocational Rehabilitation Counselor (VRC) determines that a Veteran has a Serious Employment Handicap.

What Happens after Eligibility is Established?

The veteran is scheduled to meet with a VRC for a comprehensive evaluation to determine if he/she is entitled for services. A comprehensive evaluation includes:

- An assessment of the veteran's interests, aptitudes, and abilities
- An assessment of whether service-connected disabilities impair the veteran's ability to find and/or hold a job using the occupational skills he or she has already developed
- Vocational exploration and goal development leading to employment and/or

maximum independence in the Veteran's daily living at home and in the community

What is an Entitlement Determination?

A VRC works with the veteran to complete a determination if an employment handicap exists. An employment handicap exists if the veteran's service-connected disability impairs his/her ability to obtain and maintain a job. Entitlement to services is established if the veteran has an employment handicap and is within his or her 12-year basic period of eligibility and has a 20% or greater service-connected disability rating.

If the service-connected disability rating is less than 20%, or if the veteran is beyond the 12- year basic period of eligibility, then a serious employment handicap must be found to establish entitlement to VR&E services. A serious employment handicap is based on the extent and complexity of services required to help a veteran to overcome the significant restrictions caused by his or her service and non-service-connected disabilities, permitting the return to suitable employment

What Happens after the Entitlement Determination is Made?

The veteran and VRC work together to:

- Determine transferable skills, aptitudes, and interests
- Identify viable employment and/or independent living services options
- Explore labor market and wage information
- Identify physical demands and other job characteristics
- Explore vocational options to identify a suitable employment goal
- Select a VR&E program track leading to an employment or independent living goal
- Investigate training requirements
- Identify resources needed to achieve rehabilitation
- Develop an individualized rehabilitation plan to achieve the identified employment or independent living goals

What is a Rehabilitation Plan?

A rehabilitation plan is an individualized, written plan of services, which outlines the resources and criteria that will be used to achieve employment or independent living goals. The plan is an agreement that is signed by the veteran and the VRC and is updated as needed to assist the veteran in achieving his/her goals. Depending on their circumstances, veterans will work with their VRC to select one of the following five tracks of services

- Reemployment (with a former employer)
- Direct job placement services for new employment
- Self-employment
- Employment through long term services including OJT, college, and other training

- Independent living services

What Happens after the Rehabilitation Plan is Developed?

After a plan is developed and signed, a VRC or case manager will continue to work with the veteran to implement the plan to achieve suitable employment and/or independent living. The VRC or case manager will provide ongoing counseling, assistance, and coordinate services such as tutorial assistance, training in job-seeking skills, medical and dental referrals, adjustment counseling, payment of training allowance, if applicable, and other services as required to help the veteran achieve rehabilitation.

How can I get paid the Post-9/11 GI Bill rate for my Vocational Rehabilitation program?

A veteran participating in the VR&E Program who qualifies for Post-9/11 GI Bill benefits can elect to receive the GI Bill rate of pay instead of the regular Chapter 31 subsistence allowance. In most cases, the GI Bill rate is higher than the regular Chapter 31 rate of pay. To elect the GI Bill rate, the veteran must have remaining eligibility for the Post-9/11 GI Bill, and must formally choose (or "elect") the GI Bill rate. Your VRC can help you with selection. Veterans participating in the VR&E Program who elect the Post-9/11 rate are paid at the 100% rate level for their school and training time, even if their Post-9/11 GI Bill eligibility is less than 100%. Additional benefits are also available through the VR&E Program, such as payment of all required books, fees, and supplies as well as other supportive services.

Amount of VA Payments

If a veteran needs training, VA will pay his or her training costs, such as:

Tuition and fees;

Books;

Supplies;

Equipment; and

Special services (such as prosthetic devices, lip-reading training, or signing for the deaf), if needed

While a veteran is in training, VA will also pay him or her a monthly benefit to help with living expenses, called a subsistence allowance. Details are provided in the next section of this chapter.

Subsistence Allowance

In some cases, a veteran requires additional education or training to become employable. A Subsistence Allowance may then be paid each month and is based on the rate of attendance (full-time or part-time) and the number of dependents. The below rates are effective as of October 1, 2020.

The following Subsistence Allowance rates are paid for training in an Institution of Higher Learning

Number of Dependents	Full Time	Three Quarter Time	One Half Time
No Dependents	$653.96	$491.38	$328.78
One Dependent	$811.18	$609.27	$407.36
Two Dependents	$955.92	$714.69	$478.83
Each Additional Dependent	$69.66	$53.59	$35.74

Subsistence Allowance is paid for full time training only, in the following training programs: Nonpay or nominal pay on-job training in a federal, state, local, or federally recognized Indian tribe agency; training in the home; vocational course in a rehabilitation facility or sheltered workshop; institutional non-farm cooperative.

Number of Dependents	Full Time
No Dependents	$653.96
One Dependent	$811.18
Two Dependents	$955.92
Each Additional Dependent	$69.66

The following rates are paid for Work Experience programs: Nonpay or nominal pay work experience in a federal, state, local or federally recognized Indian tribe agency.

Number of Dependents	Full Time	Three Quarter Time	One Half Time
No Dependents	$653.96	$491.38	$324.14
One Dependent	$811.18	$609.27	$407.36
Two Dependents	$955.92	$714.69	$478.83
Each Additional Dependent	$69.66	$52.83	$35.74

Subsistence Allowance is paid for full time training only in the following training programs: Farm cooperative, apprenticeship, or other on-job training

Number of Dependents	Full Time
No Dependents	$571.77
One Dependent	$691.45
Two Dependents	$796.88
Each Additional Dependent	$51.82

Subsistence Allowance is paid at the following rates for combined training programs: Combination of Institutional and On-Job Training (Full Time Rate Only).

Number of Dependents	Institutional Greater than one half	On-The-Job Greater than one half
No Dependents	$653.96	$571.77
One Dependent	$811.18	$691.45
Two Dependents	$955.18	$796.88
Additional Dependents	$69.66	$51.82

Subsistence Allowance is paid at the following rates for Non-farm Cooperative Training: Non-farm Cooperative Institutional Training and Non-farm Cooperative On-Job Training - Full Time Rate Only.

Number of Dependents	FT Non-farm Coop/Institutional	FT Non-farm Coop/On-The-Job
No Dependents	$653.96	$571.77
One Dependent	$811.18	$691.45
Two Dependents	$955.92	$796.88
Each Additional Dependent	$69.66	$51.82

Subsistence Allowance is paid at the following rates for Independent Living programs:

A subsistence allowance is paid each month during the period of enrollment in a rehabilitation facility when a veteran is pursuing an approved Independent Living Program plan. Subsistence allowance paid during a period of Independent Living Services is based on rate of pursuit and number of dependents.

Number of Dependents	Full Time	Three Quarter Time	One Half Time
No Dependents	$653.96	$491.38	$328.78
One Dependent	$811.18	$609.27	$407.36
Two Dependents	$955.92	$714.69	$478.83
Each Additional Dependent	$69.66	$53.59	$35.74

Subsistence Allowance is paid at the following rates for Extended Evaluation programs:

A subsistence allowance is paid each month during the period of enrollment in a rehabilitation facility when a veteran requires this service for the purpose of extended evaluation. Subsistence allowance during a period of extended evaluation is paid based on the rate of attendance and the number of dependents.

Number of Dependents	Full Time	Three Quarter Time	One Half Time	One Quarter Time
No Dependents	$653.96	$491.38	$328.78	$164.37
One Dependent	$811.18	$609.27	$407.36	$203.72
Two Dependents	$955.92	$714.69	$478.83	$239.42
Each Additional Dependent	$69.66	$53.59	$35.74	$17.83

Programs for Unemployable Veterans

Veterans awarded 100% disability compensation based upon unemployability may still request an evaluation, and, if found eligible, may participate in a vocational rehabilitation program and receive help in getting a job. A veteran who secures employment under the special program will continue to receive 100% disability compensation until the veteran has worked continuously for at least 12 months.

Election of Alternate Subsistence Allowance Under Public Law 111- 377

This option is included for your use in comparing subsistence allowance rates that may be available to certain Veterans participating in the Chapter 31 program.

The VA is authorized to allow a Veteran, entitled to both a Chapter 31 subsistence allowance and Post 9/11 GI Bill Chapter 33 educational assistance, to elect to receive a replacement in an alternate amount instead of the regular Chapter 31 subsistence allowance.

The alternate payment will be based on the military basic allowance for housing (BAH) for an E-5 with dependents residing in the zip code of the training facility. Training in foreign institutions and training that is solely on-line or in-home will be based on the national average BAH.

Paralympic Veteran Benefit

Some veterans in training for the U.S. Paralympics may qualify for a monthly subsistence allowance from VA. The allowance is pegged to the subsistence allowance for participants in a fulltime institutional program under chapter 31 of title 38 of the U.S. Code.

According to the new rule, the VA will pay the allowance to a veteran with a service-connected or non-service-connected disability if the veteran is invited by the U.S. Paralympics to compete for a slot on the U.S. Paralympic team or is residing at the U.S. Paralympic training center for training or competition.

Applications for the allowance must be submitted through the U.S. Paralympics. Through the program, VA will pay a monthly allowance to a veteran with a service-connected or non-service-connected disability if the veteran meets the minimum military standard or higher (e.g., Emerging, Talent Pool, National Team) in his or her respective sport at a recognized competition. Besides making the military standard, an athlete must also be nationally or internationally classified by his or her respective sport federation as eligible for Paralympic competition within six or 12 months of a qualifying performance.

Athletes must also have established training and competition plans and are responsible for turning in monthly and quarterly reports in order to continue receiving a monthly assistance allowance. The allowance base for an athlete approved for monetary assistance ranges from $566.97 up to $1,084.00 per month, depending on the number of dependent.

Vocational Training for Children with Spina Bifida

To qualify for entitlement to a vocational training program an applicant must be a child:

- To whom VA has awarded a monthly allowance for spina bifida; and
- For whom VA has determined that achievement of a vocational goal is reasonably feasible.

A vocational training program may not begin before a child's 18th birthday, or the date of completion of secondary schooling, whichever comes first. Depending on the need, a child may be provided up to 24 months of full-time training.

Vocational Training for Children of Female Vietnam Veterans Born with Certain Birth Defects

Section 401 of P.L. 106-416, which became law on November 1, 2000 directed the Secretary of VA to identify birth defects of children of female Vietnam veterans that: (1) are associated with service during the Vietnam era; and (2) result in the permanent physical or mental disability of such children. The law excludes from such defects familial or birth- related defects or injuries. The law further directs the Secretary to provide to such children a monthly monetary allowance, as well as necessary health care to address the defect and any associated disability. It authorizes the Secretary to provide vocational training to such a child if the achievement of a vocational goal is reasonably feasible.

Independent Living Services

These services can help an individual with disabilities so severe that he or she cannot work. These services can lessen the individual's need to rely on others by giving him or her the skills needed to live as independently as possible at home and in the community.

Applying for Benefits

Interested veterans can apply by filling out "VA Form 28-1900", "Disabled Veterans Application for Vocational Rehabilitation" and mailing it to the VA regional office serving his or her area.

CHAPTER 18

VET CENTERS

Vet Centers serve veterans and their families by providing a continuum of quality care that adds value for veterans, families, and communities. Care includes:

- Professional readjustment counseling;
- Professional counseling for posttraumatic stress disorder;
- Marital and family counseling;
- Substance abuse information and referral;
- Community education;
- Outreach to special populations, including disenfranchised and unserved veterans;
- The brokering of services with community agencies;
- Provides a key access link between the veteran and other services in the U.S. Department of Veterans Affairs;
- Promotion of wellness activities with veterans to help them reach quality health and life goals

Eligibility

All Veterans are encouraged to seek Vet Center services. Any veterans and current service members, including members of the National Guard and Reserve components, are eligible if they have served on active military duty in any combat theater or area of hostility, or have experienced a military sexual trauma.

> **Key Takeaways**
>
> Vet Centers are community-based counseling centers providing a wide range of social and psychological services, including professional readjustment counseling to eligible veterans, active duty servicemembers and their families.
>
> Readjustment counseling is offered to make a successful transition from military to civilian life, or after a traumatic event experienced in the military.
>
> Individual, group, marriage and family counseling are offered in addition to referrals.

Veterans and current servicemembers are also eligible if they provided direct emergent medical care or mortuary services while serving on active duty to the casualties of war or served as a member of an unmanned aerial vehicle crew providing direct support to operations in a combat zone or area of hostility. Vietnam-era veterans who have access care at a Vet Center prior to January 2, 2013 are also eligible.

Vet Center services are also provided to family members of veterans and service members for military-related issues when they aid in the adjustment of those who have served. This includes bereavement counseling for families who experienced an active-duty death.

Sexual Trauma and Harassment Counseling

Veterans of both sexes, all eras. Vet Center services include individual readjustment counseling, referral for benefits assistance, group readjustment counseling, liaison with community agencies, marital and family counseling, substance abuse information and referral, job counseling and placement, sexual trauma counseling, and community education.

At the VA, Veterans can receive free, confidential treatment for mental and physical health conditions related to Military Sexual Trauma (MST). You may be able to receive this MST-related care even if you are not eligible for other VA services. To receive these services, you do not need a VA service-connected disability rating, to have reported the incident when it happened, or have other documentation that it occurred.

Knowing that MST survivors may have special concerns, every VA healthcare facility has an MST Coordinator who can answer any questions you might have about VA's MST services. VA has a range of services available to meet Veterans where they are at in their recovery:

Every VA healthcare facility has providers knowledgeable about treatment for problems related to MST. Many have specialized outpatient mental health services focusing on sexual trauma. Vet Centers also have specially trained sexual trauma counselors. VA has almost two dozen programs nationwide that offer specialized MST treatment in residential or inpatient setting. These programs are for Veterans who need more intense treatment and support.

Because some Veterans do not feel comfortable in mixed-gender treatment settings, some facilities have separate programs for men and women. All residential and inpatient MST programs have separate sleeping areas for men and women.

Vet Center Locations

ALABAMA

Birmingham Vet Center
400 Emery Drive, Suite 200
Hoover, AL 35244
(205) 989-6415

Huntsville Vet Center
415 Church Street, Bldg H, Suite 101
Huntsville, AL 3580
(256) 539-5775

Mobile Vet Center
3221 Springhill Ave Bldg 2, Suite C
Mobile, AL 36607
(251) 478-2237

Montgomery Vet Center
4405 Atlanta Highway
Montgomery, AL 36109
(334) 273-7796

ALASKA

Anchorage Vet Center
4400 Business Park Blvd.
Suite B-34
Anchorage, AK 99503
(907) 563-6966

Fairbanks Vet Center
540 4th Avenue
Suite 100
Fairbanks, AK 99701
(907) 456-4238

Wasilla Vet Center
851 East West Point Ave,
Suite 102
Wasilla, AK 99654
(907) 376-4318

ARIZONA

Lake Havasu Vet Center
1720 Mesquite
Suite 101
Lake Havasu, AZ 86403
(928) 505-0394

Mesa Vet Center
1303 South Longmore
Suite 5
Mesa, AZ 85202
(480) 610-6727

Phoenix Vet Center
4020 North 20th St.
Suite 110
Phoenix, AZ 85016
(602) 640-2981

Prescott Vet Center
3180 Stillwater Dr.
Suite A
Prescott, AZ 86305
(928) 778-3469

Tucson Vet Center
2525 E. Broadway Blvd.
Suite 100
Tucson, AZ 85716
(520) 882-0333

West Valley Vet Center
14050 N. 83rd Ave.
Suite 170
Peoria, AZ 85381
(623) 398-8854

Yuma County Vet Center
1450 East 16th St.
Suite 103
Yuma, AZ 85365
(928) 726-1343

ARKANSAS

Fayetteville Vet Center
1416 N. Collage Ave.
Fayetteville, AR 72703
(910) 488-6252

Little Rock Vet Center
10800 Financial Centre Parkway
Suite 175
North Little Rock, AR 72703
(501) 918-1800

CALIFORNIA

Antelope Valley Vet Center
38925 Trade Center Dr.
Suites I/J
Palmdale, CA 93551
(661) 267-1026

Bakersfield Vet Center
1110 Golden State Ave.
Bakersfield, CA 93301
(661) 325-8387

Chatsworth Vet Center
20946 Devonshire St.
Suite 101
Chatsworth, CA 91311
(818) 576-0201

Chico Vet Center
280 Cohasset Road
Chico, CA 95926
(530) 899-8549

Chula Vista Vet Center
180 Otay Lakes Rd.
Suite 108
Bonita, CA 91902
(877) 618-6534

Citrus Heights Vet Center
5650 Sunrise Blvd.
Suite 150
Citrus Heights, CA 95610
(916) 535-0420

Concord Vet Center
1333 Willow Pass Rd.
Suite 106
Concord, CA 94520
(925) 680-4526

Corona Vet Center
800 Magnolia Avenue
Suite 110
Corona, CA 92879-8202
(909) 734-0525

East Los Angeles Vet Center
5400 E Olympic Blvd
Suite 140
Commerce, CA 90022
(323) 728-9966

Eureka Vet Center
2830 G Street
Suite A
Eureka, CA 95501
(707) 444-8271

Fresno Vet Center
1320 E. Shaw Ave
Suite 125
Fresno, CA 93710
(559) 487-5660

High Desert Vet Center
15095 Amargosa Rd.
Suite 107
Victorville, CA 92394
(706) 261-5925

North Bay Vet Center
6010 Commerce Blvd.
Suite 145
Rohnert Park, CA 94928
(707) 586-5966

North Orange County Vet Center
12453 Lewis St.
Suite 101
Garden Grove, CA 92840
(714) 776-0161

Los Angeles Vet Center
1045 W. Redondo Beach Blvd.,
Suite 150
Gardena, CA 90247
(310) 767-1221

Modesto Vet Center
1219 N. Carpenter Rd.,
Suite 12
Modesto, CA 95351
(209) 569-0713

Oakland Vet Center
7700 Edgewater Dr.
Suite 125
Oakland, CA 94621
(510) 562-7906

Peninsula Vet Center
345 Middlefield Rd.
Building 1
Menlo Park, CA 94025
(650) 617-4300

Sacramento Vet Center
1111 Howe Avenue
Suite 390
Sacramento, CA 95825
(916) 566-7430

San Bernardino Vet Center
356 East Vanderbilt Way
San Bernardino, CA 92408
(909) 801-5762

San Diego Vet Center
2790 Truxtun Rd.
Suite 130
San Diego, CA 92106
(858) 642-1500

San Francisco Vet Center
505 Polk Street
San Francisco, CA 94102
(415) 441-5051

San Jose Vet Center
5855 Silver Creek Valley Place
3rd Floor 3A
San Jose, CA 95138

San Luis Obispo Vet Center
1070 Southwood Dr.
San Luis Obispo, CA 93401
(805) 782-9101

San Marcos Vet Center
One Civic Center Dr.
Suite 150
San Marcos, CA 92069
(760) 744-6914

Santa Cruz County Vet Center
1350 41st Ave,
Suite 104
Capitola, CA 95010
(831) 464-4575

South Orange County Vet Center
26431 Crown Valley Parkway
Suite 100
Mission Viejo, CA 92691
(949) 348-6700

Temecula Vet Center
40935 County Center Drive
Suite A/B
Temecula, CA 92591
(951) 302-4849

Ventura Vet Center
790 E. Santa Clara St.
Suite 100
Ventura, CA 93001
(805) 585-1860

West Los Angeles Vet Center
5730 Uplander Way
Suite 100
Culver City, CA 90230
(310) 641-0326

COLORADO
Boulder Vet Center
4999 Pearl East Circle
Suite 106
Boulder, CO 80301
(303) 440-7306

Colorado Springs Vet Center
602 South Nevada Ave.
Colorado Springs, CO 80903
(719) 471-9992

Denver Vet Center
7465 East First Ave.
Suite B
Denver, CO 80230
(303) 326-0645

Ft. Collins Vet Center
702 W. Drake
Building C
Fort Collins, CO 80526
(970) 221-5176

Grand Junction Vet Center
561 25 Road
Suite 101
Grand Junction, CO 81505
(970) 245-4156

Pueblo Vet Center
1515 Fortino Blvd.
Suite 130
Pueblo, CO 81008
(719) 583-4058

CONNECTICUT
Danbury Vet Center
457 North Main St., 1st Floor
Danbury, CT 06811
(203) 790-4000

Hartford Vet Center
25 Elm St. Suite A
Rocky Hill, CT 06067
(860) 563-8800

New Haven Vet Center
291 South Lambert Rd.
Orange, CT 06477
(203) 795-0148

Norwich Vet Center
2 Cliff Street
Norwich, CT 06360
(860) 887-1755

DELAWARE
Sussex County Vet Center
20653 Dupont Blvd, Suite 1
Georgetown, DE 19947
(302) 225-9110

Wilmington Vet Center
2710 Centerville Rd. Suite 103
Wilmington, DE 19808
(302) 994-1660

DISTRICT OF COLUMBIA

Washington, D.C. Vet Center
1296 Upshsur Street Northwest
Washington, DC 20011
(202) 726-5212

FLORIDA

Bay County Vet Center
3109 Minnesota Ave, Suite 101
Panama City, FL 32405
(850) 522-6102

Clearwater Vet Center
29259 US Hwy 19 North
Clearwater, CL 33761-2102
(727) 549-3600

Clermont Vet Center
1655 East Highway 50, Suite 102
Clermont, FL 34711
(352) 536-6701

Daytona Beach Vet Center
1620 Mason Ave., Suite C
Daytona Beach, FL 32117
(386) 366-6600

Fort Lauderdale Vet Center
3666 W. Oakland Park Blvd.
Lauderdale Lakes, FL 33311
(954) 714-2381

Fort Myers Vet Center
2891 Center Point Drive, Suite 100
Ft. Myers, FL 33916
(239) 652-1861

Gainesville Vet Center
105 NW 75th Street, Suite #2
Gainesville, FL 32607
(352) 331-1408

Jacksonville Vet Center
3728 Phillips Highway, Suite 31
Jacksonville, FL 32207
(904) 399-8351

Jupiter Vet Center
6650 W. Indiantown Rd., Suite 120
Jupiter, FL 33458
(561) 422-1220

Làkeland Vet Center
1370 Ariana St.
Lakeland, FL 33803
(863) 284-0841

Melbourne Vet Center
2098 Sarno Road
Melbourne, FL 32935
(321) 254-3410

Miami Vet Center
8280 NW 27th St Suite 511
Miami, FL 33122
(305) 718-3712

Naples Vet Center
2705 Horseshoe Dr. South, Suite #204
Naples, FL 34104
(239) 403-2377

Ocala Vet Center
3300 SW 34th Avenue, Suite 140
Ocala, FL 34474
(352) 237-1947

Okaloosa County Vet Center
6 11th Avenue, Suite G-1
Shalimar, FL 32579
(850) 651-1000

Orlando Vet Center
5575 S. Semoran Blvd., Suite #30
Orlando, FL 32822
(407) 857-2800

Palm Beach Vet Center
4996 10th Ave North, Suite 6
Greenacres, FL 33463
(561) 422-1201

Pasco County Vet Center
5139 Deer Park Drive
New Port Richey, FL 34653
(727) 372-1854

Pensacola Vet Center
4504 Twin Oaks Drive
Pensacola, FL 32506
(850) 456-5886

Pompano Beach Vet Center
2300 West Sample Road, Suite 102
Pompano, FL 33073
(954) 984-1669

Sarasota Vet Center
4801 Swift Rd. Suite A
Sarasota, FL 34231
(941) 927-8285

St. Petersburg Vet Center
6798 Crosswinds Drive, Bldg A
St. Petersburg, FL 33710
(727) 549-3633

Tallahassee Vet Center
2002 Old St. Augustine Road
Bldg A/100
Tallahassee, FL 32301
(850) 942-8810

Tampa Vet Center
Fountain Oaks Business Plaza;
3637 W. Waters Ave., Suite 600
Tampa, FL 33614-2783
(813) 228-2621

GEORGIA
Atlanta Vet Center
1800 Phoenix Boulevard, Building 400,
Suite 404 Box 55
College Park, GA 30349
(404) 417-5414

Augusta Vet Center
2050 Walton Way, Suite 100
Augusta, GA 30904
(706) 729-5762

Columbus Vet Center
2601 Cross Country Drive,
Condominium B-2 Suite 900
Columbus, GA 31906
(706) 596-7170

Lawrenceville Vet Center
930 River Centre Place
Lawrenceville, GA 30043
(404) 728-4195

Macon Vet Center
750 Riverside Drive
Macon, GA 31201
(478) 477-3813

Marietta Vet Center
40 Dodd St., Suite 700
Marietta, GA 30060
(404) 327-4954

Savannah Vet Center
321 Commercial Dr
Savannah, GA 31406
(912) 961-5800

GUAM

Guam Vet Center
400 Route 8, Suite 301
Maite, GU 96910
(671) 472-7161

HAWAII

Hilo Vet Center
70 Lanihuli Street, Suite 102
Hilo, HI 96720
(808) 969-3833

Honolulu Vet Center
1680 Kapiolani Blvd. Suite F-3
Honolulu, HI 96814
(808) 973-8387

Kailua-Kona Vet Center
73-4976 Kamanu St
Kailua-Kona, HI 96740
(808) 329-0574

Kauai Vet Center
4485 Pahe'e St., Suite 101
Lihue, HI 96766
(808) 246-1163

Maui Vet Center
157 Ma'a Street
Kahului, HI 96732
(808) 242-8557

Western Oahu Vet Center
885 Kamokila Boulevard, Suite 105
Kapolei, HI 96707
(808) 674-2414

IDAHO

Boise Vet Center
2424 Bank Drive, Suite 100
Boise, ID 83705
(208) 342-3612

Pocatello Vet Center
1800 Garrett Way, Suite 47
Pocatello, ID 83201
(208) 232-0316

ILLINOIS

Aurora Vet Center
750 Shoreline Drive, Suite 150
Aurora, IL 60504
(630) 585-1853

Chicago Heights Vet Center
1010 Dixie Hwy, 2nd Floor
Chicago Heights, IL 60411
(708) 754-8885

Chicago Vet Center
3348W. 87th Street, Suite 2
Chicago, IL 60652-3767
(773) 962-3740

Metro East Vet Center
228 West Pointe Drive
Swansea, IL 62226
(618) 825-0160

Evanston Vet Center
1901 Howard St
Evanston, IL 60202
(847) 332-1019

Oak Park Vet Center
1515 South Harlem
Forest Park, IL 60130
(708) 383-3225

Orland Park Vet Center
8651 W.159th Street, Suite 1
Orland Park, IL 60462
(708) 444-0561

Peoria Vet Center
8305 N. Allen Road, Suite 1
Peoria, IL 61615
(309) 689-9708

Quad Cities Vet Center
465 42nd Ave (Avenue of the Cities)
Suite #140
East Moline, IL 61244
(309) 755-3260

Rockford Vet Center
7015 Rote Road, Suite 105
Rockford, IL 61107
(815) 395-1276

Springfield, IL Vet Center
2980 Baker Drive
Springfield, IL 62703
(217) 492-4955

INDIANA
Evansville Vet Center
1100 N. Burkhardt Rd
Evansville, IN 47715
(812) 473-5993

Fort Wayne Vet Center
3810 Coldwater Road
Fort Wayne, IN 46805
(260) 460-1456

Gary Area Vet Center
107 E. 93rd Ave
Crown Point, IN 46307
(219) 736-5633

Indianapolis Vet Center
8330 Naab Road, Suite 103
Indianapolis, IN 46260
(317) 988-1600

South Bend Vet Center
4727 Miami Street
South Bend, N 46614
(574) 231-8480

IOWA
Cedar Rapids Vet Center
4250 River Center Court NE, Suite D
Cedar Rapids, IA 52402
(319) 378-0016

Des Moines Vet Center
1821 22nd Street #115
Des Moines, IA 50266
(515) 284-4929

Sioux City Vet Center
4280 Sergeant Road, Suite 104
Sioux City, IA 51106
(712) 255-3808

KANSAS
Manhattan Vet Center
1133 College Avenue, Building C,
Suite 200
Manhattan, KS 66502
(785) 587-8257

Wichita Vet Center
251 N. Water St.
Wichita, KS 67202
(316) 265-0889

KENTUCKY
Lexington Vet Center
1500 Leestown Rd Suite 104
Lexington, KY 40511
(859) 253-0717

Louisville Vet Center
1347 South 3rd Street
Louisville, KY 40208
(502) 287-6710

LOUISIANA
Alexandria Vet Center
5803 Coliseum Blvd., Suite D
Alexandria, LA 71303
(318) 466-4327

Baton Rouge Vet Center
7850 Anselmo Lane, Suite B
Baton Rouge, LA 70810
(225) 761-3140

New Orleans Vet Center
1250 Poydras Street, 4th Floor,
Suite 400
New Orleans, LA 70113
(504) 507-4977

Shreveport Vet Center
1255 Shreveport Barksdale Highway
Shreveport, LA 71105
(318) 861-1776

MAINE
Bangor Vet Center
615 Oldin Road, Suite 3
Bangor, ME 04401
(207) 947-3391

Lewiston Vet Center
35 Westminster St.
Lewiston, ME 04240
(207) 783-0068

Northern Maine Vet Center
456 York Street
Caribou, ME 04736
(207) 496-3900

Portland Vet Center
475 Stevens Ave.
Portland, ME 04103
(503) 688-5361

Sanford Vet Center
628 Main Street
Springvale, ME 04083
(207) 490-1513

MARYLAND
Annapolis Vet Center
100 Annapolis Street
Annapolis, MD 21401
(410) 605-7826

Baltimore Vet Center
1777 Reisterstown Road Suite 199
Baltimore, MD 21208
(410) 764-9400

Dundalk Vet Center
1553 Merritt Blvd
Dundalk, MD 21222
(410) 282-6144

Elkton Vet Center
103 Chesapeake Blvd. Suite A
Elkton, MD 21921
(410) 392-4485

Prince George's County Vet Center
7905 Malcolm Road, Suite 101
Clinton, MD 20735-1734
(301) 856-7173

Silver Spring Vet Center
2900 Linden Lane Suite 100
Silver Spring, MD 20910
(301) 589-1073

MASSACHUSETTS
Boston Vet Center
7 Drydock Ave, Suite 2070
Boston, MA 02210-2303
(617) 424-0665

261

Brockton Vet Center
1041L Pearl St. Suite L
Brockton, MA 02301
(508) 580-2730

Cape Cod Vet Center
474 West Main Street
Hyannis, MA 02601
(508) 778-0124

Lowell Vet Center
10 George Street
Lowell, MA 01852
(978) 453-1151

New Bedford Vet Center
73 Huttleton Ave. Unit 2
Fairhaven, MA 02719
(508) 999-6920

Springfield Vet Center
95 Ashley Avenue, Suite A
West Springfield, MA 01089
(413) 737-5167

Worcester Vet Center
255 Park Ave Suite 900
Worcester, MA 01609
(508) 753-7902

MICHIGAN
Dearborn Vet Center
19855 Outer Drive, Suite 105 W
Dearborn, MI 48124
(313) 277-1428

Detroit Vet Center
11214 East Jefferson Avenue
Detroit, MI 48214
(313) 822-1141

Escanaba Vet Center
3500 Ludington Street, Suite # 110
Escanaba, MI 49829

(906) 233-0244
Grand Rapids Vet Center
2050 Breton Rd SE
Grand Rapids, MI 49546
(616) 285-5795

Macomb County Vet Center
42621 Garfield Rd. Suite 105
Clinton Township, MI 48038-5031
(586) 412-0107

Pontiac Vet Center
44200 Woodward Avenue, Suite 108
Pontiac, MI 48341
(248) 874-1015

Saginaw Vet Center
5360 Hampton Place
Saginaw, MI 48604
(989) 321-4650

Traverse City Vet Center
3766 N US 31 South
Traverse City, MI 49684
(231) 935-0051

MINNESOTA
Brooklyn Park Vet Center
7001 78th Avenue North, Suite 300
Brooklyn Park, MN 55445
(763) 503-2220

Duluth Vet Center
4402 Haines Road
Duluth, MN 55811
(218) 722-8654

St. Paul Vet Center
550 County Road D West, Suite 10
New Brighton, MN 55112
(651) 644-4022

262

MISSISSIPPI
Biloxi Vet Center
288 Veterans Ave
Biloxi, MS 39531
(228) 388-9938

Jackson Vet Center
1755 Lelia Dr. Suite 104
Jackson, MS 39216
(601) 985-2560

MISSOURI
Columbia Vet Center
4040 Rangeline Street, Suite 105
Columbia, MO 65202
(573) 814-6206

Kansas City Vet Center
4800 Main Street, Suite 107
Kansas City, MO 64112-2501
(816) 753-1866

Springfield, MO Vet Center
3616 S. Campbell
Springfield, MO 65807
(417) 881-4197

St. Louis Vet Center
287 N. Lindbergh Blvd
Creve Coeur, MO 63141
(314) 894-5739

MONTANA
Billings Vet Center
2795 Enterprise Ave., Suite 1
Billings, MT 59102
(406) 657-6071

Great Falls Vet Center
615 2nd Avenue North
Great Falls, MT 59401
(406) 452-9048

Kalispell Vet Center
690 North Meridian Road, Suite 101
Kalispell, MT 59901
(406) 257-7308

Missoula Vet Center
910 Brooks St.
Missoula, MT 59801
(406) 721-4918

NEBRASKA
Lincoln Vet Center
3119 O Street, Suite A
Lincoln, NE 68510
(402) 476-9736

Omaha Vet Center
3047 S 72nd Street
Omaha, NE 68124
(402) 346-6735

NEVADA
Henderson Vet Center
400 orth Stephanie, Suite 180
Henderson, NV 89014
(702) 791-9100

Las Vegas Vet Center
7455 W. Washington Ave, Suite 240
Las Vegas, NV 89128
(702) 791-9170

Reno Vet Center
5580 Mill St. Suite 600
Reno, NV 89502
(775) 323-1294

NEW HAMPSHIRE
Berlin Vet Center
515 Main Street
Gorham, NH 03581
(603) 752-2571

263

Manchester Vet Center
1461 Hooksett Rd, B7
Hooksett, NH 03106-1882
(860) 646-5170

NEW JERSEY
Bloomfield Vet Center
2 Broad St. Suite 703
Bloomfield, NJ 07003
(973) 748-0980

Lakewood Vet Center
1255 Route 70 Suite 22N
Lakewood, NJ 08701
(908) 607-6364

Secaucus Vet Center
110A Meadowlands Parkway, Suite
102
Secaucus, NJ 07094
(201) 223-7787

South Jersey Vet Center
2900 Fire Road Suite 101
Egg Harbor Township, NJ 08234
(609) 487-8387

Trenton Vet Center
934 Parkway Ave. Suite 201
Ewing, NJ 08618
(609) 882-5744

NEW MEXICO
Albuquerque Vet Center
2001 Mountain Road NW
Albuquerque, NM 87104
(505) 346-6562

Farmington Vet Center
4251 E. Main Suite A
Farmington, NM 87402
(505) 327-9684

Las Cruces Vet Center
1120 Commerce Drive, Suite B
Las Cruces, NM 88001
(575) 523-9826

Santa Fe Vet Center
2209 Brothers Road Suite 110
Santa Fe, NM 87505
(505) 988-6562

NEW YORK
Albany Vet Center
17 Computer Drive West
Albany, NY 12205
(518) 626-5130

Babylon Vet Center
100 West Main Street
Babylon, NY 11702
(631) 661-3930

Binghamton Vet Center
53 Chenango Street
Binghamton, NY 13901
(607) 722-2393

Bronx Vet Center
2471 Morris Ave., Suite 1A
Bronx, NY 10468
(718) 367-3500

Brooklyn Vet Center
25 Chapel St. Suite 604
Brooklyn, NY 11201
(718) 630-2830

Buffalo Vet Center
2372 Sweet Home Road Suite 1
Amherst, NY 14228
(716) 862-7350

Harlem Vet Center
2279 3rd Avenue 2nd Floor
New York, NY 10035
(646) 273-8139

Manhattan Vet Center
32 Broadway 2nd Floor - Suite 200
New York, NY 10004-1637
(785) 350-4920

Middletown Vet Center
726 East Main Street, Suite 203
Middletown, NY 10940
(845) 342-9917

Nassau Vet Center
970 South Broadway
Hicksville, NY 11801-5019
(516) 348-0088

Queens Vet Center
75-10B 91 Avenue
Woodhaven, NY 11421-2824
(718) 296-2871

Rochester Vet Center
2000 S. Winton Road, Bldg 5, Suite 201
Rochester, NY 14618
(585) 393-7608

Staten Island Vet Center
60 Bay Street
Staten Island, NY 10301
(718) 816-4499

Syracuse Vet Center
109 Pine Street Suite 101
Syracuse, NY 13210
(315) 478-7127

Watertown Vet Center
210 Court Street Suite 20
Watertown, NY 13601
(315) 782-5479

White Plains Vet Center
300 Hamilton Ave. Suite C 1st Floor
White Plains, NY 10601
(914) 682-6250

NORTH CAROLINA
Charlotte Vet Center
2114 Ben Craig Drive Suite 300
Charlotte, NC 28262
(704) 549-8025

Fayetteville Vet Center
2301 Robeson St., Suite 103
Fayetteville, NC 28305
(910) 488-6252

Greensboro Vet Center
3515 West Market Street Suite 120
Greensboro, NC 27406
(336) 323-2660

Greenville, NC Vet Center
1021 WH Smith Blvd. Suite 100
Greenville NC 27834
(252) 355-7920

Jacksonville Vet Center
110A Branchwood Dr
Jacksonville, NC 28345
(910) 577-1100

Raleigh Vet Center
8851 Ellstree Lane, Suite 122
Raleigh, NC 27617
(919) 361-6419

NORTH DAKOTA
Bismarck Vet Center
619 Riverwood Drive, Suite 105
Bismarck, ND 58504
(701) 224-9751

Fargo Vet Center
3310 Fiechtner Drive. Suite 100
Fargo, ND 58103-8730
(701) 237-0942

Minot Vet Center
3300 South Broadway
Minot, ND 58701
(701) 852-0177

OHIO

Cincinnati Vet Center
4545 Montgomery Road
Norwood, OH 45212
(513) 763-3500

Cleveland Vet Center
5310 1/2 Warrensville Center Rd
Maple Heights, OH 44137
(216) 707-7901

Columbus Vet Center
30 Spruce Street
Columbus, OH 43215
(614) 257-5550

Dayton Vet Center
3085 Woodman Drive Suite 180
Kettering, OH 45420
(937) 296-0489

Parma Vet Center
5700 Pearl Road Suite 102
Parma, OH 44129
(440) 845-5023

Stark County Vet Center
601 Cleveland Ave N, Suite C
Canton, OH 44702
(330) 454-3120

Toledo Vet Center
1565 S. Byrne Road, Suite 104
Toleo, OH 43614
(419) 213-7533

OKLAHOMA

Lawton Vet Center
1016 SW C Avenue, Suite B
Lawton, OK 73501
(580) 585-5880

Oklahoma City Vet Center
6804 N. Robinson Avenue
Oklahoma City, OK 73116
(405) 456-5184

Tulsa Vet Center
14002 E. 21st Street
Tulsa, OK 74134-1422
(918) 628-2760

OREGON

Central Oregon Vet Center
1645 NE Forbes Rd. Suite 105
Bend, OR 97701
(541) 749-2112

Eugene Vet Center
190 East 11th Avenue
Eugne, OR 97401
(541) 465-6918

Grants Pass Vet Center
211 S.E. 10th St.
Grants Pass, OR 97526
(541) 479-6912

Portland Vet Center
1505 NE 122nd Ave.
Portland, OR 97230
(503) 688-5361

Salem Vet Center
2645 Portland Road NE, Suite 250
Salem, OR 97301
(503) 362-9911

PENNSYLVANIA
Bucks County Vet Center
2 Canal's End Road Suite 201B
Bristol, PA 19007
(215) 823-4590

City Center Philadelphia Vet Center
801 Arch Street Suite 502
Philadelphia, PA 19107
(215) 923-2284

DuBois Vet Center
100 Meadow Lane, Suite 8
DuBois, PA 15801
(814) 372-2095

Erie Vet Center
240 West 11th Street Suite 105
Erie, PA 16501
(814) 453-7955

Harrisburg Vet Center
1500 North Second Street Suite 2
Harrisburg, PA 17102
(717) 782-3954

Lancaster Vet Center
1817 Olde Homestead Lane, Suite 207
Lancaster, PA 17601
(717) 283-0735

Norristown Vet Center
320 East Johnson Hwy, Suite 201
Norristown, PA 19401
(215) 823-5245

Northeast Philadelphia Vet Center
101 East Olney Avenue Suite C-7
Philadelphia, PA 19120
(215) 924-4670

Pittsburgh Vet Center
2500 Baldwick Rd, Suite 15
Pittsburgh, PA 15205
(412) 920-1765

Scranton Vet Center
1002 Pittston Ave.
Scranton, PA 18505
(570) 344-2676

White Oak Vet Center
2001 Lincoln Way, Suite 280
White Oak, PA 15131
(412) 678-7704

Williamsport Vet Center
49 East Fourth Street Suite 104
Williamsport, PA 17701
(570) 327-5281

PUERTO RICO
Arecibo Vet Center
50 Gonzalo Marin St
Arecio, PR 00612
+1 (787) 879-4510

Ponce Vet Center
35 Mayor Street, Suite 1
Ponce, PR 00730
+1 (787) 841-3260

San Juan Vet Center
7th Tabonuco Street Suite 4
Guaynabo, PR 00968-4702
(787) 749-4410

RHODE ISLAND
Providence Vet Center
2038 Warwick Ave
Warwick, RI 02889
(401) 739-0167

SOUTH CAROLINA
Charleston Vet Center
3625 West Montague Avenue
North Charleston, SC 29418
(843) 789-7000

Columbia Vet Center
1710 Richland Street, Suite A
Columbia, SC 29201
(803) 765-9944

Greenville, SC Vet Center
3 Caledon Court, Suite B
Greenville, SC 29615
(864) 271-2711

Myrtle Beach Vet Center
2024 Corporate Centre Dr, Suite 103
Myrtle Beach, SC 29577
(843) 232-2441

SOUTH DAKOTA
Rapid City Vet Center
621 6th St, Suite 101
Rapid City, SD 57701
(605) 348-0077

Sioux Falls Vet Center
3200 W 49th Street
Sioux Falls, SD 57106
(605) 330-4552

TENNESSEE
Chattanooga Vet Center
1300 Premier Drive, Suite 180
Chattanooga, TN 37421
(423) 855-6570

Johnson City Vet Center
2203 McKinley Road, Suite 254
Johnson City, TN 37604
(423) 928-8387

Knoxville Vet Center
1645 Downtown West Blvd #28
Knoxville, TN 37919
(865) 633-0000

Memphis Vet Center
1407 Union Ave., Suite 410
Memphis, TN 38104
(901) 522-3950

Nashville Vet Center
1420 Donelson Pike Suite A-5
Nashville, TN 37217
(615) 883-2333

TEXAS
Abilene Vet Center
3564 N. 6th St.
Abilene, TX 79603
(325) 232-7925

Amarillo Vet Center
3414 Olsen Blvd. Suite E
Amarillo, TX 79109
(806) 354-9779

Arlington Vet Center
3337 West Pioneer Parkway
Pantgo, TX 76013
(817) 274-0981

Austin Vet Center
1524 South IH 35 Suite 100
Austin, TX 78704
(512) 416-1314

Beaumont Vet Center
990 IH10 North, Suite 180
Beaumont, TX 77702
(409) 347-0124

Corpus Christi Vet Center
4646 Corona Suite 250
Corpus Christi, TX 78411
(361) 854-9961

Dallas Vet Center
8610 Greenville Ave., Suite 125
Dallas, TX 75243
(214) 361-5896

El Paso Vet Center
1155 Westmoreland Suite 121
El Paso, TX 79925
(915) 772-0013

Fort Worth Vet Center
6620 Hawk Creek Avenue
Westworth Village, TX 76114
(817) 921-9095

Houston Southwest Vet Center
10103 Fondren Road, Suite 470
Houston, TX 77096
(713) 770-1803

Houston West Vet Center
701 N. Post Oak Road Suite 102
Houston, TX 77024
(713) 682-2288

Killeen Heights Vet Center
302 Millers Crossing, Suite #4
Harker Heights, TX 76548
(254) 953-7100

Laredo Vet Center
6999 McPherson Road Suite 102
Laredo, TX 78041
(956) 723-4680

Lubbock Vet Center
3106 50th St. Suite 400
Lubbock, TX 79413
806-792-9782

McAllen Vet Center
2108 S M Street, MedPoint Plaza
Unit 2
McAllen, TX 78503
(956) 631-2147

Mesquite Vet Center
502 West Kearney, Suite 300
Mesquite, TX 75149
(972) 288-8030

Midland Vet Center
4400 N. Midland Drive, Suite 540
Midland, TX 79707
(432) 697-8222

San Antonio Northeast Vet Center
9504 IH 35 N, Suite 214
San Antonio, TX 78233
(210) 650-0422

San Antonio Northwest Vet Center
9910 W Loop 1604 N, Suite 126
San Antonio, TX 78254
(210) 688-0606

Spring Vet Center
14300 Cornerstone Village Dr.,
Suite 110
Houston, TX 77014
(281) 537-7812

UTAH

Major Brent Taylor Vet Center
Outstation
2357 N 400 E
North Ogden, UT 84414

Provo Vet Center
360 S. State Street Bldg C Suite 103
Orem, UT 84770-4494
(801) 377-1117

Saint George Vet Center
1664 South Dixie Drive, Suite C-102
St. George, UT 84770-4494
(435) 673-4494

Salt Lake City Vet Center
22 West Fireclay Avenue
Murray, UT 84107
(801) 266-1499

VERMONT

South Burlington Vet Center
19 Gregory Drive Suite 201
South Burlington, VT 05403
(802) 862-1806

White River Junction Vet Center
118 Prospect Street Suite 100
White River Junction, VT 05001
(802) 295-2908

VIRGINIA

Alexandria Vet Center
6940 South Kings Highway Suite 204
Alexandria, VA 22310
(703) 360-8633

Norfolk Vet Center
3132 Lynnhurst Blvd
Chesapeake, VA 23321
(757) 623-7584

Richmond Vet Center
4902 Fitzhugh Avenue
Richmond, VA 23230
(804) 353-8958

Roanoke Vet Center
1401 Franklin Rd SW Suite 200
Roanoke, VA 24016
(540) 342-9726

Virginia Beach Vet Center
324 Southport Circle, Suite 102
Virginia Beach, VA 23452
(757) 248-3665

WASHINGTON

Bellingham Vet Center
3800 Byron Ave Suite 124
Bellingham, WA 98229
(360) 733-9226

Everett Vet Center
1010 SE Everett Mall Way Suite 207
Everett, WA 98208
(425) 252-9701

Federal Way Vet Center
32020 32nd Ave South Suite 110
Federal Way, WA 98001
(253) 838-3090

Seattle Vet Center
305 S. Lucille St.
Seattle, WA 98108
(206) 764-5130

Spokane Vet Center
13109 E Mirabeau Parkway
Spokane, WA 99216
(509) 444-8387

Tacoma Vet Center
4916 Center St. Suite E
Tacoma, WA 98409
(253) 565-7038

Walla Walla Vet Center
1104 West Poplar
Walla Walla, WA 99362
(509) 526-8387

Yakima Valley Vet Center
2119 W. Lincoln
Yakima, WA 98302
(509) 453-7161

WEST VIRGINIA
Beckley Vet Center
201 Grey Flatts Road
Beckley, WV 25801
(877) 927-8387

Charleston Vet Center
200 Tracy Way
Charleston, WV 25311
(304) 343-3825

Huntington Vet Center
3135 16th Street Road Suite 11
Huntington, WV 25701
(304) 523-8387

Martinsburg Vet Center
300 Foxcroft Ave. Suite 100A
Martinsburg, WV 25401-5341
(304) 263-6776

Morgantown Vet Center
34 Commerce Drive Suite 101
Morgantown, WV 26501
(304) 291-4303

Princeton Vet Center
1511 North Walker Street
Princeton, WV 24740
(304) 425-8098

Wheeling Vet Center
1058 East Bethlehem Blvd.
Wheeling, WV 26003
(304) 232-0587

WISCONSIN
Green Bay Vet Center
1600 S. Ashland Ave
Green Bay, WI 54304
(920) 435-5650

La Crosse Vet Center
20 Copeland Ave.
La Crosse, WI 54603
(608) 782-4403

Madison Vet Center
1291 N. Sherman Ave
Madison, WI 53704
(608) 264-5342

Milwaukee Vet Center
7910 N. 76th Street, Suite 100
Milwaukee, WI 53223
(414) 902-5561

WYOMING
Casper Vet Center
1030 North Poplar, Suite B
Casper, WY 82601
(307) 261-5355

Cheyenne Vet Center
3219 E Pershing Blvd
Cheyenne, WY 82001
(307) 778-7370

CHAPTER 19

EDUCATION BENEFITS OVERVIEW

The Veterans Administration administers ten educational assistance programs, each with different eligibility criteria. Typically, a veteran's eligibility is based on his or her dates of active duty. Generally, only the VA can determine an applicant's eligibility. Specific information regarding educational benefits can be obtained from the Education Service of the VA (888) GI-BILL-1 or any VA regional office.

An individual can be eligible for more than one of the available education benefits. If so, he or she must elect which benefit to receive. Payments for more than one benefit at a time may not be made.

The VA strongly encourages individuals who qualify for more than one type of education benefit to discuss their educational plans with a Veterans Benefits Counselor so that all options can be explored, and maximum benefits can be paid.

Harry W. Colmery Act

Section 1. Short Title This section cites the short title of this bill as the "Harry W. Colmery Veterans Educational Assistance Act of 2017."

Key Takeaways

VA education benefits help veterans, servicemembers and their qualified family members with things such as paying college tuition, finding the right school or training program, and getting career counseling.

Since 1944 the GI Bill has helped veterans and their family members pay for training and education.

Programs under the BI Bill include the Post-9/11 GI Bill, the Montgomery GI Bill Active Duty and the Montgomery GI Bill Selected Reserve.

Section 101. Consideration of Certain Time Spent Receiving Medical Care from Secretary of Defense as Active Duty for Purposes of Eligibility for Post-9/11 Educational Assistance. This section would add time spent on active duty under orders authorized by section 12301(h) of title 10, U.S.C., as a qualifying time for the Post-9/11 GI Bill. These particular orders are used when a National Guardsman or Reservist is receiving medical care or is recovering from active-duty injuries.

Section 102. Consolidation of Eligibility Tiers under the Post-9/11 Educational Assistance Program of the Department of Veterans Affairs. This section would authorize additional GI Bill funding for members of the National Guard and Reserve. This section would increase the amount of money/eligibility that individuals receive who serve at least 90 days but less than 6 months on active duty – it would increase from 40% to 50% benefit payable.   It would also increase the amount of money/eligibility that individuals receive who serve at least 6 months but less than 12 months – it would increase from 50% to 60% benefit payable. For a student attending a private school, this would result in approximately $2300 more a year in tuition than they are receiving now and would receive more money for their housing allowance.

Section 103. Educational Assistance Under the Post-9/11 Educational Assistance Program for Members of the Armed Forces awarded the Purple Heart. This section would extend full eligibility for the Post-9/11 GI Bill to any Purple Heart recipients since September 11, 2001.

Section 104. Eligibility for Post-9/11 Educational Assistance for Certain Members of Reserve Components of Armed Forces who Lost Entitlement to Educational Assistance under Reserve Educational Assistance Program. This section would allow certain members of the Reserve component to transfer into the Post-9/11 GI Bill, who lost educational assistance benefits when Congress repealed the Reserve Educational Assistant Program (REAP).

Section 105. Calculation of Monthly House Stipend under Post-9/11 Educational Assistance Program Based on Location of Campus where Classes are Attended. This section would change the way living stipend amounts are calculated, from the current rule that says the living stipend payment is based on where the school is located to instead having the payment calculated based on where the student attends the majority of their classes.

Section 106. Charge to Entitlement for Certain Licensure and Certification Tests and National Tests under Department of Veterans' Affairs Post-9/11 Educational Assistance. This section would change the current rules that require that a veteran be charged a whole month of entitlement to pay for any national test (GMAT, GRE, SAT etc.) or test that is required for state licensing. Instead of a full month of entitlement, this bill would require that the test be pro-rated to the amount of the actual cost of the test.

Section 107. Restoration of Entitlement to Post-9/11 Educational Assistance for Veterans Affected by Closures of Educational Institution. This section would restore entitlement to individuals when their school closes in the middle of a semester. This section would also authorize additional living stipend payments to be paid to students whose school closes in the middle of the semester for no more than 4 months, or the length of the semester, where they were attending training.

Section 108. Inclusion of Fry Scholarship Recipients in Yellow Ribbon GI Education Enhancement Program. This section would extend the Yellow Ribbon Program to students receiving GI Bill payments through the Fry Scholarship program and those who received a Purple Heart after September 11, 2001. Fry recipients are surviving dependents of servicemembers who died while serving on active duty.

Section 109. Additional Authorized Transfer of Unused Post-9/11 Educational Assistance Benefits to Dependents upon Death of Originally Designated Dependent. This section would allow a veteran to transfer remaining months of GI Bill entitlement to another dependent if the dependent who originally received the transferred benefits dies before they can use all of the benefits. The section would also allow a dependent to transfer remaining months of GI Bill entitlement to another dependent after the death of the servicemember or veteran.

Section 110. Edith Nourse Rogers STEM Scholarship. This section would authorize VA to provide additional GI Bill funds to help a student veteran complete a STEM degree. They would be eligible to apply for the program, which would pay for the lesser of nine additional months of Post-9/11 GI Bill or a lump sum of $30,000. The amount of money that could be spent on this program would not exceed $100,000,000 in any one fiscal year. These additional benefits would be known as the 'Edith Nourse Rogers STEM Scholarship.'

Section 111. Honoring National Service of the Members Elimination of Time Limitation for the use of Entitlement. This section would eliminate the current time limitation to use the GI Bill for new members of the Armed Forces. Student veterans currently have 15 years from the date of their last active duty discharge to use the benefit.

Section 112. Monthly Stipend for Certain Members of the Reserve Components of the Armed Forces Receiving Post-9/11 Educational Assistance. This section would require VA to pro-rate the GI Bill housing stipend provided to Reservists who get called up for active duty during the middle of a month. Current law prohibits them from pro-rating the stipend, so if the reservist is on active duty orders for even one day of a month then they would lose the entire months' worth of VA housing allowance.

Section 113. Improvement of Information Technology of the Veterans Benefits Administration of the Department of Veterans Affairs. This section would authorize $30 million to improve GI Bill claims processing and complete their rules-based processing system for these claims.

Section 114. Department of Veterans Affairs High Technology Pilot Program. This section would authorize VA to conduct a 5-year pilot program that would provide veterans the opportunity to enroll in high technology courses (coding boot camp, IT certifications, etc.). VA would enter into contracts with these schools or programs and would provide tuition and fees payments on a sliding scale that incentivizes the schools to graduate the student and ensure they find a job in their field of study. The section would also authorize a living stipend payment equal to the Post-9/11 rate to students while they are using the benefit.

Section 201. Work-Study Allowance This section would repeal the sunset date in the law that allows VA work-study benefits for outreach to student veterans and to assist State approving agencies.

Section 202. Duration of Educational Assistance under Survivors' and Dependent' Educational Assistance Program. This section would change the number of months of entitlement for individuals who become eligible for the Survivors' and Dependents' Educational Assistance Program from 45 months to 36 months. This would re-align this program with other GI Bill programs that provide 36 months of eligibility for educational assistance. This change would only apply to individuals that become entitled to this program on or after August 1, 2018.

Section 203. Olin E. Teague Increase in the Amounts of Educational Assistance Payable Under Survivors' and Dependent' Educational Assistance Program. This section would increase the monthly payment for educational assistance provided under Survivors' and Dependent' Educational Assistance Program by $200 a month.

Section 301. State Approving Agency Funding. This section would increase the funding out VA's mandatory account for the State Approving Agencies (SAA) from $19 million a year to $21 million a year. This section would also authorize VA to provide an additional $3 million a year to the SAAs out of the Department's discretionary account. This section would also, beginning in the fiscal year 2019, require VA to provide a cost-of-living adjustment increase to the SAAs budget in an amount that equals the same percentage increase as benefits provided under the Social Security Act.

Section 302. Authorization for the use of Post-9/11 Educational Assistance to Pursue Independent Study Programs at Certain Educational Institutions that are Not Institutions of Higher Learning. This section would allow an eligible individual to use their GI Bill benefit for an accredited independent study program (including open circuit television) at an educational institution that is an area career and technical education school or a postsecondary vocational school providing postsecondary level education.

Section 303. Provision of Information on Priority Enrollment for Veterans in Certain Courses of Education. This section would require VA to include on its GI Bill Comparison Tool, information on whether a school has a priority enrollment system in place that allows veterans to enroll in courses earlier than other students attending the school.

Section. 304. Limitation on Use of Reporting Fees Payable to Educational Institutions and Sponsors of Programs of Apprenticeship. This section would allow VA to provide a fee to schools or a sponsor of a program of apprenticeship for the reports or certifications that these institutions are required to submit to VA about the individuals at their school receiving GI Bill benefits. This section would require VA to provide $16 to the institution for each individual that they certify as using GI Bill benefits at their institution. This section would also require that schools with 100 or more enrollees using GI Bill benefits, may not use the funds received by the institution from the reporting fees for the institution's general fund and that these funds may only be used for veterans programs at that institution.

Section. 305. Training for School Certifying Officials. This section would require VA, in consultation with the SAA's, to provide requirements for training for school certifying officials at educational institutions that are approved for GI Bill benefits. This section would also allow VA to disapprove a course of education if a school does not ensure that the school certifying official meets the training requirements.

Section 306. Extension of Authority for Advisory Committee on Education. This section would extend the authority for VA's Advisory Committee on Education from December of 2017 through to December of 2022.

Section 307. Department of Veterans Affairs Provision of On-Campus Educational and Vocational Counseling for Veterans. This section would codify VA's Veterans Success on Campus (VSOC) program, which is administered and overseen by the Vocational Rehabilitation and Employment Service (VS&E). There are currently 94 schools with a VSOC program, which provides a VR&E counselor at each school to assist veterans with their transition from military to college life as well as who provide the support and assistance needed to pursue their educational and employment goals.

Section 308. Provision of Information Regarding Veteran Entitlement to Educational Assistance. This section would require VA to make available to educational institutions, the ability to view the remaining benefit amount for each veteran attending that institution. This section would also allow the veteran or their dependent (if they are a beneficiary of their GI Bill benefits) to opt-out of the school's ability to receive such information from VA.

Section 309. Treatment for Purposes of Educational Assistance Administered by the Secretary of Veterans Affairs of Educational Courses that Begin Seven or Fewer Days after the First Day of an Academic Year. This section would provide more flexibility to the school certifying officials if the first day of a course does not start on the first day of an academic term, by allowing the school certifying official to certify the course as beginning on that day first day of the academic term for purposes of certifying a veteran for GI Bill benefits.

Section 401. Eligibility of Reserve Component Members for Post 9/11 Educational Assistance. This section would make individuals eligible for Post-9/11 GI Bill benefits who have served and who will serve on 12304, 12304(a), and 12304(b) orders. Any active-duty service under these Reserve component orders since the enactment of the Post-9/11 Veterans Educational Assistance Act of 2008 would apply for such benefits going forward.

Section 402. Time Limitation for Training and Rehabilitation for Veterans with Service-Connected Disabilities. This section would also make the 12304, 12304(a), and 12304(b) orders eligible for benefits under the Vocational Rehabilitation and Employment program in chapter 31 of title 38, U.S.C.

Section 501. Repeal Inapplicability of Modification of Basic Allowance for Housing to Benefits under Laws Administered by Secretary of Veterans Affairs. This section would be the offset for the package by realigning the living stipend payments for those using the Post 9/11 GI Bill (E-5 with dependents rate) to the same Basic Allowance for Housing (BAH) payments currently paid to active duty servicemembers at the E-5 with dependents rate. Several years ago, the annual percentage increase to active duty BAH payments was reduced by 1% a year for five years but GI bill payments were exempt. This bill would re-align these payments so that a GI Bill recipient would receive the same living stipend per month as an E-5 active-duty servicemember with dependents. This section also stipulates that these decreases to the annual percentage increase would only be in effect for individuals who first begin using their education benefits on or after January 1, 2018

Veterans Educational Assistance Program (VEAP)

The Post-Vietnam Veterans' Educational Assistance Program is also known as VEAP. VEAP provides education and training opportunities to eligible persons who contributed to the program while on active duty. If an individual did not contribute or received a refund of contributions, he or she is not eligible for VEAP benefits. The initial contribution must have been made by March 31, 1987. The maximum contribution by any individual participant is $2,700. A participating member's contributions are matched on a $2 for $1 basis by the Government.

Since August 1, 2011, break (or interval pay) became no longer be payable under VEAP except during periods your school is closed as a result of an Executive Order of the President or an emergency (such as a natural disaster or strike). For example, if your Fall term ends on December 15th and your Spring term begins January 10th, your January housing allowance will cover 15 days in December, and your February housing allowance will cover 21 days in January.

VEAP Eligibility

To qualify for VEAP benefits, individuals must have:
- Entered active duty for the first time between January 1, 1977, and June 30, 1985; and
- Enrolled in and contributed to VEAP before April 1, 1987; and
- Served for a continuous period of 181 days or more (Individuals may be eligible if discharged from a shorter period of active duty for a service-connected disability.);and
- Been discharged or released from service under conditions other than dishonorable; and
- Completed 24 continuous months of active duty if enlisted for the first time after September 7, 1980, or entered active duty as an officer or enlistee after October 16, 1981. (Individuals meet this requirement if they completed a shorter period of active duty to which the service department called or ordered the individual.)

Individuals may be eligible for VEAP benefits if they did not complete 24 continuous months of active duty if they:
- Received VA disability compensation or military disability retirement; or
- Served a period of at least 24 continuous months of active duty before

October 17, 1981; or

- Were discharged or released for early out, hardship, or service-connected disability.

Individuals may be eligible for VEAP benefits while still on active duty if they:

- Entered active duty for the first time after December 31, 1976, and before July 1, 1985; and
- Enrolled in and contributed to VEAP before April 1, 1987, and have at least three months of contributions available (For an elementary or high school program, at least one month of contributions must be available.); and
- Served for a continuous period of 181 days or more; and
- Completed their first active-duty commitment.

The following types of active duty do not establish eligibility:

- Time assigned by the military to a civilian institution for the same course provided to civilians;
- Time served as a cadet or midshipman at a service academy;
- Time spent on active duty for training in the National Guard or Reserve

NOTE: Individuals are not eligible for VEAP if they are eligible for the Montgomery GI Bill-Active Duty based on prior eligibility for Vietnam Era Veterans' Educational Assistance.

Approved Courses

VEAP benefits may be received for a wide variety of training, including:

- Training for a high school diploma or the equivalent
- Undergraduate or graduate degrees from a college or university
- Cooperative training programs
- Accredited independent study programs leading to standard college degrees
- Courses leading to certificates or diplomas from business, technical or vocational schools
- Vocational flight training (Individuals must have a private pilot's license and meet the medical requirements for the desired license before beginning training and throughout the flight training program)
- Apprenticeship or job training programs offered by a company or union
- Correspondence courses
- VA may approve programs offered by institutions outside of the United States, when they are pursued at educational institutions of higher learning, and lead to a college degree. Individuals must receive VA approval prior to attending or enrolling in any foreign programs.

Since March 1, 2001, benefits weren't payable for licensing or certification tests. The tests are those needed to enter, maintain, or advance into employment in a civilian vocation or profession. The eligible veteran or family member may receive payment of the fee charged for the test or $2,000, whichever is less. The tests must be approved for VA benefits.

If an individual is seeking a college degree, the school must admit him or her to a degree program by the start of the third term.

Restrictions on Training

- Bartending and personality development courses
- Non-accredited independent study courses
- Any course given by radio
- Self-improvement courses such as reading, speaking, woodworking, basic seamanship, and English as a second language
- Any course which is avocational or recreational in character
- Farm cooperative courses
- Audited courses
- Courses not leading to an educational, professional, or vocational objective
- Courses an individual has previously taken and successfully completed
- Courses taken by a Federal government employee under the Government Employees' Training Act
- Courses paid for in whole or in part by the Armed Forces while on active duty
- Courses taken while in receipt of benefits for the same program from the Office of Workers' Compensation Programs
- The VA must reduce benefits for individuals in Federal, State, or local prisons after being convicted of a felony.
- An individual may not receive benefits for a program at a proprietary school if he or she is an owner or official of the school.

Part-Time Training

Individuals unable to attend school full-time should consider going part-time. Benefit rates and entitlement charges are less than the full-time rates. For example, if a student receives full-time benefits for 12 months, the entitlement charge is 12 months. However, if the student receives ½ time benefits for 12 months, the charge is 6 months. VA will pay for less than ½ time training if the student is not receiving Tuition Assistance for those courses.

Remedial, Deficiency and Refresher Training

Remedial and deficiency courses are intended to assist a student in overcoming a deficiency in a particular area of study. In order for such courses to be approved, the courses must be deemed necessary for pursuit of a program of education.

Refresher training is for technological advances that occurred in a field of employment. The advance must have occurred while the student was on active duty or after release. There is an entitlement charge for these courses.

Tutorial Training

Students may receive a special allowance for individual tutoring if they entered school at one-half time or more. To qualify, the student must have a deficiency in a subject. The school must certify the tutor's qualifications and the hours of tutoring. Eligible students may receive a maximum monthly payment of $100.00. The maximum total benefit payable is $1,200.00. There is no entitlement charge for the first

279

$600.00 of tutorial assistance.

To apply for tutorial assistance, students must submit "VA Form 22-1990t", Application and Enrollment Certification for Individualized Tutorial Assistance. The form should be given to the certifying official in the office handling VA paperwork at the school for completion.

Months of Benefits/Entitlement Charged

Eligible members may be entitled to receive up to 36 months of VEAP benefits. Usually, the number of monthly payments for full- time training is the same as the number of months an individual contributed to VEAP.

Benefits are generally payable for 10 years following a veteran's release from active duty. Individuals qualifying for more than one VA education program may receive a maximum of 48 months of benefits. For example, if a student used 30 months of Dependents' Educational Assistance, and is eligible for chapter 1606 benefits, he or she could have a maximum of 18 months of entitlement remaining.

Individuals are charged one full day of entitlement for each day of full-time benefits paid. For correspondence and flight training, one month of entitlement is charged each time VA pays one month of benefits. For cooperative programs, one month of entitlement is used for each month of benefits paid.

For apprenticeship and job training programs, the entitlement charge changes every 6 months. During the first 6 months, the charge is 75% of full time. For the second 6 months, the charge is 55% of full time. For the remainder of the program, the charge is 35% of full time.

Rates of Educational Assistance Pay

The total dollar amount of VEAP benefits is:

An individual's total contributions, plus

Matching funds equal to 2 times the individual's contributions, plus

Any additional contributions or kickers made by the Department of Defense

The amount of money an individual receives each month depends on the type of training and the training time.

Institutional Training

The monthly benefit payment will vary depending on the amount and number of contributions. Divide the total contributions by the number of months contributed, and this equals the full-time institutional rate.

Example: Step 1:

$1,800 individual contributions

+3,600 matching funds (2 times individual contribution)

+ -0- kicker

$5,400 TOTAL ENTITLEMENT

Step 2:

$5,400 divided by 36 months of contributions = $150 monthly full-time institutional rate (No amount in excess of an individual's total entitlement can be paid.)

Correspondence Training

An individual can be reimbursed for the entire established charges paid for a correspondence course. However, no amount in excess of an individual's total entitlement can be paid.

Flight Training

Individuals taking flight training will receive 60% of the approved charges for the course, including solo hours. (VA does not pay for solo hours before October 1, 1992.) No amount in excess of an individual's total entitlement can be paid.

Apprenticeship or On-the-Job Training

The monthly benefit amount is:

- 75% of the full-time rate for the first 6 months of training;
- 55% of the full-time rate for the second 6 months of training;
- 35% of the full-time rate for the rest of the training.

Monthly payments are reduced if an individual works less than 120 hours a month.

Cooperative Training

Individuals may receive payment at 80% of the rate to which he or she is entitled for institutional training.

Eligibility Periods

Benefits end 10 years from the date of the individual's last discharge or release from active duty. VA can extend the 10-year period by the amount of time a service member was prevented from training during the period due to a disability or being held by a foreign government or power.

VA may extend the 10-year period if the individual reenters active duty for 90 days or more after becoming eligible. The extension ends 10 years from the date of discharge or release from the later period. Periods of active duty of less than 90 days can qualify for extensions only if discharge or release was due to:

A service-connected disability; or
A medical condition existing before active duty; or Hardship; or
A reduction in force.

If a discharge is upgraded by the military, the 10-year period begins on the date of the upgrade.

Misc. Information

Any change in educational, professional or vocational objectives is considered a "change of program." The law permits one change of program without prior VA approval, provided an individual's attendance, conduct and progress in the last program were satisfactory. Additional "changes of program" require prior VA approval. VA will not charge a change of program if the individual enrolls in a new program after successful completion of the immediately preceding program.

Once an individual starts receiving benefits, he must maintain satisfactory attendance, conduct and progress. The VA may stop benefits if an individual does not meet the standards set by the school. VA may later resume benefits if the individual reenters the same program at the same school, and the school approves the reentry, and certifies it to VA.

If the individual does not reenter the same program at the same school, VA may resume benefits if the cause of unsatisfactory attendance, conduct or progress has been removed; and the program that the student intends to pursue is suitable to his or her abilities, aptitudes and interests.

Application for Benefits

When the individual finds a school, program, company, apprenticeship or job-training program, there are two important steps that must be followed:

- Make sure the program is approved for VA training. Contact the local VA regional office if there are any questions.
- Compete "VA Form 22-1990", "Application for Education Benefits." The completed form should be sent to the VA regional office with jurisdiction over the State where training will occur. (See the following section for Areas of VA jurisdiction.) Individuals not on active duty should send copy 4 of Form DD-214 along with the completed "VA Form 22-1990."

Following receipt of an application, VA will review it and advise if anything else is needed. If an individual has started training, the application and Notice of Basic Eligibility should be taken to the school, employer or union. The certifying official should complete "VA Form 22-1999," Enrollment Certification, and send all the forms to VA.

Areas of VA Jurisdiction

Eastern VA Regional Office
PO Box 4616
Buffalo, NY
14240-4616

Connecticut

Delaware

District of Columbia

Maine

Maryland

Massachusetts

New Hampshire
New Jersey
New York
Ohio
Pennsylvania
Rhode Island
Vermont
Virginia
West Virginia
Foreign Schools

Southern VA Regional Office
PO Box 100022
Decatur, GA 30031-7022

Alabama
Florida
Georgia
Mississippi
North Carolina
Puerto Rico
South Carolina
Virgin Islands

Western VA Regional Office
PO Box 8888
Muskogee, OK 74402-8888

Alaska
Arizona
Arkansas
California
Hawaii
Idaho
Louisiana
New Mexico
Nevada
Oklahoma
Oregon
Philippines
Texas
Utah
Washington

American Samoa
Guam
Midway Wake Island
Any of the islands in the Federated States of the Marshall Islands,
the Republic of Micronesia, or the Republic of Palau

Central VA Regional Office
PO Box 66830
St. Louis, MO 63166-6830

Colorado
Illinois
Indiana
Iowa
Kansas
Kentucky
Michigan
Minnesota
Missouri
Montana
Nebraska
North Dakota
South Dakota
Tennessee
Wisconsin
Wyoming

Procedures for Receipt of Monthly Payments

After selecting a school and submitting an application to VA, the school official must complete an enrollment certification and submit it to the appropriate VA regional office. If a student meets the basic eligibility requirements for benefits, and the program or course is approved, VA will process the enrollment based on certified training time.

If a student is enrolled in a degree program at a college or university, he or she will receive payment after the first of each month for the training during the preceding month. If a student is enrolled in a certificate or diploma program at a business, technical, or vocational school, he or she will not receive payment until they have verified their attendance. Students will receive a "Student Verification of Enrollment Form 22-8979" each month and must complete and return it to the appropriate VA regional office. After processing, VA will release a check.

If an individual is in an apprenticeship or job-training program, he or she will receive a form to report the hours worked each month. The form must be signed and given to the certifying official for the company or union. The certifying official must complete

284

the form and send it to the appropriate VA regional office. After processing, VA will release a check.

If an individual is taking a correspondence course, he or she will receive a form each quarter, on which the student must show the number of lessons completed that quarter. The completed form should be sent to the school for certification of the number of lessons serviced during the quarter. The school will send the form to the appropriate VA regional office. After processing, VA will release a check. Payments are based on the number of lessons serviced by the school.

VA will send flight schools a supply of blank monthly certification of flight training forms. The school must complete the form by entering the number of hours, the hourly rate, and the total charges for flight training received during the month. The student should review and sign the completed form, and send it to the appropriate VA regional office. After processing, VA will release a check.

NOTE: It is against the law for schools to cash VA checks under a Power of Attorney Agreement.

Timely Receipt of Verification Forms and Checks

Once a completed verification form has been submitted, the student should receive a check within 2 weeks. If a check is not received by then, the VA should immediately be contacted so that appropriate action can be taken.

Students taking courses leading to a degree at a college or university should receive their checks for each month by the fifth of the next month. If it is not received by then, the VA should be immediately contacted so that appropriate action can be taken.

Students taking courses leading to a certificate or diploma from a business, technical, or vocational school should receive their verification forms for each month by the fifth of the following month. If it is not received by then, the VA should be immediately contacted so that another form can be issued.

Advance Payments

An advance payment for the initial month, or partial month and the following month may be made, if:

- The school agrees to handle advance payments; and
- Training is one-half time or more; and
- A request is made by the individual in writing; and
- The VA receives the enrollment certification at least 30 days prior to the start of classes.

Advance payments are made out to the individual and sent to the applicable school for delivery to the individual registration. VA cannot issue a check more than 30 days before classes start. Before requesting an advance payment, students should verify with the school certifying official that the school has agreed to process advance

285

payments.

Requests for advance payments must be on "VA Form 22-1999," Enrollment Certification, or a sheet of paper attached to the enrollment certification.

Once a student receives an advance payment at registration, the school must certify to VA that the student received the check. If a student reduces enrollment, or withdraws from all courses during the period covered by an advance payment, he or she must repay the overpayment to VA.
If an individual believes that the amount of a VA check is incorrect, the VA should be contacted before the check is cashed.

Direct Deposit

Payments can be sent directly to a student's savings or checking account through Direct Deposit (Electronic Funds Transfer). To sign up for direct deposit by phone, students must call (877) 838-2778.

Student Responsibilities

To ensure timely receipt of correct payments, students should be sure to promptly notify the VA of:
Any change in enrollment
Any change in address

In addition, students should use reasonable judgment when accepting and cashing a check. All letters from VA about monthly rates and effective dates should be read carefully. If a student thinks the amount of a VA check is wrong, VA should be contacted before cashing the check. Any incorrect checks should be returned to VA.

If a student cashes a check for the wrong amount, he or she will be liable for repayment of any resulting overpayment.

Recovery of Overpayments

VA must take prompt and aggressive action to recover overpayments. Students have the right to request a waiver of the overpayment, or verification that the amount is correct. If an overpayment is not repaid or waived, VA may add interest and collection fees to the debt. VA may also take one or more of the following actions to collect the debt:
Withhold future benefits to apply to the debt;
Refer the debt to a private collection agency;
Recover the debt from any Federal income tax refund;
Recover the debt from the salary (if student is a Federal employee);
File a lawsuit in Federal court to collect the debt;
Withhold approval of a VA home loan guarantee.

An individual's reserve component will act to collect penalties caused by unsatisfactory participation in the reserve.

Changes in Enrollment

If a student withdraws from one or more courses after the end of the school's drop period, VA will reduce or stop benefits on the date of reduction or withdrawal. Unless the student can show that the change was due to mitigating circumstances, the student may have to repay **all** benefits for the course.

VA defines mitigating circumstances as "unavoidable and unexpected events that directly interfere with the pursuit of a course, and which are beyond the student's control.

Examples of reasons VA **may accept include:**
- Extended illness;
- Severe illness or death in immediate family;
- Unscheduled changes in employment; and
- Lack of child care.

Examples of reasons VA **may not accept include:**
- Withdrawal to avoid a failing grade;
- Dislike of the instructor; and
- Too many courses attempted.

VA may ask the student to furnish evidence to support the reason for change, such as physician or employer written statements.

The first time a student withdraws from up to 6 credit hours, VA will "excuse" the withdrawal, and pay benefits for the period attended.

If a student receives a grade that does not count toward graduation, all benefits for the course may have to be repaid.

If a student receives a non-punitive grade, the school will notify VA, and VA may reduce or stop benefits. The student may not have to repay the benefits if he or she can show that the grades were due to mitigating circumstances.

Work-Study Programs

Students may be eligible for an additional allowance under a work-study program that allows students to perform work for VA in return for an hourly wage. Students may perform outreach services under VA supervision, prepare and process VA paperwork, work at a VA medical facility or National Cemetery, or perform other approved activities.

Students must attend school at the three-quarter of full-time rate.

VA will select students for the work-study program based on different factors. Such factors include:

- Disability of the student;
- Ability of the student to complete the work-study contract before the end of his or her eligibility for education benefits;
- Job availability within normal commuting distance to the student.

VA will give the highest priority to a veteran who has a service-connected disability or disabilities rated by VA at 30% or more.

The number of applicants selected will depend on the availability of VA-related work at the school or at VA facilities in the area. Students may work during or between periods of enrollment, and can arrange with VA to work any number of hours during his or her enrollment. However, the maximum number of hours a student may work is 25 times the number of weeks in the enrollment period.

Students will earn an hourly wage equal to the Federal or State minimum wage, whichever is greater. If a student works at a college or university, the school may pay the difference between the amount VA pays and the amount the school normally pays other work-study students doing the same job.

Students interested in taking part in a work-study program must complete VA Form 228691, "Application for Work-Study Allowance." Completed forms should be sent to the nearest VA regional office.

Educational Counseling

VA can provide services to help eligible individuals understand their educational and vocational strengths and weaknesses and to plan:

- An educational or training goal, and the means by which the goal can be reached; or
- An employment goal for which an individual qualifies on the basis of present training or experience.

VA can also help plan an effective job search. Counseling is available for:

- Service members eligible for VA educational assistance; or
- Service members on active duty and within 180 days of discharge; or
- Veterans with discharges that are not dishonorable, who are within one year from date of discharge.

Vocational Rehabilitation

Vocational rehabilitation helps disabled veterans become independent in daily living. Veterans may also receive assistance in selecting, preparing for, and securing employment that is compatible with their interests, talents, skills, physical capabilities, and goals.

Veterans may qualify for Training and Rehabilitation if:

- The veteran has a service- connected disability or disabilities rated by VA at 20% or more; and

- The veteran received a discharge from active duty that was not dishonorable; and
- The veteran has an employment handicap.

Veterans may also qualify with a service-connected disability or disabilities rated by VA at 10%, and:

- The veteran has a serious employment handicap; or
- The veteran first applied for vocational rehabilitation benefits before November 1, 1990, reapplied after that date, and has an employment handicap.
- To apply for vocational rehabilitation, VA form 28-1900, Disabled Veterans

Application for Vocational Rehabilitation, must be completed and sent to the nearest VA regional office.

Refund of VEAP Payments

If a service member does not wish to use his or her VEAP benefits, he or she must apply to the nearest VA regional office for a refund of his or her contributions.

Appeal of VA Decision

VA decisions on education benefits may be appealed within one year of the date an individual receives notice of a VA decision.

Educational and Assistance Test Program (Section 901)

This program was included as part of the Department of Defense Authorization Act of 1981. The test program is funded by the Department of Defense and administered by the VA. "Section 901" has been used to identify the program since its inception. However, the title "chapter 107" may also be used.

Section 901 is a noncontributory program in which an eligible participant, or in some cases his or her dependent(s), may receive an educational assistance and subsistence allowance while training at an accredited institution.

Basic eligibility to section 901 benefits was limited to a small group of servicepersons who enlisted between September 30, 1980 and October 1, 1981, met strict guidelines and were selected by the Department of Defense. The Waco Regional Office processes all section 901 payments.

Beginning August 1, 2011, break (or interval pay) was no longer be payable under the Educational Assistance Test Program except during periods your school is closed as a result of an Executive Order of the President or an emergency (such as a natural disaster or strike). For example, if your Fall term ends on December 15th and your Spring term begins January 10th, your January housing allowance will cover 15 days in December and your February housing allowance will cover 21 days in January.

Survivors and Dependents Educational Assistance Program (DEA)

The Survivors' and Dependents Educational Assistance Program (DEA) was enacted by Congress to provide education and training opportunities to eligible dependents of certain veterans. The program offers up to 45 months of education benefits.

Eligibility Requirements

To qualify, one must be the son, daughter or spouse of:

- A veteran who died, or is permanently and totally disabled as the result of a service-connected disability, which arose out of active service in the Armed Forces.
- A veteran who died from any cause while such service-connected disability was in existence.
- A service member who is missing in action or captured in the line of duty by a hostile force.
- A service member who is being forcibly detained or interned in the line of duty by a foreign power.
- A service member who is hospitalized or receiving outpatient treatment for a service-connected permanent and total disability and is likely to be discharged for that disability. This change became effective December 23, 2006.

Eligibility Period: Son or Daughter

As a son or daughter (including stepchild or adopted child), as long as the individual has entitlement left, he or she may generally receive benefits under this program from age 18 to 26 (8 years). However, in certain instances, benefits may begin before age 18 and continue after age 26. In some instances, the individual may choose among possible beginning dates.

Effect of Active Duty on Eligibility

Following are the effects of active duty on an individual's period of eligibility. (See also Effect of Active Duty on Entitlement.)

Individuals may not receive DEA benefits while on active duty in the Armed Forces. To receive DEA benefits after military service, discharge must not be under dishonorable conditions.

The eligibility period can generally extend for eight years from the date of the individual's first unconditional release from active duty, if his or her service was between ages 18 and 26. But this extension can't go beyond the individual's 31st birthday.

If, on or after September 11, 2001, an individual is called to active duty under title 10, or if he or she was involuntarily ordered to full-time National Guard duty under section 502 (f) of title 32 (State authority), in most cases VA can extend the eligibility period for

DEA by the number of months and days spent on active duty plus four months. This extension may go beyond the 31st birthday, depending on the facts in the claim.

Other Extensions of the Eligibility Period

Circumstances Beyond an Individual's Control
If evidence is provided that training had to stop because of conditions beyond an individual's control, in some cases VA can extend eligibility for the period he or she had to stop training.

Circumstances that may be considered beyond control (if verified by evidence) include:
- Service in an official missionary capacity;
- Immediate family or financial obligations that require the individual to stop training, for example, to take employment;
- Unavoidable conditions of employment that require the individual to stop training;
- The individual's illness or death; or illness in his or her immediate family.

In Training When Eligibility Ends
If an individual is enrolled in training when eligibility ends, in most cases VA can extend his or her eligibility to the end of the semester or quarter, or to the end of twelve weeks if the course isn't operated on a semester or quarter basis.

Marriage
As a son or daughter, marriage doesn't affect the period of eligibility.

Eligibility Period: Spouse
If a spouse is eligible because the veteran has a permanent and total service-connected disability, benefits generally end 10 years from one of the following dates:
- Effective date of the veteran's permanent and total disability evaluation;
- Date VA notifies the veteran of the permanent and total disability evaluation;
- Beginning date chosen by the spouse, between the date the spouse become eligible and the date VA notifies the veteran of the permanent and total disability evaluation.
- If the VA rated the veteran permanently and totally disabled with an effective date of 3 years from discharge a spouse will remain eligible for 20 years from the effective date of the rating. This change is effective October 10, 2008 and no benefits may be paid for any training taken prior to that date.

Service Member Held Captive or Missing
If a spouse is eligible because the veteran or service member is being held or is missing, as:
- A prisoner of war;
- Missing in action; or
- Forcibly held by a foreign government or power;

291

His or her 10-year period of eligibility begins on the 91st day after the date the service member was listed as a captive or missing.

If the veteran or service member is released from captivity, or is determined to be alive and no longer missing, the spouse's period of eligibility ends on that date. If the spouse is enrolled in training on that date, his or her eligibility may be extended to the end of the term or course.

Veteran Died on Active Duty
If a spouse is eligible because the veteran died on active duty, his or her eligibility period is 20 years from the date of death.

Effect of Active Duty on Eligibility
Following are the effects of active duty on the eligibility period:

- Individuals may not receive DEA benefits while on active duty in the Armed Forces.
- To receive DEA benefits after military service, his or her discharge must not be under dishonorable conditions.
- If, on or after September 11, 2001, the individual was called to active duty under title 10, or involuntarily ordered to full-time National Guard duty under section 502 (f) of title 32 (State authority), in most cases VA can extend the eligibility period for DEA by the number of months and days spent on active duty plus four months.

Effect of Divorce on Eligibility
If marriage to the veteran ends in divorce, the spouse's eligibility for DEA benefits ends on that date. But if he or she is in training, and the divorce occurs through no fault of him or her, VA can extend the eligibility as detailed in the following section "Extensions of Eligibility Period."

Extension of Eligibility Period

Disability
VA may be able to extend the 10-year eligibility period by the amount of time the spouse was prevented from training during that period because of a disability he or she incurred. WHILE IN TRAINING

If the spouse is enrolled in training when his or her eligibility ends, in most cases VA can extend eligibility to the end of the semester or quarter, or to the end of twelve weeks if the course isn't operated on a semester or quarter basis.

Effect of Remarriage

Before age 57:
- If a surviving spouse remarries before age 57, his or her eligibility ends on the date of remarriage.
- If an individual remarried after November 30, 1999, and the remarriage ends, VA may reinstate eligibility to DEA. The remarriage must be ended by death, divorce, or because the individual stopped living with his or her spouse and stopped holding him or herself out to the public as the person's spouse.
- If a surviving spouse remarried after October 31, 1990, but before November 30, 1999, VA can't reinstate eligibility, even if remarriage ends.

After age 57:
- If a surviving spouse remarries on or after January 1, 2004, and is 57 or older, he or she can still be eligible for DEA benefits. (If the surviving spouse remarried after age 57 and before December 16, 2003, **he or she must have applied in writing before December 16, 2004,** for eligibility to be reinstated.)

Note: Remarrying after age 57 doesn't extend the 10-year period of eligibility that was established before remarriage.

Example: A surviving spouse established eligibility for a 10-year period ending on November 15, 2005, which is 10 years from the date of the veteran's death. She remarried in April 2004 at age 58. She will keep her eligibility for DEA through November 15, 2005.

Months of Benefits Payable

The following applies to sons and daughters (including stepchildren and adopted children), spouses and surviving spouses.

Individuals may be entitled to receive up to 45 months of DEA benefits. They may receive a maximum of 48 months of benefits combined if they are eligible under more than one VA education program.

Individuals are charged one full day for each day of full-time benefits paid. Entitlement is charged in months and days. Each month is counted as 30 days. If he or she trains part-time, VA adjusts the entitlement charge according to the training time

Effect of Active Duty on Available Months of Benefits Payable
If an individual is called up to active duty under title 10 (federal authority) while he or she is receiving benefits, and has to drop out of school without receiving credit, VA will restore (give back) the months of benefits used for that period of training.

If called up under title 32 (State authority), VA can't restore the months of benefits used.

Pension, Compensation and DIC Programs

A son or daughter who is eligible for Chapter 35 benefits, as well as pension, compensation, or Dependency & Indemnity Compensation (DIC) based on school attendance, must elect which benefit to receive. An election of Chapter 35 benefits is a bar to further payment of pension, compensation, or DIC after the age of 18.

NOTE: If a program will last longer than 45 months, the son or daughter may find it to his or her advantage to defer Chapter 35 benefits. He or she could continue to receive pension, compensation, or DIC benefits which are payable as a result of school attendance. The VA strongly encourages individuals who qualify for more than one type of education benefit to discuss their education plans with a Veterans Benefits Counselor so that all options can be explored, and maximum benefits can be paid.

Approved Courses

A State agency or VA must approve each program offered by a school or company. Individuals may receive benefits for a wide variety of training, including:

- Undergraduate degrees from a college or university
- Graduate degrees from a college or university
- Cooperative training programs
- Accredited independent study programs leading to a college degree
- Courses leading to a certificate or diploma from business, technical, or vocational schools
- Apprenticeship or job training program offered by a company or union
- Correspondence courses (spouses only)
- Farm cooperative courses
- Secondary school programs for individuals who are not high school graduates
- Secondary school deficiency or remedial courses to qualify for admission to an educational institution
- Effective November 1, 2000, persons eligible for DEA became able to receive benefits for VA-approved preparation courses for college and graduate school entrance exams. (The law also allows children to pursue these courses before age 18.)
- Effective March 1, 2001, benefits became payable for licensing or certification tests. The tests are those needed to enter, maintain, or advance into employment in a civilian vocation or profession. The eligible veteran or family member may receive payment of the fee charged for the test or $2,000, whichever is less. The tests must be approved for VA benefits. Contact the VA for a complete list of approved certification tests.

VA may approve programs offered by institutions outside of the United States, when they are pursued at educational institutions of higher learning, and lead to a college degree. Individuals must receive VA approval prior to attending or enrolling in any foreign programs.

An eligible son or daughter who is handicapped by a physical or mental disability that prevents pursuit of an educational program may receive Special Restorative Training. This may involve speech and voice correction, language retraining, lip reading, auditory training, Braille reading and writing, etc.

An eligible spouse or son or daughter over age 14 who is handicapped by a physical or mental disability that prevents pursuit of an educational program may receive Specialized Vocational Training. This includes specialized courses, alone or in combination with other courses, leading to a vocational objective that is suitable for the person and required by reason of physical or mental handicap.

If an individual is seeking a college degree, the school must admit the individual to a degree program by the start of the individual's third term.

Restrictions on Training
Benefits are not payable for the following courses:
- Non-accredited independent study courses
- Bartending and personality development courses
- Correspondence courses (if you are a dependent or surviving child)
- Any course given by radio
- Vocational flight training
- Self-improvement courses such as reading, speaking, woodworking, basic seamanship, and English as a 2nd language
- Any course which is avocational or recreational in character
- Audited courses
- Courses not leading to an educational, professional, or vocational objective
- Courses previously taken and successfully completed
- Courses taken by a Federal government employee under the Government Employee's Training Act
- Courses taken while in receipt of benefits for the same program from the Office of
  - Workers' Compensation Programs
- VA must reduce benefits for individuals in Federal, State, or local prisons after being convicted of a felony.
- An individual may not receive benefits for a program at a proprietary school if her or she is an owner or official of the school.
- An individual may not receive benefits under this program while serving on active duty in the Armed Forces.

Part-Time Training
Individuals unable to attend school full-time should consider going part-time. Benefit rates and entitlement charges are less than the full-time rates. For example, if a

student receives full-time benefits for 12 months, the entitlement charge is 12 months. However, if the student receives ½ time benefits for 12 months, the charge is 6 months. VA will pay for less than ½ time training if the student is not receiving Tuition Assistance for those courses.

Remedial, Deficiency and Refresher Training

Remedial and deficiency courses are intended to assist a student in overcoming a deficiency in a particular area of study.

Refresher training is available only at the elementary or secondary level. It is for reviewing or updating material previously covered in a course satisfactorily completed. There is no entitlement charge for these courses for the first 5 months of training.

Tutorial Assistance

Students may receive a special allowance for individual tutoring performed after September 30, 1992, if they entered school at one-half time or more. To qualify, the student must have a deficiency in a subject. The school must certify the tutor's qualifications, and the hours of tutoring. Eligible students may receive a maximum monthly payment of $100.00. The maximum total benefit payable is $1,200.00.

There is no entitlement charge for the first $600.00 of tutorial assistance. To apply for tutorial assistance, students must submit VA Form 22-1990t, Application and Enrollment Certification for Individualized Tutorial Assistance. The form should be given to the certifying official in the office handling VA paperwork at the school for completion.

You may receive up to 45 months of education benefits. Effective October 1, 2013, some DEA beneficiaries may be eligible for up to 81 months of GI Bill benefits if they use the Survivors and Dependents Educational Assistance program in conjunction with an entitlement from other VA education programs.

Rates of Educational Assistance

The following basic monthly rates are effective October 1, 2020

Basic Monthly Rates of Survivors and Dependents Educational Assistance Program (DEA)					
Type of Training	Full-Time	Three-Quarter Time	One-Half Time	Less than ½ Time, But More Than ¼ Time	One-Quarter Time
Institutional	$1265.00	$1000.00	$734.00	Tuition & Fees, not to exceed $734.00	Tuition & Fees, not to exceed $316.25
Farm Cooperative Training	$885.00	$666.00	$442.00		
Correspondence Training	55 percent of the established charge for the number of lessons completed by the eligible spouse or surviving spouse and serviced by the school -- Allowance paid quarterly.				
Apprenticeship On-The-Job Training -	First six months: $804.00 Second six months: $604.00 Third six months: $397.00 Remainder of program: $202.00				
Special Restorative Training:	$1265.00				
Accelerated Charges: Cost of Tuition & Fees in Excess of:	$333.00				
Entitlement Reduced 1 Day for Each	$42.17 (1/30th of Full-Time Rate)				

Change of Program

Any change in educational, professional or vocational objectives is considered a "change of program." VA will not charge a change of program when a student enrolls in a new program, provided he or she successfully completed the immediately preceding program.

Spouse, Widower or Widow of Veteran

A spouse, widow, or widower of a veteran may make one change of program without prior VA approval if attendance, conduct, and progress in the last program were satisfactory. VA may approve additional changes if the proposed programs are suitable to the student's abilities, aptitudes, and interests.

Child of Veteran

VA may approve a change of program for sons or daughters if it finds that the new program is suitable to the student's abilities, aptitudes, and interests.

Attendance, Conduct and Progress

Once an individual start receiving benefits, he must maintain satisfactory attendance, conduct and progress. The VA may stop benefits if an individual does not meet the standards set by the school. VA may later resume benefits if the individual reenters the same program at the same school, and the school approves the reentry, and certifies it to VA.

If the individual does not reenter the same program at the same school, VA may resume benefits if the cause of unsatisfactory attendance, conduct or progress has been removed; and the program that the student intends to pursue is suitable to his or her abilities, aptitudes and interests.

Application for Benefits

When the individual finds a school, company or apprenticeship, there are two important steps that must be followed:

- Make sure the program is approved for VA training. Contact the local VA regional office if there are any questions.
- Complete VA Form 22-5490, "Application for Survivors' and Dependents' Educational Assistance." The completed form should be sent to the VA regional office with jurisdiction over the State where training will occur. Sons or daughters under legal age must have the application signed by a parent or guardian. Sons or daughters of age can apply alone.
- Following receipt of an application, VA will review it and advise if anything else is needed.

If an individual has started training, the application and Notice of Basic Eligibility should be taken to the school, employer or union. The certifying official should complete VA Form 22-1999, "Enrollment Certification," and send all the forms to VA.

Procedures for Receipt of Monthly Payments

After selecting a school and submitting an application to VA, the school official must complete an enrollment certification, and submit it to the appropriate VA regional office. If a student meets the basic eligibility requirements for benefits, and the program or course is approved, VA will process the enrollment based on certified training time.

If a student is enrolled in a degree program at a college or university, he or she will receive payment after the first of each month for the training during the preceding month. If a student is enrolled in a certificate or diploma program at a business, technical, or vocational school, he or she will not receive payment until they have verified their attendance. Students will receive a "Student Verification of Enrollment Form 22-8979" each month and must complete and return it to the appropriate VA regional office. After processing, VA will release a check.

If an individual is in an apprenticeship or job-training program, he or she will receive a form to report the hours worked each month. The form must be signed and given to the certifying official for the company or union. The certifying official must complete the form and send it to the appropriate VA regional office. After processing, VA will release a check.

If an individual is taking a correspondence course, he or she will receive a form each quarter, on which the student must show the number of lessons completed that quarter. The completed form should be sent to the school for certification of the number of lessons serviced during the quarter. The school will send the form to the appropriate VA regional office. After processing, VA will release a check. Payments are based on the number of lessons serviced by the school.

NOTE: It is against the law for schools to cash VA checks under a Power of Attorney Agreement.

Timely Receipt of Verification Forms and Checks

Students taking courses leading to a degree at a college or university should receive their checks for each month by the fifth of the next month. If it is not received by then, the VA should be immediately contacted so that appropriate action can be taken.

Students taking courses leading to a certificate or diploma from a business, technical, or vocational school should receive their verification forms for each month by the fifth of the following month. If it is not received by then, the VA should be immediately contacted so that another form can be issued.

One a completed verification form has been submitted, the student should receive a check within 2 weeks. If a check is not received by then, the VA should immediately be contacted so that appropriate action can be taken.

Advance Payments

An advance payment for the initial month, or partial month and the following month may be made, if:

- The school agrees to handle advance payments; and Training is one-half time or more; and
- A request is made by the individual in writing; and
- The VA receives the enrollment certification at least 30 days prior to the start of classes.

Advance payments are made out to the individual, and sent to the applicable school for delivery to the individual registration. VA cannot issue a check more than 30 days before classes start. Before requesting an advance payment, students should verify with the school certifying official that the school has agreed to process advance payments.

Requests for advance payments must be on VA Form 22-1999, "Enrollment Certification," or a sheet of paper attached to the enrollment certification.

Once a student receives an advance payment at registration, the school must certify to VA that the student received the check. If a student reduces enrollment, or withdraws from all courses during the period covered by an advance payment, he or she must repay the overpayment to VA.

If an individual believes that the amount of a VA check is incorrect, the VA should be contacted before the check is cashed.

Direct Deposit

Payments can be sent directly to a student's savings or checking account through Direct Deposit (Electronic Funds Transfer). To sign up for direct deposit by phone, students must call (877) 838-2778.

Student Responsibilities

To ensure timely receipt of correct payments, students should be sure to promptly notify the VA of:

- Any change in enrollment;
- Any change in address;
- Any change in marital status (separation from the veteran, divorce from the veteran, or remarriage following the death of the veteran).

In addition, students should use reasonable judgment when accepting and cashing a check. All letters from VA about monthly rates and effective dates should be read carefully. If a student thinks the amount of a VA check is wrong, VA should be contacted **before** cashing the check. Any incorrect checks should be returned to VA.

If a student cashes a check for the wrong amount, he or she will be liable for repayment of any resulting overpayment.

Recovery of Overpayments

VA must take prompt and aggressive action to recover overpayments. Students have the right to request a waiver of the overpayment, or verification that the amount is correct. If an overpayment is not repaid or waived, VA may add interest and collection fees to the debt. VA may also take one or more of the following actions to collect the debt:

- Withhold future benefits to apply to the debt;
- Refer the debt to a private collection agency;
- Recover the debt from any Federal income tax refund;
- Recover the debt from the salary (if student is a Federal employee);
- File a lawsuit in Federal court to collect the debt;
- Withhold approval of a VA home loan guarantee.

Changes in Enrollment

If a student withdraws from one or more courses after the end of the school's drop period, VA will reduce or stop benefits on the date of reduction or withdrawal. Unless the student can show that the change was due to mitigating circumstances, the student may have to repay **all** benefits for the course. VA defines mitigating circumstances as "unavoidable and unexpected events that directly interfere with the pursuit of a course, and which are beyond the student's control.

Examples of reasons VA may accept include:
- Extended illness;
- Severe illness or death in immediate family;
- Unscheduled changes in employment; and
- Lack of child care.

Examples of reasons VA may not accept include:
- Withdrawal to avoid a failing grade;
- Dislike of the instructor; and
- Too many courses attempted.

(VA may ask the student to furnish evidence to support the reason for change, such as physician or employer written statements.) The first time a student withdraws from up to 6 credit hours, VA will "excuse" the withdrawal, and pay benefits for the period attended.

If a student receives a grade that does not count toward graduation, all benefits for the course may have to be repaid. If a student receives a non-punitive grade, the school will notify VA, and VA may reduce or stop benefits. The student may not have to repay the benefits if he or she can show that the grades were due to mitigating circumstances.

Work-Study Programs

Students may be eligible for an additional allowance under a work-study program that allows students to perform work for VA in return for an hourly wage. Students may perform outreach services under VA supervision, prepare and process VA paperwork, work at a VA medical facility or National Cemetery, or perform other approved activities.

Students must attend school at the three-quarter of full-time rate. VA will select students for the work-study program based on different factors. Such factors include:
- Disability of the student;
- Ability of the student to complete the work-study contract before the end of his or her eligibility for education benefits;
- Job availability within normal commuting distance to the student;
- VA will give the highest priority to a veteran who has a service-connected disability or disabilities rated by VA at 30% or more.

The number of applicants selected will depend on the availability of VA-related work at the school or at VA facilities in the area. Students may work during or between periods of enrollment, and can arrange with VA to work any number of hours during his or her enrollment. However, the maximum number of hours a student may work is 25 times the number of weeks in the enrollment period.

Students will earn an hourly wage equal to the Federal or State minimum wage, whichever is greater. If a student works at a college or university, the school **may** pay the difference between the amount VA pays and the amount the school normally pays other work-study students doing the same job.

Students interested in taking part in a work-study program must complete VA Form 22,8691, "Application for Work-Study Allowance." Completed forms should be sent to the nearest VA regional office.

Educational Counseling

Upon request, VA will provide counseling services, including testing, to help qualified individuals:

- Select an educational, vocational, or professional objective;
- Develop a plan to achieve the above objective;
- Overcome any personal or academic problems that may interfere with the successful achievement of the stated objective.
- Qualified VA personnel are available to provide counseling services free of charge
- to qualified individuals. Individuals must pay the cost of any travel to and from the place at which VA provides counseling.

VA requires and provides counseling for each disabled child who needs special services to pursue a program of education and for certain other eligible children. VA requires and provides counseling for disabled spouses and those who need specialized programs of vocational training as a result of the handicapping effects of their disabilities. Individuals should contact the nearest VA regional office to make counseling appointments.

Appeal of VA Decision

VA decisions on education benefits may be appealed within one year of the date an individual receives notice of a VA decision.

Restored Entitlement Program for Survivors (REPS)

The Restored Entitlement Program for Survivors (REPS) is authorized by Section 156 of Public Law 97-377. This program restores social security benefits that were reduced or terminated by Public Law 97-35, the Omnibus Budget Reconciliation Act of 1981. This act eliminated the "parent with child in care" benefit when a surviving spouse's last child in care attained age 16. REPS restores the benefit until the youngest child in care attains 18, unless entitled to another Social Security benefit of equal or greater value. The REPS program is funded by the Department of Defense, based on Social Security rules, and administered by the VA.

REPS benefits are payable to certain spouses and children of veterans who died while on active duty before August 13, 1981 or died from disabilities incurred in active duty before August 13, 1981. If a surviving spouse remarries, his or her benefits are terminated. If the child in care leaves the parent's custody, marries or dies, REPS entitlement ends. REPS benefits are reduced by $1 for each $2 of earned income over the exempt amount for Social Security (announced by Social Security Administration at the beginning of each calendar year).

REPS benefits are payable to unmarried children between the ages of 18 and 22 who are full-time students at approved schools beyond the high school level. Benefits are awarded on a school year basis. Each year verification must be received before any additional benefits can be awarded. If the child marries or reduces to less than full-time attendance, benefits will be discontinued. If the child has earned income or wages, REPS benefits are reduced. REPS benefits are not payable based on service in the commissioned corps of the National Oceanic and Atmospheric Administration, or the Public Health Service.

To apply for REPS benefits, VA Form 21-8924, "Application of Surviving Spouse or Child for REPS Benefits" must be completed and sent to the local VA regional VA office for basic eligibility determination.

Once completed, the application will be forwarded to the St. Louis office for processing. A Student Beneficiary Report is mailed to each student receiving REPS benefits each March. The report confirms enrollment, and allows students to report any earnings. For specific information, contact the nearest regional VA office.

Omnibus Diplomatic Security and Antiterrorism Act

Public Law 99-399, The Omnibus Diplomatic Security and Antiterrorism Act of 1986 (the Antiterrorism Act) became effective January 21, 1981. This program is designed to provide educational assistance for persons held as captives, and their dependents.

Under this Act, VA may provide education benefits to:
- Former captives who were employees of the United States Government. Individuals providing personal services to the United States similar to that provided by civil service employees may also be eligible. This includes foreign nationals and resident aliens of the United States.
- Former captives taken during hostile action resulting from their relationship with the United States
- Family members of individuals in captivity or individuals who die while in captivity.
- VA will provide educational benefits to persons eligible under the Antiterrorism Act that are identical to those provided to eligible persons under Chapter 35 of title 38, U.S. Code (Survivors' and Dependents' Educational Assistance Program).

All inquiries regarding this Act should be directed to the nearest VA regional office.

CHAPTER 20

EDUCATION BENEFITS – MONTGOMERY G.I. BILL (MGIB), CHAPTER 30

The MGIB-AD Program, also called Chapter 30, is designed to provide education benefits to veterans and servicemembers with at least two years of active duty.

Assistance may be used for anything from college degree and certificate programs.

Benefits are usually payable for 10 years following your release from honorable active service.

The Montgomery G.I. Bill (MGIB) establishes education benefits for four categories of individuals, based on active-duty service. The benefits available under each category may vary depending on individual situations and lengths of active-duty service.

The eligibility requirements for each category are described below. However, the following two requirements must be met by all individuals, no matter which category his or her eligibility falls under.

Character of Discharge

To use MGIB after an individual is separated from active duty, an individual's discharge must be fully honorable. Discharges "under honorable conditions" and "general" discharges don't establish eligibility for MGIB.

Completed High School:

To use MGIB as an active-duty member, or after separation from active duty, an individual must obtain a high school diploma or equivalency certificate before applying for benefits.

Completing 12 hours toward a college degree before applying for benefits also meets this requirement. This is a change in eligibility rules that became effective November 1, 2000. If an individual wasn't previously eligible because he or she did not meet the high school requirement, the change provides a second chance.

In addition to the above requirements, individuals must meet requirements from one of the four following categories. (Individuals who entered active duty before July 1, 1985 may only qualify under Categories 2, 3, or 4.)

Category I

- The veteran must have entered active duty for the first time on or after July 1, 1985.
- The veteran must have enrolled in MGIB (didn't decline MGIB in writing upon entry into active duty). Exception: If an individual declined MGIB in writing, he or she may not change this decision at a later date unless:
  - o The individual qualifies under Category 3; or
  - o The individual withdrew his or her election not to participate during the "open period" for withdrawal (December 1, 1988 through June 30, 1989).
- Individuals who graduated from a service academy and received a commission are not eligible. Individuals who became commissioned upon completing an ROTC scholarship program are not eligible, unless one of the following exceptions applies:
  - o The individual received a commission after becoming eligible for MGIB.
  - o The individual received a commission after September 30, 1996, and received less than $3,400 during any one year of his or her ROTC program.
- Individuals who received loan repayment from the military for their education are not eligible. (Note: Individuals who received loan repayment for one period of active duty, may still be eligible based on another period of active duty, as long as they did not decline MGIB when they first entered active duty.
- To use MGIB while on active duty, an individual must serve two continuous years of active duty.

- To use MGIB after separation from active duty, the individual must have served 3 continuous years of active duty, unless discharged early for one of the following reasons:
  - Convenience of the government (veteran must have served 30 months if he had a 3-year obligation)
  - Service-connected disability
  - Hardship
  - A medical condition the individual had before service
  - A condition that interfered with performance of duty
  - Certain reductions in force (RIF)

Exception: To use MGIB after separation from active duty, the individual may only need 2 years of active duty if:

- He or she first enlisted for 2 years of active duty; or
- The individual has an obligation to serve 4 years in the Selected Reserve (the 2 X 4 program). The individual must enter the Selected Reserve within one year of release from active duty; or
- The individual was separated early for one of the following reasons:
- Convenience of the government (veteran must have served 20 months if he had a 2-year obligation)
- Service-connected disability
- Hardship
- A medical condition the individual had before service
- A condition that interfered with performance of duty
- Certain reductions in force (RIF)

Service in the National Guard or Reserve

Service in the National Guard or reserve is qualifying as active duty for MGIB benefits only under the following conditions:

- Full-time National Guard or Reserve service authorized under title 10, U.S. Code (Active Guard/Reserve, or AGR) is considered active duty for purposes of qualifying for VA education benefits, unless the service is active duty for training.
- Full-time National Guard service under title 32, U.S. Code (State authority) is considered active duty for purposes of qualifying for VA education benefits, provided the service was first performed after November 29, 1989 (with no previous active duty); and is for the purpose of organizing, administering, recruiting, instructing, or training the National Guard. Duty for the purpose of performing operations (such as drug interdiction, for example) is not considered active duty for MGIB benefits.

Category II

The veteran had remaining entitlement under the Vietnam Era Veterans' Educational

Assistance Program (chapter 34 of Title 38, U.S. Code) on December 31, 1989; and

- The veteran served on active duty for any number of days during the period October 19, 1984 to June 30, 1985, and then continued active duty without a break from July 1, 1985 through: June 30, 1988, or June 30, 1987, and then served four years in the Selected Reserve after release from active duty. The individual must have entered the Selected Reserve within one year of his or her release from active duty.
- The individual wasn't on active duty on October 19, 1984, but reentered active duty after that date, and served three continuous years on active duty on or after July 1, 1985, or two years on active duty followed by four years in the Selected Reserve on or after July 1, 1985. (This option became effective December 27, 2001.)
- Individuals who graduated from a service academy and received a commission after December 31, 1976 are not eligible.
- Individuals who received a commission after September 30, 1996 upon completing an ROTC scholarship program are not eligible, unless one of the following exceptions applies:
  - the individual received a commission after becoming eligible for MGIB.
  - The individual completed ROTC without a full scholarship.
  - The individual received a commission after September 30, 1996 and received less than $3,400 during any one year of his or her ROTC program.

Category III

A veteran may qualify if:

- The veteran was on active duty on September 30, 1990, and was involuntarily separated after February 2, 1991; or
- The veteran was involuntarily separated on or after November 30, 1993.
- Effective October 23, 1992, the law was expanded to allow the same opportunity to elect MGIB benefits before separation to members voluntarily separated under either the Voluntary Separation Incentive (VSI) or Special Separation Benefit (SSB) program.
- If the member was eligible for the Post Vietnam Era Veterans' Educational Assistance Program (VEAP), he must elect to receive MGIB benefits, and apply for a refund of contributions to Chapter 32.
- The member must have had his military pay reduced by $1,200 before discharge.
- Members qualifying under Category III based on a voluntary or involuntary separation are not eligible for MGIB benefits until the day following discharge.

(If a veteran eligible under Category 3 had a chapter 32 kicker, VA will pay the basic chapter 30 rate and an additional amount based upon the amount of the remaining kicker.)

Category IV

- Individuals may qualify under Category IV if they were on active duty on October 9, 1996 and were VEAP participants with money in the VEAP fund. These individuals must have elected MGIB, and paid $1,200 by October 9, 1997.
- Individuals may also be eligible if they served on full time active duty in the National Guard between June 10, 1985 and November 29, 1989, and elected to have their National Guard service count toward establishing eligibility for MGIB benefits by July 9, 1997.
- Effective November 1, 2000, VEAP participants, whether they had contributions in their accounts or not, could become eligible for MGIB if they:
  o Made an irrevocable election to receive MGIB; and
  o Were VEAP participants on or before October 9, 1996; and
  o Continuously served on active duty from October 9, 1996 through April 1, 2000; and
  o Made a payment of $2,700. The payment will be made by reducing their basic pay before their discharge from service. If $2,700 is not collected before discharge from pay reductions, veterans must make payments to the military service in the amount needed to bring the total to $2,700. DoD can also collect the additional amount by reducing retired or retainer pay.

(NOTE: This payment, unlike earlier contributions to VEAP is not refundable.)

The payment does not go into the VEAP account, it is deposited into the Treasury of the United States as miscellaneous receipts; and

- Met other VEAP eligibility requirements.
- VEAP participants must have made this election on or before October 31, 2001.

Transferability of GI Bill to Dependents

The transferability option under the Post-9/11 GI Bill allows Servicemembers to transfer all or some unused benefits to their spouse or dependent children. The request to transfer unused GI Bill benefits to eligible dependents must be completed while serving as an active member of the Armed Forces. The Department of Defense (DoD) determines whether or not you can transfer benefits to your family. Once the DoD approves benefits for transfer, the new beneficiaries apply for them at VA. To find out more, visit DoD's website or apply now.

Type of Assistance

Eligible Servicemembers may transfer all 36 months or the portion of unused Post-9/11 GI Bill benefits (unless DoD or the Department of Homeland Security has limited the number of transferable months). If you're eligible, you may transfer benefits to the following individuals:

- Your spouse
- One or more of your children
- Any combination of spouse and child

Available Benefits and Eligibility

Family members must be enrolled in the Defense Eligibility Enrollment Reporting System (DEERS) and be eligible for benefits at the time of transfer to receive transferred benefits.

The option to transfer is open to any member of the armed forces active duty or Selected Reserve, officer or enlisted who is eligible for the Post-9/11 GI Bill, and meets the following criteria:

- Has at least six years of service in the armed forces (active duty and/or Selected Reserve) on the date of approval and agrees to serve four additional years in the armed forces from the date of election.

- Has at least 10 years of service in the armed forces (active duty and/or Selected Reserve) on the date of approval, is precluded by either standard policy (by Service Branch or DoD) or statute from committing to four additional years, and agrees to serve for the maximum amount of time allowed by such policy or statute.

- Transfer requests are submitted and approved while the member is in the armed forces.

- Effective 7/20/19, eligibility to transfer benefits will be limited to sevicemembers with less than 16 years of active duty or selected reserve service.

Transfer Process. While in the armed forces, transferors use the Transfer of Education Benefits (TEB) website to designate, modify, and revoke a Transfer of Entitlement (TOE) request. After leaving the armed forces, transferors may provide a future effective date for use of TOE, modify the number of months transferred, or revoke entitlement transferred by submitting a written request to VA.

Upon approval, family members may apply to use transferred benefits with VA by applying online or by printing, completing, and mailing the VA Form 22-1990e to your VA Regional processing office of jurisdiction. VA Form 22-1990e should only be completed and submitted to VA by the family member after DoD has approved the request for TEB. Do not use VA Form 22-1990e to apply for transfer of education benefits.

Other Factors to Consider

Marriage and Divorce

- A child's subsequent marriage will not affect his or her eligibility to receive the educational benefit; however, after an individual has designated a child as a transferee under this section, the individual retains the right to revoke or modify the transfer at any time.

- A subsequent divorce will not affect the transferees eligibility to receive educational benefits; however, after an individual has designated a spouse as a transferee under this section, the eligible individual retains the right to revoke or modify the transfer at any time.

Reallocation of Benefits

If a Veteran or Servicemember wants to reallocate transferred benefits they can do so using the TEB Portlet in MilConnect.

Reallocation of Benefits if a Family Member Dies

The Harry W. Colmery Veterans Assistance Act of 2017 allows for designation and transfer of Post-9/11 GI Bill benefits to eligible dependents of the Veteran/servicemember upon the death of the Veteran/servicemember or of a dependent who had unused transferred benefits.

Nature of Transfer

Family member use of transferred educational benefits is subject to the following rules:

Spouses

- May start to use the benefit immediately
- May use the benefit while the member remains in the Armed Forces or after separation from active duty
- Are not eligible for the monthly housing allowance while the member is serving on active duty
- If servicemember's last discharge was before January 1, 2013, can use the benefit for up to 15 years after the last separation from active duty. If the servicemember's last discharge is after January 1, 2013, there is no time limit to use benefits

Children

- May start to use the benefit only after the individual making the transfer has completed at least 10 years of service in the armed forces
- May use the benefit while the eligible individual remains in the armed forces or after separation from active duty
- May not use the benefit until he or she has attained a secondary school diploma (or equivalency certificate), or he or she has reached age 18
- Is entitled to the monthly housing allowance stipend even though the eligible individual is on active duty
- Is not subject to the 15-year delimiting date, but may not use the benefit after reaching 26 years of age

Discharges and Separations

As previously mentioned, if the veteran is separated from active duty, the character of discharge must specifically be listed as "Honorable." "Under Honorable Conditions," or a "General" discharge do not establish eligibility. A discharge for one of the following reasons may result in a reduction of the required length of active duty to qualify for benefits under the MGIB:

- Convenience of the Government; or
- Disability; or
- Hardship; or
- Medical conditions existing before entry into Service; or
- Force reductions; or
- Medical condition which is not a disability due to misconduct, but which prevents satisfactory performance of duty.

The following types of active duty do not establish eligibility for MGIB benefits:

- Time assigned by the military to a civilian institution to take the same course provided to civilians.
- Time served as a cadet or a midshipman at a service academy.
- Time spent on active duty for training in the National Guard or Reserve.

Please note: Time assigned by the military to a civilian institution, and time served at a service academy does not break the continuity of active duty required to establish eligibility for MGIB benefits. Active duty for training does count toward the four years in the Selected Reserve under the 2 by 4 program.

Approved Courses

This program provides veterans up to 36 months of education benefits. The benefits may be used for:

- Undergraduate or graduate degrees from a college or university;
- Cooperative training programs;
- Accredited independent study programs leading to standard college degrees;
- Courses leading to certificates or diplomas from business, technical or vocational schools;
- Vocational flight training (from September 30, 1990 only – Individuals must have a private pilot's license and meet the medical requirements for a desired license before beginning training, and throughout the flight training program);
- Apprenticeship / job training programs offered by a company or union;
- Correspondence courses;

VA may approve programs offered by institutions outside of the United States, when they are pursued at educational institutions of higher learning, and lead to an associate or higher degree, or the equivalent. Individuals must receive VA approval prior to attending or enrolling in any foreign programs.

Restrictions on Training

- Bartending and personality development courses
- Non-accredited independent study courses;
- Any course given by radio;
- Self-improvement courses such as reading, speaking, woodworking, basic seamanship, and English as a second language;
- Any course which is avocational or recreational in character;
- Farm cooperative courses;

- Audited courses;
- Courses not leading to an educational, professional, or vocational objective;
- Courses an individual has previously completed;
- Courses taken by a Federal government employee under the Government Employees' Training Act;
- Courses paid for in whole or in part by the Armed Forces while on active duty;
- Courses taken while in receipt of benefits for the same program from the Office of Workers' Compensation Programs.

The VA must reduce benefits for individuals in Federal, State or local prisons after being convicted of a felony.

An individual may not receive benefits for a program at a proprietary school if he or she is an owner or official of the school. Benefits are generally payable for 10 years following a veteran's release from active duty.

Part-Time Training

Individuals unable to attend school full-time should consider going part-time. Benefit rates and entitlement charges are pro-rated as follows:

- Individuals who are on active duty or training at less than one-half time, will receive the lesser of:
- The monthly rate based on tuition and fees for the course(s); or
- The maximum monthly rate based on training time.
- Individuals training at less than one-half time will receive payment in one sum for the whole enrollment period.

Remedial, Deficiency and Refresher Training

Remedial and deficiency courses are intended to assist a student in overcoming a deficiency in a particular area of study. In order for such courses to be approved, the courses must be deemed necessary for pursuit of a program of education. Refresher training is for technological advances that occurred in a field of employment. The advance must have occurred while the student was on active duty, or after release. There is an entitlement charge for these courses.

Tutorial Assistance

Students may receive a special allowance for individual tutoring, if attending school at one-half time or more. To qualify, the student must have a deficiency in a subject. The school must certify the tutor's qualifications, and the hours of tutoring. Eligible students may receive a maximum monthly payment of $100.00. The maximum total benefit payable is $1,200.00.

There is no entitlement charge for the first $600.00 of tutorial assistance. To apply for tutorial assistance, students must submit VA Form 22-1990t, "Application and Enrollment Certification for Individualized Tutorial Assistance." The form should be given to the certifying official in the office handling VA paperwork at the school for completion.

Months of Benefits/Entitlement Charged

Individuals who complete their full period of enlistment may receive up to 36 months of MGIB benefits.

Individuals are considered to have completed their full enlistment period if they are discharged for the convenience of the government after completing 20 months of an enlistment of less than three years; or 30 months of an enlistment of three years or more Individuals will earn only one month of entitlement for each month of active duty after June 39, 1985, if they are discharged for other specific reasons (i.e. service-connected disability, reduction in force, hardship, etc.) before completing the enlistment period.

Individuals will earn one month of entitlement for each four months in the Selected Reserve after June 30, 1985. Individuals qualifying for more than one VA education program may receive a maximum of 48 months of benefits. For example, if a student used 30 months of Dependents' Educational Assistance, and is eligible for chapter 1606 benefits, he or she could have a maximum of 18 months of entitlement remaining.

Individuals are charged one full day of entitlement for each day of full-time benefits paid. For correspondence and flight training, individuals use one month of entitlement each time the VA pays the equivalent of one month of full-time benefits. Individuals pursuing a cooperative program use one month for each month of benefits paid.

For apprenticeship and job-training programs, the entitlement charge during the first 6 months is 75% of full-time. For the second six months, the charge is 55% of full-time. For the rest of the program, the charge is 35% of full-time. VA can extend entitlement to the end of a term, quarter, or semester if the ending date of an individual's entitlement falls within such period. If a school does not operate on a term basis, entitlement can be extended for 12 weeks.

Rates of Educational Assistance After Separation from Active Duty

The basic monthly rates increase October 1 every year with the Consumer Price Index (CPI) increase. While in training, students receive a letter with the current rates when the increase goes into effect each year. The rates may increase at other times by an act of Congress.

Basic Monthly Rates for College and Vocational Training

For approved programs in college and vocational or technical schools, basic payments are monthly, and the rates are based on training time. When students train at less than half time, they will be paid tuition and fees. But if tuition and fees amount to more than would be paid at the half-time rate (or the quarter-time rate if training at quarter-time or less), payments will be limited to the half time (or the quarter-time rate). For on-the-job training (OJT) and apprenticeship programs, rates are monthly and based on the length of time in the program. MGIB rates decrease as the student's wages increase according to an approved wage schedule.

Rates for Other Types of Training

For correspondence courses, students receive 55% of the approved charges for the course. For flight training, students receive 60% of the approved charges for the course. For reimbursement of tests for licenses or certifications, students receive 100% of the charges up to a maximum of $2,000 per test.

Rates of Educational Assistance While on Active Duty

If a service member goes to school while on active duty, he or she may have two options for using MGIB benefits. They may be eligible to receive:

- "Regular" MGIB; or
- Tuition Assistance plus MGIB, or
- Tuition Assistance "Top-Up"

Using "Regular" MGIB While on Active Duty

If a service member uses "regular" MGIB while on active duty, VA can pay whichever is less:

- The monthly rate based on tuition and fees for your course(s); or
- The maximum monthly MGIB rate (basic rate plus any increases he or she may qualify for).

The basic monthly rates increase October 1 every year with the Consumer Price Index (CPI) increase. While in training, students receive a letter with the current rates when the increase goes into effect each year. The rates may increase at other times by an act of Congress.

Using Tuition Assistance Top-Up

If a student is on active duty, he or she may be eligible to receive Tuition Assistance (TA) from his or her branch of service. If the student has been on active duty for two years, he or she may also be eligible to use MGIB to supplement, or "top up," the TA. Top-up covers the remaining percentage of costs approved for TA that TA alone doesn't' cover—**up to specified limits**. For example, if a student's service authorizes 75% of costs, top-up can pay the remaining 25% of costs approved for TA.

DETAILED Rates of Educational Assistance— The rates effective October 1, 2020 are detailed in the following charts:

Basic Monthly Rates Effect October 1, 2020 Montgomery G.I. Bill – Active Duty (MGIB), Chapter 30					
Type of Training	Full-Time	Three- Quarter Time	One-Half Time	Less Thank One-Half Time But More than 1/4	One- Quarter Time
Institutional	$2122.00	$1591.50	$1061.00	$1061.00	$530.50
Cooperative Training	$2122.00				
Correspondence Training	Entitlement charged at the rate of one month for each $2122.00 paid.				
Apprenticeship On-The-Job Training-	First six months: $1291.50 Second six months: $947.10 Remainder of program: $602.70				
Flight Training	Entitlement charged at the rate of one month for each $1722.00				

Basic Monthly Rates Effective October 1, 2020 For persons whose initial active duty obligation was less than three years and who served less than three years (excluding 2x4 participants)					
Type of Training	Full- Time	Three- Quarter Time	One- Half Time	Less Than ½ Time But More Than 1/4	One- Quarter Time
Institutional	$1722.00	$1291.50	$861.00	Tuition & Fees, not to exceed $861.00	$430.50
Correspondence Training	Entitlement charged at the rate of one month for each $1722.00 paid				
Apprenticeship On-The-Job Training-	First six months: $1291.00 Second six months: $947.00 Remainder of program: $602.70				
Flight Training	Entitlement charged at the rate of one month for each $1722.00 paid				
Cooperative Training	$1722.00 (Full-Time Only)				

Basic Institutional Rates Effective October 1, 2020
For persons with remaining entitlement under Chapter 34 of Title 38, U.S.C.

Time	No Dependents	One Dependent	Two Dependents	Each Add'l Dependent
Full	$2310.00	$2346.00	$2377.00	$16.00
Three-Quarter	$1733.00	$1759.50	$1783.00	$12.00
One-Half	$1155.00	$1173.00	$1188.50	$8.50
Less Than 1/2, But More Than 1/4	Tuition and fees, not to exceed the rate of $1155.00			
One-Quarter	Tuition and fees, not to exceed the rate of $577.50			
Cooperative	$2310.00	$2346.00	$2377.00	$16.00

Basic Job Training Rates Effective October 1, 2020
For persons with remaining entitlement under Chapter 34 of Title 38 U.S.C. Apprenticeship and On-the-Job Training

Time	No Dependents	One Dependent	Two Dependents	Each Add'l Dependent
First six months	$1694.25	1706.63	1717.50	$5.25
Second six months	1223.48	1232.83	1240.53	$3.85
Third six months	766.50	772.63	777.35	$2.45
Remainder	754.60	760.38	765.63	$2.45

SPECIAL NOTES:

Cooperative Training is full time only.

Individuals taking correspondence courses will receive 55% of the approved charges for the course. Individuals taking flight training will receive 60% of the approved charges for the course, including solo hours.

Increased Above Basic Rates

Individuals may qualify for the following increases above their basic monthly rates. These increases don't apply to correspondence courses, the test for a license or certification, or flight training.

College Fund

Certain branches of service may offer the College Fund. The College Fund money, or "kicker," is an additional amount of money that increases the basic MGIB monthly benefit and is included in the VA payment.

Important: Students can't receive College Fund money without receiving MGIB. A common misunderstanding is that the College Fund is a separate benefit from MGIB.

The College Fund is an add-on to the MGIB benefit.

VEAP Kicker

VA pays an additional amount, commonly known as a "kicker," if directed by the Department of Defense (DoD). If an individual is eligible under Category 3 or Category 4 and has a VEAP kicker, he or she can receive the amount of the VEAP kicker contributed by the service department divided by the total months of MGIB eligibility.

Accelerated Payments for Education Leading to Employment in High Technology

One of the provisions contained in the Veterans Education and Benefits Expansion Act of 2001 (Public Law 107-103) called for accelerated payments for education leading to employment in high technology, effective October 1, 2002. Following are questions and answers provided by the VA regarding this provision.

What is an accelerated payment?

An accelerated payment is a lump sum payment of 60% of tuition and fees for certain high cost, high tech programs. If a participant does not have sufficient entitlement to cover 60% of tuition and fees, he or she will receive pay based on the actual remaining entitlement.

VA will make accelerated payments for one term, quarter, or semester at a time. However, if the program is not offered on a term, quarter or semester basis, the accelerated payment is paid for the entire program. To qualify, a participant must be enrolled in a high-tech program and must certify that he or she intends to seek employment in a high tech industry as defined by VA. Accelerated payment is paid instead of Montgomery GI Bill benefits that would otherwise have been received.

Who qualifies for accelerated payments?

Only individuals eligible for the Montgomery GI Bill - Active Duty (Chapter 30) qualify for accelerated payments.

How high do the tuition and fees have to be?

To receive accelerated payment, the tuition and fees must be more than double the Montgomery GI Bill benefits that a participant would otherwise receive for that term. For example, if the full-time rate is $732 and a participant is enrolled in a 4-month semester, the tuition and fees must be over $5,856 (4 months x $732=$2,928; $5,856=2 x $2,928) before he or she could receive an accelerated payment.

If a participant receives $900 in monthly benefits, the tuition and fees must be over $7,200 (4 months x $900=$3,600; $7,200= 2 x $3,600).

If a participant receives $1,050 in monthly benefits, the tuition and fees must be over $8,400 (4 months x $1,050 = $4,200; 2 x $4,200 = $8,400).

317

What programs qualify for accelerated payment?

Both degree and non-degree programs qualify. A participant must be enrolled in a program in one of the following categories:
Life science or physical science (but not social science);
Engineering (all fields);
Mathematics;
Engineering and science technology;
Computer specialties; and·
Engineering, science, and computer management

What industries qualify for accelerated payments?

A participant must intend to seek employment in one of the following industries:
Biotechnology;
Life Science Technologies;
Opto-electronics;
Computers and telecommunications; Electronics;
Computer-integrated manufacturing; Material Design;
Aerospace;
Weapons;
Nuclear technology

How does a participant apply for accelerated payments?
The individual must ask the school to include his or her request for accelerated payment to VA when it sends the enrollment information to VA for processing. The individual's request must include his or her certification of intent to seek employment in a high technology industry.

How is the education entitlement charged?
VA will divide the accelerated payment by the amount of the individual's full-time monthly rate (including kickers and additional contributions) and will reduce the entitlement by the resulting number of months and days. Example: Jill received an accelerated payment of $3,600. Her full-time rate is $900. VA will charge her entitlement as follows: $3,600/$900 = 4months.

When can accelerated payments be made?
Accelerated payments may only be made for terms or other enrollment periods that begin on or after October 1, 2002.

Can school-related expenses (such as books, supplies and living expenses) be counted as tuition and fees for accelerated payments?
No. Only the school's tuition and fees can be considered for accelerated payment.

Can an individual receive accelerated payments for short, non-degree courses?
Yes, as long as they are approved for VA benefits. Short, expensive, IT courses offered by businesses typically are <u>not</u> approved for VA benefits.

Can an individual receive accelerated payments for non-technical courses when taking them as part of a high technology program?

Yes. However, the degree or certificate must require the completion of these other non- technical courses.

Is it possible to receive an accelerated payment check before a school term begins?

No. VA needs to verify that the individual has enrolled before sending out the large payment. VA will pay the student as soon after the start of the term as possible. Individuals will receive payment faster if they receive direct deposit.

Does a student have to verify enrollment each month if he or she receives an accelerated payment?

No. After the individual completes his or her enrollment, VA will ask the student to verify that he or she have received the accelerated payment. VA will also ask the individual to indicate how he or she used the accelerated payment (such as toward tuition, fees and books and supplies). VA is asking the latter question for statistical purposes only because the law requires them to collect this information. A student's answer will have no bearing on his or her entitlement to the accelerated payment. The student must respond to these questions within 60 days from the end of the enrollment period or VA will create an overpayment equal to the accelerated payment. As with any course, the student must notify VA of any change in his or her enrollment. The student's school must report any changes as well.

Is there any financial risk with accelerated payment?

Yes. If a student receives a grade, which does not count toward graduation requirements, he or she may have to repay all or part of the accelerated payment, depending on the circumstances. This could be a large amount of money.

Do the accelerated payments have to be paid back if the individual fails to find employment in a high technology industry?

No. The fact that he or she intended to find employment in a high technology industry is sufficient.

List of approved high technology programs

1.09 Animal Sciences
01.0901 Animal Sciences, General
01.0902 Agricultural Animal Breeding
01.0903 Animal Health
01.0904 Animal Nutrition
01.0905 Dairy Science
01.0906 Livestock Management
01.0907 Poultry Science

01.10 Food Science and Technology
01.1001 Food Science

01.1002 Food Technology and Processing

01.1099 Food Science and Technology

01.1101 Plant Sciences General

01.1102 Agronomy and Crop Science

01.1103 Horticultural Science

01.1104 Agricultural and Horticultural Plant Breeding

01.1105 Plant Protection and Integrated Pest Management

01.1106 Range Science Management

01.12 Soil Sciences

01.1201 Soil Science and Agronomy General

01.1202 Soil Chemistry and Physics

01.1203 Soil Microbiology

01.1299 Soil Sciences

03.01 Natural Resources Conservation and Research

03.0104 Environmental Science

03.03 Fishing and Fisheries Sciences and Management

Forestry

03.0501 Forestry, General

03.0502 Forest Sciences and Biology

03.0506 Forest Management/Forest Resources Management

03.0508 Urban Forestry

03.0509 Wood Science and Wood Products/Pulp and Paper Technology

03.0510 Forest Resources Production and Management

03.0511 Forest Technology/Technician

Wildlife and Wildlands Science and Management

09.07 Radio, Television, and Digital Communication

09.0702 Digital Communication and Media/Multimedia

11.0101 Computer and Information Sciences, General

11.0102 Artificial Intelligence and Robotics

11.0103 Information Technology

11.0199 Computer and Information Sciences

Computer Programming

11.0201 Computer Programming/Programmer General

11.0202 Computer Programming Specific Applications

Data Processing

11.0301 Data Process and Data Processing Technology/Technician

Information Science/Studies Computer Systems Analysis Computer Science

Computer Software and Media Application

11.0801 Web Page, Digital/Multimedia and Information Resources Design 11.0802 Data Modeling/Warehousing and Database Administration

11.0803 Computer Graphics

11.0899 Computer Software and Media Applications, Other.

Computer System Networking and Telecommunications Computer/Information Technology Administration and Management

11.1001 System Administration/Administrator

11.1002 System, Networking and LAN/WAN Management/Manager

11.1003 Computer and Information Systems Security

11.1004 Web/Multimedia Management and Webmaster

Engineering

Instructional program that prepare individuals to apply mathematical and scientific principles to the solution of practical problems.

*15. Engineering Technologies/Technicians.

Instructional programs that prepare individuals to apply basic engineering principles and technical skills in support of engineering and related projects.

Biological and Biomedical Sciences.

Instructional programs that focus on the biological sciences and the non-clinical biomedical sciences, and that prepare individuals for research and professional careers as biologist and biomedical scientist.

Mathematics and Statistics.

Instructional programs that focus on the systematic study of logical symbolic language and its applications.

*Military Technologies.

A program that prepares individuals to undertake advanced and specialized leadership and technical responsibilities for the armed services and related national security organizations. Includes instruction in such areas as weapons systems and technology, communications, intelligence, management, logistics and strategy.

30.01 Biological and Physical Sciences

30.06 System Science and Theory

30.08 Mathematics and Computer Science Biopsychology

Gerontology

Accounting and Computer Science Behavioral Sciences

Natural Sciences Nutrition Sciences Neuroscience Cognitive Science

*40. Physical Sciences.
Instructional programs that focus on the scientific study of inanimate objects, processes of matter and energy, and associated phenomena.

*41. Science Technologies/Technicians.
Instructional programs that prepare individuals to apply scientific principles and technical skills in support of scientific research and development.

42.11 Physiological Psychology/Psychobiology

42.19 Psychometrics and Quantitative Psychology

- 24 Psychopharmacology Forensic Psychology

*51.14 Medical Clinical Sciences/Graduate Medical Studies
51.1401 Medical Scientist (MS, PhD)

NOTE: "*" means all programs are considered high technology programs within that discipline.

Eligibility Periods
Benefits generally end 10 years from the date of an individual's last discharge or release from active duty. The VA may extend the 10-year period by the amount of time an individual is prevented from training due to a disability, or the individual is being held by a foreign government or power.

The VA may extend the 10-year period if an individual reenters active duty for 90 days or more after becoming eligible. The extension ends 10 years from the date of discharge or release from the later period. Periods of active duty of fewer than 90 days may qualify for extensions, only if the discharge or release was for:

- A service-connected disability; or
- A medical condition existing before active duty; or
- Hardship; or
- A reduction in force.

If an individual's discharge is upgraded by the military, the 10-year period begins on the date of the upgrade.

Special Note for Individuals Eligible Under the 2 by 4 Program
If an individual is eligible based upon two years of active duty followed by four years in the Selected Reserve, the individual may have 10 years from release from active duty, or 10 years from the completion of the four-year Selected Reserve obligation to use benefits, whichever is later.

Miscellaneous Information

Any change in educational, professional or vocational objectives is considered a "change of program." The law permits one change of program without prior VA approval, provided an individual's attendance, conduct and progress in the last program were satisfactory. Additional "changes of program" require prior VA approval. VA will not charge a change of program if the individual enrolls in a new program after successful completion of the immediately preceding program.

Once an individual starts receiving benefits, he must maintain satisfactory attendance, conduct and progress. The VA may stop benefits if an individual does not meet the standards set by the school. VA may later resume benefits if the individual reenters the same program at the same school, and the school approves the reentry, and certifies it to VA.

If the individual does not reenter the same program at the same school, VA may resume benefits if the cause of unsatisfactory attendance, conduct or progress has been removed; and the program that the student intends to pursue is suitable to his or her abilities, aptitudes and interests.

Application for Benefits

VA Form 22-1990, "Application for Education Benefits" must be completed. The form may be obtained from individual schools, from any VA regional office, or by calling (888) GIBILL-1.

The completed form should be sent to the VA regional office with jurisdiction over the state in which the individual will train.

If an individual is not on active duty, copy 4 of DD Form 214 ("Certificate of Release or Discharge from Active Duty"), must also be sent to the VA. If an individual is on active duty, enrollment must be approved by the Base Education Services Officer, and service must be verified by the Commanding Officer.

If training has already started, the school, employer, or union should complete VA Form 22-1999 ("Enrollment Certification") and submit it along with the application.

Procedures for Receipt of Monthly Payments

After selecting a school and submitting an application to VA, the school official must complete an enrollment certification, and submit it to the appropriate VA regional office. If a student meets the basic eligibility requirements for benefits, and the program or course is approved, VA will process the enrollment based on certified training time.

If a student is enrolled in a degree program at a college or university, or a certificate or diploma program at a business, technical, or vocational school, they will not receive payment until they have verified their attendance. Students will receive a "Student Verification of Enrollment Form 22-8979" each month, and must complete and return it to the appropriate VA regional office. After processing, VA will release a check.

If an individual is in an apprenticeship or job-training program, he or she will receive a form to report the hours worked each month. The form must be signed and given to the certifying official for the company or union. The certifying official must complete the form and send it to the appropriate VA regional office. After processing, VA will release a check.

If an individual is taking a correspondence course, he or she will receive a form each quarter, on which the student must show the number of lessons completed that quarter. The completed form should be sent to the school for certification of the number of lessons serviced during the quarter. The school will send the form to the appropriate VA regional office. After processing, VA will release a check. Payments are based on the number of lessons serviced by the school.

VA will send flight schools a supply of blank monthly certification of flight training forms. The school must complete the form by entering the number of hours, the hourly rate, and the total charges for flight training received during the month. The student should review and sign the completed form and send it to the appropriate VA regional office. After processing, VA will release a check.

NOTE: It is against the law for schools to cash VA checks under a Power of Attorney Agreement.

Timely Receipt of Verification Forms and Checks

Students should receive their verification forms for each month by the fifth of the following month. If it is not received by then, the VA should be immediately contacted so that another form can be issued.

One a completed verification form has been submitted, the student should receive a check within 2 weeks. If a check is not received by then, the VA should immediately be contacted so that appropriate action can be taken.

Advance Payments

An advance payment for the initial month, or partial month and the following month may be made, if:

- The school agrees to handle advance payments; and
- Training is one-half time or more; and
- A request is made by the individual in writing; and
- The VA receives the enrollment certification at least 30 days prior to the start of classes.
- Advance payments are made out to the individual, and sent to the applicable

324

school for delivery to the individual registration. VA cannot issue a check more than 30 days before classes start. Before requesting an advance payment, students should verify with the school certifying official that the school has agreed to process advance payments.

Requests for advance payments must be on VA Form 22-1999, "Enrollment Certification," or a sheet of paper attached to the enrollment certification.

Once a student receives an advance payment at registration, the school must certify to VA that the student received the check. If a student reduces enrollment, or withdraws from all courses during the period covered by an advance payment, he or she must repay the overpayment to VA.

If an individual believes that the amount of a VA check is incorrect, the VA should be contacted before the check is cashed.

Direct Deposit

Chapter 30 payments can be sent directly to a student's savings or checking account through Direct Deposit (Electronic Funds Transfer). To sign up for direct deposit by phone, students must call (877) 838-2778.

Student Responsibilities

To ensure timely receipt of correct payments, students should be sure to promptly notify the VA of:

- Any change in enrollment;
- Any change in address;
- Any change in selected reserve status;
- Any changes affecting a student's dependents (if a student is receiving an allowance which includes an additional amount for dependents).

In addition, students should use reasonable judgment when accepting and cashing a check. All letters from VA about monthly rates and effective dates should be read carefully. If a student thinks the amount of a VA check is wrong, VA should be contacted **before** cashing the check. Any incorrect checks should be returned to VA.

If a student cashes a check for the wrong amount, he or she will be liable for repayment of any resulting overpayment.

Recovery of Overpayments

VA must take prompt and aggressive action to recover overpayments. Students have the right to request a waiver of the overpayment, or verification that the amount is correct. If an overpayment is not repaid or waived, VA may add interest and collection fees to the debt. VA may also take one or more of the following actions to collect the debt:

- Withhold future benefits to apply to the debt;
- Refer the debt to a private collection agency;
- Recover the debt from any Federal income tax refund;

- Recover the debt from the salary (if student is a Federal employee);
- File a lawsuit in Federal court to collect the debt;
- Withhold approval of a VA home loan guarantee.

Changes in Enrollment

If a student withdraws from one or more courses after the end of the school's drop period, VA will reduce or stop benefits on the date of reduction or withdrawal. Unless the student can show that the change was due to mitigating circumstances, the student may have to repay **all** benefits for the course.

VA defines mitigating circumstances as "unavoidable and unexpected events that directly interfere with the pursuit of a course, and which are beyond the student's control. Examples of reasons VA may accept include:

- Extended illness;
- Severe illness or death in immediate family;
- Unscheduled changes in employment; and
- Lack of child care.

Examples of reasons VA may not accept include:

- Withdrawal to avoid a failing grade;
- Dislike of the instructor; and
- Too many courses attempted.

(VA may ask the student to furnish evidence to support the reason for change, such as physician or employer written statements.)

The first time a student withdraws from up to 6 credit hours, VA will "excuse" the withdrawal, and pay benefits for the period attended. If a student receives a grade that does not count toward graduation, all benefits for the course may have to be repaid. Affected students should check the school's grading policy with the office handling VA paperwork.

If a student receives a non-punitive grade, the school will notify VA, and VA may reduce or stop benefits. The student may not have to repay the benefits if he or she can show that the grades were due to mitigating circumstances.

Work-Study Programs

Students may be eligible for an additional allowance under a work-study program that allows students to perform work for VA in return for an hourly wage.

Students may perform outreach services under VA supervision, prepare and process VA paperwork, work at a VA medical facility or National Cemetery, or perform other approved activities.

Students must attend school at the three-quarter of full-time rate. VA will select students for the work study program based on different factors. Such factors include:

- Disability of the student;
- Ability of the student to complete the work-study contract before the end of his or her eligibility for education benefits;
- Job availability within normal commuting distance to the student;
- VA will give the highest priority to a veteran who has a service-connected disability or disabilities rated by VA at 30% or more.

The number of applicants selected will depend on the availability of VA-related work at the school or at VA facilities in the area.

Students may work during or between periods of enrollment, and can arrange with VA to work any number of hours during his or her enrollment. However, the maximum number of hours a student may work is 25 times the number of weeks in the enrollment period.

Students will earn an hourly wage equal to the Federal or State minimum wage, whichever is greater. If a student works at a college or university, the school **may** pay the difference between the amount VA pays and the amount the school normally pays other work-study students doing the same job.

Students may elect to be paid in advance for 40% of the number of hours in the work-study agreement, or for 50 hours, whichever is less. After completion of the hours covered by the first payment, VA will pay the student after completion of each 50 hours of service.

Students interested in taking part in a work-study program must complete VA Form 22- 8691, "Application for Work-Study Allowance." Completed forms should be sent to the nearest VA regional office.

Educational Counseling

VA can provide services to help eligible individuals understand their educational and vocational strengths and weaknesses and to plan:

- An educational or training goal, and the means by which the goal can be reached; or
- An employment goal for which an individual qualifies on the basis of present training or experience.

VA can also help plan an effective job search. Counseling is available for:

- Service members who are on active duty, and are within 180 days of discharge, and are stationed in the United States; or
- Veterans with discharges that are not dishonorable, who are within one year from date of discharge.

Vocational Rehabilitation

Veterans may qualify for Training and Rehabilitation under Chapter 31 of Title 38, United States Code, if:

- The veteran has a service-connected disability or disabilities rated by VA at 20% or more; and
- The veteran received a discharge from active duty that was not dishonorable; and
- The veteran has an employment handicap.

Veterans may also qualify with a service-connected disability or disabilities rated by VA at 10%, and:

- The veteran has a serious employment handicap; or
- The veteran first applied for vocational rehabilitation benefits before November 1, 1990, reapplied after that date, and has an employment handicap.

Vocational rehabilitation helps disabled veterans become independent in daily living. Veterans may also receive assistance in selecting, preparing for, and securing employment that is compatible with their interests, talents, skills, physical capabilities, and goals.

To apply for vocational rehabilitation, VA for 28-1900, "Disabled Veterans Application for Vocational Rehabilitation," must be completed and sent to the nearest VA regional office For detailed information on vocational rehabilitation refer to Chapter 14 of this book.

Appeal of VA Decision

VA decisions on education benefits may be appealed within one year of the date an individual receives notice of a VA decision.

CHAPTER 21

EDUCATION BENEFITS: POST-9/11 G.I. BILL, CHAPTER 33

The Post-9/11 GI Bill is for servicemembers with at least 90 days of aggregate active-duty service after September 10, 2001, whether they are still on active duty or they are an honorably discharged veteran. This education benefit also applies to veterans discharged with a service-connected disability after 30 days.

If you have eligibility for the Post-9/11 GI Bill and any other GI Bill program, you must make an irrevocable election of the Post-9/11 GI Bill before you can receive any benefits.

The Post-9/11 GI Bill has specific components unavailable in other GI Bill programs including Yellow Ribbon Program and the Transfer of Entitlement Option.

For approved programs, the Post-9/11 GI Bill provides up to 36 months of education benefits, generally payable for 15 years following release from active duty.

Key Takeaways

The Post-9/11 GI Bill (Chapter 33) helps you pay for school or job training.

If you served on active duty after September 10, 2001, you may qualify for the Post-9/11 GI Bill.

You can receive up to 36 months of benefits including tuition and fees, money for housing, money for books and supplies and money to help you move from a rural area to go to school.

Institutions of higher learning participating in the Yellow Ribbon Program may make additional funds available for education programs without an additional charge to GI Bill entitlements.

329

Purple Heart Recipients Exempt from GI Bill Transfer Policy Changes

If you're an active-duty Purple Heart recipient and you want to transfer your psot-9/11 GI Bill education benefits to your children, you're exempt from a policy change made at the start of 2018.

In July 2018, it was announced that there would be an immediate change where wounded warriors would be excluded from eligibility if they couldn't extend their service by four years. Starting in 2019, only servicemembers with 6 to 16 years of total active duty or selected reserve service would be eligible. Anyone above or below that wouldn't be able to transfer benefits.

Before the change, there was no cap on service time for transferability as long as service members could commit to four more years in the service. The changes were implemented for troop retention.

However, Defense Secretary James Mattis signed another policy immediately exempted wounded warrior Purple Heart recipients from the change. This means wounded warriors with Purple Hearts CAN transfer their benefits, regardless of their total years of service or ability to complete more service.

Veterans Educational Assistance Improvements Act of 2010

Certain National Guard members mobilized on Title 32 orders on-or-after September 11, 2001 are eligible for the Post-9/11 GI Bill and any qualifying Title 32 mobilization may be used to increase his or her percentage of eligibility.

- Limits active-duty members to the net cost for tuition and fees prorated based on the eligibility tiers (40%-100%) previously established for Veterans. (Same limitations apply to transferee spouses of active duty servicemembers.)
- The Post-9/11 GI Bill will now pay all public school in-state tuition and fees; this includes graduate training, etc.
- MGIB-AD & MGIB-SR College fund payments will now be paid on a monthly basis instead of a lump-sum at the beginning of the term.
- Reimbursement is now available for multiple Licensing and Certification Tests.
- Reimbursement is now available for fees paid to take national examinations used for admission to an institution of higher learning (e.g. SAT, LSAT, ACT, GMAT, etc).
- Vocational Rehabilitation participants may now elect the higher housing allowance offered by the Post-9/11 GI Bill if otherwise eligible for the Post-9/11 GI Bill.
- If training at greater than ½ time the housing allowance is now prorated according to the training time the individual is enrolled (rounded to the nearest tenth). So, if a student's full housing allowance is $1000, and he or she is attending ¾ time - the housing allowance would be $800 (80% of

$1000).

- Break or interval pay is no longer payable under any VA education benefit program unless under an Executive Order of the President or due to an emergency situation such as a natural disaster or strike. Entitlement which previously would have been used for break pay will be available for use during a future enrollment. This means that if the semester ends December 15, the housing allowance is paid for the first 15 days of December only. Benefits will begin again when the new semester begins (e.g. January 15), and the student will be paid for the remaining days of that month and term.
- Students using other VA education programs are included in this change. Monthly benefits will be prorated in the same manner.
- NOAA and PHS personnel are now eligible to transfer their entitlement to eligible dependents

If a student is training at greater than ½ time, his or her housing allowance is now prorated according to the training time he or she is enrolled. Housing allowance is now payable to students enrolled solely in distance learning. The housing allowance is ½ the national average BAH for an E-5 with dependents.

Non-college degree programs, on-the-job training, and flight training programs are now covered under the Post-9/11 GI Bill. The book stipend is now payable to active-duty members.

Eligibility

If an individual has served a total of at least 90 consecutive days on active duty in the Armed Forces since September 11, 2001, he or she is eligible. However, the amount of benefits received under this program is determined by the actual amount of accumulated post 9/11 service the individual has.

An individual may be eligible if he or she has served at least 90 aggregate days on active duty after September 10, 2001, and is still on active duty, or was honorably:
- Discharged from the active duty; or
- Released from active duty and placed on the retired list or temporary disability retired list; or
- Released from active duty and transferred to the Fleet Reserve or Fleet Marine Corps Reserve; or
- Released from the active duty for further service in a reserve component of the Armed Forces.

Individuals may also be eligible if they were honorably discharged from active duty for a service-connected disability, and served 30 continuous days after September 10, 2001.

Some periods of active-duty service are excluded. Periods of service under the following do not count toward qualification for the Post 9/11 GI Bill:

- NOAA, PHS, or Active Guard Reserve; ROTC under 10 U.S.C. 2107(b);
- Service academy contract period.
- Service terminated due to defective enlistment agreement.
- Service used for loan repayment; and
- Selected reserve service used to establish eligibility under the Montgomery GI Bill (MGIB chapter 30), MGIB for Selected Reserve (MGIB-SR Chapter 1606), or the Reserve Education Assistance Program (REAP chapter 1607).

Under the MGIB, officers who received their commission through a service academy, or an ROTC scholarship were ineligible. There are no such restrictions under the new program. Any officer who was previously ineligible will be eligible for the new program, assuming they have at least 90 days of post 9/11 active-duty service. Similarly, military members who previously declined the MGIB are eligible for the new program.

If, on August 1, 2009, a servicemember was eligible for MGIB-SR or REAP, and he or she qualifies for the Post-9/11 GI Bill, he or she must make an irrevocable election to receive benefits under the Post-9/11 GI Bill. The individual then loses any right to future MGIB- SR or REAP benefits.

Benefit Amount Payable

The new rates depend on the length of post 9/11 active-duty service, the state of residence, and the number of courses taken. Like the MGIB, the Post-9/11 GI Bill pays 36 months of full-time education benefits. So, if an individual goes to school full-time, he or she will receive the full benefit rates for 36 months. If he or she goes to school 1/2 time, he or she will receive half of the monthly entitlement for 72 months, etc.

Based on the length of active-duty service, eligible participants are entitled to receive a percentage of the following:

- Cost of tuition and fees, not to exceed the most expensive in-state undergraduate tuition at a public institution of higher education (paid directly to the school);
- Monthly housing allowance equal to the basic allowance for housing payable to a military E-5 with dependents, in the same zip code as the primary school (paid directly to the servicemember or veteran);
- Yearly books and supplies stipend of up to $1,000 per year (paid directly to the servicemember or veteran); and
- A one-time payment of $500 paid to certain individuals relocating from highly rural areas. (The housing allowance and books and supplies stipend are not payable to individuals on active duty. The housing allowance is not payable to those pursuing training at halftime or less or to individuals enrolled solely in distance learning programs.)

The following chart outlines the breakdown of benefits based on amount of service:

Member Serves	Percentage of Maximum Benefit Payable
At least 36 months	100%
At least 30 continuous days on active duty and must be discharged due to service-connected disability	100%
At least 30 months, but less than 36 months	90%
At least 24 months, but less than 30 months	80%
At least 18 months, but less than 24 months	70%
At least 12 months, but less than 18 months	60%
At least 06 months, but less than 12 months	50%
At least 90 days, but less than 06 months	40%

2020-2021 Maximum In-State Tuition and Fees

If an eligible student is attending a public school, they may qualify for all tuition and fee payments for an in-state student.

For private or foreign school attendees, students receive up to $25,162.14 per academic year, based on the National Maximum.

Contributions

Unlike the MGIB and VEAP, the new MGIB does not require the servicemember to elect or decline, nor make monthly contributions. Unfortunately, if someone has already contributed to the GI Bill, he or she won't get their money back, unless they use all of their new GI Bill entitlements.

If they do, the $1,200 contribution to the MGIB (or a proportional amount, if they used any of their MGIB entitlement) will be added to his or her final new GI Bill education payment. If an individual is currently paying into the MGIB, he or she can stop now, and still be eligible for the new program.

Covered Expenses

The plan covers any approved programs offered by a school in the United States that is authorized to grant an associate (or higher) degree.

You can be reimbursed up to $2,000 per test. Your entitlement will be charged one month for every $1,972.66 paid to you rounded to the nearest non-zero whole month; this means even low-cost tests are charged one month of entitlement per test.

If a servicemember transferred to the Post-9/11 GI Bill from MGIB-Active Duty, MGIB-SR, or REAP, he or she may also receive Post-9/11 benefits for flight training, apprenticeship, or on-the-job training programs, and correspondence courses.

College Funds

If the member is eligible for a "kicker," such as the Army or Navy College Fund, or a Reserve "Kicker," he or she will still receive the extra monthly benefit under the new GI bill. This monthly amount will be paid to the member, not to the university.

Collage Loan Repayment

Individuals, who were previously ineligible for the MGIB because they elected the College Loan Repayment Program (CLRP), are eligible for the new GI Bill, but only active-duty service performed after their initial active-duty service obligation counts toward the new benefits. In other words, if they were initially enlisted for five years and received the CLRP, they would have to reenlist or extend their enlistment in order to take advantage of the new GI Bill.

Transferring Benefits to Dependents

While the Post-9/11 GI Bill offers a very generous post-service education benefit, a special provision of the program allows career service members the opportunity to share their education benefits with immediate family members.

Allowing career service members to transfer their GI Bill benefits to family members has long been one of the most requested items among military family readiness and advocacy groups.

Eligible Individuals

Any member of the Armed Forces (active duty or Selected Reserve, officer or enlisted) on or after August 1, 2009, who is eligible for the Post-9/11 GI Bill, and:

- Has at least 6 years of service in the Armed Forces on the date of election and agrees to serve 4 additional years in the Armed Forces from the date of election.
- Has at least 10 years of service in the Armed Forces (active duty and/or selected reserve) on the date of election, is precluded by either standard policy (service or DoD) or statute from committing to 4 additional years, and agrees to serve for the maximum amount of time allowed by such policy or statute, or
- Is (or becomes) retirement eligible during the period from August 1, 2009, through August 1, 2013. A servicemember is considered to be retirement eligible if he or she has completed 20 years of active duty or 20 qualifying years of reserve service.
- For those individuals eligible for retirement on August 1, 2009, no additional service is required.
- For those individuals who have an approved retirement date after August 1, 2009, and before July 1, 2010, no additional service is required.
- For those individuals eligible for retirement after August 1, 2009, and before August 1, 2010, 1 year of additional service after approval of transfer is required.

- For those individuals eligible for retirement on or after August 1, 2010, and before August 1, 2011, 2 years of additional service after approval of transfer are required.
- For those individuals eligible for retirement on or after August 1, 2011, and before August 1, 2012, 3 years of additional service after approval of transfer required.

Eligible Family Members

An individual approved to transfer an entitlement to educational assistance under this section may transfer the individual's entitlement to:

- The individual's spouse.
- One or more of the individual's children.
- Any combination of spouse and child.

A family member must be enrolled in the Defense Eligibility Enrollment Reporting System (DEERS) and be eligible for benefits, at the time of transfer to receive transferred educational benefits.

A child's subsequent marriage will not affect his or her eligibility to receive the educational benefit; however, after an individual has designated a child as a transferee under this section, the individual retains the right to revoke or modify the transfer at any time.

A subsequent divorce will not affect the transferee's eligibility to receive educational benefits; however, after an individual has designated a spouse as a transferee under this section, the eligible individual retains the right to revoke or modify the transfer at any time.

Nature of Transfer

An eligible Service member may transfer up to the total months of unused Post-9/11 GI Bill benefits, or the entire 36 months if the member has used none.

Family member use of transferred educational benefits is subject to the following:

Spouse

May start to use the benefit immediately.

May use the benefit while the member remains in the Armed Forces or after separation from active duty.

Is not eligible for the monthly stipend or books and supplies stipend while the member is serving on active duty.

Can use the benefit for up to 15 years after the service member's last separation from active duty.

Child

May start to use the benefit only after the individual making the transfer has completed at least 10 years of service in the Armed Forces.

May use the benefit while the eligible individual remains in the Armed Forces or after separation from active duty.

May not use the benefit until he/she has attained a secondary school diploma (or equivalency certificate), or reached 18 years of age.

Is entitled to the monthly stipend and books and supplies stipend even though the eligible individual is on active duty.

Is not subject to the 15-year delimiting date but may not use the benefit after reaching 26 years of age.

VEAP & the Post-9/11 Benefit

If someone is eligible for both VEAP and the Post-9/11 GI Bill he or she may un-enroll from VEAP and receive a refund of contributions or leave the remaining contributions in the VEAP account and remain eligible for both benefit programs.

NOTE: Students may not receive benefits under more than one program at the same time.

Expiration Date

Eligibility for the new GI Bill expires 15 years from the last period of active duty of at least 90 consecutive days. If released for a service-connected disability after at least 30 days of continuous service, eligibility ends 15 years from when the member is released for the service-connected disability.

Yellow Ribbon Program

The Post-9/11 GI Bill pays up to the highest public in-state undergraduate tuition. Tuition and fees may exceed that amount for individuals attending a private institution, graduate school or attending in a non-resident status.

The Yellow Ribbon Program is a provision of the Post-9/11 Veterans Education Assistance Act of 2008. Its purpose is to address enrollment at institutions that cost more than the Post-9/11 GI Bill's tuition benefit cap.

This program allows institutions of higher learning (degree-granting institutions) in the United States to voluntarily enter into an agreement with VA to fund tuition expenses that exceed the highest public in-state undergraduate tuition rate. The institution can waive up to 50% of those expenses and VA will match the same amount as the institution.

To be eligible, the student must be:
- A veteran receiving benefits at the 100% benefit rate payable; A transfer-of-entitlement eligible dependent child; or
- A transfer-of-entitlement eligible spouse of a veteran. The Institution of Higher Learning (IHL) must agree to:

336

- o Provide contributions to eligible individuals who apply for the Yellow Ribbon Program on a first-come-first-served basis, regardless of the
- Rate at which the individual is pursuing training in any given academic year;
  - o Provide contributions during the current academic year and all subsequent academic years in which the student maintains satisfactory progress, conduct, and attendance; Make contributions toward the program on behalf of the individual in the form of a waiver;
  - o Choose the percentage that will be waived and waive the same percentage (up to 50%) of established charges that exceed the in-State maximum for each student eligible;
  - o State the maximum number of individuals for whom contributions will be made in any given academic year.

Work-Study Program

Veterans and eligible transfer-of-entitlement recipients who train at the three-quarter rate of pursuit or higher may be eligible for a work-study program in which they work for VA and receive hourly wages. Students under the work-study program must be supervised by a VA employee and all duties performed must relate to VA. The types of work allowable include:

- VA paperwork processing at schools or other training facilities
- Assistance with patient care at VA hospitals or domiciliary care facilities.
- Work at national or state veterans' cemeteries.
- Other VA-approved activities.

REAP Note

If you're a member of the Reserves who lost education benefits when the Reserve Educational Assistance Program (REAP) ended in November 2015, you may qualify to receive restored benefits under the Post-9/11 GI Bill.

CHAPTER 22

EDUCATION BENEFITS – MONTGOMERY G.I. BILL – SELECTED RESERVE (MGIB-SR), CHAPTER 1606

The Montgomery GI Bill-Selected Reserve Program is for members of the Selected Reserve, including the Army Reserve, Navy Reserve, Air Force Reserve, Marine Corps Reserve, Coast Guard Reserve, Army National Guard and Air National Guard. While the reserve components decide who is eligible for the program, VA makes the payments for the program. Chapter 1606 is the first educational program that does not require service in the active Armed Forces in order to qualify.

Eligibility Requirements

Member must have signed a 6-year obligation to serve in the Selected Reserve after June 30, 1985. (Officers must have agreed to serve 6 years in addition to his or her original obligation.) For some types of training, it is necessary to have a 6-year commitment that began after September 30, 1990. Call (888) GIBILL-1 for more information.

Key Takeaways

The MGIB-SR program offers up to 36 months of education and training benefits. If you are a member of the Army, Navy, Air Force, Marine Corps or Coast Guard Reserve, Army National Guard or Air National Guard, you may be eligible for the benefit.

You can currently get up to $384 a month in compensation for up to 36 months.

Member must have completed his or her Initial Active Duty for Training (IADT); Member must maintain Selected Reserve Status - Serve in a drilling Selected Reserve unit and remain in good standing;

Member must meet the requirement to receive a high school diploma or equivalency certificate before completing IADT. Member must remain in good standing while serving in an active Selected Reserve Unit;

Effective November 1, 2000, veterans and reservists can apply for MGIB-SR benefits any time after receiving their high school diploma or equivalency certificate. It no longer has to be received prior to the end of the individual's first period of active duty. If an individual enters active duty in the Selected Reserve (AGR, TAR, FTS) after November 29, 1989, he or she must have been eligible before November 29, 1989 in order to remain eligible.

Eligibility Restriction

MGIB – AD:

An individual can't be eligible for MGIB – SR if he or she elected to have his or her service in the Selected Reserve credited toward establishing eligibility under the Montgomery GI Bill – Active Duty

ROTC (Reserve Officers' Training Corps) scholarship under section 2107 of title 10, Code:

An individual can't be eligible for MGIB – SR if he or she is receiving financial assistance through the Senior ROTC program under this section of the law.

Note: However, an individual may still be eligible for MGIB – SR if he or she receives financial assistance under **Section 2107a** of title 10, U.S. Code. This financial assistance program is for specially selected members of the Army Reserve and National Guard only. Individuals should check with their ROTC advisor for more information.

Note: There's no restriction on service academy graduates receiving MGIB – SR. Service academy graduates who received a commission aren't eligible under MGIB – AD.

If an individual enters Active Guard and Reserve (AGR) status, his or her eligibility for MGIB – SR will be suspended. He or she may be eligible for MGIB – AD. The individual may resume MGIB – SR eligibility after AGR status ends.

Approved Courses

Individuals may receive benefits for a wide variety of training, including:
- Undergraduate degrees from a college or university;
- Beginning November 30, 1993, graduate degrees from a college or university;
- Accredited independent study programs leading to standard college degrees;

- Technical courses for a certificate at a college or university.

Individuals with 6-year commitments beginning after September 30, 1990 may take the following types of training:

- Courses leading to a certificate or diploma from business, technical, or vocational schools;
- Cooperative training;
- Apprenticeship or job training programs offered by companies;
- Correspondence training;
- Independent study programs;
- Flight training (Individuals must have a private pilot's license, and must meet the medical requirements for the desired license program before beginning training, and throughout the flight training program.)

VA may approve programs offered by institutions outside of the United States, when they are pursued at educational institutions of higher learning, and lead to a college degree. Individuals must receive VA approval prior to attending or enrolling in any foreign programs.

Eligibility for this program is determined by the Selected Reserve components. Payments for the program are made by the VA. A state agency or VA must approve each program offered by a school or company. If an individual is seeking a college degree, the school must admit the individual to a degree program by the start of the individual's third term.

Restrictions on Training

Benefits are not payable for the following courses:

- Courses paid by the military Tuition Assistance program, if student is enrolled at less than ½ time;
- Courses taken while student is receiving a Reserve Officers' Training Corps scholarship;
- Non-accredited independent study courses;
- Bartending and personality development courses;
- Any course given by radio;
- Self-improvement courses such as reading, speaking, woodworking, basic seamanship, and English as a 2nd language;
- Any course which is avocational or recreational in character;
- Farm-cooperative courses;
- Audited courses;
- Courses not leading to an educational, professional, or vocational objective;
- Courses previously taken and successfully completed;
- Courses taken by a Federal government employee under the Government Employee's Training Act;
- Courses taken while in receipt of benefits for the same program from the Office of Workers' Compensation Programs.

VA must reduce benefits for individuals in Federal, State, or local prisons after being convicted of a felony.

An individual may not receive benefits for a program at a proprietary school if he or she is an owner or official of the school.

Part-Time Training

Individuals unable to attend school full-time should consider going part-time. Benefit rates and entitlement charges are less than the full-time rates. For example, if a student receives full-time benefits for 12 months, the entitlement charge is 12 months. However, if the student receives ½ time benefits for 12 months, the charge is 6 months. VA will pay for less than ½ time training if the student is not receiving Tuition Assistance for those courses.

Remedial, Deficiency and Refresher Training

Remedial and deficiency courses are intended to assist a student in overcoming a deficiency in a particular area of study. Individuals may qualify for benefits for remedial, deficiency, and refresher courses if they have a 6-year commitment that began after September 30, 1990. In order for such courses to be approved, the courses must be deemed necessary for pursuit of a program of education.

Refresher training is for technological advances that occurred in a field of employment. The advance must have occurred while the student was on active duty, or after release. There is an entitlement charge for these courses.

Tutorial Assistance

Students may receive a special allowance for individual tutoring performed after September 30, 1992, if they entered school at one-half time or more. To qualify, the student must have a deficiency in a subject. The school must certify the tutor's qualifications, and the hours of tutoring. Eligible students may receive a maximum monthly payment of $100.00. The maximum total benefit payable is $1,200.00.

There is no entitlement charge for the first $600.00 of tutorial assistance.

To apply for tutorial assistance, students must submit VA Form 22-1990t, "Application and Enrollment Certification for Individualized Tutorial Assistance." The form should be given to the certifying official in the office handling VA paperwork at the school for completion.

Months of Benefits/Entitlements Charged

Eligible members may be entitled to receive up to 36 months of education benefits. Benefit entitlement ends 10 years from the date the member becomes eligible for the program, or on the day the member leaves the Selected Reserve. (If a member's Reserve or National Guard unit was deactivated during the period October 1, 1991 through September 30, 1999, or if the member was involuntarily separated from service during this same period, eligibility for MGIB-SR benefits is retained for the full 10-year eligibility period. Eligibility for MGIB-SR benefits is also retained if a member is discharged due to a disability that was not caused by misconduct. Eligibility periods may be extended if a member is ordered to active duty.)

Individuals qualifying for more than one VA education program may receive a maximum of 48 months of benefits. For example, if a student used 30 months of Dependents' Educational Assistance, and is eligible for chapter 1606 benefits, he or she could have a maximum of 18 months of entitlement remaining.

Individuals are charged one full day of entitlement for each day of full-time benefits paid. For correspondence and flight training, one month of entitlement is charged each time VA pays one month of benefits. For cooperative programs, one month of entitlement is used for each month of benefits paid.

For apprenticeship and job training programs, the entitlement charge changes every 6 months. During the first 6 months, the charge is 75% of full time. For the second 6 months, the charge is 55% of full time. For the remainder of the program, the charge is 35% of full time.

Rates of Educational Assistance Pay

The following basic monthly rates are effective October 1, 2020:

Basic Monthly Rates Montgomery GI Bill Selected Reserve (MGIB-SR), Chapter 1606				
Type of Training	Full-Time	Three-Quarter Time	One-Half Time	Less than ½ Time
Institutional	$397.00	$297.00	$198.00	$99.25
Cooperative Training	$397.00 (Full-Time Only)			
Correspondence Training	Entitlement charged at the rate of one month for each $397.00 paid (Payment for correspondence courses is made at 55% of the approved charges for the course.)			
Apprenticeship On-The-Job Training -	First six months: $297.75 Second six months: $218.35 Remainder of program: $138.95			
Flight Training	Entitlement charged at the rate of one month for each $397.00 paid (Payment for flight training is made at 60% of the approved charges for the course, including solo hours.)			

Eligibility Periods

Under previous law, benefits typically ended upon separation from the Reserves. Section 530 of the National Defense Authorization Act of 2008 **increased the time period that a reservist may use SRMGIB benefits to ten years after separation from the Reserves**, as long as the member's discharge characterization is honorable. **This revision is backdated to October 28, 2004.**

For individuals who separated from the Selected Reserve prior to 10/28/2004, generally benefits end the day of separation. For individuals who stayed in the Selected Reserve, generally benefits ended 14 years from the date the individual became eligible for the program.

Exceptions: If an individual stayed in the Selected Reserve, VA could generally extend the 14-year period if:

- The individual couldn't train due to a disability caused by Selected Reserve service; or
- The individual was activated for service in the Persian Gulf Era (which hasn't ended for purposes of VA education benefits); or
- The individual's eligibility expired during a period of his or her enrollment in training.

Miscellaneous Information

Any change in educational, professional or vocational objectives is considered a "change of program." The law permits one change of program without prior VA approval, provided an individual's attendance conduct and progress in the last program were satisfactory. Additional "changes of program" require prior VA approval. VA will not charge a change of program if the individual enrolls in a new program after successful completion of the immediately preceding program.

Once an individual starts receiving benefits, he must maintain satisfactory attendance, conduct and progress. The VA may stop benefits if an individual does not meet the standards set by the school. VA may later resume benefits if the individual reenters the same program at the same school, and the school approves the reentry, and certifies it to VA.

If the individual does not reenter the same program at the same school, VA may resume benefits if the cause of unsatisfactory attendance, conduct or progress has been removed; and the program that the student intends to pursue is suitable to his or her abilities, aptitudes and interests.

Effective November 1, 2000, VA education benefits can be paid (with some exceptions) for school breaks, if the breaks do not exceed 8 weeks; and the terms before and after the breaks are not shorter than the break. Prior to November 1 2000, VA education benefits could be paid only if the breaks did not exceed a calendar month.

Application for Benefits

When an individual becomes eligible for the program, his or her unit will provide the individual with a "Notice of Basic Eligibility, DD Form 2384," or DD Form 2384-1 (for persons who establish eligibility on or after October 1, 1990). The unit will also code the eligibility into the Department of Defense personnel system.

When the individual finds a school, program, company, apprenticeship or job-training program, there are two important steps that must be followed:
- Make sure the program is approved for VA training. Contact the local VA regional office if there are any questions.
- Complete VA Form 22-1990, "Application for Education Benefits." The completed form should be sent to the VA regional office with jurisdiction over the state where training will occur.

Following receipt of an application, VA will review it and advise if anything else is needed. If an individual has started training, the application of "Basic Eligibility" should be taken to the school, employer or union. The certifying official should complete VA Form 22- 1999, "Enrollment Certification," and send all the forms to VA.

Procedures for Receipt of Monthly Payments

After selecting a school and submitting an application to VA, the school official must complete an enrollment certification, and submit it to the appropriate VA regional office. If a student meets the basic eligibility requirements for benefits, and the program or course is approved, VA will process the enrollment based on certified training time.

VA will accept the Notice of Basic Eligibility to pay benefits for 120 days after an individual's eligibility date. If the eligibility date is more than 120 days before the training program starts, VA will not approve the claim unless the Department of Defense personnel system shows that the individual is eligible. Only a student's reserve component can update the DoD personnel system. VA cannot change an individual's eligibility record.

When VA approves a claim, it will issue a letter with the details of the benefits payable. The first payment should be received within a few days of receipt of the letter.

If a student is enrolled in a degree program at a college or university, he or she will receive payment after the first of each month for the training during the preceding month. If a student is enrolled in a certificate or diploma program at a business, technical, or vocational school, he or she will not receive payment until they have verified their attendance. Students will receive a "Student Verification of Enrollment Form 22-8979" each month and must complete and return it to the appropriate VA regional office. After processing, VA will release a check.

If an individual is in an apprenticeship or job-training program, he or she will receive a form to report the hours worked each month. The form must be signed and given to the certifying official for the company or union. The certifying official must complete the form and send it to the appropriate VA regional office. After processing, VA will release a check.

If an individual is taking a correspondence course, he or she will receive a form each quarter, on which the student must show the number of lessons completed that quarter. The completed form should be sent to the school for certification of the number of lessons serviced during the quarter. The school will send the form to the appropriate VA regional office. After processing, VA will release a check. Payments are based on the number of lessons serviced by the school.

VA will send flight schools a supply of blank monthly certification of flight training forms. The school must complete the form by entering the number of hours, the hourly rate, and the total charges for flight training received during the month. The student should review and sign the completed form, and send it to the appropriate VA regional office. After processing, VA will release a check.

NOTE: It is against the law for schools to cash VA checks under a Power of Attorney Agreement.

Timely Receipt of Verification Forms and Checks

Students taking courses leading to a degree at a college or university should receive their checks for each month by the fifth of the next month. If it is not received by then, the VA should be immediately contacted so that appropriate action can be taken.

Students taking courses leading to a certificate or diploma from a business, technical, or vocational school should receive their verification forms for each month by the fifth of the following month. If it is not received by then, the VA should be immediately contacted so that another form can be issued.

One a completed verification form has been submitted; the student should receive a check within 2 weeks. If a check is not received by then, the VA should immediately be contacted so that appropriate action can be taken.

Advance Payments

An advance payment for the initial month, or partial month and the following month may be made, if:

- The school agrees to handle advance payments; and
- Training is one-half time or more; and
- A request is made by the individual in writing; and
- The VA receives the enrollment certification at least 30 days prior to the start of classes.

Advance payments are made out to the individual, and sent to the applicable school for delivery to the individual registration. VA cannot issue a check more than 30 days before classes start. Before requesting an advance payment, students should verify with the school certifying official that the school has agreed to process advance payments.

Requests for advance payments must be on VA Form 22-1999, Enrollment Certification, or a sheet of paper attached to the enrollment certification.

Once a student receives an advance payment at registration, the school must certify to VA that the student received the check. If a student reduces enrollment, or withdraws from all courses during the period covered by an advance payment, he or she must repay the overpayment to VA.

If an individual believes that the amount of a VA check is incorrect, the VA should be contacted before the check is cashed.

Direct Deposit

Payments can be sent directly to a student's savings or checking account through

Direct Deposit (Electronic Funds Transfer). To sign up for direct deposit by phone, students must call (877) 838-2778.

Student Responsibilities

To ensure timely receipt of correct payments, students should be sure to promptly notify the VA of:

- Any change in enrollment;
- Any change in address;
- Any change in selected reserve status (If an individual changes units or components, both the old and new units must report the change to VA through the components' eligibility data systems.)

In addition, students should use reasonable judgment when accepting and cashing a check. All letters from VA about monthly rates and effective dates should be read carefully. If a student thinks the amount of a VA check is wrong, VA should be contacted **before** cashing the check. Any incorrect checks should be returned to VA.

If a student cashes a check for the wrong amount, he or she will be liable for repayment of any resulting overpayment.

If an individual does not participate satisfactorily in the Selected Reserve, his or her eligibility ends. His or her component can require that a penalty be paid, based on a portion of payments received.

Recovery of Overpayments

VA must take prompt and aggressive action to recover overpayments. Students have the right to request a waiver of the overpayment, or verification that the amount is correct. If an overpayment is not repaid or waived, VA may add interest and collection fees to the debt. VA may also take one or more of the following actions to collect the debt:

- Withhold future benefits to apply to the debt;
- Refer the debt to a private collection agency;
- Recover the debt from any Federal income tax refund;
- Recover the debt from the salary (if student is a Federal employee);
- File a lawsuit in Federal court to collect the debt;
- Withhold approval of a VA home loan guarantee.
- An individual's reserve component will act to collect penalties caused by unsatisfactory participation in the reserve.

Changes in Enrollment

If a student withdraws from one or more courses after the end of the school's drop period, VA will reduce or stop benefits on the date of reduction or withdrawal. Unless the student can show that the change was due to mitigating circumstances, the student may have to repay **all** benefits for the course.

VA defines mitigating circumstances as "unavoidable and unexpected events that directly interfere with the pursuit of a course, and which are beyond the student's control.

Examples of reasons VA **may accept include:**
- Extended illness;
- Severe illness or death in immediate family;
- Unscheduled changes in employment; and
- Lack of child care.

Examples of reasons VA **may not accept include:**
- Withdrawal to avoid a failing grade;
- Dislike of the instructor; and
- Too many courses attempted.

(VA may ask the student to furnish evidence to support the reason for change, such as physician or employer written statements.)

The first time a student withdraws from up to 6 credit hours, VA will "excuse" the withdrawal, and pay benefits for the period attended.

If a student receives a grade that does not count toward graduation, all benefits for the course may have to be repaid.

If a student receives a non-punitive grade, the school will notify VA, and VA may reduce or stop benefits. The student may not have to repay the benefits if he or she can show that the grades were due to mitigating circumstances.

Work-Study Programs

Students may be eligible for an additional allowance under a work-study program that allows students to perform work for VA in return for an hourly wage. Students may perform outreach services under VA supervision, prepare and process VA paperwork, work at a VA medical facility or National Cemetery, or perform other approved activities.

Students must attend school at the three-quarter of full-time rate. VA will select students for the work-study program based on different factors. Such factors include:
- Disability of the student;
- Ability of the student to complete the work-study contract before the end of his or her eligibility for education benefits;
- Job availability within normal commuting distance to the student

VA will give the highest priority to a veteran who has a service-connected disability or disabilities rated by VA at 30% or more.

The number of applicants selected will depend on the availability of VA-related work at the school or at VA facilities in the area. Students may work during or between periods of enrollment, and can arrange with VA to work any number of hours during his or her enrollment. However, the maximum number of hours a student may work is 25 times the number of weeks in the enrollment period.

Students will earn an hourly wage equal to the Federal or State minimum wage, whichever is greater. If a student works at a college or university, the school **may** pay the difference between the amount VA pays and the amount the school normally pays other work-study students doing the same job.

Students interested in taking part in a work-study program must complete VA Form 22- 8691, Application for Work-Study Allowance. Completed forms should be sent to the nearest VA regional office.

Educational Counseling

VA can provide services to help eligible individuals understand their educational and vocational strengths and weaknesses and to plan:

An educational or training goal, and the means by which the goal can be reached; or An employment goal for which an individual qualifies on the basis of present training or experience.

VA can also help plan an effective job search. Counseling is available for:
- Service members eligible for VA educational assistance; and
- Service members on active duty and within 180 days of discharge; or
- Veterans with discharges that are not dishonorable, who are within one year from date of discharge.

Vocational Rehabilitation

Veterans may qualify for Training and Rehabilitation under Chapter 31 of Title 38, United States Code, if:
- The veteran has a service-connected disability or disabilities rated by VA at 20% or more; and
- The veteran received a discharge from active duty that was not dishonorable; and
- The veteran has an employment handicap.

Veterans may also qualify with a service-connected disability or disabilities rated by VA at 10%, and:
- The veteran has a serious employment handicap; or
- The veteran first applied for vocational rehabilitation benefits before November 1, 1990, reapplied after that date, and has an employment handicap.

Vocational rehabilitation helps disabled veterans become independent in daily living. Veterans may also receive assistance in selecting, preparing for, and securing employment that is compatible with their interests, talents, skills, physical capabilities, and goals. To apply for vocational rehabilitation, VA for 28-1900, Disabled Veterans Application for Vocational Rehabilitation, must be completed and sent to the nearest VA regional office.

Appeal of VA Decision

VA decisions on education benefits may be appealed within one year of the date an individual receives notice of a VA decision. Examples of VA decisions include:

- Training time,
- Change of program,
- School or course approval.

If a service member disagrees with a decision about his or her basic eligibility, he or she must contact the unit, National Guard Education Officer, or Army Reserve Education Services Officer. VA does not have authority under the law to reverse eligibility determinations. If the eligibility status is corrected, VA will pay benefits for periods during which the individual was eligible.

CHAPTER 23

LIFE INSURANCE

VA insurance programs were developed to provide insurance benefits for veterans and servicemembers who may not be able to get insurance from private companies because of a service-connected disability or because of the extra risks involved in military service.

VA has responsibility for veterans' and servicemembers' life insurance programs. Listed below are the eight life insurance programs managed by VA. The first four programs listed are closed to new issues. The last four are still issuing new policies.

VA Reduces Rates for Servicemembers' Group Life Insurance

On July 1, 2019, the VA reduced Servicemembers' Group Life Insurance (SGLI) monthly premium rates from 7 cents per $1,000 to 6 cents per $1,000 of insurance, along with Family SGLI Program (FSGLI) premium rates for spousal coverage at all age brackets.

> ### Key Takeaways
>
> Different programs cover Veterans (VGLI), service members (SGLI), and family members (FSGLI). You may also be able to get short-term financial coverage through TSGLI to help you recover from a traumatic (severe) injury. And if you're disabled because of an injury or illness caused— or made worse—by your active service, you may be able to get coverage through S-DVI to continue your life insurance beyond 2 years after you leave the military.

This lowers the premium for a servicemember with the maximum coverage of $400,000 from $28 to $24 a month. (Note: Servicemembers pay an additional $1 per month for traumatic injury protection.) Additionally, the SGLI premium rate for members who participate in one-day musters or funeral honors duty is also decreasing from $.25 per $1,000 of coverage to $.20 per $1,000 of coverage. Additionally, the SGLI premium rate for members who participate in one-day musters or funeral honors duty is also decreasing from $.25 per $1,000 of coverage to $.20 per $1,000 of coverage.

The Family SGLI spousal coverage premium rates are decreasing for all age brackets on July 1, 2019. Spousal coverage premiums are based on the age and amount of coverage elected by the Servicemember for their spouse.

Service-Disabled Veterans Insurance-S-DVI (1951- Present) (Policy Prefix - RH or ARH)

The only new insurance issued between 1957 and 1965 to either servicemembers or veterans was Service-Disabled Veterans Insurance. This insurance was (and still is) available to veterans with a service-connected disability.

S-DVI, also called "RH Insurance" is available in a variety of permanent plans, as well as term insurance. Policies are issued for a maximum face amount of $10,000.

VI is open to veterans separated from the service on or after April 25, 1951, who receive a service-connected disability rating of 0% or greater. New policies are still being issued under this program.

To apply for Supplemental S-DVI, you must file "VA Form 29-4364, Application for Supplemental Service-Disabled Veterans (RH) Life Insurance" or send a letter requesting this insurance over your signature. You must apply for the coverage within one year from notice of the grant of waiver of premiums.

Eligibility for S-DVI Insurance ("RH")
Veterans are eligible to apply for S-DVI if they meet the following four criteria:
- They have received a rating for a service-connected disability (even if only 0%).
- They were released from active duty under any other condition than dishonorable on or after April 25, 1951.
- They are in good health except for any service-related condition.
- They apply for the insurance within two years from the date service-connection is established.

Eligibility for Supplemental S-DVI ("Supplemental RH")
The Veterans' Benefits Act of 2010, provided for $30,000 of supplemental coverage to S- DVI policyholders. Premiums may not be waived on this supplemental coverage. S-DVI policyholders are eligible for this supplemental coverage if:
- They are eligible for a waiver of premiums.
- They apply for the coverage within one year from notice of the grant of waiver.
- Are under age 65.

Gratuitous S-DVI ("ARH")
Congress enacted legislation in 1959 to protect veterans who become incompetent

from a service-connected disability while eligible to apply for S-DVI, but who die before an application is filed. "ARH" insurance is:

- Issued posthumously;
- Payable to a preferred class of the veteran's relatives;
- Payable in a lump sum only.

Premiums for S-DVI Insurance

The premiums charged for this coverage are:

- Based on the rates a healthy individual would have been charged when the program began in 1951.
- Insufficient to pay all of the claims because the program insures many veterans with severe disabilities.
- Waived for totally disabled veterans (27% of S-DVI policyholders).
- Supplemented on an annual basis by Congressional appropriations.

Effective November 1, 2000, the VA "capped" premium rates at the age 70 rate. This means that a term policyholder's premium will never increase over the age 70 - premium rate. There are no reserves or surplus funds in this program. Therefore, dividends are not paid.

Disability Provisions

VI policies (except supplemental coverage) provide for the following disability benefits:

- A waiver of premiums at no extra premium based on the insured's total disability lasting six months or longer and starting before age 65;
- A total disability premium waiver in cases where the disability commenced prior to the effective date of the policy, providing the disability is service-connected.
- The optional Total Disability Income Provision is not available under this program.

Filing a Death Claim

To file a death claim, the beneficiary should complete "VA Form 29-4125, Claim for One Sum Payment."

The completed form should be mailed or faxed, along with a death certificate to:
Department of Veterans Affairs Regional Office and Insurance Center
PO Box 7208
Philadelphia, PA 19101
Fax: (215) 381-3561

If the beneficiary desires monthly payments instead of one lump sum, additional information is needed. The beneficiary should call the Insurance Center at (800) 669-8477 for instructions.

Customer Service

Any questions regarding USGLI should be directed to the VA Life Insurance Program at (800) 669-8477.

Servicemembers' Group Life Insurance - SGLI (1965-PRESENT)

SGLI Online Enrollment System

Beginning October 1, 2017, Army members can manage their Servicemembers' Group Life Insurance (SGLI) coverage using the SGLI Online Enrollment System (SOES). Army members join the Navy and Air Force in using the new system. Navy began using SOES on April 5, 2017 and Air Force on August 2, 2017. Air Force, Navy, and Army members should look for information from their service about when they should access SOES to confirm and certify their SGLI elections.

SOES access for other branches of service is planned for release on the following schedule*:

Marine Corps – February 2018
Coast Guard, National Oceanic and Atmospheric Administration – March 2018
*This schedule is subject to change.

SGLI provides automatic life insurance coverage of $400,000 to Servicemembers upon enlistment. Members with SGLI also get automatic coverage for their dependent children and spouses (unless the child or spouse is insured under SGLI as a Servicemember) under the Family SGLI program and traumatic injury protection (TSGLI). Servicemembers with full-time SGLI coverage will no longer have to complete a paper SGLV-8286 to make changes to their coverage or beneficiary elections. Instead, these Servicemembers can use the online system, SOES, to manage the amount of their SGLI and spouse coverage and to designate or update beneficiaries.

To access SOES, go to www.dmdc.osd.mil/milconnect, sign in, and go to Benefits, Life Insurance SOES- SGLI Online Enrollment System. Servicemembers can log in with their CAC or with their DS Logon using Internet Explorer as soon as they receive notice that SOES access is available. Servicemembers can then make sure their SGLI coverage and beneficiaries are up-to-date.

SGLI is supervised by the Department of Veterans Affairs and is administered by the Office of Servicemembers' Group Life Insurance (OSGLI) under terms of a group insurance contract.

Effective December 1, 2005, a new program of insurance was created under SGLI, called Traumatic Servicemembers' Group Life Insurance (TSGLI). This coverage

354

provides servicemembers protection against loss due to traumatic injuries and is designed to provide financial assistance to members so their loved ones can be with them during their recovery from their injuries. The coverage ranges from $25,000 to $100,000 depending on the nature of the injury.

(See following section for further information regarding Traumatic Injury Coverage.)

Eligibility for SGLI

Full-time coverage is available for:

- Commissioned, warrant and enlisted members of the Army, Navy, Air Force, Marine Corps and Coast Guard;
- Commissioned members of the National Oceanic and Atmospheric Administration and the Public Health Service;
- Cadets or midshipmen of the four United States Service Academies;
- Ready Reservists scheduled to perform at least 12 periods of inactive training per year.
- Members of the Individual Ready Reserves who volunteer for assignment to a mobilization category.
- Part-time coverage is available for eligible members of the Reserves who do not qualify for full-time coverage.

Coverage Amounts

Effective September 1, 2005 coverage in the SGLI Program increased from $250,000 to $400,000. Coverage must be elected in $50,000 increments.

A special death gratuity of $150,000 was approved for survivors of servicemembers who:

- Died from October 7, 2001 to September 1, 2005, and
- Died while on active duty.

SGLI Coverage Is:

- Automatic at the time of entry into a period of active duty or reserve status.
- Available in $50,000 increments up to the maximum of $400,000 of insurance.

Members may decline coverage or may elect reduced coverage by contacting their personnel officer and completing "Form 8286, SGLI Election and Certificate." If such a member later wishes to obtain or increase coverage, proof of good health will be required.

NOTE: Reservists called to active duty, are **automatically** insured for $400,000 regardless of whether or not they had previously declined coverage, or elected a lesser amount of coverage while on reserve duty.

Coverage Periods

Full-time SGLI coverage for members on active duty or active duty for training and members of the Ready Reserve will terminate:

The 120th day after separation or release from duty, or separation or release from assignment to a unit or position of the Ready Reserve;

For members who are totally disabled on the date of separation or release, at the end of the last day of one year following separation or release or at the end of the day on which the insured ceases to be totally disabled, whichever is earlier, but in no event earlier than

- 120 days following separation or release from such duty; (NOTE: Refer to important updated information following #4, below.)
- At the end of the 31st day of a continuous period of: Absence without leave;
- Confinement by military authorities under a court-martial sentence involving total forfeiture of pay and allowances; or
- Confinement by civilian authorities under sentence adjudged by a civilian court.

*Note: Any insurance terminated as the result of the absence or confinement, together with any beneficiary designation in effect at the time the insurance was terminated, will be automatically restored as of the date the member returns to duty with pay.

The last day of the month in which the member files with the uniformed service, written notice of an election not to be insured.

SGLI Disability Extension Increased to Two Years

On June 15, 2006, the President signed P.L. 109-233, the Veterans' Housing Opportunity & Benefits Improvement Act of 2006. The law extends the period of Servicemembers' Group Life Insurance (SGLI) coverage for totally disabled veterans following separation from active duty or active duty for training to the earlier of:

- The date on which the insured ceases to be totally disabled; or
- The date that is two years after separation or release,

The law makes identical changes with respect to certain reserve assignments in which the individual performs active duty or volunteers for assignment to a mobilization category.

The SGLI Disability Extension is available to you if you are totally disabled at time of discharge. To be considered totally disabled, you must have a disability that prevents you from being gainfully employed OR have one of the following conditions, regardless of your employment status:

- Permanent loss of use of both hands Permanent loss of use of both feet
- Permanent loss of use of both eyes
- Permanent loss of use of one hand and one foot Permanent loss of use of one foot and one eye Permanent loss of use of one hand and one eye Total loss of hearing in both ears
- Organic loss of speech (lost ability to express oneself, both by voice and whisper, through normal organs for speech - being able to speak with an

artificial appliance is disregarded in determination of total disability)

Part-Time Coverage Terminates as Follows:

Part-time coverage is in effect only on the days of active duty or active duty for training, and the hours of inactive duty training, including period of travel to and from duty. A temporary termination of coverage occurs at the end of each such period of duty, including travel time, and coverage is resumed at the commencement of the next period of covered duty or travel.

When part-time coverage is extended for 120 days as the result of a disability, the extended coverage terminates at the end of the 120th day following the Reservist active or inactive period during which the disability was incurred or aggravated.

Unless extended for 120 days because of disability as referred to above, eligibility for part-time coverage terminates at the end of the last day of the member's obligation to perform such duty.

If a member files with the uniformed service a written notice of an election not to be insured, coverage terminates on the last day of the period of active duty or active duty for training, or at the end of the period of inactive duty training, including travel time while returning from such duty during which the election is filed. If the election is filed with a member's uniformed service other than during a period of active duty, active duty for training, or inactive duty the coverage is terminated immediately.

Beneficiary Selection

Any beneficiary can be named. If none is selected, the insurance is distributed, by law, in the following order:

- Spouse; or
- Children; or
- Parents; or
- Executor of estate; or
- Other next of kin.

An insured should designate a beneficiary by completing "Form SGVL 8286, Servicemembers' Group Life Insurance Election and Certificate." The completed form should be submitted to the individual's uniformed service.

Options for Payments of Policy Proceeds

SGLI proceeds can be paid in a lump sum **or** over a 36-month period.

Alliance Account

If the proceeds are to be paid in a lump sum, then beneficiaries of SGLI and VGLI will receive the payment of their insurance proceeds via an "Alliance Account". Rather than the traditional single check for the full amount of insurance proceeds, the beneficiary receives a checkbook for an interest-bearing account from which the beneficiary can write a check for any amount from $250 up to the full amount of the proceeds.

The Alliance Account:

Earns interest at a competitive rate; Is guaranteed by Prudential;

Gives the beneficiary time to make important financial decisions while their funds are secure and earning interest ;

Gives them instant access to their money at all times.

Accelerated Benefits

On November 11, 1998, the President signed legislation authorizing the payment of "Accelerated Benefits" in the SGLI and VGLI programs subject to the following:

- Terminally ill insureds will have access of up to 50% of the face amount of their coverage during their lifetime.
- This money will be available in increments of $5,000.
- An insured must have a medical prognosis of life expectancy of 9 months or less.

Insurance Options After Separation from Service

When released from active duty or the Reserve, members with full-time SGLI coverage can convert their coverage to Veterans Group Life Insurance **or** to an individual commercial life insurance policy with any one of 99 participating commercial insurance companies.

Filing Death Claims

A beneficiary may file a claim for VGLI proceeds by submitting Form SGLV 8283, Claim for Death Benefits, to:

Office of Servicemembers' Group Life Insurance (OSGLI)

PO Box 70173

Philadelphia, PA 19176-9912

SGLI Traumatic Injury (TSGLI) Claims

Taxation

SGLI proceeds that are payable at the death of the insured are excluded from gross income for tax purposes. (The value of the proceeds, however, may be included in determining the value of an estate, and that estate may ultimately be subject to tax.)

If SGLI proceeds are paid to a beneficiary in 36 equal installments, the interest portion included in these installments is also exempt from taxation. In addition, delayed settlement interest (interest accrued from the date of the insured's death to the date of settlement) is also exempt from taxation.

A beneficiary is not required to report to the Internal Revenue Service any installment interest or delayed settlement interest received in addition to the proceeds.

Customer Service

Any questions regarding SGLI should be directed to the Office of Servicemembers' Group Life Insurance (OSGLI) at (800) 419-1473.

Traumatic Injury Protection Under Servicemembers' Group Life Insurance (TSGLI)

TSGLI is a program that provides automatic traumatic injury coverage to all servicemembers covered under the Servicemembers' Group Life Insurance (SGLI) program. Every member who has SGLI also has TSGLI effective December 1, 2005. This coverage applies to active-duty members, reservists, funeral honors duty and one-day muster duty. The premium for TSGLI is a flat rate of $1 per month for most service members. This benefit is also provided retroactively for members who incur severe losses as a result of traumatic injury between October 7, 2001 and December 1, 2005 if the loss was the direct result of injuries incurred in Operations Enduring Freedom or Iraqi Freedom.

For the purposes of TSGLI only, "incurred in Operation Enduring Freedom or Operation Iraqi Freedom" means that the member must have been deployed outside the United States on orders in support of OEF or OIF or serving in a geographic location that qualified the service member for the Combat Zone Tax Exclusion under the Internal Revenue Service Code.

The service member is the beneficiary of TSGLI. The member cannot name someone other than himself or herself as the TSGLI beneficiary. If the member is incompetent, the benefit will be paid to his or her guardian or attorney-in-fact. If the service member is deceased, the TSGLI payment will be made to the beneficiary or beneficiaries of the member's basic SGLI.

TSGLI coverage will pay a benefit of between $25,000 and $100,000 depending on the loss directly resulting from the traumatic injury.

In 2011 the VA announced that servicemembers with severe injuries to the genitourinary organs are now eligible for Servicemembers' Group Life Insurance Traumatic Injury Protection (TSGLI). The first payments for eligible veterans and servicemembers began December 1, 2011. Eligibility is retroactive to injuries received on or after October 7, 2001.

Expansion of Covered Losses

Loss of Sight

Loss of Sight lasting 120 days or more is considered as "permanent", qualifying the service member for the same payment rate as for permanent loss of sight ($100,000 for both eyes, $50,000 for one eye).

Uniplegia

Uniplegia (complete and total paralysis of one limb) has been added to the schedule of losses with payment at $50,000.

Amputation of the Hand

The definition of amputation of the hand has been expanded to include loss of four fingers (on the same hand) or loss of thumb, with payment remaining at $50,000 for one affected hand and $100,000 for both hands.

Amputation of the Foot

The definition of amputation of the foot has been expanded to include loss of all toes, with the payment remaining at $50,000 for one affected foot and $100,000 for both feet.

Loss of Four Toes

A new category has been created for loss of four toes (on the same foot and not including the big toe) with payment at $25,000 for one affected foot and $50,000 for both feet.

Loss of Big Toe

A new category has been created for the loss of the big toe, with payment at $25,000 for one affected foot and $50,000 for both feet.

Limb Salvage

Coverage has been expanded to include limb salvage (multiple surgeries intended to save a limb rather than amputate) with payment equivalent to amputation.

Burns

The burn standard, currently 3rd degree (full thickness) burns to at least 30% of face or body, has been expanded to include 2nd degree (partial thickness) burns to at least 20% of the face or body.

Hospitalization as a Proxy for ADL Loss

Continuous 15-day inpatient hospital care is deemed a proxy for the first ADL eligibility period for OTI (Other Traumatic Injury) and TBI (Traumatic Brain Injury) claims.

Facial Reconstruction

Facial Reconstruction, required as a result of traumatic avulsion of the face or jaw that causes discontinuity defects, has been added to the schedule of losses, with payment levels of $25,000 to $75,000, depending upon the severity of the injury.

Losses to the Genitourinary System

Effective beginning in 2011, the VA amended its regulations to add certain genitourinary system injuries to the Schedule of Covered Losses. These are injuries that occur to the genitals or urinary system. Payments range from $25,000 to $50,000 and are retroactive to October 7, 2001. The new losses added to the TSGLI Schedule of Covered Losses include the following:

- Anatomical loss of penis
- Permanent loss of use of the penis
- Anatomical loss of one or both of the testicles
- Permanent loss of use of both testicles
- Anatomical loss of the vulva, uterus or vaginal canal
- Permanent loss of use of the vulva or vaginal canal
- Anatomical loss of one or both ovaries
- Permanent loss of use of both ovaries
- Total and permanent loss of urinary system function

360

Servicemembers' Group Life Insurance Family Coverage

The Veterans' Opportunities Act of 2001 extended life insurance coverage to spouses and children of members insured under the SGLI program, effective November 1, 2001.

Amount of Coverage

SGLI coverage is available in $50,000 increments up to a maximum of $400,000. Covered members receive 120 days of free coverage from their date of separation. Coverage can be extended for up to two years if the Servicemember is totally disabled at separation. Part-time coverage is also provided to Reserve members who do not qualify for full-time coverage (members covered part-time do not receive 120 days of free coverage).

If you are totally disabled at the time of separation (unable to work), you can apply for the SGLI Disability Extension, which provides free coverage for up to two years from the date of separation. At the end of the extension period, you automatically become eligible for VGLI, subject to premium payments.

Eligibility

Family coverage is available for the spouses and children of:
- Active-duty servicemembers; and
- Members of the Ready Reserve of a uniformed service.

Note: Family coverage is available only for members insured under the SGLI program. Family coverage is not available for those insured under the VGLI program.

Premiums

SGLI coverage for children is free. For monthly premiums for spouses, individuals should call (800) 419-1473.

Dependent Child Coverage Extended to Include Stillborn Children

Public law 110-389 expanded the Servicemembers' Group Life Insurance (SGLI) program to include a member's "stillborn child" as an insurable dependent. SGLI dependent coverage provides for a $10,000 payment to the insured service member upon the death of the member's dependent child. The law was enacted October 10, 2008, and on November 18, 2009, regulations implementing section 402 of the Veterans' Benefits Improvement Act of 2008, were published in the Federal Register, and immediately went into effect. This change applies only for stillbirths on or after October 10, 2008, the effective date of PL110-389.

Declining Coverage

If an individual does not want insurance coverage for a spouse or wants a reduced amount of coverage, he or she must complete "form SGLV-82861, Family Coverage Election", and submit it to his or her personnel officer.

Termination of Coverage

Coverage for a spouse ends 120 days after any of the following events:

- The date elected in writing to terminate a spouse's coverage;
- The date elected in writing to terminate the service member's own coverage;
- The date of the service member's death;
- The date the service member's coverage terminates;
- The date of divorce.

A spouse can covert his or her coverage to a policy with a commercial company within 120 days following one of the events listed above. He or she should contact the Office of Servicemembers' Group Life Insurance at (800) 419-1473.

Coverage for a service member's children ends 120 days after any of the following events:

- The date elected in writing to terminate the service member's own coverage;
- The date the service member separates from service;
- The date of the service member's death;
- The date the child is no longer the service member's dependent.

No conversion options are available to children.

Payment of Proceeds

The service member is paid the proceeds due to the death of a spouse or child. If the service member were to die before payment could be made, the proceeds of a spouse or child claim would be paid to the member's beneficiary, as designated by the member.

Veterans' Group Life Insurance – VGLI (1974- Present)

VMLI is issued to those severely disabled veterans and servicemembers who have received grants for specially adapted housing from VA. These grants are issued to veterans and servicemembers whose movement or vision is substantially impaired because of their disabilities.

Policyholders have three options for their VMLI coverage. They may decline the increase and retain their pre-October level of VMLI coverage and premium, accept the maximum amount of VMLI coverage for which they are eligible, or select a different amount of VMLI coverage. Coverage may not exceed the maximum allowed by law, or their mortgage balance, whichever is less.

VGLI, like SGLI, is supervised by the Department of Veterans Affairs, but is administered by the Office of Servicemembers' Group Life Insurance (OSGLI). VGLI provides for the conversion of Servicemembers' Group Life Insurance to a five-year renewable term policy of insurance protection after a service member's separation from service.

Effective April 11, 2011, VGLI insureds who are under age 60 and have less than $400,000 in coverage can purchase up to $25,000 of additional coverage on each five-year anniversary of their coverage, up to the maximum $400,000. No medical underwriting is required for the additional coverage.

Eligibility for VGLI

Full-time coverage is available for the following members:

- Full-time SGLI insureds that are released from active duty or the Reserves, or;
- Ready Reservists who have part-time SGLI coverage, and who, while performing active duty or inactive duty for training for a period of less than 31 days, incur a disability or aggravate a preexisting disability that makes them uninsurable at standard premium rates, or;
- Members of the Individual Ready Reserve (IRR) and Inactive National Guard (ING), or;
- A member of the Public Health Service (PHS) or Inactive Reserve Corps (IRC), or;
- A member who had part-time SGLI and who, while performing duty (or traveling directly to or from duty), suffered an injury or disability which renders him/her uninsurable at standard premium rates.

Coverage Amounts

VGLI is issued in multiples of $10,000 up to a maximum of $400,000, but not for more than the amount of SGLI coverage the member had in force at the time of separation from active duty or the reserves.

VGLI Renewal

Members may renew their VGLI coverage under the following conditions:

- Members who have separated from service may renew their VGLI coverage for life in 5-year term periods.
- Members of the IRR or ING may renew their VGLI for additional 5-year term periods, as long as they remain in the IRR or ING.

Rather than renew, a member also has the right at any time to **convert** VGLI to an individual commercial life insurance policy with any one of 99 participating commercial insurance companies.

Increasing VGLI Coverage

You can increase your VGLI coverage by up to $25,000 on the five-year anniversary date of your coverage policy if you meet all of the following criteria:

- You have an active VGLI policy.
- You currently have less than $400,000 of VGLI.
- You will be under age 60 on your next policy anniversary date.
- You must request the increase during the 120-day period prior to the 5-year anniversary of your policy

For more information on increasing your VGLI coverage, contact the Office of Servicemembers' Group Life Insurance online at osgli.osgli@prudential.com or by calling 1-800-419-1473.

How to Apply for VGLI

VGLI applications are mailed to eligible members, generally within 60 days after separation, and again shortly before the end of the 16-month application period. Applications are mailed to the address shown on the member's DD-Form 214 or equivalent separation orders. It is the member's responsibility, however, to apply within the time limits, even if they do not receive an application in the mail.

Applications should be mailed to:
Office of Servicemembers Group Life Insurance (OSGLI)
PO Box 70173
Philadelphia, PA 19176-9912

Time Limits to Apply for VGLI

To be eligible, a member must apply for VGLI within the following time limits:

Ordinarily, a member must submit an application to the OSGLI with the required premium within 120 days following separation from service.

If a member is totally disabled at the time of separation from active duty and is granted extended free SGLI coverage, he or she may apply for VGLI anytime during the one-year period of extension.

Individuals who are assigned to the IRR and ING have 120 days after assignment to apply, without evidence of good health, and one year after that with evidence of good health. If an application or the initial premium has not been submitted within the time limits above, VGLI may still be granted if an application, the initial premium and **evidence of insurability** (good health) are submitted to OSGLI within 1 year and 120 days following termination of SGLI. **Applications will not be accepted after one year and 120 days.**

An application for an incompetent member may be made by a guardian, committee, conservator or curator. In the absence of a court-appointed representative, the application may be submitted by a family member or anyone acting on the member's behalf.

VGLI Premium Rates

VGLI premium rates are determined by age group and amount of insurance. To lessen the high cost of term insurance at the older ages, a Decreasing Term Option is available, starting at age group 60 to 64. Under this option, an insured pays a level premium for life, while the insurance amount declines by 25% for three subsequent five-year renewals. At that point, coverage remains level at 25% of the original insurance amount.

Payment of Premiums

Once the VGLI application is approved, the OSGLI will send the insured a certificate and a supply of monthly premium payment coupons.

Premiums may be paid:

- Monthly;
- Quarterly;
- Semiannually;
- Annually;
- By monthly allotment from military retirement pay;
- By monthly deduction from VA compensation payments.

If the insured does not pay the premium when it is due or within a grace period of 60 days, the VGLI coverage will lapse. If VGLI lapsed due to failure to pay the premiums on time, the insured will receive a notification of the lapse and a reinstatement form. The insured may apply to reinstate coverage at any time within 5 years of the date of the unpaid premium. If the insured applies for reinstatement within 6 months from the date of lapse, the individual only needs to provide evidence that he or she is in the same state of health on the date of reinstatement as on the date of lapse. Otherwise, the individual may need to provide proof of good health.

Beneficiary Selection

Any beneficiary can be named. If none is selected, the insurance is distributed, by law, in the following order:

- Spouse, or
- Children, or
- Parents, or
- Executor of estate, or
- Other next of kin.

To name a beneficiary, the insured must submit "Form SGLV 8712, Beneficiary Designation-Veterans' Group Life Insurance." The completed form should be sent to:

Office of Servicemembers Group Life Insurance (OSGLI)
PO Box 70173
Philadelphia, PA 19176-9912

When an insured converts SGLI to VGLI following separation from service, a new beneficiary designation form must be completed. If a new form is not filed, the SGLI beneficiary designation will be considered the VGLI designation for up to 60 days after the effective date of the VGLI. If a new beneficiary is not designated after this 60-day period, the proceeds would be paid "By Law" under the order of precedence in the law

Alliance Account

VGLI proceeds can be paid in a lump sum or over a 36-month period.

If the proceeds are to be paid in a lump sum then beneficiaries of SGLI and VGLI will receive the payment of their insurance proceeds via an "Alliance Account".

Rather than the traditional single check for the full amount of insurance proceeds, the beneficiary receives a checkbook for an interest-bearing account from which the beneficiary can write a check for any amount from $250 up to the full amount of the proceeds.

The Alliance Account:
- Earns interest at a competitive rate;
- Is guaranteed by Prudential;
- Gives the beneficiary time to make important financial decisions while their funds are secure and earning interest;
- Gives them instant access to their money at all times.

Accelerated Benefits
On November 11, 1998, the President signed legislation authorizing the payment of "Accelerated Benefits" in the SGLI and VGLI programs subject to the following:
- Terminally ill insureds will have access of up to 50 percent of the face amount of their coverage during their lifetime.
- This money will be available in increments of $5,000.
- An insured must have a medical prognosis of life expectancy of 9 months or less.

Taxation
VGLI proceeds are exempt from taxation. Any installment interest or delayed settlement interest that a beneficiary receives in addition to the proceed is also exempt from taxation and does not need to be reported to the IRS.

Customer Service
Any questions regarding VGLI should be directed to the office of Servicemembers' Group Life Insurance (OSGLI) at (800) 419-1473.

Veterans' Mortgage Life Insurance – VMLI (1971- Present)

The Veterans' Mortgage Life Insurance (VMLI) program began in 1971, and is designed to provide financial protection to cover eligible veterans' home mortgages in the event of death. VMLI is issued to those severely disabled veterans, under age 70, who have received grants for Specially Adapted Housing from VA. (Refer to Chapter 6 of this book for information regarding Specially Adapted Housing.) **Veterans must apply for VMLI before their 70th birthday.** The Veterans Benefits Act of 2010 increased the maximum amount of VMLI coverage from $90,000 to $150,000, which became effective October 1, 2011. On January 1, 2012, the amount increased from $150,000 to 200,000, under the same law. The insurance is payable if the veteran dies before the mortgage is paid off. VA will pay the amount of money still owed on the mortgage up to $200,000.

The insurance is payable only to the mortgage lender. The day-to-day operations of the program are handled by the Philadelphia VAROIC.

Coverage Amounts

VMLI coverage decreases as the insured's mortgage falls below $90,000. This reduced coverage cannot be reinstated. However, if the home is sold and a new home is purchased the veteran becomes eligible once again for the maximum amount of coverage.

Payment of VMLI Proceeds

Certain conditions apply to the payment of VMLI benefits:
- The insurance is payable at the death of the veteran only to the mortgage holder.
- If the title of the property is shared with anyone other than the veteran's spouse, the insurance coverage is only for the percentage of the title that is in the veteran's name.
- No insurance is payable if the mortgage is paid off before the death of the insured or if it was paid off by other mortgage insurance before the VMLI payment is made.

The insurance will be canceled for any of the following conditions:
- The mortgage is paid in full.
- Termination of the veteran's ownership of the property securing the loan.
- The request of the veteran.
- Failure of the veteran to submit timely statements or other required information

Premiums

Premiums are determined by the insurance age of the veteran, the outstanding balance of the mortgage at the time of application, and the remaining length of time the mortgage has to run. Veterans who desire insurance will be advised of the correct premium when it is determined.

Premiums **must** be paid by deduction from the veteran's monthly compensation or pension payments if the veteran is receiving such payments. If such payments are not being received the veteran may make direct payments, on a monthly, quarterly, semiannual, or annual basis, to the VA Insurance Center in Philadelphia, Pennsylvania.

Dividend Options

If a policyholder is eligible for a dividend, he or she may choose from several dividend options that are available:

Cash paid to the policyholder by US Treasury check.

Credit, held in account for the insured with interest. Can be used to prevent policy lapse. Will be refunded upon the insured's request, or will be included in the award to the beneficiary(ies) at the time of the insured's death.

367

Paid-Up Additions (PUA'S), used as a net single premium to purchase additional paid-up insurance. Available only on "V," "RS," "W," "J," "JR," and "JS" policies. PUA's will be whole life insurance if the basic insurance is an endowment policy.

Deposit, held in account for insured with interest. Available only on permanent plan policies. Considered part of the policy's cash value for the purpose of purchasing reduced paid-up insurance, or if the policy lapses, extended insurance (except for "K" or "JS" policies). Will be refunded upon the insured's request. Will be included in the award to the beneficiary(ies) at the time of the insured's death.

Premium, applied to pay premiums in advance.

Indebtedness applied toward a loan or lien on a policy.

Net Cash used to pay an annual premium with any remainder paid to the policyholder under the cash option.

Net PUA, used to pan an annual premium with any remainder used to purchase paid-up additional insurance.

Net Loan-Lien used to pay an annual premium with any remainder used to reduce an outstanding loan or lien.

To change the method in which dividends are paid, individuals should speak with an Insurance Specialist at (800) 669-8477

Miscellaneous Information About Government Life Insurance Policies

Power of Attorney is not acceptable for executing a change of beneficiary for government life insurance, even if certain state statutes allow it. Only a court-appointed guardian that is recognized by state statutes can execute a beneficiary designation. If the state statute does not give the guardian broad powers to authorize a beneficiary change, a specific court order is needed to effectuate a change.

Assignment of government life insurance is not allowed, for any reason, nor can ownership of a policy be transferred. Only the insured can exercise the rights and privileges inherent in the ownership of the policy.

Policy Loans are available on permanent plans of insurance. The policyholder can take up to 94% of the reserve value of the policy, less any indebtedness. The policy cannot be lapsed, and premiums must be paid or waived at least one year before a policy has a loan value. Changes in interest rates are made on October 1 of each year, if warranted. Rate changes are tied to the "ten-year constant maturities", U.S. Treasury securities index.

A policyholder can apply for a loan by filing VA Form 29-1546, Application for Policy Loan.

The completed form can be faxed to (215) 381-3580, or mailed to:
Department of Veterans Affairs Regional Office and Insurance Center
PO Box 7327
Philadelphia, PA 19101

An Annual Insurance Policy Statement is mailed to the insured on the policy anniversary date of each policy. The statement provides the insured with information about his or her VA insurance. The statement should be reviewed for accuracy each year, and the VA should be contacted immediately if there are any discrepancies.

CHAPTER 24

HOME LOAN GUARANTIES

Benefits

Purchase Loans help veterans purchase a home at a competitive interest rate, often without requiring a down payment or private mortgage insurance. Cash-Out Refinance loans let eligible veterans take cash out of their home equity to pay off things such as debt, to, make home improvements or to fund education. To be eligible veterans must have satisfactory credit, sufficient income to meet the expected monthly obligations, and a valid Certificate of Eligibility (COE).

Interest Rate Reduction Refinance Loans (IRRRL) are also called the Streamline Refinance Loan, and they can help veterans obtain a lower interest rate by refinancing an existing VA loan. This can be used only for veterans with an existing VA guaranteed loan on a property.

Native American Direct Loan (NADL) Program helps eligible Native American veterans finance the purchase, construction or improvement of homes on Federal Trust Land or reduce the interest rate on a VA loan. The veterans' tribal organization must participate in VA direct loan program, and the veteran must have a valid COE.

Cash-OUT Refinance Loan is a VA-backed cash-out refinance loan that lets you replace your current loan with a new one under different terms. If you want to take cash out of your home equity or refinance a non-

> ### Key Takeaways
>
> VA helps Servicemembers, Veterans, and eligible surviving spouses become homeowners. As part of our mission to serve you, we provide a home loan guaranty benefit and other housing-related programs to help you buy, build, repair, retain, or adapt a home for your own personal occupancy.
>
> VA Home Loans are provided by private lenders, such as banks and mortgage companies. VA guarantees a portion of the loan, enabling the lender to provide you with more favorable terms.

VA loan into a VA-backed loan, a VA-backed cash-out refinance loan might be right for you. You must qualify for a VA-backed home loan Certificate of Eligibility and meet VA's and your lender's standards for credit, income and other requirements and live in the home you're refinancing.

Adapted Housing Grants help veterans with a permanent and total service-connected disability purchase or build an adapted home or to modify an existing home to account for their disability.

Other resources may be available to veterans depending on their state of residency, including property tax reductions.

General Information

The purpose of the VA loan guaranty program is to help veterans and active-duty personnel finance the purchase of homes with competitive loan terms and interest rates.

The VA does not actually lend the money to veterans. VA guaranteed loans are made by private lenders, such as banks, savings & loans, or mortgage companies. The VA guaranty means the lender is protected against loss if the veteran fails to repay the loan.

The VA Loan Guaranty Service is the organization within the VA that has the responsibility of administering the home loan program.

In 2011 the VA announced that those veterans who qualify and submit to a short sale or deed-in-lieu of foreclosure may be eligible to receive $1,500 in relocation assistance. The VA has instructed mortgage lenders to provide the funds in order to help borrowers cover the cost of moving or other expenses incurred during the process.

In 2012 Under Public Law 112-154, veterans in specially adapted housing or those in receipt of VA home loans, which have property hindered or destroyed by a natural disaster, became eligible to receive VA assistance. The law also extended the VA's authority to extend the guarantee of timely payment of principal and interest of mortgage loans. The VA's authority was also extended with regard to the collection of loan fees and adjustment of maximum home loan guarantee amounts.

PL 116-23 Changes to the VA Home Loan Program

The Blue Water Navy Vietnam Veterans Act of 2019 (PL 116-23) extended the presumption of herbicide exposure, such as Agent Orange, to veterans who served in the offshore waters of the Republic of Vietnam between January 9, 1962, and May 7, 2975. Beginning January 1, 2020, veterans who served as far as 12 nautical miles from the shore of Vietnam or who had served in the Korean Demilitarized Zone are presumed to have been exposed to herbicides. Additionally, PL 116-23 made changes to the VA Home Loan Program, including:

- VA-guaranteed home loans will no longer be limited to the Federal Housing Finance Agency Conforming Loan Limits. Veterans are now able to obtain a no-down-payment home loan in all areas, regardless of loan amount.
- The law exempts Purple Heart recipients currently serving on active duty from the VA Home Loan funding fee
- VA removed the loan limit for Native American Veterans seeking to build or purchase a home on Federal Trust Land
- At this time, there is a temporary change to the VA funding Fee, which is a congressionally mandated fee associated with the VA Home Loan. Veterans and service members will see a slight increase of 0.15 to 0,30% in their funding fee, while National Guard and Reserve members will see a slight decrease in their fee to align with the fee paid by 'Regular Military' borrowers. Veterans with service-connected disabilities, some surviving spouses and other potential borrowers are exempt from the VA loan funding fee and won't be impacted by the change.

Features of VA Guaranteed Home Loans

- Equal opportunity for all qualified veterans to obtain a VA guaranteed loan.
- No down payment (unless required by the lender or the purchase price is more than the reasonable value of the property).
- Buyer's interest rate is negotiable.
- Buyer has the ability to finance the VA funding fee (plus reduced funding fees with a down payment of at least 5% and exemption for veterans receiving VA compensation).
- Closing costs are comparable with other financing types (and may be lower).
- No mortgage insurance premiums are necessary.
- An assumable mortgage may be available.
- Buyer has the right to prepay without penalty.

VA Guaranteed Loans Do Not Do the Following:

- Guarantee that a home is free of defects
- VA only guarantees the loan. It is the veteran's responsibility to assure that he or she is satisfied with the property being purchased. Veterans should seek expert advice as necessary, before legally committing to a purchase agreement.
- If a veteran has a home built, VA cannot compel the builder to correct construction defects, although VA does have the authority to suspend a builder from further participation in the VA home loan program.
- VA cannot guarantee the veteran is making a good investment.
- VA cannot provide a veteran with legal service.

Uses for VA Loan Guarantees

VA loan guarantees can be used for the following:

- To purchase, construct, or improve a home.
- To purchase and improve a home concurrently.
- To purchase a residential condominium or townhouse unit in a VA approved project. (If one veteran is purchasing the property, the total number of separate units cannot be more than 4.)
- To purchase a manufactured home or a manufactured home and manufactured home lot.
- To purchase and improve a manufactured home lot on which to place a manufactured home which the veteran already owns and occupies.
- To refinance an existing home loan.
- To refinance an existing VA loan to reduce the interest rate and make energy-efficient improvements.
- To refinance an existing manufactured home loan in order to acquire a lot.
- To improve a home by installing a solar heating and/or cooling system or other energy-efficient improvements.

Veterans must certify that they plan to live in the home they are buying or building in order to qualify for a VA loan guaranty.

VA loan guarantees are available only for property located in the United States, its territories, or possessions (Puerto Rico, Guam, Virgin Islands, American Samoa, and Northern Mariana Islands).

VA loan guarantees are not available for farm loans unless there is a home on the property, which will be personally occupied by the veteran. Non-realty loans for the purchase of equipment, livestock, machinery, etc. are not made. Other loan programs for farm financing may be available through the Farmers Home Administration, which gives preference to veteran applicants. (Interested veterans should refer to the local telephone directory for the phone number of a local office.)

Although business loans are not available through VA, the Small Business Administration (SBA) has a number of programs designed to help foster and encourage small business enterprises, including financial and management assistance. Each SBA office has a veteran's affairs officer available to speak with. (Interested veterans should refer to the local telephone directory for the phone number of a local SBA office, or call (800) 827- 5722.)

Eligibility Requirements

Individuals may qualify for VA home loan guaranties if their service falls within any of the following categories:

Vietnam Eligibility Requirements

- Active duty on or after August 5, 1964, and prior to May 8, 1975. (For those serving in the Republic of Vietnam, the beginning date is February 28, 1961.); and

- Discharge or separation under other than dishonorable conditions; and
- At least 90 days of total service, unless discharged earlier for a service-connected disability.
- Unremarried widows of above-described eligible individuals who died as a result of service.
- Widows of above-described eligible individuals who died as a result of service who remarried after age 57.

Post-Vietnam Eligibility Requirements for Veterans with Enlisted Service Between May 8, 1975 AND September 7, 1980 (if enlisted) Or October 16, 1981 (if officer):

- At least 181 days of continuous service, all of which occurred on or after May 8, 1975, unless discharged earlier for a service-connected disability; and
- Discharge or separation under other than dishonorable conditions.
- Unremarried widows of above-described eligible individuals who died as a result of service.
- Widows of above-described eligible individuals who died as a result of service who remarried after age 57.

Post-Vietnam Eligibility Requirements for Veterans Separated from Enlisted Service between September 7, 1980 (October 17, 1981 for officers) and August 1, 1990:

- At least 24 months of continuous active duty, or the full period (at least 181 days) for which individual was called or ordered to active duty, and discharged or separated under other than dishonorable conditions; or
- At least 181 days of continuous active duty, and discharged due to:
  - a hardship; or
  - a service-connected, compensable disability; or
  - a medical condition which preexisted service, and has not been determined to be service connected; or
  - the convenience of the government as a result of a reduction in force; or
  - a physical or mental condition not characterized as a disability, and not the result of misconduct, but which did interfere with the performance of duty.
- Early discharge for a service-connected disability.
- Unremarried widows of above-described eligible persons who died as the result of service.
- Widows of above-described eligible individuals who died as a result of service who remarried after age 57.

Persian Gulf War Eligibility Requirements

- At least 24 months of continuous active duty on or after August 2, 1990, or the

374

full period for which the individual was called or ordered to active duty, and discharged or separated under other than dishonorable conditions; or

- At least 90 days of continuous active duty, and discharged due to:
  - A hardship; or
  - A service-connected, compensable disability; or
  - A medical condition which preexisted service, and has not been determined to be service-connected; or
  - The convenience of the government as a result of a reduction in force; or
  - A physical or mental condition not characterized as a disability, and not the result of misconduct, but which did interfere with the performance of duty.
- Early discharge for a service-connected disability.
- Unremarried widows of above-described eligible individuals who died as the result of service.
- Widows of above-described eligible individuals who died as a result of service who remarried after age 57.

When law or Presidential Proclamation ends the Persian Gulf War, a minimum of 181 days of continuous active duty will be required for those who did not serve during wartime.

Members of the Reserve and National Guard are eligible if activated after August 1, 1990, served at least 90 days, and discharged or separated under other than dishonorable conditions.)

Active-Duty Personnel Requirements

Individuals who are now on regular duty (not active duty for training) are eligible after having served 181 days (90 days during the Gulf War), unless discharged or separated from a previous qualifying period of active-duty service.

Eligibility Requirements for Members of the Selected Reserve

- At least 6 years in the Reserves or National Guard, or discharged earlier due to a service-connected disability; and
- Discharged or separated under other than dishonorable conditions; or
- Placed on the retired list; or
- Transferred to an element of the Ready Reserve other than the Selected Reserve; or
- Continue to serve in the Selected Reserve.
- Unremarried widows of above-described eligible persons who died as the result of service.
- Widows of above-described eligible individuals who died as a result of service who remarried after age 57.

Eligibility Requirements for Other Types of Service

- Certain U.S. citizens who served in the armed forces of a U.S. ally in World War II. Members of organizations with recognized contributions to the U.S. during World War II (Questions about this type of service eligibility can be answered at any VA regional office.)
- Spouses of American servicemen who are listed as missing-in-action, or prisoners-of-war for a total of 90 days or more.

Certificate of Eligibility

The Certificate of Eligibility is the medium by which VA certifies eligibility for A VA loan guaranty.

Individuals may request a Certificate of Eligibility by completing "VA Form 26-1880 Request for a Certificate of Eligibility for VA Home Loan Benefits." The completed form should be submitted to a VA Eligibility Center along with acceptable proof of service.

Veterans separated after January 1, 1950 should submit DD Form 214, Certificate of Release or Discharge from active Duty.

Veterans separated after October 1, 1979 should submit copy 4 of DD Form214.

Since there is no uniform document similar to the DD Form 214 for proof of service in the Selected Reserve a number of different forms may be accepted as documentation of service in the Selected Reserve:

- For those who served in the Army or Air National Guard and were discharged after at least 6 years of such service, NGB Form 22 may be sufficient.
- Those who served in the Army, Navy, Air Force, Marine Corps or Coast Guard Reserves may need to rely on a variety of forms that document at least 6 years of participation in paid training periods, or have paid active duty for training.
- Often it will be necessary to submit a combination of documents, such as an Honorable Discharge certificate together with a Retirement Points Statement. It is the reservist's responsibility to obtain and submit documentation of 6 years of honorable service.

In addition, if an individual is now on active duty, and has not been previously discharged from active-duty service, he or she must submit a statement of service that includes the name of the issuing authority (base or command), and is signed by or at the direction of an appropriate official. The statement must identify the individual, include the social security number, provide the date of entry on active duty and the duration of any lost time.

The Certificate of Eligibility should be presented to the lender when completing the loan application. (However, if an individual does not have a Certificate, the lender may have the forms necessary to apply for the Certificate of Eligibility.)

Procedures for Obtaining Loans

- Find a real estate professional to work with.
- Locate a lending institution that participates in the VA program. You may want to get "pre-qualified" at this point - that is, find out how big a loan you can afford. Lenders set their own interest rates, discount points, and closing points.
- Obtain your Certificate of Eligibility. The lender can probably get you a certificate online. Or, you can apply online yourself. To get your Certificate of Eligibility (COE) online, please go to the eBenefits portal at this link. If you need any assistance, please call the eBenefits Help Desk at 1-800-983-0937. Their hours are Monday-Friday, 8am to 8pm EST.
- You find a home you want to buy.
- When you negotiate, make sure the purchase and sales agreement contains a "VA option clause."
- You may also want the agreement to allow you to "escape" from the contract without penalty if you can't get a VA loan.
- You formally apply to the lender for a VA-backed loan. The lender will complete a loan application and gather the needed documents such as pay stubs and bank statements.
- The lender orders a VA appraisal and begins to "process" all the credit and income information.
- The lending institution reviews the appraisal and all the documentation of credit, income, and assets. The lender then decides whether the loan should be granted.
- Finally, the closing takes place and the property is transferred. The lender chooses a title company, an attorney, or one of their own representatives to conduct the closing. This person will coordinate the date and time.
- If a lender cannot be located, the local VA regional office can provide a list of lenders active in the VA program.

A VA loan guaranty does not guarantee approval of a loan. The veteran must still meet the financial institution's income and credit requirements. If a loan is approved, the VA guarantees the loan when it's closed.

VA Eligibility Centers

Regional Loan Center	Jurisdiction	Mailing Address	Telephone Number
Atlanta	Georgia North Carolina South Carolina Tennessee	Department of Veterans Affairs VA Regional Loan Center 1700 Clairmont Rd. Decatur, GA 30033-4032 (Mail: P.O. Box 100023, Decatur, GA 30031-7023)	(888) 768-2132

Cleveland	Connecticut Delaware Indiana Maine Massachusetts Michigan New Hampshire New Jersey New York Ohio Pennsylvania Rhode Island Vermont	Department of Veterans Affairs VA Regional Loan Center 1240 East Ninth Street Cleveland, OH 44199	(800) 729-5772
Denver	Alaska Colorado Idaho Montana Oregon Utah Washington Wyoming	Department of Veterans Affairs VA Regional Loan Center 155 Van Gordon Street Lakewood, CO 80228 (Mail: Box 25126, Denver, CO 80225)	(888) 349-7541
Honolulu	Hawaii Guam American Samoa Commonwealth of the Northern Marianas	Department of Veterans Affairs VA Regional Loan Center Loan Guaranty Division (26) 459 Patteson Rd. Honolulu, HI 96819 *Although not an RLC, this office is a fully functioning Loan Guaranty operation for Hawaii.	(888) 433-0481
Houston	Arkansas Louisiana Oklahoma Texas	Department of Veterans Affairs VA Regional Loan Center 6900 Almeda Road Houston, TX 77030-4200	(888) 232-2571
Phoenix	Arizona California New Mexico Nevada	Department of Veterans Affairs VA Regional Loan Center 3333 N. Central Avenue Phoenix, AZ 85012-2402	(888) 869-0194
Roanoke	District of Columbia Kentucky Maryland Virginia West Virginia	Department of Veterans Affairs VA Regional Loan Center 210 Franklin Road, SW Roanoke, VA 24011	(800) 933-5499

St. Paul	Illinois Iowa Kansas Minnesota Missouri Nebraska North Dakota South Dakota Wisconsin	Department of Veterans Affairs VA Regional Loan Center 1 Federal Drive, Ft. Snelling St. Paul, MN 55111- 4050	(800) 827-0611
St. Petersburg	Alabama Florida Mississippi Puerto Rico U.S. Virgin Islands	Department of Veterans Affairs VA Regional Loan Center 9500 Bay Pines Blvd. St. Petersburg, FL 33708 (Mail: P.O. Box 1437, St. Petersburg, FL 33731)	(888) 611-5916

Guaranty or Entitlement Amount

Eligible veterans, service members and survivors with full entitlement no longer have limits on loans over $144,000. This means you won't have to pay a down payment and the VA will guarantee to your lender if you default on a loan that's over $144,000, the VA will pay them up to 25% of the loan amount.

You have full entitlement if at least one of the following is true:
- You've never used your home loan benefit or
- You've paid a previous VA loan in full and sold the property, or
- You've used your home loan benefit, but had a foreclosure or compromise claim and repaid VA in full

If you apply and are eligible for a VA-backed home loan, you'll receive a COE. This is the document that tells private lenders you have VA home loan eligibility and entitlement. Your lender will still need to approve you for a loan. The lender will determine the size of the loan you are eligible for based on credit history, income, and assets.

With remaining entitlement, your VA home loan limit is based on the county loan limit where you live. You may need to make a down payment if you're using remaining entitlement and your loan amount is over $144,000. This is because most lenders require that your entitlement, down payment or a combination of both covers at least 24% of your total loan amount. If you're willing and able to make a down payment, as a result, you may be able to borrow more than the county loan limit with a VA-backed loan.

Hybrid Adjustable-Rate Mortgages

An Adjustable-Rate Mortgage means the interest rate changes with changes in the market. The first-year rate, which is also referred to as a teaser rate, is generally a couple of percentage points below the market rate. The "cap" is the upper limit of the interest rate. If a teaser rate is 4%, and there is a five-point cap, then the highest that an interest rate could go would be 9%. The amount that the interest rate can rise each year is usually limited to one or two percentage points per year, but the frequency at which the rate adjusts can vary. If interest rates go up, an ARM will adjust accordingly.

Down Payments

The VA does not require a down payment be made, provided that:

- The loan is not for a manufactured home or lot (a 5% down payment is required for manufactured home or lot loans); and
- The purchase price or cost does not exceed the reasonable value of the property, as determined by VA; and
- The loan does not have graduated payment features. (Because with a graduated-payment mortgage, the loan balance will be increasing during the first years of the loan, a down payment is required to keep the loan balance from going over the reasonable value or the purchase price.)

Even though the VA may not require a down payment, the lender may require one.

Closing Costs and Fees

The VA regulates the closing costs that a veteran may be charged in connection with closing a VA loan. The closing costs and origination fees must be paid in cash, and cannot be included in the loan itself, except in the case of refinancing loans. Although some additional costs are unique to certain localities, the closing costs generally include:

VA appraisal Credit report Survey
Title evidence Recording fees
A 1% loan origination fee Discount points

A veteran is charged the customary fees for title search, credit report, appraisal, and transfer fees, etc., the same as any other borrower, but he is not required to pay commission or brokerage fees for obtaining the loan. In home loans, the lender may also charge a reasonable flat charge, called a funding fee, to cover the costs of originating the loan.

Funding Fees

A VA funding fee is payable at the time of loan closing. This fee may be included in the loan and paid from the loan proceeds. The funding fee does not have to be paid by veterans receiving VA compensation for service-connected disabilities, or who but for the receipt of retirement pay, would be entitled to receive compensation for service-connected disabilities, or surviving spouses of veterans who died in service or from a service-connected disability.

The funding fee rates are as follows:

Loan Purpose	Percent of loan for veterans, active-duty service members, and National Guard and Reserve Members
Purchase or construction loan with down payment of less than 5%; or Refinancing loan; or Home improvement loan	2.3%
Purchase or construction loan with down payment between 5% and 10%	1.65%
Second or subsequent use without a down payment	3.6%
Assumption of VA guaranteed loan	0.5%
Interest rate reduction loan	0.5%
Manufactured home loan	1.0%
Purchase or construction loan with a downpayment of 10% or more	1.4%

Flood Insurance

If the dwelling is in an area identified by the Department of Housing and Urban Development as having special flood hazards, and the sale of flood insurance under the national program is available, such insurance is required on loans made since March 1, 1974. The amount of insurance must be equal to the outstanding loan balance, or the maximum limit of coverage available, whichever is less.

Interest Rates

The interest rate on VA loans varies due to changes in the prevailing rates in the mortgage market. One a loan is made, the interest rate set in the note remains the same for the life of the loan. However, if interest rates decrease, a veteran may apply for a new VA loan to refinance the previous loan at a lower interest rate.

Repayment Period

The maximum repayment period for VA home loans is 30 years and 32 days. However, the exact amortization period depends upon the contract between the lender and the borrower.

The VA will guarantee loans with the following repayment terms:

- Traditional Fixed Payment Mortgage
- Equal monthly payments for the life of the loan
- Graduated Payment Mortgage – GPM
- Smaller than normal monthly payments for the first few years – usually 5 years, which gradually increase each year, and then level off after the end of the "graduation period" to larger than normal payments for the remaining term of the loan. The reduction in the monthly payment in the early years of

381

the loan is accomplished by delaying a portion of the interest due on the loan each month, and by adding that interest to the principal balance.

Buydown

The builder of a new home or seller of an existing home may "buy down" the veteran's mortgage payments by making a large lump sum payment up front at closing that will be used to supplement the monthly payments for a certain period, usually 1 to 3 years.

Growing Equity Mortgage (GEM)

Provides for a gradual annual increase in monthly payments, with all of the increase applied to the principal balance, resulting in early payoff of the loan.

Prepayment of Loan

A veteran or serviceman may pay off his entire loan at any time without penalty or fee or make advance payments equal to one monthly installment or $100, whichever is the lesser amount. Individuals should check with the mortgage holder for the proper procedure.

Loan Defaults

If a veteran fails to make payments as agreed, the lender may foreclose on the property. If the lender takes a loss, the VA must pay the guaranty to the lender, and the individual must repay this amount to the VA. If the loan closed on or after January 1, 1990, the veteran will owe the VA in the event of default, only if there was fraud, misrepresentation, or bad faith on the veteran's part.

The US Department of Veterans Affairs urges all Veterans who are encountering problems making their mortgage payments to speak with their loan servicers as soon as possible to explore options to avoid foreclosure. Depending on a Veteran's specific situation, servicers may offer any of the following options to avoid foreclosure:

- Repayment Plan: The borrower makes regular installment each month plus part of the missed installments.
- Special Forbearance: The servicer agrees not to initiate foreclosure to allow time for borrowers to repay the missed installments. An example would be when a borrower is waiting for a tax refund.
- Loan Modification: Provides the borrower a fresh start by adding the delinquency to the loan balance and establishing a new payment schedule.
- Additional time to arrange a private sale: The servicer agrees to delay foreclosure to allow a sale to close if the loan will be paid off.
- Short Sale: When the servicer agrees to allow a borrower to sell his/her home for a lesser amount than what is currently required to payoff the loan.
- Deed-in-Lieu of Foreclosure: The borrower voluntarily agrees to deed the property to the servicer instead of going through a lengthy foreclosure process.

Release of Liability

Any veteran who sells or has sold a home purchased with a VA loan guaranty may request release from liability to the VA. (If the VA loan closed prior to March 1, 1988, the application forms for a release of liability must be requested from the VA office that guaranteed the loan. If the VA loan closed on or after March 1, 1988, then the application forms must be requested from the lender to whom the payments are made.) The loan must be current, the purchaser must assume full liability for the loan, and the purchaser must sign an Assumption of Liability Agreement. The VA must approve the purchaser from a credit standpoint.

For loans closed on or after March 1, 1988, the release of liability is not automatic. To approve the assumer and grant the veteran release from liability, the lender or VA must be notified, and release of liability must be requested.

If the loan was closed prior to March 1, 1988, the purchaser may assume the loan without approval from VA or the lender. However, the veteran is encouraged to request a release of liability from VA, regardless of the loan's closing date. If a veteran does not obtain a release of liability, and VA suffers a loss on account of a default by the assumer, or some future assumer, a debt may be established against the veteran. Also, strenuous collection efforts will be made against the veteran if a debt is established.

The release of a veteran from liability to the VA does not change the fact that the VA continues to be liable on the guaranty.

Restoration of Entitlement

Veterans who have used all or part of their entitlement may restore their entitlement amount to purchase another home, provided:

- The property has been sold, and the loan has been paid in full; or
- A qualified veteran buyer has agreed to assume the outstanding balance on the loan and agreed to substitute his entitlement for the same amount of entitlement the original veteran owner used to get the loan. (The veteran buyer must also meet the occupancy, income, and credit requirements of the VA and the lender.)
- If the veteran has repaid the VA loan in full but has not disposed of the property securing that loan, the entitlement may be restored ONE TIME ONLY.

Restoration of entitlement does not occur automatically. The veteran must apply for restoration by completing "Form 26, 1880." Completed forms may be returned to any VA regional office or center (A copy of the HUD-1, Closing Statement, or other appropriate evidence of payment in full should also be submitted with the completed Form 26, 1880.) Application forms for substitution of entitlement can be requested from the VA office that guaranteed the loan.

If the requirements for restoration of entitlement cannot be met, veterans who had a VA loan before may still have remaining entitlement to use for another VA loan. The current amount of entitlement available to eligible veterans has been increased over time by changes in the law.

For example, in 1974 the maximum guaranty entitlement was $12,500. Today the maximum guaranty entitlement is $36,000 (for most loans under $144,000). So, if a veteran used the $12,500 guaranty in 1974, even if that loan is not paid off, the veteran could use the $23,500 difference between the $12,500 entitlement originally used and the current maximum of $36,000 to buy another home with a VA loan guaranty.

Direct Home Loans

VA direct home loans are only available to:
- Native American veterans who plan to buy, build, or improve a home on Native American trust land; or
- Certain eligible veterans who have a permanent and total service-connected disability, for specially adapted homes.

Native American Veterans Living on Trust Lands

A VA direct loan can be used to purchase, construct, or improve a home on Native American trust land. These loans may also be used to simultaneously purchase and improve a home, or to refinance another VA direct loan made under this program in order to lower the interest rate. VA direct loans are generally limited to the cost of the home or $80,000, whichever is less.

To qualify for a VA direct loan, the tribal organization or other appropriate Native American group must be participating in the VA direct loan program. The tribal organization must have signed a Memorandum of Understanding with the Secretary of Veterans Affairs that includes the conditions governing its participation in the program.

Veterans should contact their regional VA office for specific information regarding direct home loans.

Resale of Repossessed Homes

The VA sells homes that it acquires after foreclosure of a VA guaranteed loan. These homes are available to veterans and non-veterans.

The properties are available for sale to the general public through the services of private sector real estate brokers. The VA cannot deal directly with purchasers. Real estate brokers receive the keys to the properties and assist prospective purchasers in finding, viewing, and offering to purchase them.

Participating brokers receive instructional material regarding the sales program, and are familiar with VA sales procedures. VA pays the sales commission. Offers to purchase VA acquired properties must be submitted on VA forms. Offers cannot be submitted on offer forms generally used in the real estate industry.

VA financing is available for most, but not all, property sales. The down payment requirements are usually very reasonable, the interest rate is established by VA based on market conditions. Any prospective purchaser who requests VA financing to purchase a VA-owned property must have sufficient income to meet the loan payments, maintain the property, and pay all other obligation. The purchaser must have acceptable credit and must also have enough funds remaining for family support.

Anyone interested should consult a local real estate agent to find out about VA-acquired properties listed for sale in the area.

HUD / FHA Loans

Veterans are not eligible for VA financing based on service in World War I, Active Duty for Training in the Reserves, or Active Duty for Training in the National Guard (unless "activated" under the authority of Title 10, U.S. Code). However, these veterans may qualify for a HUD / FHA veteran's loan.

The VA's only role in the HUD / FHA program is to determine the eligibility of the veteran, and issue a Certificate of Veteran Status, if qualified. Under this program, financing is available for veterans at terms slightly more favorable than those available to non-veterans.

A veteran may request a "Certificate of Veteran Status" by completing "VA form 26-8261a." The completed form and required attachments should be submitted to the veteran's regional VA office for a determination of eligibility.

Servicemembers Civil Relief Act (SCRA)

The Servicemembers Civil Relief Act expanded and improved the former Soldiers' and Sailors' Civil Relief Act (SSCRA). It is designed to provide a wide range of protections for people entering the military, being called to active duty, and deployed servicemembers. The goal of the SCRA is to postpone or suspend particular civil obligations, in order for the servicemember to devote full attention to service duties. It is also designed to relieve stress on family members of deployed servicemembers. Among these obligations, a servicemember may be exempt from are mortgage payments.

The new law expands the current law in place to protect servicemembers and their families from eviction from housing while the servicemember is on active duty.

Based on provisions of a recent SCRA Foreclosure Settlement completed by the Federal government, five major servicers (Bank of America, JPMorgan Chase, Ally (GMAC), CitiMortgage, and Wells Fargo) must provide the following relief to service members and veterans:

- Conduct a review of every servicemember foreclosure since 2006 and provide any who were wrongly foreclosed with compensation equal to a minimum of lost equity, plus interest and $116,785;
- Refund money lost because they were wrongfully denied the opportunity to reduce their interest rates to the 6% cap;
- Provide relief for service members who are forced to sell their homes for less than the amount they owe on their mortgage due to a Permanent Change in Station.

Extend certain foreclosure protections afforded under the Servicemember Civil Relief Act to service members serving in harm's way.

CHAPTER 25

OVERSEAS BENEFITS

Medical Benefits

The Foreign Medical Program (FMP) is a healthcare benefits program for U.S. veterans with VA-rated service-connected conditions who are residing or traveling abroad (except Canada and the Philippines). Services provided in Canada and the Philippines are under separate jurisdictions, as indicated later in this chapter.

Under the FMP, VA assumes payment responsibility for certain necessary medical services associated with the treatment of service-connected conditions.

The Foreign Medical Program, Office in Denver, Colorado, has jurisdiction over all foreign provided services, with the exception of medical services received in Canada and the Philippines. It is responsible for all aspects of the program, including application processing, verification of eligibility, authorization of benefits, and payments of claims.

In September 2011, the VA announced the creation of a new program to provide comprehensive compensation and pension (C&P) examinations to U.S. veterans living overseas. The program includes providing a

> **Key Takeaways**
> For eligible veterans living or traveling abroad, VA offers medical services through the Foreign Medical Program (FMP). Through this program, FMP will pay for health care services, medications, and durable medical equipment for service-connected conditions and conditions associated with and held to be aggravating a service-connected condition. VA may authorize foreign medical services for any condition if you are participating in the VA Vocational Rehabilitation Program (Title 38, U.S. Code, Chapter 31).

medical assessment to evaluate veterans' current disabilities that may be related to their military service. .

If VA has previously determined a veteran has a service-connected medical condition, the examination helps determine the current severity of the condition, which could affect the amount of VA disability compensation payable or entitlement to additional benefits. During this time, the VA also conducted its first C&P examinations using telehealth technology, which is designed to ease the burden of travel for U.S. veterans living overseas. The VA plans to provide these services in various locations in Europe and Asia.

Individuals who are traveling to or reside in one of the following countries should use the following number to contact the FMP Office in Denver, Colorado: (877) 345-8179: Germany; Panama; Australia; Italy; UK; Japan; Spain.

For individuals who are in Mexico or Costa Rica, first, dial the U.S.A code and then (877) 345-8179. The number also works from the United States.

Generally, as long as the service is medically necessary for the treatment of a VA rated service-connected condition, it will be covered by the FMP. Additionally, the services must be accepted by VA and / or the U.S. Medical community (such as the American Medical Association and the U.S. Food and Drug Administration.)

Exclusions to Medical Benefits

The following services are not covered by the Foreign Medical Program:
- Procedures, treatments, drugs, or devices that are experimental or investigational;
- Family planning services and sterilization;
- Infertility services;
- Plastic surgery primarily for cosmetic purposes;
- Procedures, services, and supplies related to sex transformations;
- Non-acute institutional care such as long-term inpatient psychiatric care and nursing home care;
- Day care and day hospitalization;
- Non-medical home care (aid and attendance);
- Abortions
- Travel, meals, and lodging (including transportation costs to return to the United States)

Prosthesis

If an individual residing in a foreign country requires a prosthesis for a VA rated service-connected condition, and the cost of the prosthetic appliance is less than $300 (U.S. currency), the individual may purchase the prosthetic appliance from a local healthcare provider, and send the invoice to the FMP Office for reimbursement, or the healthcare provider may bill the VA. If the cost of the prosthetic appliance exceeds $300 (U.S. currency), the individual must obtain preauthorization for the VA Foreign Medical Program Office (see address below).

Application Process—Registration

Although pre-registration for eligible veterans is not necessary, veterans who are permanently relocating to a country under the FMP's jurisdiction are encouraged to notify the FMP once a permanent foreign address is established. At that time, FMP will provide detailed program material, such as benefit coverage, benefit limitations, selecting healthcare providers, and claim filing instructions.

Veterans who are simply traveling and are not planning a permanent relocation do not need to notify the FMP of their travel plans. Program materials are available, however, upon request.

The FMP can be contacted at:
VA Health Administration Center Foreign Medical Program (FMP)
P.O. Box 65021
Denver, CO 80206-9021
Phone: (303) 331-7590
Fax: (303) 331-7803

Medical Services in Canada

The VA Medical and Regional Office Center in White River Junction, Vermont, is responsible for determining eligibility of U.S. veterans for reimbursement of medical treatment while traveling or residing in Canada. The local offices of Veterans' Affairs-Canada assists veterans in obtaining authorizations for treatment, arranging for treatment (if necessary), and providing information about the medical treatment program.

The same exclusions listed earlier in this chapter also apply to medical services in Canada, and VA assumes payment responsibility only for certain necessary medical services associated with the treatment of service-connected conditions.

To receive reimbursed medical treatment, an authorization must be obtained from the White River Junction office prior to treatment (unless an emergency situation exists).

When required by the VA to support a claim for disability benefits, Veterans Affairs-Canada will make arrangements for disability examinations for veterans residing in Canada. In some instances, arrangements will be made locally in Canada. In other instances, arrangements will be made at bordering VA medical facilities.

Information on how to obtain medical services in Canada, including procedures for filing claims, can be obtained by contacting the following office:

VAM & RO Center (136FC)
North Hartland Road
White River Junction, VT 05009-0001
Fax: (802) 296-5174
Or
Veterans Affairs-Canada Foreign Countries Operations
Room 1055
264 Wellington Street
Ottawa, Ontario, Canada K1A 0P4
(613) 943-7461

Medical Services in the Philippines

The Republic of the Philippines is the only foreign country in which the VA operates a regional office and outpatient clinic.

The same exclusions listed earlier in this chapter also apply to medical services in the Philippines, and VA assumes payment responsibility only for certain necessary medical services associated with the treatment of service-connected conditions.

To receive reimbursed medical treatment, authorization must be obtained prior to treatment (unless an emergency situation exists).

Information on how to obtain medical services in the Philippines, including procedures for filing claims, can be obtained by contacting the following office:

VA Department of Veterans Affairs Manila Regional Office & Outpatient Clinic
1501 Roxas Boulevard 1302
Pasay City, Philippines
TEL: 011-632-318-8387

Virtually all VA monetary benefits, including compensation, pension, educational assistance, and burial allowances, are payable regardless of an individual's place of residence. However, there are some program limitations in foreign jurisdictions, including:

- Home-loan guarantees are available only in the United States and selected territories and possessions.
- Educational benefits are limited to approved degree-granting programs in institutions of higher learning
- Information and assistance are available to U.S. veterans worldwide at American embassies and consulates. In Canada, the local offices of Veterans Affairs-Canada provide information and assistance. Individuals

may call toll- free within Canada, (888) 996-2242.

In the Philippines, service is available at the VA Regional Office and Outpatient Clinic in Manila:

VA Regional Office
1131 Roxas Boulevard
Manila, Philippines
TEL: 011-632-521-7521

Direct Deposit

The conventional method of direct deposit is not available outside of the U.S. However, there are foreign banks with branches in the United States, through which direct deposit can be established. Once the funds are received in the U.S. branch through electronic funds transfer, the U.S. branch transfers the money to the foreign branch.

While this process may take a few days longer than direct deposit within the United States, it is still quicker than having checks mailed overseas through the Department of State or International Priority Airmail.

CHAPTER 26

AGENT ORANGE, MUSTARD GAS, RADIATION AND PROJECT 112 / SHAD

Veterans who were exposed to Agent Orange or other herbicides during military service may be eligible for a variety of VA benefits, including disability compensation for diseases associated with exposure. Dependents and survivors may also be eligible.

Agent Orange is a blend of herbicides that were sprayed by the U.S. Military in Vietnam and around the Korean demilitarized zone to remove trees and foliage that could provide cover to the enemy. Herbicides were also used by the U.S. military to defoliate facilities domestically and in other countries dating back to the 1950s.

The VA has also determined there is evidence Air Force and Air Force Reserve members were exposed to Agent Orange if they served between 1969 and 1986, and regularly and repeatedly operated, maintained, or served onboard C-123 aircraft, which were known to have been used to spray an herbicide during the Vietnam era.

Key Takeaways
Agent Orange was a tactical herbicide the U.S. military used to clear leaves and vegetation for military operations mainly during the Vietnam War. Veterans who were exposed to Agent Orange may have certain related illnesses.

Blue Water Navy veterans who served aboard ships in the open waters off the coast of Vietnam during the Vietnam War are now presumed to be exposed to Agent Orange. If your claim was previously denied, you can file a new claim based on Public Law 116-23.

According to the VA and federal law, there is a presumption that certain diseases are a result of exposure to these herbicides. This policy of presumption intends to simplify how exposed veterans receive compensation for these diseases because the VA eliminates the normal requirements of proving an illness began during or was worsened by military service.

A veteran who believes he or she has a disease caused by exposure to Agent Orange that is not one of the conditions listed as presumptive is required to show a connection between the disease and herbicide exposure during military service.

The Bluewater (BWN) Vietnam Veterans Act 2019 (Public Law 116-23)

Public Law 116-23, The Blue Water Vietnam Veterans Act of 2019, went into effect on January 1, 2020. According to this new law, veterans who served as far as 12 nautical miles from the shore of Vietnam or who had served in the Korean Demilitarized zone, are presumed to have been exposed to herbicides such as Agent Orange and may be entitled to service compensation for any of the 14 conditions related to herbicide exposure. These conditions are:

- Chronic B-cell leukemia
- Hodgkin's disease
- Multiple myelomas
- Non-Hodgkin's lymphoma
- Prostate cancer
- Respiratory cancers including lung cancer
- Soft tissue sarcomas other than osteosarcoma, chondrosarcoma, Kaposi's sarcoma or mesothelioma
- AL amyloidosis
- Chloracne
- Diabetes mellitus type 2
- Ischemic heart disease
- Parkinson's disease
- Peripheral neuropathy
- Porphyria cutanea tarda

VA is now able to extend benefits to children with spina bifida whose BWN veteran parent may have been exposed while serving. Additionally, PL 116-23 made changes to the VA Home Loan Program. See Chapter 25 for more information about these changes. To be entitled to VA benefits, veterans must have served between January 9, 1962, and May 7, 1975 and have one or more of thee conditions listed in section 3.309€ of title 38, Code of Federal Regulations.

You can apply for initial compensation claims with VA Form 21-526EZ. For initial DIC claims, submit a VA Form 21P-534EZ. For previously denied claims, submit a VA Form 20-0995.

When filing a claim, you should state on your application that you're filing for one of the conditions related to presumed herbicide exposure such as Agent Orange. You should include any evidence you have of service in the offshore waters of the Republic of Vietnam during the required timeframe. Include the name of the vessels and the dates you served within 12 nautical miles of the Republic of Vietnam if you have that information. Provide medical evidence showing a diagnosis of a current condition related to exposure to herbicide such as Agent Orange or tell the VA where you're being treated.

Eligibility

According to the VA, eligibility is based on the facts of each veteran's claim. However, some cancers and other illnesses are assumed to be caused by Agent Orange. These are called presumptive diseases. The VA also assumes that veterans who served in certain locations were exposed to Agent Orange, which is called presumptive exposure.

Between January 9, 1962, and May 7, 1975, you must have served for any length of time in at least one of these locations:
- In the Republic of Vietnam, or
- Aboard a U.S. military vessel that operated in the inland waterways of Vietnam, or
- On a vessel operating not more than 12 nautical miles seaward from the demarcation line of the waters of Vietnam and Cambodia, or
- On regular perimeter duty on the fenced-in perimeters of a U.S. Army installation in Thailand or a Royal Thai Air Force base. These bases include U-Tapao, Ubon, Nakhon Phanom, Udorn, Takhli, Korat, or Don Muang.

Or at least one of these must be true. You:
- Served in or near the Korean DMZ for any length of time between September 1, 1967, and August 31, 1971, or
- Served on active duty in a regular Air Force unit location where a C-123 aircraft with traces of Agent Orange was assigned, and had repeated contact with this aircraft due to your flight, ground, or medical duties, or
- Were involved in transporting, testing, storing, or other uses of Agent Orange during your military service, or
- Were assigned as a Reservist to certain flight, ground, or medical crew duties at one of the below locations.

Eligible Reserve locations, time periods, and units include:
- Lockbourne/Rickenbacker Air Force Base in Ohio, 1969 to 1986 (906th and 907th Tactical Air Groups or 355th and 356th Tactical Airlift Squadrons)
- Westover Air Force Base in Massachusetts, 1972 to 1982 (731st Tactical Air Squadron and 74th Aeromedical Evacuation Squadron, or 901st Organizational Maintenance Squadron)
- Pittsburgh International Airport in Pennsylvania, 1972 to 1982 (758th Airlift Squadron)

Agent Orange Exposure from C-123 Aircraft

If you flew on—or worked with—C-123 aircraft in Vietnam or other locations, you may have had contact with Agent Orange. The U.S. military used this herbicide to clear trees and plants during the Vietnam War. C-123 aircraft sprayed Agent Orange during the war, and the planes still had traces of the chemical in them afterward while they were being used, up until 1986.

For active-duty service members, you may be able to get disability benefits if the following are true for you. First, you must have an illness the VA believes is caused by contact with Agent Orange (a presumptive disease).You also must have served in a regular Air Force unit location where a C-123 aircraft with traces of Agent Orange was assigned, and your flight, ground or medical duties must have put you in regular and repeated contact with C-123 aircraft that had traces of Agent Orange.

If you have an illness the VA determines to be caused by Agent Orange, you don't have to show your problem started during or got worse because of your military service, because it's a presumptive disease.

For reservists, you may be able to get disability benefits if you have a presumptive disease and you were assigned to certain flight, ground, or medical crew duties at one of the following locations:

You must have been assigned to one of these locations:
Lockbourne/Rickenbacker Air Force Base in Ohio, 1969-1986 (906th and 907th Tactical Air Groups or 355th and 356th Tactical Airlift Squadrons), or Westover Air Force Base in Massachusetts, 1972-1982 (731st Tactical Air Squadron and 74th Aeromedical Evacuation Squadron, or 901st Organizational Maintenance Squadron), or Pittsburgh International Airport in Pennsylvania, 1972-1982 (758th Airlift Squadron)

You'll need to file a claim for disability compensation for these benefits. Supporting documents you can include with your online application are:
- Discharge or separation papers (DD214 or other separation documents)
- USAF Form 2096 (unit where you were assigned at the time of the training action)
- USAF Form 5 (aircraft flight duties)
- USAF Form 781 (aircraft maintenance duties)
- Dependency records (marriage certificate and children's birth certificates
- Medical evidence (like a doctor's report or medical test results)

You can get help filing your claim by calling the C-123 hotline at 800-749-8387 or emailing the St. Paul regional benefit office at VSCC123.VAVBASPL@va.gov.

Veterans' Diseases Associated with Agent Orange

VA assumes that certain diseases can be related to a Veteran's qualifying military service. These are "presumptive diseases." VA has recognized certain cancers and other health problems as presumptive diseases associated with exposure to Agent Orange or other herbicides during military service. Veterans and their survivors may be eligible for benefits for these diseases.

AL Amyloidosis
A rare disease caused when an abnormal protein, amyloid, enters tissues or organs

Chronic B-cell Leukemias
A type of cancer which affects white blood cells

Chloracne (or similar acneform disease)
A skin condition that occurs soon after exposure to chemicals and looks like common forms of acne seen in teenagers. Under VA's rating regulations, it must be at least 10 percent disabling within one year of exposure to herbicides.

Diabetes Mellitus Type 2
A disease characterized by high blood sugar levels resulting from the body's inability to respond properly to the hormone insulin

Hodgkin's Disease
A malignant lymphoma (cancer) characterized by progressive enlargement of the lymph nodes, liver, and spleen, and by progressive anemia

Ischemic Heart Disease
A disease characterized by a reduced supply of blood to the heart, that leads to chest pain

Multiple Myeloma
A cancer of plasma cells, a type of white blood cell in bone marrow

Non-Hodgkin's Lymphoma
A group of cancers that affect the lymph glands and other lymphatic tissue

Parkinson's Disease
A progressive disorder of the nervous system that affects muscle movement

Peripheral Neuropathy, Early-Onset
A nervous system condition that causes numbness, tingling, and motor weakness. Under VA's rating regulations, it must be at least 10 percent disabling within one year of herbicide exposure.

Porphyria Cutanea Tarda
A disorder characterized by liver dysfunction and by thinning and blistering of the skin in sun-exposed areas. Under VA's rating regulations, it must be at least 10 percent disabling within one year of exposure to herbicides.

Prostate Cancer
Cancer of the prostate; one of the most common cancers among men

Respiratory Cancers (includes lung cancer)
Cancers of the lung, larynx, trachea, and bronchus

Soft Tissue Sarcomas (other than osteosarcoma, chondrosarcoma, Kaposi's sarcoma, or mesothelioma)
A group of different types of cancers in body tissues such as muscle, fat, blood and lymph vessels, and connective tissues

Veterans with Lou Gehrig's Disease
VA presumes Lou Gehrig's Disease (amyotrophic lateral sclerosis or ALS) diagnosed in ALL veterans who had 90 days or more continuous active military service is related to their service, although ALS is not related to Agent Orange Exposure.

396

Evidence Needed

If you are seeking service connection for one of the diseases presumed by the VA to be associated with herbicide exposure during service, the VA needs the following:
- A medical diagnosis of a disease which the VA recognizes as being associated with Agent Orange
- Competent evidence of service in Vietnam or at or near the Korean demilitarized zone during the dates shown above or exposure to herbicides in a location other than the Vietnam or the Korean demilitarized zone
- Competent medical evidence that the disease began within the deadline

If you believe you have a disease caused by exposure to herbicides but it's not listed on the presumptive diseases for Agent Orange, you will need all of the following to apply for service connection:
- Competent medical evidence of a current disability
- Competent medical evidence of an actual connection between herbicide exposure and the current disability and
- Competent evidence of service in Vietnam at or near the Korean demilitarized zone during the dates shown above or exposure to herbicides in a location other than Vietnam or the Korean demilitarized zone

Mustard Gas Exposure and Long-Term Health Effects

In 1991, the Department of Veterans Affairs (VA) relaxed requirements for evaluating mustard gas-related compensation claims because of the confidentiality of some of the World War II testing and a lack of military medical records and follow-up. At that time, a review of studies of the effects of mustard gas exposure led VA to publish regulations authorizing service-connection and disability compensation payments to veterans who were exposed to significant levels of mustard gas and who suffer from chronic forms of certain diseases.

An estimated 4,000 servicemen participated in tests using significant concentrations of mustard gas either in chambers or field exercises in contaminated areas during World War II. This secret testing was conducted in order to develop better protective clothing, masks and skin ointments. There is no central roster of World War II participants in either the laboratory or field tests. The Army conducted tests on Army personnel in the laboratory and in the field.

The test sites included:
Edgewood Arsenal, Maryland;
Camp Sibert, Alabama;
Bushnell, Florida;
Dugway Proving Ground, Utah;
and San Jose Island, Panama Canal Zone
Military personnel from the U.S. Navy Training Center Bainbridge, Maryland. also were sent to the Naval Research Lab in Washington, D.C., to participate in tests. Gas testing

facilities also were located at Great Lakes Naval Training Center in Illinois and Camp Lejeune, North Carolina.

Veterans Who May be Eligible for Compensation

VA policies generally authorize service-connection and compensation payments to veterans who were exposed to mustard gas and/or Lewisite and who suffer from a number of diseases or conditions, including:

- Full-body exposure to nitrogen or sulfur mustard together with the subsequent development of chronic conjunctivitis, keratitis, corneal opacities, scar formation, or the following cancers: nasopharyngeal; laryngeal; lung (except mesothelioma); or squamous cell carcinoma of the skin;

- Full-body exposure to nitrogen or sulfur mustard -- or exposure to Lewisite -- and the subsequent development of a chronic form of laryngitis, bronchitis, emphysema, asthma or chronic obstructive pulmonary disease;

- Full-body exposure to nitrogen mustard with the subsequent development of acute nonlymphocytic leukemia.

Service-connection is not allowed if the claimed condition is due to the veteran's own willful misconduct or if there is affirmative evidence that establishes some other nonservice-related condition or event as the cause of the claimed disability.

Veterans who were exposed to significant amounts of mustard gas and have health problems that may be compensable (or their survivors) may contact the nearest VA regional office at (800) 827-1000 for more information about benefits.

VA Programs for Veterans Exposed to Radiation

VA provides special priority for enrollment for health-care services to any veteran exposed to ionizing radiation in connection with:

- Onsite participation in a test involving the atmospheric detonation of a nuclear device (without regard to whether the nation conducting the test was the United States or another nation).

- The American occupation of Hiroshima and Nagasaki, Japan, during the period beginning August 6, 1945, and ending July 1, 1946.

- Internment as a prisoner of war in Japan (or service on active duty in Japan immediately following such internment) during World War II which (as determined by the Secretary of the VA) resulted in an opportunity for exposure to ionizing radiation comparable to that of veterans described above.

- The definition of radiation-risk activities was expanded in March 2002 to include service at Amchitka Island, Alaska, prior to January 1, 1974, if a veteran was exposed while performing duties related to certain underground nuclear tests.

- The new definition also includes service at gaseous diffusion plants located in Paducah, Ky., Portsmouth, Ohio, and an area known as K25 at Oak Ridge, Tenn.

In addition, these veterans are eligible to participate in the VA ionizing radiation registry examination program. VA also pays compensation to veterans and their survivors if the veteran is determined to have a disability due to radiation exposure while in service.

Radiation Statistics

Some 195,000 service members have been identified as participants in the post-World War II occupation of Hiroshima and Nagasaki, Japan. In addition, approximately 210,000 mostly military members are confirmed as participants in U.S. atmospheric nuclear tests between 1945 and 1962 in the United States and the Pacific and Atlantic oceans prior to the 1963 Limited Test Ban Treaty. The Defense Threat Reduction Agency's Nuclear Test Personnel Review program since 1978 has maintained a database of participants in atmospheric nuclear test activities. About one-fourth of the participants received no measurable dose of ionizing radiation, with fewer than one percent of the nuclear test participants identified as having a dose of 5 rem or higher. (The current federal guideline for U.S. workplace exposure is 5 rem per year.)

Determination of Service-Connected Diseases

VA may pay compensation for radiogenic diseases under two programs specific to radiation-exposed veterans and their survivors:

Statutory List

Veterans who participated in nuclear tests by the U.S. or its allies, who served with the occupation forces in Hiroshima or Nagasaki, Japan, between August 1945 and July 1946, or who were similarly exposed to ionizing radiation while a prisoner of war in Japan, are eligible for compensation for cancers specified in legislation.

The types of cancer covered by these laws are:

All forms of leukemia;
Cancer of the thyroid;
Cancer of the breast;
Cancer of the pharynx;
Cancer of the esophagus;
Cancer of the stomach;
Cancer of the small intestine;
Cancer of the pancreas;
Cancer of the bile ducts;
Cancer of the gall bladder;
Cancer of the salivary gland;
Cancer of the urinary tract;
Lymphomas (except Hodgkin's disease);

Multiple myelomas;
Primary liver cancer;
Bone Cancer;
Brain Cancer;
Lung Cancer;
Colon Cancer;
Ovary Cancer

In 2011, the VA expanded the definition of non-Hodgkin's lymphoma to include:

Chronic lymphocytic leukemia;
Small-cell lymphocytic lymphoma

The new rules apply to those veterans who participated in "radiation-risk activities" while on active duty, during active duty for training or inactive duty training as a member of a reserve component.

Regulatory List

Disability compensation claims of veterans who were exposed to radiation in service and who develop a disease within specified time periods not specified in the statutory list are governed by regulation. Under the regulations, various additional factors must be considered in determining service-connection, including amount of radiation exposure, duration of exposure, and elapsed time between exposure and onset of the disease. VA regulations identify all cancers as potentially radiogenic, as well as certain other non- malignant conditions: posterior subcapsular cataracts; non-malignant thyroid nodular disease; parathyroid adenoma; and tumors of the brain and central nervous system.

A final rule that expanded the regulatory list from more than a dozen specific cancers to add "any other cancer" (any malignancy) was published September 24, 1998. The rulemaking began following a 1995 review of the radiogenicity of cancer generally by the Veterans Advisory Committee on Environmental Hazards. It concluded that, on the basis of current scientific knowledge, exposure to ionizing radiation can be a contributing factor in the development of any malignancy. VA also will consider evidence that diseases other those specified in regulation may be caused by radiation exposure.

Rates of Disability Compensation

Rates of compensation depend upon the degree of disability and follow a payment schedule that is adjusted annually and applies to all veterans. Please refer to the charts in Chapter 4 of this book.

Ionizing Radiation Registry

In addition to special eligibility to enroll for VA healthcare for radiation-related conditions, atomic veterans are eligible to participate in VA's Ionizing Radiation

Registry examination. Under the Ionizing Radiation Registry program, VA will perform a complete physical examination, including all necessary tests, for each veteran who requests it if the veteran was exposed to ionizing radiation while participating in the nuclear weapons testing program, or if he or she served with the U.S. occupation forces in Hiroshima or Nagasaki. Veterans need not be enrolled for general VA care to be eligible for the Ionizing Radiation Registry.

Project 112 / Project Shad Veterans

Project SHAD, an acronym for Shipboard Hazard and Defense, was part of a larger effort called Project 112, which was a comprehensive program initiated in 1962 by the Department of Defense (DoD).

Project SHAD encompassed a series of tests by DoD to determine the vulnerability of U.S. warships to attacks with chemical and biological warfare agents, and the potential risk to American forces posed by these agents.

Project 112 tests involved similar tests conducted on land rather than aboard ships.

Project SHAD involved service members from the Navy and Army and may have involved a small number of personnel from the Marine Corps and Air Force. Service members were not test subjects, but rather were involved in conducting the tests. Animals were used in some, but not most, tests.

DoD continues to release declassified reports about sea- and land- based tests of chemical and biological materials known collectively as "Project 112." The Department of Veterans Affairs (VA) is working with DoD to obtain information as to the nature and availability of the tests, who participated, duration and agents used.

To date, there is no clear evidence of specific, long-term health problems associated with a veteran's participation in Project SHAD, but the VA is conducting a follow-up study to a 2007 Institute of Medicine Study.

Veterans who believe their health may have been affected by these tests should contact the SHAD helpline at (800) 749-8387.

CHAPTER 27

SPINA BIFIDA PROGRAM

Spina bifida is the most frequently occurring permanently disabling birth defect. It affects approximately one of every 1,000 newborns in the United States. Neural tube defects (NTD) are birth defects that involve incomplete development of the brain, spinal cord, and/or protective coverings for these organs. Spina bifida, the most common NTD, results from the failure of the spine to close properly during the first month of pregnancy. (Anencephaly and encephalocele are less common types of NTDs). In severe cases, the spinal cord protrudes through the back of and may be covered by skin or a thin membrane.

The Department of Veterans Affairs (VA) provides monetary allowances, vocational training and rehabilitation and VA-financed health care benefits to certain Korea and Vietnam Veterans' birth children who have been diagnosed with spina bifida (SB). If you are the birth child of a Vietnam Veteran and you have been diagnosed with spina bifida, you may already be receiving monetary allowances, vocational training or rehabilitation due to your condition. For the purpose of the VA SB Health Care Benefits Program, spina bifida is defined as all forms or manifestations of spina bifida (except spina bifida occulta).

> **Key Takeaways**
>
> Spina Bifida is a type of neural tube birth defect.
>
> Some Vietnam veterans and other certain veterans have children with Spina Bifida.
>
> The VA pays a monthly allowance based on the level of disability to or for a child with Spina Bifida who is a child of a Vietnam Veteran.
>
> Vocational training programs may also be available as well as healthcare benefits.

The Veterans Health Administration Office of Community Care (VHA OCC) in Denver, Colo., manages the SB Health Care Benefits Program, including authorization of benefits and the subsequent processing and payment of health care claims after a determination of eligibility has been made by the Denver VA Regional Office (VARO).

For the purpose of the Spina Bifida Program, the term **Vietnam Veteran** means an individual who performed active military, naval, or air service in the Republic of Vietnam during the period beginning on January 9, 1962, and ending May 7, 1975, without regard to the characterization of the individual's service. Service in the Republic of Vietnam includes service in the waters offshore and service in other locations if the conditions of service involved duty or visitation in the Republic of Vietnam.

Please note, the Spina Bifida Program does not include spina bifida occult.

People born with spina bifida and meet the following requirements may be eligible for VA benefits, including healthcare, compensation, and vocational training:
- Are biological children of Veterans who served:
- In Vietnam during the period from January 9, 1962, through May 7, 1975, or
- In or near the Korean demilitarized zone, between September 1, 1967 and August 31, 1971 and were exposed to herbicides. Veterans who served in a unit in or near the Korean demilitarized zone anytime between April 1, 1968 and August 31, 1971 are presumed to have been exposed to herbicides.
- Were conceived after the date on which the Veteran first entered Vietnam or the Korean demilitarized zone during the qualifying service period
- The term "herbicide agent" means a chemical in a herbicide used in support of United States and military operations in or near the Korean demilitarized zone, during the period beginning on September 1, 1967, and ending on August 31, 1971.

Spina Bifida Hotline

In June 2001, VA opened a hot line for Vietnam veterans with questions about health care benefits for their children who have spina bifida.
The number for the hot line is (888) 820-1756.

Callers can speak to a benefits advisor Monday through Friday, from 10:00 a.m. to 1:30 p.m., and from 2:30 p.m. to 4:30 p.m., Eastern time. An after-hours phone message will allow callers to leave their names and telephone numbers for a return call the next business day. The hotline is managed by VA's Health Administration Center in Denver, Colorado.

Monetary Benefits

VA shall pay a monthly allowance based upon the level of disability to or for a child who is suffering from spina bifida, and who is a child of a Vietnam veteran. Receipt of this allowance shall not affect the right of the child, or the right of any individual based on the child's relationship to that individual, to receive any other benefit to which the child, or that individual, may be entitled under any law administered by VA. If a child suffering from spina bifida is the natural child of two Vietnam veterans, he or she is entitled to only one monthly allowance. The monthly allowance is set at three levels, depending upon the degree of disability suffered by the child. VA shall determine the level of disability suffered by the child in accordance with the following criteria:

Level I

- The child is able to walk without braces or other external support (although gait may be impaired); and
- Has no sensory or motor impairment of upper extremities; and
- Has an IQ of 90 or higher; and
- Is continent of urine and feces.

Level II

Provided that none of the child's disabilities are severe enough to be evaluated at Level III, and the child is:

- Ambulatory, but only with braces or other external support; or
- Has sensory or motor impairment of upper extremities but is able to grasp pen, feed self, and perform self-care; or
- Has an IQ of at least 70 but less than 90; or
- Requires drugs or intermittent catheterization or other mechanical means to maintain proper urinary bladder function, or mechanisms for proper bowel function.

Level III

- The child is unable to ambulate; or
- Has sensory or motor impairment of upper extremities severe enough to prevent grasping a pen, feeding self, and performing self-care; or
- Has an IQ of 69 or less; or
- Has complete urinary or fecal incontinence

Spina Bifida Rate Table Effective December 1, 2020	
Disability Level	Monthly Allowance
Level I	$341.00
Level II	$1162.00
Level III	$1,979.00

Vocational Training for Children with Spina Bifida

To qualify for entitlement to a vocational training program, an applicant must be a child:

- To whom VA has awarded a monthly allowance for spina bifida and;
- For whom VA has determined that achievement of a vocational goal is reasonably feasible.
- A vocational training program may not begin before a child's 18th birthday or the date of completion of secondary schooling, whichever comes first. Depending on the need, a child may be provided up to 24 months of full-time training

Healthcare Benefits

In addition to monetary allowances, vocational training and rehabilitation, the Department of Veterans Affairs (VA) also provides VA-financed healthcare benefits to Vietnam veterans' birth children diagnosed with spina bifida. For the purpose of this program, spina bifida is defined as all forms or manifestations of spina bifida (except spina bifida occulta), including complications or associated medical conditions related to spina bifida according to the scientific literature.

Healthcare benefits available under this program are limited to those necessary for the treatment of spina bifida and related medical conditions. Beneficiaries should be aware that this program is not a comprehensive healthcare plan and does not cover care that is unrelated to spina bifida.

The administration of the program is centralized to VA's Health Administration Center (HAC) in Denver, Colorado. HAC is responsible for all aspects of the spina bifida healthcare program, including the authorization of benefits and the subsequent processing and payment of claims. All inquiries regarding healthcare benefits should be made directly to HAC.

Healthcare benefits may be claimed for services and supplies starting on the effective date specified in the VA regional office award letter.

Beneficiaries in receipt of a VA regional office spina bifida award will receive an identification card from the Health Administration Center.

There are no beneficiary co-payments or deductibles. VA is the exclusive payer for services provided to beneficiaries under this program, and billing should be sent directly to the Health Administration Center. The determined allowable amount for payment is considered payment in full, and the provider may not bill the beneficiary for the difference between the billed amount and the VA-determined allowed amount.

Covered Benefits

This program provides comprehensive health care for covered services and supplies that are considered medically necessary and appropriate.

General Exclusions

- Care as part of a grant study or research program
- Care considered experimental or investigational
- Care that is not medically necessary or appropriate
- Drugs not approved by the FDA for commercial marketing
- Services provided outside the scope of the provider's license or certification
- Services rendered by providers suspended or sanctioned by a federal agency
- Services, procedures or supplies for which the beneficiary has no legal obligation to pay, such as services obtained at a health fair
- Treatment for spina bifida occulta

Preauthorization Requirements

Although most health care services and supplies do not require approval in advance (preauthorization), some do. Preauthorization is NOT required for routine health care services and supplies. Preauthorization IS required for:

- Attendants Dental services
- Durable medical equipment (DME) with a total rental or purchase price in excess of $2,000
- Mental health services Hospice care
- Substance abuse treatment Training of family members
- Transplantation services
- Travel (other than mileage for privately owned automobiles for local travel) Note: When in doubt, contact the HAC.

Selecting Healthcare Providers

Beneficiaries may select the provider of their choice, as long as the provider is an approved health care provider. The provider must be approved by the Centers for Medicare and Medicaid Services (CMS), Department of Defense TRICARE program, CHAMPVA, JCAHO or may be a health care provider approved for providing services pursuant to a state license or certificate. A provider is not required to contract with the HAC; the HAC does not maintain a list of providers.

Claims

Claims are to be mailed directly to VA's Health Administration Center at the following address.

VA Health Administration Center
PO Box 469065
Denver CO 80246-906

As a safeguard against claims getting lost in the mail, beneficiaries should keep copies of all claim documents submitted.

Filing Deadlines

Claims must be filed with the Health Administration Center no later than:

- One year after the date of service; or
- In the case of inpatient care, one year after the date of discharge; or
- In the case of a VA regional office award for retroactive eligibility, 180 days following beneficiary notification of the award.

Payments

Approved healthcare providers will be paid 100% of the VA-determined allowable charge for covered services. VA payment for covered services constitutes payment in full. Federal regulations prohibit providers from seeking any additional monies from beneficiaries and third-party payers such as private insurers, for services paid by VA.

Note: If the beneficiary pays for care and subsequently files a claim for reimbursement, VA payment to the beneficiary will be limited to the VA-allowed amount. For this reason, beneficiaries are advised not to pay their providers-but instead, have the providers bill HAC directly.

Other Health Insurance

While VA assumes full responsibility for the cost of services related to the treatment of spina bifida and associated conditions, third-party insurers including Medicare and Medicaid, assume payment responsibility for services unrelated to the VA-covered conditions.

Explanation of Benefits

Upon completion of claim processing, an EOB will be mailed to the beneficiary. If a provider files the claim, an EOB will be mailed to them also. The EOB is a summarization of the action taken on the claim and contains, at a minimum, the following information.

- Beneficiary name;
- Description of services and/or supplies provided; Dates of service or supplies provided;
- Amount billed;
- VA-allowed amount;
- To whom payment, if any, was made; Reasons for denial (if applicable).

Reconsideration of Claims/Appeals

If a healthcare provider, beneficiary or beneficiary's representative disagrees with a claim determination, including the VA-allowed amount, a request for reconsideration of the disputed determination may be made. To do so, the request must:

- Be in writing;
- Be accompanied by a copy of the EOB in question; and

- State the specific issue that is being disputed, why the VA determination is considered to be in error, and include any new and relevant information not previously considered.

To meet the filing deadline, requests for reconsideration are to be mailed to the following address within one year of the date of the initial EOB:

VA Health Administration Center Reconsideration/Appeals
PO Box 460948
Denver CO 80246-0948

Upon complete review of the request and all the relevant documentation and evidence, a written determination will be mailed to the claimant.

CHAPTER 28

MENTAL HEALTH

According to the RAND Center for Military Health Policy Research, 20 percent of veterans who served in Iraq or Afghanistan suffer from either major depression or post-traumatic stress disorder.

19.5 percent of veterans in these categories have experienced a traumatic brain injury. Veterans mental health services are available to help those individuals struggling with mental health issues related to their service.

According to the Government Accountability Office, 2.1 million veterans received mental health treatment from the VA during the period from 2006 to 2010. According to a study from the Substance Abuse and Mental Health Services Administration, only 50 percent of returning veterans who need mental health treatment receive the services they need.

> **Key Takeaways**
>
> If you need support for a specific mental health problem, services are available through the VA. Services include peer support, therapy, medication or a combination approach.
>
> If you are already using VA medical services, you can ask your primary care provider to help you make an appointment with your VA mental health provider.
>
> If you aren't already using VA medical services, you should contact your nearest VA medical center or VET center.

Some of the barriers cited as reasons veterans might not seek help and treatment for mental health issues include:
- They are embarrassed to have service-related mental disabilities
- There are long wait times to receive treatment
- They feel shame over the need to get mental health care

- A fear of being viewed as weak
- The stigma surrounding mental health issues
- A lack of understanding about mental health

While post-traumatic stress disorder is often associated with veterans and mental health care, substance abuse is also a significant issue. According to the National Institute of Drug Abuse, substance abuse among veterans shows a strong link to their combat exposure. It's estimated that 25 percent of veterans who return from Iraq and Afghanistan have signs of substance abuse disorder.

Same-Day Care for Mental Health Needs

In January 2018, the VA announced that all of their more than 1,000 medical facilities around the country offer same-day services for urgent mental and physical health care needs.

Same-day services allow a veteran with an urgent need for primary care and mental health care to receive care in different formats, depending on the situation. This could include a face-to-face visit with a clinician, a phone call with a nurse, a telehealth or video care visit, an appointment with a specialist could be scheduled, or a prescription could be filled the same day.

AMVETS Health Program

In August 2018, American Veterans (AMVETS) and the Department of Veterans Affairs signed a Memorandum of Agreement, as part of their efforts to eliminate risk factors contributing to veteran suicide and to establish programs and practices to offer at-risk veterans the necessary interventions to avert a potential suicide risk.

The agreement is part of a partnership between the AMVETS HEAL program and the VA, through the VHA Office of Suicide Prevention. The program provides ways for AMVETS and VA to identify and eliminate the barriers veterans face in accessing healthcare, enroll more at-risk veterans into the VA healthcare system, and provide training for professionals who work with veterans so that intervention begins when red flags are identified.

The partnership follows a January 2018 executive order signed by then-President Donald Trump that directed the VA, Department of Defense, and Department of Homeland Security to collaborate in providing seamless access to mental health care and suicide prevention resources for veterans who have recently separated from military service.

AMVETS hired a team of clinical experts with experience in eliminating barriers to access in healthcare for veterans nationwide. HEAL, which stands for healthcare, evaluation, advocacy, legislation, encompasses all necessary steps the team will take to intervene directly on behalf of veterans, service members, families, and caregivers to reduce veteran suicide, unemployment, homelessness, and hopelessness. The support services can be accessed via the toll-free 1-833 VET-HEAL (1-833-838-4325)

410

or email VETHEAL@amvets.org.

Veterans in crisis or having thoughts of suicide — and those who know a Veteran in crisis — should call the Veterans Crisis Line for confidential support 24 hours a day and 365 days a year. Call 800-273-8255 and press 1, chat online at VeteransCrisisLine.net/Chat, or text to 838255.

VA Launches Telehealth Program for Rural Veterans with PTSD

In 2018, the VA announced the launch of a pilot telehealth program that gives rural veterans with post-traumatic stress disorder (PTSD), remote access to psychotherapy, and related services. The VA Office of Rural Health in partnership with the Quality Enhancement Research Initiative is supporting the Telemedicine Outreach for PTSD (TOP) program to deliver therapy and other care services through phone and video contact.

According to a VA representative, long-distance travel to urban areas can be a major barrier to care for rural veterans.

Veterans participating in the program receive frequent phone calls from a care manager who helps them access services provided by off-site psychiatrists and psychologists. The psychotherapy is delivered via interactive video from a VA medical center to a community-based outpatient clinic (CBOC) or to the veteran's home. The telephone care manager also monitors the veterans' progress and helps them overcome barriers to care.

The program includes 12 CBOCs across the nation in Charleston, South Carolina; Iowa City, Iowa; Little Rock, Arkansas; Denver, Colorado; San Diego, California; and Seattle. The results, which will be available in 2020, will lay the groundwork for national implementation of the TOP program.

Coaching into Care

Coaching Into Care is a national telephone service operated by the VA. The Goal of Coaching Into Care is to help educate, support, and empower family members, friends and loved ones who need care or services for a veteran. The goal of Coaching Into Care is to help veterans and their loved ones find the right services for them either at their local VA or in their community. There is also coaching available for the loved ones of a veteran who is having a difficult time transitioning into civilian life.

Coaching is provided by licensed psychologists or social workers free-of-charge. Coaching services include helping callers figure out the best ways to motivate a veteran to seek treatment. The calls with a coach can vary in length but are usually anywhere from 10 to 30 minutes. The same coach may work with someone over several calls.

Coaching Into Care is available by calling 888-823-7458. The hours of operation for this service from Monday through Friday from 8am to 8pm EST.

Depression

Everyone occasionally feels blue or sad, but these feelings are usually fleeting and pass within a couple of days. When a person has a depressive disorder, it interferes with daily life, normal functioning, and causes pain for both the person with the disorder and those who care about him or her. Depression is a common but serious illness, and most who experience it need treatment to get better. The good news is that depression, even the most severe cases, is a highly treatable disorder.

Treating Depression

A number of depression treatments are available. Medication and psychological counseling (psychotherapy) are very effective for most people. There are also many types of professionals who treat depression. A good place to start is with your primary care physician. In some cases, a primary care physician can prescribe medication to relieve depression symptoms. However, if treatment by your physician does not help you, the next step is to see a mental health professional.

In addition to medications, psychotherapy can be very effective in the treatment of depression. In fact, evidence-based psychotherapies are among the most effective treatments for depression. The following evidence-based psychotherapies have been found to be effective in treating depression. One or more of them can be found at your local VA Medical Center.

- Cognitive Behavioral Therapy (CBT-D): CBT is a structured, time-limited psychotherapy that helps individuals develop more balanced and helpful thoughts about themselves, others, and the future. CBT also helps individuals spend more time engaging in pleasurable or productive activities. CBT helps individuals to achieve personal goals and solve problems by learning and practicing new skills.
- Acceptance and Commitment Therapy: ACT is a psychotherapy based on the relationship between thoughts, feelings, and behaviors, which help individuals overcome their struggle with emotional pain and worry by encouraging them to take active steps to move forward. ACT helps individuals recognize, commit to, and achieve what matters most to them in life.
- Interpersonal Psychotherapy: Interpersonal Psychotherapy (IPT) is a treatment for depression that focuses on the relationships that may be the cause or the result of depression. IPT helps individuals to understand the connection between their depression and current relationship problems. It also helps individuals build social skills to deal better with problems. This helps to improve how someone feels as well and the quality of their life.

Anxiety

Anxiety and fear are basic emotions that are experienced by everyone and are necessary for survival. Anxiety is important because it helps people prepare for a threat. Fear is important because it helps people fight or escape.

The experiences of anxiety and fear are normal responses to threat or danger and are usually helpful. Anxiety and fear may be unhelpful if they interfere with a person's daily routine or prevent a person from doing things that he/she normally does. If the anxiety or fear is long-lasting and without relief, it may be a sign that a person has developed a more significant problem with anxiety, often called an "anxiety disorder."

Anxiety disorders are common. Almost one-third of adults will have experienced an anxiety disorder at some point in their lifetime. The good news is there are effective treatments for anxiety disorders.

Treating Anxiety

Every VA Medical Center offers mental health services. If you would like to learn more about anxiety or anxiety disorders or if you would like more information about what programs or services are available to you, please contact your local VA facility and ask to be connected to the mental health clinic. Your primary care provider may also be able to provide additional information or refer you to a mental health clinician.

There are a number of treatments for anxiety that are available at your local VA medical center or community-based outpatient clinic (CBOC). Research studies have shown that medication, psychotherapy (talk therapy), and the combination of medication and psychotherapy are very effective for most people who seek treatment for anxiety. There are many types of professionals who treat anxiety. A visit with your primary care provider may be a good place to start. Your primary care provider may be able to prescribe medication to relieve symptoms of anxiety and may refer you to a behavioral health provider for additional evaluation and treatment.

One of the most effective treatments for anxiety disorders is a kind of talk therapy known as cognitive-behavioral therapy (CBT). In general, CBT is a short-term treatment that helps people with anxiety learn new ways of coping with or managing their anxiety. The CBT provider typically teaches people different ways of thinking about things that make them anxious and guides them in changing their behavior so that they are not avoiding things that feel scary but are not dangerous. The goal of CBT is to teach the person with anxiety new ways of responding to the anxiety so that it no longer gets in the way of routine activities. Your primary care or mental health provider can refer you to a VA clinician who is trained to provide CBT.

Alcohol and Drug Misuse

Alcohol and drug misuse can lead to serious health, relationship, employment, and legal problems. Problematic alcohol or drug use can also lead to substance use

413

disorders (SUD). Symptoms of SUD include tolerance, the ability to drink or use greater quantities over time, inability to stop drinking or using in spite of negative consequences, and withdrawal, feeling sick when trying to quit drinking, or using drugs.

Problems with drinking or drug use may occur in response to stress, or in combination with posttraumatic stress disorder, depression, or other medical conditions. Fortunately, there are proven methods to help Veterans recover from alcohol or drug misuse, including mutual help groups and other effective treatments.

VHA has many resources to help Veterans and their loved ones answer questions, find support, get treatment, and recover. Please click on the tabs above to find information on some of these resources.

Treating Substance Use Disorders

Many veterans have problems with use of alcohol, tobacco, or drugs. This can include use of street drugs as well as using prescription medications in ways they weren't prescribed. Such substance use can harm health, cause mood and behavior problems, hurt social relationships, and cause financial problems. Many people find it difficult to cut down or stop using substances on their own. Effective treatments for substance use problems are available at VA. Available treatments address all types of problems related to substance use, from unhealthy use of alcohol to life-threatening addictions.

The VA provides effective, scientifically proven services for all eligible veterans, no matter where they come for services. VA providers know that in many cases substance use problems are continuing conditions that require care over a long period of time. For other veterans, the substance use problems may be resolved more quickly with attention paid to related problems. Such related problems could be posttraumatic stress disorder (PTSD), depression, pain, disturbed sleep, irritability, and/or relationship problems.

The VA offers a number of options for those seeking treatment for substance use problems. These options include therapy, either alone with the therapist or in a group, as well as medications to help veterans reduce their use of alcohol, tobacco and drugs.

Treatments that do not involve medications involve one or more of the following:

- Increasing and making clearer the veteran's motivation for change
- Helping veterans to improve their skills for spotting and dealing with triggers and relapse risks
- Counseling couples together on how to recover from substance abuse and how to improve relationships
- Getting outside support for recovery, including programs like Alcoholics

414

Anonymous (AA)

- Looking at how substance use problems may relate to other problems such as PTSD and depression.

VA providers may use medications to treat alcohol dependence. Effective medications can help manage withdrawal symptoms, reduce craving, and promote abstinence, which is not drinking any alcohol. Several medications for stopping tobacco can be effective alone or in combination:

- a nicotine replacement skin patch, gum or lozenge
- the medication bupropion, that has also been effective with depression
- the newest choice, varenicline, that has a very different way of working than the other medicines.

There are three different medications to treat addiction to opioid drugs like heroin, oxycodone or other pain killers. Methadone is an effective approach for chronic opioid addiction that can be provided only within a special program. Buprenorphine / naloxone and naltrexone can be part of treatment plans in a variety of clinical settings.

To help make sure that veterans can attend VA treatment services, programs offer evening and weekend hours. Residential (live-in) options are available for veterans who live far away from a VA clinic or have unstable housing. Special programs are often offered for patients with special concerns, such as women, OEF/OIF veterans, and homeless patients.

A patient coming to VA can expect to find the following types of care:

- first-time screening for alcohol or tobacco use in all care locations
- short outpatient counseling including focus on motivation
- intensive outpatient treatment
- residential (live-in) care
- medically managed detoxification (stopping substance use safely) and services to get stable
- continuing care and relapse prevention
- marriage and family counseling
- self-help groups
- drug substitution therapies and newer medicines to reduce cravings

Decisions as to which services are provided and how intense they are will be based on the patient's needs and desires.

Getting Help

- Speak with your existing VA healthcare provider
- Contact the OEF/OIF Coordinator at your local VA Medical Center
- Contact your local Vet Center

- Call 1-800-827-1000, VA's general information hotline

Veterans Alcohol and Drug Dependence Rehabilitation Program

The Department of Veterans Affairs (VA) Alcohol and Drug Dependence Rehabilitation Program provides social, vocational, and rehabilitation therapies to eligible alcohol and drug-dependent veterans. The programs include different forms of treatment such as detoxification, rehabilitation and psychiatric care. These treatment programs are located in VA medical centers and clinics.

To be eligible, you need to be enrolled in the VA healthcare system or qualify based on the exceptions in the law. To receive VA benefits and services, a veteran generally needs a character of discharge or service that's under other than dishonorable conditions.

For more information, veterans can contact their nearest VA medical facility.

Suicide Prevention

The challenges of life can feel overwhelming, and like there's no way for them to get better. If a veteran feels like they can't bear with their life anymore or if they're thinking of ending it, there are resources available.

The Veterans Crisis Line is available at 1-800-273-8255. You can also send a text message to 838255, and there is an online chat option available as well.

Suicide is a national health concern that affects all Americans regardless of whether not they have served in the military. According to the VA, everyone has a role to play in preventing suicide. That's why the VA works with partners across the country to prevent suicide among all veterans, including the ones who don't come to the VA for care.

The VA recently launched something called S.A.V.E. online suicide prevention training as part of a collaboration with PsychArmor Institute. S.A.V.E stands for "Signs, Ask, Validate, and Encourage and Expedite."

Suicide Warning Signs

- Hopelessness; feeling like there's no way out
- Anxiety, agitation, sleeplessness, or mood swings
- Feeling like there is no reason to live
- Rage or anger
- Engaging in risky activities without thinking
- Increasing alcohol or drug misuse
- Withdrawing from family and friends

The presence of the following signs requires immediate attention:

- Thinking about hurting or killing yourself
- Looking for ways to kill yourself
- Talking about death, dying, or suicide
- Self-destructive behavior such as drug misuse, carelessly handling weapons, etc.

If you or the veteran in your life is feeling depressed, anxious, hopeless, or as if life has no purpose, but is **not** in immediate danger, the following are things you can do:

- Visit VeteransCrisisLine.net to learn about support that is available to you.
- Use the VA's resource locator to discover the suicide prevention resources in your area, including VA medical centers and Suicide Prevention Coordinators.
- Visit **MakeTheConnection.net** to hear from veterans and their family members who have coped with challenges like yours.

Post-Traumatic Stress Disorder (PTSD)

PTSD is a condition resulting from exposure to direct or indirect threat of death, serious injury, or a physical threat. The events that can cause PTSD are called "stressors" and may include combat or war exposure, sexual or physical abuse, terrorist attacks, serious accidents or natural disasters such as fire, tornado, hurricane, flood or earthquake.

Symptoms of PTSD can include recurrent thoughts of the traumatic event, reduced involvement in work or outside interests, emotional numbing, hyper-alertness, anxiety and irritability. The disorder can be more severe and longer-lasting when the stress is human initiated action (example: war, rape, terrorism).

There are many types of treatment for PTSD, including counseling and medicines known as SSRIs.

According to the National Center for PTSD, it's normal to have upsetting memories, feel on edge, or have trouble sleeping after a traumatic event. At first, it may be hard to do normal daily activities, like go to work, go to school, or spend time with people you care about. But most people start to feel better after a few weeks or months.

If it's been longer than a few months and you're still having symptoms, you may have PTSD. For some people, PTSD symptoms may start later on, or they may come and go over time.

Anyone can develop PTSD at any age. A number of factors can increase the chance that someone will have PTSD, many of which are not under that person's control. For example, having a very intense or long-lasting traumatic event or getting injured during the event can make it more likely that a person will develop PTSD. PTSD is

417

also more common after certain types of trauma, like combat and sexual assault.

Personal factors, like previous traumatic exposure, age, and gender, can affect whether or not a person will develop PTSD. What happens after the traumatic event is also important. Stress can make PTSD more likely, while social support can make it less likely.

PTSD Treatment Programs

No matter where you live, PTSD treatment in the Department of Veterans Affairs is available. Each medical center within VA has PTSD specialists who provide treatment for Veterans with PTSD and there are nearly 200 specialized PTSD treatment programs throughout the country.

Some large Community-Based Outpatient Clinics (CBOCs) also offer PTSD care. When there are no nearby facilities, smaller CBOCs provide needed treatment services by telemental health (using technology to communicate) or by referral to Vet Centers or community clinicians. This page describes the specialized PTSD programs and these other options within VA for getting PTSD treatment.

You can use this VA PTSD Program Locator to see if there is a specialized program near you.

Who Is Covered for VA Care?

VA services are provided to all Veterans who:
- Completed active military service in the Army, Navy, Air Force, Marines, or Coast Guard (or Merchant Marines during WWII)
- Were discharged under other than dishonorable conditions
- Were National Guard members or Reservists who have completed a federal deployment to a combat zone
- At times, the VA has special agreements to provide care to Active Duty service members and family.

What services are offered?

Each PTSD program offers education, evaluation, and treatment. Program services include:
- One-to-one mental health assessment and testing Medications
- One-to-one psychotherapy and family therapy
- Group therapy (covers topics such as anger and stress, combat support, partners, etc.) or groups for Veterans of specific conflicts or specific traumas

Clay Hunt Act

The Clay Hunt Suicide Prevention for American Veterans (SAV) Act will help reduce military and veteran suicides and improve access to quality mental health care. The following are goals of the legislation.
- Increase access to mental health care by, among other things, creating a peer support and community outreach pilot program to assist transitioning

servicemembers as well as a one-stop, interactive website of available resources.

- Better meet the demand for mental health care by starting a pilot program to repay the loan debt of students in psychiatry so it is easier to recruit them to work at the VA.

- Boost the accountability of mental health care by requiring an annual evaluation of VA mental health and suicide-prevention programs.

Presumptive Eligibility for Psychosis and Other Mental Illness

Certain Veterans who experienced psychosis within a specified time-frame are to have their psychosis presumed to be service-connected for purposes of VA medical benefits. In addition, VA will presume that Persian Gulf War Veterans are service-connected for purposes of VA medical benefits if such Veterans develop mental illness other than psychosis within two years after discharge or release from service and before the end of the 2-year period beginning on the last day of the Persian Gulf War. Under this authority veterans who are not otherwise eligible for VA health care and meet the description stated can receive treatment only for psychosis or mental illness and other conditions directly related to psychosis or mental illness at no cost.

Psychosis

Eligibility for treatment of psychosis, and such condition is exempted from copayments for any Veteran who served in the United States active-duty military, naval, or air service and developed such psychosis within two years after discharge or release from the active military duty, naval or air service; and before the following date associated with the war or conflict in which the Veteran served:

- **World War II** July 26, 1949
- **Korean Conflict** February 1, 1957
- **Vietnam Era** May 8, 1977
- **Persian Gulf War** Date To Be Determined

Mental Illness (other than Psychosis)

Eligibility for benefits is established for treatment of an active mental illness (other than psychosis), and such condition is exempted from copayments for any Veteran of the Persian Gulf War who developed such mental illness:

- Within two years after discharge or release from the active-duty military, naval, or air service; and
- Before the end of the two-year period beginning on the last day of the Persian Gulf War (end date not yet determined).

Disability Compensation

The Veterans Service Organizations provide Service Officers at no cost to help veterans and family members pursue VA disability claims. Service Officers are familiar with every step in the application and interview process and can provide both technical guidance and moral support. In addition, some Service Officers particularly specialize in assisting veterans with PTSD disability claims. Even if a veteran has not been a member of a specific Veterans Service Organization, the veteran still can request the assistance of a Service Officer working for that organization. In order to get representation by a qualified and helpful Service Officer, you can directly contact the local office of any Veterans Service Organization or ask for recommendations from other veterans who have applied for VA disability, or from a PTSD specialist at a VA PTSD clinic or a VetCenter.

Once the VA has awarded service connection for PTSD, it will then review the most current clinical evidence of record to determine how the severity of your symptoms impairs your social and industrial (ability to work) capacity.

The VA has a schedule of rating disabilities, located in title 38 C.F.R., Part 4. The VA has established "Diagnostic Codes" (DC) for various medical and psychiatric disorders, which include a description of the severity of related symptoms and a corresponding disability percentage (called a "rating" or "evaluation").

Although there are different DCs for covered psychiatric disorders, the VA evaluates the level of disability due to psychiatric disorders under the same criteria, regardless of the actual diagnosis. 38 C.F.R. §4.130, DC 9411, governs PTSD ratings. This regulation provides graduated ratings of 0%, 10%, 30%, 50%, 70% or 100%. A 0% rating is noncompensable this means that you have service-connected PTSD, however, there is little or no impairment as a result. VA compensation payments begin at 10% and increase at each rating level.

In July 2010, VA simplified the process for a veteran to claim service connection for PTSD. VA reduced the evidence needed if the trauma claimed by a veteran is related to "fear of hostile military or terrorist activity," and is consistent with the places, types, and circumstances of the veteran's service.

Previously, unless the veteran was a combat veteran, claims adjudicators were required to undertake extensive record development to corroborate whether a veteran actually experienced the claimed in-service stressor.

The rule applies to claims:
- Received by VA on or after July 13, 2010;
- Received before July 13, 2010 but not yet decided by a VA regional office;
- Appealed to the Board of Veterans' Appeals on or after July 13, 2010;
- Appealed to the Board before July 13, 2010, but not yet decided by the Board; and
- Pending before VA on or after July 13, 2010, because the Court of Appeals for Veterans Claims vacated a Board decision and remanded for re-adjudication.

General Rating Formula for Mental Disorders

Disability Rating	Description of Disability
100%	Total occupational and social impairment, due to such symptoms as: gross impairment in thought process or communication; persistent delusions or hallucinations; grossly inappropriate behavior; persistent danger of hurting self or others; intermittent inability to perform activities of daily living (including maintenance of minimal personal hygiene); disorientation to time or place; memory loss for names of close relatives, own occupation, or own name
70%	Occupational and social impairment, with deficiencies in most areas, such as work, school, family relations, judgment, thinking, or mood, due to such symptoms as: suicidal ideation; obsessional rituals which interfere with routine activities; speech intermittently illogical, obscure, or irrelevant; near-continuous panic or depression affecting the ability to function independently, appropriately and effectively; impaired impulse control (such as unprovoked irritability with periods of violence); spatial disorientation; neglect of personal appearance and hygiene; difficulty in adapting to stressful circumstances (including work or a work-like setting); inability to establish and maintain effective relationships
50%	Occupational and social impairment with reduced reliability and productivity due to such symptoms as: flattened affect; circumstantial, circumlocutory, or stereotyped speech; panic attacks more than once a week; difficulty in understanding complex commands; impairment of short- and long-term memory (e.g., retention of only highly learned material, forgetting to complete tasks); impaired judgment; impaired abstract thinking; disturbances of motivation and mood; difficulty in establishing and maintaining effective work and social relationships

30%	Occupational and social impairment with Occasional decrease in work efficiency and intermittent periods of inability to perform occupational tasks (although generally functioning satisfactorily, with routine behavior, self-care, and conversation normal), due to such symptoms as: depressed mood, anxiety, suspiciousness, panic attacks (weekly or less often), chronic sleep impairment, mild memory loss (such as forgetting names, directions, recent events)
10%	Occupational and social impairment due to mild or transient symptoms which decrease work efficiency and ability to perform occupational tasks only during periods of significant stress, or; symptoms controlled by continuous medication
0%	A mental condition has been formally diagnosed, but symptoms are not severe enough either to interfere with occupational and social functioning or to require continuous medication

VA Medical Center Programs

While PTSD treatment is available through all of VA's 171 medical centers, a VA network of 124 facilities offers specialized inpatient and outpatient treatment. One notable program consists of PTSD clinical teams that provide outpatient treatment but also work closely with other VA treatment programs, including Vet Centers, to coordinate services and provide information on PTSD throughout the medical center and the community.

In addition to 83 PTSD clinical teams, VA operates 22 specialized inpatient units around the country, plus 13 brief-treatment units, 11 residential rehabilitation programs, and four PTSD day hospitals. There also are four outpatient Women's Stress Disorder and Treatment Teams and eight outpatient-based PTSD Teams Substance Use Disorder demonstration projects. A special focus in the program expansions has included underserved and minority populations, such as African Americans, Hispanics and Native Americans. A specialized PTSD inpatient treatment unit serves women veterans at the Palo Alto, Calif., VA Medical Center's Menlo Park Division.

Each PTSD program offers education, evaluation, and treatment. Program services include:
- One-to-one mental health assessment and testing
- Medicines
- One-to-one psychotherapy and also family therapy
- Group therapy (covers topics such as anger and stress, combat support, partners, or groups for Veterans of specific conflicts)

- The VA provides treatments shown by research to be effective in treating Veterans
- Services are conducted by mental health care workers

Help for Families

In 2011, the Department of Veterans' Affairs launched a new telephone service to assist family members and friends of veterans to encourage them to seek healthcare for readjustment and mental health issues. The telephone service is called Coaching Into Care and is available by calling **(888) 823-7458**.

Military Sexual Trauma (MST)

Both women and men can experience sexual harassment or sexual assault during their military service. VA refers to these experiences as military sexual trauma, or MST. Like other types of trauma, MST can negatively impact a person's mental and physical health, even many years later. Some problems associated with MST include:

Disturbing memories or nightmares;
Difficulty feeling safe;
Feelings of depression or numbness;
Problems with alcohol or other drugs;
Feeling isolated from other people;
Problems with anger or irritability;
Problems with sleep;
Physical health problems.

VA defines sexual trauma as any lingering physical, emotional, or psychological symptoms resulting from a physical assault of a sexual nature, or battery of a sexual nature. Examples of this are:
- Rape;
- Physical assault;
- Domestic Battering; and
- Stalking.

Treatment for MST

People can recover from trauma. To help veterans do this, VA provides free, confidential counseling and treatment for mental and physical health conditions related to experiences of MST. You do not need to be service-connected and may be able to receive this benefit even if you are not eligible for other VA care. You do not need to have reported the incidents when they happened or have other documentation that they occurred.

Every VA facility has a designated MST Coordinator who serves as a contact person for MST-related issues. This person is your advocate and can help you find and access VA services and programs, state and federal benefits, and community resources.

Every VA facility has providers knowledgeable about treatment for the aftereffects of MST. Many have specialized outpatient mental health services focusing on sexual trauma. Vet Centers also have specially trained sexual trauma counselors.

Nationwide, there are programs that offer specialized sexual trauma treatment in residential or inpatient settings. These are programs for Veterans who need more intense treatment and support.

To accommodate veterans who do not feel comfortable in mixed-gender treatment settings, some facilities throughout VA have separate programs for men and women. All residential and inpatient MST programs have separate sleeping areas for men and women.

Disability Compensation is a monthly payment to a veteran disabled by an injury or a disease incurred or aggravated on active service. The veteran must have been discharged under other than dishonorable conditions to be eligible. The individual must currently be suffering from disabling symptoms to receive compensation. Refer to Chapter 4 of this book for information regarding Disability Compensation.

Early Identification, Screening and Intervention in Primary Care Settings

Early identification, accurate diagnosis, and effective treatment of mental health conditions improve the chances for recovery, so VA primary care providers screen veterans for depression, posttraumatic stress disorder (PTSD), problematic alcohol use, and difficulties related to military sexual trauma (MST).

Many veterans who receive care in VA clinics have been diagnosed with mental health conditions:

- In fiscal year (FY) 2017, more than 1.7 million veterans received mental health treatment in a VA mental health program; this number has risen each year from about 900,000 in FY2006.
- Nearly one-third (29.2 percent) of these patients received care from a mental health care provider working in the primary care clinic, while 350,000 (70.8 percent) had their depression documented by providers who exclusively practice primary care.
- Other mental health conditions such as PTSD, substance use disorders (SUD), and anxiety are also commonly diagnosed in VA primary care patients.

The integration of mental health services into primary care settings is designed in part to help overcome some Veterans' reservations about seeking mental health treatment. It also provides an opportunity to deliver mental health services to those who may otherwise not seek them and to identify, prevent, and treat mental health conditions at the earliest opportunity. VA provided more than 1.2 million mental health visits in primary care settings in FY2017, an increase of 4 percent from FY2016 and up 20 percent from FY2014. In most cases, mental health professionals embedded in the primary care team can effectively treat the patient. If warranted, the patient can be referred to specialty care.

Full Range of Medical Health Care Services

VA provides a continuum of outpatient, residential, and inpatient mental health services. The Veterans Health Administration (VHA) has 168 medical centers, 1,053 community-based outpatient clinics, 300 Vet Centers, 80 mobile Vet Centers, and VA staff working on college and university campuses. In FY2017, more than 1.7 million Veterans received mental health treatment in a VA mental health specialty program; this number has risen each year from over 900,000 in FY2006.

VA believes this increase is partly due to proactive screening to identify Veterans who may have symptoms of depression, PTSD, or problematic use of alcohol, or who have experienced MST. In addition, the introduction of Peer Specialists to the mental health workforce provides unique opportunities for engaging Veterans in care.

As of the end of FY2017, there were almost 1,100 peers providing services at VA medical centers (VAMC) and community-based outpatient clinics. VA has also developed useful web and mobile tools to help connect Veterans and their families to mental health resources.

Nonmedical Determinants of Health

VA delivers a broad range of services that contribute to a veteran's overall psychological resilience and ability to recover from mental health conditions — recognizing that recovery requires a holistic approach to care. Whether veterans are having legal problems, experiencing homelessness, living without a positive social support system, or lacking job training, VA staff members work with them to tailor evidence-based treatment and services to the challenges in their lives that may hamper their recovery. For example, we know that homelessness and the need for job skills contribute to economic instability, and these circumstances make it less likely that a veteran in need of mental health care will seek care or continue to be engaged.

VA also recognizes that many veterans who have been arrested or prosecuted have a mental illness or behavioral health condition that increases their risk of future legal troubles if they do not receive support and treatment services. Veterans who are employed, have a stable place to live, and are affiliated with a community of Veterans and others for support are more likely than others to be optimistic about their future.

Outpatient Mental Health Services

Outpatient mental health services comprise a broad range of services delivered in individual or group settings. In response to the growing Veteran need for mental health services, VA doubled the number of outpatient mental health encounters, or treatment visits, from 10.7 million in FY2006 to 21.3 million in FY2017. Each Veteran receiving ongoing VA specialty mental health care is assigned a Mental Health Treatment Coordinator (MHTC), who ensures continuity of care and provides the Veteran with a consistent and reliable point of contact, especially during times of care transitions. The MHTC serves as a clinical resource for the Veteran and staff, generally as part of the Veteran's assigned mental health care team.

As of January 30, 2018, 1,347,189 Veterans had an assigned MHTC. In addition, VA facilities throughout the country are utilizing teams to promote Veteran-centered, coordinated care to support recovery. One model for this team-based care is the Behavioral Health Interdisciplinary Program (BHIP), which coordinates collaborative, evidence-based, Veteran-centered care by an interdisciplinary team of providers and clerical staff in outpatient mental health clinics at all VAMCs. BHIP is guided by the evidence-based Collaborative Care Model, which focuses on six core elements: providing organizational and leadership support, anticipating care needs through process redesign, enhancing Veteran self-management skills, offering decision support for providers, managing clinical information about Veterans, and accessing support for Veterans in the community.

Through its emphasis on team building, communication, and coordination, BHIP is demonstrating a meaningful, positive impact on patient care and teamwork — including improved staff relationships, job satisfaction, and Veteran access to care.

Psychosocial Rehabilitation and Recovery Centers (PRRC)

PRRCs help veterans challenged with SMI and significant functional impairment acquire the skills necessary to integrate into meaningful self-determined roles in the community.

In support of this goal, PRRCs provides a transitional educational center that inspires and helps Veterans to reclaim their lives, instills hope, validates strengths, teaches life skills, and facilitates community integration into the roles they desire. PRRCs provide Veterans with SMIs an avenue to define and pursue a personal mission and vision for their future based on their strengths and self-identified values, In Veterans' own words Cognitive behavioral therapy, or CBT, can be an effective treatment for PTSD, anxiety, depression, and other conditions.

Nonprofits That Deliver Mental Health Resources to Veterans

The Soldier's Project helps service members, their spouses, parents, children, friends, colleagues and other relatives. There are mental health professionals who work

426

through The Soldier's Project, and it's completely free and confidential. There are local chapters of the Soldier's Project available throughout the country.

Give An Hour is a nonprofit that's mission is to develop a national network of volunteers who can respond to acute and chronic conditions that arise in society. The focus of the organization is currently on meeting the mental health needs of troops who have served in Iraq and Afghanistan, as well as their families. The group provides counseling and treatment for anxiety, depression, substance abuse, PTSD, traumatic brain injury, loss and grieving and more. They can help people by putting them in contact with a provider who will offer services free of charge. There is no insurance information required to receive access to help.

The Camaraderie Foundation offers counseling assistance for military service members and their immediate family members who actively served in the Armed Forces after September 11, 2001. According to the organization, their goal is to help heal the invisible wounds of war through counseling, emotional and spiritual support. For services you have to fill out an application for assistance. If you qualify, the Camaraderie Foundation will provide completely free counseling services to supplement what's provided by the military. There is private counseling which is conducted by licensed professionals.

CHAPTER 29

BENEFITS FOR FORMER PRISONERS OF WAR (POWS)

Former prisoners of war (POW) are veterans who, while on active duty in the military, air, or naval service, were forcibly detained or interned in the line of duty by an enemy government or its agents or a hostile force. Periods of war include World War II, the Korean War, the Vietnam War, and the Persian Gulf War (service after August 2, 1990).

Veterans who, while on active duty during peacetime, were forcibly detained or interned by a foreign government or its agents or a hostile force are also considered former POWs if the circumstances of the internment were comparable to wartime internment (for example Iran, Somalia or Kosovo). A POW Coordinator has been designated at each VA regional office. The POW Coordinator can furnish former POWs with information about the benefits and services available to them.

Key Takeaways

More than one-half million Americans have been captured and interned as POWs since the American revolution.

Each VA Regional Office has a POW Veterans Outreach Coordinator.

Former POWs are eligible for VA disability compensation, and certain conditions are presumed to be related to time in captivity.

Healthcare

Former POWs are recognized as a special category of veterans and will be placed on one of the top three Priority Groups established for VA healthcare by Congress. Those who have a service-connected disability are eligible for VA health care. This includes hospital, nursing home, and outpatient treatment. Former POWs who do not have a service- connected disability are eligible for VA hospital and nursing home care, regardless of the veterans' ability to provide payment. They are also eligible for outpatient care on a priority basis. Public Law 108-170, which became law December 6, 2003, eliminated prescription drug co-payments for former POWs.

Veterans who were POWs may receive complete dental care.

Former POWs are eligible for any prosthetic item, including eyeglasses and hearing aids. A VA physician must order the prosthetic items, when medically indicated, for eligible veterans.

Veterans may enroll in VA healthcare by completing VA Form 10-10EZR, "Application for Medical Benefits."

Disability Compensation

Veterans are encouraged to apply for VA Disability Compensation for any disabilities related to service, whether they were a POW or not. Some disabilities are presumptive, which means that if a veteran is diagnosed with certain conditions, and the veteran was a POW for at least 30 days (certain conditions do not include the 30-day requirement), the VA presumes the captivity caused the disability.

Presumptions of Service Connection Relating to Certain Diseases and Disabilities for Former Prisoners of War

Public Law 108-183, The Veterans Benefits Act of 2003, eliminated the requirement that a veteran was a POW for at least 30 days for certain conditions. Therefore, there are now two categories of presumptive conditions – those that include the 30-day requirement, and those that do not.

In the case of any veteran who is a former prisoner of war, and who was detained or interned for thirty days or more, any of the following which became manifest to a degree of 10% or more after active military, naval or air service, shall be considered to have been incurred in or aggravated by such service, notwithstanding that there is no record of such disease during the period of service:

- Avitaminosis
- Beriberi (Including beriberi heart disease, which includes Ischemic Heart Disease- coronary artery disease-for former POWs who suffered during captivity from edema- swelling of the legs or feet- also known as "wet" beriberi)
- Chronic dysentery Helminthiasis
- Malnutrition (including optic atrophy associated with malnutrition)
- Pellagra
- Any other nutritional deficiency
- Peripheral neuropathy, except where directly related to infectious causes Irritable bowel syndrome
- Peptic ulcer disease Cirrhosis of the liver
- Osteoporosis, on or after September 28, 2009

In the case of any veteran who is a former prisoner of war, and who was detained or interned for any period of time, any of the following which became manifest to a degree of 10% or more after active military, naval or air service, shall be considered to have been incurred in or aggravated by such service, notwithstanding that there is no record of such disease during the period of service:

- Psychosis
- Dysthymic disorder, or depressive neurosis
- Post-traumatic osteoarthritis
- Any of the Anxiety States Cold Injury
- Stroke and complications
- Heart Disease and complications
- Osteoporosis, on or after October 10, 2008, when Post Traumatic Stress Disorder is diagnosed

Former POWs should file a claim by completing "VA Form 21-526, Application for Compensation or Pension." The VA also offers a POW protocol exam. This is a one-time exam available to all former POWs and is conducted at a VA medical facility to help determine if any presumptive disabilities exist.

Survivors of POWS

There are benefits for survivors of POWs. The major benefit is Dependency and Indemnity Compensation (DIC) which is a monthly benefit payable to the surviving spouse (and the former POW's children and parents in some cases) when the former POW:

- Was a service member who died on active duty; or
- Died from service-related disabilities; or
- Died on or before September 30, 1999 and was continuously rated totally disabled for a service-connected condition (including individual unemployability) for at least 10 years immediately preceding death; or
- Died after September 30, 1999 and was continuously rated totally disabled for a service-connected condition (including individual unemployability) for at least 1 year immediately preceding death.

DIC is terminated for a surviving spouse who remarries but can be resumed if the remarriage ends in death, divorce, or annulment. However, a surviving spouse who remarries on or after attaining age 57, and on or after December 16, 2003, can continue to receive DIC.

Prisoner of War Medal

A Prisoner of War Medal is available to any member of the U.S. Armed Forces taken prisoner during any armed conflict dating from World War I.

CHAPTER 30

CAREGIVERS

According to the VA, as a family caregiver, you play an important role in caring for the veteran at home and in the community. The VA has two programs for caregivers. The first is the Program of General Caregiver Support Services, which is available for eligible veterans of all eras. There's also the Program of Comprehensive Assistance for Family Caregivers, for eligible post-9/11 veterans. The recent MISSION Act gives veterans greater access to health care and expands services for caregivers. Another update from 2019 is the expansion of commissary and military exchange access to approved Primary Family Caregivers under the Program of Comprehensive Assistance for Family Caregivers.

2020 Update: VA Publishes Final Regulation for its Program of Comprehensive Assistance for Family Caregivers

The U.S. Department of Veterans Affairs (VA) published on July 31, 2020 its final regulation to improve and expand the VA Program of

Key Takeaways
As part of the VA MISSION Act, more family caregivers now have access to the program.

There are two phases of access expansion.

On October 1, 2020, the VA expanded the program to include family caregivers of eligible veterans who were injured in the line of duty on or before May 7, 1975.

Two years from that date, the VA will further expand the program to include family caregivers of eligible veterans from all eras who were seriously injured in the line of duty.

Comprehensive Assistance for Family Caregivers (PCAFC) with the final regulation which went into effect on October 1, 2020.

Under the final regulation, PCAFC will include eligible Veterans that have a single or combined service-connected disability rating by VA of 70% or higher, regardless of whether it resulted from an injury, illness or disease.

This is a notable change to the definition of serious injury from the current regulations, among other improvements aimed at standardizing the PCAFC and improving transparency in the program.

Expansion of VA's PCAFC to eligible veterans of earlier eras will occur in two phases. The first phase began October 2020 and will include eligible veterans who incurred or aggravated a serious injury in the line of duty in the active, military, naval or air service on or before May 7, 1975. Phase two will go into effect two years later and include eligible veterans of all eras.

Additionally, the new regulation changes the PCAFC stipend payment methodology, defines new procedures for revocation and discharge, and includes certain advance notice requirements aimed at improving communication between VA and PCAFC participants as well as include information for current program participants. VA is also standardizing operating procedures for the Caregiver Support Program, providing new training for staff and caregivers, and boosting operational capacity by hiring additional staff. With this expansion, Primary Family Caregivers in PCAFC will also have access to financial planning and legal services. VA is also working to fully implement the new information technology system required by the VA MISSION Act of 2018 by October 2020.

VA's Caregiver Support Program offers support services for caregivers including training, peer mentoring, respite care, a telephone support line, and self-care courses for caregivers of covered Veterans enrolled in VA health care who need personal care services.

Caregivers can visit VA Caregiver support website or call the Caregiver Support Line at 855-260-3274 for questions.

Am I a Caregiver?

Often people don't identify themselves as a caregiver. A caregiver can be a daughter, wife, husband, son, grandchild, niece, nephew, partner, or friend. Consider the following in determining whether you are a caregiver. Do you help a veteran:

- Make medical appointments?
- Drive to the doctor?
- Get to the pharmacy to get medications?

- Get dressed, take a shower, or take medicine?
- Get in or out of bed?
- Complete physical therapy?
- Administer injections?
- Feed self with feeding tubes or complete similar procedures at home?
- Talk with doctors, nurses, and social works to understand medical care or benefits?

If you answered yes to any of these questions, you are a caregiver and may be eligible for caregiver services at VA.

VA Caregiver Support

As a caregiver, the best thing you can do for people who depend on you is taking care of yourself. There are a variety of resources from the VA that provide general support services to family caregivers. These include:

Caregiver Support Line

The VA Caregiver Support Line is available at 1-855-260-3274. There are licensed professionals who staff the support line, and they can connect you with VA services, a Caregiver Support Coordinator at your nearest VA medical center or just listen. Caregivers can participate in monthly telephone education groups where they can discuss self-care tips and ask questions on different topics.

Peer Support Mentoring

Caregivers of veterans are eligible to participate in the VA Caregiver Peer Support Mentoring Program, both as mentors and mentees. Mentors and mentees communicate using email, telephone, and letter writing. Mentors receive training before being paired with another caregiver and are volunteers with their local VA medical center Voluntary Services department. Caregivers participating in the Caregiver Peer Support Mentoring Program agree to participate for six months, but many participate for much longer.

REACH VA

Mentoring in the areas of caregiving, stress management, mood management, and problem-solving is available through REACH VA. The program is available for caregivers of veterans diagnosed with ALS, dementia, MS, PTSD or spinal cord injury/disorder.

The REACH VA program is an opportunity for caregivers of veterans to take better care of themselves and their loved ones by providing them with important information in the areas of caregiving and building their skills in stress management and problem-solving.

The trained and certified REACH VA program coach usually provides four individual sessions with the caregiver over a period of two to three months, extending the session if both the coach and caregiver feel they need to do more work.

To be eligible for the REACH VA program, the caregiver must be caring for a veteran or a veteran caring for a loved one where the veteran is receiving services at the VA. Caregivers receive a Caregiver Notebook, which is the first resource for caregiver issues and challenges.

What is the VA Caregiver Support Program?

The VA Caregiver Support Program was established under Public Law 11-163, the Caregivers and Veterans Omnibus Health Services Act of 2010, established 38 U.S.C. 1720G, directing the VA to establish a Program of Comprehensive Assistance for Family Caregivers and a Program of General Caregiver Support Services. These two programs are collectively referred to as the caregiver support program.

The Program of Comprehensive Assistance for Family Caregivers provides education and training, respite care, mental health services, beneficiary travel, a monthly stipend payment and access to health care if qualified through the Civilian Health and Medical Program of the Department of Veterans Affairs (CAMPVA).

The Program of General Caregiver Support Services provides education, training, and support on the care of disabled veterans in need of personal care services, the use of telehealth and other available technologies, specified counseling, and respite care to caregivers of quality veterans of all ears.

VA establishes between three types of caregivers based upon the requirements of law. The assistance and support available to the caregiver are dependent upon which program the veteran is participating in and their associated caregiver's designation.

Veteran Eligibility

The Program of Comprehensive Assistance for Family Caregivers involves both primary and secondary family caregivers. Pursuant to 38 CFR 71.20, an individual is eligible for a primary or secondary family caregiver if all the following requirements are met:
The individual is either:
- A veteran; or
- A member of the Armed Forces who has been found unfit for duty due to a medical condition by their Service's Physical Evaluation Board and has been issued a date for medical discharge from the Armed forces.
- The individual has a serious injury (including traumatic brain injury, psychological trauma, or other mental disorder) incurred or aggravated in the line of duty in the active military, naval or air service on or after September 11, 2001.

- Such serious injury renders the individual in need of personal care services from another individual (a caregiver) for a minimum of six continuous months based on any of the following criteria:
    - An inability to perform one or more activities of daily living;
    - A need for supervision or protection based on symptoms or residuals of neurological or other impairment or injury;
    - The individual is a veteran who is service-connected for a serious injury that was incurred or aggravated in the line of duty in the active military, naval or air service on or after September 11, 2001 and has been rated 100% disabled for that serious injury and has been award special monthly compensation that includes and aid and attendance allowance
- A clinical determination—authorized by the individual's primary care team—has been made that it is in the best interest of the individual to participate in the program.
- Personal care services that would be provided by the family caregiver will not be simultaneously and regularly provided by or through another individual or entity.
- The individual agrees to receive care at home after VA designates a family caregiver.
- The individual agrees to receive ongoing care from a primary care team after VA designates a family caregiver.

Approval and Designation of Primary and Secondary Family Caregivers

A veteran's eligibility for the Program of Comprehensive Assistance for Family Caregivers may be determined by the VA Caregiver Support Coordinator, who receives the application or the Caregiver Support Coordinator who will refer the application to the veteran's VA primary care team to complete eligibility determinations.

Alternatively, a VA Caregiver Support Program multidisciplinary Clinical Eligibility Team or an individual VA provider may be designated to complete eligibility determinations with input from the veteran's primary care team.

Application Requirements

The veteran, and individuals who wish to be considered for designation by VA as primary or secondary family caregivers must complete, sign, and submit VA Form 10-10CG, or successor form, to VA. Individuals interested in serving as family caregivers must be identified as such on the joint application, and no more than 3 individuals may serve as family caregivers at one time for a veteran, with no more than one serving as the primary family caregiver. NOTE: Caregiver benefits, including the stipend provided to primary family caregivers, are effective as of the date the application was received by VA or when the veteran begins receiving care at home, whichever occurs later

Upon receiving the application, a VA Caregiver Support Coordinator will evaluate eligibility by identifying a potentially qualifying injury that was incurred or aggravated in the line of duty in the active military, naval, or air service on or after September 11, 2001, and assessing whether the potentially qualifying injury may render the Veteran in need of personal care services from a caregiver.

In performing this initial eligibility evaluation, the Caregiver Support Coordinator will consider input from the caregiver and the Veteran or Veterans' representative, as applicable. If the Caregiver Support Coordinator determines that the Veteran does not have a potentially qualifying injury that was incurred or aggravated in the line of duty in the active military, naval, or air service on or after September 11, 2001, or the potentially qualifying injury does not render the Veteran in need of personal care services from a caregiver, the Caregiver Support Coordinator will issue the applicant a determination that the applicant is not eligible for the Program of Comprehensive Assistance for Family Caregivers.

If the Coordinator does not issue such a determination, the Caregiver Support Coordinator will refer the application to the Veteran's VA primary care team, a VA Caregiver Support Program multidisciplinary Clinical Eligibility Team or an individual VA provider to perform the required clinical evaluations, including evaluating the Veteran's level of dependency for purposes of determining the applicable stipend.

Caregiver Eligibility

In order to serve as a primary or secondary family caregiver and for VA to approve the application, the applicant must meet all of the following requirements:
- Be at least 18 years of age.
- Be either:
  - The veteran's spouse, son, daughter, parent, step-family member or extended family member; or
  - Someone who lives with the veteran full-time or will do so if designated as a family caregiver.
- There must be no determination by VA of abuse or neglect of the veteran by the family caregiver applicant.

Before VA approves an application for an applicant to serve as a primary or secondary family caregiver, all of the following requirements must be met:
- The applicant must be initially assessed by a VA primary care team as being able to complete caregiver education and training. NOTE: The Veterans Transportation Service may be available for purposes of this assessment in accordance with 38 CFR Part 70 Subpart B.
- The assessment must consider relevant information specific to the veteran as well. For example, whether the applicant can communicate and understand details of the treatment plan and specific instructions related to

436

the care of the veteran and whether the applicant will be able to follow, without supervision, a treatment plan listing the specific care needs of the veteran.

- For purpose of the VA directive, caregiver training is part of a program of education and training designed and approved by VA that consists of issues generally applicable to family caregivers, as well as issues specific to the needs of the veteran.

- No later than ten business days after VA certifies completion of caregiver education and training, or should a veteran be hospitalized during this process, no later than ten days from the date the veteran returns home, a VA clinician or a clinical team will visit the veteran's home to assess the caregiver's completion of training and competence to provide personal care services and to measure the veteran's well-being.

- If the VA determines the veteran and at least one family caregiver applicant meets the applicable eligibility requirements, VA will approve the application and designate primary and/or secondary family caregivers. The approval and designation is a clinical decision.

Caregiver Benefits

One approved, the following benefits may be available to participating secondary family caregivers:

- Education and training: VA provides education and training offerings to all caregivers of veterans to maintain or improve personal care services. Referrals are made to VA-provided training and education as well as to community services and supports.

- Mental health services: Mental health services are available to family caregivers, including individual and group therapy, individual counseling and peer support groups, but this is limited to outpatient care and doesn't include medication or medication management. If a caregiver requires medication management or psychiatric inpatient hospitalization, the Caregiver Support Coordinator can assist the caregiver with identifying a provider using the caregiver's health insurance or other coverage or community health resources.

- Beneficiary travel: During the caregiver's education and training, family caregiver applicants are eligible for beneficiary travel. Approved and designated primary and secondary family caregivers are eligible for beneficiary travel during the period in which the veteran is traveling to and from medical examination, treatment, or care and for the duration of such examination, treatment or care as long as the veteran is eligible for beneficiary travel.

- Stipend payments: A monthly stipend is paid directly to the primary family caregiver. The amount of the monthly stipend is tied to the veteran's assigned tier level and is calculated based on the veteran's geographic area of residence. The tier level is based on the personal care needs of the veteran, not specific duties performed by caregivers that are not directly related to assistance with activities of daily living or providing supervision or protection based on symptoms or residuals of neurological or other impairment or injury in the home.

Requirements of Primary Family Caregivers

Primary caregivers are expected to:

- Work closely with the veteran/servicemember's team to support, promote, and encourage the veteran/servicemember in attaining the highest level of independence possible.
- Promptly inform the veteran/servicemember's primary care team of any changes in their physical or mental health condition.
- Provide a written statement to the Caregiver Support Coordinator when the veteran/servicemember's address changes, to avoid disruption of stipend payment. This notification should be made anytime the veteran/servicemember moves.
- Demonstrate flexibility in scheduling home visits --- be physically present and participate during home visits and monitoring required by the Program of Comprehensive Assistance for Family Caregivers.
- Promptly inform the Caregiver Support Coordinator if you're no longer able to serve as the Primary Family Caregiver, or if the veteran/servicemember is admitted to the hospital or a long-term treatment facility.
- The stipend is not an entitle—instead, it recognizes the care and support provided by the caregiver to the veteran/servicemember.

Caregiver Access to Military Commissaries, Exchanges and Recreation Facilities

According to the Department of Defense, starting January 1, 2020, all service-connected veterans Purple Heart recipients, former prisoners of war and individuals approved and designated as the primary family caregivers of eligible veterans under the Department of Veterans Affairs Program of Comprehensive Assistance for Family Caregivers can use commissaries, exchanges, and morale, welfare and recreational (MWR) retail facilities in-person and online.

Eligible caregivers will receive an eligibility letter from the VA Office of Community Care. Primary family caregivers who lose their eligibility letter can call 1-877-733-7927 to request a replacement.

Stipend Benefit for the Primary Family Caregiver

A Primary Family Caregiver stipend is monetary compensation paid for providing personal care services to an eligible veteran. The stipend benefit is not meant to replace career earnings, and the stipend payment doesn't create an employment relationship between the VA and the Primary Family Caregiver. Only the designated

Primary Family Caregiver of an eligible veteran is entitled to receive a stipend. There can be only one Primary Family Caregiver designated at a time. The stipend is a VA enhanced service and is not considered taxable income.

The veteran's Patient Aligned Care Team at your assigned VA Medical Center makes a determination as far as the number of hours of personal care services a veteran requires. The PACT provides a clinical evaluation of the veteran's level of dependency, based on the degree to which the veteran is in need of supervision or protection based on symptoms or residuals of neurological or other impairment or injury.

As a result of the clinical evaluation and score, eligible veterans are rated as follows:
- High Tier: Equates to a maximum of 40 hours of care per week
- Medium Tier: Equates to a maximum of 25 hours of care per week
- Low Tier: Equates to a maximum of 10 hours of care per week

The stipend amount is based on the weekly number of hours of personal care services that an eligible veteran requires. It is calculated by multiplying the Bureau of Labor Statistics hourly wage for home health aides, Skill code 311011, for the geographic region in which the eligible veteran resides by the Consumer Price Index Cost of Living Adjustment (COLA), and then multiplying that total by the number of weekly hours of caregiver assistance required. This is then multiplied by the average number of weeks in each month.

An Example: If an eligible veteran requires 10 hours of personal care services weekly (Tier 1) and the caregiver's hourly wage (including COLA) is $10 per hour, then the monthly stipend would be: (10 hours x $10) X 4.35=435.

The stipend is paid monthly for personal care services that a Primary Family Caregiver provided in the prior month. Once an application is approved, the stipend will be retroactive to the date the application was received at the VAMC.

The Caregiver Support Line can provide more information at 1-855-260-3274 Monday through Friday, 8 a.m. to 8 p.m. Eastern Standard Time. You can learn more by mail by contacting:
VHA Office of Community Care
Caregiver Support Program
PO Box 460637
Denver CO 80246-0637

CHAMPVA Benefits for Primary Family Caregivers

CHAMPVA for the Primary Family Caregiver is a health care benefits program in which the Department of Veterans Affairs shares the cost of certain health care services and supplies with the Primary Family Caregiver, who is not entitled to care or services under a health-plan contract, including a health insurance plan, TRICARE, Medicare or Medicaid. CHAMPVA is managed by the VHA Office of Community Care. Not all caregivers are eligible for CHAMPVA medical benefits. Only the designated Primary Family Caregiver who is without health insurance coverage is eligible for CHAMPVA benefits.

The Primary Family Caregiver is also eligible to receive health care at a VA facility through the CHAMPVA In-House Treatment Initiative Program if the VA facility has the excess capacity to provide care. Medical care and supplies received through a participating VA facility are not subject to cost shares or deductibles.

CHAPTER 31

VETERAN FEDERAL HIRING

Veterans' Preference gives eligible veterans preference in appointment over many other applicants. Veterans' preference applies to almost all new appointments in both the competitive and excepted service. Veterans' preference does, not guarantee veterans a job and it does not apply to internal agency actions like promotions, transfers, reinstatements, and reassignments.

In accordance with Title 5, U.S. Code, Section 2108 (5 USC 2108), veterans' preference eligibility is based on dates of active-duty service, receipt of a campaign badge, Purple Heart, or a service-connected disability. Not all active-duty service may qualify for veterans' preference.

Only veterans discharged or released from active duty in the armed forces under honorable conditions are eligible for veterans' preference. That means you must have been discharged under honorable or general discharge. If you are a "retired member of the armed forces" you are not included in the definition of preference eligible unless you are a disabled veteran OR you retire below the rank of major or its equivalent.

> **Key Takeaways**
>
> OPM works with the Federal government to offer hiring programs that benefit veterans, transitioning servicemembers and their families.
>
> Veterans may be given preference during the hiring process when applying to OPM positions at USAJOBS and depending on eligibility they may also quality for special hiring authorities.

There are three types of preference eligible, disabled (10-point preference eligible), non-disabled (5-point preference eligible), and sole survivorship preference (0-point preference eligible).

You are 0-point Preference eligible—no points are added to the passing score or rating of a veteran who is the only surviving child in a family in which the father or mother or one more sibling:

- Served in the armed forces; and
- Was killed, died as a result of wounds, accident or disease, is in captured or missing in action status, was permanently 100 percent disabled or hospitalized on a continuing basis and is not gainfully employed because of the disability or hospitalization where the death, status or disability did not result from the intentional misconduct or willful neglect of the parent or sibling and was not incurred during a period of unauthorized absence.

You are a 5-point preference eligible if your active-duty service meets any of the following:

- For more than 180 consecutive days, other than for training, any part of which occurred during the period beginning September 11, 2001, and ending on August 31, 2010, the last day of Operation Iraqi Freedom, OR
- Between August 2, 1990, and January 2, 1992, OR
- For more than 180 consecutive days, other than for training, any part of which occurred after January 31, 1955, and before October 15, 1976, OR
- In a war, campaign or expedition for which a campaign badge has been authorized or between April 28, 1952, and July 1, 1955.

You are 10-point preference eligible if you served at any time and you:

- Have a service-connected disability, OR
- Received a Purple Heart.

Preference eligibles are divided into five basic groups, as follows:

CPS - Disability rating of 30% or more (10 points)

CP - Disability rating of at least 10% but less than 30% (10 points)

XP - Disability rating less than 10% (10 points)

TP - Preference eligibles with no disability rating (5 points)

SSP – Sole Survivorship Preference (0 points)

Disabled veterans receive 10 points, regardless of their disability rating.

When agencies use a numerical rating and ranking system to determine the best-qualified applicants for a position, an additional 5 or 10 points are added to the numerical score of qualified preference eligible veterans.

When an agency does not use a numerical rating system, preference eligibles who have a compensable service-connected disability of 10 percent or more (CPS, CP) are placed at the top of the highest category on the referral list (except for scientific or professional positions at the GS-9 level or higher). XP and TP preference eligibles are placed above non-preference eligibles within their assigned category.

You must provide acceptable documentation of your preference or appointment eligibility. Acceptable documentation may be:

- A copy of your DD-214, "Certificate of Release or Discharge from Active Duty," which shows dates of service and discharge under honorable conditions.
- A "certification" that is a written document from the armed forces that certifies the service member is expected to be discharged or released from active duty service in the armed forces under honorable conditions not later than 120 days after the date the certification is signed.

You may obtain a letter from the Department of Veterans Affairs reflecting your level of disability for preference eligibility by visiting a VA Regional Office, contacting a VA call center, or online.

NOTE: Prior to appointment, an agency will require the service member to provide a copy of the DD-214.

If claiming 10-point preference, you will need to submit a Standard Form (SF-15Adobe Acrobat Version [152 KB]) "Application for 10-point Veterans' Preference."

VOW (Veterans Opportunity to Work Act)

On November 21, 2011, the President signed the VOW (Veterans Opportunity to Work) Act. (Public Law 112-56). The VOW Act amends chapter 21 of title 5, United States Code (U.S.C.) by adding section 2108a, "Treatment of certain individuals as veterans, disabled veterans, and preference eligibles." This new section requires Federal agencies to treat certain active-duty service members as preference eligibles for purposes of an appointment in the competitive or excepted service, even though the service members have not been discharged or released from active duty.

Because many service members begin their civilian job search prior to being discharged or released from active-duty service, they may not have a DD Form 214, Certificate of Release or Discharge from Active Duty, when applying for Federal jobs. The VOW Act was enacted to ensure these individuals do not lose the opportunity to be considered for Federal service (and awarded their veterans' preference entitlements if applicable) despite not having a DD form 214 to submit along with their résumés.

Agencies are required to accept, process, and grant tentative veterans' preference to those active-duty service members who submit a certification (in lieu of a DD-form 214) along with their job application materials. Agencies must verify the individual meets the definition of 'preference eligible' under 5 U.S.C. 2108 prior to appointment.

A "certification" is any written document from the armed forces that certifies the service member is expected to be discharged or released from active-duty service in the armed forces under honorable conditions within 120 days after the certification is submitted by the applicant. The certification letter should be on letterhead of the appropriate military branch of the service and contain (1) the military service dates including the expected discharge or release date, and (2) the character of service.

If the certification has expired, an agency must request other documentation (e.g., a copy of the DD form 214) that demonstrates the service member is a preference-eligible per 5 U.S.C. 2108, before veterans' preference can be awarded.

Filling a Position Through the Competitive Examining Process

Announcing the Vacancy

To fill a vacancy by selection through the competitive examining process, the selecting official requests a list of eligibles from the examining office. The examining office must announce the competitive examining process through USAJOBS. OPM will notify the State employment service where the job is being filled. Subsequently, the examining office determines which applicants are qualified, rates and ranks them based on their qualifications, and issues a certificate of eligibles, which is a list of eligibles with the highest scores from the top of the appropriate register. A certificate of eligibles may be used for permanent, term, or temporary appointment.

Category Rating

Category rating is an alternative ranking and selection procedure authorized under the Chief Human Capital Officers Act of 2002 (Title XIII of the Homeland Security Act of 2002) and codified at 5 U.S.C. § 3319. Category rating is part of the competitive examining process. Under category rating, applicants who meet basic minimum qualification requirements established for the position and whose job-related competencies or knowledge, skills and abilities (KSAs) have been assessed are ranked by being placed in one of two or more predefined quality categories instead of being ranked in numeric score order. Preference eligibles are listed ahead of non-preference eligibles within each quality category. Veterans' preference is absolute within each quality category. For more detailed information on Category Rating please visit Chapter 5 of the Delegated Examining Operations Handbook.

The "Rule of Three" and Veteran pass overs

Selection must be made from the highest three eligibles on the certificate who are available for the job--the "rule of three." However, an agency may not pass over a preference eligible to select a lower-ranking nonpreference eligible or nonpreference eligible with the same or lower score.

Example: If the top person on a certificate is a 10-point disabled veteran (CP or CPS) and the second and third persons are 5-point preference eligibles, the appointing authority may choose any of the three.

Example: If the top person on a certificate is a 10-point disabled veteran (CP or CPS), the second person is not a preference eligible, and the third person is a 5-point preference eligible, the appointing authority may choose either of the preference eligibles. The appointing authority may not pass over the 10-point disabled veteran to select the nonpreference eligible unless an objection has been sustained.

Disqualification of Preference Eligibles

A preference eligible can be eliminated from consideration only if the examining office sustains the agency's objection to the preference eligible for adequate reason. These reasons, which must be recorded, include medical disqualification under 5 CFR Part 339, suitability disqualification under 5 CFR Part 731, or other reasons considered by the Office of Personnel Management (OPM) or an agency under delegated examining authority to be disqualifying .

OPM must approve the sufficiency of an agency reason to medically disqualify or pass over a preference eligible on a certificate based on medical reasons to select a nonpreference eligible. Special provisions apply to the proposed disqualification or pass over for any reason of a preference eligible with a 30 percent or more compensable disability. See Disqualification of 30 Percent or more Disabled Veterans below.

Agencies have delegated authority for determining suitability in accordance with 5 CFR Part 731.

The preference eligible (or his or her representative) is entitled on request to a copy of the agency's reasons for the proposed pass over and the examining office's response.

An appointing official is not required to consider a person who has three times been passed over with appropriate approval or who has already been considered for three separate appointments from the same or different certificates for the same position. But in each of these considerations, the person must have been within reach under the rule of three and a selection must have been made from that group of three. Further, the preference eligible is entitled to advance notice of discontinuance of certification.

U.S.C. 3317, 3318 and 5 CFR 332.402, 332.404, 332.405, 332.406, and Parts 339 and 731

Disqualification of a 30 Percent or More Disabled Veteran

- If an agency proposes to pass over a disabled veteran on a certificate to select a person who is not a preference eligible, or to disqualify a disabled veteran based on the physical requirements of the position, it must at the same time notify both the Office of Personnel Management (OPM) and the disabled veteran of the reasons for the determination and of the veteran's right to respond to OPM within 15 days of the date of the notification.

- The agency must provide evidence to OPM that the notice was timely sent to the disabled veteran's last known address.
- OPM must make a determination on the disabled veteran's physical ability to perform the duties of the position, taking into account any additional information provided by the veteran.
- OPM will notify the agency and the disabled veteran of its decision, with which the agency must comply. If OPM agrees that the veteran cannot fulfill the physical requirements of the position, the agency may select another person from the certificate of eligibles. If OPM finds the veteran able to perform the job, the agency may not pass over the veteran.
- OPM is prohibited by law from delegating this function to any agency. U.S.C. 3312, 3318.

Filing Late Applications

A veteran may file a late application under the following circumstances by contacting the employing agency. Agencies are responsible for accepting, retaining, and considering their applications as required by law and regulation regardless of whether the agency uses case examining or maintains a continuing register of eligibles.

- Applications from 10-point preference eligibles must be accepted, as described below, for future vacancies that may arise after a case examining register or continuing register is closed. Agencies must accept applications from other individuals who are eligible to file on a delayed basis only as long as a case examining register exists.
- A 10-point preference eligible may file a job application with an agency at any time. If the applicant is qualified for positions filled from a register, the agency must add the candidate to the register, even if the register is closed to other applicants. If the applicant is qualified for positions filled through case examining, the agency will ensure that the applicant is referred on a certificate as soon as possible. If there is no immediate opening, the agency must retain the application in a special file for referral on certificates for future vacancies for up to three years. The Office of Personnel Management's Delegated Examining Operations Handbook provides detailed instructions.
- A preference eligible is entitled to be reentered on each register (or its successor) where previously listed if he or she applies within 90 days after resignation without delinquency or misconduct from a career or career-conditional appointment.
- A preference eligible is entitled to be entered on an appropriate existing register if he or she applies within 90 days after furlough or separation without delinquency or misconduct from a career or career-conditional appointment or if found eligible to apply after successfully appealing a furlough or discharge from career or career-conditional appointment.
- A person who lost eligibility for appointment from a register because of active duty in the Armed Forces is entitled to be restored to the register (or its

successor) and receive priority consideration when certain conditions are met. See 5 CFR 332.322 for more details.

- A person who was unable to file for an open competitive examination or appear for a test because of service in the Armed Forces or hospitalization continuing for up to 1 year following discharge may file after the closing date if the register of eligibles still exists.

- A Federal employee who was unable to file for an open competitive examination or appear for a test because of active Reserve duty continuing beyond 15 days may file after the closing date of an existing register. 5 U.S.C. 3305, 3314, 3315, and 5 CFR 332.311, 332.312, 332.321, 332.322

Preference in Federal Employment

Veterans' preference is a tool to assist in the placement of veterans in federal government positions, providing a "first consideration." Veterans' preference was established by the Veterans' Preference Act of 1944, as amended and is found in certain provisions of 5 U.S.C. 2108.

Veterans' preference applies to permanent and temporary positions in both the competitive and excepted services, which are two class of jobs in the federal government. For the competitive service, applicants must compete with other individuals for positions that are posted on the USAJOBS website through a structured process. In the excepted service, applicants such as veterans with disabilities may be noncompetitively considered and hired through special appointing authorities that agencies may utilize to fill jobs. The excepted service contains certain agencies and entitles groups of individuals and positions that are outside the competitive service.

The methods used for the competitive and excepted services differ.

For competitive service, veterans' preference gives eligible veterans additional points toward passing examination score or rating. Eligible veterans are also placed at the top of hiring certificates for positions, except for professional and scientific positions at grate GS-09 and above. Eligible veterans who apply for professional or scientific positions still receive points and are listed ahead of other applicants having the same rating.

Regarding Excepted Service, veterans' preference allows eligible veterans to apply noncompetitively under special appointing authorities.

Veterans must be discharged from active duty under an honorable or general discharge to be eligible for veteran's preference. Veterans preference does not guarantee a veteran will be selected for employment, apply to internal agency agencies, or apply to Senior Executive Service, positions in the legislative and judicial

447

branches of the federal government, or positions in certain exempted agencies like the Central Intelligence Agency.

VA partners with the Vocational Rehabilitation and Employment Office and its Regional Veteran Employment Coordinators (RVECs) to support the Department's National Veterans Employment Program. VESO was designed to be a strategic management program that oversees VA Veteran employment initiatives and manages VA for Vets, its flagship initiative. VA for Vets is a comprehensive ,career support and management program for Veterans, National Guard, Reserve members and VA employees. Services include employment counseling, assistance in identifying transferable military skills (skills matching), qualifications and career assessment, assistance in drafting competitive resumes, instruction in developing comprehensive job search strategies, and direct job placement assistance. RVECs also advocate on behalf of Veterans, promoting the values, work ethic, leadership, dedication, skills, and qualifications Veterans possess, all of which make them ideal candidates to fill any position in the federal sector.

VR&E staff members must be thoroughly familiar and current with Veterans' preference regulations and documentation requirements.

Vocational Rehabilitation Counselors (VRCs) and Employment Coordinators (ECs) act as resources to perform the following tasks:
- Provide guidance on Veterans' preference and assist job ready Veterans in completing federal vacancy applications.
- Review applications and ensure Veterans have complete packages including appropriate Veterans' preference and required documentation.
- Educate Human Resources (HR) personnel and managers on the importance of hiring Veterans with disabilities and Veterans' preference regulations and rules. Hiring managers have at their discretion the ability to select applicants from various lists, some of which may not contain any Veteran applicants.
- Develop a basic understanding of the Office of Personnel Management's (OPM) Delegated Examining Operating Handbook (DEOH) and its regularly occurring memoranda, which provide updated information on Veterans' preference. The DEOH provides operational procedures for agencies to use in the staffing and placement process for competitive examining of positions.

OPM Role

The Office of Personnel Management is responsible for prescribing and enforcing regulations in the administration of veterans' preference in the competitive and excepted services. OPM is the deciding agency in requests for selecting non-veterans over veterans in the job selection process.

Required Documentation

Veterans who claim veterans' preference must submit the following documentation with their federal job applications. If a veteran doesn't submit the required documentation, the veterans' preference doesn't apply.

For Claiming 5-Points Preference

DD214, Certificate of Release or Discharge from Active Duty (must show Veteran's character of service upon discharge).

For Claiming 10-Points Preference

- DD214, Certificate of Release or Discharge from Active Duty (must show Veteran's character of service upon discharge).
- Purple Heart Recipients, which is listed on the DD214 or other official documentation
- SF-15, Application for 10-Point Veteran' Preference form
- Letter from the VA Regional Office or on eBenefits stating the veteran's percentage of disability

For Claiming To Be a Spouse or Child of a Qualifying Veteran (10-Points Preference)

- DD214, Certificate of Release or Discharge from Active Duty (must
- show the Veteran's character of service upon discharge)
- SF-15, Application for 10-Point Veterans' Preference form
- Letter from the VA Regional Office or on eBenefits showing that the veteran is unemployable or 100-percent service-connected
- If veteran is deceased, a copy of the death certificate

Veterans must contact their local VA Regional Office to obtain a veterans' preference letter at 800-827-1000, or the letter can be obtained on eBenefits.

Special Appointing Authorities

Special appointing authorities are non-competitive and excepted service appointing authorities, which federal agencies can use entirely at their discretion. These authorities provide flexibility in staffing hard-to-fill positions and overcoming underrepresentation and allow for quick and easy hiring. The following is a chart showing the overview of authorities.

VRA	VRA gives agencies the discretion to appoint eligible Veterans to positions in the federal government without competition. Veterans may be appointed to any grade level in the General Schedule through GS-11 or equivalent. This authority also allows applicants with disabilities rated at 30 percent or more or rated at 10 or 20 percent and determined to have a "serious employment handicap" to be employed by VA as Veterans benefits counselors, Veterans claims examiners, Veterans representatives at educational institutions and counselors at readjustment centers. Applicants must meet the basic qualifications for the position to be filled.
30 Percent or More Disabled Veterans' Authority	Veterans may be initially appointed noncompetitively to a temporary or term position. Then, as early as day 61 of employment under this authority, hiring managers may convert veterans to a career or career-conditional appointment. There is no grade-level limitation for this authority. Applicants must meet all qualification requirements for the position to be filled.
Disabled Veterans Enrolled in a VA Training Authority	This authority is the equivalent to the Non-Paid Work Experience (NPWE) program. Veterans eligible for training through VR&E may enroll in training or work experience under an agreement between any government agency (local, state or federal) and VA. Veterans are not considered government employees for most purposes. Training is tailored to the individual's needs and goals. Certificates of Training are provided at the end of the training/work experience, which allows agencies to appoint Veterans noncompetitively

	under status quo appointments. Those appointments may be converted to career or career conditional at any time
VEOA	This authority, unique to the competitive service, allows Veterans to apply to positions under merit promotion procedures (inside the federal government) when the agency is recruiting outside of its own workforce. Veterans' preference is not a consideration when selections are made for these appointments.
Schedule A for Persons with Disabilities	This excepted service authority is an alternative to authorities specifically designed for Veterans. Schedule A provides a way to hire individuals with physical, psychiatric or cognitive impairments without competition. Schedule A employees can be converted to permanent positions in the competitive service after completing two years on the job demonstrating satisfactory performance, with or without reasonable accommodation
Employment of Veterans with Disabilities Who Have Completed a Training Course Under Chapter 31	This authority, unique to the competitive service, allows any agency to appoint a Veteran with a disability noncompetitively to positions or class of positions for which he/she is trained. Veterans with disabilities must satisfactorily complete an approved course of training prescribed by VR&E.

Noncompetitive Hiring

Eligible veterans may be appointed to federal positions without competing with the general public and federal agencies can hire veterans without posting a vacancy announcements. Veterans who are eligible for Special Hiring Authorities may be noncompetitively hired if they meet eligibility and qualification requirements for the position. The following highlights the differences between competitive and noncompetitive hiring.

Competitive Hiring	Noncompetitive Hiring
Positions must be announced to a pool of job seekers in USAJOBS	Positions don't require public announcement
The applicant doesn't have to meet the same eligibility requirements as a noncompetitive job posting	The applicant must meet the requirements for noncompetitive status and be able to perform the essential duties of the job with or

	without reasonable accommodation
The applicant is rated based on qualifications	The applicant will not be subject to the usual requirement to determine the most qualified candidate and rating of qualification
All veterans have the option to apply	Veterans must provide proof of eligibility for Veterans' Preference or special appointments in order to be considered for noncompetitive placement. Documents may include SF-15, Application for 10-Point Veterans Preference, DD214, Certification of Job Readiness, and other medical documentation as requested

Veterans Recruitment Appointment (VRA) Authority

The VRA is a special authority by which agencies can, if they wish, appoint eligible veterans without competition to positions at any grade level through General Schedule (GS) 11 or equivalent. (The promotion potential of the position is not a factor.) VRA appointees are hired under excepted appointments to positions that are otherwise in the competitive service. There is no limitation to the number of VRA appointments an individual may receive, provided the individual is otherwise eligible.

If the agency has more than one VRA candidate for the same job and one (or more) is a preference eligible, the agency must apply the Veterans' preference procedures prescribed in 5 CFR Part 302 in making VRA appointments. A veteran who is eligible for a VRA appointment is not automatically eligible for Veterans' preference.

After two years of satisfactory service, the agency must convert the veteran to career or career-conditional appointment, as appropriate.

Eligibility Criteria

The Jobs for Veterans Act, Public Law 107-288, amended title 38 U.S.C. 4214 by making a major change in the eligibility criteria for obtaining a Veterans Recruitment Appointment (VRA). Those who are eligible:

- Disabled veterans; or
- Veterans who served on active duty in the Armed Forces during a war, or in a campaign or expedition for which a campaign badge has been authorized; or

452

- Veterans who, while serving on active duty in the Armed Forces, participated in a United States military operation for which an Armed Forces Service Medal was awarded; or
- Recently separated veterans.
- Veterans claiming eligibility on the basis of service in a campaign or expedition for which a medal was awarded must be in receipt of the campaign badge or medal.

In addition to meeting the criteria above, eligible veterans must have been separated under honorable conditions (i.e., the individual must have received either an honorable or general discharge).

Note: Under the eligibility criteria, not all 5-point preference eligible veterans may be eligible for a VRA appointment. For example, a veteran who served during the Vietnam era (i.e., for more than 180 consecutive days, after January 31, 1955, and before October 15, 1976) but did not receive a service-connected disability or an Armed Forces Service medal or campaign or expeditionary medal would be entitled to 5 pt. veterans' preference. This veteran, however, would not be eligible for a VRA appointment under the above criteria.

As another example, a veteran who served during the Gulf War from August 2, 1990, through January 2, 1992, would be eligible for veterans' preference solely on the basis of that service. However, service during that time period, in and of itself, does not confer VRA eligibility on the veteran unless one of the above VRA eligibility criteria is met.

Lastly, if an agency has 2 or more VRA candidates and 1 or more is a preference eligible, the agency must apply Veterans' preference. For example, one applicant is VRA eligible on the basis of receiving an Armed Forces Service Medal (this medal does not confer veterans' preference eligibility). The second applicant is VRA eligible on the basis of being a disabled veteran (which does confer veterans' preference eligibility). In this example, both individuals are VRA eligible, but only one of them is eligible for Veterans' preference. As a result, agencies must apply the procedures of 5 CFR 302 when considering VRA candidates for appointment.

Making Appointments

Ordinarily, an agency may simply appoint any VRA eligible who meets the basic qualifications requirements for the position to be filled without having to announce the job or rate and rank applicants. However, as noted, Veterans' preference applies in making appointments under the VRA authority. This means that if an agency has 2 or more VRA candidates and 1 or more is a preference eligible, the agency must apply Veterans' preference. Furthermore, an agency must consider all VRA candidates on file who are qualified for the position and could reasonably expect to be considered for the opportunity; it cannot place VRA candidates in separate groups or consider them as separate sources in order to avoid applying preference or to reach a favored candidate.

Terms and Conditions of Employment

A VRA appointee may be promoted, demoted, reassigned, or transferred in the same way as a career employee. As with other competitive service employees, the time in grade requirement applies to the promotion of VRAs. If a VRA-eligible employee is qualified for a higher grade, an agency may, at its discretion, give the employee a new VRA appointment at a higher grade up through GS-11 (or equivalent) without regard to time-in-grade.

Agencies must establish a training or education program for any VRA appointee who has less than 15 years of education. This program should meet the needs of both the agency and the employee.
Appeal Rights

During their first year of employment, VRA appointees have the same limited appeal rights as competitive service probationers, but otherwise, they have the appeal rights of excepted service employees. This means that VRA employees who are preference eligibles have adverse action protections after one year (see Chapter 7). VRA's who are not preference eligibles do not get this protection until they have completed 2 years of current continuous employment in the same or similar position.

Nonpermanent Appointment Based on VRA Eligibility

Agencies may make a noncompetitive temporary or term appointment based on an individual's eligibility for VRA appointment. The temporary or term appointment must be at the grades authorized for VRA appointment but is not a VRA appointment itself and does not lead to conversion to career-conditional. Refer To: 38 U.S.C. 4214; Pub. L. 107-288; 5 CFR Part 307; 5 CFR 752.401 (c)(3)

Protected Veteran Status

Protected veteran status was created through the Vietnam Era Veterans' Readjustment Act in 1974. It protects veterans from discrimination based on their military service. The act specifically protects workers working for federal contractors and other companies that do business with the U.S. government. As a protected veteran, workers are able to request reasonable accommodation to perform their job duties and other things. Protected veterans are provided with Affirmative Action-type requirements for certain employers to hire vets who fall under protected status. A protected veteran is considered to be:

- Disabled veterans
- Veterans who served on active duty during a war, campaign, or expedition for which a campaign badge has been authorized
- Veterans with an Armed Forces Service Medial pursuant to Executive

Order 12985
- Recently separated veterans

All of the above must have a military discharge not characterized as dishonorable.

Under VEVRAA, employers doing business with the federal government must recruit, hire and provide upward mobility for those with protected status. This applies to both contractors and subcontractor s doing business with the government. An employer can't, under VEVRAA, refuse protected veterans any reasonable accommodations in the workplace for disabilities or related issues.

Those who feel they have been discriminated against as protected veterans should file a complaint with the Office of Federal Contract Compliance Programs (OFCCP). You cannot be legally retaliated against for filing a complaint including harassment, threats, coercion, etc. Companies that violate protected veteran laws risk being prohibited from receiving future contracts with the federal government, and that includes violation of the anti-retaliation laws designed to protect veterans who file complaints.

CHAPTER 32

HOMELESS VETERANS

Approximately one-third of the adult homeless population living on the streets or in shelters has served their country in the armed services. Many other veterans are considered at risk because of poverty, lack of support from family and friends and precarious living conditions in overcrowded or substandard housing.

The VA describes its mission to end veteran homelessness as having three core goals and approaches. First, the VA conducts outreach to seek out veterans proactively if they might need assistance. The VA also works to connect homeless and at-risk veterans with housing, health care, community employment services and other support services. The VA also collaborates with federal, state and local agencies, employers, housing providers, faith-based and community non-profits with the goal of expanding employment and affordable housing options for veterans who are exiting homelessness.

> **Key Takeaways**
>
> Veterans who are homeless or at imminent risk of becoming homeless can call or visit their local VA Medical Center or Community Resource and Referral Center, so VA staff can help.
>
> Veterans and their families can also call 1-877-424-3838 to access VA services.

In 2012 as part of Public Law 112-154, there were a number of changes in homeless and housing programs for veterans. These include:

- Authorization of grant funds for the construction of transitional housing for homeless veterans. It also ensures the matching of funds from private and public sources for transitional housing.
- Extension of funding for programs designed to assist homeless veterans, including homeless veterans' reintegration programs and support services for

low-income veteran families.

- Public Law 112-154 increases case management and coordination of care for homeless veterans through state and local agencies.

Homeless Providers Grant and Per Diem Program

VA's Homeless Providers Grant and Per Diem Program are offered annually (as funding permits) by the Department of Veterans Affairs Health Care for Homeless Veterans (HCHV) Programs to fund community agencies providing services to homeless veterans. The purpose is to promote the development and provision of supportive housing and/or supportive services with the goal of helping homeless veterans achieve residential stability, increase their skill levels and/or income, and obtain greater self-determination.

Hotline for Homeless Veterans

In March 2010, VA announced a new hotline for homeless veterans: **(877) 4AID-VET.**

Well-trained expert responders will staff the hotline 24 hours a day, seven days a week. Responders can provide emergency support and resources to homeless veterans, as well as family members, community agencies and non-VA providers.

Loan Guarantee Program for Homeless Veterans Multifamily Housing

This initiative authorizes VA to guarantee no more than 15 loans with an aggregate value of $100 million within 5 years for construction, renovation of an existing property and refinancing of existing loans, facility furnishing or working capital. No more than 5 loans could be guaranteed under this program prior to November 11, 2001. The amount financed is a maximum of 90% of project costs.

Legislation allows the Secretary to issue a loan guarantee for large-scale self-sustaining multifamily loans. Eligible transitional project are those that:

1) Provide supportive services including job counseling;
2) Require veteran to seek and maintain employment;
3) Require veteran to pay reasonable rent;
4) Require sobriety as a condition of occupancy; and,
5) Serves other veterans in need of housing on a space-available basis.

Stand Downs

Stand Downs are one part of the Department of Veterans Affairs' efforts to provide services to homeless veterans. Stand Downs are typically one to three day events providing services to homeless veterans such as food, shelter, clothing, health screenings, VA and Social Security benefits counseling, and referrals to a variety of other necessary services, such as housing, employment and substance abuse treatment. Stand Downs are collaborative events, coordinated between local VAs,

457

other government agencies, and community agencies who serve the homeless.

For additional information on Stand Down dates and locations, please contact the Homeless Veterans Programs Office at (202) 273-5764.

Compensated Work Therapy/Transitional Residence (CWT/TR) Program

In VA's Compensated Work Therapy/Transitional Residence (CWT/TR) Program, disadvantaged, at-risk, and homeless veterans live in CWT/TR community-based supervised group homes while working for pay in VA's Compensated Work Therapy Program (also known as Veterans Industries). Veterans in the CWT/TR program work about 33 hours per week, with approximate earnings of $732 per month, and pay an average of $186 per month toward maintenance and up-keep of the residence. The average length of stay is about 174 days. VA contracts with private industry and the public sector for work done by these veterans, who learn new job skills, relearn successful work habits, and regain a sense of self- esteem and self-worth.

CHALENG

Community Homelessness Assessment, Local Education, and Networking Groups (CHALENG) for veterans is a nationwide initiative in which VA medical center and regional office directors work with other federal, state, and local agencies and nonprofit organizations to assess the needs of homeless veterans, develop action plans to meet identified needs, and develop directories that contain local community resources to be used by homeless veterans.

More than 10,000 representatives from non-VA organizations have participated in Project CHALENG initiatives, which include holding conferences at VA medical centers to raise awareness of the needs of homeless veterans, creating new partnerships in the fight against homelessness, and developing new strategies for future action.

For more information, please contact CHALENG at (404) 327-4033.

DCHV

The Domiciliary Care for Homeless Veterans (DCHV) Program provides biopsychosocial treatment and rehabilitation to homeless veterans. The program provides residential treatment to approximately 5,000 homeless veterans with health problems each year and the average length of stay in the program is 4 months. The domiciliaries conduct outreach and referral; vocational counseling and rehabilitation; and post-discharge community support.

Drop-In Centers

These programs provide a daytime sanctuary where homeless veterans can clean up, wash their clothes, and participate in a variety of therapeutic and rehabilitative activities. Linkages with longer-term assistance are also available.

Comprehensive Homeless Centers

VA's Comprehensive Homeless Centers (CHCs) place the full range of VA homeless efforts in a single medical center's catchment area and coordinate administration within a centralized framework. With extensive collaboration among non-VA service providers, VA's CHCs in Anchorage, AK; Brooklyn, NY; Cleveland, OH; Dallas, TX; Little Rock, AR; Pittsburgh, PA; San Francisco, CA; and West Los Angeles, CA, provide a comprehensive continuum of care that reaches out to homeless veterans and helps them escape homelessness.

VBA-VHA Special Outreach and Benefits Assistance

VHA has provided specialized funding to support twelve Veterans Benefits Counselors as members of HCMI and Homeless Domiciliary Programs as authorized by Public Law 102-590. These specially funded staff provides dedicated outreach, benefits counseling, referral, and additional assistance to eligible veterans applying for VA benefits. This specially funded initiative complements VBA's ongoing efforts to target homeless veterans for special attention. To reach more homeless veterans, designated homeless veterans coordinators at VBA's 58 regional offices annually make over 4,700 visits to homeless facilities and over 9,000 contacts with non-VA agencies working with the homeless and provide over 24,000 homeless veterans with benefits counseling and referrals to other VA programs. These special outreach efforts are assumed as part of ongoing duties and responsibilities. VBA has also instituted new procedures to reduce the processing times for homeless veterans' benefits claims.

VBA'S Acquired Property Sales for Homeless Veterans

This program makes all the properties VA obtains through foreclosures on VA-insured mortgages available for sale to homeless provider organizations at a discount of 20 to 50 percent, depending on time of the market.

VA Excess Property for Homeless Veterans Initiative

This initiative provides for the distribution of federal excess personal property, such as hats, parkas, footwear, socks, sleeping bags, and other items to homeless veterans and homeless veteran programs. A Compensated Work Therapy Program employing formerly homeless veterans has been established at the Medical Center in Lyons, NJ to receive, warehouse, and ship these goods to VA homeless programs across the country.

Supportive Services for Veteran Families (SSVF)

In July 2011, the VA announced the award of $60 million in grants to serve homeless and at-risk veterans and their families as part of the Supportive Services for Veteran Families (SSVF) program. The SSVF program awards grants to private non-profits and consumer cooperatives that provide a range of services to eligible low-income

459

veteran families.

VA has been authorized to offer community-based grants through the Supportive Services for Veteran Families (SSVF) Program, which will provide supportive services to very low-income Veteran families in or transitioning to permanent housing. Funds are granted to private non- profit organizations and consumer cooperatives who will assist very low- income veteran families by providing a range of supportive services designed to promote housing stability.

Through the SSVF Program, VA aims to improve very low-income Veteran families' housing stability. Grantees (private non-profit organizations and consumer cooperatives) will provide eligible Veteran families with outreach, case management, and assistance in obtaining VA and other benefits, which may include:

- Health care services
- Daily living services
- Personal financial planning services
- Transportation services
- Fiduciary and payee services
- Legal services
- Childcare services
- Housing counseling services

In addition, grantees may also provide time-limited payments to third parties (e.g., landlords, utility companies, moving companies, and licensed child care providers) if these payments help Veterans' families stay in or acquire permanent housing on a sustainable basis.

Healthcare for Homeless Veterans Program (HCHV)

HCHV programs now serve as the hub for a myriad of housing and other services which provide VA a way to outreach and assist homeless Veterans by offering them entry to VA care.

Outreach is the core of the HCHV program. The central goal is to reduce homelessness among Veterans by conducting outreach to those who are the most vulnerable and are not currently receiving services and reengaging them in treatment and rehabilitative programs.

Contract Residential Treatment Program ensures that Veterans with serious mental health diagnoses can be placed in community-based programs that provide quality housing and services.

Program Monitoring and Evaluation

VA has built program monitoring and evaluation into all of its homeless veterans' treatment initiatives and it serves as an integral component of each program. Designed, implemented, and maintained by the Northeast Program Evaluation Center (NEPEC) at VAMC West Haven, CT, these evaluation efforts provide important information about the veterans served and the therapeutic value and cost-effectiveness of the specialized programs. Information from these evaluations also helps program managers determine new directions to pursue in order to expand and improve services to homeless veterans.

CHAPTER 33

BENEFITS FOR FEMALE VETERANS

Females veterans are entitled to the same benefits that are available to male veterans (see below list), and the VA has also designed a number of programs aimed specifically at female veterans, including healthcare benefits and programs.

Female veterans are entitled to all of the benefits available to male veterans, including:

- Disability Compensation For Service-Related Disabilities;
- Disability Pension For Non-Service Related Disabilities;
- Education Assistance Programs;
- Work-Study Allowance;
- Vocational Rehabilitation And Counseling;
- Insurance;
- Home Loan Benefits;
- Medical Inpatient And Outpatient C
- Substance Abuse Treatment And Counseling;
- Sexual Trauma And Assault Counseling;
- Nursing Home Care;

Burial Benefits;
- Burial in A VA National Cemetery
- Employment Assistance;
- Survivors' Benefit Programs

> **Key Takeaways**
> Women veterans may be eligible for a wide variety of benefits available to all veterans including disability compensation, pension, education and training, health care, home loans and more.
>
> The VA's Center for Women Veterans monitors and coordinates VA's administration of services and programs for women veterans. There are Women Veteran Coordinators located in every regional office who serve as the primary contact for women veterans.

Healthcare for Female Veterans

In the spring of 2012, the VA announced a new partnership with the American Heart Association to combat heart disease in female veterans. The program, entitled "Go Red for Women," is working to actively address the issues associated with heart disease in women, including smoking, poor diet and obesity, all of which are risk factors. Heart disease has been identified as the leading cause of death among women, and a third of female veterans suffer from high cholesterol or high blood pressure.

Women Veterans Health Care works to make certain that all eligible women Veterans requesting VA care are assured of:

- Comprehensive primary care by a proficient and interested primary care provider
- Privacy, safety, dignity, and sensitivity to gender-specific needs
- The right care in the right place and time
- State-of-the-art health care equipment and technology
- High-quality preventive and clinical care, equal to that provided to male veterans

Services Provided to Women Veterans Include:

Primary Care
General care includes health evaluation and counseling, disease prevention, nutrition counseling, weight control, smoking cessation, and substance abuse counseling and treatment as well as gender-specific primary care, e.g., cervical cancer screens (Pap smears), breast cancer screens (mammograms), birth control, preconception counseling, Human Papillomavirus (HPV) vaccine, menopausal support (hormone replacement therapy).

Mental Health Care
Mental health includes evaluation and assistance for issues such as depression, mood, and anxiety disorders; intimate partner and domestic violence; sexual trauma; elder abuse or neglect; parenting and anger management; marital, caregiver, or family-related stress; and post-deployment adjustment or post-traumatic stress disorder (PTSD).

Sexual Trauma
Military Sexual Trauma (MST). Women—and men as well—may experience repeated sexual harassment or sexual assault during their military service. Special services are available to women who have experienced MST. VA provides free, confidential counseling and treatment for mental and physical health conditions related to MST.

Specialty Care
Management and screening of chronic conditions include heart disease, diabetes, cancer, glandular disorders, osteoporosis, and fibromyalgia as well as sexually

463

transmitted diseases such as HIV/AIDS and hepatitis.

Reproductive health care includes maternity care, infertility evaluation, and limited treatment, sexual problems, tubal ligation, urinary incontinence, and others. VA is prohibited by legislative authority from providing either in-vitro fertilization or abortion services.

Rehabilitation, homebound, and long-term care. VA referrals are given to those in need of rehabilitation therapies such as physical therapy, occupational therapy, speech-language therapy, exercise therapy, recreational therapy, and vocational therapy. Homebound and long-term care services are available as well, limited to those meeting specific requirements

The VA has placed a strategic priority on six pillars, which are designed to give women veterans the best possible health care services. These include:
Comprehensive Primary Care: Women Veterans Health Care works closely with Primary Care Services to redesign the way primary care is delivered, which tailors it to the specific needs of women.

Women's Health Education: Women Veterans Health Care has partnered with the VA Employee Education Services to create mini-residencies in women's health, which will allow providers to be more educated in the advanced topics regarding women's health.

Reproductive Health: Women Veterans Health Care is working to implement safe prescribing measures for female veterans of childbearing age. Other efforts include improving follow-up of abnormal mammograms, tracking the timeliness of breast cancer treatment, and ensuring the care women receive from non-VA, maternity and emergency department care.

Communication and Partnerships: Women Veterans Health Care is working to develop a VA-wide communication plan to enhance the language, practice, and culture of the VA to be more inclusive of female veterans.

Women's Health Research: Women Veterans Health Care has partnered with the Women's Health Evaluation Initiative, based in Palo Alto, CA to develop a series of Sourcebooks with key descriptive information about women Veterans including demographics, population growth over time, diagnoses, utilization and cost of care.

Special Women Veteran Populations: The Women's Veteran Health Strategic Healthcare Group (WVHSHG) is working to ensure that the needs of all women Veterans are addressed, including those populations that require special attention.

Rural and homebound veterans can benefit from emerging technology that will deliver care remotely through "e-clinics," mobile clinics, and home-based care services.

Women veterans with mental illnesses can benefit through integration of mental health services within primary care so that necessary treatment is provided in a comprehensive and coordinated way. Women Veterans Health Care is also working to enhance the availability of woman-safe inpatient psychiatric acute units.

Aging women veterans can benefit from the latest advances in medical science and technology to identify and address cardiovascular disease as well as advances in treatments for diabetes, osteoporosis, and menopause.

Referrals are made for services that VA is unable to provide. Women Veterans Program Managers are available in a private setting at all VA facilities to assist women veterans seeking treatment and benefits.

VA has also established a division within the National Center for Post-Traumatic Stress Disorder, the Women's Health Science Division. The center is based at the Boston VA Medical Center and conducts clinical research addressing trauma-related problems of female veterans. Veterans may contact the Center at:

VA Medical Center Women's Health Sciences Division
150 South Huntington Avenue
Boston, MA 02130
(617) 232-9500

Women Veterans Comprehensive Health Centers

Eight Women Veterans Comprehensive Health Centers have been established to develop and enhance programs focusing on the gender-specific healthcare needs of female veterans. The locations are as follows:

Boston VA **Medical Center** Boston, Massachusetts (617) 232-9500, extension 4276
Chicago Area Network (Hines, Lakeside, North Chicago, and West Side VA Medical Centers) (312) 569-6168
Durham VA **Medical Center** Durham, NC (919) 286-0411
Minneapolis VA **Medical Center** Minneapolis, Minnesota (612) 725-2030
Southeast Pennsylvania Network (Coatesville, Lebanon, Philadelphia and Wilmington VA Medical Centers) (215) 823-44496
San Francisco VA **Medical Center** San Francisco, California (415) 221-4810, extension 2174
Sepulveda / West Los Angeles VA **Medical Centers** Sepulveda, California and Los

Angeles, California (415) 221-4810

Tampa VA Medical Center Tampa, Florida (813) 972-2000, extension 3678

State Women Veterans Coordinators

In addition to the Department of Veterans Affairs' Women Veterans Coordinators that are located at local, regional offices and medical centers, there may be an Office of State Veterans Affairs or a State Commission for Veterans Coordinator available within the State government veterans program. These State offices are part of the veteran-advocate community and their staff may assist female veterans in accessing State and Federal entitlements. For specific information on availability in your state, contact your local VA office.

CHAPTER 34

BENEFITS FOR GULF WAR VETERANS

The first Gulf War, an offensive led by U.S. and coalition troops in January 1991, followed the August 1990 Iraqi invasion of Kuwait. The war was over on February 28, 1991, and an official cease-fire was signed in April 1991. The last U.S. troops who participated in the ground war returned home on June 13, 1991. In all, about 697,000 U.S. troops had been deployed to the Gulf region during the conflict.

Operation Iraqi Freedom, a military campaign that began on March 20, 2003, and Operation New Dawn, named for the reduced role of U.S. troops in Iraq, has created a new group of Gulf War veterans.

With variation in exposures and veterans' concerns ranging from oil well fire smoke to possible contamination from Iraqi chemical/biological agents, VA has initiated wide-ranging research projects evaluating illnesses as well as environmental risk factors.

The Department of Veterans Affairs (VA) offers Gulf War veterans physical examinations and special eligibility for follow-up care, and it operates a toll-free hotline at (800) 749-8387 to inform these veterans of the program and their benefits. Operators are trained to help veterans with general questions about medical

Key Takeaways

For the purpose of VA benefits, the Gulf War period is still in effect.

Any veteran who served on active military service for any period from August 2, 1990 to the present meets the wartime service requirement.

Certain illnesses and diseases are presumed by VA to be related to your military service in designated areas of Southwest Asia. For Gulf War Veterans, these presumptive diseases include medically unexplained diseases, certain infectious diseases and amyotrophic lateral sclerosis (ALS).

care and other benefits. It also provides recorded messages that enable callers to obtain information 24 hours a day. Beginning in 2012, it was announced Veterans of the Persian Gulf War, with an undiagnosed illness, will have an additional five years to qualify for benefits from the VA. These changes also affect veterans of the Southwest Asia conflict. The change will apply to those veterans who may be eligible to claim VA disability compensation, as well as the ability of survivors to qualify for Dependency and Indemnity Compensation. Under previous VA guidelines, any undiagnosed illness used to establish eligibility for VA benefits had to be apparent by December 31, 2011. The change in rules pushed this date to December 31, 2016.

Gulf War Service

Gulf War service is active duty in any of the following areas in Southwest Asia during the Gulf War, which began in 1990 and continues to the present:

Iraq

Kuwait

Saudi Arabia
The neutral zone (between Iraq and Saudi Arabia)

Bahrain

Qatar
The United Arab Emirates Oman

Gulf of Aden Gulf of Oman

Waters of the Persian Gulf, the Arabian Sea, and the Red Sea

The airspace above these locations

Persian Gulf Registry Program

A free, complete physical examination with basic lab studies is offered to every Gulf War veteran, whether or not the veteran is ill. Veterans do not have to be enrolled in VA healthcare to participate in registry examinations. Results of the examinations, which include review of the veteran's military service and exposure history, are entered into special, computerized registries. The registries enable VA to update veterans on research findings or new compensation policies through periodic newsletters. The registries could also suggest areas to be explored in future scientific research. Registry participants are advised of the results of their examinations in personal consultations and by letters.

Special Access to Follow-Up Care

VA has designated a physician at every VA medical center to coordinate the special registry examination program and to receive updated educational materials and information as experience is gained nationally. Where an illness possibly related to military service in the Southwest Asia Theater of operations during the Gulf War is detected during the examination, follow-up care is provided on a higher-eligibility basis than most non-service-connected care.

Standardized Exam Protocols

VA has expanded its special registry examination protocol as more experience has been gained with the health of Gulf veterans. The protocol elicits information about symptoms and exposures, calls the clinician's attention to diseases common to the Gulf region, and directs baseline laboratory studies including chest X-ray (if one has not been done recently), blood count, urinalysis, and a set of blood chemistry and enzyme analyses that detect the "biochemical fingerprints" of certain diseases. In addition to this core laboratory work for every veteran undergoing the Gulf War program exam, physicians order additional tests and specialty consults as they would normally in following a diagnostic trail -- as symptoms dictate. If a diagnosis is not apparent, facilities follow the "comprehensive clinical evaluation protocol." The protocol suggests 22 additional baseline tests and additional specialty consultations, outlining dozens of further diagnostic procedures to be considered, depending on symptoms.

Gulf War Illness

Gulf War veterans have reported a variety of medically unexplained symptoms, such as fatigue, headache, joint pains, sleep disturbances and memory problems since serving in the Gulf. VA has recognized certain health problems as associated with Gulf War service or military service.

VA has recognized that certain health problems for Gulf War Veterans are associated with Gulf War service or military service. These Veterans may be eligible for disability compensation and health care for these illnesses. Surviving spouses, children and dependent parents of Gulf War Veterans who died as the result of illnesses associated with Gulf War service may be eligible for survivors' benefits.

For the purposes of these benefits, Gulf War Veterans are Veterans who served on active duty in the Southwest Asia theater of operations any time during the first Gulf War starting August 2, 1990, through the current conflict in Iraq. This includes Veterans who served in Operation Iraqi Freedom (2003-2010) and Operation New Dawn (2010 and continuing).

Illnesses that are associated with Gulf War service include:
* Medically Unexplained Chronic Multi-Symptom Illnesses
* Gulf War Veterans have reported a variety of medically unexplained symptoms, such as fatigue, headache, joint pains, sleep disturbances and memory problems since serving in the Gulf. VA presumes certain medically unexplained symptoms existing for six months or more are associated with military service in the Gulf. The illnesses must have appeared during active duty in the Southwest Asia theater of operations or by December 31, 2016 and be at least 10 percent disabling.
* Illnesses include medically unexplained multi-symptom illnesses that have

existed for six months or more, such as:

- Chronic fatigue syndrome
- Fibromyalgia

- Functional gastrointestinal disorders, a group of conditions marked by chronic or recurrent symptoms related to any part of the gastrointestinal tract. Functional condition refers to an abnormal function of an organ, without a structural alteration in the tissues. Examples include irritable bowel syndrome (IBS),
- functional dyspepsia, and functional abdominal pain syndrome. VA's final rule specifying that functional gastrointestinal disorders are covered as presumptive illnesses took effect on August 15, 2011.
- Undiagnosed illnesses with symptoms that may include but are not limited to: abnormal weight loss, cardiovascular symptoms, fatigues, gastrointestinal symptoms, headache, joint pain, menstrual disorders, muscle pain, neurologic symptoms, neuropsychological symptoms, skin conditions, upper and lower respiratory system symptoms, and sleep disturbances
- Infectious Diseases

In late 2010, VA established new presumptions of service connection for nine specific infectious diseases associated with military service in Southwest Asia during the first Gulf War starting August 2, 1990, through the conflict in Iraq and on or after September 19, 2001, in Afghanistan. Veterans must have the diseases within the time frames shown below and have a current disability as a result of that disease in order to receive disability compensation:

- Brucellosis
- Campylobacter jejuni
- Coxiella burnetii (Q fever)
- Malaria
- Mycobacterium tuberculosis
- Nontyphoid Salmonella
- Shigella
- Visceral leishmaniasis
- West Nile virus

A veteran now only has to show service in Southwest Asia or Afghanistan and that he or she had one of the nine diseases within a certain time after service, and has a current disability as a result of that disease, subject to certain time limits for seven of the diseases.

Amyotrophic Lateral Sclerosis (ALS)

VA does not presume that amyotrophic lateral sclerosis (ALS) is associated with hazardous exposures during the Gulf War. However, VA has recognized ALS diagnosed in Veterans with 90 days or more of continuously active service in the military was caused by their military service.

Obtaining Copies of Hospital Records

A program is in place to help Gulf War veterans obtain copies of their in-patient hospital records from hospitals established during the Persian Gulf War.

Although these records were always located in the National Personnel Records Center in St. Louis, MO, they were stored only by the name of the hospital and the date of treatment.

An electronic database has been created to cross-reference patient names and social security numbers with their theater hospitals and admission dates.

Veterans may call (800) 497-6261 to find out if their inpatient record has been added to the database and to obtain the paperwork necessary to request a copy.

CHAPTER 35

SERVICEMEMBERS' CIVIL RELIEF ACT

Congress and state legislatures have long recognized that military service can often place an economic and legal burden on servicemembers. The Soldiers' and Sailors' Civil Relief Act of 1918 was passed in order to protect the rights of service members while serving on active duty.

Servicemembers were protected from such things as repossession of property, bankruptcy, foreclosure or other such actions while serving in the military. This Act remained in effect until shortly after World War I when it expired. The Soldiers' and Sailors' Civil Relief Act of 1940 (SSCRA) was passed in order to protect the rights of the millions of service members activated for World War II. The SSCRA has remained in effect until the present day and has been amended many times since 1940 to keep pace with the changing military.

> **Key Takeaways**
>
> Veteran borrowers who are called to active duty may be able to request relief pursuant to the Servicemembers Civil Relief Act.
>
> The SCRA provides eligible servicemembers with a variety of rights and benefits.
>
> The SCRA protects servicemembers and their families from eviction if they leave a house or apartment and can't make rent.

In December 2003, Congress passed legislation renaming SSCRA as the Servicemembers' Civil Relief Act (SCRA). The SCRA updates and strengthens the civil protections enacted during World War II.

The SCRA is designed to protect active-duty military members, reservists who are in active federal service, and National Guardsmen who are in active federal service. Some of the benefits under the SCRA extend to dependents of active duty military members as well.

Public Law 107-330 extended protections under the SCRA to members of the National Guard who are called to active service authorized by the President or the Secretary of Defense, or a state governor for a period of more than 30 consecutive days, for purposes of responding to a national emergency declared by the President and supported by Federal funds.

The SCRA can provide many forms of relief to military members. Below are some of the most common forms of relief.

Protection from Eviction

If a military member is leasing a house or apartment and his or her rent is below a certain amount, the SCRA can protect the individual from being evicted for a period of time, usually three months. The dwelling place must be occupied by either the active-duty member or his or her dependents and the rent on the premises cannot exceed $4,089.62 month (rate as of 2021). This rent ceiling will be adjusted annually for consumer price index (CPI) changes. Additionally, the military member must show that military service materially affects his or her ability to pay rent. If a landlord continues to try to evict the military member or does actually evict the member, he or she is subject to criminal sanctions such as fines or even imprisonment.

Termination of Pre-Service Residential Leases

The SCRA also allows military members who are just entering active duty service to lawfully terminate a lease without repercussions. To do this, the service member needs to show that the lease was entered into prior to the commencement of active duty service, that the lease was signed by or on behalf of the service member, and that the service member is currently in military service or was called to active-duty service for a period of 180 days or more. Proper written notice with a copy of orders must be provided to the landlord.

Termination of Residential Leases During Military Service

The SCRA allows military members who receive permanent change of station (PCS) orders or are deployed for a period of 90 days or more to terminate a lease by providing written notice to the landlord along with a copy of the military orders. The termination of a lease that provides for monthly payment of rent will occur 30 days after the first date on which the next rental payment is due and payable after the landlord receives proper written notice.

Mortgages

The SCRA can also provide military members temporary relief from paying their mortgage. To obtain relief, a military member must show that their mortgage was entered into prior to beginning active duty, that the property was owned prior to entry into military service, that the property is still owned by the military member, and that military service materially affects the member's ability to pay the mortgage.

473

Mortgage foreclosures or lien actions initiated during your military service or within nine months after the end of your military service must be stayed upon your request. This applies only to obligations that you have undertaken before entering active duty. A court may instead "adjust the obligations in a way that preserves the interests of all parties." Note that the nine-month period reverts to 90 days as of January 1, 2013, unless further extended.

No sale, foreclosure, or seizure of property for a breach of a pre-service mortgage-type obligation is valid if made during or within 9 months after the period of active duty, unless pursuant to a valid court order. This provides the service member tremendous protections from foreclosure in the many states that permit foreclosures to proceed without involvement of the courts. Service members who miss any mortgage payments should immediately see a legal assistance attorney.

Maximum Rate of Interest

Under the SCRA, a military member can cap the interest rate at 6% for all obligations entered into before beginning active duty if the military service materially affects his or her ability to meet the obligations. This can include interest rates on credit cards, mortgages, and even some student loans (except for Federally guaranteed student loans), to name a few. To qualify for the interest rate cap the military member has to show that he or she is now on active duty, that the obligation or debt was incurred prior to entry on active duty, and that military service materially affects the members' ability to pay. To begin the process, the military member needs to send a letter along with a copy of current military orders to the lender requesting relief under the SCRA. The interest rate cap lasts for the duration of active duty service. The interest rate cap will apply from the first date of active-duty service. The military member must provide written notice to the creditor and a copy of military orders not later than 180 days after the servicemember's termination or release from military service.

Termination of Automobile Leases During Military Service

The SCRA allows military members to terminate pre-service automobile leases if they are called up for military service of 180 days or longer. Members who sign automobile leases while on active duty may be able to terminate an automobile lease if they are given orders for a permanent change of station outside the continental United States or to deploy with a military unit for a period of 180 days or longer.

Stay of Proceedings

If a military member is served with a complaint indicating that they are being sued for some reason, they can obtain a "stay" or postponement of those proceedings if the military service materially affects their ability to proceed in the case. A stay can be used to stop the action altogether or to hold up some phase of it. According to the SCRA, military members can request a "stay" during any stage of the proceedings. However, the burden is on the military member to show that their military service has materially affected their ability to appear in court. In general, individuals can request a stay of the proceedings for a reasonable period of time (30-60 days). For example, if they are being sued for divorce, they can put off the hearing for some period of time, but it is unlikely that a court will allow the proceedings to be put off indefinitely. The stay can be granted in administrative proceedings.

Default Judgments

A default judgment is entered against a party who has failed to defend against a claim that has been brought by another party. To obtain a default judgment, a plaintiff must file an affidavit (written declaration of fact) stating that the defendant is not in the military service and has not requested a stay. If someone is sued while on active duty and fails to respond, and as a result a default judgment is obtained against them, they can reopen the default judgment by taking several steps. First, they must show that the judgment was entered during their military service or within 30 days after they've left the service. Second, they must write to the court requesting that the default judgment be reopened while they are still on active duty or within 90 days of leaving the service. Third, they must not have made any kind of appearance in court, through filing an answer or otherwise, prior to the default judgment being entered. Finally, they must indicate that their military service prejudiced their ability to defend their case and show that they had a valid defense to the action against them.

Insurance

Under SCRA, the U.S. Department of Veterans Affairs (VA) will protect, from default for nonpayment of premiums, up to $250,000 of life insurance for servicemembers called to active duty. (This amount was previously $10,000.) The protection provided by this legislation applies during the insured's period of military service and for a period of two years thereafter. The following are conditions for eligibility for protection:
- The policy must be whole life, endowment, universal life or term insurance.
- The policy must have been in force on a premium-paying basis for at least six months at the time the servicemember applies for benefits.
- Benefits from the policy cannot be limited, reduced or excluded because of military service.
- Policies for which an additional amount of premium is charged due to military service are not eligible for protection under SCRA.

The servicemember must apply for protection of their life insurance by filing "VA Form 29-380 "Application For Protection Of Commercial Life Insurance Policy" with his/her insurance company and forwarding a copy of the application to VA.

Benefits of SCRA Life Insurance Protection

Once the servicemember has applied for protection of their life insurance policy and VA determines that the policy is eligible for protection under SCRA:
- The servicemember is still responsible for making premium payments. However, the policy will not lapse, terminate, or be forfeited because of the servicemember's failure to make premium payments or to pay any indebtedness or interest due during their period of military service or for a

period of two years thereafter.
- The rights of the servicemember to change their beneficiary designation or select an optional settlement for a beneficiary are not affected by the provisions of this Act.

Limitations of SCRA Life Insurance Protection

Once the servicemember has applied for protection of their life insurance policy and VA determines that the policy is eligible for protection under SCRA:
- Premium payments are deferred only, not waived. During this period, the government does not pay the premiums on the policy but simply guarantees that the premiums will be paid at the end of the servicemember's period of active duty.
- A servicemember cannot receive dividends, take out a loan, or surrender the policy for cash without the approval of VA. (Dividends or other monetary benefits shall be added to the value of the policy and will be used as a credit when final settlement is made with the insurer.)
- If the policy matures as a result of the insured's death, or any other means, during the protected period, the insurance company will deduct any unpaid premiums and interest due from the settlement amount.

Termination of Period Under SCRA

The servicemember has up to two years after their military service terminates to repay the unpaid premiums and interest to the insurer. If the amount owed is not paid before the end of the two years, then:
- The insurer treats the unpaid premiums as a loan against the policy.
- The government will pay the insurer the difference between the amount due and the cash surrender value (if the cash surrender value of the policy is less than the amount owed.)
- The amount the United States government pays to the insurance company under the SCRA Act becomes a debt due the government by the insured.
- If the policy matures as a result of the insured's death, or any other means, during the protected period, the insurance company will deduct any unpaid premiums and interest due from the settlement amount.

Taxation

A service member's state of legal residence may tax military pay and personal property. A member does not lose residence solely because of a transfer to another state pursuant to military orders.

For example, if an Illinois resident who is a member of Illinois Army National Guard is activated to federal military service and sent to California for duty, that person remains an Illinois resident while in California. The service member is not subject to California's authority to tax his/her military income. However, if the service member has a part-time civilian job in California, California will tax his/her non-military income earned in the state.

The Servicemembers Civil Relief Act also contains a provision preventing servicemembers from a form of double taxation that can occur when they have a spouse who works and is taxed in a state other than the state in which they maintain their permanent legal residence. The law prevents states from using the income earned by a servicemember in determining the spouse's tax rate when they do not maintain their permanent legal residence in that state. Public Law 111-98, which became law on November 11, 2009, provides that when a service member leaves his or her home state in accord with military or naval orders, the service member's spouse may retain residency in his or her home state for voting and tax purposes, after relocating from that state to accompany the service member.

Right to Vote

In addition to the protections involving debt payments and civil litigation, the act guarantees service members the right to vote in the state of their home of record and protects them from paying taxes in two different states.

Caution

The SSCRA does not wipe out any of an individual's obligations. Rather, it temporarily suspends the right of creditors to use a court to compel an individual to pay, only if the court finds that the inability to pay is due to military service. The obligation to honor existing debts remains, and some day the individual must "pay up."

It is important to remember that the SSCRA affords no relief to persons in the Service against the collection of debts or other obligations contracted or assumed by them after entering such Service.

The Servicemembers' Civil Relief Act is highly technical. The above summary is intended only to give a general overview of the protection available. The specific nature of all the relief provided under the law is a matter about which an individual may need to contact an attorney. The Act is designed to deal fairly with military personnel and their creditors. While relief is very often available, individuals are expected and required to show good faith in repayment of all debts.

Veterans Benefits Act of 2010

Amends the Servicemembers Civil Relief Act (SCRA) to prohibit lessors from charging early termination fees with respect to residential, business, agricultural, or motor vehicle leases entered into by servicemembers who subsequently enter military service or receive orders for a permanent change of station or deployment in support of a military operation.

Allows a servicemember to terminate a contract for cellular or home telephone service at any time after receiving military orders to deploy for at least 90 days to a location that does not support the contract. Requires the return of any advance payments made by a deploying servicemember under such a contract.

Allows the Attorney General to bring a civil suit against any violator of the SCRA. Also gives servicemembers a "private right of action" to file their own lawsuits against those who violate their legal rights.

CHAPTER 36

APPEALS

Veterans and other claimants for VA benefits have the right to appeal decisions made by a VA regional office or medical center.

Veteran Appeals Improvement and Modernization Act of 2017

The Veteran Appeals Improvement and Modernization Act of 2017 became law in August 2017. It's also known as the Appeals Modernization Act, and in 2019 aspects of this law were implemented, changing the veteran appeals process. The new law achieves several things, including:

- It modernizes the current claims and appeals process
- Includes three review options for disagreements with decisions
- Requires improved notification of VA decisions
- Provides earlier claim resolution
- Ensures veterans get the earliest effective date possible

The implementation of the law means there are three options for review.

Option One: Higher-Level Review

With this option, your claim is reviewed by a more senior claims adjudicator. It involves a higher level de novo review of the decision, meaning a new look. You aren't allowed to submit new evidence, and there is a possibility for the decision to be overturned based on a difference of opinion or a clear and unmistakable error. The reviewer can return the claim to the regional office for correction. The veteran or their representative can request an informal phone call to identify specific issues.

You should use VA Form 20-0996: Higher-Level Review. You can request a Higher-Level Review of an initial claim or supplemental claim decision. This option isn't available after a Higher-Level Review or Board Appeal.

You have one year from the date on your decision letter to request a higher-level review.

Option Two: A Supplemental Claim Line

With this option, you can submit or identify new and relevant evidence to support your claim. VA provides assistance in developing the evidence.

To file a supplemental claim, you should use VA Form 20-0995. The goal for completing supplemental claims, according to the VA, is anywhere from four to five months. You can't file a supplemental claim if you have a fiduciary claim or a multiple party or contested claim.

You can file anytime if you have new evidence, but the VA recommends you file within one year from the date on your decision letter. This protects the best possible effective date for you if you are ultimately eligible for retroactive benefit payments.

Option Three: Appeal Lane for Appeals to the Board

This option lets you appeal directly to the Board of Veterans' Appeals. You can choose between three options:
- Direct review: You have no new evidence and don't want a hearing
- Evidence submission: You have new evidence but don't want a hearing
- Hearing: You have new evidence and want to testify before a Veterans Law Judge

If you choose this option you'll use VA Form 10182: Board Appeal. The goal for deciding appeals with no new evidence and no hearing is about a year.

If you receive an initial claim decision after February 2019 and you disagree, you can choose one of three lanes.

If you disagree with a decision from the Supplemental Claim Line, you can choose to resubmit the claim as another supplemental claim with new evidence, as a higher-level review or as an appeal to the Board of Veterans' Appeals.

If you disagree with a decision from the Higher-Level Review Lane, you may resubmit the claim as a supplemental claim or as an appeal to the Board of Veterans' Appeals. If you disagree with a Board decision, you may either resubmit as a supplement claim or through an appeal to the U.S. Court of Appeals for Veterans Claims.

Under AMA, veterans keep their effective dates if they decide to appeal their original decision. The effective date is the date from which benefits begin accruing, which is often determined by the date of the initial filing of the claim.

Please note, the appeals process has changed. For VA decisions you received on or after February 19, 2019, you need to follow the new process above. For decisions you received before February 19, 2019, you can keep reading the below information to find out how to appeal your disability compensation decision.

RAMP Eligibility

You are eligible if you have a disability compensation appeal pending in one of the following legacy appeal stages:

- Notice of Disagreement (NOD)
- Form 9, Appeal to Board of Veterans' Appeals
- Certified to the Board but not yet activated for a Board decision
- Remand from the Board to VBA
- Those who have been waiting the longest in each of the above appeal stages for a resolution of their appeal will receive a letter giving them the opportunity to participate in RAMP first.

Docket

A veteran's VA Form 9-Substantive Appeal becomes part of his or her claims folder, and is the basis for adding the appeal to the Board's docket.

The Board's docket is the record of all appeals awaiting review by the Board, listed in the order that appeals (VA Form 9) are received.

When an appeal is placed on the Board's docket, it is assigned the next higher number than the one received before it. The Board reviews appeals in the order in which they were placed on the docket. Thus, the lower the docket number, the sooner the appeal will be reviewed.

Lawyers and Other Representatives

A veteran may represent himself or herself. However, over 90% of all people who appeal to the Board of Veterans' Appeals obtain representation. The majority choose to be represented by Veterans' Service Organizations (VSOs) or their state's veterans department.

A lawyer may also be hired for representation. There are strict guidelines about what a lawyer may charge for services, as well as restrictions on fees that a lawyer may charge for work performed prior to issuance of the Board's final decision.

In addition to VSOs and attorneys, some other agents are recognized by VA to represent appellants.

To authorize a VSO for representation, VA Form 21-22 must be completed. To authorize an attorney or recognized agent for representation, VA Form 22a must be completed. Both forms are available at all VA offices.

Personal Hearings

A personal hearing is a meeting between the veteran (and his/her representative) and an official from VA who will decide the case. During the hearing, the veteran presents testimony and other evidence supporting the case. There are two types of personal hearings:

- Regional office hearings (also called RO hearing or local office hearings); and BVA hearings.
- A regional office hearing is a meeting held at a local VA office with a "hearing officer" from the local office's staff. To arrange a regional office hearing, a veteran should contact the local VA office or appeal representative as early in the appeal process as possible.
- In a BVA hearing, the veteran presents his or her case in-person to a member of the Board. Appellants in most areas of the country can choose whether to hold the BVA hearing at the local VA regional office, called a "Travel Board Hearing," or at the BVA office in Washington, D.C. Some regional offices are also equipped to hold BVA hearings by videoconference. (Check with the regional office for availability.)

Checking on the Status of an Appeal

To check on the status of an appeal, veterans or their representatives should contact the office where the claims folder is located (see previous section).

If a claims file is at the Board, veterans or their representatives may call (202) 565-5436 to check on its status (be sure to have the claim number available).

The Board Review Process

When the VBA receives an appeal from a local VA office, the veteran and/or representative will be notified in writing. The Board will then examine the claims folder for completeness and will provide an opportunity to submit additional written arguments. The case is then assigned to a Board member for review. If a BVA hearing was requested, the Board member assigned the case will conduct the hearing prior to reaching a decision.

When the docket number for an appeal is reached, the file will be reviewed by a

Board member and a staff attorney, who will check for completeness, review all evidence and arguments, as well as the regional office's Statement of the Case (and Supplement Statement of the Case, if applicable), the transcript of the hearing (if applicable), the statement of any representative, and any other information included in the claims folder. The staff attorney, if directed to do so by the Board member, may also conduct additional research and prepare recommendations for the Board member's review.

When, in the judgment of the Board member, expert medical opinion, in addition to that available within the VA, is warranted by the medical complexity or controversy involved in an appeal, the Board may secure an advisory medical opinion from one or more independent medical experts who are not employees of the VA.

The VA shall make necessary arrangements with recognized medical schools, universities, or clinics to furnish such advisory medical opinions at the request of the Chairman of the Board. Any such arrangement shall provide that the actual selection of the expert or experts to give the advisory opinion in an individual case shall be made by an appropriate official of such institution.

The Board shall furnish a claimant with notice that an advisory medical opinion has been requested, and shall furnish the claimant with a copy of such opinion when it is received by the Board.

Prior to reaching a decision, the Board member must thoroughly review all materials and recommendations. The Board member will then issue a decision.

The Board member's decision will be mailed to the home address that the Board has on file, so it is extremely important that the VA be kept informed of any address changes.

The BVA must attempt to make its decisions as understandable as possible. However, due to the nature of legal documents, laws, court cases, and medical discussions, decisions can be confusing. If an appeal is denied , the Board will send a "Notice of Appellate Rights" that describes additional actions that can be taken.

The Board annually produces a CD-ROM with the text of its decisions. Most VA regional offices have these CD-ROMS available for review, or the CD-Rom may be purchased from the Government Printing Office. For further information, contact:

REMANDS
Department of Veterans Affairs
Board of Veterans' Appeals (01B)
Washington, D.C. 20420

Sometimes when reviewing a claims folder, the Board member determines additional development of the case is necessary. The appeal is then returned to the local VA office. This is called a "remand." After performing the additional work, the regional office may issue a new decision. If the claim is still denied, the case is returned to the Board for a final decision. (The case keeps its original place on the Board's docket, so it is reviewed soon after it is returned to the Board.)

Depending on the reason for the remand, the regional office may provide the veteran with a Supplement Statement of the Case (SSOC). The claimant then has 60 days from the date the local VA office mails the SSOC to comment on it.

Appealing the Board of Veterans' Affairs Decisions
Motion for Reconsideration

If it can be demonstrated that the Board made an obvious error of fact or law in its decision, a written "motion to reconsider" can be filed. Any such motions should be sent directed to the Board, not to the local VA office. A motion to reconsider should not be submitted simply because of disagreement with the BVA's decision. The claimant must be able to show that the Board made a mistake and that the Board's decision would have been different if the mistake had not been made. A motion to reconsider should be sent directly to the Board, not to the local VA office.

Reopening

If a claimant has "new and material evidence," he or she can request that the case be reopened. To be considered "new and material," the evidence submitted must be information related to the case that was not included in the claims folder when the case was decided.

To re-open an appeal, the claimant must submit the new evidence directly to the local VA office that handled the claim.

Cue Motion

The law was amended in 1997 to provide one more way to challenge a Board decision.
A Board decision can be reversed or revised if the claimant is able to show that the decision contained "clear and unmistakable error" (CUE).

The written request for the Board to review its decision for CUE is called a "motion." CUE motions should be filed directly with the Board, and not with the local VA office.

Because CUE is a very complicated area of law, most claimants seek help from a representative to file a CUE motion.

A motion for CUE review of a prior Board decision must meet some very specific requirements, described in the Board's Rules of Practice. If the motion is denied a

484

claimant can't ask for another CUE review of the way the Board decided the issues raised in the first CUE motion, so it is very important that the motion be prepared properly the first time out.

Not many CUE motions are successful because CUE is a very rare kind of error, the kind that compels a conclusion that the Board would have decided the claimant's case differently but for the error. A difference of opinion is not enough.

A motion to review a Board decision for CUE can be filed at any time, but if it is filed after filing a timely Notice of Appeal with the Court, the Board will not be able to rule on your CUE motion.

United States Court of Veterans' Appeals

The United States Court of Veterans' Appeals was created under Public Law 100-687, on November 18, 1988. The Court has seven judges, appointed by the President and confirmed by the Senate. Judges are appointed for a 15-year term.

If a claimant is not satisfied with the Board of Veterans' Appeals decision, an appeal can be filed with the United States Court of Veterans Appeals (referred to as the "Court"). The Court is an independent court that is not part of the Department of Veterans Affairs. The Court does not hold trials, receive new evidence, or hear witnesses. It reviews the BVA decision, the written record, and the briefs of the parties. Claimants do not need to appear in Washington, D.C. for an appeal. (In approximately 1% of decided cases, the Court holds oral arguments in its Washington courtroom, or occasionally, by telephone conference call.)

A claimant may represent himself or herself, but may want to get advice from an attorney or from a service officer in a veterans organization or a state or county veterans' affairs office. The VA will be represented by its attorney, and a claimant's case may be better presented if he or she is represented.

The Court does not recommend or appoint attorneys to represent claimants. However, the Court does have a Public List of Practitioners which shows who is allowed to represent appellants in the Court and have said that they are available. Most attorneys charge a fee.

To appeal a Board of Veterans' Appeals decision, a claimant must file a "Notice of Appeal" with the Court within 120 days from the date the Board's decision is mailed. (The first day of the 120 days a claimant has to file an appeal to the Court is the day the BVA's decision is postmarked, not the day the decision is signed.)

If a claimant filed a motion to reconsider with the Board of Veterans' Appeals within the 120 day time-frame, and that motion was denied, the claimant has an additional

120 days to file the "Notice of Appeal" with the Court. (This 120 day period begins on the date the Board mails a notification that it has denied the motion to reconsider.) If the Board denies the motion to reconsider, a "Notice of Appellate Rights" will be mailed to the claimant.

In addition to the above 120 day limit, in order for the Court to consider an appeal, a Notice of Disagreement must have been filed with the VA regional office handling the case on or after November 18, 1988.

An original "Notice of Appeal" must be filed directed with the Court at:
United States Court of Veterans Appeals

625 Indiana Avenue, NW, Suite 900
Washington, D.C. 20004
Fax: (202) 501-5848
(Appeals cannot be filed by e-mail)

The fee for an appeal is $50.00, and should be included with the "Notice of Appeal." If a claimant is unable to pay this fee, a "Motion to Waive Filing Fee" form must be completed and returned with the "Notice of Appeal." If a claimant appeals to the Court, a copy of the "Notice of Appeal" must also be filed with the VA General Counsel at:

Office of the General Counsel (027)
Department of Veterans Affairs
810 Vermont Avenue, NW
Washington, D.C. 20420

Please note that the original "Notice of Appeal" that is filed with the Court is the only document that protects a claimants right to appeal a BVA decision. The copy sent to the VA General Counsel does not protect that right, or serve as an official filing.

If the Court accepts an appeal, it will send a printed copy of the rules of practice and procedure to the claimant and his/her representative, if applicable.

To obtain more specific information about the "Notice of Appeal," the methods for filing with the Court, Court filing fees, and other matters covered by the Court's rules, a claimant should contact the Court directly at:

United States Court of Veterans Appeals
625 Indiana Avenue, NW, Suite 900
Washington, D.C. 20004
(800) 869-8654

If either party disagrees with the Court's ruling, an appeal may be filed with the U.S. Court of Appeals for the Federal Circuit, and, thereafter, may seek review in the Supreme Court of the United States.

Death of Appellant

According to the law, the death of an appellant generally ends the appellant's appeal, and the Board normally dismisses the appeal without issuing a decision. The rights of a deceased appellant's survivors are not affected by this action. Survivors may still file a claim at the regional office for any benefits to which they may be entitled.

General Guidelines for Efficient Processing of Claims

The following guidelines may help ensure that an appeal is not unnecessarily delayed:

- Consider having an appeal representative assist with the filing of the appeal.
- Be as specific as possible when identifying the issues the Board should consider.
- Be as specific as possible when identifying sources of evidence for the VA to obtain. (For example, provide the full names and addresses of physicians, along with dates of treatment, and reasons for treatment.)
- Keep VA informed of current address, phone number, and number of dependents.
- When possible, provide clinical treatment records, rather than simply a statement from a physician.
- Include the claim number on any correspondence with the VA.
- Do not submit material that is not pertinent to the claim. This will only delay the process.
- Do not use the VA Form 9 to raise new claims for the first time. (VA Form 9 is only to be used to appeal decisions on previously submitted claims.)
- Do not use the VA Form 9 to request a local office hearing.
- Do not raise additional issues for the Board's review late in the appeal process. This may cause the appeal to be sent back to the regional office for additional work, and may result in a longer delay.
- Do not submit evidence directly to the Board unless a written or typed statement is included, stating that consideration by the regional office is waived. The statement must clearly indicate that the Board is to review the evidence, even though the regional office has not seen it. If a waiver is not included with any additional evidence submitted directly to the Board, the case may be remanded to the regional office for review, and may result in further delays.
- Do not submit a last minute request for a hearing or a last minute change to the type or location of a hearing unless it is unavoidable. Such a request will likely result in a delay in reaching a final decision.
- Do not miss a scheduled VA examination or hearing.

CHAPTER 37

VA REGIONAL OFFICES & BENEFITS OFFICES

Department of Veterans Affairs
Headquarters
810 Vermont Avenue NW
Washington, DC 20420
(202) 273-5400

Alabama (SDN 5) Montgomery RO
345 Perry Hill Road
Montgomery, AL 36109

Alaska (SDN 8) Anchorage RO
1201 North Muldoon Road
Anchorage, AK 99504

Arizona (SDN 9) Phoenix RO
3333 North Central Avenue
Phoenix, AZ 85012

Arkansas (SDN 7)
North Little Rock RO
2200 Fort Roots Drive Building 65
North Little Rock, AR 72114

California (SDN 9)
Los Angeles RO Federal Building
11000 Wilshire Boulevard
Los Angeles, CA 90024

Oakland RO
1301 Clay Street
Room 1400 North
Oakland, CA 94612

San Diego RO
8810 Rio San Diego Drive
San Diego, CA 92108

Colorado (SDN 8) Denver RO
155 Van Gordon Street
Lakewood, CO 80228

Connecticut (SDN 1) Hartford RO
555 Willard Avenue
Newington, CT 06111
Mailing Address:
P.O. Box 310909
Newington , CT 06131

Delaware (SDN 3) Wilmington RO
1601 Kirkwood Highway
Wilmington, DE 19805

Florida (SDN 5) St. Petersburg RO
9500 Bay Pines Boulevard Bay Pines,
FL 33708 Mailing Address:
P.O. Box 1437
St. Petersburg, FL 33731

Georgia (SDN 4) Atlanta RO
1700 Clairmont Road
Decatur, GA 30033
Mailing Address:
P.O. BOX 100026
Decatur, GA 30031-7026

Hawaii (SDN 9) Honolulu RO
459 Patterson Road E-Wing
Honolulu, HI 96819-1522

Idaho (SDN 8) Boise RO
444 W. Fort Street
Boise, ID 83702-4531

Illinois (SDN 6) Chicago RO
2122 West Taylor Street
Chicago, IL 60612

Indiana (SDN 2) Indianapolis RO
575 North Pennsylvania Street
Indianapolis, IN 46204

Iowa (SDN 6) Des Moines RO
210 Walnut Street
Des Moines, IA 50309

Kansas (SDN 6) Wichita RO
5500 East Kellogg
Wichita, KS 67211

Kentucky (SDN 3) Louisville RO
321 West Main Street, Suite 390
Louisville, KY 40202

Louisiana (SDN 7) New Orleans RO
1250 Poydras Street
New Orleans, LA 70113

Maine (SDN 1) Togus VA Med/RO
1 VA Center
Augusta, ME 04330

Maryland (SDN 3) Baltimore RO
31 Hopkins Plaza Federal Bldg
Baltimore, MD 21201

Massachusetts (SDN 1) Boston RO
JFK Federal Building
15 New Sudbury St. Government
Center
Boston, MA 02114

Michigan (SDN 2) Detroit RO
Federal Building
477 Michigan Avenue
Detroit, MI 48226

Minnesota (SDN 6) St. Paul RO
1 Federal Drive
Fort Snelling
St. Paul, MN 55111-4050

Mississippi (SDN 5) Jackson RO
1600 East Woodrow Wilson Ave.
Jackson, MS 39216

Missouri (SDN 6)St. Louis RO
Federal Building
400 South, 18th Street
St. Louis, MO 63103

Montana (SDN 8) Fort Harrison RO
3633 Veterans Drive
Fort Harrison, MT 59636-0188

Nebraska (SDN 6) Lincoln RO
3800 Village Drive
Lincoln, NE 68516
Mailing Address: PO Box 85816
Lincoln, NE 68501-5816

New Hampshire (SDN 1) Manchester
RO
Norris Cotton Federal Bldg
275 Chestnut Street
Manchester, NH 03101

New Jersey (SDN 2) Newark RO
20 Washington Place
Newark, NJ 07102

New Mexico (SDN 8) Albuquerque
RO
Dennis Chavez Federal Building
 500 Gold Avenue,
S.W. Albuquerque, NM 87102

Nevada (SDN 9) Reno RO
5460 Reno Corporate Dr.
Reno, NV 89511-2250

New York (SDN1) Buffalo RO
130 South Elmwood Avenue
Buffalo, NY 14202

New York RO
245 West Houston Street
New York, NY 10014

North Carolina (SDN 4) Winston-
Salem RO
Federal Building
251 North Main Street
Winston-Salem, NC 27155

North Dakota (SDN 6) Fargo RO
2101 Elm Street
Fargo, ND 58102

Ohio (SDN 2) Cleveland RO
A.J. Celebrezze Federal Building
1240 East 9th Street
Cleveland, OH 44199

Oklahoma (SDN 7) Muskogee RO
125 South Main Street
Muskogee, OK 74401

Oregon (SDN 8) Portland RO
100 SW Main Street, Floor 2
Portland, OR 97204
Mailing Address:
100 SW Main St FL 2
Portland, OR 97204

Pennsylvania (SDN 2) Philadelphia
RO
5000 Wissahickon Avenue
Philadelphia, PA 19101

Pittsburgh RO
1000 Liberty Avenue
Pittsburgh, PA 15222

Rhode Island (SDN 1) Providence RO
380 Westminster St.
Providence, RI 02903

South Carolina (SDN 4) Columbia RO
6437 Garners Ferry Road
Columbia, SC 29209

South Dakota (SDN 6) Sioux Falls RO
2501 West 22nd Street
Sioux Falls, SD 57117

Tennessee (SDN 4) Nashville RO
110 9th Avenue South
Nashville, TN 37203

Southern Area Office
3322 West End, Suite 408
Nashville, TN 37203

Texas (SDN 7) Houston RO
6900 Almeda Road
Houston, TX 77030

Waco RO
1 Veterans Plaza
701 Clay Avenue
Waco, TX 76799

Utah (SDN 8) Salt Lake City RO
550 Foothill Drive
Salt Lake City, UT 84158

Vermont (SDN 1) White River
Junction RO
215 N. Main St.
White River Junction, VT 05009

Virginia (SDN 3) Roanoke RO
116 N. Jefferson St.
Roanoke, VA 24016

Washington (SDN 8) Seattle RO
Federal Building
915 2nd Avenue
Seattle, WA 98174

West Virginia (SDN 3) Huntington RO
640 Fourth Avenue
Huntington, WV 25701

Wisconsin (SDN 6) Milwaukee RO
5400 West National Avenue
Milwaukee, WI 53214

Wyoming (SDN 8) Cheyenne RO
2360 East Pershing Blvd.
Cheyenne, WY 82001

District of Columbia (SDN 3)
Washington DC RO
1722 I Street N.W.
Washington, DC 20421

Puerto Rico (SDN 5) San Juan RO
50 Carr 165
Guaynabo, PR 00968-8024

Philippines (SDN 9) Manila RO
1501 Roxas Boulevard
Pasay City, PI 1302
Note: SDN = Service Delivery Network

*In order to reach any of the above offices by phone, call (800) 827-1000 and your call will be directed appropriately.

CHAPTER 38

STATE BENEFITS

Many states offer services and benefits to veterans in addition to those offered by the Department of Veterans' Affairs. To find out more about a particular state's programs, individuals should contact the following

Alabama VA
RZA Plaza
770 Washington Ave,
Suite 530
Montgomery, AL 36102-1509
(334) 242-5077

Alaska VA
P.O. Box 5800
Fort Richardson, AK 99505- 5800
(907) 428-6031

Arizona VA Services
3839 North Third
Street, Suite 209
Phoenix, AZ 85012
(602) 248-1554

Arkansas VA
2200 Fort Roots Drive
Room 119 – Bldg 65
North Little Rock, AR 72114
(501) 370-3820

California VA
1227 O Street, Suite 300
Sacramento, CA 95814
(800) 952-5626

Colorado VA
6848 South Revere Parkway
Centennial, CO 80112
(720) 250-1500

Connecticut VA
287 West Street
Rocky Hill, CT 06067
(860) 616-3603

Delaware VA
Robbins Building
802 Silverlake Blvd, Suite 100
Dover, DE 19904
(302) 739-2792
(800) 344-9900 (in-state only)

Florida VA
Mary Grizzle Building, Room 311-K
11351 Ulmerton Road
Largo, FL 33778
(727) 518-3202

Georgia VA
Floyd Veterans Memorial Building
Suite E-970
Atlanta, GA 30334
(404) 656-2300

Hawaii VA
 Mailing Address:
459 Patterson Road
E-Wing, Room 1-A103
Honolulu, HI 96819-1522
Location:
Tripler Army Med Center (Ward Road)
VAMROC, E-Wing, Room 1-A103
Honolulu, HI 96819
(808) 433-0420

Idaho VA
351 Collins Road
Boise, ID 83702
(208) 577-2310

Illinois VA
362 North Linwood Rd.
Galesburg, IL 61401
(309) 343-2510

Indiana VA
302 West Washington, Room E120
Indianapolis, IN 46204-2738
(317) 232-3910

Iowa Commission of Veterans' Affairs
7105 N.W. 70th Avenue Camp
Dodge - Building 3663
Johnston, IA 50131-1824
(515) 242-5331

Kansas Commission on Veterans'
Affairs
Jayhawk Towers Suite 1004
700 S.W. Jackson Street
Topeka, KS 66603-3714
(785) 296-3976

Kentucky VA
1111 Louisville Road NGAKY Building
Frankfort, KY 40601
(502) 564-9203

Louisiana VA
P.O. Box 94095 Capitol Station
1885 Wooddale Blvd. 10th Floor,
Room 1013
Baton Rouge, LA 70806
(225) 219-5000

Maine Bureau of Veterans' Services
117 State House Station
Camp Keyes Building 7, Room 115
Augusta, ME 04333
(207) 430-6035

Maryland VA
16 Francis St. 4th Floor
Annapolis, MD 21401
(410) 260-3838

Massachusetts Department of
Veterans' Services
600 Washington Street,
Suite 1100
Boston, MA 02111
(617) 210-5480

Michigan VA
7109 W. Saginaw
Lansing, MI 48913
(517) 335-6523

Minnesota VA
State Veterans Service Building
20 West 12th Street, 2nd Floor Rm.
206 St. Paul, MN 55155-2079
(651) 296-2562

Mississippi State Veterans' Affairs
Board
3466 Highway 80 East
P.O. Box 5947
Pearl, MS 39288-5947
(601) 576-4850

Missouri Veterans' Commission
Mailing Address:
205 Jefferson Street
12th Floor Jefferson Building
P.O. Drawer 147
Jefferson City, MO 65102
(573) 751-3779

Montana Veterans' Affairs Division
P.O. Box 5715
1900 Williams Street
Helena, MT 59604
(406) 324-3740

Nebraska VA
State Office Building
301 Centennial Mall South
P.O. Box 95083
Lincoln, NE 68509-5083
(402) 471-2458

Nevada Commission for Veterans'
Affairs
5460 Reno Corporate Dr.
Suite 131
Reno, NV 89511
(775) 688-1656

New Hampshire Office of Veterans'
Service
275 Chestnut Street Room 517
Manchester, NH 03101-2411
(603) 624-9230
1-800-622-9230 (in-state only)

New Jersey VA
Eggert Crossing Road PO Box 340
Trenton, NJ 08625-0508
(800) 624-0508

New Mexico Veterans' Service
Commission
Bataan Memorial Building
407 Galisteo St. Rm. 142
Santa Fe, NM 87504
(866) 433-8387

New York Division of Veterans' Affairs
2 Empire State Plaza 17th Floor
Albany, NY 12223-1551
(518) 474-6114

North Carolina Division of Veterans'
Affairs
325 N. Salisbury Street
Raleigh, NC 27601
(919) 807-4250

North Dakota VA
4201 38th St S # 104
Fargo, ND 58104
(701) 239-7165

Ohio Governor's Office of Veterans'
Affairs
77 South High Street
Columbus, OH 43215
(614) 644-0898

Oklahoma VA
2311 N. Central Avenue
Oklahoma City, OK 73105
(405) 521-3684

Oregon VA
100 South Main St.
Portland, OR 97204
(503) 412-4777

Pennsylvania VA
Fort Indiantown Gap Building S-O-47
Annville, PA 17003-5002
(717) 861-2000

Rhode Island Division of Veterans'
Affairs
480 Metacom Avenue
Bristol, RI 02809
(401) 462-0324

South Carolina Office of Veterans'
Affairs
1205 Pendleton Street, Suite 463
Columbia, SC 29201
(803) 734-0200

South Dakota Division of Veterans'
Affairs
425 East Capitol Avenue
c/o 500 East Capitol Avenue
Pierre, SD 57501
(605) 773-3269

Tennessee VA
312 Rosa Parks Ave.
Nashville, TN 37243-1010
(615) 741-2931

Texas Veterans' Commission
1700 Congress Ave.

Austin, TX 78701
(512) 463-5538
Utah Division of Veterans' Affairs
550 Foothill Blvd, Room 202
Salt Lake City, UT 84113
(801) 326-2372

Vermont State Veterans' Affairs
118 State Street
Montpelier, VT 05602
(802) 828-3379

Virginia VA
900 East Main Street
Richmond, VA 23219
(804) 786-0286

Washington VA
P.O. Box 41150
1011 Plum Street
Olympia, WA 98504-1150
(800) 562-0132

West Virginia Division of Veterans'
Affairs
1514-B Kanawha Blvd.
Charleston, WV 25311
(304) 558-3661

Wisconsin VA
201 West Washington Avenue
Madison, WI 53703
(800) 947-8387

Wyoming Veterans' Affairs
Commission
Wyoming ANG Armory
5905 CY Avenue - Room 101
Casper, WY 82604
(307) 265-7372

American Samoa Veterans' Affairs
P.O. Box 982942

Pago Pago, American Samoa 96799
(001) 684-633-4206
Guam Veterans' Affairs Office Mailing
Address:
770 East Sunset Blvd., Suite 165
Tamuning, GU 96913
(671) 475-4222

Puerto Rico Public Advocate for
Veterans' Affairs
Mailing Address:
Apartado 11737 Fernandez Juncos
Station
San Juan, PR 00910-1737
Location:
Mercantile Plaza Bldg, Fourth Floor,
Suite 4021
Hato Rey, PR 00918-1625
(787) 758-5760

Government of the Virgin Islands
Division of Veterans' Affairs
1013 Estate Richmond Christiansted
St. Croix VI 00820-4349
(340) 773-6663

CHAPTER 39

MILITARY PERSONNEL RECORDS

Note: The U.S. Department of Veterans Affairs does not maintain veterans' military service records.

The personnel records of individuals currently in the military service, in the reserve forces, and those completely separated from military service are located in different offices. A nominal fee is charged for certain types of service. In most instances service fees cannot be determined in advance. If your request involves a service fee you will be notified as soon as that determination is made.

A veteran and spouse should be aware of the location of the veteran's discharge and separation papers. If a veteran cannot locate discharge and separation papers, duplicate copies may be obtained (further information regarding who to contact is included later in this chapter).

Use "Standard Form 180, Request Pertaining to Military Records," which is available from VA offices and veterans organizations. Specify that a duplicate separation document or discharge is needed. The veteran's full name should be printed or typed so that it can be read clearly, but the request must also contain the signature of the veteran or the signature of the next of kin if the veteran is deceased. Include branch of service, service number or Social Security number and

> **Key Takeaways**
>
> If you've been discharged from military service, your personnel files are stored at the National Archives and Record Administration.
>
> Recent military service and medical records are not online, but most veterans and their next-of-kin can get free copies of their DD Form 214 and other records by using the eVetRecs System to create a request or mailing a fax or standard form SF-180.

exact or approximate date and years of service.

It is not necessary to request a duplicate copy of a veteran's discharge or separation papers solely for the purpose of filing a claim for VA benefits. If complete information about the veteran's service is furnished on the application, VA will obtain verification of service from the National Personnel Records Center or the service department concerned.

Who to Contact

The various categories of military personnel records are described in the tables below. Please read the following notes carefully, to make sure an inquiry is sent to the right address. Please note especially that the record is not sent to the National Personnel Records Center as long as the person retains any sort of reserve obligation, whether drilling or non-drilling.

Locations of Medical Records—National Personnel Records Center

Veterans who plan to file a claim for medical benefits with the **Department of Veterans Affairs (VA)** do not need to request a copy of their military health record from the NPRC. After a claim is filed, the VA will obtain the original health record from the NPRC. In addition, many health records were lent to the Department of Veterans Affairs prior to the **1973 Fire**. Veterans who filed a medical claim should contact the Department of Veterans Affairs (VA) in order to determine if their record is already on file. The VA Toll Free number is: 1-800-827-1000 - it will connect the caller to the nearest VA office.

In the 1990s, the military services discontinued the practice of filing health records with the personnel record portion at the NPRC. In 1992, the Army began retiring most of its former members' health records to the Department of Veterans Affairs (VA). Over the next six years, the other services followed suit:

Branch	Status	Health Record to VA
Army	Discharged, retired or separated from any component	October 16, 1992
Navy	Discharged, retired or separated from any component	January 31, 1994
Air Force	Discharged, retired or separated from Active Duty/Discharged or retired from Reserves or National	May 1, 1994

June 1, 1994 |

	Guard	
Marine Corps	Discharged, retired or separated from any component	May 1, 1994
Coast Guard	Discharged, retired or separated from Active Duty/Reservists with 90 days active duty for training	April 1, 1998

After the dates listed above, the Department of Veterans Affairs (VA), Records Management Center, in St. Louis, MO, became responsible for maintaining active duty health records and managing their whereabouts when on loan within the VA. Call the VA toll free number at 1-800-827-1000 to identify the current location of specific health records and to find out how to obtain releasable documents or information.

Location of Army Personnel Records (Includes Army Air Corps and Army Air Forces)

Dates of Service	Rank	Personnel Record Location	Health Record Location
1789 to November 1, 1912	Enlisted	NARA, Washington, DC	N/A
1789 to July 1, 1917	Officer	NARA, Washington, DC	N/A
November 1, 1912 to October 15, 1992 *Note: Many records were destroyed by the 1973 fire	Enlisted	National Personnel Records Center *Note: Personnel records are Archival 62 years after the service member's separation	
July 1, 1917 to October 15,1992	Officer	National Personnel Records Center *Note: personnel records are Archival 62 years after the service member's separation	

October 16, 992 to September 30, 2002	All Personnel	National Personnel Records Center	Department of Veterans Affairs
Discharged, deceased or retired on or after October 1, 2002 to December 31, 2013	All Personnel	U.S. Army Human Resources Command *Note: all records are stored electronically at AHRC but requests are serviced by National Personnel Records Center	Department of Veterans Affairs
Discharged, deceased or retired on or after January 1, 2014	All Personnel	U.S. Army Human Resources Command *Note: records are stored electronically at AHRC but requests are served by National Personnel Records Center	AMEDD Record Processing Center
All active duty, including active Army Reserve	All Personnel	U.S. Army Human Resources Command	
All active and non-active duty National Guard	All Personnel	The Adjutant General (of the appropriate state, DC or Puerto Rico)	

Location of Air Force Personnel Records

Dates of Service	Rank	Personnel Record Location	Health Record Location
September 24, 1947 to May 1, 1994 *Note: Many records were destroyed by the 1973 Fire	All Personnel	National Personnel Records Center *Note: Personnel records are Archival 62 years after the service member's separation	

May 1, 1994 to September 30, 2004	All Personnel	National Personnel Records Center	Department of Veterans Affairs
Discharged, deceased or retired from active duty on or after October 1, 2004 to December 31, 2013	All Personnel	Air Force Personnel Center HQ AFPC/DPSSRP	Department of Veterans Affairs
Discharged, deceased or retired from active duty on or after January 1, 2014	All Personnel	Air Force Personnel Center HQ AFPC/DPSSRP	AF STR Processing Center
Active (including National Guard on active duty in the Air Force), TDRL, or general officers retired with pay	All Personnel	Air Force Personnel Center HQ AFPC/DPSSRP	
Reserve, retired reserve in non-pay status, current National Guard officers not on active duty in the Air Force or National Guard released from active duty in the Air Force	Various Personnel	Air Reserve Personnel Center HQ ARPC/DPTOCW (Contact Center)	
Current National Guard enlisted not on active duty in the Air Force	All Personnel	The Adjutant General (of the appropriate state, DC, or Puerto Rico)	

Location of Navy Personnel Records

Dates of Service	Rank	Personnel Record Location	Health Record Location
1798 to 1885	Enlisted	NARA, Washington DC	N/A
1798 to 1902	Officer	NARA, Washington DC	N/A
1885 to January 30, 1994	Enlisted	National Personnel Records Center *Note: Personnel records are Archival 62 years after the servicemember's separation	
1902 to January 30, 1994	Officer	National Personnel Records Center *Note: Personnel records are Archival 62 years after the service member's separation	
January 31, 1994 to December 31, 1994	All Personnel	National Personnel Records Center	Department of Veterans Affairs
Discharged, deceased or retired on or after January 1, 1995 to December 31, 2013	All Personnel	Navy Personnel Command	Department of Veterans Affairs
Discharged, deceased or retired on or after January 1, 2014	All Personnel	National Personnel Records Center	BUMED Navy Medicine Records Activity
Active, reserve or TDRL	All Personnel	Navy Personnel Command	

Location of Marine Corps Personnel Records

Dates of Service	Rank	Personnel Record Location	Health Record Location
1798 to 1904	All Personnel	NARA, Washington DC	N/A
1905 to April 30, 1994	All Personnel	National Personnel Records Center *Note: Personnel records are Archival 62 years after the servicemember's separation	
May 1, 1994 to December 31, 1998	All Personnel	National Personnel Record Center	Department of Veterans Affairs
Discharged, deceased or retired on or after January 1, 1999 to December 31, 2013	All Personnel	HQ U.S. Marine Corps	Department of Veterans Affairs
Discharged, deceased or retired on or after January 1, 2014	All Personnel	HQ U.S. Marine Corps	BUMED Navy Medicine Records Activity
Individual Ready Reserve	All Personnel	Marine Forces Reserve	
Active, Selected Marine Corps Reserve TDRL	All Personnel	HQ U.S. Marine Corps	

Location of Coast Guard Personnel Records—Including Revenue Cutter Service, Life-Saving Service and Lighthouse Service

Dates of Service	Rank	Personnel Record Location	Health Record Location
Discharged, deceased or retired prior to December 31, 1897	All Personnel	NARA, Washington DC	N/A
January 1, 1898 to March 31, 1998	All Personnel	National Personnel Records Center *Note: Personnel records are Archival 62 years after the service member's separation	
Discharged, deceased or retired from active duty from April 1, 998 to September 30, 2014	All Personnel	National Personnel Records Center	Department of Veterans Affairs
Discharged deceased or retired from active duty on or after October 1, 2014	All Personnel	National Personnel Records Center	
Active, Reserve or TDRL	All personnel	USCG Personnel Command	

Address List

Army

U.S. Army Human Resources Command
Attn: AHRC-PDR-VIB
1600 Spearhead Division Avenue Dept 420
Fort Knox, KY 40122-5402

Telephone: 1-888-276-9472

AMEDD Record Processing Center
3370 Nacogdoches Road, Suite 116
San Antonio, TX 78217

Air Force

Air Force Personnel Center
HQ AFPC/DPSSRP
550 C Street West, Suite 19
Randolph AFB, TX 78150-4721

Telephone: 1-800-525-0102

Air Reserve Personnel Center
HQ ARPC/DPTOCW (Contact Center)
18420 E Silver Creek Ave Bldg 390 MS 68
Buckley AFB, CO 80011

Telephone: 1-800-525-0102

AF STR Processing Center
ATTN: Release of Information
3370 Nacogdoches Road, Suite 116
San Antonio, TX 78217

Navy

Navy Personnel Command
(PERS-312E)
5720 Integrity Drive
Millington, TN 38055-3120

Telephone: 901-874-4885

Navy Medicine Records Activity (NMRA)
BUMED Detachment St. Louis
4300 Goodfellow Blvd., Building 103
St. Louis, MO 63120

Marine Corps

Headquarters U.S. Marine Corps
Personnel Management Support Branch
(MMSB-10)
2008 Elliot Road
Quantico, VA 22134-5030

Telephone: 1-800-268-3710

Marine Forces Reserve
4400 Dauphine St.
New Orleans, LA 70146-5400

Telephone: 1-800-255-5082

Coast Guard

Commander CG PSC-bobs-mr
USCG Personnel Command
4200 Wilson Blvd., Suite 1100
Arlington, VA 22203-1804

Telephone: 1-703-872-6392

Other Agencies

The Adjutant General
(of the appropriate state, DC, or Puerto Rico)

Department of Veterans Affairs
Records Management Center (VARMC)
P.O. Box 5020
St. Louis, MO 63115-5020

Telephone: 1-888-533-4558

Division of Commissioned Personnel and Readiness
ATTN: Records Officer
1101 Wootton Parkway, Plaza Level, Suite 100
Rockville, MD 20852

Telephone: 240-453-6041

National Archives & Records Administration
Old Military and Civil Records (NWCTB-Military)
Textual Services Division
700 Pennsylvania Ave., N.W.
Washington, DC 20408-0001

Telephone: 202-357-5000

Customer Service Center Telephone: 1-866-272-6272

National Personnel Records Center, NARA
1 Archives Drive
St. Louis, MO 63138

Request records online, or
Telephone: 314-801-0800

Selective Service System
Data Management Center
P.O Box 94638
Palatine, IL 60094-4638

Telephone: 847-688-6888 or toll-free: 1-888-655-1825

Facts About the 1973 ST. Louis Fire and Lost Records

A fire at the NPRC in St. Louis on July 12, 1973, destroyed about 80 percent of the records for Army personnel discharged between November 1, 1912, and January 1, 1960. About 75 percent of the records for Air Force personnel with surnames from "Hubbard" through "Z" discharged between September 25, 1947, and January 1, 1964, were also destroyed

What Was Lost

It is hard to determine exactly what was lost in the fire, because:

- There were no indices to the blocks of records involved. The records were merely filed in alphabetical order for the following groups:

    o World War I: Army November 1, 1912 - September 7, 1939

    o World War II: Army September 8, 1939 - December 31, 1946

    o Post World War II: Army January 1, 1947 - December 31, 1959

    o Air Force September 25, 1947 - December 31, 1963

- Millions of records, especially medical records, had been withdrawn from all three groups and loaned to the Department of Veterans Affairs (VA) before the fire. The fact that one's records are not in NPRC files at a particular time does not mean the records were destroyed in the fire.

Reconstruction of Lost Records

If veterans learn that their records may have been lost in the fire, they may send photocopies of any documents they possess -- especially separation documents -- to the NPRC at:

National Personnel Records Center
Military Personnel Records
9700 Page Blvd.
St. Louis, MO 63132-5100.

Alternate Sources

When veterans don't have copies of their military records and their NPRC files may have been lost in the St. Louis fire, essential information about their military service may be available from a number of other sources including:

The Department of Veterans Affairs (VA) maintains records on veterans whose military records were affected by the fire if the veteran or a beneficiary filed a claim before July 1973.

Service information may also be found in various kinds of "organizational" records such as unit morning reports, payrolls and military orders on file at the NPRC or other National Archives and Records Administration facilities.
There also is a great deal of information available in records of the State Adjutants General, and other state "veterans services" offices.

By using alternate sources, NPRC often can reconstruct a veteran's beginning and ending dates of active service, the character of service, rank, time lost on active duty, and periods of hospitalization. NPRC can issue NA Form 13038, "Certification of Military Service," considered the equivalent of a Form DD-214, "Report of Separation From Active Duty," to use in establishing eligibility for veterans benefits.

Necessary Information for File Reconstruction
The key to reconstructing military data is to give the NPRC enough specific information so the staff can properly search the various sources. The following information is normally required:
- Full name used during military service;
- Place of entry into service;
- Branch of service;
- Last unit of assignment;
- Approximate dates of service;
- Place of discharge;
- Service number or Social Security number.

CHAPTER 40

CORRECTION OF RECORDS BY CORRECTION BOARDS

Retirees may feel that their records need correcting or amending for any number of reasons. Correction boards consider formal applications for corrections of military records. Each service department has a permanent Board for Correction of Military (Naval) records, composed of civilians, to act on applications for correction of records.

In order to justify the correction of a military record, the applicant must prove to a Corrections Board that the alleged entry or omission in the record was in error or unjust. This board considers all applications and makes recommendations to the appropriate branch Secretary.

An application for correction of record must be filed within three years after discovering the error or injustice. If filed after the three-year deadline, the applicant must include in the application reasons the board should find it in the interest of justice to accept the late application. Evidence may include affidavits or signed testimony executed under oath, and a brief of arguments supporting the application. All evidence not already included in one's record must be submitted. The responsibility for securing new evidence rests with the applicant.

> ## Key Takeaways
>
> The secretary of a military department has the authority to change any military record when necessary to correct an error or remove an injustice.
>
> A correction board may consider applications for correction of a military record including a review of a discharge issued by courts martial.
>
> The veteran, survivor or legal representative must file a request for correction within three years after the discovery of error or injustice.

To justify any correction, it is necessary to show to the satisfaction of the board that the alleged entry or omission in the records was in error or unjust. Applications should include all available evidence, such as signed statements of witnesses or a brief of arguments supporting the requested correction. Application is made with DD Form 149, available at VA offices, from veterans organizations or from the internet. Each of the military services maintains a discharge review board with authority to change, correct or modify discharges or dismissals that are not issued by a sentence of a general courts-martial. The board has no authority to address medical discharges. The veteran or, if the veteran is deceased or incompetent, the surviving spouse, next of kin or legal representative may apply for a review of discharge by writing to the military department concerned, using DoD Form 293. This form may be obtained at a VA regional office, from veterans organizations or from the Internet. However, if the discharge was more than 15 years ago, a veteran must petition the appropriate service Board for Correction of Military Records using DoD Form 149, which is discussed in the "Correction of Military Records" section of this booklet. A discharge review is conducted by a review of an applicant's record and, if requested, by a hearing before the board.

Discharges awarded as a result of a continuous period of unauthorized absence in excess of 180 days make persons ineligible for VA benefits regardless of action taken by discharge review boards unless VA determines there were compelling circumstances for the absence. Boards for the correction of military records also may consider such cases.

Veterans with disabilities incurred or aggravated during active military service may qualify for medical or related benefits regardless of separation and characterization of service. Veterans separated administratively under other than honorable conditions may request that their discharge be reviewed for possible recharacterization, provided they file their appeal within 15 years of the date of separation. Questions regarding the review of a discharge should be addressed to the appropriate discharge review board at the address listed on DoD Form 293.

Jurisdiction

Correction boards are empowered to deal with all matters relating to error or injustice in official records. The boards cannot act until all other administrative avenues of relief have been exhausted. Discharges by sentence of Special Court-Martial and administrative discharges cannot be considered by correction boards unless:

- Application to the appropriate Discharge Review Board has been denied and rehearing is barred; or
- Application cannot be made to the Discharge Review Board because the time limit has expired.

Application

DD Form 149, Application for Correction of Military or Naval record, must be used to apply for the correction of military records. It should be submitted, along with supporting evidence, to one of the review boards listed below:

Army
Army Review Boards Agency (ARBA)
ATTN: Client Information and Quality Assurance
251 18th Street South, Suite 385
Arlington, VA 22202

Navy & Marine Corps
Board for Correction of Naval Records
701 S. Courthouse Road
Bldg 12, Suite 1001
Arlington, VA 22204-2490
(703) 604-6884

Coast Guard
DHS Office of the General Counsel
Board for Correction of Military Records
245 Murray Lane, Stop 0485
Washington, DC 20528
(202) 447-4099

Air Force
Board for Correction of Air Force Records
SAF/MRBR
550-C Street West, Suite 40
Randolph AFB, TX 78150-4742

Decisions

In the absence of new and material evidence the decision of a correction board, as approved or modified by the Secretary of the Service Department, is final. Adverse decisions are subject to judicial review in a U.S. District Court. Decisions of the Boards for Correction of Military or Naval Records must be made available for public inspection. Copies of the decisional documents will be provided on request.

CHAPTER 41

DISCHARGE REVIEW

Discharge Review Boards

Each branch of service has discharge review boards to review the discharge or dismissal of former service members. (The Navy Board considers Marine Corps cases.)

Online Tool for Discharge Upgrade Process

The Department of Defense (DoD), through a joint program with the VA, has launched a new web-based tool that provides customized guidance to veterans who want to upgrade or change the conditions of their military discharge.

By answering questions, veterans can receive information on the specific armed services board to contact, the forms to fill out, special guidance applicable to their case, where to send their application, and helpful tips for appealing their discharge.

The military has estimated that tens of thousands of veterans with less than honorable discharges are especially likely to have unjust discharges deserving of upgrades. These are veterans who were discharged due to incidents relating to post-traumatic stress disorder, traumatic brain injury or sexual orientation. Fragmented and confusing information has historically deterred

> **Key Takeaways**
> All branches of the military consider you to have a strong case for a discharge upgrade if you can show your discharge was connected to any of these categories:
> Mental health conditions, including posttraumatic stress disorder (PTSD)
> Traumatic brain injury (TBI)
> Sexual assault or harassment during military service (at VA, we refer to this as military sexual trauma or MST)
> Sexual orientation (including under the Don't Ask, Don't Tell policy)

veterans from obtaining crucial information and — in many cases — necessary benefits.

The discharge upgrade tool is available at https://www.vets.gov/discharge-upgrade-instructions.

Consideration for Veterans' Discharge Upgrade Requests

The Defense Department released guidance in 2017 to clarify the liberal consideration given to veterans who request upgrades of their discharge saying they had mental health conditions or were victims of sexual assault or sexual harassment.

The new guidance clarifies that the liberal consideration policy includes conditions resulting from post-traumatic stress disorder, traumatic brain injury, sexual assault or sexual harassment.

The policy is meant to ease the burden on veterans and give them a reasonable opportunity to establish the extenuating circumstances of their discharge.

Under new guidance, the following are some of the key things involved in discharge relief:

- Evidence may come from sources other than a veteran's service record and may include records from the DoD Sexual Assault Prevention and Response Program (DD Form 2910, Victim Reporting Preference Statement), and/or DD Form 2911 (DoD Sexual Assault Forensic SAFE Report), law enforcement authorities, rape crisis centers, mental health counseling centers, hospitals, physicians, pregnancy tests, tests for sexually transmitted diseases, and statements from family members, friends, roommates, co-workers, fellow servicemembers, or clergy.
- Evidence may also include changes in behavior, requests for transfer to another military duty assignment, deterioration in performance, inability of the individual to conform their behavior to the expectations of a military environment, substance abuse, periods of depression, panic attacks or anxiety without an identifiable cause, unexplained economic or social behavior changes, relationship issues or sexual dysfunction
- Evidence of misconduct, including any misconduct underlying a veteran's discharge may be evidence of a mental health condition, including PTSD, TBI or of behavior consistent with experiencing sexual assault or sexual harassment
- The veteran's testimony alone, written or oral, may establish the existence of a condition or experience, that the condition or experience existing during or was aggravated by military service, and that the condition or experience causes or mitigates the discharge

- Absent clear evidence to the contrary, a diagnosis from a licensed psychiatrist or psychologist is evidence the veteran had a condition that could excuse or mitigate the discharge
- Evidence that may reasonably support more than one diagnosis should be liberally considered as supporting a diagnosis, where applicable, that could excuse or mitigate the discharge
- A veteran asserting a mental health condition without a corresponding diagnosis of such condition from a licensed psychiatrist or psychologist will receive liberal consideration of evidence that may support the evidence of such a condition
- Review Boards are not required to find that a crime of sexual assault or an incident of sexual harassment occurred in order to grant liberal consideration to a veteran that the experience happened during military service, was aggravated by military service, or that it excuses or mitigates the discharge

Authority

Discharge review boards can based on the official records and such other evidence as may be presented, upgrade a discharge or change the reason and authority for discharge. Discharge review boards cannot grant disability retirement, revoke a discharge, reinstate any person in the service, recall any person to active duty, act on requests for re-enlistment code changes or review a discharge issued by sentence of a general court-martial. Discharge review boards have no authority to address medical discharges.

Discharges awarded as a result of a continuous period of unauthorized absence in excess of 180 days make persons ineligible for VA benefits regardless of action taken by discharge review boards, unless VA determines there were compelling circumstances for the absence. Boards for the correction of military records also may consider such cases.

Application

DD Form 293, "Application for Review of Discharge or Dismissal from the Armed Forces of the United States," is used to apply for review of discharge. (If more than 15 years have passed since discharge, DD Form 149 should be used.) The individual or, if legal proof of death is provided, the surviving spouse, next-of-kin, or legal representative can apply. If the individual is mentally incompetent, the spouse, next-of-kin, or legal representative can sign the application, but must provide legal proof of incompetence. The instruction for completing DD Form 293 must be read and complied with.

Time Limitation

Initial application to a discharge review board must be made within 15 years after the date of discharge.

514

Personal Appearance

A personal appearance before the Discharge Review Board is a legal right. A minimum 30-day notice of the scheduled hearing date is given unless the applicant waives the advance notice in writing. Reasonable postponements can be arranged if circumstances preclude appearance on the scheduled date. All expenses of appearing before the board must be paid by the applicant. If no postponement of a scheduled hearing date is requested and the applicant does not appear on the date scheduled, the right to a personal hearing is forfeited and the case will be considered on the evidence of record.

Hearings

Discharge review boards conduct hearings at various locations in the U.S. Information concerning hearing locations and availability of counsel can be obtained by writing to the appropriate board at the address shown on DD Form 293. Those addresses are listed at the end of this chapter.

Published Uniform Standards for Discharge Review

A review of discharge is conducted to determine if an individual was properly and equitably discharged. Each case is considered on its own merits. A discharge is considered to have been proper unless the discharge review determines:

- That there is an error of fact, law, procedures, or discretion which prejudiced the rights of the individual, or
- That there has been a change of policy which requires a change of discharge

A discharge is considered to have been equitable unless the discharge review determines:

- That the policies and procedures under which the individual was discharged are materially different from current policies and procedures and that the individual probably would have received a better discharge if the current policies and procedures had been in effect at the time of discharge; or
- That the discharge was inconsistent with the standards of discipline; or
- That the overall evidence before the review board warrants a change of discharge. In arriving at this determination, the discharge review board will consider the quality and the length of the service performed, the individual's physical and mental capability to serve satisfactorily, abuses of authority which may have contributed to the character of the discharge issued, and documented discriminatory acts against the individual.

An authenticated decisional document is prepared and a copy provided to each applicant and council. A copy of each decisional document, with identifying details of the applicant and other persons deleted to protect personal privacy, must be made available for public inspection and copying. These are located in a reading room in the Pentagon, Washington, DC.

To provide access to the documents by persons outside the Washington, D.C. area, the documents have been indexed. The index includes case number of each case;

the date, authority and reason for, and character if the discharge, and the issues addressed in the statement of findings, conclusions and reasons.

Interested parties may contact the DVARO or the State veterans Agency for the location of an index. A copy of the index will be made available at the sites of traveling board hearings during the period the board is present.

An individual can go through the index and identify cases in which the circumstances leading to discharge are similar to those in the individual's case. A copy of these case decisional documents can be requested by writing to:

DA Military Review Boards Agency
ATTN: SFBA (Reading Room) Room 1E520
The Pentagon Washington, D.C. 20310

Examination of decisional documents may help to identify the kind of evidence that was used in the case, and may indicate why relief was granted or denied. Decisional documents do not set precedence - each case is considered on its own merits.

Reconsideration
An application that has been denied can be reopened if:

- The applicant submits newly discovered evidence that was not available at the time of the original consideration.
- The applicant did not request a personal hearing in the original application and now desires to appear before the board. If the applicant fails to appear at the hearings, the case will be closed with no further action.
- The applicant was not represented by counsel in the original consideration and now desires counsel and the application for reconsideration is submitted within 15 years following the date of discharge.
- Changes in policy, law or regulations have occurred or federal court orders have been issued which substantially enhances the rights of the applicant.

Service Department Discharge Review Board Addresses
Army
ARMY DISCHARGE REVIEW BOARD
Attention: SFMR-RBB
251 18th St. South Suite 385
Arlington, VA 22202-4508

Navy & USMC
Secretary of the Navy Council of Review Boards
720 Kennon St. SE Suite 309
Washington, DC 20374

Air Force
Air Force Military Personnel Center Attention: DP-MDOA1
Randolph AFB, TX 78150-6001

Coast Guard
DHS Office of the General Counsel Board for Correction of Military Records
Mailstop # 485
245 Murray Lane
Washington, DC 20528

CHAPTER 42

PENAL AND FORFEITURE PROVISIONS

The first section of this chapter outlines basic information for veterans with questions concerning the effect of incarceration on VA benefits. The later sections of this chapter provide detailed information regarding misappropriation by fiduciaries, fraudulent acceptance of payments, forfeiture for fraud, forfeiture for treason, and forfeiture for subversive activities.

> **Key Takeaways**
>
> VA benefits are restricted if a veteran, surviving spouse, dependent parent or child is convicted of a felony and imprisoned more than 60 days.
>
> Any person who fraudulently accepts money is fined or may be imprisoned for a maximum of one year.

Basic Information

VA benefits are restricted if a veteran, surviving spouse, child, or dependent parent is convicted of a felony and imprisoned for more than 60 days. VA may still pay certain benefits, however, the amount paid depends on the type of benefit and reason for imprisonment. Following is information about the benefits most commonly affected by imprisonment.

Please note that overpayments due to failure to notify VA of a veteran's incarceration results in the loss of all financial benefits until the overpayment is recovered.

VA Disability Compensation

VA disability compensation payments are reduced if a veteran is convicted of a felony and imprisoned for more than 60 days. Veterans rated 20 percent or more are limited to the 10 percent disability rate. For a veteran whose disability rating is 10 percent, the payment is reduced by one-half. Once a veteran is released from prison, compensation payments may be reinstated based upon the severity of the service-connected disability(ies) at that time.

The disability compensation paid to a veteran incarcerated because of a felony is limited to the 10% disability rate, beginning with the 61st day of imprisonment. For a surviving spouse, child, dependent parent or veteran whose disability rating is 10%, the payment is at the 5% rate. This means that if a veteran was receiving $188 or more prior to incarceration, the new payment amount will be $98. If a veteran was receiving $98 before incarceration, the new payment amount will be $49.

If a veteran resides in a halfway house, participates in a work release program, or is on parole, compensation payments will not be reduced.

*Increased compensation during incarceration - the amount of any increased compensation awarded to an incarcerated veteran that results from other than a statutory rate increase may be subject to reduction due to incarceration.

VA Disability Pension
VA will stop a veteran's pension payments beginning on the 61st day of imprisonment for conviction of either a felony or misdemeanor. Payments may be resumed upon release from prison if the veteran meets VA eligibility requirements.

VA Medical Care

While incarcerated veterans do not forfeit their eligibility for medical care, current regulations restrict VA from providing hospital and outpatient care to an incarcerated veteran who is an inmate in an institution of another government agency when that agency has a duty to give the care or services.

However, VA may provide care once the veteran has been unconditionally released from the penal institution. Veterans interested in applying for enrollment into the VA health care system should contact the nearest VA health care facility upon their release.

Educational Assistance / Subsistence Allowance
Beneficiaries incarcerated for other than a felony can receive full monthly benefits, if otherwise entitled. Convicted felons residing in halfway houses (also known as "residential re-entry centers") or participating in work-release programs also can receive full monthly benefits.

Claimants incarcerated for a felony conviction can be paid only the costs of tuition, fees, and necessary books, equipment, and supplies.

VA cannot make payments for tuition, fees, books, equipment, or supplies if another Federal State, or local program pays these costs in full.

If another government program pays only a part of the cost of tuition, fees, books, equipment, or supplies, VA can authorize the incarcerated claimant payment for the remaining part of the costs.

Clothing Allowance

In the case of a veteran who is incarcerated in a Federal, State, or local penal institution for a period in excess of 60 days and who is furnished clothing without charge by the institution, the amount of any annual clothing allowance payable to the veteran shall be reduced by an amount equal to 1/365 of the amount of the allowance otherwise payable under that section for each day on which the veteran was so incarcerated during the 12- month period preceding the date on which payment of the allowance would be due.

Payments to Dependents

VA may be able to take part of the amount that the incarcerated veteran is not receiving and pay it to his or her dependents, if they can show need. Interested dependents should contact the nearest VA regional office for details on how to apply. They will be asked to provide income information as part of the application process.

VA will inform a veteran whose benefits are subject to reduction of the right of the veteran's dependents to an apportionment while the veteran is incarcerated, and the conditions under which payments to the veteran may be resumed upon release from incarceration.

VA will also notify the dependents of their right to an apportionment if the VA is aware of their existence and can obtain their addresses.

No apportionment may be made to or on behalf of any person who is incarcerated in a Federal, State, or local penal institution for conviction of a felony.

An apportionment of an incarcerated veteran's VA benefits is not granted automatically to the veteran's dependents. The dependent(s) must file a claim for an apportionment.

Restoration of Benefits

When a veteran is released from prison, his or her compensation or pension benefits may be restored. Depending on the type of disability, the VA may schedule a medical examination to see if the veteran's disability has improved or worsened.

Misappropriation by Fiduciaries

Whoever, being a guardian, curator, conservator, committee, or person legally vested with the responsibility or care of a claimant or a claimant's estate, or any other person having charge and custody in a fiduciary capacity of money heretofore or hereafter paid under any of the laws administered by the VA for the benefit of any minor, incompetent, or other beneficiary, shall lend, borrow, pledge, hypothecate, use, or exchange for other funds or property, except as authorized by law, or embezzle or in any manner misappropriate any such money or property derived wherefrom in whole or in part, and coming into such fiduciary's control in any matter whatever in the execution of such fiduciary's trust, or under color of such fiduciary's office or service as such fiduciary, shall be fined in accordance with Title 18, or imprisoned not more than 5 years, or both.

Any willful neglect or refusal to make and file proper accountings or reports concerning such money or property as required by law shall be taken to be sufficient evidence prima facie of such embezzlement or misappropriation.

Fraudulent Acceptance of Payments

Any person entitled to monetary benefits under any of the laws administered by the VA whose right to payment ceases upon the happening of any contingency, who thereafter fraudulently accepts any such payment, shall be fined in accordance with Title 18, or imprisoned not more than one year, or both.

Whoever obtains or receives any money or check under any of the laws administered by the VA without being entitled to it, and with intent to defraud the United States or any beneficiary of the United States, shall be fined in accordance with Title 18, or imprisoned not more than one year, or both.

Forfeiture for Fraud

Whoever knowingly makes or causes to be made or conspires, combines, aids, or assists in, agrees to, arranges for, or in any way procures the making or presentation of a false or fraudulent affidavit, declaration, certificate, statement, voucher, or paper, concerning any claim for benefits under any of the laws administered by the VA (except laws pertaining to insurance benefits) shall forfeit all rights, claims, and benefits under all laws administered by the VA (except laws pertaining to insurance benefits).

Whenever a veteran entitled to disability compensation has forfeited the right to such compensation under this chapter, the compensation payable but for the forfeiture shall thereafter be paid to the veteran's spouse, children, and parents. Payments made to a spouse, children, and parents under the preceding sentence shall not exceed the amounts payable to each if the veteran had died from service-connected disability. No spouse, child, or parent who participated in the fraud for which forfeiture was imposed shall receive any payment by reason of this subsection. Any apportionment award under this subsection may not be made in any case after September 1, 1959.

Forfeiture of benefits by a veteran shall not prohibit payment of the burial allowance, death compensation, dependency and indemnity compensation, or death pension in the event of the veteran's death.

After September 1, 1959, no forfeiture of benefits may be imposed under the rules outlined in this chapter upon any individual who was a resident of, or domiciled in, a State at the time the act or acts occurred on account of which benefits would, but not for this subsection, be forfeited unless such individual ceases to be a resident of, or domiciled in, a State before the expiration of the period during which criminal prosecution could be instituted. The paragraph shall not apply with respect to:

- Any forfeiture occurring before September 1, 1959; or
- An act or acts that occurred in the Philippine Islands before July 4, 1946.

The VA is authorized and directed to review all cases in which, because of a false or fraudulent affidavit, declaration, certificate, statement, voucher, or paper, a forfeiture of gratuitous benefits under laws administered by the VA was imposed, pursuant to this section or prior provisions of the law, on or before September 1, 1959. In any such case in which the VA determines that the forfeiture would not have been imposed under the provisions of this section in effect after September 1, 1959, the VA shall remit the forfeiture, effective June 30, 1972. Benefits to which the individual concerned becomes eligible by virtue of any such remission may be awarded, upon application for, and the effective date of any award of compensation, dependency and indemnity compensation, or pension made in such a case shall be fixed in accordance with the facts found, but shall not be earlier than the effective date of the Act or administrative issue. In no event shall such award or increase be retroactive for more than one year from the date of application, or the date of administrative determination of entitlement, whichever is earlier.

Forfeiture for Treason

Any person shown by evidence satisfactory to the VA to be guilty of mutiny, treason, sabotage, or rendering assistance to an enemy of the United States or its allies shall forfeit all accrued or future gratuitous benefits under laws administered by the VA.

The VA, in its discretion, may apportion and pay any part of benefits forfeited under the preceding paragraph to the dependents of the person forfeiting such benefits. No dependent of any person shall receive benefits by reason of this subsection in excess of the amount to which the dependent would be entitled if such person were dead.

In the case of any forfeiture under this chapter, there shall be no authority after September 1, 1959 to:

- Make an apportionment award pursuant to the preceding paragraph; or
- Make an award to any person of gratuitous benefits based on any period of military, naval, or air service commencing before the date of commission of the offense.

Forfeiture for Subversive Activities

Any individual who is convicted after September 1, 1959, of any offense listed below shall, from and after the date of commission of such offense, have no right to gratuitous benefits (including the right to burial in a national cemetery) under laws administered by the VA based on periods of military, naval, or air service commencing before the date of commission of such offense, and no other person shall be entitled to such benefits on account of such individual. After receipt of notice of the return of an indictment for such an offense, the VA shall suspend payment of such gratuitous benefits pending disposition of the criminal proceedings. If any individual whose rights to benefits has been terminated pursuant to this section, is granted a pardon of the offense by the President of the United States, the right to such benefits shall be restored as of the date of such pardon.

The offenses referred to in the previous paragraph are:

Sections 894, 904 and 906 of Title 10 (articles 94, 104, and 106 of the Uniform Code of Military Justice);

Sections 792, 793, 794, 798, 2381, 2382, 2383, 2384, 2385, 2387, 2388, 2389, 2390, and chapter 105 of Title 18;

Sections 222, 223, 224, 225 and 226 of the Atomic Energy Act of 1954 (42 U.S.C. 2272, 2273, 2274, 2275, and 2276);

Section 4 of the Internal Security Act of 1950 (50 U.S.C. 783).

The Secretary of Defense, the Secretary of Transportation, or the Attorney General, as appropriate, shall notify the VA in each case in which an individual is convicted of an offense mentioned in this chapter.

CHAPTER 43

PERIODS OF WAR

Military service is classified either as wartime or peacetime service. This is important because there are significant advantages specifically accruing only to veterans with wartime service. The following list sets out the periods of wartime designated by Congress for pension purposes. To be considered by the VA to have served during wartime, a veteran need not have served in a combat zone, but simply during one of these designated periods.

Indian Wars:
The period January 1, 1817 through December 31, 1898. Service must have been rendered with the United States military forces against Indian tribes or nations.

Spanish-American War:
The period April 21, 1898 through July 4, 1902. In the case of a veteran who served with the United States military forces engaged in hostilities in the Moro Province the ending date is July 15, 1903.

Mexican Border Period:
The period May 9, 1916 through April 5, 1917, in the case of a veteran who during such period served in Mexico, on the borders thereof, or in the waters adjacent thereto.

World War I:
The period April 6, 1917, through November 11, 1918. In the case of a veteran who served with the United States military forces in Russia, the ending date is April 1, 1920. Service after November 11, 1918 and before July 2, 1921 is considered World War I for compensation or pension purposes, if the veteran served in the active military, naval, or air service after April 5, 1917 and before November 12, 1918.

World War II:
The period December 7, 1941 through December 31, 1946. If the veteran was in service on December 31, 1946, continuous service before July 26, 1947 is considered World War II service.

Korean Conflict:
The period June 27, 1950 through January 31, 1955.

Vietnam Era:
The period August 5, 1964 (February 28, 1961 for Veterans who served "in country" before August 5, 1964), and ending May 7, 1975.

Persian Gulf War:

The period August 2, 1990 through a date to be set by law or Presidential Proclamation.

Future Dates:

The period beginning on the date of any future declaration of war by the Congress, and ending on a date prescribed by Presidential Proclamation or concurrent resolution of the Congress. (Title U.S.C. 10)

CHAPTER 44

COMMON FORMS

General Administration Forms		
Form #	**Purpose**	
20-572	Request For Change Of Address / Cancellation Of Direct Deposit	
Compensation and Pension Forms		
Form #	**Purpose**	
21-22	Appointment Of Veterans Service Organization As Claimant's Representative	
21-0304	Application For Spina Bifida Benefits	
21P-534EZ	Application for DIC, Death Pension, and/or Accrued Benefits	
21-526EZ	Application for Disability Compensation Benefits	
21-526c	Pre-Discharge Compensation Claim	
21P-527EZ	Application for Pension	
21P-530	Application for Burial Benefits	
21P-601	Application for Accrued Amounts Due a Deceased Beneficiary	
21-686c	Declaration of Status of Dependents	
Form 9	Appeal to Board of Veterans Appeals	
21-0958	Notice of Disagreement	
21-0966	Intent to File a VA Claim	
21-2680	Request for Aid and Attendance/Housebound Status	
21-4138	Statement in Support of Claim	
21-4142	Authorization for Release of Information	

21-8940	Application for Increased Compensation Due Unemployability

Vocational Rehabilitation and Employment Forms	
Form #	Purpose
22-1190	Application for VA Education Benefits
22-5490	Dependent's Application for VA Education Benefits
28-1900	Disabled Veterans Application for Vocational Rehabilitation

VA Insurance Forms	
Form #	Purpose
29-336	Designation Of Beneficiary – Government Life Insurance
29-1546	Application For Cash Surrender Value / Application For Policy Loan
29-4125	Claim For One Sum Payment
29-4364	Application For Service-Disabled Insurance

Finance and Budget Forms	
Form #	Purpose
24-0296	Direct Deposit Enrollment

Miscellaneous Forms	
Form #	Purpose
DD 149	Application For Correction Of Military Record
DD 214	Report of Separation From Active Duty
DD 293	Application For The Review Of Discharge OR Dismissal From The Armed Forces Of The United States
SF 15	Application For 10-Point Veteran's Preference
SF 180	Request Pertaining To Military Records
SGLV8283	Claim For Death Benefits – Form Returned To Office Of Servicemembers' Group Life Insurance
SGLV8285	Request For Insurance (Servicemembers' Group Life Insurance)
SGLV8286	Servicemembers' Group Life Insurance Election And Certificate
SGLV8714	Application For Veterans' Group Life Insurance
VAF 8	Certification To Appeal

VAF 9	Appeal To Board Of Veterans' Appeals
10 –10ez	Instructions For Completing Application For Health Benefits
VAF 3288	Request For And Consent To Release Of Information From Claimant's Records
VAF 4107	Notice Of Procedural And Appellate Rights
VAF 4107b	Notice Of Procedural And Appellate Rights (Spanish Version)
40-1330M	Application For Standard Government Headstone Or Marker For Installation In A Private Or State Veterans' Cemetery

Discharge Documents
DD214 and Other Department of Defense Documents

Form	Title
DD 214	Certificate of Release or Discharge from Active Duty
DD 13	Statement of Service
DA 1569	Transcript of Military Record
DD 2A	Armed Forces Identification Card (Active)
DD 2AF	Armed Forces Identification Card (Active)
DD 2CG	Armed Forces Identification Card (Active)
DD 2MC	Armed Forces Identification Card (Active)
DD 2N	Armed Forces Identification Card (Active)
DD 2NOAA	Armed Forces Identification Card (Active)
DD 2 (Retired)	US Uniformed Services Identification Card
DD 214	Certificate of Release or Discharge from Active Duty
DD 217	Discharge Certificate
DD 303	Certificate in Lieu of Lost or Destroyed Discharge
DD 303AF	Certificate in Lieu of Lost or Destroyed Discharge
DD 303CG	Certificate in Lieu of Lost or Destroyed Discharge
DD 303MC	Certificate in Lieu of Lost or Destroyed Discharge
DD 303N	Certificate in Lieu of Lost or Destroyed Discharge
DD 1300	Report of Casualty

CHAPTER 45

APPLICATION AND CHARACTER OF DISCHARGE

Applying for Benefits and Your Character of Discharge

Generally, in order to receive VA benefits and services, the Veteran's character of discharge or service must be under other than dishonorable conditions (e.g., honorable, under honorable conditions, general). However, individuals receiving undesirable, bad conduct, and other types of dishonorable discharges may qualify for VA benefits depending on a determination made by VA.

Basic eligibility for Department of Veterans Affairs (VA) benefits depends upon the type of military service performed, the duration of the service, and the character of discharge or separation. VA looks at the "character of discharge" to determine whether a person meets the basic eligibility requirements for receipt of VA benefits under title 38 of the United States Code. Any discharge under honorable conditions satisfies the character of discharge requirement for basic eligibility for VA benefits. Certain types of discharges, along with the circumstances surrounding those discharges, bar an individual from basic eligibility for VA benefits. Other types of discharges require VA to make a character of discharge determination in order to assess basic eligibility for VA benefits.

> **Key Takeaways**
>
> Generally, to receive VA benefits and services the veteran's character of discharge must be under other than honorable discharge.
>
> Discharge requirements for compensation benefits and services include discharge under other than dishonorable conditions including honorable, under honorable conditions, or general.

Under the law (38 U.S.C. § 5303), a release or discharge for any of the following reasons constitutes a statutory bar to benefits, unless it is determined that the Servicemember was insane at the time he/she committed the offense that resulted in the discharge:

- Sentence of a general court-martial
- Being a conscientious objector who refused to perform military duty, wear the uniform, or otherwise comply with lawful orders of competent military authority
- Desertion
- Absence without official leave (AWOL) for a continuous period of 180 days or more, without compelling circumstances to warrant such prolonged unauthorized absence (as determined by VA)
- Requesting release from service as an alien during a period of hostilities, or This means that if an individual is discharged for any of the above reasons, the law prohibits VA from providing any benefits
- Resignation by an officer for the good of the service

VA reviews military service records, including facts and circumstances surrounding the incident(s) leading to the discharge. VA also considers the following when making its determination:

- Any mitigating or extenuating circumstances presented by the claimant
- Any supporting evidence provided by third parties who were familiar with the circumstances surrounding the incident(s) in question
- Length of service
- Performance and accomplishments during service
- Nature of the infraction(s), and
- Character of service preceding the incident(s) resulting in the discharge.

VA considers whether an individual was insane when determining whether a statutory bar to benefits exists. When no statutory bar to benefits exists, the impact of disabilities may be considered during the analysis of any mitigating or extenuating circumstances that may have contributed to the discharge.

Specific Benefit Program Character of Discharge Requirements

Compensation Benefits

To receive VA compensation benefits and services, the Veteran's character of discharge or service must be under other tan dishonorable conditions (e.g., honorable, under honorable conditions, general).

Education Benefits

To receive VA education benefits and services through the Montgomery GI Bill program or Post-9/11 GI Bill program, the Veteran's character of discharge or service must be honorable.

To receive VA education benefits and services through any other VA educational benefits program, including the Survivors' and Dependents' Educational Assistance (DEA) program, the Veteran's character of discharge or service must be under other than dishonorable conditions (e.g., honorable, under honorable conditions, general).

Home Loan Benefits

To receive VA home loan benefits and services, the Veteran's character of discharge or service must be under other than dishonorable conditions (e.g., honorable, under honorable conditions, general).

Insurance Benefits

Generally, there is no character of discharge bar to benefits to Veterans' Group Life Insurance. However, for Service-Disabled Veterans Insurance and Veterans' Mortgage Life Insurance benefits, the Veteran's character of discharge must be other than dishonorable.

Pension Benefits

To receive VA pension benefits and services, the Veteran's character of discharge or service must be under other than dishonorable conditions (e.g., honorable, under honorable conditions, general).

Review of Discharge from Military Service

Each of the military services maintains a discharge review board with authority to change, correct or modify discharges or dismissals not issued by a sentence of a general court- martial. The board has no authority to address medical discharges.

The Veteran or, if the Veteran is deceased or incompetent, the surviving spouse, next of kin or legal representative, may apply for a review of discharge by writing to the military department concerned, using DD Form 293, "Application for the Review of Discharge from the Armed Forces of the United States." This form may be obtained at a VA regional office, or from Veterans organizations.

However, if the discharge was more than 15 years ago, a Veteran must petition the appropriate Service's Board for Correction of Military Records using DD Form 149, "Application for Correction of Military Records Under the Provisions of Title 10, U.S. Code, Section 1552." A discharge review is conducted by a review of an applicant's record and, if requested, by a hearing before the board.

Discharge Related to Mental Health Conditions, Sexual Assault, or Sexual Harassment

In December 2016, the Department announced a renewed effort to ensure that veterans are aware of the opportunity to have discharges and military records reviewed. Following a review, it was determined that clarifications were needed regarding mental health conditions, sexual assault and sexual harassment. New guidance was issued.

Clarifying Guidance to Military Discharge Review Boards and Boards for Correction Requests by Veterans for Modification of Their Discharge Due to Mental Health Conditions, Traumatic Brain Injury, Sexual Assault or Sexual Harassment

Requests for discharge relief usually involve four questions, which include:
- Did the veteran have a condition or experience that may excuse or mitigate the discharge?
- Did that condition exist/experience occur during military service?
- Does that condition or experience actually excuse or mitigate the discharge?
- Does that condition or experience outweigh the discharge?

Liberal consideration will be given to veterans for petitioning for discharge relief when the application for relief is based in whole or in part on matters relating to mental health conditions including PTSD, TBI, sexual assault or sexual harassment.

Evidence may come from sources other than a veteran's service record and may include records from the DoD Sexual Assault Prevention and Response Program (DD Form 2910, Victim Reporting Preference Statement) and/or DD Form 2911, DoD Sexual Assault Forensic Examination (SAFE) Report, law enforcement authorities, rape crisis centers, mental health and counseling centers, hospitals, physicians, pregnancy tests, tests for sexually transmitted diseases and statements from family members, friends, roommates, co-workers, and fellow servicemembers or clergy.

Evidence may also include changes in behavior, requests for transfer to another military assignment, deterioration in work performance, inability of the individual to conform their behavior to expectations of a military environment, substance abuse, episodes of depression or panic attacks, anxiety without an identifiable cause, unexplained economic or social behavior changes, relationship issues, or sexual dysfunction.

Evidence of misconduct, including any misconduct underlying a veteran's discharge may be evidence of a mental health condition, including PTSD, TBI or behavior consistent with experience sexual assault or sexual harassment.

The veteran's testimony alone, oral or written, may establish the existence of a condition or experience, that the condition or experience existed during or was aggravated by military service, and that the condition or experience excuses or mitigates the discharge.

The Department of Defense today announced a renewed effort to ensure veterans are aware of the opportunity to have their discharges and military records reviewed. Through enhanced public outreach, engagement with Veterans Service Organizations (VSOs), Military Service Organizations (MSOs), and other outside groups, as well as direct outreach to individual veterans, the department encourages all veterans who believe they have experienced an error or injustice to request relief from their service's Board for Correction of Military/Naval Records (BCM/NR) or Discharge Review Board (DRB).

Additionally, all veterans, VSOs, MSOs, and other interested organizations are invited to offer feedback on their experiences with the BCM/NR or DRB processes, including how the policies and processes can be improved.

In the past few years, the department has issued guidance for consideration of post-traumatic stress disorder (PTSD), as well as the repealed "Don't Ask, Don't Tell" and its predecessor policies. Additionally, supplemental guidance for separations involving victims of sexual assault is currently being considered.

The department is reviewing and consolidating all of the related policies to reinforce the department's commitment to ensuring fair and equitable review of separations for all veterans. Whether the discharge or other correction is the result of PTSD, sexual orientation, sexual assault, or some other consideration, the department is committed to rectifying errors or injustices and treating all veterans with dignity and respect.

To request an upgrade or correction:
Veterans who desire a correction to their service record or who believe their discharge was unjust, erroneous, or warrants an upgrade, are encouraged to apply for review.

For discharge upgrades, if the discharge was less than 15 years ago, the veteran should complete DD Form 293 and send it to their service's DRB (the address is on the form). For discharges over 15 years ago, the veteran should complete the DD Form 149 and send it to their service's BCM/NR (the address is on the form).

For corrections of records other than discharges, veterans should complete the DD Form 149 and submit their request to their service's BCM/NR (the address is on the form).

Key information to include in requests:
There are three keys to successful applications for upgrade or correction. First, it is very important to explain why the veteran's discharge or other record was unjust or erroneous—for example, how it is connected to, or resulted from unjust policies, a physical or mental health condition related to military service, or some other explainable or justifiable circumstance.

Second, it is important to provide support, where applicable, for key facts. If a veteran has a relevant medical diagnosis, for example, it would be very helpful to include medical records that reflect that diagnosis.

Third, it is helpful, but not always required, to submit copies of the veteran's applicable service records. The more information provided, the better the boards can understand the circumstances of the discharge.

BCM/NRs are also authorized to grant relief on the basis of clemency. Veterans who believe their post-service conduct and contributions to society support an upgrade or correction should describe their post-service activity and provide any appropriate letters or other documentation of support.

Personnel records for veterans who served after 1997 should be accessible online and are usually retrievable within hours of a request through the Defense Personnel Records Information Retrieval System (DPRIS). Those who served prior to 1997 or for whom electronic records are not available from DPRIS, can request their records from the National Personnel Records Center (NPRC).

CHAPTER 46

VETERAN ENTREPRENEURSHIP

According to data from the U.S. Small Business Administration (SBA), there is about one veteran-owned firm for every ten veterans. Veteran-owned firms employ 5.8 million individuals. A recent SBA study also found that military service exhibits one of the largest effects on self-employment. Veterans are 45 percent more likely to be self-employed than non-veterans.

Resources

The office of Veterans Business Development's mission is to maximize the availability, applicability and usability of all administration small business programs for veterans, service-disabled veterans, reserve component members and their dependents or survivors.

OVBD is SBA's liaison with the veterans' business community; provides policy analysis and reporting, and is as an Ombudsman for veteran entrepreneurs. OVBD has a number of programs and services to assist aspiring and existing veteran entrepreneurs such as training, counseling and mentorship, and oversight of Federal procurement programs for Veteran-Owned and Service-Disabled Veteran-Owned Small Businesses.

> **Key Takeaways**
>
> Federal, private and non-profit resources are available for veterans who want to start a business.
>
> The VA works with the Small Business Administration on Funding and other resources for veteran entrepreneurs.
>
> The Veteran Entrepreneur portal is also available from the VA and it serves as a way for veterans to get streamlined access to resources related to beginning or growing a business.

Veterans Business Outreach Center

The Veterans Business Outreach Center (VBOC) Program is designed to provide entrepreneurial development services such as business training, counseling and resource partner referrals to transitioning service members, veterans, National Guard & Reserve members and military spouses interested in starting or growing a small business. The SBA has 22 organizations participating in this cooperative agreement and serving as Veterans Business Outreach Centers (VBOC).

Services Provided by the Centers

Pre-Business Plan Workshops

VBOCs conduct entrepreneurial development workshops dealing specifically with the major issues of self-employment. An important segment of these workshops entails the usage of the Internet as a tool for developing and expanding businesses. Each client is afforded the opportunity to work directly with a business counselor.

Concept Assessments

VBOCs assist clients in assessing their entrepreneurial needs and requirements.

Business Plan Preparations

VBOCs assist clients in developing and maintaining a five-year business plan. The business plan includes such elements as the legal form of the business, equipment requirements and cost, organizational structure, a strategic plan, market analysis, and a financial plan. Financial plans include financial projections, budget projections, and funding requirements.

Comprehensive Feasibility Analysis

VBOCs provide assistance in identifying and analyzing the strengths and weaknesses of the business plan to increase the probability of success. The results of the analysis are utilized to revise the strategic planning portion of the business plan.

Entrepreneurial Training and Counseling

VBOCs, working with other SBA resource partners, target entrepreneurial training projects and counseling sessions tailored specifically to address the needs and concerns of the service-disabled veteran entrepreneur.

Mentorship

VBOCs conduct, as appropriate, on-site visits with clients to ensure adherence to their business plans. Additionally, VBOCs review monthly financial statements to determine whether a revision of the business plan is warranted or that desired results are being attained.

Other Business Developmental Related Services

VBOCs also provide assistance and training in such areas as international trade, franchising, Internet marketing, accounting, and more.

Center Locations and Areas of Coverage

Region I

- Veterans Business Outreach Center of New England
    - Coverage: Connecticut, Maine, Massachusetts, New Hampshire,

Rhode Island, Vermont
- o Address: 132 George M Cohan Blvd, 2nd Fl, Providence, RI 02903
- o Website: www.VBOCNewEngland.org
- o Telephone: (401) 427-6536
- o Email: koneill@cweonline.org

Region II
- Arsenal Business and Technology Partnership
  - o Coverage: New Jersey, New York, Puerto Rico, U.S. Virgin Islands
  - o Address: 44 Dalliba Ave, Watervliet, NY 12189
  - o Website: www.vbocregion2.com
  - o Telephone: (518) 326-6328
  - o Email: aamoroso@arsenalpartnership.com

Region III
- Old Dominion University Veterans Business Outreach Center
  - o Coverage: Virginia, West Virginia
  - o Address: 4111 Monarch Way, Suite 106, Norfolk, VA 23508
  - o Website: www.odu.edu/vboc
  - o Telephone: (757) 683-5505
  - o Email: d1miller@odu.edu
- Community Business Partnership
  - o Coverage: District of Columbia, Maryland, Northern Virginia, Delaware, Pennsylvania
  - o Address: 6564 Loisdale Court, Suite 600, Springfield, VA 22150
  - o Website: www.cbponline.org
  - o Telephone: (703) 768-1440
  - o Email: charles@cbponline.org

Region IV
- Veterans Business Outreach Center at Gulf Coast State College
  - o Coverage: Florida
  - o Address: 5230 US Hwy 98, Panama City, FL 32401
  - o Website: www.vboc.org
  - o Telephone: (800) 542-7232 | (850) 769-1551, ext. 3327
  - o Email: bpeacock@gulfcoast.edu
- Veterans Business Outreach Center at Fayetteville State University
  - o Coverage: North Carolina
  - o Address: 1200 Murchison Rd, Fayetteville, NC 28301
  - o Website: www.fsuvboc.com
  - o Telephone: (910) 672-2683
  - o Email: tcbryant@uncfsu.edu
- Veterans Business Outreach Center at Pathway Lending
  - o Coverage: Tennessee, Kentucky
  - o Address: 201 Venture Circle, Nashville, TN 37228

- o Website: www.pathwaylending.org/vboc
- o Telephone: (615) 425-7171
- o Email: reggie.ordonez@pathwaylending.org
- Veterans Business Outreach Center at Mississippi State University
  - o Coverage: Alabama, Louisiana, Mississippi
  - o Address: 60 Technology Blvd, Ste 105 D, Starkville, MS 39759
  - o Website: www.vboc.msstate.edu
  - o Telephone: (662) 325-4990
  - o Email: rseitz@business.msstate.edu
- VECTR Center (Veterans Education Career Transition Resource Center – CGTC)
  - o Coverage: Georgia, South Carolina
  - o Address: 1001 S. Armed Forces Blvd., Warner Robins, GA 31088
  - o Website: www.gavectr.org/vboc
  - o Telephone: 1-833-44VECTR (83287)
  - o Email: VBOC@gavectr.org

Region V

- VetBiz Central, Inc
  - o Coverage: Indiana, Michigan, Ohio
  - o Address: 1401 East Court Street, Flint Michigan 48503
  - o Website: www.vetbizcentral.org
  - o Telephone: (810) 767-8387
  - o Email: matt@vetbizcentral.org
- Wisconsin Women's Business Initiative Corporation (WWBIC)
  - o Coverage: Illinois, Minnesota, Wisconsin
  - o Address: 1533 N Rivercenter Dr, Milwaukee, WI 53212
  - o Website: www.wwbic.com
  - o Telephone: (414) 395-4555
  - o Email: lisa.taylor@wwbic.com

Region VI

- Veterans Business Outreach Center at University of Texas Rio Grande Valley
  - o Coverage: Central, West & Southern Texas
  - o Address: 1407 E Freddy Gonzalez Dr, Ste 1200, Edinburg, TX 78539
  - o Website: www.utrgv.edu/vboc
  - o Telephone: (956) 665-8931
  - o Email: juan.santosflores01@utrgv.edu
- Veterans Business Outreach Center at University of Texas Arlington College of Business
  - o Coverage: Arkansas, Northern Texas, Oklahoma
  - o Address: 701 S West St, Ste 635, Arlington, TX 76019
  - o Website: www.uta.edu/vboc
  - o Telephone: (817) 272-6789

- o Email: utavboc@uta.edu
- New Mexico Veterans Business Outreach Center
  - o Coverage: Colorado, New Mexico
  - o Address: 5201 Eagle Rock Ave NE, Ste 2A, Albuquerque, NM 87113
  - o Website: www.nmvboc.org
  - o Telephone: (505) 383-2401
  - o Email: RichardL.Coffel@state.nm.us

Region VII

- Veterans Business Resource Center
  - o Coverage: Iowa, Kansas, Missouri, Nebraska
  - o Addresses:
    - 911 Washington Ave, St. Louis, MO 63101
    - 2700 N 14th St, St. Louis, MO 63106
    - 1000 Walnut 5th Floor, Kansas City, MO 64101
  - o Website: www.vetbiz.com
  - o Telephone: (314) 531-8387 for HQ | (314) 532-8387 for Kansas City ONLY
  - o Fax: (877) 825-4190
  - o Email: Info@vetbiz.com(link sends e-mail)

Region VIII

- Big Sky Economic Development Authority
  - o Coverage: Montana, Utah, Wyoming
  - o Address: 222 N 32nd St, Ste 200, Billings, MT 59101
  - o Website: www.bigskyeconomicdevelopment.org/veterans-business-outreach-centers
  - o Telephone: (406) 869-8411
  - o Email: dustin@bigskyeda.org
- University of North Dakota (UND)
  - o Coverage: North Dakota, South Dakota
  - o Address: 4200 James Ray Dr., Room 203, Stop 8372, Grand Forks, ND 58202
  - o Website: www.und.edu/dakotasvboc
  - o Telephone: (701) 777-3700
  - o Email: dakotas.vboc@und.edu

Region IX

- VBOC IX
  - o Coverage: Nevada, Northern California
  - o Address: 4608 Duckhorn Dr, Sacramento, CA 95834
  - o Website: www.vbocix.org
  - o Telephone: (916) 527-8400
  - o Email: admin@vbocix.org
- SoCal Veterans Business Outreach Center

539

- o Coverage: Southern California
- o Address: 2075 Las Palmas Dr, Carlsbad, CA 92011
- o Website: www.socalvboc.org
- o Telephone: (760) 795-8739
- o Email: socalvboc@miracosta.edu
- A New Leaf, Inc. - AWEEc
  - o Coverage: Arizona
  - o Address: 750 E Bartow Dr., Suite 9, Sierra Vista, AZ 85635
  - o Website: www.aweecenter.org
  - o Telephone: (480) 322-4634
  - o Email: mevangelesta@turnanewleaf.org
- Veterans Business Outreach Center of the Pacific
  - o Coverage: American Samoa, Guam, Hawaii
  - o Address: 2800 Woodlawn Dr, Ste 146, Honolulu, HI 96822
  - o Website: www.hilo.hawaii.edu/vboc
  - o Telephone: (808) 988-1236
  - o Email: vboc@hawaii.edu

Region X
- Business Impact NW
  - o Coverage: Washington, Alaska, Idaho, Oregon
  - o Address: 1437 S Jackson St, Seattle, WA 98144
  - o Website: https://businessimpactnw.org/vboc/
  - o Telephone: (206) 324-4330, ext.136
  - o Email: DomoniqueJ@businessimpactnw.org

VA Entrepreneurship Training

Entrepreneurship training allows eligible service members and veterans to use VA education benefits to take courses offered by the Small Business Development Centers (SBDCs). Individual courses must be specifically approved for VA purposes to use your benefits.

Am I Eligible?

You may receive reimbursement for approved entrepreneurship courses if you're eligible for any of the following VA education programs:
- Montgomery GI Bill
- Active Duty Montgomery GI Bill
- Selected Reserve Veterans' Educational Assistance Program
- The Post-9/11 GI Bill

Dependents Educational Assistance (DEA) participants aren't eligible for this benefit.

Owning or operating your own business will not disqualify you from using your benefits for these courses. You can use your benefits more than once to take approved entrepreneurship courses.

To find a course you can contact the Small Business Development Center directly by phone at 800-8-Ask SBA. You can also contact the VA at 888-442-4551 for local training sites where you are planning to attend to see what courses are approved for VA purposes.

You can get and submit an application for benefits (VA Form 22 1990) online or submit a printed copy to apply.

Non-Paid Work Experience Program

The VA Non-Paid Work Experience (NPWE) program provides eligible veterans and servicemembers with training and practical job experience. This program is well-suited to veterans and servicemembers with clear career goals, and those who learn well in a hands-on setting but might have a hard time finding employment because of a lack of experience. The NPWE program can only be set up in federal, state or local government agencies. The employer can hire a veteran or service member at any point during his or her participation in the program.

An employer can take the following steps to set up a NPWE program:
- Provide a training outline. List required tools, equipment, uniforms and supplies. This identifies items a Veteran or Servicemember will need before entering training.
- Identify specific job objectives for the Veteran or Servicemember to accomplish. You may receive help identifying goals from the vocational rehabilitation counselor (VRC) or employment coordinator (EC). You decide the length of time each objective should take.
- Sign the form designating certifying officials. This form lists staff authorized to sign NPWE-related documents.
- Sign a Department of Veterans Affairs Statement of Assurance of Compliance with Equal Opportunity Laws.
- Fill out the Monthly Record of Training and Wages form for each Veteran or Servicemember. This form must be submitted to the VRC or EC every month.

When you participate in an NPWE program, the VA, VRC or the EC will help complete all required forms. This reduces the amount of time it takes to complete the paperwork for the NPWE. Please contact an employment coordinator at 202-461-9600 for more information.

Funding for Veteran-Owned Small Business

There are different tools and resources available from the SBA including Lender Match that connects veteran entrepreneurs with lenders. The SBA also makes special consideration for veterans through certain programs.

SBA Loan Programs

The U.S Small Business Administration (SBA) has implemented a new measure to help get small business loans into the hands of veterans. This new measure sets the borrower upfront fee to zero for all veteran loans authorized under the SBA Express program up to $350,000. This initiative started on January 1st, and will continue through the end of the fiscal year.

Of all SBA loans that go to veterans, 73 percent are $350,000 and below. The SBA Express Loan Program, which supports loans under $350,000, is SBA's most popular loan delivery method, with nearly 60 percent of all 7(a) loans over the past decade being authorized through the program. Since the program's inception, it has also been one of the most popular delivery methods for getting capital into the hands of veteran borrowers.

This policy announcement means that veteran borrowers will no longer have to pay an upfront fee for any loan up to $350,000 under the SBA Express program. This will make the loans cheaper for the borrower, another way SBA is looking to serve small business owners as they look for ways to access capital.

SBA provides veterans access to business counseling and training, capital and business development opportunities through government contracts. In FY 2013, SBA supported $1.86 billion in loans for 3,094 veteran-owned small businesses. And since 2009, the dollar amount of SBA lending support to veteran-owned firms has nearly doubled.

Guaranty Fee Reduction
Currently, SBA Express loans of $150,001 to $350,000 have an up-front guaranty fee of 3%. To continue supporting America's veterans, the SBA Veterans Advantage reduces the up-front guaranty fee from 3% to 0% for SBA Express loans over $150,000 approved to small businesses owned by qualified veterans. This will encourage greater participation in SBA lending programs with a direct benefit to veteran-owned small businesses.

SBA Veterans Advantage Qualifications
In order to qualify for this, businesses must be 51% or more owned and controlled by an individual or individuals in one or more of the following groups:
- Veterans (other than dishonorably discharged);
- Service-Disabled Veterans;
- Active Duty Military service member participating in the military's Transition Assistance Program (TAP);
- Reservists and National Guard Members; or
- Current spouse of any Veteran, Active Duty service member, or any Reservist or National Guard member; or widowed spouse of a service member who died while in service or of a service-connected disability.

SBA Veterans Advantage Documentation Requirements
Lenders must document in their loan file a borrower's eligibility using the following documentation must present copies of that documentation with any request to SBA to purchase.

1) Veteran: Copy of Form DD 214, which is provided for other than dishonorably discharged veterans.

2) Service-Disabled Veteran: Copy of Form DD 214 or documentation from the DVA that the veteran has been determined as having a service-connected disability.

3) Transitioning Active Duty Military Member: DD Form 2, "U.S. Armed Forces Identification Card (Active)," or DD Form 2, "Armed Forces of the United States Geneva Conventions Identification Card (Active)" and, DD Form 2648 (Active Duty Military member) or DD Form 2648-1 (Reserve Component member).

4) Reservists and National Guard: DD Form 2, Armed Forces of the United States Identification Card (Reserve).

5) Current Spouse of Veteran: The veteran's Form DD 214 and evidence of status as a current spouse.

6) Current Spouse of Transitioning Active Duty Military Member or Current Reservist/National Guard Member: DD Form 1173, Department of Defense Guard Reserve Family Member Identification Card and evidence of status as the current spouse.

7) Widow of Active Duty Service Member who died in service or Widowed Spouse of Veteran who died of a service connected disability: Documentation from DOD or from DVA clearly showing this to be the case.

In the event that the veteran's DD 214 is unavailable, a "Certification of Military Service" (NA Form 13038) is an acceptable equivalent.

For any category listed above that requires a photocopy of a military ID, as an alternative to photocopying the military ID, the servicemember may provide a "statement of service" signed by, or by the direction of, the adjutant, personnel office, or commander of the unit or higher headquarters they are attached to. There is no one unique form used by the military for a statement of service. While statements of service are typically on military letterhead, some may be computer-generated. The statement of service must clearly show:

- The Servicemember's full name;
- The Servicemember's Social Security Number (SSN) or the last 4 digits of SSN;
- The entry date on active duty or the entry date of applicant's Reserve/Guard duty, as applicable (depending on whether the applicant is on active duty or is a current member of the Reserves or National Guard);
- The duration of lost time, if any (for active duty); and
- The name of the command providing the information.

Note for Current Reserve/Guard Members: The statement must clearly indicate that the applicant is an "active" reservist and not just in a control group (inactive status).

Military Reservist Economic Injury Disaster Loan Program

The purpose of the Military Reservist Economic Injury Disaster Loan program (MREIDL) is to provide funds to eligible small businesses to meet its ordinary and necessary operating expenses that it could have met, but is unable to meet, because an essential employee was "called-up" to active duty in their role as a military reservist. These loans are intended only to provide the amount of working capital needed by a small business to pay its necessary obligations as they mature until operations return to normal after the essential employee is released from active military duty. The purpose of these loans is not to cover lost income or lost profits. MREIDL funds cannot be used to take the place of regular commercial debt, to refinance long-term debt or to expand the business. Federal law requires SBA to determine whether credit in an amount needed to accomplish full recovery is available from non-government sources without creating an undue financial hardship to the applicant. The law calls this credit available elsewhere. Because the Military Reservist economic injury loans are taxpayer-subsidized, Congress intended that applicants with the financial capacity to fund their own recovery should do so and therefore are not eligible for MREIDL assistance.

Credit Requirements: SBA's assistance is in the form of loans, as such SBA must have a reasonable assurance that such loans can and will be repaid.

Collateral Requirements: Collateral is required for all MREIDLs over $50,000. SBA takes real estate as collateral when it is available. SBA will not decline a loan for lack of collateral, but SBA will require the borrower to pledge collateral that is available.

The interest rate on MREIDL loans is no more than 4% per year. The maximum maturity for such business disaster loans is 30 years. However, the actual maturity is based on your ability to repay the loan. The maximum loan amount is $2.0 million.

Boots to Business

The Boots to Business program is offered by the U.S. Small Business Administration as a training track within the U.S. Department of Defense's Transition Assistance Program (TAP), and it's open to transitioning service members and their spouses on military installations throughout the world. This also extends to the National Guard and Reserve. The Boots to Business program starts with the "Introduction to Entrepreneurship: course. This is a two-day in-person course that provides an introduction to business ownership.

Once someone completes the Introduction to Entrepreneurship course, participants can continue their study through online courses that are specific to certain skillsets. Participants in this program are encouraged to take advantage of other resources offered by the SBA and the Veterans Business Outreach Centers.

Vets First Verification Program

The Veterans Benefits, Health Care, and Information Technology Act of 2006 (Public Law 109-461) provides the U.S. Department of Veterans Affairs (VA) with unique authority for Service-Disabled Veteran-Owned Small Business (SDVOSB) and Veteran-Owned Small Business (VOSB) set-aside and sole source contracts.

This procurement authority, and its subsequent implementation, is a logical extension of VA's mission to care for our Nation's Veterans. VA refers to this program as the Veterans First Contracting Program.

The Vets First Verification Program affords verified firms owned and controlled by Veterans and Service-disabled Veterans the opportunity to compete for VA set-asides. During Verification, the Center for Verification and Evaluation (CVE) verifies SDVOSBs/VOSBs according to the tenets found in Title 38 Code of Federal Regulations (CFR) Part 74 that address Veteran eligibility, ownership, and control. In order to qualify for participation in the Veterans First Contracting Program, **eligible SDVOSBs/VOSBs must first be verified**.

As part of the Vets First Verification Program, applicants move through four stages: Intake, Assessment, Federal Review, and Decision.

CHAPTER 47

VETERANS SERVICE ORGANIZATIONS AND STATE DIRECTORS FOR VETERANS' AFFAIRS

The following are some of the veterans and military service organizations in the U.S. and their contact information. There is also contact information for all the directors of state veterans' affairs. If you see any updates or corrections, please contact us at the phone number listed in the front of this book.

American Ex-Prisoners of War
National Headquarters
3201 East Pioneer Parkway, #40
Arlington, TX 76010
(817) 649-2979

Primary Contact
Clydie Morgan, Executive
Director/Treasurer
Phone Number
(202) 861-2786

The American Legion
National Headquarters
PO Box 1055
Indianapolis, IN 46206

Primary Contact
Peter S. Gaytan
Executive Director
Phone Number
(202) 861-2783

American Red Cross
National Headquarters
430 17th St. NW
Washington DC 2006
(202) 632-5844

Primary Contact:
Ronald Williams
National Service Director
425 I Street, NW
Room 2W240K
Washington, DC 20001
(202) 632-4612

AMVETS
National Headquarters
4647 Forbes Blvd.
Lanham, MD 20706
(301) 459-9600
Primary Contact
Joseph Chenelly
National Executive Director

4647 Forbes Blvd.
Lanham, MD 20706
(301) 459-9600

Blinded Veterans Association
National Headquarters
477 H Street, NW
Washington, DC 20001
(202) 371-8880

Primary Contact
Joseph Bogart
Executive Director
Blinded Veterans Association
477 H Street NW
Washington, DC 20001

Disabled American Veterans
National Headquarters
3725 Alexandria Pike
Cold Spring, KY 41076
(859) 441-7300

Primary Contact
Garry Augustine, Executive director
Washington Headquarters
Disabled American Veterans
807 Maine Ave. SW
Washington, DC 20024
(202) 554-3501

Gold Star Wives of America, Inc.
National Headquarters
PO Box 361986
Birmingham, AL 35236
(202) 823-1778
info@goldstarwives.org

Primary Contact
Harriet Boyden,
National President/
Washington Representative
200 N. Glebe Rd. Suite 425
Arlington, VA 22203
(703) 351-6246

Legion of Valor of the USA, Inc.
National Headquarters
4706 Calle Reina

Santa Barbara, CA 93110
(805) 692-2244

Primary Contact
Donald Marx
Legion of Valor
3927 Rust Hill Place
Fairfax, VA 22030
(202) 320-3295

Military Officers Association of American (MOAA)
National Headquarters
201 N. Washington St.
Alexandria, VA 22314
(703) 549-2311 or (800) 234-6622

Primary Contact
Lt. General Dana Atkins, USAF (RET)
President and CEO
(703) 838-8173

National Association of County Veterans Service Officers, Inc.
National Headquarters
660 North Capital St. NW
Suite 400
Washington, DC 20001
(937) 206-2806

Primary Contact
Kim Shalloo
Washington Liaison
kshalloo@nacvso.org

National Veterans Legal Services Program
National Headquarters
PO Box 65762
Washington, DC 20035
(202) 265-8305

Phone Number
(202) 265-8305

Paralyzed Veterans of America
National Headquarters
801 18th St. NW
Washington DC 20006
(202) 872-1300

Primary Contact
Sherman Gillums Jr.
Executive Director
801 18th St. NW
Washington DC 20006
(202) 872-1300

Veterans of Foreign Wars of the United States
National Headquarters
406 West 34th St.
Kansas City, MO 64111
(816) 561-8655

Primary Contact
Robert E Wallace
Executive Director
200 Maryland Ave. NE
Washington, DC 20002
(202) 543-2239

Vietnam Veterans of America
National Headquarters
8719 Colesville Rd.
Suite 100
Silver Spring, MD 20910
(301) 585-4000

Primary Contact
John Rowan
8719 Colesville Rd.
Suite 100
Silver Spring MD 20910

(301) 585-4000

Wounded Warrior Project
National Headquarters
4899 Belfort Rd.
Suite 300
Jacksonville, FL 32256
(904) 296-7350

Primary Contact
Michael Linnington
CEO
4899 Belfort Rd.
Suite 300
Jacksonville, FL 32256
(904) 296-7350

Armed Forces Service Corporation
National Headquarters
2800 S. Shirlington Rd.
Suite 350
Arlington, VA 22206
(888) 237-2872

Primary Contact
Goeffrey J. Deutsch
President & CEO
2800 S. Shirlington Rd.
Suite 350
Arlington, VA 22206

The following is the contact information for the State Directors' of Veterans Affairs

Alabama
RADM W. Clyde Marsh, USN (Ret)
Commissioner Alabama VA
RSA Union, 100 South Union,
Suite 850
Montgomery, AL 36130
Phone: (334) 242-5077
Fax: (334) 242-5102
clyde.marsh@va.alabama.gov

Alaska
Mr. Verdie Bowen, Director
Division of Veterans Affairs Alaska VA
4600 Debarr Road, Suite 180
Anchorage, AK 99508
Toll Free: 888-248-3682
(main) (907) 334-0874
(desk) (907) 334-0870
(fax) (907) 334-0869
verdie.bowen@alaska.gov

Arizona
Col. Wanda Wright, Director, Arizona VA
3839 North Third Street, Suite 200
Phoenix, AZ 85012
Phone: 602-234-8415
Fax: 602-255-1038
wwright@azdvs.gov

Arkansas
Mr. Nate Todd, Director
Arkansas VA
501 Woodlane Drive, Suite 230C
Little Rock, AR 72201
Phone: (501) 683-1376
Fax: (501) 682-4833
Nate.Todd@arkansas.gov

California
Dr. Vito Imbasciani,
Secretary California VA
1227 O Street, Room 300
Sacramento, CA 95814
Phone: (916) 653-2158
Fax: (916) 653-2456
vito.imbasciani@calvet.ca.gov

Colorado
Mr. Ben Mestas, Director
Colorado Division of Veteran Affairs
1355 South Colorado Blvd. Suite 113
Denver, CO 80222
Phone: 303-284-6077
Fax: 303-284-3163
reuben.mestas@dmva.state.co.us

Connecticut
Mr. Sean Connolly, Commissioner
Connecticut VA
287 West Street
Rocky Hill, CT 06067
Phone: (860) 616-3603
Fax: (860) 616-3532
Sean.Connolly@ct.gov

Delaware
Mr. Lawrence Kirby,Executive Director
Delaware Commission of Veterans Affairs
Robbins Building
802 Silver Lake Blvd, Suite 100
Dover, DE 19904
In State Toll Free: (800) 344-9900
Phone: (302) 739-2792
Fax: (302) 739-2794
lawrence.kirby@state.de.us

Florida
Glenn Sutphin, Executive Director
Florida Department of Veterans Affairs
11351 Ulmerton Road, Rm 311-K
Largo, FL 33778-1630
Phone: (727) 518-3202 ext 5594
Fax: (727)518-3403
exdir@fdva.state.fl.us

Georgia
Mr. Mike Roby, Commissioner
Georgia Department of Veterans Service
Floyd Veterans Memorial Building
Suite E-966
Atlanta, GA 30334-4800
Phone: 404-656-2312
Fax: 404-656-7006
mroby@vs.state.ga.us

Hawaii
COL-R Ronald P. Han Jr., Director
Office of Veterans Services
Tripler Army Medical Center
459 Patterson Road
E-Wing, Room 1-A103
Honolulu, HI 96819-1522
Phone: (808) 433-0420
Fax: (808) 433-0385
TTD/Relay Service: 1-711
Ronald.han@va.gov

Idaho
David Brasuell, Col., USMC (Ret), Administrator
Idaho Division of Veterans Services
351 Collins Road
Boise, Idaho 83702
Phone: (208) 780-1300
Fax: (208) 780-1301

David.Brasuell@veterans.idaho.gov

Illinois
Ms. Erica Jeffries, Director
Illinois Department of Veterans' Affairs
P.O. Box 19432
833 S. Spring Street
Springfield, IL 62794
Springfield Office: (217) 785-4114
Fax: (217) 524-0344
IDVA.Director@illinois.gov

Indiana
Mr. James M. Brown, Director
Indiana VA
302 W. Washington Street
Room E-120
Indianapolis, IN 46204
Phone: (317) 232-3910
Fax: (317) 232-7721
TOLL FREE (In State) 1-800-400-4520
jambrown@dva.in.gov

Iowa
Colonel Robert C. King (Ret)
Executive Director
Iowa VA
Camp Dodge, Building 3465
7105 NW 70th Avenue
Johnston, IA 50131-1824
Phone: (515) 727-3444
Fax: (515) 727-3713
robert.king@iowa.gov

Kansas
Mr. Gregg Burden, Director
Kansas Commission on Veterans
Affairs Office
Jayhawk Tower, Suite 1004
700 S.W. Jackson Street
Topeka, KS 66603-3150
Phone: (785) 296-3976
Fax: (785) 296-1462
gburden@kcva.ks.gov

Kentucky
Norman E. Arflack, Commissioner
Kentucky VA
NGAKY Bldg.

1111B Louisville Road
Frankfort, KY 40601
Phone: (502) 564-9203
Fax: (502) 564-9240
NormanE.Arflack@ky.gov

Louisiana
Mr. Joey Strickland, Secretary
Louisiana VA
602 North 5th Street (70802)
PO Box 94095, Capitol Station
Baton Rouge, LA 70804
Phone: (225) 219-5001
Fax: (225) 922-0511
Joey.Strickland@la.gov

Massachusetts
Mr. Francisco Ureña, Secretary
Massachusetts VA
600 Washington Street, 7th Floor
Boston, MA 02111
Phone: (617) 210-5767
Fax: (617) 210-5755
Francisco.urena@state.ma.us

Michigan
Mr. James R. Redford, Director
Michigan Veterans Affairs Agency
222 Washington Square North
PO Box 30104
Lansing, MI 48909
Phone: (517) 284-5217
Fax: (517) 284-5295
RedfordJ1@michigan.gov

Minnesota
Mr. Larry W. Shellito, Commissioner
Minnesota VA
Veterans Service Building
20 West 12th Street, 2nd Floor
St. Paul, MN 55155
Phone: (651) 757-1555
Fax: (651) 757-1539
larry.shellito@state.mn.us

Mississippi
Mr. Randy Reeves, Executive Director
Mississippi State Veterans Affairs
Board

550

3466 Highway 80 East
Post Office Box 5947
Pearl, MS 39288-5947
Phone: (601) 576-4850
Fax: 601-576-4868
rreeves@vab.ms.gov
Missouri
Mr. Larry D. Kay, Executive Director
Missouri Veterans Commission
Post Office Drawer 147
Jefferson City, MO 65102-0147
Phone: (573) 751-3779
Fax: (573)751-6836
Larry.kay@mvc.dps.mo.gov
Montana
Mr. Joe Foster, Administrator
Montana Veterans Affairs Division
Post Office Box 5715
Helena, MT 59604
Phone: (406) 324-3740
Fax: (406) 324-3745
jofoster@mt.gov
Nebraska
Mr. John Hilgert, Director
Nebraska VA
Post Office 95026
Lincoln, NE 68509-5026
Phone: (402) 471-3156
Fax: (402) 471-2491
John.Hilgert@nebraska.gov
Nevada
Ms. Katherine "Kat" Miller, Director
Nevada Department of Veterans
Services
6880 S. McCarran Blvd., Suite 2
Reno, NV 89509
Phone: (775) 688-1653
Fax: (775) 688-1656
millerk@veterans.nv.gov

New Hampshire
Bobby Broneske, Director
New Hampshire Office of Veterans
Services

275 Chestnut Street, Room 517
Manchester, NH 03101-2411
Phone: (603) 624-9230, X 302
Fax: (603) 624-9236
Bobby.Broneske@va.gov
New Jersey
Mr. Raymond Zawacki, Deputy
Commissioner for Veterans Affairs
New Jersey Dept of Military &
Veterans Affairs
Eggerts Crossing Road,
P.O. Box 340
Trenton, NJ 08625-0340
Phone: (609) 530-7045
Fax: (609) 530-7191
raymond.zawacki@dmava.nj.gov
New Mexico
BG Jack R. Fox (Ret. U.S. Army/NM
National Guard), Secretary
New Mexico Department of Veterans
Services
Post Office Box 2324
Santa Fe, NM 87509
Phone: (505) 827-6300
Fax: (505) 827-6372
jackr.fox@state.nm.us
New York
COL. Eric J. Hesse, (Ret), Director
New York State VA
5 Empire State Plaza, Suite 2836
Albany, NY 12223-1551
Phone: (518) 474-6114
FAX: (518) 474-6924
EHesse@veterans.ny.gov

North Carolina
Mr. James (Jim) Prosser, Assistant
Secretary for Veterans Affairs
Department of Military & Veterans
Affairs
413 North Salisbury Street
Raleigh, NC 27603
Phone: (984) 204-2982
Fax: (919) 807-4260

James.Prosser@nc.gov
North Dakota
Mr. Lonnie Wangen, Commissioner
VA
P.O. Box 9003
Fargo, ND 58106
Phone: (701) 239-7165
Fax: (701) 239-7166
LWangen@nd.gov
Ohio
Mr. Chip Tansill, Director
Ohio Department of Veterans
Services
77 South High Street, 7th Floor
Columbus, OH 43215
Phone: (614) 644-0898
Fax: (614) 728-9498
chip.tansill@dvs.ohio.gov
Oklahoma
Mr. Myles Deering, Secretary
Oklahoma VA
Post Office Box 53067
Oklahoma City, Oklahoma 73152
Phone: (405) 521-3684
Fax: (405) 521-6533
mdeering@odva.state.ok.us
Oregon
Mr. Cameron Smith, Director
Oregon VA
Oregon Veterans' Building
700 Summer Street, NE
Salem, Oregon 97310-1285
Phone: (503-373-2388
Toll Free: 1 (800) 828-8801
Cameron.Smith@state.or.us
Pennsylvania
Eric Weller
Deputy Adjutant General VA
Pennsylvania Dept of Military &
Veterans Affairs
Fort Indiantown Gap, Building S-O-47
Annville, Pennsylvania 17003-5002
Phone: (717) 861-8902
Fax: (717) 861-8589

Eriweller@pa.gov
Rhode Island
Kasim Yarn, Director
Office of Veterans Affairs
560 Jefferson Blvd, Suite 206
Warwick, RI 02886
Phone: (401) 921-2119 x3
Fax: (401) 254-2320
Kasim.Yarn@vets.ri.gov
South Carolina
Mr. Howard Metcalf, Director
South Carolina Division of Veterans
Affairs
1205 Pendleton Street, Suite 463
Columbia, SC 29201
Phone: (803) 734-0200/0203
Fax: (803) 734-0241
HMetcalf@oepp.sc.gov
South Dakota
Mr. Larry Zimmerman, Secretary
South Dakota VA
Soldiers and Sailors Memorial
Building
425 E. Capitol Ave.
Pierre, SD 57501
Phone: (605) 773-3269
Fax: (605) 773-5380
larry.zimmerman@state.sd.us
Tennessee
COL (Ret.) Many-Bears Grinder,
Commissioner
Tennessee VA
312 Rosa L. Parks Avenue
William R. Snodgrass TN Tower, 13th
Floor
Nashville, TN 37243
Phone: (615) 741-1959
Fax: (615) 741-5056
many-bears.grinder@tn.gov
Texas
Mr. Thomas P. Palladino, Col. USA
(Ret)
Executive Director
Texas Veterans Commission

1700 North Congress, Suite 800
Post Office Box 12277
Austin, Texas 78711-2277
Phone: (512) 463-656
Fax: (512) 475-2395
Thomas.Palladino@tvc.texas.gov
Utah
Mr. Gary Harter, Executive Director
Department of Veterans & Military Affairs
550 Foothill Boulevard, Room 105
Salt Lake City, UT 84113
Phone: (801) 326-2372
Fax: (801) 326-2369
Toll Free: 1-800-894-9497
gharter@utah.gov
Vermont
Mr. Robert E. Burke, Director
Vermont Office of Veterans Affairs
118 State Street
Montpelier, VT 05620-4401
Phone: (802) 828-3379
Fax: (802) 828-5932
Robert.Burke@state.vt.us
Virginia
Mr. John L. Newby II, Commissioner
Virginia Department of Veterans Services
900 East Main Street
Sixth Floor, West Wing
Richmond, VA 23219
Phone: (804) 786-0286
Fax: (804) 786-0302
john.newby@dvs.virginia.gov

Washington
Ms. Lourdes (Alfie) Alvarado Ramos, CSM (Ret.), Director
Washington VA
1102 Quince St. SE
Post Office Box 41150
Olympia, WA 98504-1150
Phone: (360) 725-2155
Mobile: (360) 791-4339

Fax: (360) 586-4393
alfie@dva.wa.gov
West Virginia
Dennis E. Davis, Secretary
West Virginia Department of Veterans Assistance
1514-B Kanawha Blvd. East
Charleston, WV 25311
Phone: (304) 558-3661
Fax: (304) 558-3662
Dennis.E.Davis@wv.gov
Wisconsin
Daniel Zimmerman, Secretary
Wisconsin VA
201 W. Washington Ave.
PO Box 7843
Madison, Wisconsin 53707
Phone: (608) 266-1315
Fax: (608) 264-7616
Daniel.Zimmerman@dva.wisconsin.gov
Wyoming
Mr. Larry Barttelbort, Col. USA (Ret.)
Director
Wyoming Veterans' Commission
5410 Bishop Boulevard
Cheyenne, WY 82009
Phone: (307) 777-8151
Fax: (307) 777-8150
larry.barttelbort@wyo.gov
District of Columbia
Ely Ross, Director
DC Office of Veterans Affairs
1 Judiciary Square
441 4th St NW, Suite 870 North
Washington DC, 20001
Phone: (202) 724-4010
Fax: (202) 724-7117
Ely.Ross@dc.gov
American Samoa
Mr. Anthony Fu'e Allen
Veterans Affairs Officer
American Samoa Government
Office of the Governor
P.O. Box 2586

Pago Pago, American Samoa 96799
Phone (684) 633-4206
Fax: (001) (684) 633-2269
AnthonyAllen_644@yahoo.com

Guam

Jose San Agustin, Administrator
Guam Office of Veterans Affairs
172 West Marine Corp Drive
PO Box 2950
Hagatna, GU 96932
Phone: (671) 487-8505
Fax: (671) 475-8396
Joe.San.Agustin@gvao.guam.gov

Northern Mariana Islands

Vincente Camacho, Director
Division of Veterans Affairs-DC&CA
P.O. Box 503416 CK
Commonwealth of the Northern
Mariana Islands
Saipan MP 96950
Phone: (670) 664-2650
Fax: (670) 664-2660
Vicente.Camacho@gov.mpi

Puerto Rico

Mr. Augustin Montanez-Allman
Interim Director
Veterans and Military Affairs
P.O. Box 11737
San Juan, Puerto Rico 00918-1737
Phone: (787) 758-5760
Fax: (787) 772-2090
A.Montanez.Allman@gmail.com

Virgin Islands

Mr. Patrick Farrell, Director
Virgin Islands VA
3241 Estate Contant; Suite #5
St. Thomas, VI 00802
Phone: (340) 774-8387
Fax: (340) 714-0589
patrick.farrell@va.vi.gov

T

Y

Would You Like Additional Copies Of
What Every Veteran Should Know?
Simply tear out this form, and:
Phone 309-757-7760 or Fax 309-278-5304
Mail To: VETERANS INFORMATION SERVICE
P.O. Box 111
East Moline, IL 61244-0111
ORDER ONLINE AT: www.vetsinfoservice.com

☐ Yes! Send me _____ copies of "*What Every Veteran Should Know*", at $28.00 each (shipping & handling included). I request the _____ (specify: current already released 2020, or pre-reserve 2021) edition. New annual books are published every March 1st.

☐ Yes! I would like to subscribe to "*What Every Veteran Should Know*" monthly supplement (an 8-page newsletter which keeps your book up-to-date), and receive _____ copies of all 12 monthly issues (1 year) for $36.00 per subscription (shipping & handling included).

☐ Yes! I want to save money, and receive both the book and the monthly supplement. I would like _____ sets, at $60 per set (shipping & handling included).

Name   Current Customer ID?

Address

City / State / Zip Code

Telephone Number   E-mail Address

Amount Enclosed   Daytime Phone # (including area code)

Method of Payment:

☐ Check   ☐ Visa   ☐ MasterCard   ☐ Money Order

Credit Card # 3-digit CVV   Expiration Date (Month/Year)

Signature

Thank you for your order!
If you have any questions, feel free to contact us at
(309) 757-7760
www.vetsinfoservice.com - Email: help@vetsinfoservice.com

Would You Like Additional Copies Of
What Every Veteran Should Know?
Simply tear out this form, and:
Phone 309-757-7760 or Fax 309-278-5304
Mail To: VETERANS INFORMATION SERVICE
P.O. Box 111
East Moline, IL 61244-0111
ORDER ONLINE AT: www.vetsinfoservice.com

☐ Yes! Send me _____ copies of "*What Every Veteran Should Know*", at $28.00 each (shipping & handling included). I request the _____ (specify: current already released 2020, or pre-reserve 2021) edition. New annual books are published every March 1ˢᵗ.

☐ Yes! I would like to subscribe to "*What Every Veteran Should Know*" monthly supplement (an 8-page newsletter which keeps your book up-to-date), and receive _____ copies of all 12 monthly issues (1 year) for $36.00 per subscription (shipping & handling included).

☐ Yes! I want to save money, and receive both the book and the monthly supplement. I would like _____ sets, at $60 per set (shipping & handling included).

Name   Current Customer ID?

Address

City / State / Zip Code

Telephone Number   E-mail Address

Amount Enclosed   Daytime Phone # (including area code)

Method of Payment:

☐ Check   ☐ Visa   ☐ MasterCard   ☐ Money Order

Credit Card # 3-digit CVV   Expiration Date (Month/Year)

Signature

Thank you for your order!
If you have any questions, feel free to contact us at
(309) 757-7760
www.vetsinfoservice.com - Email: help@vetsinfoservice.com

Would You Like Additional Copies Of
What Every Veteran Should Know?
Simply tear out this form, and:
Phone 309-757-7760 or Fax 309-278-5304
Mail To: VETERANS INFORMATION SERVICE
P.O. Box 111
East Moline, IL 61244-0111
ORDER ONLINE AT: www.vetsinfoservice.com

☐ Yes! Send me _____ copies of "*What Every Veteran Should Know*", at $28.00 each (shipping & handling included). I request the _____ (specify: current already released 2020, or pre-reserve 2021) edition. New annual books are published every March 1st.

☐ Yes! I would like to subscribe to "*What Every Veteran Should Know*" monthly supplement (an 8-page newsletter which keeps your book up-to-date), and receive _____ copies of all 12 monthly issues (1 year) for $36.00 per subscription (shipping & handling included).

☐ Yes! I want to save money, and receive both the book and the monthly supplement. I would like _____ sets, at $60 per set (shipping & handling included).

Name   Current Customer ID?

Address

City / State / Zip Code

Telephone Number   E-mail Address

Amount Enclosed   Daytime Phone # (including area code)

Method of Payment:

☐ Check   ☐ Visa   ☐ MasterCard   ☐ Money Order

Credit Card # 3-digit CVV   Expiration Date (Month/Year)

Signature

Thank you for your order!
If you have any questions, feel free to contact us at
(309) 757-7760
www.vetsinfoservice.com - Email: help@vetsinfoservice.com

Would You Like Additional Copies Of
What Every Veteran Should Know?
Simply tear out this form, and:
Phone 309-757-7760 or Fax 309-278-5304
Mail To: VETERANS INFORMATION SERVICE
P.O. Box 111
East Moline, IL 61244-0111
ORDER ONLINE AT: www.vetsinfoservice.com

☐ Yes! Send me _____ copies of "*What Every Veteran Should Know*", at $28.00 each (shipping & handling included). I request the _____ (specify: current already released 2020, or pre-reserve 2021) edition. New annual books are published every March 1ˢᵗ.

☐ Yes! I would like to subscribe to "*What Every Veteran Should Know*" monthly supplement (an 8-page newsletter which keeps your book up-to-date), and receive _____ copies of all 12 monthly issues (1 year) for $36.00 per subscription (shipping & handling included).

☐ Yes! I want to save money, and receive both the book and the monthly supplement. I would like _____ sets, at $60 per set (shipping & handling included).

Name   Current Customer ID?

Address

City / State / Zip Code

Telephone Number   E-mail Address

Amount Enclosed   Daytime Phone # (including area code)

Method of Payment:

☐ Check   ☐ Visa   ☐ MasterCard   ☐ Money Order

Credit Card # 3-digit CVV   Expiration Date (Month/Year)

Signature

Thank you for your order!
If you have any questions, feel free to contact us at
(309) 757-7760
www.vetsinfoservice.com - Email: help@vetsinfoservice.com

Reference Standing Order

REF 355.115 WHAT

**What every veteran should
know.**

LAKE COUNTY PUBLIC LIBRARY
INDIANA

FOR REFERENCE ONLY

Black Oak	Highland
Cedar Lake	Hobart
Central	Lake Station/New Chicago
Dyer-Schererville	Munster
Griffith	St. John

Some materials may be renewed by phone, in person, or through the online catalog
if there are no reserves or fines due.

www.lcplin.org   LibraryLine: (219) 756-9356